THE (COMP) SOLUTION

D0999075

STUDENT RESOURCES

- Interactive eBook
- Graded Quizzes
- New Practice Quiz Generator
- Writer Interviews
- Trackable Activities
- Flashcards
- Text and Digital English Composition Handbook
- Tutorials
- Glossary
- Chapter Review Cards

Students sign in at **www.cengagebrain.com**

INSTRUCTOR RESOURCES

- All Student Resources
- Engagement Tracker
- LMS Integration
- Instructor's Manual
- New PowerPoint® Slides
- Instructor Prep Cards
- Discussion Questions

Instructors log in at **www.cengage.com/login**

Print

COMP3 delivers all the key terms and all the content for the **English Composition** course through a visually engaging and easy-to-reference print experience.

CourseMate

CourseMate provides access to the full **COMP3** narrative, alongside a rich assortment of quizzing, flashcards, and interactive resources for convenient reading and studying.

CENGAGE
Learning®

COMP3

John Van Rys
Redeemer University College
Verne Meyer
Dordt College
Randall VanderMey
Westmont College
Pat Sebranek

Vice President, General Manager, 4LTR Press and the Student Experience: Neil Marquardt

Product Director, 4LTR Press: Steven E. Joos

Product Manager: Laura A. Redden

Content Developer: Patricia Hempel

Product Assistant: Mandira Jacob

Marketing Manager: Kristen Davis

Content Project Manager: Rosemary Winfield

Manufacturing Planner: Doug Bertke

Production Service: Sebranek, Inc.

Art Director: Bethany Casey

Cover Designer: 4LTR Press

Cover Image: © J. P. Nodier / Getty Images

Intellectual Property Analyst: Ann Hoffman

Intellectual Project Manager: Farah Fard

Compositor: Sebranek Inc.

Sebranek Inc: Steven J. Augustyn, Chris Erickson, Dave Kemper, Tim Kemper, Rob King, Chris Krenzke, Lois Krenzke, Mark Lalumondier, Janae Sebranek, Lester Smith

Library of Congress Control Number: 2014957977

ISBN: 978-1-305-11276-6

Student Edition with CourseMate:

ISBN: 978-1-305-11280-3

Cengage Learning
20 Channel Center Street
Boston, MA 02210
USA

Cengage Learning is a leading provider of customized learning solutions with office locations around the globe, including Singapore, the United Kingdom, Australia, Mexico, Brazil, and Japan. Locate your local office at: **www.cengage.com/global**.

Cengage Learning products are represented in Canada by Nelson Education, Ltd.

To learn more about Cengage Learning Solutions, visit **www.cengage.com**.

Purchase any of our products at your local college store or at our preferred online store **www.cengagebrain.com**.

Printed in the United States of America
Print Number: 01   Print Year: 2015

VAN RYS/MEYER/VANDERMEY/SEBRANEK

COMP³

BRIEF CONTENTS

J.P. Nodier / Getty Images

CONTENTS

Part 2
FORMS OF WRITING
Narrative, Descriptive, and Reflective Writing

Analytical Writing

Zastolskiy Victor, 2014 / Used under license from Shutterstock.com

Research Writing

Bonus Online Chapters

Africa Studio, 2014 / Used under license from Shutterstock.com

Part 3
HANDBOOK

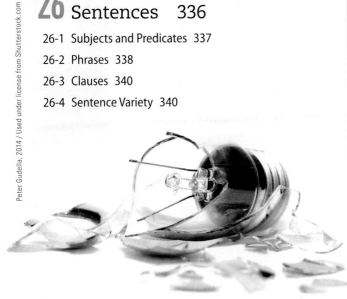

THEMATIC CONTENTS

1 | Understanding the Reading-Writing Connection

"LITERACY IS NOT A LUXURY; IT IS A RIGHT AND A RESPONSIBILITY."

BILL CLINTON

tobkatrina, 2014 / Used under license from Shutterstock.com

LEARNING OBJECTIVES

1-1 Use the SQ3R reading strategy.

1-2 Read actively.

1-3 Respond to a text.

1-4 Summarize a text.

1-5 Effectively analyze images.

1-6 Think critically through writing.

After you finish
this chapter
go to
PAGE 11 for STUDY TOOLS

When you write, you are sending a message into the world. But here's the thing: Before you could write, you needed to read. And your writing needs a reader if it is to be something more than static words on a page or a screen. Whether it's a poem or a novel, a tweet or an essay, a blog or a lab report, reading and writing work symbiotically—in a close relationship where one depends on the other.

In your college work (and even beyond), you'll do plenty of reading and writing, and *COMP* aims to help you improve both of these abilities in its attention to the writing process, its presentation of student and professional essays, its instruction in different forms of writing, its attention to research, and its focus on grammar. However, this first chapter looks directly at the reading-writing connection so that you can begin to strengthen those ties in your own work.

Now more than ever, reading and writing involve not only words but also visual images. For that reason, this chapter also asks you to pull visuals into view as part of the reading-writing connection.

1-1 USE THE SQ3R READING STRATEGY

Obviously, reading a novel, a textbook, and a Web page are all different activities. Nevertheless, all college reading assignments can be approached systematically, especially when your goal is to absorb and engage the text. One strategy for critical reading, especially of information-rich texts, is called SQ3R: Survey, Question, Read, Recite, and Review. Here is how SQ3R works.

1-1a Survey

The first step in SQ3R is to preview the material. Check for clues to each part of the rhetorical situation:

Rhetorical Situation

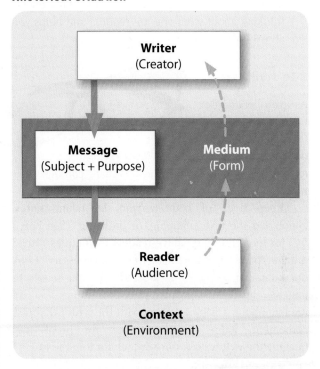

Read about the author. Then read the title and the opening and closing paragraphs to get a sense of the main points. Glance at all other pages, noting headings, topic sentences in paragraphs, boldface type, illustrations, charts, and other cues to the content and organization.

▸ **Benefits:** Surveying helps you (1) focus on the writer's message, (2) identify its organization, and (3) anticipate how the text will develop.

1-1b Question

As you survey, begin to ask questions that you hope to answer as you read.

- **Read any questions that accompany the reading.** Look at the end of the reading or in a study guide.
- **Turn headings into questions.** If a subhead says, "The Study," ask, "How was the study conducted?"
- **Imagine test questions for major points.** If the reading draws conclusions about self-control, ask, "What conclusions does the author draw about self-control?"

- **Ask the journalist's questions:** Ask *who, what, where, when, why,* and *how?* Whose attitudes are changing? What are their attitudes? Where is the change strongest? When is it occurring? Why is it happening? How?

  ▸ **Benefits:** Asking questions keeps you actively thinking about what you are reading and helps you absorb information.

1-1c Read

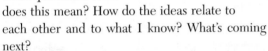

As you encounter facts and ideas, ask these questions: What does this mean? How do the ideas relate to each other and to what I know? What's coming next?

Keep track of your answers by taking notes, annotating the text, mapping, or outlining. (See pages 5–7 for more on these active-reading techniques.) Read difficult parts slowly; reread them if necessary. Look up unfamiliar words or ideas, and use your senses to imagine the events, people, places, or things you are reading about. Imagine talking with the writer. Express agreement, lodge complaints, ask for proof—and imagine the writer's response or look for it in the text.

  ▸ **Benefits:** Engaging actively with the text in this way will draw you deeper into the world of the writing. You'll trigger memories and make surprising connections.

1-1d Recite

After finishing a page, section, or chapter, recite the key points aloud. Answering *Who? What? When? Where? Why?* and *How?* questions is a quick way of testing yourself on how well you understood what you read. You can also recite the key points by listing them or writing a summary (see pages 7–8).

  ▸ **Benefits:** Reciting tests your comprehension, drives the material deeper into your long-term memory, and helps you connect the content with what you already know.

1-1e Review

As soon as you finish reading the material, double-check the questions you posed in the "question" stage of SQ3R. Can you answer them? Glance over any notes you made as well. But don't stop there if the reading is especially

important. You will remember the material much better by spacing out your reviews; spend a few minutes reviewing each text over the next few days. Consider the following helpful memory techniques:

- **Visualize the concepts in concrete ways.** *Example:* If a text discusses a study about self-control, imagine a television panel discussing the topic.
- **Draw diagrams or develop clusters.** *Example:* See the cluster on page 6.
- **Put the material in your own words.** *Example:* See the summary on pages 7–8.
- **Teach it to someone.** *Example:* For a study about self-control, explain the main points to a friend or relative—in person, on the phone, or by email.
- **Use acronyms or rhymes.** *Example:* "*i* before *e* except after *c*"

  ▸ **Benefits:** Research shows that reviewing within 24 hours helps considerably to move information from your short-term memory to your long-term memory. You will also improve your memory if you create a network of associations with the information you want to remember, if you link the memory to two or more senses, or if you reorganize the material while still retaining the substance with accuracy.

1-2 READ ACTIVELY

Truly active reading is a kind of mental dialogue with the writer. Use these strategies to read actively:

- **Pace yourself.** Read in stretches of 30 to 45 minutes, followed by short breaks.
- **Anticipate.** When you break, think about what is coming next and why.
- **Read difficult parts aloud.** Or take turns reading aloud with a partner.
- **Take thoughtful notes.** Find a note-taking system that works for you. (See pages 262–264.) This is especially true for research projects.
- **Annotate the text.** Mark up the text (if you own it) or a photocopy. Underline or highlight key points. Write a "?" beside puzzling parts. Write key words in the margin and add personal observations.

1-2a Read, Annotate, and Respond to a Text

The following article first appeared on June 2, 2010, in a monthly column in the *Fast Company* newsletter. The author, Dan Heath, is also coauthor (with his brother) of the best-selling business books *Made to Stick* and *Switch*. He is currently a consultant to the Policy Programs at the Aspen Institute. Read the following article, using SQ3R and active-reading strategies.

Why Change Is So Hard: Self-Control Is Exhaustible

SQ3R   Survey • Question • Read • Recite • Review

1   You hear something a lot about change: People won't change because they're too lazy. Well, I'm here to stick up for the lazy people. In fact, I want to argue that what looks like laziness is actually exhaustion. The proof comes from a psychology study that is absolutely fascinating.

The Study

2   So picture this: Students come into a lab. It smells amazing—someone has just baked chocolate-chip cookies. On a table in front of them, there are two bowls. One has the fresh-baked cookies. The other has a bunch of radishes. Some of the students are asked to eat some cookies but no radishes. Others are told to eat radishes but no cookies, and while they sit there, nibbling on rabbit food, the researchers leave the room—which is intended to tempt them and is frankly kind of sadistic. But in the study none of the radish-eaters slipped— they showed admirable self-control. And meanwhile, it probably goes without saying that the people gorging on cookies didn't experience much temptation.

3   Then, the two groups are asked to do a second, seemingly unrelated task—basically a kind of logic puzzle where they have to trace out a complicated geometric pattern without raising their pencil. Unbeknownst to them, the puzzle can't be solved. The scientists are curious how long they'll persist at a difficult task. So the cookie-eaters try again and again, for an average of 19 minutes, before they give up. But the radish-eaters—

they only last an average of 8 minutes. What gives?

The Results

4   The answer may surprise you: They ran out of self-control. Psychologists have discovered that self-control is an exhaustible resource. And I don't mean self-control only in the sense of turning down cookies or alcohol; I mean a broader sense of self-supervision—any time you're paying close attention to your actions, like when you're having a tough conversation or trying to stay focused on a paper you're writing. This helps to explain why, after a long hard day at the office, we're more likely to snap at our spouses or have one drink too many— we've depleted our self-control.

5   And here's why this matters for change: In almost all change situations, you're substituting new, unfamiliar behaviors for old, comfortable ones, and that burns self-control. Let's say I present a new morning routine to you that specifies how you'll shower and brush your teeth. You'll understand it and you might even agree with my process. But to pull it off, you'll have to supervise yourself very carefully. Every fiber of your being will want to go back to the old way of doing things. Inevitably, you'll slip. And if I were uncharitable, I'd see you going back to the old way and I'd say, You're so lazy. Why can't you just change?

6   This brings us back to the point I promised I'd make: that what looks like laziness is often exhaustion. Change wears people out—even well-intentioned people will simply run out of fuel.

Reading for Better Writing

1. In a single sentence, state the thesis of the essay.

2. In a few sentences, tell how the findings of the study help explain why change is difficult.

3. Compare your notes and annotations with a partner. Which parts of your notes and annotations are the same? Which parts are different? How does discussing the content of the essay reinforce or otherwise alter your understanding of the essay?

4. Think about your own life. What sorts of activities require you to exert a great deal of self-control? What sorts of activities do you find too tempting to resist when you have run out of self-control? How could this information help you avoid temptation?

 TIP Reading actively also involves evaluating texts. For help, see pages 259–260, where you'll find instruction on evaluating sources for research.

1-2b Map the Text

If you are visually oriented, you may understand a text best by mapping out its important parts. One way to do so is by clustering. Start by naming the main topic in an oval at the center of the page. Then branch out using lines and "balloons," where each balloon contains a word or phrase for one major subtopic. Branch out in further layers of balloons to show even more subpoints.

1-2c Outline the Text

Outlining is the traditional way of showing all the major parts, points, and subpoints in a text. An outline uses parallel structure to show main points and subordinate points. See pages 43–45 for more on outlines.

Sample Outline for "Why Change Is So Hard: Self-Control Is Exhaustible"

1. Introduction: Change is hard not because of laziness but because of exhaustion.
2. A study tests self-control.
   a. Some students must eat only cookies—using little self-control.
   b. Some students must eat only radishes—using much self-control.
   c. Both sets of students have to trace a pattern without lifting the pencil—an unsolvable puzzle.
      - Cookie-only students last an average of 19 minutes before quitting.
      - Radish-only students last an average of 8 minutes before quitting.
3. Results show that self-control is exhaustible.
   a. Avoiding temptation and working in a hard, focused way require self-control.
   b. Change requires self-control.
   c. Failure to change often results from exhaustion of self-control.

1-3 RESPOND TO A TEXT

In a sense, when you read a text, you enter into a dialogue with it. Your response expresses your turn in the dialogue. Such a response can take varied forms, from a journal entry to a blog to a discussion-group posting.

1-3a Follow These Guidelines for Response Writing

On the surface, responding to a text seems perfectly natural—just let it happen. But it can be a bit more complicated. A written response typically is not the same as a private diary entry but is instead shared with other readers, whether your instructor or a class. You develop your response keeping in mind your instructor's requirements and the response's role in the course. Therefore, follow these guidelines:

1. **Be honest.** Although you want to remain sensitive to the context in which you will share your response, be bold enough to be honest about your reaction to the text—what it makes you think, feel, and question. To that end, a response usually allows you to express yourself directly using the pronoun "I."

2. **Be fluid.** Let the flow of your thoughts guide you in what you write. Don't stop to worry about grammar, punctuation, mechanics, and spelling. These can be quickly cleaned up before you share or submit your response.

3. **Be reflective.** Generally, the goal of a response is to offer thoughtful reflection as opposed to knee-jerk reaction. Show, then, that you are engaging the text's ideas, relating them to your own experience, looking both inward and outward. Avoid a shallow reaction that comes from skimming the text or misreading it.

4. **Be selective.** By nature, a response must limit its focus; it cannot exhaust all your reactions to the text. So zero in on one or two elements of your response, and run with those to see where they take you in your dialogue with the text.

Sample Response

Here is part of a student's response to Dan Heath's "Why Change Is So Hard" on page 5. Note the informality and explanatory tone.

> Heath's report of the psychological experiment is very vivid, referring to the smell of chocolate-chip cookies and hungry students "gorging" on them. He uses the term "sadistic" to refer to making the radish-eaters sit and watch this go on. I wonder if this mild torment plays into the student's readiness to give up on the later test. If I'd been rewarded with cookies, I'd feel indebted to the testers and would stick with it longer. If I'd been punished with radishes, I might give up sooner just to spite the testers.
>
> Now that I think of it, the digestion of all that sugar and fat in the cookies, as opposed to the digestion of roughage from the radishes, might also affect concentration and performance. Maybe the sugar "high" gives students the focus to keep going?

corund, 2014 / Used under license from Shutterstock.com

1-4 SUMMARIZE A TEXT

Writing a summary disciplines you by making you pull only essentials from a reading—the main points, the thread of the argument. By doing so, you create a brief record of the text's contents and exercise your ability to comprehend, analyze, and synthesize.

1-4a Follow These Guidelines for Summary Writing

Writing a summary requires sifting out the least important points, sorting the essential ones to show their relationships, and stating those points in your own words. Follow these guidelines:

1. **Skim first; then read closely.** First, get a sense of the whole, including the main idea and strategies for support. Then read carefully, taking notes as you do.

2. **Capture the text's argument.** Review your notes and annotations, looking for main points and clear connections. State these briefly and clearly, in your own words. Include only what is essential, excluding most examples and details. Don't say simply that the text talks about its subject; tell what it says about that subject.

3. **Test your summary.** Aim to objectively provide the heart of the text; avoid interjecting your own opinions and presence as a writer. Don't confuse an objective summary of a text with a response to it (shown on the left). Check your summary against the original text for accuracy and consistency.

Sample Summary

Below is a student's summary of Dan Heath's "Why Change Is So Hard," on page 5. Note how the summary writer includes only main points and phrases them in her own words. She departs from the precise order of details, but records them accurately.

> In the article "Why Change Is So Hard," Dan Heath argues that people who have trouble changing are not lazy but have simply exhausted their self-control. Heath refers to a study in which

one group of students was asked to eat cookies and not radishes while another group in the same room was asked to eat radishes and not cookies. Afterward, both groups of students were asked to trace an endless geometric design without lifting their pencils. The cookie-only group traced on average 19 minutes before giving up, but the radish-only group traced on average only 8 minutes. They had already used up their self-control. Heath says that any behavioral change requires self-control, an exhaustible resource. Reverting to old behavior is what happens due not to laziness but to exhaustion.

1-5 EFFECTIVELY ANALYZE IMAGES

Images communicate, just as words do. Most images are made to communicate quickly—magazine covers, ads, signs, social-media photos, and so on. Other images require contemplation, such as the Mona Lisa. When you view an image, analyze through careful viewing and interpreting.

1-5a Actively View Images

When you look at an image, follow these steps:

▶ **Survey the image.** See it as a whole, but also study the focal point, the background-foreground relationship, left and right content, and colors.

▶ **Inspect the image.** Examine all the details and the relationships between parts.

▶ **Question the image.** Who created the image, and why? What is the image's subject and message? Who is the intended viewer? In what medium and context does the image appear (e.g., magazine, academic report, Web page)?

▶ **Understand the purpose.** What is this image meant to do? Arouse curiosity? Entertain? Inform? Illustrate a concept? Persuade?

1-5b Actively Interpret Images

Interpreting an image follows naturally from viewing or "reading" the image. Interpreting means figuring out what the image is meant to do, say, or show. Interpreting requires you to think more deeply about each element of the rhetorical situation and complications with each element.

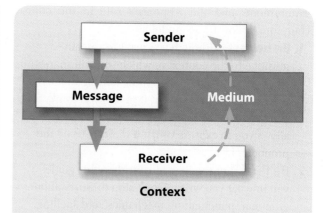

- **Sender:** Who created the image—a photographer, a painter, a Web designer? Why did the person create it? What other people might have been involved—editors, patrons?

  Complications: The sender might be unknown or a group.

- **Message:** What is the subject of the image? How is the subject portrayed? What is the main purpose of the image—to entertain, to inform, to persuade, to entice, to shock?

  Complications: The message might be mixed, implied, ironic, unwelcome, or distorted. The subject might be vague, unfamiliar, complex, or disturbing.

- **Medium:** What is the image—a painting, a cartoon panel, a photo? How might the image have been modified over time? What visual language has the sender used?

  Complications: The medium might be unusual, unfamiliar, or multiple. The visual languages might be literal, stylized, numeric, symbolic, and so on.

- **Receiver:** Whom was the image made for? Are you part of the intended audience? What is your relationship with the sender? Do you agree with the message? How comfortable are you with the medium? What is your overall response to the image?

  Complications: You might be uninterested in, unfamiliar with, or biased toward the message.

- **Context:** What was the context in which the image was first presented? What context surrounds the image now? Does the image fit its context or fight it?

  Complications: The context might be disconnected, ironic, changing, or multilayered.

1-5c Interpret an Image

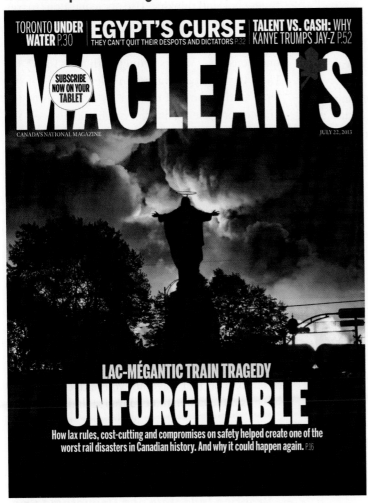

Discussion

This vivid color photograph captures a moment in the unfolding disaster that took place in the small town of Lac Mégantic in the Canadian province of Quebec. On July 6, 2013, a train derailed in the center of the town, resulting in the deaths of 47 people, widespread destruction of property, and environmental damage.

The power of this image is found in both the sharp contrasts and the suggestive symbolism. In the background, the bright yellows and reds of the exploding tanker cars flare up into the sky, throwing everything in the foreground into dark relief. The result is an image that captures something of the destructive force of the night-time explosions, their violence and their extent within the quiet town. The religious symbolism, too, is clear and vivid. The explosions, hellish and deadly in nature and appearance, outline sharply the religious statue. Likely a figure of Christ, the statue—haloed and arms

outstretched to suggest welcome, love, and care—offers both a contrast to the violence behind it and a commentary on the moral failure represented by the tragedy. In a way, the image elevates the events to the level of enduring spiritual concerns about human caring and human destructiveness at war with each other.

Sender: Photographer David Charron, cover designer for *Maclean's*

Message: The cover reads "Unforgiveable" in big, bold letters. The message is that the train derailment, explosions, and fire that killed dozens of people and destroyed the center of Lac Mégantic on July 6, 2013, represent a moral failure, not just an accidental disaster.

Medium: Digital color photograph

Receiver: The intended viewer is anyone who subscribes to the magazine, but also people scanning magazine racks and reading the story online, meaning that the image serves a persuasive purpose along with its message.

Context: As part of the cover, this photograph serves as the first statement about the disaster, a statement that is then followed up by the story within the magazine, a story that reports and analyzes what happened, supplying several more powerful photographs to capture the nature and scope of the disaster.

1-6 THINK CRITICALLY THROUGH WRITING

Reading, viewing, and writing can all be means of critical thinking. In college, you often need to show your ability to think critically about topics and issues by analyzing complex processes, synthesizing concepts, weighing the value of opposing perspectives, and applying principles. To think critically through your writing, practice the strategies that follow.

1-6a Ask Probing Questions

Every field uses questions to trigger critical thinking. For example, scientific questions generate hypotheses, sociological questions lead to studies, mathematical questions call for proofs, and literary criticism questions call for interpretations. A good question opens up a problem and guides you all the way to its solution. But not all questions are created equal. Consider the differences:

- **Rhetorical questions** aren't meant to be answered. They're asked for effect.
  Example: Who would want to be caught in an earthquake?

- **Closed questions** seek a limited response and can be answered with "yes," "no," or a simple fact.
  Example: Would I feel an earthquake measuring 3.0 on the Richter scale?

- **Open questions** invite brainstorming and discussion.
  Example: How might a major earthquake affect this urban area?

- **Theoretical questions** call for organization and explanation of an entire field of knowledge.
  Example: What might cause a sudden fracturing of Earth's crust along fault lines?

To improve the critical thinking in your writing, ask better questions. The strategies that follow will help you think freely, respond to reading, study for a test, or collect your thoughts for an essay.

- ▶ **Ask open questions.** Closed questions sometimes choke off thinking. Use open questions to trigger a flow of ideas.

- ▶ **Ask "educated" questions.** Compare these questions: (A) What's wrong with television? (B) Does the 16.3 percent rise in televised acts of violence during the past three years signal a rising tolerance for violence in the viewing audience? You have a better chance of expanding the "educated" question—question B—into an essay because the question is clearer and suggests debatable issues.

- ▶ **Keep a question journal.** Divide a notebook page or split a computer screen. On one side, write any questions that come to mind about the topic that you want to explore. On the other side, write answers and any thoughts that flow from them.

- ▶ **Write Q & A drafts.** To write a thoughtful first draft, write quickly, then look it over. Turn the main idea into a question and write again, answering your question. For example, if your main idea is that TV viewers watch far more violence than they did 10 years ago, ask *Which viewers? Why?* and *What's the result?* Go on that way until you find a key idea to serve as the main point of your next draft.

FYI For more help with critical-thinking skills, see "Strategies for Argumentation and Persuasion," pages 182–193.

1-6b Practice Inductive and Deductive Logic

Questions invite thinking; reasoning responds to that challenge in an organized way. Will the organization of your thoughts be inductive or deductive? Inductive logic reasons from specific information toward general conclusions. Deductive logic reasons from general principles toward specific applications. Notice in the diagram that inductive reasoning starts with specific details or observations (as shown at the base) and then moves "up" to broader ideas and eventually to a concluding generalization. In contrast, deduction starts with general principles at the top and works down, applying the principles to explain particular instances.

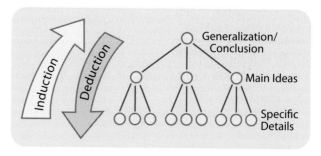

Example

The paragraphs below are an excerpt from "A Fear Born of Sorrow," an editorial that student Anita Brinkman wrote in the days following the 9/11 attacks. The first paragraph works inductively, the second paragraph deductively. Notice how the idea at the end of the first paragraph (the inductive conclusion) leads naturally into the contrasting idea (a deductive principle) at the beginning of the second paragraph.

1
(A) More than 100 people were killed in the tragic bombing of the Oklahoma Federal Building in 1995. About 6,000 die of AIDS in Africa each day. Between 8,000 and 10,000 people worldwide die of starvation daily. Tragedies occur all around us, and we accept them out of necessity as a part of life.

2
(B) But sometimes the horror of a tragedy affects us in a new way: It overwhelms a nation and stuns the international community. This is what happened last week when two hijacked planes hit the Twin Towers of the World Trade Center and their resulting collapse killed thousands of people from several countries. News of the tragedy flashed around the globe. Everywhere, it seemed, people in uncomprehending horror listened to reports on their radios or watched endless replays on their televisions. Several countries declared days of mourning and scheduled services of remembrance. Now, one week after the attack, tokens of grief and letters of condolence still flood U.S. embassies and government offices worldwide. But why is the outpouring of grief so much deeper for this tragedy than for others? Why isn't the attack considered just a large-scale repeat of the Oklahoma bombing? Could it be that our grief is more than sorrow, and that our loss is much more than what lies in the rubble?

(A) Induction: specific details to generalization
(B) Deduction: generalization to specific details

⚙ Critical-Thinking and Writing Activities

1. Northrop Frye has argued that "[n]obody is capable of free speech unless he [or she] knows how to use language, and such knowledge is not a gift: It has to be learned and worked at." How does Frye's claim relate to the discussions of reading, viewing, and writing in this chapter?

2. In a news source (print or online), find a brief article that discusses a recent scientific study (similar to Dan Heath's article on page 5). Read your selected article by practicing the SQ3R method. Then do the following: Map the text, write a response to it, and summarize it. If the article has visual content, view and interpret any images. Finally, generate a list of probing questions and speculative answers related to the article's topic.

3. In a print or digital publication, find an image that is striking. Using the instruction on effectively analyzing images, draft an interpretation of the image.

4. Read three or four articles on a current issue that interests you. Using what you've learned, draft two paragraphs on the issue—one patterned deductively and the other inductively.

STUDY TOOLS 1

LOCATED AT BACK OF THE TEXTBOOK
☐ Tear-Out Chapter Review Card

LOCATED AT WWW.CENGAGE.COM/LOGIN
☐ Chapter eBook

☐ Graded quizzes and a practice quiz generator

☐ Videos: Writer Interviews

☐ Tutorials

☐ Flashcards

☐ Cengage Learning Write Experience

☐ Interactive activities

2 | One Writer's Process

"ESSAYS ARE EXPERIMENTS IN MAKING SENSE OF THINGS."

SCOTT RUSSELL SANDERS

Brian A Jackson, 2014. Used under license from Shutterstock.com

LEARNING OBJECTIVES

2-1 Understand the assignment.

2-2 Explore your topic and plan the writing.

2-3 Write a first draft.

2-4 Revise the draft.

2-5 Seek a reviewer's response.

2-6 Edit the writing for style.

2-7 Edit the writing for correctness.

2-8 Check for documentation and page-design problems.

After you finish this chapter go to PAGE 27 for STUDY TOOLS

An essay is an attempt to understand a topic more deeply and clearly. That's one of the reasons this basic form of writing is essential in many college courses. It's a tool for both discovering and communicating.

How do you move from an assignment to a finished, polished essay? The best strategy is to take matters one step at a time, from understanding the assignment to submitting the final draft. Don't try to churn out the essay the night before it's due.

This chapter shows how student writer Angela Franco followed the writing process outlined in chapters 3 through 8.

2-1 UNDERSTAND THE ASSIGNMENT

In this chapter, you will follow student Angela Franco as she writes an assigned essay for her Environmental Policies class. Start by carefully reading the assignment and discussion below, noting how she thinks through the rhetorical situation.

2-1a Angela Examined the Assignment

Angela carefully read her assignment and responded with the notes.

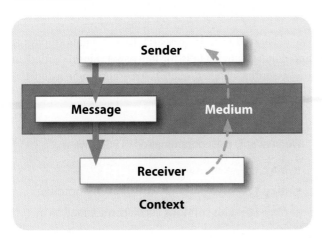

"Explain in a two- to three-page essay how a local environmental issue is relevant to the world community. The issue you examine should be one that has arisen in the last 20 years. Using *COMP* as your guide, format the paper and document sources in APA style, but omit the title page and abstract. You may seek revising help from a classmate or from the writing center."

▶ **Role**
I'm writing as a student in Environmental Policies and as a resident of Ontario.

▶ **Subject**
The subject is a local environmental issue—something that's happened in the last 20 years.

▶ **Purpose**
My purpose is to explain how the issue is relevant to all people. That means I must show how this issue affects my audience—both positively and negatively.

▶ **Form**
I need to write a two- to three-page essay—that sounds formal. This is a serious topic, so my voice should sound knowledgable and academic.

I'll need to include a thesis statement, as well as references to my sources using APA style.

▶ **Audience**
My audience will be people like me—neighbors, classmates, and community members.

I'll need to keep in mind what they already know and what they need to know.

▶ **Context**
I'll use the guidelines and checklists in *COMP* to evaluate and revise my writing.

I'll get editing feedback from Jeanie and from the writing center.

TIP For each step in the writing process, choose strategies that fit your writing situation. For example, a personal essay or response to literature in an English class might require significant time getting started, whereas a lab report in a chemistry or biology class might require little or none.

2-1b Angela Explored Topic Possibilities

Angela explored her assignment and narrowed its focus by clustering and freewriting.

Cluster

When she considered environmental issues, Angela first thought of water pollution as a possible topic for her essay. After writing the phrase in the center of her page, she drew from memories, experiences, and readings to list related ideas and details. Notice how she used three different-colored inks to distinguish the topic (blue) from ideas (red) and details (green).

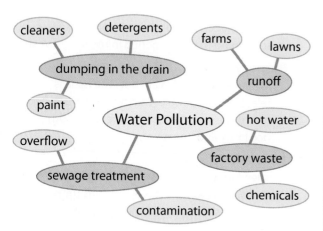

Freewriting

Angela decided to freewrite about the water pollution caused a few years earlier by improper sewage treatment in a small Canadian town.

> I remember reading an article about problems in a small Ontario town about a decade ago. People actually died. The water they drank was contaminated. This is becoming a problem in developed countries like ours. I thought for a long time this was a problem only in developing countries. So who is responsible for sewage treatment? Who guarantees the safety of our drinking water? How does water get contaminated? Are there solutions for every kind of contamination: mercury, PCBs, sewage?

Narrowed Topic

Based on her freewriting, Angela rephrased her assignment to narrow its focus.

> Explain in a two- to three-page essay how a water pollution problem last decade in a small Ontario town is relevant to the world community.

2-2 EXPLORE YOUR TOPIC AND PLAN THE WRITING

Once she had narrowed her topic sufficiently, Angela proceeded to think about the topic more thoroughly and deeply while carefully researching it. That thinking and research prepared her to then plan her essay.

2-2a Angela Explored Her Topic

To explore her topic, Angela used a range of strategies, including reflection and periodic freewriting. As shown below, she also answered the journalistic questions (five W's and H).

Topic: Water pollution in a small Ontario town

Who?	• Farm operators, wastewater officials, Walkerton residents
What?	• Water supply contaminated • Spread bacteria (E. coli) • Caused disease • Clean, fresh water depleted
Where?	• Walkerton, Ontario
When?	• May 2000
Why?	• Improper regulation; human error
How?	• Groundwater from irrigation, untreated sewage, and runoff

2-2b Angela Researched the Topic

Angela also did careful research to understand the topic and collect more details for her paper. She recorded all the essential data on each source and then listed the specific details related to her topic. Here's one source:

> CBC News. (2010, May 17) "Inside Walkerton: Canada's worst ever E. coli contamination." CBC News.
>
> • **May 15**—water sampled
> • **May 17**—first patients with flu-like symptoms
> • **May 18**—Lab confirms E. coli contamination in

water, but Public Utilities Commission (PUC) does not report information.

- **May 19**—Medical Health Office (MHO) discovers E. coli outbreak but is assured by the PUC that the water is safe.
- **May 20**—At least 40 people treated at hospital with bloody diarrhea, but PUC says twice that water is safe.
- **May 21**—MHO tells people not to drink water, runs their own test.
- **May 23**—MHO finds E. coli, learns of May 18 memo and that chlorinator not working for some time.
- **May 24**—Three adults and a baby die of E. coli.

2-2c Angela Decided How to Organize Her Writing

Some assignments specify an organizing pattern in their instructions. Other assignments require writers to choose a pattern that best suits their writing purpose. Common organizational patterns include chronological, logical, spatial, cause-effect, classification, comparison-contrast, and problem-solution. Each pattern serves a different purpose (see pages 53–58).

With her research and thinking in mind, Angela was able to consider a plan for her essay. Specifically, she used the three guidelines below to choose the best organization.

Quick Guide:
Organization Pattern

1. Review your assignment and record your response.

> **Assignment:** Explain in a two- to three-page essay how a local environmental issue is relevant to the world community.
> **Response:** My assignment clearly states that I need to explain my topic, so I have a general idea of how my paper will be organized.

2. Decide on your thesis statement and think about your essay's possible content and organization.

> **Thesis Statement:** The water pollution incident in Walkerton, Ontario, had a devastating effect that every town should learn from.
> **Response:** After reading my thesis statement, it's obvious that I'm going to be writing about a problem and its causes.

3. Choose an overall method and reflect on its potential effectiveness.

> **Response:** Looking at the list of methods, I see that I can use cause/effect or problem/solution. After making two quick lists of my main points using both approaches, I decided to use a problem/solution approach. I will still talk about causes and effects in my essay—they just won't be front and center.

> With problem/solution, I need to first present the problem clearly so that readers can fully understand it and see why it's important. Then I need to explore solutions to the problem—maybe what they did in Walkerton and what we all need to do to make water safe.

 TIP Many essays you write will be organized according to one basic method or approach. However, within that basic structure you may want to include other methods. For example, while developing a comparison essay you may do some describing or classifying. In other words, you should choose methods of development that (1) help you understand the topic and (2) help your readers understand your thinking.

2-3 WRITE A FIRST DRAFT

By composing her opening, middle, and closing paragraphs, Angela put together her first draft. She then added a working title.

chaythawin, 2014 / Used under license from Shutterstock.com

The writer uses a series of images to get the reader's attention.

The thesis statement (red) introduces the subject.

The writer describes the cause of the problem.

The writer indicates some of her source material with a citation.

The writer covers the solutions that were used to resolve the problem.

Water Woes

It's a hot day. Several people just finished mowing their lawns. A group of bicyclists—more than 3,000—have been passing through your picturesque town all afternoon. Dozens of Little Leaguers are batting, running, and sweating. What do all these people have in common? They all drinks lots of tap water, especially on hot summer days. They also take for granted that the water is clean and safe. But in reality, the water they drink could be contaminated and pose a serious health risk. That's just what happened in Walkerton, Ontario, where a water pollution incident had a devastating effect that every town can learn from.

What happened in Walkerton Ontario? Heavy rains fell on May 12. It wasn't until May 21 that the townspeople were advised to boil their drinking water. The rains washed cattle manure into the town well. The manure contained E coli, a type of bacteria. E coli is harmless to cattle. It can make people sick. Seven days after the heavy rains, people began calling public health officials. The warning came too late. Two people had already died ("Inside Walkerton," 2010).

Once Walkerton's problem was identified, the solutions were known. The government acted quickly to help the community and to clean the water supply. One Canadian newspaper reported that a $100,000 emergency fund was set up to help families with expenses. Bottled water for drinking and containers of bleach for sanitizing and cleaning were donated by local businesses.

So what messed up Walkerton? Basically, people screwed up! According to one news story, a flaw in the water treatment system allowed the bacteria-infested water to enter the well. The manure washed into the well, but the chlorine should have killed the deadly bacteria. In Walkerton, the PUC group fell asleep at the wheel.

At last, the Provincial Clean Water Agency restored the main water and sewage systems by flushing out all of the town's pipes and wells. The ban on drinking Walkerton's water was finally lifted seven months after the water became contaminated.

The concluding paragraph stresses the importance of public awareness.

Could any good come from Walkerton's tragedy? Does it have a silver lining? It is possible that more people are aware that water may be contaminated. Today people are beginning to take responsibility for the purity of the water they and their families drink. In the end, more and more people will know about the dangers of contaminated water—without learning it the hard way.

2-3a Angela Kept a Working Bibliography

As she researched her topic, Angela kept a working bibliography—a list of resources that she thought might offer information helpful to her essay. During the writing process, she deleted some resources, added others, and edited the document that became the references page shown on page 27.

The writer creates a working bibliography of APA references.

Working References

CBC News. (2010, May 17). "Inside Walkerton: Canada's worst ever E.coli contamination." CBC News.

Phone interview with Alex Johnson, Walkerton Police Department, 23 September 2014.

Blackwell, Thomas (2001, January 9). Walkerton doctor defends response. *The Edmonton Journal.* http://edmontonjournal.com.

REVISE THE DRAFT

After finishing the first draft, Angela set it aside. When she was ready to revise it, she looked carefully at global issues—ideas, organization, and voice. She wrote notes to herself to help keep her thoughts together.

Angela's Comments

I need to give my opening more energy.

Does my thesis still fit the paper?—Yes.

Using time sequence, put this paragraph in better order.

Move this paragraph—it interrupts the discussion of causes.

Water Woes

It's a hot day. [an unusually] [Saturday afternoon] Several people just finished mowing their lawns. A group of bicyclists—more than 3,000—have been passing through your picturesque town all afternoon. [pedal up the street] Dozens of Little Leaguers are batting, running, and sweating. What do all these people have in common? They all drinks lots of tap water, especially on hot summer days. They also take for granted that the water is clean and safe. But in reality, the water they drink could be contaminated and pose a serious health risk. That's just what happened in Walkerton, Ontario, where a water pollution incident had a devastating effect that every town can learn from.

What happened in Walkerton Ontario? Heavy rains fell on May 12. It wasn't until May 21 that the townspeople were advised to boil their drinking water. The rains washed cattle manure into the town well. The manure contained E coli, a type of bacteria. E coli is harmless to cattle. It can make people sick. Seven days after the heavy rains, people began calling public health officials. The warning came too late. Two people had already died ("Inside Walkerton," 2010).

Once Walkerton's problem was identified, the solutions were known. The government acted quickly to help the community and to clean the water supply. One Canadian newspaper reported that a $100,000 emergency fund was set up to help families with expenses. Bottled water for drinking and containers of bleach for sanitizing and cleaning were donated by local businesses.

My voice here is too informal.

Explain "fell asleep." Move paragraph three here and combine.

Cut the clichés.

So what ~~messed up~~ *went wrong in* Walkerton? ~~Basically, people screwed up!~~ *Human error was a critical factor.*
First, According to one news story, a flaw in the water treatment system allowed the bacteria-infested water to enter the well. *Even after* ~~The~~ the manure washed into the well, ~~but~~ the chlorine should have killed the deadly bacteria. In Walkerton, the ~~PUC group fell asleep at the wheel.~~

~~At last,~~ *In addition* the Provincial Clean Water Agency restored the main water and sewage systems by flushing out all of the town's pipes and wells. The ban on drinking Walkerton's water was finally lifted seven months after the water became contaminated.

Could any good come from Walkerton's tragedy? ~~Does it have a silver lining?~~ It is possible that more people are aware that water may be contaminated. Today people are beginning to take responsibility for the purity of the water they and their families drink. In the end, more and more people will know about the dangers of contaminated water—without learning it the hard way.

Public Utilities Commission was responsible for overseeing the testing and treating of the town's water, but they failed to monitor it properly. Apparently, shortcuts were taken when tracking the water's chlorine level, and as a result, some of the water samples were mislabeled. There was also a significant delay between the time that the contamination was identified and the time it was reported.

2-5 SEEK A REVIEWER'S RESPONSE

Next, Angela asked a peer to review her work. His comments are in the margin. Angela used them to make additional changes, including writing a new opening and closing.

Angela's Changes

Reviewer's Comments

> Could you make the opening more relevant and urgent?

> Could you clarify your focus on the topic?

> Add the year and other specific details.

> Make sure you document all source material—you have just one citation in your draft.

Water Woes

WARNING: City tap water is polluted with animal waste. Using the water for drinking, cooking, or bathing could cause sickness or death.

According to the Seirra Club, run-off pollutants from farm cites are steadily seeping into our streams, lakes, reservoirs and wells. Because much of our drinking water comes from these resources, warnings like the one above are already posted in a number of U.S. and Canadian communities, and many more postings will be needed (Sierra Club, 2013). As the Seirra Club argues, the pollution and related warnings are serious, and failure to take them seriously could be deadly. For example, a few years ago the citizens of Walkerton Ontario learned that the water that they believed to be clean was actually poisoned.

The events began
~~What happened~~ in Walkerton, ~~Ontario? Heavy rains fell~~ on May , 2000, when heavy rains
12. ~~The rains~~ washed cattle manure into the town well. The manure contained E coli, a type of bacteria. E coli is harmless to cattle.

It can make people sick. Seven days after the heavy rains, people
to complain of nausea and diarrhea
began calling public health officials. It wasn't until May 21 that the townspeople were advised to boil their drinking water. The warning
and more than 2,000 were ill
came too late. Two people had already died, ("Inside Walkerton," 2010).
Several factors contributed to the terrible tragedy in Walkerton,
~~So what went wrong in Walkerton? Human error was a critical~~
including human error. The Edmonton Journal
~~factor.~~ First, according to ~~one news story,~~ a flaw in the water treatment
(Blackwell, 2001)
system allowed the bacteria-infested water to enter the well. Even after the manure washed into the well, the chlorine should have killed

Monkey Business Images, 2014 / Used under license from Shutterstock.com

the deadly bacteria. In Walkerton, the Public Utilities Commission was responsible for overseeing the testing and treating of the town's water, but it failed to monitor it properly. Apparently, shortcuts were taken when tracking the water's chlorine level, and as a result, some of the water samples were mislabeled. There was also a significant delay between the time that the contamination was identified and the time it was reported.

Use active voice.

Once Walkerton's problem was identified, ~~the solutions were known.~~ The government acted quickly to help the community~~, and to clean the~~ The Edmonton Journal ~~water supply. One Canadian newspaper~~ reported a $100,000 emergency fund was set up to help families with expenses. Local businesses donated ~~B~~ottled water for drinking and containers of bleach for basic sanitizing and cleaning ~~were~~ ~~donated by local businesses.~~ In addition, the Provincial Clean Water Agency restored the main water and sewage systems by flushing out all of the town's pipes and wells. The ban on drinking Walkerton's water was finally lifted seven months after the water became contaminated.

Consider adding details—maybe an entire paragraph—calling readers to action, and stating your thesis clearly.

As the Sierra Club warned and the citizens of Walkerton learned, water purity is a life-and-death issue. Fortunately, both the United States and Canada have been addressing the problem. For example, since 2001, more states and provinces are tightening their clean-water standards, more communities have begun monitoring their water quality, and more individuals have been using water-filtration systems, bottled water, or boiled tap water. However, a tragedy like that in Walkerton could happen again. To avoid such horror, all of us must get involved by demanding clean tap water in our communities and by promoting the polices and procedures needed to achieve that goal.

EDIT THE WRITING FOR STYLE

When Angela began editing, she read each of her sentences aloud to check for clarity and smoothness. The first page of Angela's edited copy is shown below.

The writer revises the title.

in Walkerton
Water Woes∧

> **Warning:** City tap water is polluted with animal waste. Using the water for drinking, cooking, or bathing could cause sickness or death.

According to the Seirra Club, run-off pollutants from farm cites are steadily seeping into our streams, lakes, reservoirs∧and wells. Because much of our drinking water comes from these resources, warnings like the one above are already posted in a number of U.S.

She qualifies her statement, replacing "will" with "might."

and Canadian communities, and many more postings ~~will~~ be needed (Sierra Club, 2013). As the Seirra Club argues, the pollution and related warnings are serious, and failure to take them seriously could be deadly. For example, a few years ago the citizens of Walkerton Ontario learned that the water that they believed to be clean was

tragically∧
∧~~actually~~ poisoned.

She rewrites and combines several choppy sentences.

The events in Walkerton began on May 12, 2000, when heavy rains washed cattle manure into the town well. The manure contained

commonly called   While E coli
~~E coli.~~ a bacteria∧E col∧is harmless to cattle∧It can make people sick.

Seven days after the heavy rains, people began calling public health officials to complain of nausea and diarrhea. It wasn't until May 21 that the townspeople were advised to boil their drinking water. The warning came too late. Two people had already died, and more than 2,000 were ill ("Inside Walkerton," 2010).

Angela deletes unnecessary words.

Several factors contributed to the ~~terrible~~ tragedy in Walkerton, including human error. First, according to The Edmonton Journal, a flaw in the water treatment ~~system~~ allowed the bacteria-infested water to enter the well (Blackwell, 2001). Even after the manure washed into the well, the chlorine . . .

EDIT THE WRITING FOR CORRECTNESS

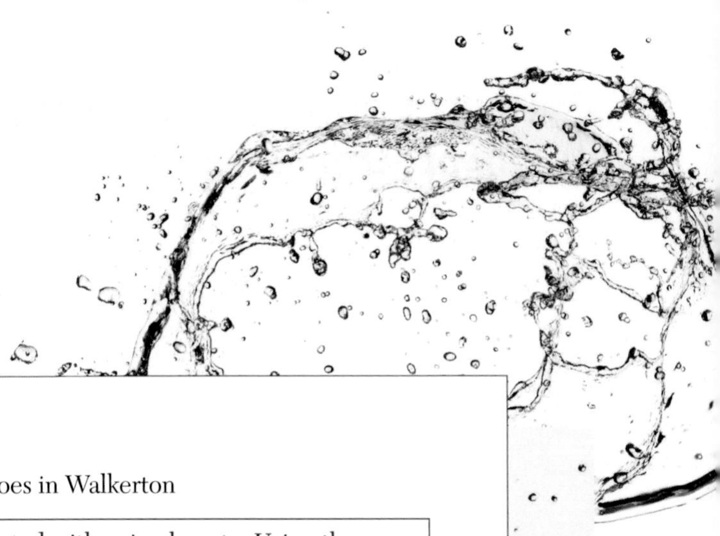

Angela reviewed her edited copy for punctuation, agreement issues, and spelling. The first page of Angela's proofread essay is shown below.

Jag_cz, 2014 / Used under license from Shutterstock.com

The writer corrects errors that the spell checker did not pick up.

She adds a comma between the city and province.

She adds periods and italicizes "E. coli" to show that it is a scientific term.

She adds a word for clarity.

Water Woes in Walkerton

Warning: City tap water is polluted with animal waste. Using the water for drinking, cooking, or bathing could cause sickness or death.

According to the Sierra Club, run-off pollutants from farm sites are steadily seeping into our streams, lakes, reservoirs, and wells. Because much of our drinking water comes from these resources, warnings like the one above are already posted in a number of U.S. and Canadian communities, and many more postings might be needed in the future (Sierra Club, 2013). As the Sierra Club argues, the pollution and related warnings are serious, and failure to take them seriously could be deadly. For example, a few years ago the citizens of Walkerton, Ontario, learned that the water that they believed to be clean was tragically poisoned.

The events in Walkerton began on May 12, 2000, when heavy rains washed cattle manure into the town well. The manure contained bacteria commonly called E. coli. While E. coli is harmless to cattle, it can make people sick. Seven days after the heavy rains, people began calling public health officials to complain of nausea and diarrhea. It wasn't until May 21 that the townspeople were advised to boil their drinking water. The warning came too late. Two people had already died, and more than 2,000 were ill ("Inside Walkerton," 2010).

Several factors contributed to the tragedy in Walkerton, including human error. First, according to The Edmonton Journal, a flaw in the water treatment system allowed the bacteria-infested water to enter Walkerton's the well (Blackwell, 2001). Even after the manure washed into the well, the chlorine should have . . .

2-8 CHECK FOR DOCUMENTATION AND PAGE-DESIGN PROBLEMS

After proofreading and formatting her essay, Angela added a heading and page numbers. She also added more documentation and a references page at the end. As assigned, she omitted the title page and abstract.

The writer revises the title.

The warning is emphasized with red print.

An appropriate font and type size are used.

Running Head: Clean Water Is Everyone's Business   1

Angela Franco

Professor Kim Van Es

Environmental Policies 105

October 18, 2014

Clean Water Is Everyone's Business

> **Warning:** City tap water is polluted with animal waste.
> Using the water for drinking, cooking, or bathing could
> cause sickness or death.

According to the Sierra Club, run-off pollutants from farm sites are steadily seeping into our streams, lakes, reservoirs, and wells. Because much of our drinking water comes from these resources, warnings like the one above are already posted in a number of U.S. and Canadian communities, and many more postings might be needed in the future (Sierra Club, 2013). As the Sierra Club argues, the pollution and related warnings are serious, and failure to take them seriously could be deadly. For example, a few years ago the citizens of Walkerton, Ontario, learned that the water that they believed to be clean was tragically poisoned.

The events in Walkerton began on May 12, 2000, when heavy rains washed cattle manure into the town well. The manure contained bacteria commonly called E. coli. While E. coli is harmless to cattle, it

Title and page number are used on each page.

can make people sick. Seven days after the heavy rains, people began calling public health officials to complain of nausea and diarrhea. It wasn't until May 21 that the townspeople were advised to boil their drinking water. The warning came too late. Two people had already died, and more than 2,000 were ill ("Inside Walkerton," 2010).

Each claim or supporting point is backed up with reasoning and evidence.

Several factors contributed to the tragedy in Walkerton, including human error. First, according to the *Edmonton Journal*, a flaw in the water treatment system allowed the bacteria-infested water to enter Walkerton's well (Blackwell, 2001). Even after the manure washed into the well, the chlorine should have killed the deadly bacteria. In Walkerton, the Public Utilities Commission was responsible for overseeing the testing and treating of the town's water, but it failed to monitor the procedure properly ("Walkerton's water-safety," 2000). Apparently, shortcuts were taken when tracking the water's chlorine level, and as a result, some of the water samples were mislabeled. There was also a significant delay between the time that the contamination was identified and the time it was reported.

The writer continues to give credit throughout the essay.

Once Walkerton's problem was identified, the government acted quickly to help the community. In its December 7, 2000, edition, the *Edmonton Journal* reported that a $100,000 emergency fund was set up to help families with expenses. Local businesses donated bottled water for drinking and containers of bleach for basic sanitizing and cleaning. In addition, the Provincial Clean Water Agency restored the main water and sewage systems by flushing out all of the town's pipes and wells. Seven months after the water became contaminated, the ban on drinking Walkerton's water was finally lifted.

As the Sierra Club warns and the citizens of Walkerton learned, water purity is a life-and-death issue. Fortunately, both the United States and Canada have been addressing the problem. For example, since 2001, more states and provinces have been tightening their clean-water standards, more communities have been monitoring their water quality, and more individuals have been using water-filtration systems, bottled water, or boiled tap water. However, a tragedy like that in Walkerton could happen again. To avoid such horror, all of us must get involved by demanding clean tap water in our communities and by promoting the policies and procedures needed to achieve that goal.

> The writer restates her thesis in the last sentence.

 ## Cross-Curricular Connections

Angela used APA style, which is standard for the social sciences: psychology, sociology, political science, and education. MLA style is standard for English and some humanities. Make sure to find out what documentation style your instructor requires. For more on documentation systems, see pages 288–321.

 ## Critical-Thinking and Writing Activities

1. Scott Russell Sanders suggests that "essays are experiments in making sense of things." Does Sanders' statement ring true? What makes such experiments fail or succeed? What kinds of "sense" do essays create?

2. Review Angela's writing process. How does it compare with your own writing process on a recent assignment?

3. Review the peer-editing instructions in "Revising Collaboratively" (pages 72–73). Then reread the reviewer's comments in the margins of Angela's second revision (pages 20–21). Do the comments reflect the instructions? Explain.

Running Head: Clean Water Is Everyone's Business   4

References

Blackwell, T. (2001, January 9). Walkerton doctor defends response. *Edmonton Journal.* Retrieved September 22, 2014, from <http://edmontonjournal.com>.

Inside Walkerton: Canada's worst ever E.coli contamination. (2010, May 17). CBC News. Retrieved September 14, 2014, from http://www.cbc.ca/news/canada/inside-walkerton-canada-s-worst-ever-e-coli-contamination-1.887200

Sierra Club. (2005) Water sentinels: Keeping it clean around the U.S.A. Retrieved September 24, 2014, from <http://sierraclub.org/watersentinels/>.

Walkerton's water-safety tests falsified regularly, utility official admits. (2000, December 7). *Edmonton Journal.* Retrieved April 2, 2014, from <http://edmontonjournal.com>.

Wickens, B. (2000, June 5). Tragedy in Walkerton. *Maclean's, 113*(23), 34–36.

STUDY TOOLS 2

LOCATED AT BACK OF THE TEXTBOOK
☐ Tear-Out Chapter Review Card

LOCATED AT WWW.CENGAGEBRAIN.COM/LOGIN
☐ Chapter eBook
☐ Graded quizzes and a practice quiz generator
☐ Videos: Writer Interviews
☐ Tutorials
☐ Flashcards
☐ Cengage Learning Write Experience
☐ Interactive activities

3 | Starting

> "I THINK I DID PRETTY WELL, CONSIDERING I STARTED OUT WITH NOTHING BUT A BUNCH OF BLANK PAPER."
>
> STEVE MARTIN

Evgeny Atamanenko, 2014 / Used under license from Shutterstock.com

LEARNING OBJECTIVES

3-1 Discover your process.

3-2 Understand the rhetorical situation.

3-3 Understand the assignment.

3-4 Select, limit, and explore your topic.

3-5 Research your topic.

After you finish
this chapter
go to
PAGE 38 for STUDY TOOLS

The blank page or screen can be daunting for any writer. That's because writing doesn't go from nothing to a masterpiece in one step. Writing is a process, much like painting.

The aim of the writing process is discovery—along the way and in the finished text, both for the writer and for the reader. As Peter Stillman argues, "Writing is the most powerful means of discovery available to all of us throughout life." Discovery happens when you give ample time to each step, and when you follow strategies that encourage your thinking to deepen and your writing to sharpen.

This chapter introduces the writing process and then focuses on getting started on any writing project through prewriting. It provides numerous concrete strategies for understanding writing assignments, deciding on a topic, and exploring it. The very act of writing generates ideas and creates new connections that will make it easy to fill the blank page.

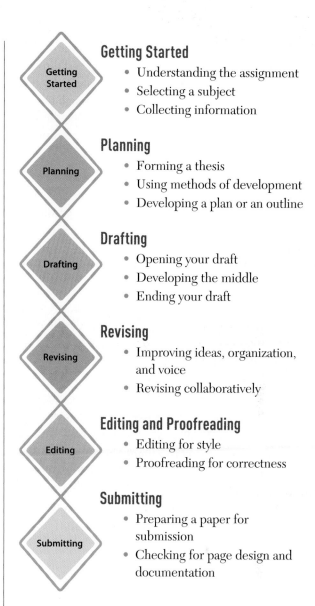

Getting Started
- Understanding the assignment
- Selecting a subject
- Collecting information

Planning
- Forming a thesis
- Using methods of development
- Developing a plan or an outline

Drafting
- Opening your draft
- Developing the middle
- Ending your draft

Revising
- Improving ideas, organization, and voice
- Revising collaboratively

Editing and Proofreading
- Editing for style
- Proofreading for correctness

Submitting
- Preparing a paper for submission
- Checking for page design and documentation

3-1 DISCOVER YOUR PROCESS

It's easy to feel overwhelmed by a writing project—especially if the form of writing is new to you, the topic is complex, or the paper must be long. However, using the writing *process* will relieve some of that pressure by breaking down the task into manageable steps. An overview of those steps is shown in the flow chart in the next column, followed by key principles.

3-1a Consider the Writing Process

The flowchart maps out the basic steps in the writing process. As you work on your writing project, periodically review this diagram to keep yourself on task.

3-1b Adapt the Process to Your Project

The writing process shown in the flow chart is flexible, not rigid. As a writer, you need to adapt the process to your situation and assignment. To do so, consider these essential principles.

▶ **Writing tends not to follow a straight path.** While writing begins with an assignment or a need and ends with a reader, the journey in between is often indirect. The steps in the writing process are recursive, meaning you will sometimes move back and forth between them. For example, during the revision phase, you may discover that you need to draft a new paragraph or do more research.

- **Each assignment presents distinct challenges.** A personal essay may develop best through clustering or freewriting; a literary analysis through close reading of a story; a lab report through the experimental method; and a position paper through reading of books and journal articles, as well as through careful and balanced reasoning.

- **Writing can involve collaboration.** From using your roommate as a sounding board for your topic choice to working with a group to produce a major report, college writing is not solitary writing. In fact, many colleges have a writing center to help you refine your writing assignments. (See page 74 for more.)

- **Each writer works differently.** Some writers do extensive prewriting before drafting, while others do not. You might develop a detailed outline, whereas someone else might draft a brief list of topics. Experiment with the strategies introduced in chapters 3–8, adopting those that help you.

- **Good writing can't be rushed.** Although some students regard pulling an all-nighter as a badge of honor, good writing takes time. A steady, disciplined approach will generally produce the best results. For example, by brainstorming or reading early in a project, you stimulate your subconscious mind to mull over issues, identify problems, and project solutions—even while your conscious mind is working on other things. Similarly, completing a first draft early enough gives you time to revise objectively.

- **Different steps call for attention to different writing issues.** As you use the writing process, at each stage keep your focus where it belongs:

  1. While getting started, planning, and drafting, focus on global issues: ideas, structure, voice, format, and design.

  2. During revising, fix big content problems by cutting, adding, and thoroughly reworking material. (Our experience is that students benefit the most from revising—but spend the least time doing it!)

  3. While editing and proofreading, pay attention to small, local issues—word choice, sentence smoothness, and grammatical correctness. Worrying about these issues early in the writing process interrupts the flow of drafting and wastes time on material that later may be deleted.

UNDERSTAND THE RHETORICAL SITUATION

Rhetoric is the art of using language effectively. As Aristotle, Quintilian, and others have explained, your language is effective when all aspects of your message fit the rhetorical situation:

Rhetorical Situation

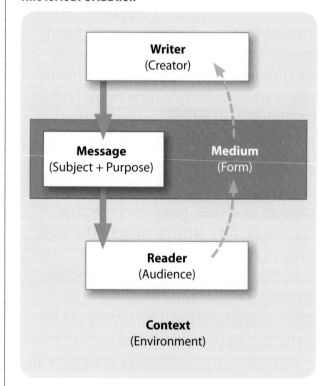

3-2a Think of Your Role as the Writer

Are you writing as a concerned citizen, as a student in a class, as a friend relating a story, as a reporter providing news, as a blogger giving an opinion? Your role in writing and otherwise communicating affects the level of language you use, the voice you use, the types of details you include, and so on.

3-2b Understand Your Subject

To truly understand your subject, you need to gather and assimilate all relevant details about it, including its history, makeup, function, and impact on people and culture. Knowing those details will help you narrow your focus to a specific thesis and support it well.

3-2c Understand Your Purpose

Key words in an assignment—such as *analyze, explain, defend,* or *describe*—tell you what the purpose of the writing is supposed to be. Understanding why you are writing helps you choose an organizational strategy, such as classification, definition, or process. (See the "Key Words" list at the bottom of this page and on page 32.)

3-2d Understand Your Audience

For any writing task, you must understand your audience in order to develop writing that meets their needs. To assess your audience, answer questions like these:

- Who are my readers: instructor? classmates? Web users?
- What do they know about my topic, and what do they need to know?
- How well do they understand the terminology involved?
- What are their attitudes toward the topic and toward me?
- How well do they read written English—or visuals such as graphs and charts?
- How will they use my writing (as entertainment or to complete a task)?

Note: Answers to such questions will help you develop meaningful sentences (pages 78–82), choose appropriate words (pages 82–86), and select relevant visuals.

3-2e Understand the Medium (Form)

Many communication options are available for every message. Academic forms include essays, analyses, reports, proposals, research papers, reviews, and so on. It is important to understand the form of the assignment. What works well in a narrative about a past experience would not work as well in a lab report. Also, each of these forms can contain multiple media: written elements, graphics, photos, drawings, videos, audios, links, and so on. Understanding the overall medium and the media within it will help you succeed.

3-2f Think About the Context

Think about how this assignment relates to others in the course. Consider these issues:

- **Weight:** Is this an everyday assignment, a weekly or biweekly one, or the big one?
- **Assessment:** Find out how the assignment will

be graded. What rubric will be used?
- **Intent:** Make certain that you understand the goals of the assignment and understand what your instructor wants you to get out of it.

Note: If the writing you are doing is not in response to an assignment, think about the environment in which the message will be read. What is the history of this issue? What is the current climate like? What might the future be?

3-3 UNDERSTAND THE ASSIGNMENT

Each college instructor has a way of personalizing a writing assignment, but most assignments will spell out (1) the objective, (2) the task, (3) the formal requirements, and (4) suggested approaches and topics. Your first step, therefore, is to read the assignment carefully, noting the options and restrictions that are part of it. The suggestions below will help you do that. (Also see pages 12–27 for one writer's approach.)

3-3a Read the Assignment

Certain words in the assignment explain what main action you must perform. Here are some words that signal what you are to do:

Key Words

Analyze:	Break down a topic into subparts, showing how those parts relate.
Argue:	Defend a claim with logical arguments.
Classify:	Divide a large group into well-defined subgroups.
Compare/contrast:	Point out similarities and/or differences.
Define:	Give a clear, thoughtful definition or meaning of something.

alphaspirit, 2014 / Used under license from Shutterstock.com

Describe:	Show in detail what something is like.
Evaluate:	Weigh the truth, quality, or usefulness of something.
Explain:	Give reasons, list steps, or discuss the causes of something.
Interpret:	Tell in your own words what something means.
Reflect:	Share your well-considered thoughts about a subject.
Summarize:	Restate someone else's ideas very briefly in your own words.
Synthesize:	Connect facts or ideas to create something new.

Options and Restrictions

The assignment often gives you some choice of your topic or approach but may restrict your options to suit the instructor's purpose. Note the options and restrictions in the following short sample assignment:

Reflect on the way a natural disaster or major historical event has altered your understanding of the past, the present, or the future.

Options:	1.	You may choose any natural disaster or historical event.
	2.	You may focus on the past, present, or future.
	3.	You may examine any kind of alteration.
Restrictions:	1.	You must reflect on a change in your understanding.
	2.	The disaster must be natural.
	3.	The historical event must be major.

3-3b Relate the Assignment to the Goals of the Course

1. How much value does the instructor give the assignment? (The value is often expressed as a percentage of the course grade.)

2. What benefit does your instructor want you to receive?
   - Strengthen your comprehension?
   - Improve your research skills?

- Deepen your ability to explain, prove, or persuade?
- Expand your style?
- Increase your creativity?

3. How will this assignment contribute to your overall performance in the course? What course goals (often listed in the syllabus) does it address?

3-3c Relate the Assignment to Other Assignments

1. Does it build on previous assignments?
2. Does it prepare you for the next assignment?

3-3d Relate the Assignment to Your Own Interests

1. Does it connect with a topic that already interests you?
2. Does it connect with work in your other courses?
3. Does it connect with the work you may do in your chosen field?
4. Does it connect with life outside school?

3-3e Reflect on the Assignment

1. **First impulses:** How did you feel when you first read the assignment?

2. **Approaches:** What's the usual approach for an assignment like this? What's a better way of tackling it?

3. **Quality of performance:** What would it take to produce an excellent piece of writing?

4. **Benefits:** What are the benefits to your education? to you personally? to the class? to society?

5. **Features:** Reflect further on four key features of any writing assignment.

   Purpose: What is the overall purpose of the assignment—to inform, to explain, to analyze, to entertain? What is the desired outcome?

   Audience: Should you address your instructor? your classmates? a general reader? How much does the reader already know about the topic? What type of language should you use?

   Form: What are the requirements concerning length, format, and due date?

   Assessment: How will the assignment be evaluated? How can you be sure that you are completing the assignment correctly?

3-4 SELECT, LIMIT, AND EXPLORE YOUR TOPIC

For some assignments, finding a suitable subject (or topic) may require little thinking on your part. If an instructor asks you to summarize an article in a professional journal, you know what you will write about—the article in question. But suppose the instructor asks you to analyze a feature of popular culture in terms of its impact on society. You won't be sure of a specific writing topic until you explore the possibilities. Keep the following points in mind when you conduct a topic search. Your topic must . . .

- meet the requirements of the assignment.
- be limited in scope.
- seem reasonable (that is, be within your means to research).
- genuinely interest you.

3-4a Limit the Subject Area

Many of your writing assignments may relate to general subject areas you are currently studying. Your task, then, is to select a specific topic related to the general area of study—a topic limited enough that you can treat it with some depth in the length allowed for the assignment. The following examples show the difference between general subjects and limited topics:

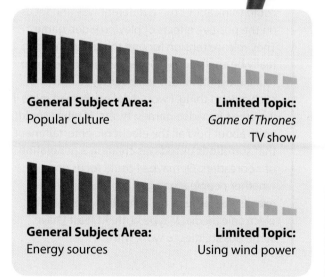

General Subject Area:
Popular culture

Limited Topic:
Game of Thrones TV show

General Subject Area:
Energy sources

Limited Topic:
Using wind power

3-4b Conduct a Search for Ideas

Finding a writing idea that meets the requirements of the assignment should not be difficult if you know how and where to look. Follow these steps:

1. Check your class notes and handouts for ideas related to the assignment.
2. Search the Internet. Type in a keyword or phrase (the general subject stated in the assignment) and mine the results. You could also follow a subject tree to narrow a subject. (See pages 250–252.)
3. Consult indexes, guides, and other library references. For example, subscription databases list current articles published on specific topics and indicate where to find them. (See pages 246–247.)
4. Discuss the assignment with your instructor or an information specialist such as a reference librarian.
5. Use one or more of the prewriting strategies described on the following pages to generate possible writing ideas.

3-4c Explore Possible Topics

You can generate possible writing ideas by using the following strategies. These same strategies can be used when you've chosen a topic and want to develop it further.

Journal Writing

Write in a journal on a regular basis. Reflect on your personal feelings, develop your thoughts, and record the happenings of each day. Periodically go back and underline ideas that you would like to explore in writing assignments. In the following journal-writing sample, the writer came up with an idea for a writing assignment about the societal impacts of popular culture.

> I read a really disturbing news story this morning. I've been thinking about it all day. In California a little girl was killed when she was struck by a car driven by a man distracted by a billboard ad for lingerie featuring a scantily clothed woman. Not only is it a horrifying thing to happen, but it also seems to me all too symbolic of the way that sexually charged images in the media are putting children, and especially girls, in danger. That reminds me of another news story I read this week about

preteen girls wanting to wear the kinds of revealing outfits that they see in music videos, TV shows, and magazines aimed at teenagers. Too many of today's media images give young people the impression that sexuality should begin at an early age. This is definitely a dangerous message.

Freewriting

Freewriting is the writing you do without having a specific outcome in mind. You simply write down whatever pops into your head as you explore your topic. Freewriting can serve as a starting point for your writing, or it can be combined with any of the other prewriting strategies to help you select, explore, focus, or organize your writing. If you get stuck at any point during the composing process, you can return to freewriting as a way of generating new ideas.

Review the following information about freewriting, including key reminders, steps in the process, and results. Then read the freewriting sample on popular culture.

Reminders

- **Freewriting helps you get your thoughts down on paper.** (Thoughts are constantly passing through your mind.)
- **Freewriting helps you develop and organize these thoughts.**
- **Freewriting helps you make sense of things** that you may be studying or researching.
- **Freewriting may seem awkward at times,** but just stick with it.

The Process

- **Write nonstop and record whatever comes into your mind.** Follow your thoughts instead of trying to direct them.

- **If you have a particular topic or assignment to complete, use it as a starting point.** Otherwise, begin with anything that comes to mind.
- **Don't stop to judge, edit, or correct your writing;** that will come later.
- **Keep writing even when you think you have exhausted all of your ideas.** Switch to another angle or voice, but keep writing.
- **Watch for a promising writing idea to emerge.** Learn to recognize the beginnings of a good idea, and then expand that idea by recording as many specific details as possible.

The Result

- **Review your writing and underline the ideas you like.** These ideas will often serve as the basis for future writings.
- **Determine exactly what you need to write about.** Once you've figured out what you are required to do, you may then decide to do a second freewriting exercise.
- **Listen to and read the freewriting of others;** learn from your peers.

Popular culture. What does that include? Television obviously but that's a pretty boring subject. What else? Movies, pop music, YouTube, video games. Is there a connection between playing violent video games and acting out violent behavior? Most video players I know would say no but sometimes news reports suggest a connection. Is this something I'd want to write about? Not really. What then? Maybe I could think about this a different way and focus on the positive effects of playing video games. They release tension for one thing and they can really be challenging. Other benefits? They help to kill time, that's for sure, but maybe that's not such a good thing. I would definitely read more if it weren't for video games, tv, etc. Maybe I could write about how all the electronic entertainment that surrounds us today is creating a generation of nonreaders. Or maybe I could focus on whether people aren't getting much physical exercise because of the time they spend with electronic media. Maybe both. At least I have some possibilities to work with.

Listing

Freely list ideas as they come to mind, beginning with a key concept related to the assignment. (Brainstorming— listing ideas in conjunction with members of a group—is often an effective way to extend your lists.) The following is an example of a student's list of ideas for possible topics on the subject of news reporting:

Aspect of popular culture: News reporting

- Sensationalism
- Sound bites rather than in-depth analysis
- Focus on the negative
- Shock radio
- Shouting matches pretending to be debates
- Press leaks that damage national security, etc.
- Lack of observation of people's privacy
- Bias
- Contradictory health news confusing to readers
- Little focus on "unappealing" issues like poverty
- Acclaim of "celebrity"
- Online news and "filter bubbles"

Clustering

To begin the clustering process, write a key word or phrase related to the assignment in the center of your paper. Circle it, and then cluster ideas around it. Circle each idea as you record it, and draw a line connecting it to the closest related idea. Keep going until you run out of ideas and connections. The following is a student's cluster on the subject of sports:

 After four or five minutes of listing or clustering, scan your work for an idea to explore through freewriting. A writing idea should begin to emerge during this freewriting session.

3-5 RESEARCH YOUR TOPIC

Writer and instructor Donald Murray said that "writers write with information. If there is no information, there will be no effective writing." How true! Before you can develop a thoughtful piece of writing, you must gain a thorough understanding of your topic; to do so, you must carry out the necessary reading, reflecting, and researching. Writing becomes a satisfying experience once you can speak with authority about your topic. Use the guidelines that follow when you start collecting information. (Also see "Research and Writing" in this book.)

3-5a Find Out What You Already Know

Use one or more of the following strategies to determine what you already know about a writing topic.

1. **Focused freewriting:** At this point, you can focus your freewriting by (1) exploring your limited topic from different angles or (2) approaching your freewriting as if it were a quick draft of the actual paper. A quick version will tell you how much you know about your topic and what you need to find out.

2. **Clustering:** Try clustering with your topic serving as the nucleus word. Your clustering should focus on what you already know.

3. **Five W's of writing:** Answer the five W's— *Who? What? When? Where?* and *Why?*—to identify basic information on your subject. Add *How?* to the list for better coverage.

4. **Directed writing:** Write whatever comes to mind about your topic, using one of the modes listed on the next page.

Repeat the directed writing process as often as you need to, selecting a different mode each time.

- **Describe it:** What do you see, hear, feel, smell, and taste?
- **Compare it:** What is it similar to? What is it different from?
- **Associate it:** What connections between this topic and others come to mind?
- **Analyze it:** What parts does it have? How do they work together?
- **Argue it:** What do you like about the topic? What do you not like about it? What are its strengths and weaknesses? What's your position on it, and why?
- **Apply it:** What can you do with it? How can you use it?

3-5b Ask Questions

To guide your collecting and researching, you may find it helpful to list questions about your topic that you would like to answer. Alternatively, you can refer to the questions below. These questions address problems, policies, and concepts. Most topics will fall under one of these categories. Use those questions that seem helpful as a guide to your research.

3-5c Identify Possible Sources

Finding meaningful sources is one of the most important steps you will take as you prepare to write. Listed below are tips that will help you identify good sources:

1. **Give yourself enough time.** Finding good sources of information may be time-consuming. Books and periodicals you need may be checked out, your computer service may be down, and so on.
2. **Know where to find information.** While the Internet often provides a good starting point for doing research, your school or public library also contains many useful research resources, including scholarly books, journals, and periodicals. In addition, many libraries store primary documents.
3. **Be aware of the limits of your resources.** Print material may be out of date. Online information may be more current, but it may not always be reliable. (See pages 259–261 for ways to help you evaluate information.)

	Problems	Policies	Concepts
Description	What is the problem? What type of problem is it? What are its parts? What are the signs of the problem?	What is the policy? How broad is it? What are its parts? What are its most important features?	What is the concept? What are its parts? What is its main feature? Whom or what is it related to?
Function	Who or what is affected by it? What new problems might it cause in the future?	What is the policy designed to do? What is needed to make it work? What are or will be its effects?	Who has been influenced by this concept? Why is it important? How does it work?
History	What is the current status of the problem? What or who caused it? What or who contributed to it?	What brought about this policy? What are the alternatives?	When did it originate? How has it changed over the years? How might it change in the future?
Value	What is its significance? Why? Why is it more (or less) important than other problems? What does it symbolize or illustrate?	Is the policy workable? What are its advantages and disadvantages? Is it practical? Is it a good policy? Why or why not?	What practical value does it have? Why is it superior (or inferior) to similar concepts? What is its social worth?

4. **Use your existing resources to find additional sources of information.** Pay attention to books, articles, and individuals mentioned in reliable initial sources of information.

5. **Ask for help.** The specialists in your school library can help you find information that is reliable and relevant. These people are trained to find information; don't hesitate to ask for their help. (See page 243.)

6. **Bookmark useful Web sites.** Include reference works and academic resources related to your major.

Explore Different Sources of Information

Of course, books and Web sites are not the only possible sources of information. Primary sources such as interviews, observations, and surveys may lead you to a more thorough and meaningful understanding of a topic. (See pages 240–242.)

1	**2**
Primary Sources	**Secondary Sources**
Interviews	News articles
Observations	Academic journals
Participation	Reference book entries
Surveys	Books
Original documents	Web sites
Original artifacts	Databases

Carry Out Your Research

As you conduct your research, try to use a variety of reliable sources. It's also a good idea to choose an efficient note-taking method before you start. You will want to take good notes on the information you find and record all the publishing information necessary for citing your sources. (See pages 262–264.)

Reserve a special part of a notebook to question, evaluate, and reflect on your research as it develops. The record of your thoughts and actions created during this process will mean a great deal to you—as much as or more than the actual information you uncover. Reflection helps you make sense of new ideas, refocus your thinking, and evaluate your progress.

WRITING WITH SOURCES

Many of your writing assignments will challenge you to do good research and to work well with the sources you find. While chapters 20–24 offer a full treatment of research writing, the material below explains how to address source-related issues linked to each step in the writing process.

For example, at the getting-started phase, you should think through broad source-use issues like these:

1. Which types of research does my assignment require?
2. Which types of research would help me explore my topic?
3. Which record-keeping and note-taking strategies would help me use source information effectively and avoid plagiarism?

Think Rhetorically

To help you resolve questions like those above, remember the rhetorical situation behind your project:

- Given the **subject** of your writing, what sources of information would offer reliable, relevant information? (See "Consider Possible Information Resources and Sites," page 235.) In your assignment, what types of sources are recommended or expected? What sources should be avoided?

- Given your **audience**, what types of sources will readers understand and respect? What sources will add to your credibility?

- Given your **purpose** (to entertain, inform, analyze, or persuade), what information will help you achieve that goal, and which types of sources contain those details?

Track Resources in a Working Bibliography

A working bibliography lists sources that you have used or intend to use. Once you find a useful book, journal article, news story, or Web page, record identifying information for the source on note cards, a designated notebook, or a computer. For more help, see page 261.

Use a Note-Taking System That Respects Sources

Essentially, your note-taking system should help you keep an accurate record of useful information and ideas from sources while also allowing you to engage those sources with your own thinking. For a discussion of possible systems, see pages 262–264.

Distinguish Summaries, Paraphrases, and Quotations

As you read sources, you will find material that answers your questions and helps you achieve your writing purpose. At that point, decide whether to summarize, paraphrase, or quote the material:

- A **summary** pulls just the main points out of a passage and puts them in your own words: Summarize source material when it contains relevant ideas and information that you can boil down.
- A **paraphrase** rewrites a passage point by point in your own words: Paraphrase source material when all the information is important but the actual phrasing isn't especially important or memorable.
- A **quotation** records a passage from the source word for word: Quote when the source states something crucial and says it well. Note: In your notes, always identify quoted material by putting quotation marks around it. The quoted material will need to be set off by quotation marks in the paper itself.

Summarizing, paraphrasing, and quoting are treated more fully on pages 264–266. Here is a brief example, with the original passage coming from Coral Ann Howells' *Alice Munro*.

Original:

"To read Munro's stories is to discover the delights of seeing two worlds at once: an ordinary everyday world and the shadowy map of another imaginary or secret world laid over the real one, so that in reading we slip from one world into the other in an unassuming domestic sort of way."

Summary: Munro's fiction moves readers from recognizable reality into a hidden world.

Paraphrase: Reading Munro's fiction gives readers the enjoyment of experiencing a double world: day-to-day reality and on top of that a more mysterious, fantastic world, with the result that readers move smoothly between the worlds in a seamless, ordinary way.

Quotation: Munro's fiction takes us into "the shadowy map of another imaginary or secret world laid over the real one."

 ## Cross-Curricular Connections

Different academic disciplines require different methods of research note taking. Investigate the styles of research note taking used in your discipline.

Critical-Thinking and Writing Activities

1. Writer Ralph Fletcher shares, "When I write, I am always struck at how magical and unexpected the process turns out to be." Would you describe the writing process you follow as "magical" and "unexpected"? Why or why not?

2. Reread one of your recent essays. Does the writing show that you thoroughly understood your subject, met the needs of your audience, and achieved your purpose?

3. Below is a list of general subject areas. Select one that interests you and do the following: Using the strategies on pages 33–35, brainstorm possible topics and select one. Then use the strategies on pages 35–37 to explore what you know about that topic and what you need to learn.

Arts/music	Environment
Health/medicine	Work/occupation

STUDY TOOLS 3

LOCATED AT BACK OF THE TEXTBOOK
- ☐ Tear-Out Chapter Review Card

LOCATED AT WWW.CENGAGE.COM/LOGIN
- ☐ Chapter eBook
- ☐ Graded quizzes and a practice quiz generator
- ☐ Videos: Writer Interviews
- ☐ Tutorials
- ☐ Flashcards
- ☐ Cengage Learning Write Experience
- ☐ Interactive activities

USE THE TOOLS.

• Rip out the Review Cards in the back of your book to study.
Or Visit CourseMate to:
• Read, search, highlight, and take notes in the Interactive eBook
• Review Flashcards (Print or Online) to master key terms
• Test yourself with Auto-Graded Quizzes
• Bring concepts to life with Games, Videos,
   and Animations!

Go to CourseMate for **COMP3** to begin using these tools.
Access at **www.cengagebrain.com**

Complete the Speak Up
survey in CourseMate at
www.cengagebrain.com

f **Follow us at**
www.facebook.com/4ltrpress

©iStockphoto.com/A-Digit | © Cengage Learning 2011

4 | Planning

Sergey Nivens, 2014 / Used under license from Shutterstock.com

"GIVE ME SIX HOURS TO CHOP DOWN A TREE AND I WILL SPEND THE FIRST FOUR SHARPENING THE AXE."

ABRAHAM LINCOLN

LEARNING OBJECTIVES

4-1 Revisit the rhetorical situation.

4-2 Form your thesis statement.

4-3 Select a method of development.

4-4 Develop a plan or an outline.

After you finish
this chapter
go to
PAGE 49 for STUDY TOOLS

Some of us are meticulous planners. We organize our lives in advance and formulate strategies for completing every task. Others of us live more in the moment, believing that whatever needs to get done will get done, with or without a plan.

In writing, author and instructor Ken Macrorie calls for a blend of these two approaches: "Good writing," says Macrorie, "is formed partly through plan and partly through accident." In other words, too much early planning can get in the way of the discovery aspect of writing, while not enough planning can harm the focus and coherence of your writing.

 ## 4-1 REVISIT THE RHETORICAL SITUATION

Use the following planning checklist to help you decide whether to move ahead with your planning or reconsider your topic.

Rhetorical Checklist for Planning

Writer
___ Am I interested in this topic?
___ How much do I now know about this topic, and is it enough?

Subject
___ Does the topic I have developed still fit with the subject requirements of the assignment?
___ Has my research sufficiently deepened my understanding of the topic?

Purpose
___ Are my goals clear enough for me to proceed with planning my writing?
___ Am I writing to entertain, inform, explain, analyze, persuade, reflect?

Form
___ What form should I create: essay, proposal, report, review?

Audience
___ Will my readers be interested in this topic? How can I interest them, given what I have learned?
___ What do they know and need to know about it? What opinions do they have?

Context
___ What weight does this assignment have in terms of my grade?
___ How will the assignment be assessed?

 ## 4-2 FORM YOUR THESIS STATEMENT

As you gain knowledge about your topic, you should concurrently develop a more focused interest in it. If all goes well, this narrowed focus will bring to mind a thesis. A thesis statement identifies the central idea for your writing. It usually highlights a special condition or feature of the topic, expresses a specific claim about it, or takes a stand.

State your thesis in a sentence that effectively expresses what you want to explore or explain in your essay. Sometimes a thesis statement develops early and easily; at other times, the true focus of your writing will emerge only after you've done some initial writing.

4-2a Find a Focus

A general subject area is typically built into your writing assignments. Your task, then, is to find a limited writing topic and examine it from a particular angle or perspective. (You will use this focus to form your thesis statement.)

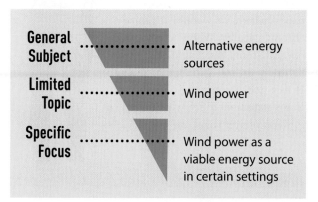

General Subject ········ Alternative energy sources

Limited Topic ········ Wind power

Specific Focus ········ Wind power as a viable energy source in certain settings

4-2b State Your Thesis

You can use the following formula to write a thesis statement for your essay. A **thesis statement** sets the tone and direction for your writing. Keep in mind that at this point you're writing a *working* thesis statement—a statement in progress, so to speak. You may change it as your thinking on the topic evolves.

| limited topic | wind power |

+

| specific focus | wind power as a viable energy source in certain settings |

| an effective thesis statement | Wind power provides a viable energy source **in the plains states**. |

4-3 SELECT A METHOD OF DEVELOPMENT

In his classic book *On Writing Well*, William Zinsser identifies "striving for order" as one of the keys to effective writing. For some assignments, this is not a problem because an **organizing pattern** is built right into the assignment. For example, you might be asked to develop a process paper, which you would organize chronologically. When a pattern is not apparent, one might still evolve naturally as you gather information. If this doesn't happen, examine your thesis statement to see what method of development it suggests.

thesis statement the central idea in a piece of writing
organizing pattern the overall pattern or structure that directs the flow of writing

michaeljung, 2014; marimedi, 2014 / Used under license from Shutterstock.com

4-3a Let Your Thesis Guide You

An effective thesis will often suggest an organizing pattern. Notice how the thesis statements below direct and shape the writing to follow. (Also see page 43.)

▸ **Thesis (Focus) for a Personal Narrative**

Writers of personal narratives do not always state a thesis directly, but they will generally have in mind an implied theme or main idea that governs the way they develop their writing. The thesis below introduces a theme related to the writer's mental illness, a theme that she unfolds as she explores her life. (See pages 100–101.)

> Being a functional member of society and having a mental disorder is an intricate balancing act.

▸ **Thesis for an Essay of Definition**

An essay of definition explores the denotation, connotation, and history of a term. In the following thesis statement, the writer names the two words he will explore—*deft* and *daft*—and provides an overview of the definition essay. (See pages 114–115.)

> Let me see if I can explain the original meaning and also how *daft* and *deft* came to part company.

▸ **Thesis for an Essay of Classification**

An essay of classification identifies the main parts or categories of a topic and then examines each one. In the thesis below, the writer identifies four ways to discuss literature, and he examines each one in turn. (See pages 168–170.)

> There are four main perspectives, or approaches, that readers can use to converse about literature.

▸ **Thesis for a Process Essay**

Process essays are organized chronologically. As indicated in the thesis below, the writer of this essay will explain how cancer cells multiply and affect the body. (See pages 132–133.)

> When a cell begins to function abnormally, it can initiate a process that results in cancer.

▸ **Thesis for an Essay of Comparison**

Some comparisons treat one subject before the other (subject by subject); others discuss the subjects point by point; and some treat similarities and then differences. The writer of the thesis below introduces her comparison and contrast of two different views of Islamic dress—both of which she holds. (See pages 148–149.)

> To wear *hijab*—Islamic covering—is to invite contradiction. Sometimes I hate it. Sometimes I value it.

▶ **Thesis for a Cause-and-Effect Essay**

A cause-and-effect essay usually begins with one or more causes followed by an explanation of the effects, or with a primary effect followed by an explanation of the causes. In the thesis below, the writer enumerates the causes of anorexia nervosa and related eating disorders, causes that she then explores in turn within the body of the essay. (See pages 156–157.)

> To cause such a fearsome and potentially fatal condition, the influencing factors must be powerful indeed. And they are powerful: the psychological pressures of adolescence, the inescapable expectations of family and peers, and the potent influence of the media.

▶ **Thesis for a Position Essay**

A position paper first introduces a topic and then states a position in its thesis. The thesis statement below defines the writer's position on nuclear energy. (See pages 196–198.)

> However, the risks of nuclear power far outweigh its benefits, making fossil fuels the safer and more environmentally responsible option.

▶ **Thesis for an Essay Proposing a Solution**

A problem-solution essay usually begins with a discussion of the problem and its causes and then examines possible solutions. In the following thesis statement, the writer argues for the seriousness of a specific problem within American families, a problem he discusses fully in the essay prior to proposing solutions. (See pages 221–224.)

> Fatherlessness is the most harmful demographic trend of this generation. Yet, despite its scale and social consequences, fatherlessness is a problem that is frequently ignored or denied.

DEVELOP A PLAN OR AN OUTLINE

After writing a working thesis and reviewing the methods of development (pages 42–43), you should be ready to organize your thoughts and the information you have collected. Remember, organizing your research and background information before you start writing can make the drafting stage less of a hassle. Here are five strategies for effective organizing, each of which is explained more fully in the pages that follow.

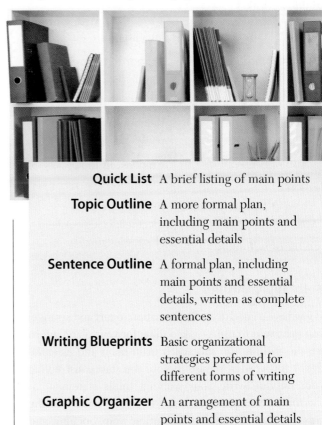

Quick List	A brief listing of main points
Topic Outline	A more formal plan, including main points and essential details
Sentence Outline	A formal plan, including main points and essential details, written as complete sentences
Writing Blueprints	Basic organizational strategies preferred for different forms of writing
Graphic Organizer	An arrangement of main points and essential details in an appropriate chart or diagram

4-4a Quick Lists

Though listing is the simplest of all the methods of organization, it can help you take stock of your main ideas and get a sense of what further research or planning needs to be done. There is no right or wrong way to go about listing. The key is to come up with a system that works best for you. Here are two examples that you may consider: the basic bulleted list, which briefly lists the main points you will discuss, and a T Chart, which lists the main points on one side and a supporting detail on the other side.

Sample Basic List

Topic: Different ways to discuss literature — Topic
- Focus on the text itself
- Focus on the text and the reader
- Focus on the author of the text
- Focus on ideas outside of literature

Main Points

Sample T Chart

Topic: Different ways to discuss literature — Topic

Main Points	Supporting Details
Text-centered approach	Emphasizes structure and rules
Audience-centered approach	Relationship between reader and text
Author-centered approach	Emphasizes the writer's life
Idea-centered approach	Interpretation via specific ideology or field of knowledge

4-4b Topic Outline

If you have a good deal of information to sort and arrange, you may want to use a topic outline for your planning. In a topic outline, you state each main point and essential detail as a word or phrase. Before you start constructing your outline, write your working thesis statement at the top of your paper to help keep you focused on the subject. (Do not attempt to outline your opening and closing paragraphs unless you are specifically asked to do so.)

Some writers prefer to generate an outline before they begin writing, while others prefer to make a more detailed outline after having written a draft. In the latter strategy, an outline can serve as a tool for evaluating the

sentence outline parallel list of main points and essential details written as sentences

logic and completeness of the paper's organization.

An effective topic outline is parallel in structure, meaning the main points (I, II, III) and essential details (A, B, C) are stated in the same way. Notice how the sample outline below uses a parallel structure, making it easy to follow.

Sample Topic Outline

Thesis: There are four main perspectives, — Thesis or approaches, that readers can use to converse about literature.

I. Text-centered approaches —————— Main Point
   A. Also called formalist criticism
   B. Emphasis on structure of text and rules of genre — Supporting Details
   C. Importance placed on key literary elements

II. Audience-centered approaches
   A. Also called rhetorical or reader-response criticism
   B. Emphasis on interaction between reader and text

III. Author-centered approaches
   A. Emphasis on writer's life
   B. Importance placed on historical perspective
   C. Connections made between texts

IV. Ideological approaches
   A. Psychological analysis of text
   B. Myth or archetype criticism
   C. Moral criticism
   D. Ecocriticism
   E. Sociological Analysis

TIP The outline on this page and the next display the organization of "Four Ways to Talk About Literature" (pages 168–170).

4-4c Sentence Outline

A sentence outline is a more formal method of arrangement in which you state each main point and essential detail as a sentence. Writing a **sentence outline** helps you determine how you will express your ideas in the actual writing. Here is an example.

bopav, 2014 / Used under license from Shutterstock.com

Sample Sentence Outline

Thesis: There are four main perspectives, — Thesis or approaches, that readers can use to converse about literature.

I. A text-centered approach focuses — Main Point on the literary piece itself.

   A. This approach is often called formalist criticism.

   B. This method of criticism examines text structure and the genre's rules. — Supporting Details

   C. A formalist critic determines how key literary elements reinforce meaning.

II. An audience-centered approach focuses on the "transaction" between text and reader.

   A. This approach is often called rhetorical or reader-response criticism.

   B. Each reader's interaction with a text is unique.

III. An author-centered approach focuses on the origin of a text.

   A. An author-centered critic examines the writer's life.

   B. This method of criticism may include a historical look at a text.

   C. Connections may be made between the text and related works.

IV. The ideological approach applies ideas outside of literature.

   A. Some critics apply psychological theories to a literary work.

   B. Myth or archetype criticism applies anthropology and classical studies to a text.

   C. Moral criticism explores the ethical dilemmas in literature.

   D. Ecocriticism examines the environmental implications of a text.

   E. Sociological approaches include Marxist, feminist, minority, and postcolonial criticism.

4-4d Writing Blueprints

The writing blueprints that follow lay out basic organizational strategies for different forms of writing. The blueprints may help you arrange the details of your essay or even find holes in your research.

Classification Blueprint

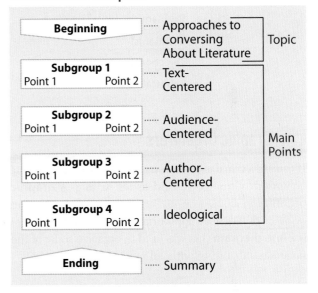

Comparison–Contrast Blueprint

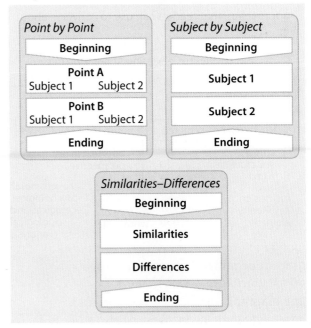

Cause–Effect Blueprint

Cause-Focused	Effect-Focused
Beginning	**Beginning**
Cause	Effect
Cause	Effect
Cause	Effect
Effect(s)	Cause(s)
Ending	**Ending**

Problem–Solution Blueprint

Problem(s)
Solution(s)
Objection(s)
Rebuttal(s)

4-4e Graphic Organizers

If you are a visual learner, you may prefer using a graphic organizer to arrange your ideas for writing. A **graphic organizer** allows you to arrange main points and essential details in an appropriate chart or diagram. Here is a **line diagram** that was used to organize some of the same ideas that were outlined previously.

Line Diagram

Thesis: There are four main perspectives, or approaches, that readers can use to converse about literature.

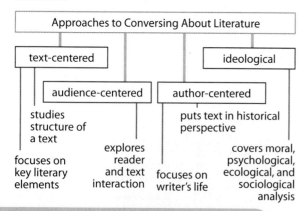

graphic organizer that maps out the overall structure of writing

line diagram a graphic organizer that uses branches to show the relationship between ideas

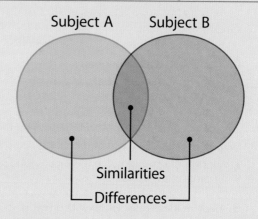

Quick Guide: Graphic Organizers

The following graphic organizers relate to the methods of development discussed on pages 42–43. Each one will help you collect and organize information for expository or persuasive writing. Adapt the organizers as necessary to fit your particular needs or personal style.

Comparison/Contrast (Venn Diagram)

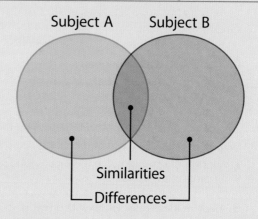

Process Analysis

Subject _____

Steps (Chronological Order)

Step 1
Step 2
Step 3

Comparison

Qualities	Subject A	Subject B

graphic organizer graphic that maps out the overall structure of writing

line diagram a graphic organizer that uses branches to show the relationship between ideas

Cause–Effect

Subject (Object of Study)

Causes (Because of . . .)	Effects (. . . these conditions resulted)
•	•
•	•
•	•
•	

Classification

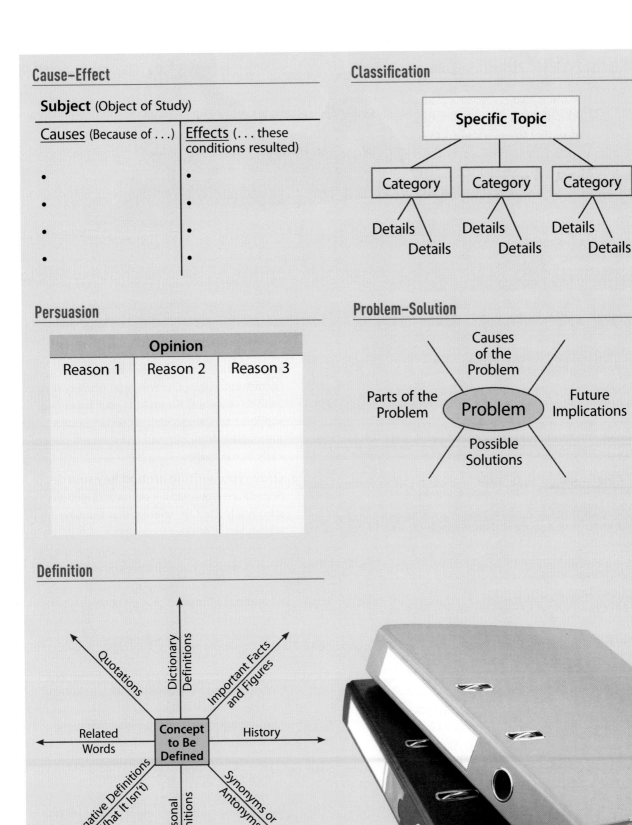

Specific Topic

Category — Details, Details

Category — Details, Details

Category — Details, Details

Persuasion

Opinion		
Reason 1	Reason 2	Reason 3

Problem–Solution

Causes of the Problem

Parts of the Problem

Problem

Future Implications

Possible Solutions

Definition

Quotations

Dictionary Definitions

Important Facts and Figures

Related Words

Concept to Be Defined

History

Negative Definitions (What It Isn't)

Personal Definitions

Synonyms or Antonyms

WRITING WITH SOURCES

When your writing project involves working with sources, the planning phase will involve a great deal of sorting through and sorting out sources as they relate to your own thinking. To advance your writing toward a first draft, thoughtfully review and order your source notes, using them to stimulate your thinking and planning. In addition, consider these strategies:.

Think Rhetorically

At the start of this chapter, you were encouraged to review the rhetorical situation in order to plan your first draft. For projects that involve research, consider these rhetorical questions as well:

- For your subject, which of the sources that you read offer a deep analysis of the topic? Which sources offer the most reliable information and analysis—analysis that has most shaped your thinking and pointed you toward a working thesis?
- Given your audience, which resources will help you create credibility with readers and clarify the topic for them?
- To achieve your purpose (to entertain, inform, analyze, and/or persuade), which resources should be featured in your writing?

Practice Planning Strategies

When you are ready to plan your first draft, use some of the source-focused strategies below to develop a working thesis, choose a method of development, and form an outline. (For more on planning your research writing, see pages 230–237.)

1. **Let your research notes speak to you.** Read and reread your research notes to let key ideas develop. What discoveries have you made? What conclusions have you reached? What questions have you answered? Those discoveries, conclusions, and answers will point toward a thesis and supporting points.

2. **Consider where to position primary and secondary sources.** Different writing projects require different approaches to using, balancing, and integrating primary and secondary sources. (See pages 236–237 for more on the distinction.)

As you plan your writing, ask these questions: Where and how should I work in primary sources—interview material, survey data, textual and artifact analysis, observation results, experiment results? Where and how should I bring in secondary sources—scholarly books, journal articles, and the like? Example: In a literary analysis, you may rely on primary textual analysis of a novel throughout your paper but support that analysis with secondary-source information from biographical research placed early in your paper.

3. **Order your writing around key sources.** Sometimes, your writing can take direction specifically from the sources that you have researched. Consider these options:

- *Make your thesis a response to a specific source.* Did a particular source stand out as especially strong or especially contrary to your own thinking? Shape your thesis as an affirmation of the strong source's authority or as a rebuttal to the contrary source's claims.
- *Structure your paper around a dialogue with sources.* Do your sources offer multiple, divergent, even contradictory perspectives on your topic? If they do, consider organizing your paper around a dialogue with these sources—a he says, she says, and here's my two cents approach. This dialogic approach may work especially well with writing that is looking at a particularly complex or controversial topic where you need to present multiple dimensions or views.

4. **Put your discussion in context.** Often, the early part of your paper will involve establishing a certain context for exploring your topic. Consider, then, tapping your sources to present

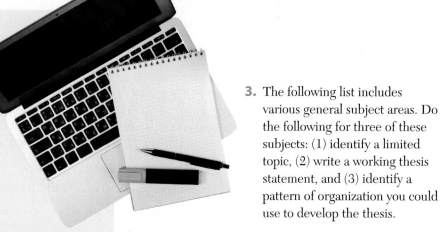

necessary background, explain key terms, describe the big picture, set out key principles, or establish a theoretical framework for your discussion. For example, if your paper will explore the problem of teen homelessness in Atlanta, you might put that analysis in context with information on national trends, general causes of homelessness, sociological definitions of homelessness, and so on.

 ## Cross-Curricular Connections

In most disciplines, it is common practice early in the paper to "survey the literature" on the topic. In a literary analysis, you might survey common interpretations of a key concept before you relay your view. In classes in the social or natural sciences, you might write a report called a literature review—a report that surveys, summarizes, and synthesizes the studies on a specific topic. To plan a literature review,

1. Identify the studies that should be included in the review.
2. Categorize studies by approach or arrange them chronologically.
3. Summarize and synthesize the studies.

Critical-Thinking and Writing Activities

1. As noted at the beginning of this chapter, author Ken Macrorie claims that "good writing is formed partly through plan and partly through accident." Do you agree? Why or why not? Relate Macrorie's idea to your own writing experiences. How carefully do you plan? How much do you leave to accident?
2. A number of organizational patterns are discussed on pages 42–43. Choose one of these patterns and select a model essay from chapters 9–19 that follows the pattern. Read the essay, note the thesis, and explain how the writer develops it.

3. The following list includes various general subject areas. Do the following for three of these subjects: (1) identify a limited topic, (2) write a working thesis statement, and (3) identify a pattern of organization you could use to develop the thesis.

Afghanistan	Family
Agriculture	Freedom
Careers	Iraq
Communications	Medicine
Community	Renewable Energy
Education	Olympics
Entertainment	U.S. Courts

Evgeny Karandaev, 2014 / Used under license from Shutterstock.com

STUDY TOOLS 4

LOCATED AT BACK OF THE TEXTBOOK
☐ Tear-Out Chapter Review Card

LOCATED AT WWW.CENGAGEBRAIN.COM/LOGIN
☐ Chapter eBook

☐ Graded quizzes and a practice quiz generator

☐ Videos: Writer Interviews

☐ Tutorials

☐ Flashcards

☐ Cengage Learning Write Experience

☐ Interactive activities

5 | Drafting

"FIRST DRAFTS ARE CONCERNED WITH IDEAS, WITH GETTING THE DIRECTION AND CONCEPT OF THE PIECE OF WRITING CLEAR."

TOBY FULWILER

karamysh, 2014 / Used under license from Shutterstock.com

LEARNING OBJECTIVES

5-1 Review your writing situation.

5-2 Opening: Introduce your topic and line of thinking.

5-3 Middle: Develop and support your main points.

5-4 Closing: Complete, clarify, and unify your message.

After you finish
this chapter
go to
PAGE 61 for STUDY TOOLS

French novelist Anatole France once said that his first drafts could have been written by a schoolboy, his next draft by a bright college student, his third draft by a superior graduate, and his final draft "only by Anatole France." Think in those terms as you write your first draft. Your main objective is to get ideas down; you'll have a chance later to improve your writing.

This chapter provides information and advice about drafting a college-level essay. You'll find specific advice for creating the three main parts and arranging information.

 ## 5-1 REVIEW YOUR WRITING SITUATION

If you have invested time in planning your writing, you are likely ready to draft your piece. Before you get started, however, spend a few minutes revisiting the rhetorical situation and reminding yourself of the basic structure of an essay.

5-1a The Rhetorical Situation for Drafting

By this point, the rhetorical situation should be well settled in your mind, but the steps below will ensure that your drafting stays on the right track.

▶ **Think about your role.** Are you writing as a student, a citizen, a friend, a member of a scholarly community or discipline? Use a voice that represents you well.

▶ **Focus on your subject.** As you develop your first draft, these strategies can help you keep your subject in focus.

- Use your outline or writing plan as a general guide. Try to develop your main points, but allow new ideas to emerge naturally.
- Write freely without concentrating on neatness and correctness. Concentrate on developing your ideas, not on producing a final copy.
- Include as much detail as possible, continuing until you reach a logical stopping point.

- Use your writing plan or any charts, lists, or diagrams you've produced, but don't feel absolutely bound by them.
- Complete your first draft in one or two sittings.
- Use the most natural voice you can so that the writing will flow smoothly. If your voice is too formal during drafting, you'll be tempted to stop and edit your words.

▶ **Reconsider your purpose.** Briefly review (1) what you want your writing to do (your task), (2) what you want it to say (your thesis), and (3) how you want to say it.

▶ **Reconsider your audience.** Review who your readers are, including their knowledge of and attitude toward your topic.

▶ **Review the form and context.** Make sure you understand the type of writing you should do, the weight of the assignment, and any assessment issues.

5-1b Basic Essay Structure: Major Moves

The following chart lists the main writing moves that occur during the development of a piece of writing. Use it as a general guide for all of your drafting. Remember to keep your purpose and audience in mind throughout the drafting process.

Opening
- **Engage your reader.** Stimulate and direct the reader's attention.
- **Establish your direction.** Identify the topic and put it in perspective.
- **Get to the point.** Narrow your focus and state your thesis.

Middle
- **Advance your thesis.** Provide background information and cover your main points.
- **Test your ideas.** Raise questions and consider alternatives.
- **Support your main points.** Add substance and build interest.
- **Build a coherent structure.** Start new paragraphs and arrange the support.
- **Use different levels of detail.** Clarify and complete each main point.

Ending
- **Reassert the main point.** Remind the reader of the purpose and rephrase the thesis.
- **Urge the reader.** Gain the reader's acceptance and look ahead.

OPENING: INTRODUCE YOUR TOPIC AND LINE OF THINKING

The opening paragraph is one of the most important elements in any composition. It should accomplish at least three essential things: (1) engage the reader; (2) establish your direction, tone, and level of language; and (3) introduce your line of thought.

> **Advice:** The conventional way of approaching the first paragraph is to view it as a kind of "funnel" that draws a reader in and narrows to a main point. Often, the final sentence explicitly states your thesis.
>
> **Cautions:** Don't feel bound by the conventional pattern, which may sound stale if not handled well.
>
> Don't let the importance of the first paragraph paralyze you. Relax and write.

The information on the next two pages will help you develop your opening. You can also refer to the sample essays in chapters 9–19 for ideas.

5-2a Engage Your Reader

Your reader will be preoccupied with other thoughts until you seize, stimulate, and direct his or her attention. Here are some effective ways to "hook" the reader:

▶ **Mention little-known facts about the topic.**
Beads may have been what separated human ancestors from their Neanderthal cousins. Yes, beads.

▶ **Pose a challenging question.**
Why would human ancestors spend days carving something as frivolous as beads while Neanderthals spent days hunting mammoths?

▶ **Offer a thought-provoking quotation.**
"A key thing in human evolution happened when people started devoting just ridiculous amounts of time to making these [beads]," says archeologist John Shea of Stonybrook University.

▶ **Tell a brief, illuminating story.**
When I walked into the room, I had only to show my hand to be accepted in the group of strangers there. The Phi Delta Kappa ring on my finger—and on all of our fingers—bound us across space and time as a group. Our ancestors discovered the power of such ornamentation forty thousand years ago.

5-2b Establish Your Direction

The direction of your line of thought should become clear in the opening part of your writing. Here are some moves you might make to set the right course:

- **Identify the topic (issue).** Show a problem, a need, or an opportunity.
- **Deepen the issue.** Connect the topic, showing its importance.
- **Acknowledge other views.** Tell what others say or think about the topic.

5-2c Get to the Point

You may choose to state your main point up front, or you may wait until later to introduce your thesis. For example, you could work inductively by establishing an issue, a problem, or a question in your opening and then build toward the answer—your thesis—in your conclusion. (See pages 10 and 187 for more on inductive reasoning.) Sometimes, in fact, your thesis may simply be implied. In any case, the opening should at least hint at the central issue or thesis of your paper. Here are three ways to get to the point:

1. **Narrow your focus.** Point to what interests you about the topic.
2. **Raise a question.** Answer the question in the rest of the essay.
3. **State your thesis.** If appropriate, craft a sentence that boils down your thinking to a central claim. You can use the thesis sentence as a "map" for the organization of the rest of the essay. (See pages 42–43, 55–58, and 233.)

rangizzz, 2014 / Used under license from Shutterstock.com

Weak Opening

Although the opening below introduces the topic, the writing states the obvious, lacks interesting details, and establishes no clear focus for the essay. At no point does the writer hint at a central issue or idea that will be unpacked further in the essay. For readers, the opening fails to present a compelling case for continuing to read the essay.

> I would like to talk about the TV show *The Simpsons*. It's about this weird family of five people who look kind of strange and act even stranger. In fact, the characters aren't even real—they're just cartoons. People have watched it for more than 25 seasons and can't seem it get enough of it.

Strong Opening

In the essay opener below, the writer uses his first paragraph to get his readers' attention, describe his subject, and provide contextual background information. He uses the second paragraph to raise a question that leads him to a statement of his thesis (underlined).

Note how, after stating the thesis, the writer forecasts the method of developing the thesis by outlining four key points that will be further developed in the essay. The noteworthy background information and clear focus make a compelling case for continuing to read the essay.

> *The Simpsons*, stars of the TV show by the same name, are a typical American family—or at least a parody of one. Homer, Marge, Bart, Lisa, and Maggie Simpson live in Springfield, U.S.A. Homer, the father, is a boorish, obese oaf who works in a nuclear power plant. Marge is an overprotective, nagging mother with an outrageous blue hairdo. Ten-year-old Bart is an obnoxious, "spiky-haired demon." Lisa is eight and a prodigy on the tenor saxophone and in class. The infant Maggie never speaks but only sucks on her pacifier.
>
> What is the attraction of this yellow-skinned family that stars on a show in which all of the characters have pronounced overbites and only four fingers on each hand? Viewers see a little bit of themselves in everything the Simpsons do. The world of Springfield is a parody of the viewer's world, and even after more than 25 seasons and 550 episodes, Americans can't get enough of it. Viewers experience this parody in the show's explanations of family, education, workplace, and politics.

5-3 MIDDLE: DEVELOP AND SUPPORT YOUR MAIN POINTS

The middle of the essay is where you do the "heavy lifting." In this part you develop the main points that support your thesis statement.

> **Advice:** As you write, you will likely make choices that were unforeseen when you began. Use "scratch outlines" (temporary jottings) along the way to show where your new ideas may take you.
>
> **Cautions:** Writing that lacks effective detail gives only a vague image of the writer's intent. Writing that wanders loses its hold on the essay's purpose.

For both of these reasons, always keep your thesis in mind when you develop the main part of your writing. For help, refer to the guidelines and models on the next five pages. You can refer to the sample essays in this book for additional ideas.

5-3a Advance Your Thesis

If you stated a thesis in the opening, you can advance it in the middle paragraphs by covering your main points and supporting them in these ways.

- ▶ **Explain:** Provide important facts, details, and examples.
- ▶ **Narrate:** Share a brief story or re-create an experience to illustrate an idea.
- ▶ **Describe:** Tell in detail how someone appears or how something works.
- ▶ **Define:** Identify or clarify the meaning of a specific term or idea.
- ▶ **Analyze:** Examine the parts of something to better understand the whole.
- ▶ **Compare:** Provide examples to show how two things are alike or different.
- ▶ **Argue:** Use logic and evidence to prove that something is true.
- ▶ **Reflect:** Express your thoughts or feelings about something.
- ▶ **Cite authorities:** Add expert analysis or personal commentary.

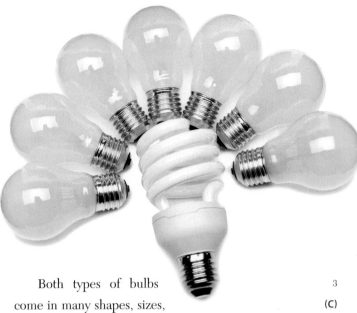

5-3b Test Your Ideas

When you write a first draft, you're testing your initial thinking about your topic. You're determining whether your thesis is valid and whether you have enough compelling reasoning and information to support it. Here are ways to test your line of thinking as you write:

▶ **Raise questions.** Try to anticipate your readers' questions.

▶ **Consider alternatives.** Look at your ideas from different angles; weigh various options; re-evaluate your thesis.

▶ **Answer objections.** Directly or indirectly deal with possible problems that a skeptical reader might point out.

5-3c Build a Coherent Structure

Design paragraphs as units of thought that develop and advance your thesis clearly and logically. For example, look at the brief essay that follows, noting how each body paragraph presents ideas with supporting details that build on and deepen the main idea.

Seeing the Light

1
(A)   All lightbulbs make light, so they're all the same, right? Not quite. You have many choices regarding how to light up your life. Two types of bulbs are the traditional incandescent and the compact fluorescent. By checking out how they're different, you can better choose which one to buy.

2
(B)   While either incandescent or compact fluorescent bulbs can help you read or find the bathroom at night, each bulb makes light differently. In an incandescent bulb, electricity heats up a tungsten filament (thin wire) to 450 degrees, causing it to glow with a warm, yellow light. A compact fluorescent is a glass tube filled with mercury vapor and argon gas. Electricity causes the mercury to give off ultraviolet radiation. That radiation then causes phosphors coating the inside of the tube to give off light.

Both types of bulbs come in many shapes, sizes, and brightnesses, but compacts have some restrictions. Because of their odd shape, compacts may not fit well in all lamps. Compacts also may not work well in very cold temperatures, and they can't be used with a dimmer switch.
  3 (C)

On the other hand, while compact fluorescents are less flexible than incandescents, compacts are four times more efficient. For example, a 15-watt compact produces as many lumens of light as a 60-watt incandescent! Why? Incandescents turn only about 5 percent of electricity into light and give off the other 95 percent as heat.
  4 (D)

But are compacts less expensive than incandescents? In the short run, no. Whereas a 60-watt incandescent costs about $1.00, a comparable compact can cost about $5.00. However, because compacts burn less electricity— and last 7 to 10 times longer—in the long run, compacts are less expensive.
  5 (E)

Now that you're no longer in the dark about lightbulbs, take a look at the lamp you're using to read this essay. Think about the watts (electricity used), lumens (light produced), efficiency, purchase price, and lamplife. Then decide how to light up your life in the future.
  6 (F)

(A) The writer introduces the topic and states his thesis.
(B) The writer starts with a basic explanation of how the two types of lightbulbs function differently.

(C) The writer shifts his attention to weaknesses of compact bulbs.
(D) He next explains the strengths of compacts.
(E) He acknowledges that compacts cost more, but he justifies the cost.
(F) The writer rephrases his thesis as a challenge.

5-3d Arrange Supporting Details

Organizing information in a logical pattern within a paragraph strengthens its coherence. The following pages explain and illustrate organizational strategies, providing suggested transitions to go with them. (See also pages 70–72.)

Definition

A definition provides the denotation (dictionary meaning) and connotation (implied meaning) of a given term. It often provides examples, gives anecdotes, and offers negative definitions—what the thing is not. In the paragraph below, the writer begins his definition by posing a question.

> First of all, what is the *grotesque*—in visual art and in literature? A term originally applied to Roman cave art that distorted the normal, the grotesque presents the body and mind so that they appear abnormal— different from the bodies and minds that we think belong in our world. Both spiritual and physical, bizarre and familiar, ugly and alluring, the grotesque shocks us, and we respond with laughter and fear. We laugh because the grotesque seems bizarre enough to belong only outside our world; we fear because it feels familiar enough to be part of it. Seeing the grotesque version of life as it is portrayed in art stretches our vision of reality. As Bernard McElroy argues, "The grotesque transforms the world from what we 'know' it to be to what we fear it might be. It distorts and exaggerates the surface of reality in order to tell a qualitative truth about it."
>
> —John Van Rys

Illustration

An illustration supports a general idea with specific reasons, facts, and details.

> As the years passed, my obsession grew. Every fiber and cell of my body was obsessed with the number on the scale and how much fat I could pinch on my thigh. No matter how thin I was, I thought I could never be thin enough. I fought my sisters for control of the TV and VCR to do my exercise programs and videos. The cupboards were stacked with cans of diet mixes, the refrigerator full of diet drinks. Hidden in my underwear drawer were stacks of diet pills that I popped along with my vitamins. At my worst, I would quietly excuse myself from family activities to turn on the bathroom faucet full blast and vomit into the toilet. Every day I stood in front of the mirror, a ritual not unlike brushing my teeth, and scrutinized my body. My face, arms, stomach, buttocks, hips, and thighs could never be small enough.
>
> —Paula Treick

Illustration/Elaboration

additionally	as well	in other
again	besides	words
along with	finally	moreover
also	for example	next
and	for instance	other
another	in addition	that is

Analogy

An analogy is a comparison that a writer uses to explain a complex or unfamiliar phenomenon (how the immune system works) in terms of a familiar one (how mall security works).

> The human body is like a mall, and the immune system is like mall security. Because the mall has hundreds of employees and thousands of customers, security guards must rely on photo IDs, name tags, and uniforms to decide who should be allowed to open cash registers and who should have access to the vault. In the same way, white blood cells and antibodies need to use DNA cues to recognize which cells belong in a body and which do not. Occasionally security guards make mistakes, wrestling Kookie the Klown to the ground while 40-inch flatscreen TVs "walk" out of the service entrance, but these problems amount only to allergic reactions or little infections. If security guards become hypervigilant, detaining every customer and employee, the situation is akin to leukemia, in which white blood cells attack healthy cells. If security guards become corrupt, letting thieves take a "five-finger discount," the situation is akin to AIDS. Both systems—mall security and human immunity—work by correctly differentiating friend from foe.
>
> —Rob King

Cause and Effect

Cause-and-effect organization shows how events are linked to their results. If you start with effects, follow with specific causes; if you begin with causes, follow with specific effects. The example below discusses the effects of hypothermia on the human body.

> Even a slight drop in the normal human body temperature of 98.6 degrees Fahrenheit causes hypothermia. Often produced by accidental or prolonged exposure to cold, the condition forces all bodily functions to slow down. The heart rate and blood pressure decrease. Breathing becomes slower and shallower. As the body temperature drops, these effects become even more dramatic until it reaches somewhere between 86 and 82 degrees Fahrenheit and the person lapses into unconsciousness. When the temperature reaches between 65 and 59 degrees Fahrenheit, heart action, blood flow, and electrical brain activity stop. Normally such a condition would be fatal. However, as the body cools down, the need for oxygen also slows down. A person can survive in a deep hypothermic state for an hour or longer and be revived without serious complications.
>
> —Laura Black

Cause and Effect

as a result	inevitably
because	resulting in
consequently	since
due to the fact that	therefore
every time that	

Narration

In the paragraph below, the writer uses narration and chronological order to relate an anecdote—a short, illustrative story.

> When I was six or seven years old, growing up in Pittsburgh, I used to take a precious penny of my own and hide it for someone else to find. It was a curious compulsion; sadly, I've never been seized by it since. For some reason I always "hid" the penny along the same stretch of sidewalk up the street. I would cradle it at the roots of a sycamore, say, or in a hole left by a chipped-off piece of sidewalk. Then I would take a piece of chalk, and, starting at either end of the block, draw huge arrows leading up to the penny from both directions. After I learned to write I labeled the arrows: surprise ahead or money this way. I was greatly excited, during all this arrow-drawing, at the thought of the first lucky passer-by who would receive in this way, regardless of merit, a free gift from the universe. But I never lurked about. I would go straight home and not give the matter another thought, until, some months later, I would be gripped again by the impulse to hide another penny.
>
> —Annie Dillard, *Pilgrim at Tinker Creek*

Process

In the paragraph that follows, a student writer describes the process of entering the "tube," or "green room," while surfing.

> At this point you are slightly ahead of the barreling part of the wave, and you need to "stall," or slow yourself, to get into the tube. There are three methods of stalling used in different situations. If you are slightly ahead of the tube, you can drag your inside hand along the water to stall. If you are a couple of feet in front of the barrel, apply all your weight onto your back foot and sink the tail of the board into the water. This is known as a "tail stall" for obvious reasons, and its purpose is to decrease your board speed. If you are moving faster than the wave is breaking, you need to do what is called a "wrap-around." To accomplish this maneuver, lean back away from the wave while applying pressure on the tail. This shifts your forward momentum away from the wave and slows you down. When the wave comes, turn toward the wave and place yourself in the barrel.
>
> —Luke Sunukjian, "Entering the Green Room"

Chronological Order

Chronological (time) order helps you tell a story or present steps in a process. For example, the following paragraph describes how cement is made. Notice how the writer explains every step and uses transitional words to lead readers through the process.

The production of cement is a complicated process. The raw materials that go into cement consist of about 60 percent lime, 25 percent silica, and 5 percent alumina. The remaining 10 percent is a varying combination of gypsum and iron oxide (because the amount of gypsum determines the drying time of the cement). First, this mixture is ground up into very fine particles and fed into a kiln. Cement kilns, the largest pieces of moving machinery used by any industry, are colossal steel cylinders lined with firebricks. They can be 25 feet in diameter and up to 750 feet long. The kiln is built at a slant and turns slowly as the cement mix makes its way down from the top end. A flame at the bottom heats the kiln to temperatures of up to 3,000 degrees Fahrenheit. When the melted cement compound emerges from the kiln, it cools into little marble-like balls called clinker. Finally, the clinker is ground to a consistency finer than flour and packaged as cement.

—Kevin Maas

Narration/Process/Chronological

a day before	during	second
about	finally	soon
after	first	then
afterward	in the end	today
as soon as	later	tomorrow
at	meanwhile	until
before	next	yesterday

Classification

When classifying a subject, place the subject in its appropriate category and then show how this subject is different from other subjects in the same category. In the following paragraph, a student writer uses classification to describe the theory of temperament.

Medieval doctors believed that "four temperaments rule mankind wholly." According to this theory, each person has a distinctive temperament or personality (sanguine, phlegmatic, melancholy, or choleric) based on the balance of four elements in the body, a balance peculiar to the individual. The theory was built on Galen's and Hippocrates' notion of "humors," which stated that the body contains blood, phlegm, black bile, and yellow bile—four fluids that maintain the balance within the body. The sanguine person was dominated by blood, associated with fire: Blood was hot and moist, and the person was fat and prone to laughter. The phlegmatic person was dominated by phlegm (associated with earth) and was squarish and slothful—a sleepy type. The melancholy person was dominated by cold, black bile (connected with the element of water) and as a result was pensive, peevish, and solitary. The choleric person was dominated by hot, yellow bile (air) and thus was inclined to anger.

—Jessica Radsma

Classification

a typical type	rarest of all
another kind	the third variety
a second variety	the most common
in one category	the most popular
one type	

Climax

Climax is a method in which you first present details and then provide a general climactic statement or conclusion drawn from the details.

As I walked home, I glanced across the road to see a troubling scene unfold. A burly man strode along the curb, shoulders rounded and face clenched in anger or grief. Behind him, a slim little girl sat on her heels on the sidewalk, hands in her lap and tears streaming down white cheeks. I glanced back at that brute, who climbed into his big black truck and started up the engine. I almost ran across the road to stop him, to set right whatever he'd done. But then I spotted the little dog lying very still in the gutter. The man in the truck must have hit the poor creature, stopped to see if he could help, realized he couldn't, apologized, and left the little girl to grieve. There was nothing I could do, either. Face clenched, I looked back to my side of the street and walked on.

—Jamal Kendal

Compare-Contrast

To compare and contrast, show how two or more subjects are similar and different.

The old man behind the counter is no doubt Pappy, after which Pappy's Grocery is named. He leans on the glass display case, world weary and watchful, tracking the youth by the snack display. The folds deepen around Pappy's intense eyes as the young customer picks lightly at a bag of potato chips, lifts a can of cashews, runs lithe fingers over the packs of gum. He crouches for a better look at the snack cakes, his pants sliding below colorful boxers. Pappy hitches his own belt higher over his tucked-in shirt. "You gonna buy anything?" The young customer startles, looks up with a smooth face and wide eyes, stands, and walks from Pappy's Grocery.

—Tina Jacobs

Comparison/Contrast

as	like
also	likewise
although	one way
both	on the one hand
but	on the other hand
by contrast	otherwise
even though	similarly
however	still
in the same way	yet

5-4 CLOSING: COMPLETE, CLARIFY, AND UNIFY YOUR MESSAGE

Closing paragraphs can be important for tying up loose ends, clarifying key points, or signing off with the reader. In a sense, the entire essay is a preparation for an effective ending; the ending helps the reader look back over the essay with new understanding and appreciation.

> **Advice:** Because the ending can be so important, draft a variety of possible endings. Choose the one that flows best from a sense of the whole.
>
> **Cautions:** If your thesis is weak or unclear, you will have a difficult time writing a satisfactory ending. To strengthen the ending, strengthen the thesis.
>
> You may have heard this formula for writing an essay: "Say what you're going to say, say it, then say what you've just said." Remember, though, if you need to "say what you've just said," say it in new words.

The information that follows will help you develop your ending. For additional strategies, refer to the sample essays elsewhere in this book.

5-4a Reassert the Main Point

If an essay is complicated, the reader may need reclarification at the end. Show that you are fulfilling the promises you made in the beginning.

▸ **Remind the reader.** Recall what you first set out to do; check off the key points you've covered; or answer any questions left unanswered.

▸ **Rephrase the thesis.** Restate your thesis in light of the most important support you've given. Deepen and expand your original thesis.

5-4b Urge the Reader

Your reader may still be reluctant to accept your ideas or argument. The ending is your last chance to gain the reader's acceptance. When your writing comes to an effective stopping point, conclude the essay. Don't tack on another idea. Here are some possible strategies:

▸ **Show the implications.** Follow further possibilities raised by your train of thought; be reasonable and convincing.

▸ **Look ahead.** Suggest possible connections between your topic and the larger context. Project where the topic may be going or where it may lead.

- ▸ **List the benefits.** Show the reader the benefits of accepting or applying the things you've said.

5-4c Complete and Unify Your Message

Your final paragraphs are your last opportunity to refocus, unify, and otherwise reinforce your message. Draft the closing carefully, not merely to finish the essay but to further advance your purpose and thesis.

popular business, 2014 / Used under license from Shutterstock.com

Weak Ending

The ending below does not focus on and show commitment to the essay's main idea. Rather than reinforcing this idea, the writing leads off in a new direction.

> I realize I've got to catch my bus. I've spent too much time talking to this woman whose life is a wreck. I give her some spare change and then head off. She doesn't follow me. It's kind of a relief. Toronto is a great city, but sometimes you have weird experiences there. Once a street vendor gave me a free falafel. I didn't want to eat it because maybe something was wrong with it. What a weird city!

Strong Endings

Below are final paragraphs from three essays in this book. Listen to their tone, watch how they reconsider the essay's ideas, and note how they offer further food for thought. (The first example is a revision of the weak paragraph above.)

> I tell her I need to get going. She should go, too, or she'll be late for the hearing. Before getting up, I reach into my wallet and give her two TTC passes and some spare change. I walk her to the street and point her toward Old City Hall. She never thanks me, only looks at me one last time with immense vulnerability and helplessness. Then she walks away.
>
> I wonder as I hurry toward the station if she'll be okay, if her boyfriend really will get out of jail, and if

her grandmother will ever take her back. Either way, I think as I cross Bay Street, what more can I do? I have a bus to catch.

(See the full essay on pages 98–100.)

Analysis: This ending vividly narrates the conclusion of the encounter between the writer and the young woman. The phrase "spare change" reminds readers of the essay's title; the writer's reflection and questions capture the impact of the encounter; and the final sentence provides an exit for both the writer and the reader.

> Passion and power permeate all of Latin America's music. The four major types of music—indigenous, Iberian and Mestizo folk, Afro-American, and popular urban—are as diverse as the people of Latin America, and each style serves a valued need or function in Latinos' everyday lives. As a result, those listening to Latin American music—whether it is a Peruvian Indian's chant, a Venezuelan farmer's whistled tune, a Cuban mambo drummer's vivacious beat, or the Bogotá rock concert's compelling rhythms—are hearing much more than music. They are hearing the passion and power of the Latin American people.

(See the full essay on pages 124–125.)

Analysis: This ending effectively ties together the writer's analysis of Latin American music by recounting the four categories of this music, emphasizing the shared character of the music, and stressing the phrase "passion and power."

> In essence, Lincoln asked the nation to confront unblinkingly the legacy of slavery. What were the requirements of justice in the face of this reality? What would be necessary to enable former slaves and their descendants to enjoy fully the pursuit of happiness? Lincoln did not live to provide an answer. A century and a half later, we have yet to do so.

(See the full essay on pages 198–201.)

Analysis: In this ending, the writer effectively summarizes the challenge of Abraham Lincoln's Emancipation Proclamation. Two questions press readers to think concretely of those challenges, and the closing sentence connects the historical discussion with the present moment of race relations in the United States.

Writing with Sources

When your writing project involves working with sources, writing the first draft involves exploring your own thinking in relation to the ideas and information that you have discovered through research. Developing this relationship requires both creativity and care—the creativity to see connections and to trace lines of thinking, and the care to respect ideas and information that you are borrowing from sources. While drafting strategies for research papers are covered more fully on pages 274–276, start with the issues outlined below.

Think Rhetorically

When you are drafting with sources, focus particularly on your role as the writer. In research writing, you are not only using sources to support your own ideas but also conversing with those sources. Essentially, while showing respect for your sources, you want to avoid being intimidated by them.

Practice Drafting Strategies

To work well with your sources during your drafting, try strategies like those below:

1. **Keep your sources handy.** While drafting, have source material at your fingertips, whether in paper or electronic form, so that you can integrate summaries, paraphrases, and quotations without disrupting the flow and energy of your drafting. Doing so also allows you to track borrowed material in your draft.

2. **Try starting your draft with a strong source reference.** Could something from a source get your paper off to an engaging start? Consider a pithy, thought-provoking, or startling quotation; a problematic or controversial statement or fact from a source; or an anecdote (a brief example, story, or case study) that makes the issue concrete.

3. **Save the best for last. Consider using an especially thought-provoking or summarizing statement, quotation, or detail in your conclusion.** Doing so clinches your point and leaves your reader with provocative food for thought.

4. **Take care not to overwhelm your draft with source material.** As you write, keep the focus on your own ideas:
   - Avoid strings of references and chunks of source material with no discussion, explanation, or interpretation on your part in between.
   - Don't offer entire paragraphs of material from a source (whether paraphrased or quoted) with a single in-text citation at the end. When you do so, your thinking disappears.
   - Be careful not to overload your draft with complex information and dense data lacking explanation.
   - Resist the urge to simply copy and paste big chunks from sources. Even if you document the sources, your paper will quickly become a patchwork of source material with a few weak stitches (your contribution) holding it together.

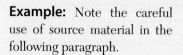

Example: Note the careful use of source material in the following paragraph.

Sample Paragraph Showing Integration of Source Material

Antibiotics are effective only against infections caused by bacteria and should never be used against infections caused by viruses. Using an antibiotic against a viral infection is like throwing water on a grease fire—water may normally put out fires but will only worsen the situation for a grease fire. In the same way, antibiotics fight infections, but they cause the body harm when they are used to fight infections caused by viruses. Viruses cause the common cold, the flu, and most sore

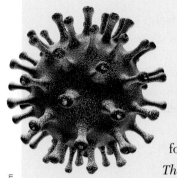

Lightspring, 2014 / Used under license from Shutterstock.com

throats, sinus infections, coughs, and bronchitis. Yet antibiotics are commonly prescribed for these viral infections. *The New England Journal of Medicine* reports that 22.7 million kilograms (25,000 tons) of antibiotics is prescribed each year in the United States alone (Wenzel and Edmond, 1962). Meanwhile, the **(C)** CDC reports that approximately 50 percent of those prescriptions are completely unnecessary ("Antibiotic Overuse" 25). "Every year, tens of millions of prescriptions for antibiotics are written to treat viral illnesses for which these antibiotics offer no benefits," says the CDC's antimicrobial resistance director David Bell, M.D. (qtd. in Bren 30). Such mis-prescribing is simply bad medical **(D)** practice that contributes to the problem of growing bacterial infection.

(A) Topic sentence: idea elaborating and supporting thesis
(B) Development of idea through reasoning
(C) Support of idea through reference to source material
(D) Concluding statement of idea

 Cross-Curricular Connections

Referring to sources is handled differently from one discipline to the next. For example, in humanities disciplines, a source reference might foreground the author's name, his or her credentials, and the source's title; conversely, a source reference in the social or natural sciences might foreground the year that the study was done or published.

 Critical-Thinking and Writing Activities

1. Patricia T. O'Connor says, "All writing begins life as a first draft, and first drafts are never any good. They're not supposed to be." Is this claim true? Why or why not? What do you hope to accomplish with a first draft?

2. Study the opening paragraphs of any three essays included in this book. Write a brief analysis of each opening based on the information on pages 52–53.

3. Read the final paragraphs of any three essays included in this book. Write a brief analysis of each ending based on the information on pages 58–59.

4. Study the body of any essay included in this book. Using the information on pages 53–58, write a brief analysis of the drafting strategies that the author used within the essay, including the body's relationship to the opening and closing.

5. Imagine that you are a journalist who has been asked to write an article about a wedding, a funeral, or another significant event you have experienced. Choose an event and sketch out a plan for your article. Include the main writing moves and the type of information at each stage of your writing.

STUDY TOOLS 5

LOCATED AT BACK OF THE TEXTBOOK
☐ Tear-Out Chapter Review Card

LOCATED AT WWW.CENGAGEBRAIN.COM/LOGIN
☐ Chapter eBook

☐ Graded quizzes and a practice quiz generator

☐ Videos: Writer Interviews

☐ Tutorials

☐ Flashcards

☐ Cengage Learning Write Experience

☐ Interactive activities

6 | Revising

"To achieve style, begin by affecting none—that is, begin by placing yourself in the background."

E. B. WHITE

Syda Productions, 2014 / Used under license from Shutterstock.com

LEARNING OBJECTIVES

6-1 Assess the state of your draft.

6-2 Revise for ideas and organization.

6-3 Revise for voice and style.

6-4 Address paragraph issues.

6-5 Revise collaboratively.

6-6 Use the writing center.

After you finish
this chapter
go to
PAGE 75 for STUDY TOOLS

The word *revising* means "taking another look," so revising is best done after a brief break. Set aside your writing and return to it later with fresh eyes. Also, enlist the fresh eyes of another reader, whether a roommate, a classmate, or someone at the writing center. Revising is all about getting perspective.

Of course, once you have perspective, you need to figure out how to make improvements. This chapter provides numerous strategies for focusing on the global traits of your writing—ideas, organization, and voice. The changes you make should improve the work significantly, perhaps even reshaping it.

 # 6-1 ASSESS THE STATE OF YOUR DRAFT

Once you've finished a first draft, set it aside (ideally for a few days) until you can look at the draft objectively and make needed changes. If you drafted on paper, photocopy the draft. If you drafted on a computer, print your paper (double-spaced). Then make changes with a good pencil or colored pen. If you prefer revising on the computer, consider using your software editing program. In all cases, save your first draft for reference.

When revising, first look at the big picture. Take it all in. Determine whether the content is interesting, informative, and worth sharing. Note any gaps or soft spots in your line of thinking. Ask yourself how you can improve what you have done so far. The information that follows will help you address whole-paper issues such as these.

6-1a Revisit the Rhetorical Situation for Revising

Just as the rhetorical situation helped you to set your direction in writing, it can help you make course corrections. Think about each part of the rhetorical situation.

▶ **Consider your role.** How are you coming across in this draft? Do you sound authoritative, engaged,

knowledgeable, confident? How do you want to come across?

▶ **Think about your subject.** Have you stated a clear focus? Have you supported it with a variety of details? Have you explored the subject fully?

▶ **Remember your purpose.** Are you trying to analyze, describe, explain, propose? Does the writing succeed? Do the ideas promote your purpose? Does your organization support the purpose? Is your writing voice helpful in achieving your purpose?

▶ **Check the form.** Have you created writing that matches the form that your instructor requested? Have you taken best advantage of the form, including graphics or other media, if appropriate?

▶ **Consider your audience.** Have you captured their attention and interest? Have you provided them the information they need to understand your writing? Have you considered their values, needs, and opinions and used them to connect?

▶ **Think about the context.** Is this piece of writing the correct length and level of seriousness for the assignment? Is it on schedule? How does it match up to what others are doing?

6-1b Consider Your Overall Approach

Sometimes it's better to start fresh if your writing contains stretches of uninspired ideas. Consider a fresh start if your first draft shows one of these problems:

▶ **The topic is worn out.** An essay titled "Lead Poisoning" may not sound very interesting. Unless you can approach it with a new twist ("Get the Lead Out!"), consider cutting your losses and finding a fresh topic.

▶ **The approach is stale.** If you've been writing primarily to get a good grade, finish the assignment, or sound cool, start again. Try writing to learn something, prompt real thinking in readers, or touch a chord.

▶ **Your voice is predictable or fake.** Avoid the bland "A good time was had by all" or the phony, academic "When one studies this significant problem in considerable depth . . ." Be real. Be honest.

▶ **The draft sounds boring.** Maybe it's boring because you pay an equal amount of attention to everything and hence stress nothing. Try condensing less important material and expanding what's important.

▶ **The essay is formulaic.** In other words, it follows the "five-paragraph" format. This handy organizing frame may prevent you from doing justice to your topic and thinking. If your draft is dragged down by rigid adherence to a formula, try a more original approach.

6-1c Think Globally

When revising, focus on the big picture—the overall strength of the ideas, organization, and voice. (These elements are briefly explained below and then addressed more fully in the rest of this chapter.)

▶ **Ideas:** Check your thesis, focus, or theme. Has your thinking on your topic changed? Also think about your readers' most pressing questions concerning this topic. Have you answered these questions? Finally, consider your reasoning and support. Are both complete and sound?

▶ **Organization:** Check the overall design of your writing, making sure that ideas move smoothly and logically from one point to the next in well-crafted paragraphs. Does your essay build effectively? Do you shift directions cleanly? Fix structural problems in one of these ways:
  • Reorder material to improve the sequence.
  • Cut information that doesn't support the thesis.
  • Add details where the draft is thin.
  • Rewrite parts that seem unclear.
  • Improve links between points by using transitions.

▶ **Voice:** Voice is your personal presence on the page, the tone and attitude that others hear when reading your work. In other words, voice is the between-the-lines message your readers get (whether you want them to or not). When revising, make sure that the tone of your message matches your purpose, whether it is serious, playful, or satiric.

Insight: Don't pay undue attention to spelling, grammar, and punctuation at this early stage in the process. Otherwise, you may become distracted from the task at hand: improving the content of your writing. Editing and proofreading come later.

REVISE FOR IDEAS AND ORGANIZATION

As you review your draft for content, make sure the ideas are fully developed and the organization is clear. From your main claim or thesis to your reasoning and your evidence, strengthen your thinking and sequencing.

6-2a Examine Your Ideas

Review the ideas in your writing, making sure that each point is logical, complete, and clear. To test the logic in your writing, see pages 188–191.

Complete Thinking

Have you answered readers' basic questions? Have you supported the thesis? The original passage below is too general; the revision is clearly more complete.

Original Passage
(Too general)

As soon as you receive a minor cut, the body's healing process begins to work. Blood from tiny vessels fills the wound and begins to clot. In less than 24 hours, a scab forms.

Revised Version *(More specific)*

As soon as you receive a minor cut, the body's healing process begins to work. In a simple wound, the first and second layers of skin are severed along with tiny blood vessels called capillaries. As these vessels bleed into the wound, minute structures called platelets help stop the bleeding by sticking to the edges of the cut and to one another, forming a plug. The platelets then release chemicals that react with certain proteins in the blood to form a clot. The blood clot, with its fiber network, begins to join the edges of the wound together. As the clot dries out, a scab forms, usually in less than 24 hours.

Clear Thesis

Make sure that your writing centers on one main issue or thesis. Although this next original passage lacks a thesis, the revision has a clear one.

> **Original Passage** *(Lacks a thesis)*
>
> Teen magazines are popular with young girls. These magazines contain a lot of how-to articles about self-image, fashion, and boy-girl relationships. Girls read them to get advice on how to act and how to look. Girls who don't really know what they want are the most eager readers.

> **Revised Version** *(Identifies a specific thesis statement)*
>
> Adolescent girls often see teen magazines as handbooks on how to be teenagers. These magazines influence the ways they act and the ways they look. For girls who are unsure of themselves, these magazines can exert an enormous amount of influence. Unfortunately, the advice these magazines give about self-image, fashion, and boys may do more harm than good.

6-2b Examine Your Organization

Good writing has structure. It leads readers logically and clearly from one point to the next. When revising for organization, consider four areas: the overall plan, the opening, the flow of ideas, and the closing.

Overall Plan

Look closely at the sequence of ideas or events that you share. Does that sequence advance your thesis? Do the points build effectively? Are there gaps in the support or points that stray from your original purpose? If you find such problems, consider the following actions:

- Refine the focus or emphasis by rearranging material within the text.
- Fill in the gaps with new material. Go back to your planning notes.
- Delete material that wanders away from your purpose.

Use an additional (or different) method of organization. For example, if you are comparing two subjects, add depth to your analysis by contrasting them as well. If you are describing a complex subject, show the subject more clearly and fully by distinguishing and classifying its parts.

The writing you are doing will usually determine the best method of organization for your essay. As you know, a personal narrative is often organized by time. Typically, however, you combine and customize methods to develop a writing idea. For example, within a comparison essay you may do some describing or classifying. See pages 53 and 55–58 for more on the common methods of development.

Opening Ideas

Reread your opening paragraph(s). Is the opening organized effectively? Does it engage readers, establish a direction for your writing, and express your thesis or focus? The original opening below doesn't build to a compelling thesis statement, but the revised version engages the reader and leads to the thesis.

> **Original Opening** *(Lacks interest and direction)*
>
> The lack of student motivation is a common subject in the news. Educators want to know how to get students to learn. Today's higher standards mean that students will be expected to learn even more. Another problem in urban areas is that large numbers of students are dropping out. How to interest students is a challenge.

> **Revised Version** *(Effectively leads readers into the essay)*
>
> How can we motivate students to learn? How can we get them to meet today's rising standards of excellence? How can we, in fact, keep students in school long enough to learn? The answer to these problems is quite simple. Give them money. Pay students to study and learn and stay in school.

Flow of Ideas

Look closely at the beginnings and endings of each paragraph. Have you connected your thoughts clearly? Transitional words and phrases can help (see pages 70–72 for a list of common transitions). The original opening words of the paragraph sequence that follows, from an essay of description, offer no links for readers. The revised versions use strong transitions indicating spatial organization (order by location). Note how much easier it is to follow the flow of ideas—or in this case location of ideas—when the transitions are included.

Original First Words in the Four Middle Paragraphs

There was a huge, steep hill . . .

Buffalo Creek ran . . .

A dense "jungle" covering . . .

Within walking distance from my house . . .

Revised Versions *(Words and phrases connect ideas)*

Behind the house, there was a huge, steep hill . . .

Across the road from the house, Buffalo Creek ran . . .

On the far side of the creek bank was a dense "jungle" covering . . .

Up the road, within walking distance from my house . . .

Another necessary step for revising ideas is to check the strength of your supporting details. If any ideas in your writing have weak or convincing support, you may need to add or reorder information. Review pages 184–188) for strategies for strengthening your support.

Closing Ideas

Reread your closing paragraph(s). Do you offer an effective summary, reassert your main point in a fresh way, and provide readers with food for thought as they leave your writing? Or is your ending abrupt, repetitive, or directionless? The original ending that follows adds little to the main part of the writing. The revision summarizes the main points in the essay and then urges the reader to think again about the overall point of writing.

Original Ending *(Sketchy and flat)*

Native Son deals with a young man's struggle against racism. It shows the effects of prejudice. Everyone should read this book.

Revised Version *(Effectively ends the writing)*

Native Son deals with a young man's struggle in a racist society but also with so much more. It shows how prejudice affects people, how it closes in on them, and what some people will do to find a way out. Anyone who wants to better understand racism in the United States should read this book.

 To generate fresh ideas for your closing, freewrite answers to questions like these: What should my readers have learned? What evidence or appeal will help readers remember my message and act on it? How does the topic relate to broader issues in society, history, or life?

6-3 REVISE FOR VOICE AND STYLE

Generally, readers more fully trust writing that speaks in an informed voice and a clear, natural style. To develop an informed voice, make sure that your details are correct and complete; to develop a clear style, make sure that your writing is well organized and unpretentious. Check the issues below.

6-3a Check the Level of Commitment

Consider how and to what degree your writing shows that you care about the topic and reader. For example, note how the following original passage lacks a personal voice, revealing nothing about the writer's connection to—or interest in—the topic. In contrast, the revision shows that the writer cares about the topic.

Original Passage *(Lacks voice)*

Cemeteries can teach us a lot about history. They make history seem more real. There is an old grave of a Revolutionary War veteran in the Union Grove Cemetery. . . .

Revised Version *(Personal, sincere voice)*

I've always had a special feeling for cemeteries. It's hard to explain any further than that except to say history never seems quite as real as it does when I walk among many old gravestones. One day I discovered the grave of a Revolutionary War veteran. . . .

6-3b Check the Intensity of Your Writing

All writing—including academic writing—is enriched by an appropriate level of intensity or even passion. In the original passage below, the writer's concern for the topic is unclear because the piece sounds neutral. In contrast, the revised version exudes energy.

Original Passage *(Lacks feeling and energy)*

The Dream Act could make a difference for people. It just takes a long time to get any bill through Congress. This bill probably will never get approved. Instead of passing the Dream Act, the country will probably just deport high school students from other countries.

Revised Passage *(Expresses real feelings)*

Given such debates, it might be a long time before the bill becomes law, thereby dashing the dreams of nearly 65,000 high school students like Maria who can't wait another year because they may already be in deportation proceedings. We need to step up and educate our representatives and senators about the importance of passing the Dream Act on its own instead of including the bill along with CIR. We need to urge them to debate and approve the Dream Act now, thereby making Maria's dreams—and the dreams of thousands of students like her—a reality!

6-3c Develop an Academic Style

Most college writing requires an academic style. Such a style isn't stuffy; you're not trying to impress readers with ten-dollar words. Rather, you are using language that facilitates a thoughtful, engaged discussion of the topic. To choose the best words for such a conversation, consider the issues that follow.

Personal Pronouns

In some academic writing, personal pronouns are acceptable. This is the case in informal writing, such as reading responses; personal essays involving narration, description, and reflection; and opinion-editorial essays written for a broad audience. In addition, *I* is correctly used in academic writing rooted in personal research, sometimes called an *I-search paper.*

Generally, however, avoid using *I, we,* and *you* in traditional academic writing. The concept, instead, is to focus on the topic itself and let your attitude be revealed indirectly. As E. B. White puts it, "To achieve style, begin by affecting none—that is, begin by placing yourself in the background."

No: I really think that the problem of the homeless in Chicago is serious, given the number of people who are dying, as I know from my experience where I grew up.

Yes: Homelessness in Chicago often leads to death. This fact demands the attention of more than lawmakers and social workers; all citizens must address the problems of their suffering neighbors.

 TIP Use the pronoun *one* carefully in academic prose. When it means "a person," *one* can lead to a stilted style if overused. In addition, the pronoun *their* (a plural pronoun) should not be used with *one* (a singular pronoun).

Technical Terms and Jargon

Technical terms and jargon—"insider" words—can be the specialized vocabulary of a subject, a discipline, a profession, or a social group. As such, jargon can be difficult to read for "outsiders." Follow these guidelines:

- Use technical terms to communicate with people within the profession or discipline as a kind of shorthand. However, be careful that such jargon doesn't devolve into meaningless buzzwords and catchphrases.

- Avoid jargon when writing for readers outside the profession or discipline. Use simpler terms and define technical terms that must be used.

Technical: Bin's Douser power washer delivers 2200 psi p.r., runs off standard a.c. lines, comes with 100 ft. h.d. synthetic-rubber tubing, and features variable pulsation options through three adjustable s.s. tips.

Simple: Bin's Douser power washer has a pressure rating of 2200 psi (pounds per square inch), runs off a common 200-volt electrical circuit, comes with 100 feet of hose, and includes three nozzles.

Level of Formality

Most academic writing (especially research papers, literary analyses, lab reports, and argumentative essays) should meet the standards of formal English. Formal English is characterized by a serious tone; careful attention to word choice; longer and more complex sentences reflecting complex thinking; strict adherence to traditional conventions of grammar, mechanics, and punctuation; and avoidance of contractions.

Formal English, modeled in this sentence, is worded correctly and carefully so that it can withstand repeated readings without seeming tiresome, sloppy, or cute.

You may write other papers (personal essays, commentaries, journals, and reviews) in which informal English is appropriate. Informal English is characterized by a personal tone, the occasional use of popular expressions, shorter sentences with slightly looser syntax, contractions, and personal references (*I, we, you*), but it still adheres to basic conventions.

> Informal English sounds like one person talking to another person (in a somewhat relaxed setting). It's the type of language that you're reading now. It sounds comfortable and real, not affected or breezy.

 TIP In academic writing, generally avoid slang—words considered outside standard English—because they are faddish, familiar to few people, and sometimes insulting.

Unnecessary Qualifiers

Using qualifiers (such as *mostly, often, likely,* or *tends to*) is an appropriate strategy for developing defendable claims in argumentative writing. (See pages 184–186.) However, when you "overqualify" your ideas or add intensifiers (*really, truly*), the result is insecurity—the impression that you lack confidence in your ideas. The cure? Say what you mean, and mean what you say.

> **Insecure:** I totally and completely agree with the new security measures at sporting events, but that's only my opinion.

> **Secure:** I agree with the new security measures at sporting events.

FYI Each academic discipline has its own vocabulary and its own vocabulary resources. Such resources include dictionaries, glossaries, or handbooks. Check your library for the vocabulary resources in your discipline. Use them regularly to deepen your grasp of that vocabulary.

6-3d Know When to Use the Passive Voice

Most verbs can be in either the active or the passive voice. When a verb is active, the sentence's subject performs the action. When the verb is passive, the subject is acted upon.

> **Active:** If you *can't attend* the meeting, *notify* Richard by Thursday.

> **Passive:** If a meeting *can't be attended* by you, Richard *must be notified* by Thursday.

▸ **Weaknesses of Passive Voice:** The passive voice tends to be wordy and sluggish because the verb's action is directed backward, not ahead. In addition, passive constructions tend to be impersonal, making people disappear.

> **Passive:** The sound system *can* now *be used* to listen in on sessions in the therapy room. Parents *can be helped* by having constructive one-on-one communication methods with children modeled by therapists.

> **Active:** Parents *can* now *use* the sound system to listen in on sessions in the therapy room. Therapists *can help* parents by modeling constructive one-on-one communication methods with children.

Also avoid using the passive voice unethically to hide responsibility. For example, an instructor who says "Your assignments could not be graded because of scheduling difficulties" might be trying to evade the truth: "I did not finish grading your assignments because I was watching *The Voice*."

▸ **Strengths of Passive Voice:** Using the passive voice isn't always wrong. In fact, the passive voice has some important uses: (1) when you need to be tactful (say, in a bad-news letter), (2) if you wish to stress the object or person acted upon, and (3) if the actual actor is understood, unknown, or unimportant.

> **Active:** Our engineers determined that you bent the bar at the midpoint.

> **Passive:** Our engineers determined that the bar had been bent at the midpoint. (tactful)

> **Active:** Congratulations! We *have approved* your scholarship for $2,500.

> **Passive:** Congratulations! Your scholarship for $2,500 has been *approved*. (emphasis on receiver; actor understood)

6-4 ADDRESS PARAGRAPH ISSUES

While drafting, you may have constructed paragraphs that are loosely held together, poorly developed, or unclear. When you revise, take a close look at your paragraphs for focus, unity, and coherence.

6-4a Remember the Basics

A paragraph should be a concise unit of thought. Revise a paragraph until it . . .

- is organized around a controlling idea—often stated in a topic sentence.
- consists of supporting sentences that develop the controlling idea.
- concludes with a sentence that summarizes the main point and prepares readers for the next paragraph or main point.
- serves a specific function in a piece of writing—opening, supporting, developing, illustrating, countering, describing, or closing.

Sample Paragraph

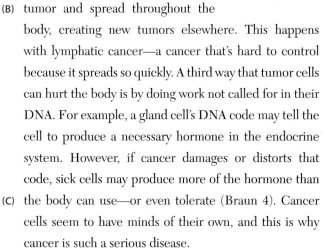

(A)　　Tumor cells can hurt the body in a number of ways. First, a tumor can grow so big that it takes up space needed by other organs. Second, some cells may detach from the original

(B) tumor and spread throughout the body, creating new tumors elsewhere. This happens with lymphatic cancer—a cancer that's hard to control because it spreads so quickly. A third way that tumor cells can hurt the body is by doing work not called for in their DNA. For example, a gland cell's DNA code may tell the cell to produce a necessary hormone in the endocrine system. However, if cancer damages or distorts that code, sick cells may produce more of the hormone than the body can use—or even tolerate (Braun 4). Cancer

(C) cells seem to have minds of their own, and this is why cancer is such a serious disease.

(A) Topic sentence　　　　(C) Closing sentence
(B) Supporting sentences

6-4b Keep the Purpose in Mind

Use these questions to evaluate the purpose and function of each paragraph:

- What function does the paragraph fulfill? How does it add to your line of reasoning or the development of your thesis?
- Would the paragraph work better if it were divided in two—or combined with another paragraph?
- Does the paragraph flow smoothly from the previous paragraph, and does it lead effectively into the next one?

6-4c Check for Unity

A unified paragraph is one in which all the details help to develop a single main topic or achieve a single main effect. Test for unity by following these guidelines.

Topic Sentence

Very often the topic of a paragraph is stated in a single sentence called a "topic sentence." Check whether your paragraph needs a topic sentence. If the paragraph has a topic sentence, determine whether it is clear, specific, and well focused. Here is a formula for writing good topic sentences:

> **Formula:** A topic sentence = a limited topic + a specific feeling or thought about it.
>
> ---
>
> **Example:** The fear that Americans feel (limited topic) comes partly from the uncertainty related to this attack (a specific thought).

Placement of the Topic Sentence

Normally the topic sentence is the first sentence in the paragraph. However, it can appear elsewhere in a paragraph.

▶ **Middle Placement:** Place a topic sentence in the middle when you want to build up to and then lead away from the key idea.

> During the making of *Apocalypse Now*, Eleanor Coppola created a documentary about the filming called *Hearts of Darkness: A Filmmaker's Apocalypse*. In the first film, the insane Colonel Kurtz has disappeared into the Cambodian jungle. As Captain Willard searches for Kurtz, the screen fills with horror.

> **However, as *Hearts of Darkness* relates, the horror portrayed in the fictional movie was being lived out by the production company.** For example, in the documentary, actor Larry Fishburne shockingly says, "War is fun. . . . Vietnam must have been so much fun." Then toward the end of the filming, actor Martin Sheen suffered a heart attack. When an assistant informed investors, the director exploded, "He's not dead unless I say he's dead."

▸ **End Placement:** Place a topic sentence at the end when you want to build to a climax, as in a passage of narration or persuasion.

> When sportsmen stop to reflect on why they find fishing so enjoyable, most realize that what they love is the feel of a fish on the end of the line, not necessarily the weight of the fillets in their coolers. Fishing has undergone a slow evolution over the last century. While fishing used to be a way of putting food on the table, most of today's fishermen do so only for the relaxation that it provides. The barbed hook was invented to increase the quantity of fish a man could land so that he could better feed his family. **This need no longer exists, so barbed hooks are no longer necessary.**

Use Supporting Sentences

All the sentences in the body of a paragraph should support the topic sentence. The closing sentence, for instance, will often summarize the paragraph's main point or emphasize a key detail. If any sentences shift the focus away from the topic, revise the paragraph in one of the following ways:

- Delete the material from the paragraph.
- Rewrite the material so that it clearly supports the topic sentence.
- Create a separate paragraph based on the odd-man-out material.
- Revise the topic sentence so that it relates more closely to the support.

Consistent Focus

Paragraphs that contain unrelated ideas lack unity and are hard to follow. As you review each paragraph for unity, ask yourself these questions: Is the topic of the paragraph clear? Does each sentence relate to the topic? Are the sentences organized in the best possible order? Examine the following paragraph about fishing hooks.

The original topic sentence focuses on the point that some anglers prefer smooth hooks. However, the writer leaves this initial idea unfinished and turns to the issue of the cost of new hooks. In the revised version, unity is restored: The first paragraph completes the point about anglers who prefer smooth hooks; the second paragraph addresses the issue of replacement costs.

Original Paragraph *(Lacks unity)*

> According to some anglers who do use smooth hooks, their lures perform better than barbed lures as long as they maintain a constant tension on the line. Smooth hooks can bite deeper than barbed hooks, actually providing a stronger hold on the fish. Some people have argued that replacing all of the barbed hooks in their tackle would be a costly operation.

Revised Version *(Unified)*

> According to some anglers who do use smooth hooks, their lures perform better than barbed lures as long as the anglers maintain a constant tension on the line. Smooth hooks can bite deeper than barbed hooks, actually providing a stronger hold on the fish. These anglers testify that switching from barbed hooks has not noticeably reduced the number of fish that they are able to land. In their experience, and in my own, enjoyment of the sport is actually heightened by adding another challenge to playing the fish (maintaining line tension).

> Some people have argued that replacing all of the barbed hooks in their tackle would be a costly operation. While this is certainly a concern, barbed hooks do not necessarily require replacement. With a simple set of pliers, the barbs on most conventional hooks can be bent down, providing a cost-free method of modifying one's existing tackle.

6-4d Check for Coherence

When a paragraph is coherent, the parts stay together. A coherent paragraph flows smoothly because each sentence is connected to others by patterns in the language, such as repetition and transitions. To strengthen the coherence in your paragraphs, check for the issues discussed on the following page.

Effective Repetition

To achieve coherence in your paragraphs, consider using repetition—repeating words or synonyms where necessary to remind readers of what you have already said. You can also use parallelism—repeating phrase or sentence structures to show the relationships among ideas. At the same time, you will add a unifying rhythm to your writing.

> **Ineffective:** The floor was littered with discarded soda cans, newspapers that were crumpled, and wrinkled clothes.
>
> **Effective:** The floor was littered with discarded soda cans, crumpled newspapers, and wrinkled clothes. (Three parallel phrases are used.)
>
> **Ineffective:** Reading the book was enjoyable; to write the critique was difficult.
>
> **Effective:** Reading the book was enjoyable; writing the critique was difficult. (Two similar structures are repeated.)

Clear Transitions

Linking words and phrases like "next," "on the other hand," and "in addition" connect ideas by showing the relationship among them. There are transitions that show location and time, compare and contrast things, emphasize a point, conclude or summarize, and add or clarify information. Note the use of transitions in the examples that follow. Then study the table of linking words and phrases after the examples.

> The paradox of Scotland is that violence had long been the norm in this now-peaceful land. In fact, the country was born, bred, and came of age in war.
>
> (The transition is used to emphasize a point.)
>
> The production of cement is a complicated process. First, the mixture of lime, silica, alumina, and gypsum is ground into very fine particles.
>
> (The transition is used to show time or order.)

 TIP Another way to achieve coherence in your paragraphs is to use pronouns effectively. A pronoun forms a link to the noun it replaces and ties that noun (idea) to the ideas that follow. As always, don't overuse pronouns or rely too heavily on them in establishing coherence in your paragraphs.

Transitions and Linking Words

The words and phrases that follow can help you tie together words, phrases, sentences, and paragraphs. Use transitions to link, expand, or intensify an idea, but don't add elements carelessly, creating run-on or rambling sentences (pages 346–347).

Show location: above, behind, down, on top of, across, below, in back of, onto, against, beneath, in front of, outside, along, beside, inside, over, among, between, into, throughout, around, beyond, near, to the right, away from, by, off, under

Show time: about, during, next, today, after, finally, next week, tomorrow, afterward, first, second, until, as soon as, immediately, soon, when, at, later, then, yesterday, before, meanwhile, third

Show similarities: also, in the same way, likewise, as, like, similarly

Show differences: although, even though, on the other hand, still, but, however, otherwise, yet

Emphasize a point: again, for this reason, particularly, to repeat, even, in fact, to emphasize, truly

Conclude or summarize: all in all, finally, in summary, therefore, as a result, in conclusion, last, to sum up

Add information: additionally, and, equally important, in addition, again, another, finally, likewise, along with, as well, for example, next, also, besides, for instance, second

Clarify: for instance, in other words, put another way, that is

6-4e Check for Completeness

The sentences in a paragraph should support and expand on the main point. If your paragraph does not seem complete, you will need to add information.

Supporting Details

If some of your paragraphs are incomplete, they may lack details. There are numerous kinds of details, including the following:

facts	anecdotes	analyses	paraphrases
statistics	quotations	explanations	comparisons
examples	definitions	summaries	analogies

Add details based on the type of writing you are engaged in.

Describing: Add details that help readers see, smell, taste, touch, or hear it.

Narrating: Add details that help readers understand the events and actions.

Explaining: Add details that help readers understand what it means, how it works, or what it does.

Persuading: Add details that strengthen the logic of your argument.

Specific Details

The original paragraph below fails to answer fully the question posed by the topic sentence. In the revised paragraph, the writer uses an anecdote to answer the question.

Original Paragraph *(Lacks completeness)*

So what is stress? Actually, the physiological characteristics of stress are some of the body's potentially good self-defense mechanisms. People experience stress when they are in danger. In fact, stress can be healthy.

Revised Version *(Full development)*

So what is stress? Actually, the physiological characteristics of stress are some of the body's potentially good self-defense mechanisms. Take, for example, a man who is crossing a busy intersection when he spots an oncoming car. Immediately his brain releases a flood of adrenaline into his bloodstream. As a result, his muscles contract, his eyes dilate, his heart pounds faster, his breathing quickens, and his blood clots more readily. Each one of these responses helps the man leap out of the car's path. His muscles contract to give him exceptional strength. His eyes dilate so that he can see more clearly. His heart pumps more blood and his lungs exchange more air—both to increase his metabolism. If the man were injured, his blood would clot faster, ensuring a smaller amount of blood loss. In this situation and many more like it, stress symptoms are good (Curtis 25–26).

If you feel that a paragraph is getting too long when you are adding details, divide it at a natural stopping point. The topic sentence can then function as the thesis for that part of your essay or paper.

6-5 REVISE COLLABORATIVELY

Every writer can benefit from feedback from an interested audience, especially one that offers constructive and honest advice during a writing project. Members of an existing writing group already know how valuable it is for writers to share their work. Others might want to start a writing group to experience the benefits. Your group might collaborate online or in person. In either case, the information on the next two pages will help you get started.

6-5a Know Your Role

Writers and reviewers should know their roles and fulfill their responsibilities during revising sessions. Essentially, the writer should briefly introduce the draft and solicit honest responses. Reviewers should make constructive comments in response to the writing.

6-5b Provide Appropriate Feedback

Feedback can take many forms, including the three approaches described here.

▶ **Basic Description:** In this simple response, the reviewer listens or reads attentively and then simply describes what she or he hears or sees happening in the piece. The reviewer offers no criticism of the writing.

> **Ineffective:** "That was interesting. The piece was informative."

> **Effective:** "First, the essay introduced the challenge of your birth defect and how you have had to cope with it. Then in the next part you . . ."

▶ **Summary Evaluation:** Here the reviewer reads or listens to the piece and then provides a specific evaluation of the draft.

Ineffective: "Gee, I really liked it!" or "It was boring."

Effective: "Your story at the beginning really pulled me in, and the middle explained the issue strongly, but the ending felt a bit flat."

▸ **Thorough Critique:** The reviewer assesses the ideas, organization, and voice in the writing. Feedback should be detailed and constructive. Such a critique may also be completed with the aid of a review sheet or checklist. As a reviewer, be prepared to share specific responses, suggestions, and questions. But also be sure to focus your comments on the writing rather than the writer.

Ineffective: "You really need to fix that opening! What were you thinking?"

Effective: "Let's look closely at the opening. Could you rewrite the first sentence so it grabs the reader's attention? Also, I'm somewhat confused about the thesis statement. Could you rephrase it so it states your position more clearly?"

6-5c Respond According to a Plan

Using a specific plan or scheme like the following will help you give clear, helpful, and complete feedback.

▸ **OAQS Method:** Use this simple four-step scheme —Observe, Appreciate, Question, and Suggest—to respond to your peers' writing.

1. **Observe** means to notice what another person's essay is designed to do and then say something about its design or purpose. For example, you might say, "Even though you are writing about your boyfriend, it appears that you are trying to get a message across to your parents."

2. **Appreciate** means to praise something in the writing that impresses or pleases you. You can find something to appreciate in any piece of writing. For example, you might say, "You make a very convincing point" or "With your description, I can actually see his broken tooth."

3. **Question** means to ask whatever you want to know after you've read the essay. You might ask for background information, a definition, an interpretation, or an explanation. For example, you might say, "Can you tell us what happened when you got to the emergency room?"

4. **Suggest** means to give helpful advice about possible changes. For example, you might say, "With a little more physical detail—especially more sounds and smells—your third paragraph could be the highlight of the whole essay. What do you think?"

Asking the Writer Questions

Reviewers should ask the following types of questions while reviewing a piece of writing:

- **To help writers reflect on their purpose and audience . . .**

  Why are you writing this?

  Who will read this, and what do they need to know?

- **To help writers focus their thoughts . . .**

  What message are you trying to get across?

  Do you have more than one main point?

  What are the most important examples?

- **To help writers think about their information . . .**

  What do you know about the subject?

  Does this part say enough?

  Does your writing cover all of the basics (*Who? What? Where? When? Why?* and *How?*)?

- **To help writers with their openings and closings . . .**

  What are you trying to say in the opening?

  How else could you start your writing?

  How do you want your readers to feel at the end?

6-6 USE THE WRITING CENTER

A college writing center or lab is a place where a trained adviser will help you develop and strengthen a piece of writing. You can expect the writing center adviser to do certain things; other things only you can do. For quick reference, refer to the chart below.

Adviser's Job	Your Job
Make you feel at home	Be respectful
Discuss your needs	Be ready to work
Help you choose a topic	Decide on a topic
Discuss your purpose and audience	Know your purpose and audience
Help you generate ideas	Embrace the best ideas
Help you develop your logic	Consider other points of view; stretch your own perspective
Help you understand how to research your material	Do the research
Read your draft	Share your writing
Identify problems in organization, logic, expression, and format	Recognize and fix problems
Teach ways to correct weaknesses	Learn important principles
Help you with grammar, usage, diction, vocabulary, and mechanics	Correct all errors

 TIP To get the most out of the writing center:
- Visit the center at least several days before your paper is due.
- Take your assignment sheet with you to each advising session.
- Read your work aloud, slowly.
- Expect to rethink your writing from scratch.
- Do not defend your wording—if it needs defense, it needs revision.
- Ask questions. (No question is "too dumb.")
- Request clarification of anything you don't understand.
- Ask for examples or illustrations of important points.
- Write down all practical suggestions.
- Ask the adviser to summarize his or her remarks.
- Rewrite as soon as possible after—or even during—the advising session.

WRITING WITH SOURCES

When your writing project involves working with sources, test your first draft for effective use of researched material by examining how well references to sources advance your thesis and enrich your ideas. The strategies that follow will help you do this.

Think Rhetorically

Consider how well your sources help you achieve your purpose, reach your audience, and thoroughly address your subject. Specifically, assess your first draft with questions like these:

- Will readers accept my sources and how I used them, or will they question my reasoning and evidence? What alternatives, objections, or questions might they raise?
- Does my writing encourage readers to think thoroughly about my topic? Do I need to add more background details, definitions, and contextual information?
- Do my sources get at essential, deep truths about my subject, or do they simply offer basic data or common knowledge?

Depending on your answers to these questions, you may have to reread your notes and sources, or you may have to look for additional information.

Test the Balance of Reasoning and Support

Examine the big picture of how you have used source material—summaries, paraphrases, and quotations—in relation to your own discussion of the issue. If your draft is thin on the support side (filled with big claims that lack adequate support), you need to either scale back your claims or beef up the support with more information and evidence. Conversely, your draft may be dominated by source material, not your own thinking. If your paper reads like a series of source summaries or quotations, if it contains big patches of copy-and-paste material, if your paragraphs all seem to start and end with source material, or if your writing is dense with detailed but almost incomprehensible data, you may need to deepen your own contribution to the paper. Do so by trying the following:

1. Before diving into source material within a paragraph or section of your paper, flesh out your thinking more fully. Offer reasoning that elaborates the claim and effectively leads into the evidence.

2. As you present evidence from source material, build on it by explaining what it means. Evidence doesn't typically speak for itself: through analysis, synthesis, illustration, etc., you need to show how or why your sources advance your thesis.

3. After you have presented evidence that elaborates and supports your idea, extend your thoughts by answering the reader's "So what?" or "Why does this matter?"

Test Your Evidence

Examine how well your researched information elaborates and backs up your points or claims. That evidence should be solid enough to encourage readers to accept your ideas; conversely, weak evidence will lead readers to reject your analysis or argument. Specifically, the evidence should be

- **accurate:** The information is all correct.
- **precise:** The data are concrete and specific, not vague and general.
- **substantial:** The amount of evidence reaches a critical mass—enough to convey the idea and convince readers of its validity.
- **authoritative:** The evidence comes from a reliable source. Moreover, the information is as close to the origin as possible; it is not a report conveying information third-hand.
- **representative:** The information fairly represents the range of data on the issue. Your presentation of evidence is balanced.
- **fitting:** Given your subject, purpose, and reader, the evidence is appropriate and relevant for the topic you are addressing.

Test the Flow of Information

Generally, writing using source material should follow the known/new principle. Because audiences "build" meaning as they read, your paper's overall structure, sections, and paragraphs should all be built so that new information comes gradually and links to information that the reader already knows.

Test for Plagiarism

Reviewing your notes and sources as needed, check that you have clearly indicated what material in your draft is summarized, paraphrased, or quoted from a source. In particular, check that your attributive phrases and citations set off all source material except for common knowledge. (For help, see pages 269–274.)

 Cross-Curricular Connections

Different disciplines value certain types of evidence more highly than other types. For example, humanities disciplines might value close interpretations of texts, while natural sciences would value quantitative evidence gathered through the scientific method. As you write in your major, use types of evidence and methods of analysis that this research community accepts and respects.

Critical-Thinking and Writing Activities

1. Doris Lessing said that when it comes to writing, "The more a thing cooks, the better." In what sense is revision a crucial stage in that "cooking" process? Using Lessing's cooking metaphor as a starting point, explore how revision should function in your own writing.

2. Review the opening and closing paragraphs of one of your essays. Then come up with fresh and different approaches for those paragraphs using the information on pages 66–72 for help.

3. For your current writing assignment, ask a peer to provide detailed feedback using the information in this chapter as a guide. Then take a fresh copy of your paper to the writing center and work through your draft with an adviser. Revise the draft as needed.

STUDY TOOLS 6

LOCATED AT BACK OF THE TEXTBOOK
☐ Tear-Out Chapter Review Card

LOCATED AT WWW.CENGAGE.COM/LOGIN
☐ Chapter eBook
☐ Graded quizzes and a practice quiz generator
☐ Videos: Writer Interviews
☐ Tutorials
☐ Flashcards
☐ Cengage Learning Write Experience
☐ Interactive activities

7 | Editing

spiber.de, 2014 / Used under license from Shutterstock.com

"MISTAKES ARE A FACT OF LIFE. IT IS THE RESPONSE TO THE ERROR THAT COUNTS."

NIKKI GIOVANNI

LEARNING OBJECTIVES

7-1 Adopt strategies for polishing your writing.

7-2 Combine short, simplistic sentences.

7-3 Expand sentences to add details.

7-4 Edit sentences for variety and style.

7-5 Eliminate wordiness.

7-6 Avoid vague, weak, and biased words.

7-7 Edit and proofread for correctness.

After you finish
this chapter
go to
PAGE 87 for STUDY TOOLS

Editing and proofreading allow you to fine-tune your writing, making it ready to hand in. When you edit, look first for words, phrases, and sentences that sound awkward, uninteresting, or unclear. When you proofread, check your writing for spelling, mechanics, usage, and grammar errors. Ask one of your writing peers to help you.

The guidelines and strategies given in this chapter will help you edit your writing for style and clarity and proofread it for errors.

However, if you need more complete instruction on correctness issues, see Part 3, the handbook section of *COMP*.

 7-1

ADOPT STRATEGIES FOR POLISHING YOUR WRITING

When you have thoroughly revised your writing, you need to edit it so that it is clear, concise, energetic, varied, and correct. Start with the strategies below.

7-1a Review the Overall Style of Your Writing

How does your writing sound? Is it mature, thoughtful, and direct? To answer these questions, consider the following:

1. **Check that your style fits the rhetorical situation.**
   - **Goal:** Does your writing sound as if you wrote it with a clear aim in mind? Does your prose seem filled with purpose?
   - **Reader:** Does the writing sound authentic and honest? Is the language fitting for your audience?
   - **Subject:** Does the writing suit the subject and your treatment of it in terms of seriousness or playfulness, complexity or simplicity?

2. **Check that your style carries the right authority.** Nineteenth-century British author

Matthew Arnold puts it this way: "Have something to say, and say it as clearly as you can. That is the only secret of style." Does your writing straightforwardly communicate a clear message? Does it avoid a false sense of authority, such as the following sentence? "Upon serious consideration, I have purposively determined without a doubt that talk radio programs are decidedly biased." Conversely, do you avoid speaking with little or no sense of authority, like this sentence? "I really just flipped when I read that *Life of Pi* story!"

3. **Check your sentence style and word choice.** At its heart, your style is about the sentences you create and the words crafted into those sentences. For that reason, this chapter focuses to a large degree on these issues:
   - Combining sentences (78), expanding them (78), varying sentence structures (80), using parallel structure (81), and avoiding weak constructions (82)
   - Avoiding wordiness (82), as well as imprecise, misleading, and biased wording (83)

7-1b Use Tools and Methods That Work

Here are three tips that will help you edit effectively:

1. **Do it at the right time, and give yourself the time.** Just as you should leave time between drafting and revising your paper, you should leave time between revising and editing it, at least 24 hours. This time lapse allows you a fresh view of your writing. In addition, don't rush through editing, as doing it well takes patience and concentration.

2. **Review your draft from multiple points of view.** While reading print on screen is generally more difficult than doing so on paper, on-screen editing offers you tremendous power and flexibility. Then again, at some point in your editing, you need to see your words in print on a page. As needed, increase the print size and line spacing to create "white space" that makes it easier to both "see" your writing and insert any changes. Finally, consider reading your paper aloud or having a classmate do so while you listen: Hearing your words will help you sense where your sentences fall flat or your grammar needs work.

3. **Use software editing tools as an aid.** Your writing software likely has several helpful tools:

spell check, grammar check, find-and-replace functions, track-changes tools, and so on. The key is to use these tools wisely while not relying on them exclusively. For example, spell check will not catch usage errors such as *it's* versus *its*. In the end, you need to manage the editing process, including your writing tools.

7-2 COMBINE SHORT, SIMPLISTIC SENTENCES

Effective sentences often contain several basic ideas that work together to show relationships and make connections. Here are five basic ideas followed by seven examples of how the ideas can be combined into effective sentences.

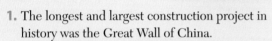

1. The longest and largest construction project in history was the Great Wall of China.
2. The project took 1,700 years to complete.
3. The Great Wall of China is 1,400 miles long.
4. It is between 18 and 30 feet high.
5. It is up to 32 feet wide.

7-2a Edit Sentences for Clarity and Style

Combine your short, simplistic sentences into longer, more detailed sentences. Sentence combining is generally carried out in the following ways:

- Use a **series** to combine three or more similar ideas.

  > The Great Wall of China is 1,400 miles long, between 18 and 30 feet high, and up to 32 feet wide.

- Use a **relative pronoun** (*who, whose, that, which*) to introduce subordinate (less important) ideas.

  > The Great Wall of China, which is 1,400 miles long and between 18 and 30 feet high, took 1,700 years to complete.

- Use an **introductory phrase** or **clause**.

  > Having taken 1,700 years to complete, the Great Wall of China was the longest construction project in history.

- Use a **semicolon** (and a conjunctive adverb if appropriate).

  > The Great Wall took 1,700 years to complete; it is 1,400 miles long and up to 30 feet high and 32 feet wide.

- Repeat a **key word** or **phrase** to emphasize an idea.

  > The Great Wall of China was the longest construction project in history, a project that took 1,700 years to complete.

- Use **correlative conjunctions** (*either, or; not only, but also*) to compare or contrast two ideas in a sentence.

  > The Great Wall of China was not only the longest construction project in history, but also the largest.

- Use an **appositive** (a word or phrase that renames) to emphasize an idea.

  > The Great Wall of China—the largest construction project in history—is 1,400 miles long, 32 feet wide, and up to 30 feet high.

7-3 EXPAND SENTENCES TO ADD DETAILS

Expand sentences when you edit so as to connect related ideas and make room for new information. Length has no value in and of itself: The best sentence is still the shortest one that says all it has to say. An expanded sentence, however, is capable of saying more—and saying it more expressively.

7-3a Use Cumulative Sentences

Modern writers often use an expressive sentence form called the cumulative sentence. A cumulative sentence is made of a general "base clause" that is expanded by adding modifying words, phrases, or clauses. In such a sentence, details are added before, within, and after the main clause, creating an image-rich thought. Here's an example of a cumulative sentence, with the base clause or main idea in red:

> In preparation for her Spanish exam, Julie was studying at the kitchen table, completely focused, memorizing a list of vocabulary words.

Discussion: Notice how each new modifier adds to the richness of the final sentence. Also notice that each of these modifying phrases is set off by a comma. Here's another sample sentence:

> With his hands on his face, Tony was laughing halfheartedly, looking puzzled and embarrassed.

Discussion: Such a cumulative sentence provides a way to write description that is rich in detail, without rambling. Notice how each modifier changes the flow or rhythm of the sentence.

7-3b Expand with Details

Here are seven basic ways to expand a main idea:

1. **Adjectives and Adverbs:**
   halfheartedly, once again
2. **Prepositional Phrases:**
   with his hands on his face
3. **Absolute Phrases:**
   his head tilted to one side
4. **Participial** (*ing* or *ed*) **Phrases:**
   looking puzzled
5. **Infinitive Phrases:**
   to hide his embarrassment
6. **Subordinate Clauses:**
   while his friend talks
7. **Relative Clauses:**
   who isn't laughing at all

To edit sentences for more expressive style, it is best to (1) know your grammar and punctuation (especially commas); (2) practice tightening, combining, and expanding sentences using the guidelines in this chapter; and (3) read carefully, looking for models of well-constructed sentences.

7-4 EDIT SENTENCES FOR VARIETY AND STYLE

Writer E. B. White advised young writers to "approach sentence style by way of simplicity, plainness, orderliness, and sincerity." That's good advice from a writer steeped in style. It's also important to know what to look for when editing your sentences. The information that follows will help you edit your sentences for style.

7-4a Avoid Sentence Problems

Always check for and correct the following types of sentence problems. Turn to the pages listed below for guidelines and examples when attempting to fix problems in your sentences.

▸ **Short, Choppy Sentences:** Combine or expand any short, choppy sentences; use the examples and guidelines on pages 78–79.

▸ **Flat, Predictable Sentences:** Rewrite any sentences that sound predictable and uninteresting by varying their structures and expanding them with modifying words, phrases, and clauses. (See pages 79–82.)

▸ **Incorrect Sentences:** Look for and correct fragments, run-ons, and comma splices. (See pages 346–347.)

▸ **Unclear Sentences:** Edit any sentences that contain unclear wording, misplaced modifiers, dangling modifiers, or incomplete comparisons. (See pages 348–349.)

▸ **Unacceptable Sentences:** Change sentences that include nonstandard language, double negatives, or unparallel constructions. (See page 349.)

7-4b Review Your Writing for Sentence Variety

Use the following strategy to review your writing for variety in terms of sentence beginnings, lengths, and types.

- In one column on a piece of paper, list the opening words in each of your sentences. Then decide if you need to vary some of your sentence beginnings.
- In another column, identify the number of words in each sentence. Then decide if you need to change the lengths of some of your sentences.
- In a third column, list the kinds of sentences used (exclamatory, declarative, interrogative, and so on). Then, based on your analysis, use the instructions on the next two pages to edit your sentences as needed.

7-4c Vary Sentence Structures

To energize your sentences, vary their structures using one or more of the methods that follow.

1. **Vary sentence openings.** Move a modifying word, phrase, or clause to the front of the sentence to stress that modifier. However, avoid creating dangling or misplaced modifiers.

   > Unvaried: The problem is not just about wasteful irrigation, though. The problem is also about resistance to change. The problem is that many people have fought against restrictions when governments have tried to pass regulations.

   > Varied: However, the problem is not just about wasteful irrigation. It's about resistance to change. When governments have tried to pass regulations controlling water use, many people have fought against restrictions.

2. **Vary sentence lengths.** Short sentences (10 words or fewer) are ideal for making points crisply. Medium sentences (10 to 20 words) should carry the bulk of your information. When they are well crafted, occasional long sentences (more than 20 words) can develop and expand your ideas.

   > Short: Museum exhibitions have become increasingly commercial in nature.

   > Medium: To the extent that "access" is an adequate measure of museum performance, art as entertainment "has proven a resounding triumph."

   > Long: Shows featuring motorcycles, automobiles, the treasures of King Tutankhamen, the works of Van Gogh, and other blockbuster favorites not only have proven immensely popular but have also offered the promise of corporate underwriting and ample commercial tie-ins.

3. **Vary sentence kinds.** The most common sentence is declarative—it states a point. For variety, try exclamatory, imperative, interrogative, and conditional statements.

   > Declarative: Historical records indicate that the lost colonists of Roanoke may have been harboring a dangerous virus: influenza.

   > Conditional: If the influenza virus was not present in the New World before the arrival of Europeans, then it is highly probable that the lost colonists of Roanoke made contact with the indigenous groups of North Carolina and served as vectors for the influenza disease.

   > Interrogative: That being said, we must now turn to a different question: What happened to those lost colonists? (Note: do not overuse rhetorical questions.)

   > Imperative: Let us take steps to ensure that the Lumbee People do not share the fate of the colonists who disappeared from the island of Roanoke.

   > Exclamatory: Just as John White found upon his belated return to the deserted colony over 400 years ago, something is terribly wrong! (Note: generally avoid exclamatory sentences in traditional academic writing.)

   In creative writing (stories, novels, plays), writers occasionally use fragments to vary the rhythm of their prose, emphasize a point, or create dialogue. Avoid fragments in academic or business writing.

4. **Vary sentence arrangements.** Where do you want to place the main point of your sentence? You make that choice by arranging sentence parts into loose, periodic, balanced, or cumulative patterns. Each pattern creates a specific effect.

   > Loose Sentence: Men are frequently mystified by women, with their unfamiliar rituals, their emotional vitality, and their biological clocks—issues often addressed in romantic comedies.

   > *Analysis:* This pattern is direct. It states the main point immediately (red), and then tacks on extra information.

   > Periodic Sentence: While Western culture celebrates and idolizes romantic and sexual forms of love, seen powerfully in the films that it creates and the romance novels it produces, such attraction between a man and a woman, no matter how strong initially, in the end fails to sustain a relationship for a lifetime.

   > *Analysis:* This pattern postpones the main point (red) until the end. The sentence builds to the point, creating an indirect, dramatic effect.

Balanced Sentence: The modern romantic comedy often portrays male characters as resistant to or hopelessly clueless about love; however, in Jane Austen's narratives, while male characters do exhibit these features to a degree, men's behavior is complicated by traditional codes of honor that have now largely vanished.

Analysis: This pattern gives equal weight to complementary or contrasting points (red); the balance is often signaled by a comma and a conjunction (and, but) or by a semicolon. Often a conjunctive adverb (however, nevertheless) or a transitional phrase (in addition, even so) will follow the semicolon to further clarify the relationship.

Cumulative Sentence: In spite of his initially limiting pride, Mr. Darcy, now properly proud and still handsome, emerges finally as the consummate romantic hero, the anonymous savior of Elizabeth's family, a true gentleman.

Analysis: This pattern puts the main idea (red) in the middle of the sentence, surrounding it with modifying words, phrases, and clauses.

5. Use positive repetition. Although you should avoid needless repetition, you might use emphatic repetition to repeat a key word to stress a point.

Repetitive Sentence: Each year, more than a million young people who read poorly leave high school unable to read well, functionally illiterate.

Emphatic Sentence: Each year, more than a million young people leave high school functionally illiterate, so illiterate that they can't read daily newspapers, job ads, or safety instructions.

7-4d Use Parallel Structure

Coordinated sentence elements should be parallel—that is, they should be written in the same grammatical forms. Parallel structures save words, clarify relationships, and present the information in the correct sequence. Follow these guidelines.

1. For words, phrases, or clauses in a series, keep elements consistent.

Not parallel: I have tutored students in Biology 101, also Chemistry 102, not to mention Physics 200.

Parallel: I have tutored students in *Biology 101, Chemistry 102, and Physics 200.*

Not parallel: I have volunteered as a hospital receptionist, have been a hospice volunteer, and as an emergency medical technician.

Parallel: I have done volunteer work as a *hospital receptionist, a hospice counselor, and an emergency medical technician.*

2. Use both parts of correlative conjunctions (*either, or; neither, nor; not only, but also; as, so; whether, so; both, and*) so that both segments of the sentence are balanced.

Not parallel: *Not only* did Blake College turn 20 this year. Its enrollment grew by 16 percent.

Parallel: *Not only* did Blake College turn 20 this year, *but* its enrollment *also* grew by 16 percent.

Not parallel: *Either* finish your thesis proposal by November 22. Ask for a week's extension.

Parallel: *Either* finish your thesis proposal by November 22 *or* ask for a week's extension.

3. Place a modifier correctly so that it clearly indicates the word or words to which it refers.

Confusing: MADD promotes *severely* punishing and eliminating drunk driving because this offense leads to a *great number* of deaths and sorrow.

Parallel: MADD promotes eliminating and *severely* punishing drunk driving because this offense leads to *many* deaths and *untold* sorrow.

4. Place contrasting details in parallel structures (*words, phrases,* or *clauses*) to stress a contrast.

Weak contrast: On average child watches 24 hours of TV a week and reads for 36 minutes.

Strong contrast: Each week, the average child watches TV for 24 hours but reads for only about half an hour.

7-4e Avoid Weak Constructions

Avoid constructions (like those below) that weaken your writing.

Nominal Constructions

The nominal construction is both sluggish and wordy. Avoid it by changing the noun form of a verb (*description* or *instructions*) to a verb (*describe* or *instruct*). At the same time, delete the weak verb that preceded the noun.

Nominal Constructions (noun form underlined)	Strong Verbs
• Tim gave a description ...	• Tim *described* ...
• Lydia provided instructions ...	• Lydia *instructed* ...

Sluggish: In her study of Austen film adaptations, Lydia Balm provides an explanation for the narrative power of dance scenes. Dances offer a symbolization and visualization of characters in situations of mutual attraction but nonverbalization.

Energetic: In her study of Austen film adaptations, Lydia Balm explains the narrative power of dance scenes. Dances symbolize visually the attraction characters feel for each other but cannot verbalize.

Expletives

Expletives such as "it is" and "there are" are fillers that serve no purpose in most sentences—except to make them wordy and unnatural.

Sluggish: It is believed by some people that childhood vaccinations can cause autism. There are several Web sites that promote this point of view quite forcefully. In fact, it is also the case that some celebrities advocate this cause.

Energetic: Some people believe that childhood vaccinations can cause autism. Several Web sites, along with some celebrities, promote this point of view forcefully.

Negative Constructions

Sentences constructed upon the negatives *no*, *not*, *neither/nor* can be wordy and difficult to understand. It's simpler to state what *is* the case.

Negative: Hybrid vehicles are not completely different from traditional cars, as hybrids cannot run without gas and cannot rely only on battery power that has not been created by the gasoline engine.

Positive: Hybrid vehicles are similar to traditional cars, as hybrids do require gas in order to power an internal-combustion engine that in turn powers batteries.

7-5 ELIMINATE WORDINESS

Wordy writing taxes the reader's attention. While your paper itself may be long, the writing itself should be concise—tightly phrased so that each word counts. To tighten your writing, cut the types of wordiness described below.

7-5a Cut Deadwood

Deadwood is filler material—verbal "lumber" that you can remove without harming the sentence. Look for irrelevant information and obvious statements.

Deadwood: GM must undergo a thorough retooling process if it is to be competitive in the fast-paced, rapidly changing world of today's global marketplace.

Concise: GM must change to meet global challenges.

7-5b Eliminate Redundancy

Redundancy refers to unnecessary repetition. Check your sentences for words and phrases that say the same thing, doubling up the meaning.

Redundant: Avoid the construction site, and be sure to pick a different route if you want to avoid riding over nails and risking a flat tire.

Concise: If you want to avoid a flat tire, don't drive through the construction site.

Check your writing especially for these common redundancies:

- Using *together* with verbs such as *combine*, *join*, *unite*, and *merge*
- Using *new* before *discovery*, *fad*, and *innovation*
- Using *up* after *connect*, *divide*, *eat*, *lift*, and *mix*
- Using *in color* with a color (*green in color*)
- Using *in shape* with a shape (*round in shape*)
- Using these phrases: *plan ahead*, *descend down*, *end result*, *visible to the eye*, *resume again*, *very unique*, *small in size*, and *repeat again*

7-5c Cut Unnecessary Modifiers

Adjectives and adverbs typically clarify nouns and verbs; however, excessive modifiers make prose dense. Edit by following these principles:

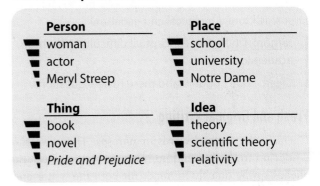

- Don't use two modifiers when one will do.
- Use precise nouns and verbs to avoid the need for modifiers.
- Generally avoid intensifying adverbs (*very, extremely, intensely, awfully, especially*).
- Delete meaningless modifiers (*kind of, sort of*).

Wordy: To ensure *very healthy, properly* growing trees, whether *deciduous* or *coniferous*, hire a *licensed*, professional tree surgeon.

Concise: To ensure healthy trees, hire a professional tree surgeon.

7-5d Replace Long Phrases and Clauses

Often, a long phrase or clause can be replaced by a shorter phrase or even a single word. For example, replace *in many cases* with *often*, *aware of the fact that* with *aware that*, *in a rapid manner* with *rapidly*, and *of a dangerous nature* with *dangerous*. In addition, locate prepositional phrases (*at the beginning of the project*) and relative clauses (*who, which, that* clauses) and replace them when possible with simpler words.

Wordy: Among a variety of different devices that could possibly perform the task of preventing the wastage of water, an interesting one is LEPA, also known by many as low-energy precision application, hence the acronym.

Concise: A second device that prevents water waste is LEPA, or low-energy precision application.

7-6 AVOID VAGUE, WEAK, AND BIASED WORDS

As you edit your writing, check your choice of words carefully. The information on the next four pages will help you edit for word choice.

7-6a Substitute Specific Words

Replace vague nouns and verbs with words that generate clarity and energy.

Specific Nouns

Make it a habit to use specific nouns for subjects. General nouns (*woman, school*) give the reader a vague, uninteresting picture. More specific nouns (*actress, university*) give the reader a better picture. Finally, very specific nouns (*Meryl Streep, Notre Dame*) are the types that can make your writing clear and colorful.

General to Specific Nouns

Person	Place
woman	school
actor	university
Meryl Streep	Notre Dame

Thing	Idea
book	theory
novel	scientific theory
Pride and Prejudice	relativity

Vivid Verbs

Like nouns, verbs can be too general to create a vivid word picture. For example, the verb *looked* does not say the same thing as *stared, glared, glanced,* or *peeked*.

- Whenever possible, use a verb that is strong enough to stand alone without the help of an adverb.

  Verb and adverb: John *fell down* in the student lounge.

  Vivid verb: John collapsed in the student lounge.

- Avoid overusing the "be" verbs (is, are, was, were) and helping verbs. Often a main verb can be made from another word in the same sentence.

  A "be" verb: Cole *is* someone who follows international news.

  A stronger verb: Cole follows international news.

- Use active rather than passive verbs. (Use passive verbs only if you want to downplay who is performing the action in a sentence. See page 68.)

  Passive verb: Another provocative essay *was submitted* by Kim.

  Active verb: Kim submitted another provocative essay.

- Use verbs that show rather than tell.

  | A verb that tells: Dr. Lewis *is* very thorough.

  | A verb that shows: Dr. Lewis prepares detailed, interactive lectures.

7-6b Replace Jargon and Clichés

Replace language that is overly technical or difficult to understand. Also replace overused, worn-out words.

Understandable Language

Jargon is language used in a certain profession or by a particular group of people. It may be acceptable to use if your audience is that group of people, but to most ears jargon will sound technical and unnatural.

| Jargon: I'm having conceptual difficulty with these academic queries.

| Clear: I don't understand these review questions.

Fresh and Original Writing

Clichés are overused words or phrases. They give the reader no fresh view and no concrete picture. Because clichés spring quickly to mind (for both the writer and the reader), they are easy to write and often remain unedited.

an axe to grind	piece of cake
as good as dead	planting the seed
beat around the bush	rearing its ugly head
between a rock and a hard place	stick your neck out
	throwing your weight around
burning bridges	
easy as pie	up a creek

Unpretentious Language

Pretentious language aims to sound intelligent but comes off sounding phony. Such language calls attention to itself rather than its meaning; in fact, pretentious words can be so high-blown that meaning is obscured altogether.

| Pretentious: Liquid precipitation in the Iberian Peninsula's nation-state of most prominent size experiences altitudinal descent as a matter of course primarily in the region characterized by minimal topographical variation.

| Plain: The rain in Spain falls mainly on the plain.

7-6c Strive for Plain English

In many ways, plain English is the product of the principles discussed earlier: avoiding jargon, technical language, clichés, flowery phrasing, and pretentious wording. However, plain English also counters these ethically questionable uses of language:

Obfuscation

Obfuscation involves using fuzzy terms, such as *throughput* and *downlink*, which muddy the issue. These words may make simple ideas sound more profound than they really are, or they may make false ideas sound true.

| Example: Through the fully functional developmental process of a streamlined target-refractory system, the military will successfully reprioritize its data throughputs. (***Objection:*** What does this mean?)

Ambiguity

Ambiguity (especially when deliberate) makes a statement open to multiple interpretations. While desirable in some forms of writing (such as poetry and fiction), ambiguity is usually disruptive in academic writing because it obscures the meaning of the words.

| Example: Many women need to work to support their children through school, but they would be better off at home. (***Objection:*** Does *they* refer to *children* or *women*? What does *better off* mean? These words and phrases are unclear.)

Euphemisms

Euphemisms are overly polite expressions that avoid stating an uncomfortable truth. In academic writing, you generally want to choose neutral, tactful phrasing, but avoid euphemisms.

| Example: This economically challenged neighborhood faces some issues concerning mind-enhancing substances and scuffles between youths. (***Translation:*** This impoverished neighborhood is being destroyed by drugs and gangs.)

Doublespeak

Doublespeak is phrasing that deliberately seeks either to hide the truth from readers or to understate the situation. Such slippery language is especially tempting when the writer holds authority, power, or privilege in a negative situation Avoid doublespeak by choosing precise, transparent, and honest phrasing.

Example: The doctor executed a nonfacile manipulation of newborn. (***Translation:*** The doctor dropped the baby during delivery.)

7-6d Change Biased Words

When depicting individuals or groups according to their differences, use language that implies equal value and respect for all people.

Words Referring to Ethnicity

General Terms	Specific Terms
American Indians, Native Americans	Cherokee people, Inuit people, and so forth
Asian Americans (not Orientals)	Chinese Americans, Japanese Americans, and so forth
Latinos, Latinas, Hispanics	Mexican Americans, Cuban Americans, and so forth

African Americans, blacks: "African American" has come into wide acceptance, though the term "black" is preferred by some individuals.

Not Recommended	Preferred
Eurasian, mulatto	person of mixed ancestry
nonwhite	person of color
Caucasian	white
American (to mean U.S. citizen internationally)	U.S. citizen

Words Referring to Age

Age Group	Acceptable Terms
up to age 13 or 14	boys, girls
between 13 and 19	teens, youth, young people, young men, young women
late teens and 20s	young adults, young women, young men
30s to age 60	adults, men, women
60 and older	older adults, older people (not elderly)
66 and older	seniors, senior citizens

Words Referring to Disabilities or Impairments

Whenever you write about a person with a disability, an impairment, or other special condition, give the person and your readers the utmost respect. An insensitive reference reflects poorly on the writer.

In the recent past, some writers were choosing alternatives to the term *disabled*, including *physically challenged*, *exceptional*, or *special*. However, it is not generally held that these new terms are precise enough to serve those who live with disabilities. Of course, degrading labels such as *crippled*, *invalid*, and *maimed*, as well as overly negative terminology, must be avoided.

Not Recommended	Preferred
handicapped	disabled
birth defect	congenital disability
stutter, stammer, lisp	speech impairment
an AIDS victim	person with AIDS
suffering from cancer	person who has cancer
mechanical foot	prosthetic foot
false teeth	dentures

Words Referring to Conditions

People with various disabilities and conditions have sometimes been referred to as though they were their condition (*quadriplegics, depressives, epileptics*) instead of people who happen to have a particular disability. As much as possible, remember to refer to the person first, the disability second.

Not Recommended	Preferred
the disabled	people with disabilities
cripples	people who have difficulty walking
the retarded	people with a developmental disability
dyslexics	students with dyslexia
neurotics	patients with neuroses
subjects, cases	participants, patients
quadriplegics	people who are quadriplegic
wheelchair users	people who use wheelchairs

Make sure you understand the following terms that address specific impairments:

hearing impairment ➡ partial hearing loss, hard of hearing (not deaf, which is total loss of hearing)

visual impairment ➡ partially sighted (not blind, which is total loss of vision)

communicative disorder ➡ speech, hearing, and learning disabilities affecting communication

Words Referring to Gender

▶ **Use parallel language for both sexes:**

> The men and the women worked together.
> Hank and Marie
> Mr. Robert Gumble, Mrs. Joy Gumble

Note: The courtesy titles *Mr., Ms., Mrs.,* and *Miss* ought to be used according to the person's preference.

▶ **Use nonsexist alternatives** to words with masculine connotations:

> humanity (not *mankind*)
> synthetic (not *man-made*)

▶ **Do not use masculine-only or feminine-only pronouns** (*he, she, his, her*) when you want to refer to a human being in general:

> A politician can kiss privacy good-bye when he runs for office. (*not recommended*)

Instead, use *he* or *she*, change the sentence to plural, or eliminate the pronoun:

> A politician can kiss privacy good-bye when he or she runs for office.
> Politicians can kiss privacy good-bye when they run for office.
> A politician can kiss privacy good-bye when running for office.

▶ **Do not use gender-specific references** in the salutation when you don't know the person's name:

> ▌ Dear Sir:

Instead, address a position:

> ▌ Dear Personnel Officer:

Occupational Issues

Not Recommended	Preferred
chairman	chair, presiding officer
salesman	sales representative, salesperson

Not Recommended	Preferred
male/female nurse/doctor	nurse
male/female doctor	doctor, physician
mailman	mail carrier, postal worker
insurance man	insurance agent
fireman	firefighter
businessman	executive, manager, businessperson
congressman	member of Congress, representative, senator
steward, stewardess	flight attendant
policeman, policewoman	police officer

7-7 EDIT AND PROOFREAD FOR CORRECTNESS

Correct errors in spelling, mechanics, usage, grammar, and form. (See Part 3, the handbook, for specific rules.)

Review Punctuation and Mechanics

1. Check for proper use of commas before coordinating conjunctions in compound sentences, after introductory clauses and long introductory phrases, between items in a series, and so on.
2. Look for apostrophes in contractions, plurals, and possessive nouns.
3. Examine quotation marks in quoted information, titles, or dialogue.
4. Watch for proper use of capital letters for first words in written conversation and for proper names of people, places, and things.

Look for Usage and Grammar Errors

1. Look for words that writers commonly misuse: *there/their/they're; accept/except.*
2. Check for verb use. Subjects and verbs should agree in number. Verb tenses should be consistent.
3. Edit for pronoun/antecedent agreement problems. A pronoun and its antecedent must agree in number.

Check for Spelling Errors

1. Use a spell checker and dictionary.
2. Check each spelling you are unsure of. Especially check proper names and other special words.
3. Check for correct page design. (See page 89.)

WRITING WITH SOURCES

When you edit writing, you sweat the small stuff—sentence style and word choice, grammatical correctness and punctuation, usage and spelling. When you are writing with sources, you need to sweat additional stuff—documentation, for example. For help, follow the guidelines that follow.

Correct Summaries, Paraphrases, and Quotations

Check your use of sources for accuracy. Are summaries and paraphrases true to the original? Are your quotations word-for-word the same as the original? Have you attributed source material to the right source, with the author's name spelled correctly? Is the page number correct?

Correct Grammar with Quotations and Citations

Quotations need to be integrated into your sentences so that the syntax and punctuation are correct. Check especially for these issues:

- **Proper use of commas and colons before source material,** as well as end punctuation after source material.
- **Proper pronoun reference:** Using a direct quotation within your sentence sometimes creates a pronoun shift in that the pronouns in the quotation don't match in person the nouns and pronouns in the first part of the sentence.
- **Proper content, format, and punctuation for citations.** (For MLA and APA rules, see pages 288–320.)

Incorrect: As she explores her spiritual attraction to monasteries, Kathleen Norris clarifies that: "I am not a monk, although I have a formal relationship with the Benedictines as an oblate." (page 17)

Correct: As she explores her spiritual attraction to monasteries, Kathleen Norris states, "I am not a monk, although I have a formal relationship with the Benedictines as an oblate" (17).

Cross-Curricular Connections

Different disciplines and their preferred documentation systems refer to sources differently, using different conventions, formats, and punctuation practices. For example, check the differences between the MLA and APA in-text citations below:

MLA: Some child prodigies "are not necessarily retarded or autistic—there have been itinerant calculators of normal intelligence as well" (Sacks 191).

APA: Some child prodigies "are not necessarily retarded or autistic—there have been itinerant calculators of normal intelligence as well" (Sacks, 1995, p.191).

Critical-Thinking and Writing Activities

1. British writer Matthew Arnold offers this advice to writers about refining their writing: "Have something to say, and say it as clearly as you can. That is the only secret of style." Does your own writing clearly communicate a meaningful message? Explain why or why not.

2. Choose a writing assignment that you have recently completed. Edit the sentences in this writing for style and correctness using pages 77–82 as a guide. Then use pages 83–86 in this chapter to edit the piece of writing for vague words, jargon, clichés, and biased language.

STUDY TOOLS 7

LOCATED AT BACK OF THE TEXTBOOK
- ☐ Tear-Out Chapter Review Card

LOCATED AT WWW.CENGAGEBRAIN.COM/LOGIN
- ☐ Chapter eBook
- ☐ Graded quizzes and a practice quiz generator
- ☐ Videos: Writer Interviews
- ☐ Tutorials
- ☐ Flashcards
- ☐ Cengage Learning Write Experience
- ☐ Interactive activities

8 | Publishing

"START WITH SOMETHING INTERESTING AND PROMISING; WIND UP WITH SOMETHING THE READER WILL REMEMBER."

RUDOLF FLESCH

Nyvlt-art, 2014 / Used under license from Shutterstock.com

LEARNING OBJECTIVES

 8-1 Format your writing.

 8-2 Create a writing portfolio.

After you finish
this chapter
go to
PAGE 91 for STUDY TOOLS

Submitting your writing might be as simple as handing it in to your instructor or posting it as a blog, or it might be as involved as submitting it to a journal in your area of study or assembling it with your other works to publish in a portfolio. Whatever the case, sharing your writing makes all the work you have done worthwhile. As writer Tom Liner states, "You learn ways to improve your writing by seeing its effect on others."

This chapter will help you prepare your writing for submission and sharing. When you make your writing public—in whatever form—you are *publishing* it.

8-1 FORMAT YOUR WRITING

A good page design makes your writing clear and easy to follow. Keep that in mind when you produce a final copy of your writing.

8-1a Strive for Clarity in Page Design

Examine the following design elements, making sure that each is appropriate and clear in your project and in your writing.

Format and Documentation

▸ **Keep the design clear and uncluttered.** Aim for a sharp, polished look in all your assigned writing.

▸ **Use the designated documentation form.** Follow all of the requirements outlined in the MLA or APA style guides (see pages 288–320).

Typography

▸ **Use an easy-to-read serif font for the main text.** Serif type, like this, has "tails" at the tops and bottoms of the letters. For most types of writing, use a 10- or 12-point type size.

▸ **Consider using a sans serif font for the title and headings.** Sans serif type, like this, does not have "tails." Use larger, perhaps 18-point, type for your title and 14-point type for any headings. You can also use boldface for headings if they seem to get lost on the page. (Follow your instructor's formatting guidelines.)

Because most people find a sans serif font easier to read on screen, consider a sans serif font for the body and a serif font for the titles and headings in any writing you publish online.

Spacing

▸ **Follow all requirements for indents and margins.** This usually means indenting the first line of each paragraph five spaces, maintaining a one-inch margin around each page, and double-spacing throughout the paper.

▸ **Avoid widows and orphans.** Avoid leaving headings, hyphenated words, or single lines of new paragraphs (orphans) alone at the bottom of a page. Also avoid carrying single words or short last lines of paragraphs (widows) to the top of a new page.

Graphic Devices

▸ **Create bulleted or numbered lists to highlight individual items in a list.** However, be selective, using traditional paragraphs when they help you more effectively communicate your message. Writing should not include too many lists.

▸ **Include charts or other graphics.** Graphics should be neither so small that they get lost on the page, nor so large that they overpower the page.

8-1b Examine a Sample Paper

Study the design choices in the following pages. The design elements make the paper easy to read and follow.

◀ 1-inch margins are used on all sides of the page.

PARADIGM MINI PAPER   Steven J. Augustyn (422.02)   2

▼ The title is centered.

Definition of a Paradigm

Shani, Gross, and Barilan (2010) describe Kuhn's (1962) seminal work on scientific paradigm by first exploring his description of a paradigm shift. Over time, knowledge is developed and questions arise that do not conform to the universally accepted thinking put forth by "normal science." Normal science is accepted knowledge that is advanced through steady research and the gathering of information (Kuhn, 1962). The evolving discrepancies and problems create dissatisfaction, conflict, and pressure that lead to "revolutionary" change—or, paradigm shi[ft]. The recursive nature of scientific questioning and rese[arch] questions that challenge the existing universally accep[ted]

◀ Times New Roman 12-point font

▼ The writer uses proper indentation.

Describing paradigm shift while examining a[n] noteworthy approach, as Kuhn himself challenged the["normal] science" in his seminal work *The Structure of Scientif[ic]* the revolutionary process of paradigm shift. Kuhn put [forth that] changes occur when normal science is stressed by inc[onsistencies in] the accepted explanation, model, or worldview (parad[igm) to form a] new and better model or framework (paradigm shift).

A paradigm, or period of normal science, is di[stinguished by a] position that the scientific community is reluctant to c[hange. They] skeptically approach paradigm shift even when seriou[s problems with a] paradigm are identified (Shani, Gross, & Barilan, 201[0). An existing] paradigm will not face rejection from the scientific co[mmunity until a] better paradigm is ready to take the existing paradigm['s place.]

PARADIGM MINI PAPER   Steven J. Augustyn (422.02)   3

acknowledged or proven problems with the existing paradigm are not necessarily enough to create a paradigm shift. There must be an alternative set of questions, research, and evidence that forms the new paradigm in order for the shift to take place. In the case where a problem or set of problems is enough to derail a paradigm, but does not provide a better paradigm, the scientific community marks the problem for future generations to explore (e.g. the "XYY Chromosome Paradigm") (Kuhn, 1970).

Defining and describing paradigm shift is essential to defining, describing, and understanding paradigm. The scientific community conducts research and presents answers or findings that either support the established and accepted paradigm or challenge it by identifying problems or contradictions that pressure the paradigm. So, another way to describe a paradigm is that it is the theoretical context the scientific community accepts between scientific revolutions—paradigm shifts (Shani, Gross, & Barilan, 2010).

◀ The text is double-spaced.

◀ The paper follows an academic documentation style, in this case, APA style.

Steve Augustyn's Definition of *Paradigm*: Paradigm is the scientifically accepted and replicable view, pattern, or model that frames thinking, research, and understanding for a broad scientific discipline that provides understanding for worldly phenomena.

▼ A bold heading signals a shift in discussion.

Qualities of a Paradigm

A paradigm portrays or defines an entire scientific arena, not just a specific phenomenon. It establishes which problems exist and the parameters for how they can be solved (Shani, Gross, & Barilan, 2010). Paradigms are universally understood and accepted by the discipline's community; define the range, conventions, and problems of a particular discipline; must offer good questions for researchers to consider and answer;

CREATE A WRITING PORTFOLIO

Once you have formatted and proofread your final draft, you should be ready to share your writing. For college assignments, you will often simply turn in your paper to your instructor. However, you should also think about sharing your writing with other audiences, including those who will want to see your writing portfolio.

8-2a Consider Potential Audiences

You could receive helpful feedback by taking any of the following steps:

- Share your writing with peers or family members.
- Submit your work to a local publication or an online journal.
- Post your writing on an appropriate Web site, including your own.
- Turn in your writing to your instructor.

8-2b Select Appropriate Submission Methods

There are two basic methods for submitting your work.

- **Paper submission:** Print an error-free copy on quality paper.
- **Electronic submission:** If allowed, send your writing as an e-mail attachment.

8-2c Use a Writing Portfolio

There are two basic types of writing portfolios: (1) a working portfolio in which you store documents at various stages of development, and (2) a showcase portfolio with which you share appropriate finished work. For example, you could submit a portfolio to complete course requirements or to apply for a scholarship, graduate program, or job. The documents below are commonly included in a showcase portfolio:

- **A table of contents** listing the pieces included in your portfolio
- **An opening essay or letter** detailing the story behind your portfolio (how you compiled it and why it features the qualities expected by the intended reader)
- **A specified number of—and types of— finished pieces**

- **A cover sheet attached to each piece of writing,** discussing the reason for its selection, the amount of work that went into it, and so on
- **Evaluation sheets or checklists** charting the progress or experience you want to show related to issues of interest to the reader

Critical-Thinking and Writing Activities

1. Catherine Drinker Bowen has argued the following: "Writing is not apart from living. Writing is a kind of double living." As you think about sharing your own writing and adding it to your writing portfolio, does this claim ring true? Why or why not?

2. Choose one of your recent writing assignments and use the instructions on page 89 to assess the quality of your formatting and page design. Edit and redesign the paper as needed.

3. For the class in which you are using this book, begin two writing portfolios: (1) an electronic portfolio on your computer and (2) a paper portfolio in a folder or binder. In the electronic portfolio, store all drafts of your assignments, as well as all related electronic correspondence with your instructor. In your paper portfolio, store all printed drafts of your work.

STUDY TOOLS 8

LOCATED AT BACK OF THE TEXTBOOK
- ☐ Tear-Out Chapter Review Card

LOCATED AT WWW.CENGAGEBRAIN.COM/LOGIN
- ☐ Chapter eBook
- ☐ Graded quizzes and a practice quiz generator
- ☐ Videos: Writer Interviews
- ☐ Tutorials
- ☐ Flashcards
- ☐ Cengage Learning Write Experience
- ☐ Interactive activities

9 | Narration, Description, and Reflection

"IF YOU DON'T UNDERSTAND YOURSELF, YOU DON'T UNDERSTAND ANYBODY ELSE."

NIKKI GIOVANNI

LoloStock, 2014 / Used under license from Shutterstock.com

LEARNING OBJECTIVES

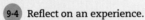

9-1 Understand how to read personal essays.

9-2 Understand how to use anecdotes.

9-3 Establish setting, describe people, and narrate action.

9-4 Reflect on an experience.

9-5 Use narration, description, and reflection to write a personal essay.

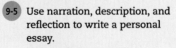

After you finish
this chapter
go to
PAGE 105 for STUDY TOOLS

Personal narratives tell stories—not ones that the writers made up, but ones that they lived. Whatever the topics, the stories should help readers see, hear, touch, and taste those details that make the experiences come alive. To do that, writers must carefully describe key aspects of the experience. But they might also reflect on why the experiences are important—exploring their personal and shared meanings.

When reading such personal essays, do so with an open mind—seeking to go where writers guide you, to experience what they carefully describe, and to analyze how they craft their work.

As you prepare to write your own story, get ready to relive it yourself—to re-experience all that you felt, thought, or sensed during the event. In addition, be ready to learn something new about the experience and about yourself.

9-1 UNDERSTAND HOW TO READ PERSONAL ESSAYS

The strategies below will help you read personal essays—writing that blends narration, description, and reflection.

9-1a Consider the Rhetorical Situation for Personal Essays

Think about the writer's purpose, audience, and topic and how these might be linked.

▶ **Purpose:** Writers develop personal essays to explore meaningful aspects of life—people, experiences, and things that they care for and are shaped by.

▶ **Audience:** Most personal essays are written for a general audience, with the writer hoping that readers will empathize with and connect to the writer's experience.

▶ **Topic:** In personal essays, writers address any topics that they find meaningful and worth exploring through the lens of personal reflection.

9-1b Consider the Writer's Strategies

For personal essays, writers primarily use **narration**, **description**, and **reflection**, but they often combine these strategies with others, such as compare/contrast and definition.

▶ **Narration:** Well-written narratives are stories that include the following:
  • **Characters** who are well developed, often complex, and engaging
  • **Dialogue** that indicates who characters are and what they think and say about themselves, others, and life itself
  • **Action** that includes conflicts and shows what characters do; usually it is organized chronologically, though it may start in the middle or flash back; often the action reveals that characters are not who they think or say they are
  • **Settings** that often influence—and sometimes reflect—the characters and action; time and place anchor the experience naturally and culturally

▶ **Description:** Effective descriptive passages offer precise details that help readers sensually and thoughtfully experience the topic. In addition, figurative language such as metaphors, similes, and symbols commonly enrich the text.

▶ **Reflection:** Strong reflective passages relay the writers' observations and insights regarding the nature, impact, and value of their experiences.

> ### Reading Guide: Personal Essays
>
> ✔ Why does the writer care about the topic, and how is he or she affected by it?
> ✔ What ideas or themes evolve from the story? Explain.
> ✔ Are the characters' actions and dialogue believable and consistent?
> ✔ Is the description concise, precise, informing, and engaging?

9-2 UNDERSTAND HOW TO USE ANECDOTES

A common narrative is the anecdote—a brief story that enlivens your writing while introducing a topic or illustrating an idea. Read the anecdotes below, along with the essays from which they are taken. Then assess the anecdotes' effectiveness.

9-2a Anecdote Introducing a Topic

In 1925, a young American physicist was doing graduate work at Cambridge University, in England. He was depressed. He was fighting with his mother and had just broken up with his girlfriend. His strength was in theoretical physics, but he was being forced to sit in a laboratory making thin films of beryllium. In the fall of that year, he dosed an apple with noxious chemicals from the lab and put it on the desk of his tutor, Patrick Blackett. Blackett, luckily, didn't eat the apple. But school officials found out what happened, and arrived at a punishment: the student was to be put on probation and ordered to go to London for regular sessions with a psychiatrist.

From "No Mercy" by Malcolm Gladwell

9-2b Anecdote Illustrating a Process

Imagine a room containing a large group of people all working hard toward the same goal. Each person knows his or her job, does it carefully, and cooperates with other group members. Together, they function smoothly—like a well-oiled machine.

Then something goes wrong. One guy suddenly drops his task, steps into another person's workstation, grabs the material that she's working with, and begins something very different—he uses the material to make little reproductions of himself, thousands of them. These look-alikes imitate him—grabbing material and making reproductions of themselves. Soon the bunch gets so big that they spill into other people's workstations, getting in their way, and interrupting their work. As the number of look-alikes grows, the work group's activity slows, stutters, and finally stops.

A human body is like this room, and the body's cells are like these workers. . . .

From "Wayward Cells," pages 132–133

9-2c Anecdote Illustrating a Problem

Attending college, joining the military, creating a career path: these are dreams for most U.S. high school graduates. But for Maria Lopez, a senior at San Marshall High School who has lived in the U.S for seven years, there is only one legal option: return to Mexico. She is one of nearly 65,000 high school students each year who do not have the opportunity to pursue their dreams because they arrived in the U.S. illegally. Like many of these students, Maria is highly motivated, hard working, and excited to be involved in her high school. However, Maria's parents brought her to this country without going through the legal immigration process. As a result, by law she is an undocumented alien who has no method to achieve legal residency while living in the U.S.

From "Dream Act May Help . . . ," pages 220–224

9-3 ESTABLISH SETTING, DESCRIBE PEOPLE, AND NARRATE ACTION

In this essay, student writer Robert Minto recalls a series of events through which he learned something about his community, himself, and the nature of life. Note how the details he cites help you visualize places, people, and events. Note also how direct dialogue reveals personalities and feelings.

Essay Outline

Introduction: Setting, key characters, and conflict: moths (such as Ryan) vs. spiders (such as Old Jack)

1. Narrator goes to Ryan's house.
2. They stop at narrator's house, pass church, arrive at cemetery.
3. They explore cemetery and discuss spirits.
4. They hear moaning and move toward it.
5. They see Old Jack's grandson and a girl.
6. They return to bikes and ride past church to Ryan's house.

Closing: Narrator tells Old Jack about grandson and girl and then reflects on the moth/spider conflict.

(A) The Entomology of Village Life

SQ3R   Survey · Question · Read · Recite · Review

1 Buddy didn't know that we were clichés. I knew. I
(B) liked it that way. We spent our days together—me too inquisitive and his tail always wagging. My neighbor, Old Jack, who was forever pulling weeds in his garden, self-exiled from a sharp-tongued wife, was a cliché too. So was the grange on the other side of my house. Most of the men in Naymari, Pennsylvania, never missed a grange meeting, mainly to supervise the village's one employee, Pedro, who mowed the grass in the park. Within this small web of places and personalities, life abounded. Some people were the moths, tied down and struggling; some were the spiders, growing fat on gossip.

2 One of the moths lived across the street. He was my
(C) friend Ryan. Ryan lived in the dirtiest house I've ever seen. His mother cared for him and for two younger, mentally disabled boys as well. She had a big heart but too few hands and no husband. In the winter, they all huddled around a kerosene heater, wearing most of the clothing they owned, the two youngest boys often licking the snot that dripped from their cold noses. They couldn't afford oil. Through a government program,

---

(A) The title forecasts a study of insects.
(B) Introduction: setting, key characters, and conflict: moths (such as Ryan) vs. spiders (such as Old Jack)
(C) Ryan, a moth

Ryan had received an old IBM computer. He spent most of his time playing Tetris on it in his room. Sometimes when Buddy and I got up early in the morning to roam the village, we'd stop outside Ryan's window, and I'd toss pebbles at it. (His mother and I had this understanding that I could get him up to play, but because she slept in later than we did, I couldn't yell.) Soon his bleary eyes would peer over the sill. Eventually he'd come out, and I'd lead him off on some adventure.

3 Old Jack, on the other hand, was one of Naymeri's
(D) spiders. His garden wasn't merely a refuge from his wife, but it was also the epicenter of his web. At the slightest hint of gossip, he'd scurry down the street with a twine-wrapped bundle of asparagus, his specialty, to gain entry into whatever home promised the best information. With most people, me included, Jack gossiped on a strictly business model. He'd tell me his latest and juiciest stories, and in return, I'd offer him—as keeper of the town's skeleton closet—whatever my wandering uncovered. It was Jack who told me, with relish, the acrimonious story of how Ryan's family had broken apart. He enjoyed the telling.

4 Old Jack also hated abortion, but not because of religion—he hated that too. One time, standing in his asparagus and gesturing with a weed, he told me why.

5 "You seen those hooded graves?" he asked.

6 "What graves?" I said, holding Buddy so he wouldn't pee on Jack's onions.

7 "You haven't seen 'em? The graves with cages across the way at the Methodist church?"

8 "Oh, *those*. Sure, I've seen 'em."

9 "Do you know why they got cages?"

10 "Why?"

11 Jack shook his weed again, and a little shower of dirt crumbled off it. "Because," he said, "if you go over there at night and listen, you can hear the spirits of aborted children screaming to get out and hurt the people who killed 'em!"

12 I shivered. Buddy licked my face.

13 A few minutes later I was tossing pebbles at Ryan's

(D) Old Jack, a spider

(E) window. Eventually he staggered out of the house.

14 "Hey Ryan," I said quietly, "want an adventure?"

15 Ryan thought that was a good idea, but he wanted to know if he should bring anything. Last adventure we got all wet in a stream, and he wished he'd brought some boots.

16 "Nah," I told him, "we're just gonna listen to some
(F) spirits."

17 We stopped by my house to get a paper bag filled with Swiss-and-ham-on-rye and a smoked pig's ear for Buddy. Then we grabbed our bikes and headed east toward the park, the cemetery, and the Methodist church. We left our bikes in the gravel parking lot by the church. We could see the pastor in the big glass window of his study. He had his head on his arms, sleeping.

18 The hooded graves were at the far edge of the
(G) cemetery, right beside the woods that harbored our park. The unmowed grass beside these graves suggested that they might not be part of the cemetery. Ryan and I waded through the grass and peered past the wire mesh that caged the white stones. Because they were worn smooth by rain, any carved writing on the stones was long gone. I tugged on one of the cages until Ryan nervously told me to stop. He needn't have—I couldn't budge it. It was firmly planted in the hard earth.

19 "When do we hear the spirits?" asked Ryan.

20 "When the sun goes down," I told him, "I think." We walked over to a big oak tree on the edge of the woods where we could see the graves better. The tree had several nice boles to sit in. I told

---

(E) Narrator goes to Ryan's house.
(F) They stop at narrator's house, pass the church, and arrive at cemetery.
(G) They explore cemetery and discuss spirits.

Ryan the rest of what Jack had told me. We agreed that the children's spirits might want to get even, but Ryan doubted that the spirits could really do that.

21 "Don't you believe in spirits?" I asked. Of course he did—he went to the Presbyterian church.

22 "I've *seen* one, too!" said Ryan. "I was in my room when we lived in Florida. That was before we left my dad. I slept upstairs in the attic there, just like here. I was lying in bed when I heard something coming up the stairs and scratching at the door. Then the door opened, and a big white thing came in and stood by the bed. I closed my eyes and prayed, and when I opened 'em, the thing was gone."

23 I told him it was probably just his dad. Or maybe his mom.

24 "No," he said, "because I got really cold when it came in, and I felt like I couldn't move." We were silent, me imagining, him remembering.

25 "Then why don't you believe that we'll hear the spirits?" I asked.

26 "Why don't you believe in the ghost I saw?" he replied.

27 I saw his point. But somehow his story just didn't seem as vivid as Old Jack's story about children's spirits out for revenge. Now *that* one would give me nightmares!

28 Suddenly I noticed that I couldn't hear Buddy. He'd been nosing around the trees, scratching at the dirt, sniffing at mole-holes, snapping at dandelions. I looked around and saw him standing, stiff. He was staring into (H) the woods. As I turned to follow his gaze I heard a moan.

29 Ryan jumped. We looked at each other. The moan again. We looked at the hooded graves, but there was nothing to see.

30 "Did you let it out when you pulled on the cage?" asked Ryan. Then he added, "But didn't you say we wouldn't hear 'em til the sun went *down*?"

31 The moan again. It seemed to be coming from the grove of trees at our backs. We turned toward the sound, and I started to worm forward on my belly into the trees. "Stay," I told Buddy. Ryan obeyed the command as well

---

(H) They hear moaning and move toward it.

for about 10 seconds, and then he started worming forward too, grumbling quietly. The damp earth was covered with crunchy leaves, but we were small and had practice sneaking.

32   As we neared the sound, it became more frequent, and then we heard a sort of ragged breathing joining in, like a duet. But it didn't sound like spirits.

33
(I)   Then we came to a place where we could see something through the trees. It was a zebra-striped car with spinners on the wheels. On top of the car, awkwardly straddling a dark-haired girl, Old Jack's grandson, Jim, was doing his best to make her moan louder. The ragged breathing was his. He jerked up and down, and I could see the silver flash of the car's antenna between them each time they separated. Ryan and I froze for a few seconds before comprehension struck. Glancing wildly at each other, we squirmed away.

34
(J)   When we reached the edge of the wood, we stood up and made our way back to our bikes. Somehow, waiting for the spirits had lost its appeal. I glanced at the Methodist church and saw the pastor was awake, waving at us through the window. We pedaled quietly back to town. I imagined that even Buddy seemed subdued. When we reached Ryan's house, he stopped and laid his bike on the grass. We could hear his mom inside, talking to his brothers.

35   Ryan began to walk up the lawn, back to his Tetris. Then he stopped, turned around, and asked, "What are you gonna do?"

36   I thought for a moment. Then I told him.

37
(K)   About an hour later, I finished telling Old Jack what we'd seen. He was watering his tomatoes, and as I talked, I noticed that one of the plants was nearly floating even though he was staring right at it. I finished up, and he went right on watering that same plant.

38   Then he glanced over at me and said, "That's very interesting." He contemplated the drowning plant again and added, "But this isn't something to get around town,

you know. You wouldn't tell anybody else, would ya?"

39   I thought for a moment. Then I smiled.

40   Somewhere, a spider was about to become a moth.

Reading for Better Writing

1. Review the title, "The Entomology of Village Life." Then explain what entomology is and why it is (or is not) a good choice for this essay.

2. In the opening paragraph, the writer refers to himself and other village residents as clichés. Explain why the writer might use this term. Does the essay show the characters to be clichés? Explain.

3. In the second paragraph, the writer refers to village residents as moths and spiders. Explain what he might mean by these metaphors and the effect of his using them to open and close the essay.

4. Identify a narrative passage, a descriptive passage, and a reflective passage that you consider well written. Explain why.

5. What is the essay's main idea or theme? How does the writer introduce the idea and develop it?

6. Reread the essay's last sentence and explain why it is (or is not) an effective closing.

9-4   **REFLECT ON AN EXPERIENCE**

Often, the meaning of an experience can simply be implied through the action and descriptions. Sometimes, however, such meaning can be accented through reflection. Study how descriptive and reflective passages are used in the following essays.

(I) They see Old Jack's grandson and a girl.
(J) They return to bikes and ride past church to Ryan's house.
(K) Closing: Narrator tells Old Jack about grandson and girl and then reflects on the moth/spider conflict.

9-4a Reflecting on an Encounter

"Spare Change" is the first part of student writer Teresa Zsuffa's "A Diary of Chance Encounters," an essay that explores her experiences of living in Toronto. The piece below recounts a challenging encounter with the face of poverty.

"Spare Change"

SQ3R Survey · Question · Read · Recite · Review

1 (A) This grime is infectious. The smell of old cigarettes and expired perfume is constricting my throat and turning my stomach. But here I am again on the underground subway platform, changing trains at Bloor-Yonge in Toronto, the weight of my backpack thrusting me forward with the Friday morning rush-hour crowd. When the subway doors open, I hurry inside and look around frantically, as usual. There is an empty seat to my left, but everyone is keeping a safe four-foot distance, as if the seat will suck them in and destroy them if they sit down. Or at least destroy the facade put on with a Ralph Lauren suit, a Coach handbag, or a pair of authentic Gucci sunglasses. Not like the fake five-dollar ones I picked up from a Chinatown vendor just yesterday. The others keep their starry distance; when I sit down, I see why.

2 (B) She must be about 29. Her orange track-pants are worn and faded, her T-shirt is far too big, and her powder-blue sweatshirt is tied around her waist. Her face and teeth are stained, hair greasy and unkempt. A part of me feels sorry for her. Another part follows the crowd and is careful not to make eye contact.

3 "Excuse me," she says, perching on the edge of her seat, leaning forward and clasping the metal pole with two hands. No one turns. "Excuse me, which stop do I take to the Old City Hall?" One man shrugs and shakes his head while pretending to check his phone. I feel guilt, but it's easily subdued. After all, she wasn't asking me.

4 I am deeply engrossed in my Nicholas Sparks novel by the time the driver announces "Dundas Station." As I stuff the book back into my purse and make my way toward the doorway, I'm irritated to see that she also stands up—one stop early for Old City Hall. Doesn't she know she should stay on until Queen? Oh well, she'll figure it out, I reason. The Toronto Transit Commission officers can help her.

5 I let her off the subway before me. Finally I'm free.

6 (C) But then she stops on the platform and turns her head, like a puppy making sure her owner is following close behind. No eye contact, I remind myself, and try to walk past, but she falls into step with me.

7 "Can I help you carry your bag?"

8 I may look like a tourist, but I'm smarter. "No, thanks," I reply.

9 "Well, it just looks pretty heavy." We reach the escalator and the staircase, and I take the left side, where I can climb the steps and go up twice as fast as those just standing there on the right and enjoying the ride. But it doesn't work; the woman is still at my heels.

10 "Are you going somewhere?" she asks.

11 "Yeah, I have to get to the Greyhound station; I'm going out of town."

12 (D) "Oh." Now we are standing in front of the underground entrance to the Eaton Center. The Atrium on Bay is to my right, on the other side of which is the bus station and my ticket out of this alien city that is now my home. The woman stands frozen and looks around trying to get her bearings. I start to walk away but hesitate. Looking back, I see her blinking and flinching as people shove past her. She reminds me of a small child lost at a summer carnival.

13 I check my watch—quarter past eight. I just missed an express shuttle, and the next bus to Niagara Falls, where my father lives, won't be leaving for another 45 minutes. Something pulls me back to the woman, and

(A) The writer describes an urban setting and a common situation.
(B) She introduces the central person through concrete details, her words, and the reactions of others (including the writer's own mixed feelings).

(C) The writer narrates the events and dialogue that lead her to offer help.
(D) Details describe the urban setting and the writer's acclimation to it.

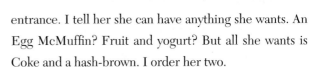

(E) against all sworn Torontonian rules, I ask if she needs help.

14   Her dull brown eyes light up. "I need to find the Old City Hall."

15   "Okay," I nod. "I'll take you." I lead her through the glass doors into the city's busiest mall. It's the fastest way from Dundas to Queen Street, and from there she will need to walk only a few blocks west. As we're walking, I'm aware of the stares I'm getting from people I'll never see again.

16   "So where are you from?" I ask.

17   "Sudbury." And I'm instantly speechless. What is **(F)** this woman doing so far from home? How did she get here? I ask why she's in the city.

18   "My boyfriend. He's in jail, and they're letting him go today. I came to take him back home with me after his hearing."

19   While we walk past Mexx, Aritzia, and Abercrombie, I learn that she had taken a bus from Sudbury the day before and spent the night on a hard and cold park bench. Her boyfriend is 42 years old and has been in jail for the past 10 months. I don't ask why. She proudly tells me she was a crack addict and that she's been clean for three months.

20   "I just got out of rehab," she says. "Now maybe my **(G)** grandma will take me back in."

21   "Back in?"

22   "Yeah, she kicked me out. She told me I wasn't allowed to be a hooker anymore, but I got caught bringing someone home once."

23   I have no idea how to talk to a prostitute, never mind **(H)** one who is so open about everything she's done, but this woman seems to like me and trust me. The next thing I know, I'm offering to buy her breakfast before she meets up with her boyfriend.

24   There's a McDonald's at the southernmost side of the Eaton Centre, overlooking the Queen Street

---

(E) She refers to the city's cultural "rules."
(F) The writer uses dialogue to describe the woman's life and her journey.
(G) Short quotes create a tensive rhythm.
(H) The writer describes her confusion, sympathy, and guilt.

---

entrance. I tell her she can have anything she wants. An Egg McMuffin? Fruit and yogurt? But all she wants is Coke and a hash-brown. I order her two.

25   We sit down at a freshly wiped table by the window. Beside us, two men in grey suits sip coffee over an array of files and spreadsheets. They pause in their conversation to stare at us—the student traveler and the **(I)** bedraggled prostitute. I tell the woman a little about my life and ask more about hers and her grandmother. She says that they used to go to church together when she was little, but she hasn't been since. She takes another bite of her hash-brown and tells me she's now 21. Only 21, and her boyfriend is 42. She talks about the drugs and the providence of God.

26   "I know that he helped me stop," she says. "I've been clean for three months; can you believe that? That's a miracle! It has to be a miracle."

27   At this point all I can do is smile.

28   "I wish I could get my boyfriend to quit," she says, staring off. Then she suddenly leans forward and asks, "Do you know how hard it is? Have you ever done crack?"

29   "No."

30   "Pot, at least?"

31   "No. Sorry." I'm not sure why I'm apologizing for **(J)** never having tried drugs, but the way her face drops and she shifts her eyes makes me feel guilty, as though I can never fully understand her because I've never experienced the things she has.

32   "Well, you should try it," she urges. "It's really good."

33   "Maybe one day." I glance at my watch. It's now

(I) A dash accents the irony of this unlikely pair sharing personal time and stories.
(J) The writer acknowledges her own inexperience and confusion.

quarter-to, and I still need to stand in line to buy my ticket and get to the right platform. I wonder why I'm not panicking yet.

34 I tell her I need to get going. She should go, too,
(K) or she'll be late for the hearing. Before getting up, I reach into my wallet and give her two TTC passes and some spare change. I walk her to the street and point her toward Old City Hall. She never thanks me, only looks at me one last time with immense vulnerability and helplessness. Then she walks away.

35 I wonder as I hurry toward the station if she'll be okay, if her boyfriend really will get out of jail, and if her grandmother will ever take her back. Either way, I think as I cross Bay Street, what more can I do? I have a bus to catch.

(K) The writer offers spare change, a gift that is cited in the title and that symbolizes the women's distanced relationship.

Reading for Better Writing

1. Teresa's essay focuses on an urban setting. What does she evoke about the city, and what descriptions create that feeling?

2. The central character in the essay is presented primarily through description, comparisons, and dialogue. Identify such passages, exploring what they communicate about the woman and how effectively they work.

3. One focus of the essay is the writer's experience of the city and of her encounter with the prostitute. Describe Teresa's reflections and feelings about both. How does she communicate these? Identify and analyze specific passages, sentences, and phrases.

9-4b Reflecting on an Illness

Mary Seymour reflects on her experience with bipolar disorder, which is sometimes called manic depression.

Call Me Crazy, But I Have to Be Myself

SQ3R Survey • Question • Read • Recite • Review

1   Nearly every day, without thinking, I say things
(A) like "So-and-so is driving me crazy" or "That's nuts!" Sometimes I catch myself and realize that I'm not being sensitive toward people with mental illness. Then I remember I'm one of the mentally ill. If I can't throw those words around, who can?

2   Being a functional member of society and having
(B) a mental disorder is an intricate balancing act. Every morning I send my son to junior high school, put on professional garb, and drive off to my job as alumni-magazine editor at a prep school, where I've worked for six years. Only a few people at work know I'm manic-depressive, or bipolar, as it's sometimes called.

3   Sometimes I'm not sure myself what I am. I blend
(C) in easily with "normal" people. You'd never know that seven years ago, fueled by the stress of a failing marriage and fanned by the genetic inheritance of a manic-depressive grandfather, I had a psychotic break. To look at me, you'd never guess I once ran naked through my yard or shuffled down the hallways of a psychiatric ward. To hear me, you'd never guess God channeled messages to me through my computer. After my breakdown at 36, I was diagnosed as bipolar, a condition marked by moods that swing between elation and despair.

4   It took a second, less-severe psychotic episode in 1997, followed by a period of deep depression, to convince me I truly was bipolar. Admitting I had a disorder that I'd have to manage for life was the hardest thing I've ever done. Since then, a combination of therapy, visits to a psychiatrist, medication, and inner calibration have helped me find an even keel. Now I manage my moods

---

(A) The writer labels herself "mentally ill."
(B) An example illustrates the extent of the illness.
(C) More examples show the difficulties the writer faces.

with the vigilance of a mother hen, nudging them back to center whenever they wander too far. Eating wisely, sleeping well, and exercising regularly keep me balanced from day to day. Ironically, my disorder has taught me to be healthier and happier than I was before.

5   Most of the time, I feel lucky to blend in with the crowd. Things that most people grumble about—paying bills, maintaining a car, working 9 to 5—strike me as incredible privileges. I'll never forget gazing through the barred windows of the psychiatric ward into the parking lot, watching people come and go effortlessly, wondering if I'd ever be like them again. There's nothing like a stint in a locked ward to make one grateful for the freedoms and burdens of full citizenship.

6   Yet sometimes I feel like an impostor. Sometimes I
(D) wish I could sit at the lunch table and talk about lithium and Celexa instead of *Will & Grace*. While everyone talks about her fitness routine, I want to brag how it took five orderlies to hold me down and shoot me full of sedatives when I was admitted to the hospital, and how for a brief moment I knew the answers to every infinite mystery of the blazingly bright universe. I yearn for people to know me—the real me—in all my complexity, but I'm afraid it would scare the bejesus out of them.

7   Every now and then, I feel like I'm truly being myself. Like the time the school chaplain, in whom
(E) I'd confided my past, asked me to help counsel a severely bipolar student. This young woman had tried to commit suicide, had been hospitalized many times, and sometimes locked herself in her dorm room to keep the "voices" from overwhelming her. I walked and talked with her, sharing stories about medication and psychosis. I hoped to show by example that manic-depression did not necessarily mean

(D) Each sentence begins with a similar phrase that reveals the writer's feelings.
(E) An extended example illustrates the point.

a diminished life. At commencement, I watched her proudly accept her diploma; despite ongoing struggles with her illness, she's continuing her education.

8   I'm able to be fully myself with my closest friends, all of whom have similar schisms between private and public selves. We didn't set out to befriend each other— we just all speak the same language, of hardship and spiritual discovery and psychological awareness.

9   What I yearn for most is to integrate both sides of myself. I want to be part of the normal world, but I also want to own my identity as bipolar. I want people to know what I've been through so I can help those traveling a similar path. Fear has kept me from telling my story: fear of being stigmatized, of making people uncomfortable, of being reduced to a label. But hiding the truth has become more uncomfortable than letting it out. It's time for me to own up to who I am, complicated psychiatric history and all. Call me crazy, but I think it's (F) the right thing to do.

(F) The final line echoes the title.

Reading for Better Writing

1. What purpose does Seymour identify for writing the essay? What other purposes might be served by publishing this piece for *Newsweek's* readers?

2. The writer starts with one category label for herself ("mentally ill") and then quickly adds another ("functional member of society"). How does the second label redefine the first?

3. Description is used to support many other kinds of writing, including the types of analytical and persuasive writing outlined here in *COMP*. In what other chapters could this essay have been included, and how do you know?

4. Review the "Editing and Proofreading" chapter of this book (pages 76–87), especially the portion on biased words. Why does Seymour use the phrase "call me crazy"? Is her use of the word biased or insulting? Explain.

9-4c Reflecting on a Cultural Practice

The following essay by Barbara Kingsolver is taken from her book *High Tide in Tucson*. In the essay, she describes her brief experience as a bodybuilding wannabe, and she reflects on how she "outgrew" her need to buff up. Study not only her use of narration and description to present her experiences but also her comic reflections on bodybuilding practices.

The Muscle Mystique

SQ3R   Survey · Question · Read · Recite · Review

1   The baby-sitter surely thought I was having an affair. Years ago, for a period of three whole months, I would dash in to pick up my daughter after "work" with my cheeks flushed, my heart pounding, my hair damp from a quick shower. I'm loath to admit where I'd really been for that last hour of the afternoon. But it's time to come clean.

2   I joined a health club.

3   I went downtown and sweated with the masses. I rode a bike that goes nowhere at the rate of five hundred calories per hour. I even pumped a little iron. I can't deny the place was a lekking ground: guys stalking around the weight room like prairie chickens, nervously eyeing each other's pectorals. Over by the abdominal machines I heard some of the frankest pickup lines since eighth grade ("You've got real defined deltoids for a girl"). A truck perpetually parked out front had vanity plates that read: LFT WTS. Another one, PRSS 250, I didn't recognize as a vanity plate until I understood the prestige of bench pressing 250 pounds.

4   I personally couldn't bench press a fully loaded steam iron. I didn't join the health club to lose weight, or to meet the young Adonis who admired my (dubiously defined) deltoids. I am content with my lot in life, save for one irksome affliction: I am what's known in comic-book jargon as the ninety-eight-pound weakling. I finally tipped the scales into three digits my last year of high school, but "weakling" I've remained, pretty much since birth. In polite terminology I'm cerebral; the muscles between my ears are what I get by on. The last great

body in my family was my Grandfather Henry. He wore muscle shirts in the days when they were known as BVDs, under his cotton work shirt, and his bronze tan stopped mid-biceps. He got those biceps by hauling floor joists and hammering up roof beams every day of his life, including his last. How he would have guffawed to see a roomful of nearly naked bankers and attorneys, pale as plucked geese, heads down, eyes fixed on a horizon beyond the water cooler, pedaling like bats out of hell on bolted-down bicycles. I expect he'd offer us all a job. If we'd pay our thirty dollars a month to *him*, we could come out to the construction site and run up and down ladders bringing him nails. That's why I'm embarrassed about all this. I'm afraid I share his opinion of unproductive sweat.

5   Actually, he'd be more amazed than scornful. His idea of fun was watching Ed Sullivan or snoozing in a recliner, or ideally, both at once. Why work like a maniac on your day off? To keep your heart and lungs in shape. Of course. But I haven't noticed any vanity plates that say GD LNGS. The operative word here is vanity.

6   Standards of beauty in every era are things that advertise, usually falsely: "I'm rich and I don't have to work." How could you be a useful farmhand, or even an efficient clerk-typist, if you have long, painted fingernails? Four-inch high heels, like the bound feet of Chinese aristocrats, suggest you don't have to do *anything* efficiently, except maybe put up your tootsies on an ottoman and eat bonbons. (And I'll point out here that aristocratic *men* wore the first high heels.) In my grandmother's day, women of all classes lived in dread of getting a tan, since that betrayed a field worker's station in life. But now that the field hand's station is occupied by the office worker, a tan, I suppose, advertises that Florida and Maui are within your reach. Fat is another peculiar cultural flip-flop: in places where food is scarce, beauty is three inches of

subcutaneous fat deep. But here and now, jobs are sedentary and calories are relatively cheap, while the luxury of time to work them off is very dear. It still gives me pause to see an ad for a weight-loss program that boldly enlists: "First ten pounds come off free!" But that is about the size of it, in the strange food-drenched land of ours. After those first ten, it gets expensive.

7   As a writer I could probably do my job fine with no deltoids at all, or biceps or triceps, so long as you left me those vermicelli-sized muscles that lift the fingers to the keyboard. (My vermicellis are very well defined.) So when I've writ my piece, off I should merrily go to build a body that says I don't really have a financial obligation to sit here in video-terminal bondage.

8   Well, yes. But to tell the truth, the leisure body and even the GD LNGS are not really what I was after when I signed up at Pecs-R-Us. What I craved, and long for still, is to be *strong*. I've never been strong. In childhood, team sports were my most reliable source of humiliation. I've been knocked breathless to the ground by softballs, basketballs, volleyballs, and once, during a wildly out-of-hand game of Red Rover, a sneaker. In every case I knew my teammates were counting on me for a volley or a double play or anyhow something more than clutching my stomach and rolling upon the grass. By the time I reached junior high I wasn't even the last one picked anymore. I'd slunk away long before they got to the bottom of the barrel.

9   Even now, the great mortification of my life is that visitors to my home sometimes screw the mustard and pickle jar lids back on so tightly *I can't get them open!* (The visitors probably think they are just closing them enough to keep the bugs out.) Sure, I can use a pipe wrench, but it's embarrassing. Once, my front gate stuck, and for several days I could only leave home by clambering furtively through the bougainvilleas and over the garden wall. When a young man knocked on my door to deliver flowers one sunny morning, I threw my arms around him. He thought that was pretty emotional, for florists' mums. He had no idea he'd just casually pushed open the Berlin Wall.

My inspiration down at the health club was a woman firefighter who could have knocked down my garden gate with a karate chop. I still dream about her triceps. But I've mostly gotten over my brief fit of muscle envy. Oh, I still make my ongoing, creative stabs at bodybuilding: I do "girl pushups," and some of the low-impact things from Jane Fonda's pregnant-lady workout book, even if I'm not. I love to run, because it always seems like there's a chance you might actually get somewhere, so I'll sometimes cover a familiar mile or so of our county road after I see my daughter onto the school bus. (The driver confessed that for weeks he thought I was chasing him; he never stopped.) And finally, my friends have given me an official item of exercise equipment that looks like a glob of blue putty, which you're supposed to squeeze a million times daily to improve your grip. That's my current program. The so-called noncompetitive atmosphere of the health club whipped me, hands down. Realistically, I've always known I was born to be a "before" picture. So I won't be seen driving around with plates that boast: PRSS 250.

Maybe: OPN JRS. 11

Reading for Better Writing

1. Kingsolver entitles her essay "The Muscle Mystique." What does "mystique" mean, and in what sense are muscles or bodybuilding a "mystique"?

2. Review the opening few paragraphs and explain how the writer introduces her subject and sets the tone for the essay. Cite words and phrases that you find interesting, engaging, or funny.

3. In paragraph 3, Kingsolver describes a health club as a "lekking ground." What does this phrase suggest about the "muscle mystique"?

4. Reread paragraph 4, in which the writer compares her own physique with that of her grandfather's. Cite details that help you envision each.

5. Find two or three passages that you consider reflective writing. and explain how they enrich the text.

9-5 USE NARRATION, DESCRIPTION, AND REFLECTION TO WRITE A PERSONAL ESSAY

Writing Guidelines

Planning

❶ Select a topic. The most promising topics are experiences that gave you insights into yourself and possibly into others as well. To identify such topics, consider the categories below and then list whatever experiences come to mind:

- Times when you felt *secure, hopeful, distraught, appreciated, confident, frightened, exploited,* or *misunderstood*
- Times when you made a decision about *lifestyles, careers, education,* or *religion*
- Events that tested your *will, patience, self-concept,* or *goals*
- Events that changed or confirmed your assessment of a *person, a group,* or *an institution*

TIP List topics in response to the following statement: Reflect on times when you first discovered that the world was strange, wonderful, complex, frightening, small, full, or empty. How did these experiences affect you?

❷ Get the big picture. Once you have chosen a topic, gather your thoughts by brainstorming or freewriting in response to questions like these:

- Where did the experience take place, and what specific sights, sounds, and smells distinguish the place?
- Who else was involved, and what did they look like, act like, do, and say?
- What were the key or pivotal points in your experiences, and why?
- What led to these key moments, and what resulted from them?
- How did your or others' comments or actions affect what happened?
- What did others learn from this experience—and what did you learn?

- Did the experience end as you had hoped? Why or why not?
- What themes, conflicts, and insights arose from the experience?
- How do your feelings now differ from your feelings then? Why?

> To find out more details about the event or people involved, sort through photo albums and home videos to trigger memories; talk to someone who shared your experiences; consult your journal, old letters, and saved email.

❸ Probe the topic and reveal what you find. The mind-searching aspect of writing this essay happens while asking so-why questions: *So why does this picture still make me smile?* or *Why does his comment still hurt?* or *Why did I do that when I knew better—or did I know better?* Your readers need to experience what you experienced, so don't hide what's embarrassing or painful or still unclear.

❹ Get organized. Review your brainstorming or freewriting, and highlight key details, quotations, or episodes. Then list the main events in chronological order, or use a cluster to help you gather details related to your experiences.

Drafting

❺ Write the first draft. Rough out the first draft. Then test your narration and description by asking whether the quotations, details, and events are accurate and clear. Test your reflection by asking whether it explains how the experience affected you. If appropriate, integrate photos or other images into the draft.

Revising

❻ Review the draft. After taking a break, read your essay for truthfulness and completeness. Does it include needed details and questions?

❼ Get feedback. Ask a classmate to read your paper and respond to it.

❽ Improve the ideas, organization, and voice. Use your own review and peer review to address these issues:

Ideas: Does the essay offer readers an engaging, informative look into your life, personality, and perspective?

Organization: Does the essay include (1) an inviting opening that pictures the setting, introduces the characters, and forecasts the themes; (2) a rich middle that develops a clear series of events, nuanced characters, and descriptions; and (3) a satisfying closing that completes the experience and unifies the essay's ideas?

Voice: Is the tone fair, and does it fit the experience? Is your voice genuine, thoughtful, and inviting?

Editing

9 **Edit and proofread your essay.** Polish your writing by addressing these items:

Words: The words in descriptive and narrative passages show instead of tell about; they are precise and rich, helping readers imagine the setting, envision the characters, and vicariously experience the action. The words in reflective passages are insightful and measured.

Sentences: The sentences in descriptive and reflective passages are clear, varied in structure, and smooth. The sentences in dialogue accurately reflect the characters' personalities, regional diction, and current idioms.

Correctness: The copy includes no errors in spelling, mechanics, punctuation, or grammar.

Page Design: The design is attractive and follows assigned guidelines. If photos are used, they are effectively reproduced and positioned in the text.

Publishing

10 **Publish your writing** by sharing your essay with friends and family, posting it on a Web site, or submitting it to a journal or newspaper.

⚙ Critical-Thinking and Writing Activities

As directed by your instructor, complete the following activities.

1. Review "The Entomology of Village Life," noting how the essay centers on what the writer and his friend witness. Think about what it means to be a witness—to a crime, a tragedy, a triumph, an encounter, and so on. Then write an essay in which you explore a time that you were a witness.

2. In "Spare Change," Teresa Zsuffa describes her encounter with someone whose qualities, experiences, and values are different from her own. Write a personal essay in which you explore such an encounter in your life.

3. In "Call Me Crazy, But I Have to Be Myself," Mary Seymour describes her illness and reflects on how it has impacted her life and others. Analyze a challenge in your life, describe how and why it was challenging, and reflect on how it has affected you.

4. Barbara Kingsolver in "The Muscle Mystique" writes about herself with self-deprecating humor. As readers, we laugh with her because we also have had experiences in which we made mistakes, did something silly, or found that we didn't measure up to our own or others' standards. Choose such an experience that you feel comfortable sharing with others. Then write an essay in which you describe what happened and reflect on its impact.

STUDY TOOLS **9**

LOCATED AT BACK OF THE TEXTBOOK
☐ Tear-Out Chapter Review Card

LOCATED AT WWW.CENGAGEBRAIN.COM/LOGIN
☐ Chapter eBook

☐ Graded quizzes and a practice quiz generator

☐ Videos: Writer Interviews

☐ Tutorials

☐ Flashcards

☐ Cengage Learning Write Experience

☐ Interactive activities

10 | Definition

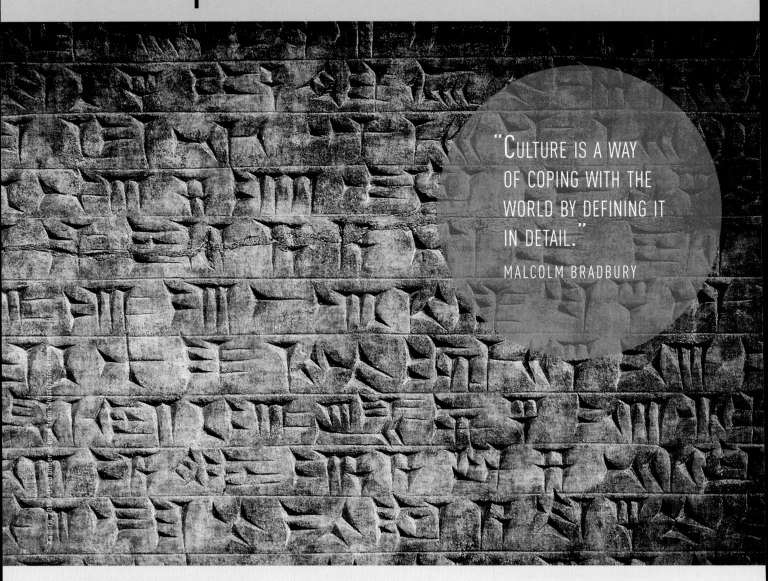

"CULTURE IS A WAY OF COPING WITH THE WORLD BY DEFINING IT IN DETAIL."

MALCOLM BRADBURY

LEARNING OBJECTIVES

10-1 Understand how to read definition essays.

10-2 Define a term through distinction from related terms.

10-3 Define a term by examining denotation and connotation.

10-4 Define a term through etymology.

10-5 Define a term through cultural and philosophical analysis.

10-6 Write, revise, and edit a definition essay.

After you finish
this chapter
go to
PAGE 119 for STUDY TOOLS

[handwritten notes at top: "Double Space   14 Point font   3-5 pgs   # Essay — ..."]

Most forms of academic and workplace writing—from essays and reports to proposals and literature reviews—include brief (one- or two-sentence) definitions of terms. Although this chapter will help you read and write those, its main purpose is to help you understand and write longer, essay-length pieces sometimes called "extended definitions."

Such definitions clarify and deepen readers' understanding of a term—whether the term refers to something concrete or abstract. When reading such essays, consider how the writers "extend" your understanding of their topics, often using examples, illustrations, comparisons, anecdotes, historical information, and cultural analysis to do so.

10-1 UNDERSTAND HOW TO READ DEFINITION ESSAYS

To effectively read extended definitions, consider the essays' rhetorical situation and the specific definition strategies the writers use—and why.

10-1a Consider the Rhetorical Situation for Definition Writing

To understand a definition, consider the writer's purpose, audience, and topic.

▶ **Purpose:** Writers compose definition essays for many reasons—to correctly define a misunderstood term, to deepen or redirect its meaning, to plumb a term's history, to define its cultural or philosophical legacy, or to entertain readers. Look for the point of the definition.

▶ **Audience:** For some readers, the term may be new; while for others, the term may be familiar but misunderstood. Determine the target audience and

think through its relationship to the term being defined.

▶ **Topic:** For any definition essay, the topic is a term. But what terms do writers typically focus on? Terms may be technical, unusual, complex, comical, or new. They may have changed through time. They may be crucial to a larger analysis or argument. As you read a definition, ask "Why this term?"

10-1b Consider Definition-Writing Strategies

To understand a definition, identify the writer's strategies. Consider, for example, what the writer conveys about the term's denotative (or literal) meaning, its connotative (or suggested) meaning, and its etymological (or historical) meaning. Examine, as well, the use of anecdotes, comparisons, contrasts, and visuals. All supporting details should derive from reliable, accurate, and authoritative resources.

Consider the Following

The writers whose essays are included in this chapter make the following choices:

- **Chase Viss** explores the meaning of *mathematics* and argues that its common definition is inadequate.
- **Paige Louter** analyzes the meaning of *asceticism* by comparing and contrasting why and how individuals have practiced the concept at different times and in different cultures.
- **David Schelhaas** explains the meanings of *deft* and *daft* by sharing a funny anecdote and analyzing the words' *etymology*, or historical development.
- **Camila Domonoske** explores the evolving history of the word *ghetto*, from its mysterious etymological origins to its 19th-century meaning as a segregated Jewish community—which later gave way to an ominous role in World War II—and finally its evolving meaning in poor, black communities.

Reading Guide: Definitions

✔ Precisely what does the writer claim about the term's meaning?

✔ Is the definition current, relevant, complete, and clear?

✔ Is the definition accurate in terms of its past and current usage?

DEFINE A TERM THROUGH DISTINCTION FROM RELATED TERMS

In his essay "The Philosophy of Mathematics," student writer Chase Viss wrote the following definition of *mathematics*. Note how he organizes the passage by first analyzing a common definition that he finds inadequate and then developing his own, more scholarly definition.

Defining Mathematics

SQ3R Survey · Question · Read · Recite · Review

1   Throughout elementary, middle, and high school, most students experience mathematics solely through classes that involve the manipulation of numbers; variables that represent numbers; figures that can be represented by numbers; and functions, which act on numbers to **(A)** produce more numbers. Given this experience, these students might define *mathematics* as "the study of numbers and their applications"—a definition that would **(B)** suit their needs. However, students enrolled in college-level mathematics courses soon learn that mathematics has a much more general foundation. For example, classes like Discrete Structures and Abstract Algebra address systems such as Sentential Logic, Set Theory, and Group Theory—systems that often intersect the world of numbers. However, numbers are by no means necessary for their study. Set Theory, for instance, involves sets of numbers such as the Rationals and the Reals, but the foundation of Set Theory is a set of axioms and definitions about objects, sets, and operations that do not emphasize numbers at all. Should this deviation exclude basic Set Theory from mathematics? Similarly, the study of Group Theory often involves numbers, but its axioms certainly do not require that members of a group actually be numbers. Clearly, if these abstract systems are to be included in the study of mathematics, then the prerequisite of numbers must be removed from its definition.

So, if not numbers, then what do all mathematical 2 systems have in common? After studying various **(C)** mathematical topics, students will begin to see that every area of mathematics has its own foundation of axioms—general assumptions used to derive necessary conclusions using accepted rules of logic and calculation. Sometimes, these axioms and rules are clearly laid out like those in Euclid's Elements, in which each assumed definition, common notion, and postulate is stated and then used in logical proofs to determine more complex, necessary propositions. In other systems, starting axioms, definitions, and deduction rules are less obvious. For example, the Ancient Mesopotamians did not explicitly write out the foundational assumptions of their mathematical system, but does this imply that none were present? The Babylonians must have shared a set of assumptions such as the definition of numbers and operations, accepted algorithms for arithmetic, and rules for solving equations and calculating the area/volume of figures. These general principles can be inferred from the particular examples given in their scrolls. Without these universal assumptions, the practice of Babylonian mathematics would have varied from scribe to scribe. The consistency of their system required that while teaching mathematics, the instructor must have shared with the student, whether explicitly or implicitly, the basic assumptions/axioms and rules for calculation from which their entire system was derived. In this same way, all mathematical systems must have a starting set of axioms and accepted methods for deducing new propositions.

If this is true, should mathematics be defined as 3 "the practice of deduction from a set of axioms using **(D)** accepted forms of logic"? While this is a characteristic of any mathematical system, the study

---

(A) The writer presents a common definition.
(B) The definition is inadequate.

(C) A transition is followed by a claim and supporting evidence.
(D) A conditional phrase introduces a second transitional question.

intuition must provide the starting points for the system and propositions for which it is designed to prove.

Finally, if mathematics is the study of certain deductive systems, something in its **(E)** definition must differentiate mathematics from other axiomatically presented sciences, such as physics. The distinguishing characteristic of mathematics is that it emphasizes the properties, relationships, and interactions of abstract concepts, such as quantity, magnitude, functions, sets, or geometric figures. Some of these concepts, like quantity, seem like fairly concrete ideas, but the study of mathematics does not involve physical instances of quantities as much as it explores the concept of quantity abstracted away from any physical representation. Similarly, the study of shapes in geometry does not usually involve actual, concrete figures but rather the idealized shapes abstracted away from these figures. Of course, just because mathematics involves primarily the abstract does not mean it cannot be applied to physical situations. Because its concepts are derived from physical phenomena and their properties/relationships are formed by intuition, mathematics can be used to make accurate predictions about the natural world and, therefore, can be applied in countless practical situations.

When studying and describing these mathematical concepts, teachers and students generally represent them and their relationships using symbols or words. However, notation is only a secondary characteristic of any mathematical system, as symbolism for certain concepts can vary from culture to culture. Mathematics, therefore, is not a study of symbols, but the abstract concepts the symbols represent.

Once students have explored areas of mathematics outside the traditional, calculus-based curriculum of middle and high school, they will be prepared to give mathematics a much more appropriate definition than

and practice of mathematics generally requires more than just deducing propositions. In order for students to deduce anything, they must first have an idea about the concept they are trying to prove. But how can they already have knowledge about a proposition if they have not yet derived it through deduction? Additionally, the starting axioms of any mathematical system are, by nature, assumed and therefore impossible to achieve through deduction. Where do they come from, and why are they chosen? Typically, foundational axioms, along with all necessary definitions, are chosen through mathematical intuition, the theorizing of general principles based on the observation of particular instances. For example, after combining two sets of objects, one might observe that if an object belonged to either of the first two sets, then it would belong to the resulting combined set. Based on this physical phenomenon, the definition of *set union*, one of the foundational operations of set theory, is formed. This example may seem incredibly obvious, but it demonstrates that axioms and definitions are chosen because they seem "true" in real life. Discovering mathematical propositions that are not starting axioms is usually more difficult. Archimedes discovered many of his propositions through "The Method," or by investigating mathematical relationships mechanically before attempting to formally deduce them. Nevertheless, it is clear that before deduction can be done in any mathematical system,

---

(E) A conditional phrase introduces another claim.

(F) just "the study of numbers." One reasonable definition would be "the study of any formal deductive system, formed and guided by intuition, involving the properties, relationships, and interactions of abstract concepts." This definition includes all areas of advanced mathematics instead of just restricting it to numerical studies. Also, this definition allows for a greater appreciation of mathematics. Reducing mathematics to numbers can easily cause students to value it exclusively due to its practical applications. However, with a broader definition in mind, students at all levels will see that another significant reason to study mathematics is that it expands and sharpens both their deductive and their intuitive capabilities—tools that will prove valuable in every possible field of study.

(F) The writer offers his definition and supporting rationale.

Reading for Better Writing

1. In his opening paragraph, Viss presents a common definition of *mathematics* and then points out weaknesses. Explain why he finds this definition weak.

2. Describe how Viss uses questions in paragraphs 2 and 3 to develop his definition. Explain why this strategy is or is not effective.

3. Explain how the opening sentence in paragraph 4 functions as a transition and as a topic sentence.

4. Explain why paragraph 6 does or does not effectively clarify Viss's definition and unify his argument.

5. Explain how Viss's essay has enriched or diminished your understanding of mathematics as an academic discipline.

DEFINE A TERM BY EXAMINING DENOTATION AND CONNOTATION

In this essay, student writer Paige Louter analyzes how the denotative and connotative meanings of *asceticism* are linked to the religious and philosophical perspectives of those who practice asceticism.

Hipsters and Hobos: Asceticism for a New Generation

SQ3R Survey • Question • Read • Recite • Review

In August 1992, a young man's remains were discovered in an abandoned bus in the Alaskan wilderness. He appeared to have starved to death. Eventually, he was identified as Christopher Johnson McCandless, a graduate of Emory University, who had disappeared two years earlier with no contact with his family since. McCandless had given $25,000 in savings to a charity dedicated to eradicating world hunger just before leaving, and he had spent the next years hitchhiking (after abandoning his car and most of his belongings) across the United States, eventually hiking into Alaska in April 1992. McCandless, or as he dubbed himself during his odyssey, Alexander Supertramp, left an indelible record of his life in many people he met as he journeyed, and in 1996 a writer named Jon Krakauer published a book called *Into the Wild*. In it, Krakauer details McCandless's travels and eventual death with a combination of interviews from the people the young man met and writings from McCandless himself (a journal of sorts was discovered with his body). The book was made into a film, which premiered in 2007. Beyond simply presenting a fascinating account of a fascinating individual, however, *Into the Wild* (and its subsequent success) represents an increasing interest, especially among young people, in an alternative lifestyle that rather than being concerned with worldly possessions and experiences, is focused

1

(A)

(A) The writer introduces the concept of asceticism with an anecdote.

upon self-denial, simplicity, and ultimately some sort of transcendence. This movement, called *asceticism*, is not a new one: John the

(B) Baptist, medieval monastic orders, Buddhists, and Jains all practiced some form of an ascetic lifestyle. But a contemporary manifestation of such a philosophy is necessarily going to look quite different from a historical manifestation. So what does a formerly well-to-do, well-educated young man like Chris McCandless have in common with a fifth-century monk, for example? Asceticism, in ways both subtle and more overt, is on the rise today, but the implications of the current cultural context may be affecting this movement in ways not immediately apparent.

2   Asceticism is a difficult concept to fully wrap one's head around. A straightforward, objective analysis might define it as "the practice or lifestyle of denying oneself

(C) physical excesses, even going to Spartan extremes, in order to achieve some revelation or higher state of being." However, ascetics historically have deviated from this pattern. Some have tended toward self-flagellation, rejecting not only excessive behavior but also physical comfort; while others do not match the end-goal of the definition above, denying any nebulous desire for enlightenment as motivation. Perhaps it is the lack of a "perfect ascetic" as a model that contributes to the difficulty of definition. There is no rule book for asceticism and ultimately perhaps no fixed set of guidelines against which the aspiring can be measured. Given this uncertainty, considering the modern manifestations of asceticism—and the degree to which these manifestations conform or differ from "true asceticism"—will be difficult. However, one element of asceticism that deals less with

the manifestation and more with the motivation for such behavior, without which a lifestyle cannot be truly considered ascetic, is intentionality. If people are not intentionally (and informed about) choosing their ascetic actions, then they are ascetics in appearance only.

3   Today, asceticism is explored and practiced in several different forms or incarnations. The first category is that **(D)** of incidental, unintentional, even completely unaware adherence; essentially, these are not truly ascetics. From the viewpoint of diet alone, most of the world could be considered ascetic, through no choice of their own. Others who choose to limit themselves from excessive purchasing, for example, without a clear idea of why they are making this choice, would also fall into this category.

4   The second form of contemporary asceticism is admiration and a kind of distorted, even ironic, mimicry. Into this category would fit most members of the current hipster movement, a movement that professes to be counter-cultural but that in reality rejects societal norms in little but clothing and music choice. Breaking away from the status quo in order to live radically different, usually dramatically simplified lives has been the goal of many a counter-cultural group. However, a lack of deeper philosophical understanding on the part of the movement's members suggests that to describe the lives of these people as ascetic would be to misuse the word. Although ascetics would likely be admired by the hipster movement in general, asceticism would more properly

---

(B) An informal definition plus historical examples offer a starting point for understanding the term.

(C) A formal definition is stated and then complicated, with the writer zeroing in on a key element of the definition.

(D) The writer turns to current manifestations of asceticism, categorizing them and testing them against the definition established.

be seen as an informed, intentional, fulfilled version of "hipsterism" (and the opposite could also be taken as true). Forrest Perry explains, in his article "Why Hipsters Aren't All that Hip," that "what unifies the diverse strategies of those who position themselves as cool, then, is the image of the nonconforming individual" (57). He goes on to argue that the materialistic focus of hipsters essentially devalues their "message," as they purchase clothes, rather than make actual lifestyle changes, to fulfill their surface-only philosophy. Other ironic forms of asceticism today include an alarming manifestation of self-flagellation, "cutting," in which a person (usually a teen or young adult) cuts his or her skin with the intention of causing pain but not death, as well as dieting and weight-loss regimens in the name of conforming to some vague societal ideal of a perfect body.

5   Partial intentional adherence makes up the third method of contemporary exploration of asceticism. This category includes many Christians, who strive to (E) embody the ideal of "being in the world, but not of it." Interestingly, this phrase never actually appears in the Bible—the closest match would be a paraphrase of John 17:13-16. (The phrase does, however, appear in Sufi teachings.) However, though the word-for-word quotation is absent, the concept remains and is supported throughout Scripture. In "The Ascetic Impulse in Ancient Christianity," Vincent L. Wimbush says this:

> Both in its origins as the Jesus movement in Palestine, Syria, and Egypt and in its later development into conventicles resembling (some argue) Jewish synagogues, Hellenistic mysteries, or philosophical schools—even in its turn toward the ethos of

(E) In the third category, the writer distinguishes modern religious asceticism from historical religious practices.

the Greco-Roman urban petit bourgeois—early Christianity generally shared the impulse toward cultural criticism or resistance. It is very difficult to account for its origins other than as a critique of resistance to different circles of establishment power and tradition. (421)

This concept of asceticism as a form of resistance against popular culture is one that is definitely present in contemporary Christianity, as well as many other counter-cultural groups. However, most Christians today do not go to the extremes of, for example, the medieval monastic orders, so while they conform to a moderate type of asceticism, they do not represent the most dedicated group of ascetics. Partial adherence is not limited to Christianity, however, or any other religious group. It is not unheard of for, as previously mentioned in the first category (unintentional adherence), a person to forgo unnecessary shopping. However, when that decision is made consciously in order to abstain from consumerism, or to live simply, that person is engaging a true, if limited, form of asceticism (whether or not the person him- or herself would identify it as such).

Finally, the fourth category is that of strict, extreme adherence to an ascetic lifestyle. Into this category are placed the most compelling examples: the people whose lives were unyieldingly dedicated to asceticism in one form or another. One example, arguably the most well-known in the history of asceticism, is that of Saint Simeon Stylites, a fifth-century monk who lived for more than 40 years on top of a pillar. Saint Simeon's extreme self-denial, which reportedly included standing for entire days and fasting for weeks on end, attracted thousands of followers and even converted the emperor to asceticism. It is also this category that contains Chris McCandless and others like him, men and women who choose to reject material belongings and easy lives in order to search for something more authentic.

6

7　Perhaps the most logical next question, however, is
(F) "why?" What would drive someone to give up comfort and ease in favor of discomfort, hardship, and even pain and death? One Internet blogger offers a potential explanation for the actions, historically, of monastic orders:

> The spirit of monasticism [. . .] emphasized a withdrawing from the world in order to create this community. This does not mean that monks did not care about the world, they sincerely did— but rather they believed that the only way to live out the Christian life was to depart from secular society. It was an attempt to create an alternative culture rather than reform the dominant one. It was only through this kind of asceticism and purity that the secular world could ever see what the Kingdom of God was. (Gonzaga par. 5)

This summary provides a good view of the motivation for monks and likely other religious ascetics as well. In fact, historically, asceticism seems consistently to have been motivated by spiritual ideals. For God, in whatever form he might take, men and women have been willing to deprive themselves of sleep, starve and beat themselves, give away all their worldly possessions, and live in isolation and separation from the world. And in a historical context, this appears to make sense. But what of ascetics today? How can a seemingly barbaric and anachronistic philosophy be a relevant and powerful movement in the twenty-first-century, post-modern (and increasingly secular) world?

8　Perhaps, as it has been historically, contemporary asceticism is mainly a reactionary philosophy. It would not be a stretch, for instance, to credit the increasingly consumerist society with motivating the

> Armed with only a vague idea rather than a deep understanding of a philosophy like asceticism, contemporary would-be adherents cannot hope to truly experience the transcendence that would have been the ultimate goal of the historical ascetic.

anti-establishment movements in the 1950s, which (G) in turn spawned the watered-down hipster culture of the twenty-first century. Likewise, Chris McCandless abandoned his primary identity in order to live apart from a society that he felt was excessive and cut off from the truly important aspects of life. This is not a reaction exclusive to asceticism, however; it is a common feature, in fact, of North Americans to be drawn to the unique or the exclusive, and a common conceit that goes along with this is to believe that, by bucking mainstream trends, a person is made automatically superior.

9　Unfortunately, it is this arrogance, as opposed to the greater-than-self awareness of the previous centuries, that best seems to characterize the contemporary manifestations of not only asceticism but also many other philosophies (and religions) as well. Armed with only a vague idea rather than a deep understanding of a philosophy like asceticism, contemporary would-be adherents cannot hope to truly experience the transcendence that would have been the ultimate goal of the historical ascetic.

10　Today, asceticism is clearly less grounded in intentionality and spiritual meaning than it has been in the past. Because true asceticism is necessarily also intentional asceticism, the possibility even arises that asceticism in its truest form no longer exists—outside (H) of certain religious groups. Perhaps, then, the definition of an ascetic life must be modified, or perhaps a new philosophy has arisen today that is valid in its own right. Or perhaps the longing for authenticity that dwells in many young people today will eventually drive them beyond a self-reliant, isolated philosophy to deeply engage with the true spirit of asceticism. Arguably,

---

(F) After looking at strict asceticism (the fourth category), the writer deepens her definition by exploring the motivation behind the practice.

(G) She contrasts motivations of past ascetics with those of current ascetics.
(H) Bringing her extended definition to a conclusion, the writer speculates that true asceticism may no longer exist and that the definition may need to be changed.

Chris McCandless may have been one of the first of this movement. While one respondent to McCandless's story accused him of adhering to an arrogant and "contrived asceticism" (Krakauer 72), McCandless himself did, ultimately, live out what he believed, rejecting materialism, consumerism, and mainstream society, all in the name of truly living. Essentially, perhaps this is what living as an ascetic is really about.

Note: The Works-Cited page is not shown. For sample pages, see MLA (page 286) or APA (page 320).

Reading for Better Writing

1. Paige Louter frames her essay with the story of Chris McCandless. Besides the opening, where else does she refer to McCandless? How does his story help her define asceticism?

2. Early in the essay (late in paragraph 1 and through paragraph 2), Louter is direct in her definition of asceticism. What strategies does she use? How effective are these strategies in clarifying asceticism?

3. To extend her definition, Louter analyzes different types of asceticism (paragraphs 3–6). How does she distinguish the categories, and how does her discussion of each category deepen your understanding of asceticism?

4. In the last part of her essay, Paige explores people's motivations for adopting an ascetic lifestyle. What conclusions does she draw, based on what thinking?

5. In the end, what does this essay encourage you to think and feel about asceticism? What does the essay ask of you?

6. Carefully review Paige's essay, looking for strengths and weaknesses in her argument. Then write your own extended definition of *asceticism* in which you cite individuals whom you believe to be legitimate ascetics.

10-4 DEFINE A TERM THROUGH ETYMOLOGY

Professor David Schelhaas delivered the following definition on his weekly radio program, *What's the Good Word?* Watch how he defines *deft* and *daft* by examining their roots.

Deft or Daft

SQ3R   Survey · Question · Read · Recite · Review

The other day, my wife, watching our son-in-law with his large hands gracefully tie the shoelaces of his little daughter, remarked, "You really are *deft*." Ever the cynic, I remarked, "He's not only *deft*, he's *daft*." I talk that sort of nonsense frequently, but as I said this, I began to wonder. What if *deft* and *daft* come from the same root and once meant the same thing? A quick trip to the dictionary showed that, indeed, they did once mean the same thing (though my wife thought me *daft* when I first suggested it).   1 (A)

Let me see if I can explain the original meaning and also how *daft* and *deft* came to part company. *Daft* originally meant *mild* or *gentle*. The Middle English *dafte* comes from the Old English *gadaefte*, which has as its underlying sense *fit* or *suitable*. Quite likely, mild or gentle people were seen as behaving in a way that was fit and suitable.   2 (B)

Gradually, however, the mild, gentle meaning descended in connotation to mean *crazy* or *foolish*. First, animals were described as *daft*—that is, without reason—and eventually people also. The word *silly*, which once meant *happy* or *blessed*, slid down the same slope. So that explains where *daft* got its present meaning.   3

But how does *deft*, meaning *skillful* or *dexterous*, fit into the picture? Again, if we start with the Old English meaning of *fit* or *suitable*, we can see a connection to *skillful*. In fact, the root of *gadaefte*, which is *dhabh, to fit*, carries with it the sense of a joiner or an artisan, someone who skillfully made the ends or corners of a cupboard or   4 (C)

(A) The writer introduces the topic with an anecdote.
(B) He describes the history of *daft*.
(C) He compares and contrasts the two words.

piece of furniture fit neatly together. From *fit* to *skillful* to *dexterous*. Thus we see how one root word meaning *fit* or *suitable* went in two different directions—one meaning *crazy*, the other meaning *skillful*.

5 These days it is usually considered much better to be *deft* than to be *daft*. But don't be too sure. It is good to remind ourselves that one person's deftness might very well appear as daftness to another.

6 This is David Schelhaas asking, "What's the Good (D) Word?"

(D) He closes with a reflection and his usual sign-off.

Reading for Better Writing

1. Explain how the opening attempts to engage the reader. In what ways does it succeed?
2. Describe how the writer cites root meanings and shows that the meanings have changed. Is his explanation clear? Why or why not?
4. Describe the writer's tone. Is it effective for a radio program? Explain.
5. Imagine turning this radio broadcast into a short video. What film would you create to deepen the definition? Explain.

DEFINE A TERM THROUGH CULTURAL AND PHILOSOPHICAL ANALYSIS

The following extended definition comes from National Public Radio's "Code Switch" blog, which is dedicated to exploring the role of language in race and culture. In this entry from April 2014, writer Camila Domonoske analyzes the evolution of the word *ghetto*, including the word's historical and cultural meaning.

Segregated from Its History, How "Ghetto" Lost Its Meaning

SQ3R Survey · Question · Read · Recite · Review

1 The word "ghetto" is an etymological mystery. Is it from the Hebrew *get*, or "bill of divorce"? From the Venetian *ghèto*, or "foundry"? From the Yiddish *gehektes*, "enclosed"? From Latin *Giudaicetum*, for "Jewish"? From the Italian *borghetto*, "little town"? From the Old French *guect*, "guard"?

2 In his etymology column for the Oxford University Press, Anatoly Liberman took a look at each of these possibilities. He considered ever more improbable origins — Latin for "ribbon"? German for "street"? Latin for "to throw"? —before declaring the word a stubborn mystery.

3 But whatever the root language, the word's original meaning was clear: "the quarter in a city, chiefly in Italy, to which the Jews were restricted," as the OED [Oxford English Dictionary] puts it. In the 16th and 17th centuries, cities like Venice, Frankfurt, Prague and Rome forcibly segregated their Jewish populations, often walling them off and submitting them to onerous restrictions.

4 By the late 19th century, these ghettos had been steadily dismantled. But instead of vanishing from history, ghettos reappeared—with a purpose more ominous than segregation—under Nazi Germany. German forces established ghettos in over a thousand cities across Europe. They were isolated, strictly controlled and

resource-deprived—but unlike the ghettos of history, they weren't meant to last.

5   Reviving the Jewish ghetto made genocide a much simpler project. As the Holocaust proceeded, ghettos were emptied by the trainload. The prisoners of the enormous Warsaw ghetto, which at one point held 400,000 Jews, famously fought their deportation to death camps. They were outnumbered and undersupplied, but some managed to die on their own terms; thousands of Jews were killed within the walls of the ghetto, rather than in the camps.

6   Jewish ghettos were finally abolished after the end of World War II. But the word lived on, redefined as a poor, urban black community.

From Anti-Semitism to Race and Poverty

7   As early as 1908, "ghetto" was sometimes used metaphorically to describe slum areas that weren't mandated by law but that were limited to a single group of people because of other constraints. That year, Jack London wrote of "the working-class ghetto." Immigrant groups and American Jews were also identified as living in these unofficial "ghettos."

8   Even as those areas were identified, they were already transforming. A 1928 study of American Jewish ghettos explained why such communities were being "invaded" by people of color: "the Negro, like the immigrant, is segregated in the city into a racial colony. Economic considerations, race prejudice and cultural differences combine to set him apart." "Race prejudice" included laws and lending practices, from redlining to restrictive covenants, explicitly designed to separate white and nonwhite city dwellers.

9   After World War II, "white flight" from inner cities further exacerbated racial segregation. By the '60s and '70s, so-called "negro ghettos" in cities like Chicago, New York and Detroit were central to the cultural conversation about poverty. "Something must be done, and done soon, to build a strong and stable family structure among Negro ghetto dwellers," an *Ebony* editorial contended in 1966; countless academic articles argued about the causes of ghetto poverty.

10   And in 1969, Elvis—in his late-career comeback—took a turn for the mournful with "In the Ghetto." Elvis (and many cover singers after him) sings about Chicago's crowded black ghettos with an outsider's concern: "People, don't you understand / the child needs a helping hand / or he'll grow to be an angry young man some day."

11   Almost half a century later, Busta Rhymes used the same song title to celebrate the ghetto as a source of identity.

12   Busta Rhymes doesn't ignore the painful effects of intergenerational poverty. The ghetto is where "crackhead chicks still smoke with babies in they belly." But he's not calling for help or claiming that all ghetto-dwellers are miserable. The ghetto is also "where you find beautiful women and rugrats / and some of the most powerful people, I love that!"

Anastasia Petrova, 2014 / Used under license from Shutterstock.com

Ghetto Not-So-Fabulous?

13   Ghettos were always defined by lack of choice—they were places inhabitants were forced to live, whether by anti-Semitic governments, discriminating neighbors or racist practices like redlining. Sociologist Mario Small argues that these limits have largely been lifted, such

that researchers should no longer consider "ghetto" a useful word for urban slums.

14 And indeed, use of the word "ghetto" in print has been declining since the early '70s. But slang variants have been rising in popularity since before the turn of the millennium. And a quick glance at social media suggests they're not going away; on a recent weekday, twitter users referenced "ghetto" almost 20

> And a quick glance at social media suggests they're not going away; on a recent weekday, twitter users referenced "ghetto" almost 20 times per minute.

15 times per minute.

"Being ghetto," or behaving in a low-class manner (see also: "ratchet"). "Ghetto fabulous," flashy glamour without the wealth. "Ghetto" as an adjective, roughly synonymous with "jury-rigged," for anything cobbled together out of subpar materials.

16 Many commentators have objected to these terms. Using *ghetto* as an insult is, as National Public Radio's Karen Grigsby Bates has pointed out, inherently classist. Ta-Nehisi Coates once wrote that "ghetto, in its most unironic usage, is a word for people you don't know. It's a word that allows you to erase individuals and create boxes." And arguments that the terms are race-neutral are, well, unconvincing.

17 This current use of "ghetto" is also curiously mismatched to the history of ghettos. Venice's ghettos were home to prosperous merchants. Warsaw's ghettos housed resistance fighters. Harlem was a ghetto when it hosted a transformative literary and cultural movement. Chicago's Bronzeville was home to the black professional class—ghettos, by removing citizens' freedom to live where they want, force schoolteachers next to drug dealers, working families next to whorehouses.

18 But slang references to "ghetto culture" don't refer to any of those legacies, or to the perseverance it takes to survive under such limitations. ("You surviving in the ghetto," raps Busta Rhymes, "you can make it anywhere.") Instead, they reduce ghetto life to poverty and poor behavior. *Acting* ghetto. *Being* ghetto. *Dressing* ghetto.

19 Ghetto, in slang usage, has entirely lost the sense of forced segregation—the meaning it held for centuries. In a rapid about-face, it's become an indictment of individual choices.

Reading for Better Writing

1. What does the essay's title convey about the essay's topic and purpose?

2. How does the writer compare and contrast the historical meaning of the word *ghetto* with its current use as a slang term for poverty and poor behavior?

3. What final conclusion does the writer make about the evolution of the meaning of *ghetto*? Cite examples from the essay that support the author's conclusion.

4. Near the end of paragraph 8, the author mentions but does not define the terms "redlining" and "restrictive covenants." Research the terms, define them, and explain how they relate to the meaning of *ghetto*.

5. How would you have defined the term *ghetto* before you read the essay? Did your understanding of the term evolve from reading the essay? How so?

WRITE, REVISE, AND EDIT A DEFINITION ESSAY

Writing Guidelines

Planning

❶ Select a topic. Beneath headings like these, list words that you'd like to explore:

Words that . . .

- are related to an art or a sport
- are in the news (or should be)
- are overused, underused, or abused
- make you chuckle, frown, or fret
- do or do not describe you

 TIP The best topics are abstract nouns (truth, individualism), complex terms (code blue, dementia), or words connected to a personal experience (excellence, deft, daft).

❷ Identify what you know. To discern what you already know about the topic, write freely about the word, letting your writing go where it chooses. Explore both your personal and your academic connections with the word.

❸ Gather information. To find information about the word's history, usage, and grammatical form, use strategies such as these:

- **Consult a general dictionary,** preferably an unabridged dictionary; list both denotative (literal) and connotative (associated) meanings for the word.
- **Consult specialized dictionaries** that define words from specific disciplines or occupations: music, literature, law, medicine, and so on.
- If helpful, **interview experts** on your topic.
- **Check reference resources** such as Bartlett's Familiar Quotations (bartleby.com/100/) to see how famous speakers and writers have used the word.
- **Research the word's etymology** and usage by consulting appropriate Web sources such as dictionary.com, m-w.com, or xrefer.com.
- **Do a general search on the Web** to see where the word pops up in titles of songs, books, or films; company names, products, and ads; nonprofit organizations' names, campaigns, and programs; and topics in the news.

- **List synonyms** (words meaning the same or nearly the same) and antonyms (words meaning the opposite).
- **Identify graphics** that could clarify the term visually.

❹ Compress what you know. Based on your freewriting and research, try writing a formal one-sentence definition that satisfies the following equation:

Equation:

Term = larger class + distinguishing characteristics

Examples:

Swedish pimple = fishing lure + silver surface, tubular body, three hooks

melodrama = stage play + flat characters, contrived plot, moralistic theme

Alzheimer's = dementia + increasing loss of memory, hygiene, social skills

❺ Get organized. To organize the information that you have and to identify details that you may want to add, fill out a graphic organizer like the one on page 47.

jannoon028, 2014 / Used under license from Shutterstock.com

Drafting

❻ Draft the essay. Review your outline as needed to write the first draft.

- **Opening:** Get the reader's attention and introduce the term. If you are organizing the essay from general to specific, consider using an anecdote, an illustration, or a quotation to set the context. If you are organizing the essay from specific to general, consider including an interesting detail from the word's history or usage. When using a dictionary definition, avoid the phrase "According to Webster . . ."

- **Middle:** Show your readers precisely what the word means. Build the definition in paragraphs that address distinct aspects of the word: common definitions, etymology, usage by professional writers, and so on. Link paragraphs so that the essay unfolds the word's meaning layer by layer.
- **Closing:** Review your main point and close your essay. (You might, for example, conclude by encouraging readers to use—or not use—the word.)

Revising

7 **Improve the ideas, organization, and voice.** Ask a classmate or someone from the college's writing center to read your essay for the following:

- **Ideas:** Is each facet of the definition clear, showing precisely what the word does and does not mean? Is the definition complete, telling the reader all that she or he needs to know in order to understand and use the word? Are the ideas well researched, coming from reliable, accurate, and authoritative resources?
- **Organization:** Does the opening identify the word and set the context for what follows? Are the middle paragraphs cohesive, each offering a unit of meaningful information? Does the closing wrap up the message and refocus on the word's core meaning?
- **Voice:** Is the voice informed, engaging, instructive, and courteous?

Editing

8 **Edit the essay** by addressing these issues:

- **Words:** The words are precise and clear to the essay's audience.
- **Sentences:** The sentences are complete, varied in structure, and readable.
- **Correctness:** The copy includes no errors in spelling, usage, punctuation, grammar, or mechanics.
- **Design:** The page design is correctly formatted and attractive. Visuals and diagrams are clearly presented and effectively integrated.

Publishing

9 **Publish the essay.** Share your writing with interested readers. Submit the essay to your instructor.

If appropriate, use what you learned to edit a wiki article on your topic.

Critical-Thinking and Writing Activities

1. In "Defining Mathematics" Chase Viss defines a key word that distinguishes his major or field of study. Choose, research, and define a key word in your major.
2. Review "Deft or Daft" and "Hipsters and Hobos." Then choose a pair of words that similarly mirror each other's meaning. Research the words, and write an essay comparing and contrasting their etymologies and meanings.
3. "Segregated from Its History, How 'Ghetto' Lost Its Meaning" explores how the cultural meaning of the term *ghetto* evolved through time. Write an extended definition exploring the evolution in meaning of another term that is culturally relevant today. Write for an audience of your age. If possible, clear up any misconceptions your peers may have about the word.
4. Write an essay defining a word or phrase that is understood by people in a particular field of study but not by "outsiders." Write for the audience of outsiders.

STUDY TOOLS 10

LOCATED AT BACK OF THE TEXTBOOK
☐ Tear-Out Chapter Review Card

LOCATED AT WWW.CENGAGEBRAIN.COM/LOGIN
☐ Chapter eBook

☐ Graded quizzes and a practice quiz generator

☐ Videos: Writer Interviews

☐ Tutorials

☐ Flashcards

☐ Cengage Learning Write Experience

☐ Interactive activities

11 | Classification

"NOTHING IN LIFE IS TO BE FEARED. IT IS ONLY TO BE UNDERSTOOD."

MADAME CURIE

LEARNING OBJECTIVES

11-1 Understand how to read classification essays.

11-2 Devise a classification scheme suitable for your writing situation.

11-3 Create categories that are consistent, exclusive, and complete.

11-4 Title categories clearly.

11-5 Illustrate distinctive and shared traits of categories.

11-6 Write, revise, and edit a classification essay.

After you finish
this chapter
go to
PAGE 129 for STUDY TOOLS

Classification is an organizational strategy that helps writers make sense of large or complex sets of things. A writer using this strategy breaks the topic into individual items or members that can be sorted into clearly distinguishable groups or categories. For example, if writing about the types of residents who live in assisted-care facilities, a nursing student might classify them according to various physical and/or mental limitations.

By sorting residents in this way, the writer can discuss them as individuals, as representatives of a group, or as members of the body as a whole. By using an additional strategy such as compare-contrast, she or he can show both similarities and differences between individuals within a group or between one group and another.

11-1 UNDERSTAND HOW TO READ CLASSIFICATION ESSAYS

Use the information that follows as a basic guide when reading and analyzing classification essays.

11-1a Consider the Rhetorical Situation for Classification Writing

When reading classification essays, examine the writers' classification schemes—how they break their subjects into groups and why they sort them as they do. Explore whether the classification schemes fit the writer's purpose, audience, and topic.

- **Purpose:** Writers classify a body of information to explain its order, to clarify relationships, and to "locate" specific items within a larger structure. For example, in her essay, "Latin American Music . . ." (pages 124–125), Kathleen Kropp wants to explain how the music reflects Latinos' cultural identity and impacts social change.

- **Audience:** While readership can vary greatly, writers using classification are seeking to illuminate the deeper order of a topic, either to enhance readers' understanding or to support an argument. For example, Kropp's criteria instruct her college-student audience about the history and diversity of Latin American music.

- **Topic:** Writers typically use classification with topics that include a complex body of individual items or members. For example, Kropp's classification takes the large body of Latin American music (made up of many individual songs) and makes sense of it all through four categories that clarify music's role in Latino culture.

11-1b Consider Classification Principles

The principles that follow help writers sort items into unified and distinct categories.

- **Consistency:** The same criteria should be used in the same way when one sorts items into groups. For example, Kathleen Kropp sorts forms of Latin music into four types based on one criterion: what each type contributes to Latin American society (see "Latin American Music . . . ," pages 124–125).

- **Exclusivity:** Groups should be distinct. In her essay, Kropp identifies four types of Latin American music, and whereas they do share some traits, each type is substantially different from the others.

- **Completeness:** All individual items or members of the larger body should fit into a category with no items left over. For example, any common form of Latin American music will fit into one of Kropp's four categories.

> **Reading Guide:**
> **Classification Writing**
>
> ✔ Does the writer's classification scheme effectively explain the order of this topic for the target audience?
> ✔ Are the categories consistent, exclusive, and complete?
> ✔ Do the writer's classification strategies help you understand the subject?

LitDenis, 2014 / Used under license from Shutterstock.com

11-2 DEVISE A CLASSIFICATION SCHEME SUITABLE FOR YOUR WRITING SITUATION

In the following essay, student writer Hillary Gammons seeks to identify the diverse bunch of college students working out in the weight room. To clarify who they are and why they lift weights, she sorts them into four groups: health enthusiasts, toners, athletes, and body builders. As you read the essay, assess whether Hillary's classification plan helps her analyze her topic, address her college readers, and achieve her writing purpose.

Essay Outline

Introduction: combatting the "freshman 15" by going to the weight room

1. Some students lift weights as part of an exercise program directed toward health.
2. Other students lift to tone muscles.
3. Athletes lift weights as part of training for their sports.
4. Bodybuilders lift to create muscle bulk for strength and show.

Closing: limits of categories, but success with the "freshman 15"

Why We Lift

SQ3R   Survey · Question · Read · Recite · Review

1

(A) I had heard rumors about it before I ever left for college, and once I moved into the dorm, I realized it was not just a rumor. I needed a way to combat the "freshman 15," that dreaded poundage resulting from a combination of late-night pizzas, care-package cookies, and cafeteria cheesecakes. So, my roommate and I headed to the university gym, where the weight-training rooms are filled with student "chain gangs" sweating and clanging their way through a series of mechanical monsters. As I looked around, it became obvious that

people work out for quite different reasons. Health enthusiasts, toning devotees, athletes, and bodybuilders seem to be the main categories of those lifting weights.

2 Some students lift weights as part of an exercise **(B)** program aimed at maintaining or improving health. They have heard how strong abdominals reduce lower-back problems. They have learned that improved flexibility can help to reduce tension buildup and prevent headaches and other problems related to prolonged periods of sitting or studying. They know that combining weights with aerobic exercise is an efficient way to lose weight. A person who exercises can lose weight while continuing to eat well because increased muscle mass burns more calories. Typical weight-lifting routines for health enthusiasts are around 20 minutes, three times a week.

3 The toners' routine is different because they want **(C)** smoothly defined muscles. Not surprisingly, this group includes many young women. Lifting weights can target problem spots and help shape up the body. To develop solid arms, these people use dumbbells and a bench press. Other equipment focuses on achieving toned legs, abdominals, and buttocks. Toning workouts must be done more often than three times a week. I talked to a few young women who lift weights (after aerobic activity of some kind) for about 30 minutes, five times a week.

4 Athletes also lift weights. Volleyball, rowing, basketball, football—all of these sports require weight training. It may seem obvious that a football player needs to be muscular and strong, but how do other athletes

---

(A) The writer provides a personal introduction to the topic, gives her criterion for classifying (why students lift), and identifies the categories.

(B) Each category of lifter is described in turn.
(C) Paragraph topic sentences distinguish and relate the categories.

benefit from weight lifting? Muscles are a lot like brains: The more they are used, the more they can do. Strong muscles can increase a person's speed, flexibility, endurance, and coordination. Consider the competition required in various sports—different muscle groups matter more to different athletes. For example, while runners, especially sprinters, need bulging thighs for quick starts and speed, basketball players need powerful arms and shoulders for endless shots and passes. And while gymnasts want overall muscle strength for balance and coordination, football players develop large muscles for strength, speed, and agility. For all members of this group, however, weight lifting is a vital part of their training.

5
(D) One last group that cannot be ignored are the people who lift weights to become as big and strong as possible. I worked out with a guy who is about 6 feet 2 inches tall and weighs more than 200 pounds. He bench-presses more than I weigh. In a room devoted to dumbbells and barbells (also known as free weights), bodybuilders roar bulk-boosting battle cries as they struggle to lift super heavy bars. After you spend only a short time in this grunt room, it is clear that the goal for bodybuilders is not simply to be healthy, toned, or strong. These lifters want muscles for both strength and show—muscles that lift and bulge. For this reason, many participants spend little time on aerobic activity and most of their time lifting very heavy weights that build bulk and strength. My partner works out for an hour or more, five days a week.

6
(E) Not everyone fits neatly into these four categories. I work out to be healthy and toned, and I find that I can benefit from lifting only three times a week. Weight lifting has become more and more popular among college students who appreciate exercise as a great stress reliever. And for me, the gym proves to be the best place to combat the dreaded "freshman 15."

(D) The writer explains the motivation of each group through observations, examples, and illustrations.
(E) The conclusion, like the opening, includes a personal note.

Reading for Better Writing

1. Hillary Gammons opens and closes her essay by describing her own interest in weight lifting. What are the strengths and weaknesses of this approach?

2. The writer classifies weight lifters according to their reasons for lifting. Does the criterion effectively organize the topic? What other criteria could be used, and for what purposes?

3. The essay moves from health enthusiasts to toners to athletes to bodybuilders. Is there a particular logic to the sequence? Would a different order have created a different essay?

4. Based on your own knowledge of the topic, does the essay accurately describe the people who work out in a weight room? In other words, is the classification consistent, exclusive, and complete? Explain.

11-3 CREATE CATEGORIES THAT ARE CONSISTENT, EXCLUSIVE, AND COMPLETE

In the essay below, student writer Kathleen Kropp uses classification strategies to describe the nature of Latin American music and to explain how the music both reflects and affects Latin American culture. As you read, assess whether she creates consistent, exclusive, and complete categories.

Essay Outline

Introduction: Latin American music's unifying power
1. Category 1: indigenous music
2. Category 2: Iberian and Mestizo folk music
3. Category 3: Afro-American music
4. Category 4: urban popular music

Closing: These diverse types together express the passion and power of Latin American people.

^(A) # Latin American Music: A Diverse and Unifying Force

SQ3R Survey · Question · Read · Recite · Review

1   On September 20, 2009, Latin pop, rock, and salsa
^(B) rhythms danced through the air in Havana's Plaza de la Revolución as more than one million people gathered to witness Paz Sin Fronteras II (Peace Without Borders II). These benefit concerts brought together performers from Cuba, Puerto Rico, Ecuador, and Venezuela. Juanes, a popular Colombian singer who headlined the concerts, explained the event's passion and power like this: "Music becomes an excuse to send a message that we're all here together building peace, that we are here as citizens and this is what we want, and we have to be heard" (Hispanic 17). His statement demonstrates Latinos' belief that their music has the power to unify Latin American people, synthesize their cultural activities, and address their diverse needs. To understand how the music (which is as diverse as Latin America's people) can do this, it is helpful to sort the many forms of music into four major types and consider what each type contributes to Latin American society.

2   One type is indigenous music, a group of musical
^(C) forms that connect the human and the spiritual. Archeological evidence indicates that indigenous musical cultures of the Americas began over 30,000 years ago. Over time the first instruments, which were stone and clay sound-producing objects, evolved into wind instruments such as flutes and windpipes. An example of indigenous music connecting the human and spiritual is found among Aymara-speaking musicians in the Lake Titicaca Region of Peru. The people of this region use music to mesh pre-Columbian agricultural rites with current Catholic practices. For instance, during feasts such as the annual Fiesta de la Candelaria (Candlemas Feast), celebrants use Sicus (panpipes), pincullos (vertical duct flutes), cajas (drums), chants, dances, and costumes—in combination with Catholic symbolism—to celebrate the gift of staple crops such as corn and potatoes (Indigenous 328, 330).

3   A second type, Iberian and Mestizo (mixed) folk
^(D) music, enriches Latinos' everyday lives in a variety of forms, including liturgical music, working songs, and mariachi tunes. For example, whereas the traditional Catholic mass featured organ music, more recent Catholic services such as the Nicaraguan Peasant Mass use the acoustic guitar along with the colorful sounds of the marimba, maracas, and melodies from popular festivals. As a result, worshipers find the music inviting and the passionate lyrics (like those that follow, translated by Mike Yoder, October 2, 1989) socially relevant:

4   You are the God of the poor, the simple and human God, the God who sweats in the street;

You eat food scrapings there in the park. I've seen you in a corner grocery working behind the counter.

5   Another form of folk music known as tonadas (or tunes) are used as serenades and working songs. For example, in Venezuela, workers might whistle or sing tonadas while milking, plowing, or fishing (Tonadas). These vocal duets, which also can be accompanied by guitar, have pleasant harmonies, two main melodies, and faster tempos ("Iberian and mestizo folk music" 338, 341).

6   The mariachi band, a final form of folk music, adds festivity to Mexicans' many celebrations. With its six to eight violins, two trumpets, and a guitar, the band creates a vibrant, engaging

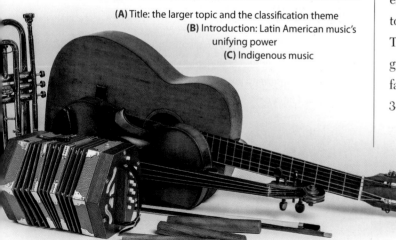

(A) Title: the larger topic and the classification theme
(B) Introduction: Latin American music's unifying power
(C) Indigenous music

(D) Liberian and Mestizo (mixed) folk music

sound. During birthdays or feast days, these bands commonly set up on streets and below windows where they awaken the residents above to the sounds of "Las Mañ Anitas," the traditional song for such days. Mariachis are also hired for baptisms, weddings, quinceañeras (the fifteenth birthday for a Mexican girl), patriotic holidays, and funerals (History of the Mariachi).

7
(E) Afro-American music, the third type of Latin American music, infuses passion and power in its percussion-driven dances and complex rhythm structures. These songs and dances, performed throughout the Caribbean, function as an entertaining, unifying force among Latin people ("Afro-American"). The energy of Afro-American music is clear in genres such as the mambo and the rumba dances. The rumba, an Afro-Caribbean dance, is highly improvisational and exciting. The quinto (a high-pitched drum) establishes a dialogue with a solo voice and challenges the male dancer, while the tumbadora and palitos (sticks on woodblock) provide a contrast with regular, unchanging rhythm patterns.

8 The mambo, an Afro-Cuban dance, became popular in Havana, Cuba. In the 1940s, nightclubs throughout Latin America caught the energy of this fast-tempo song and dance. Arsenio Rodríguez' "Bruca Managuá" exemplifies this form. Because of the song's sound and lyrics, many black Cubans consider the piece to be an anthem of Afro-Cuban pride and resistance:

9 I am Calabrí, black by birth/nation,

Without freedom, I can't live,

Too much abuse, the body is going to die.

(*Oxford Encyclopedia for Latinos and Latinas in the United States* 218)

(E) Afro-American music

10
(F) Urban popular music, the fourth type of Latin American music, combines a dynamic sound with poignant appeals for social change, appeals that resonate with many listeners. The styles of this type of music include rock, heavy metal, punk, hip-hop, jazz, reggae, and R & B. During the September 20, 2009, Paz Sin Fronteras II concerts described earlier, urban popular music was common fare. As U.S. Representative Jim McGovern observed, the message of the concerts was to "circumvent politics . . . using the medium of music to speak directly to young people, to change their way of thinking and leave behind the old politics, hatred, prejudices, and national enmities that have locked too many people in patterns of conflict, violence, poverty, and despair. It is an attempt to break down barriers and ask people to join in common purpose" (Paz Sin Fronteras II). Popular urban musicians such as Juanes utilize music not only to entertain but also to unite Latinos in a universal cause.

11
(G) Passion and power permeate all of Latin America's music. The four major types of music—indigenous, Iberian and Mestizo folk, Afro-American, and popular urban—are as diverse as the people of Latin America, and each style serves a valued need or function in Latinos' everyday lives. As a result, those listening to Latin American music—whether it is a Peruvian Indian's chant, a Venezuelan farmer's whistled tune, a Cuban mambo drummer's vivacious beat, or the Bogotá rock concert's compelling rhythms—are hearing much more than music. They are hearing the passion and power of the Latin American people.

Note: The Works Cited page is not shown. For sample pages, see MLA (page 286) and APA (page 320).

(F) Urban popular music
(G) Conclusion: passion and power of Latin American music and culture

Reading for Better Writing

1. Review the opening, in which Kropp introduces her topic, thesis, and choice to sort the music into four categories. Then explain (a) why the passage is clear or unclear and (b) whether sorting forms into categories seems necessary or helpful.

2. Cite three strategies that Kropp uses to distinguish the four types of music and the various forms within those groups. Are the strategies effective? Why?

3. Identify language that Kropp uses to help you imagine the tone and tenor of the music. Is the word choice helpful? Why?

4. In the last sentence, Kropp re-states—and re-phrases—her thesis. Review the sentence: Is it an effective closing? Why or why not?

5. Using Kropp's essay as a guide, research your own music library and other sources to find representative pieces of music for each category. Then create an audio mix that captures the diversity of Latin American music.

11-4   TITLE CATEGORIES CLEARLY

Jessica Seigel is an award-winning, widely published journalist. In the essay below, she explains how readers should respond to nuanced literary devices such as symbols, themes, and allegories. Note how Seigel clarifies her argument by sorting readers into two categories: adventurers and believers.

The Lion, the Witch, and the Metaphor

SQ3R   Survey · Question · Read · Recite · Review

1   Though it's fashionable nowadays to come out of the closet, lately folks are piling in—into the wardrobe, that is, to battle over who owns Narnia: secular or Christian lovers of C. S. Lewis's stories.

2   Children, of course, have been slipping through the magic cupboard into the mythical land for 50 years without assistance from pundits or preachers (though fauns and talking badgers have been helpful). But now that the chronicles' first book, *The Lion, the Witch and the Wardrobe,* has been made into a Disney movie, adults are fighting to claim the action. And that means analyzing it. Or not.

3   The 7-year-old who sat next to me during a recent showing said, "This is really scary." It was scary when the White Witch kills the lion Aslan, who dies to save the loathsome Edmund before rising to help him and his siblings vanquish evil. But adults reducing the story to one note—their own—are even scarier. One side dismisses the hidden Jesus figure as silly or trivial, while the other insists the lion is Jesus in a story meant to proselytize. They're both wrong.

4   As a child, I never knew that Aslan was "Jesus." And that's a good thing. My mother recently remarked that if she'd known the stories were Christian, she wouldn't have given me the books—which are among my dearest childhood memories.

5   But parents today will not be innocent of the religious subtext, considering the drumbeat of news coverage and Disney's huge campaign to remind churchgoing audiences of the film's religious themes. The marketing is so intense that the religious Web site HollywoodJesus.com even worried that ham-fisted promotion might ruin it for non-Christians.

6   But a brief foray into Criticism 101 shows that the wardrobe is big enough for everyone. Symbolism, for example, is when one thing stands for another but is not the thing itself. Psychoanalysts, for instance, have interpreted *The Wonderful Wizard of Oz* as Dorothy's quest for a penis—that is, retrieving the witch's broomstick. Does that symbolism—if you buy it—make Dorothy a pervert? No, because it's hidden. That's the point. Overt and covert meaning can exist independently.

7   Those with a fiduciary, rather than phallic, bent might prefer the theory that L. Frank Baum's Oz stories are a Populist manifesto, with the yellow brick road as the gold standard, the Tin Man as alienated labor, Scarecrow as oppressed farmers, and so on. (And surely some Jungian theory about the collective unconscious

explains why both Oz and Narnia are populated by four heroic characters fighting an evil witch.)

8   Yes, it's allegory land, a place that strings symbols together to create levels of meaning, which a determined scholar has actually quantified as ranging from two to seven layers. (No word on why not eight.) Allegory, the oldest narrative technique, often involves talking animals, from Aesop's fox with the grapes to Dr. Seuss's Yertle the Turtle, supposedly a Hitler figure.

9   Does that twist the Seuss tale into a political treatise on fascism? No, it adds another level for adults, it teaches morals (even the meekest can unseat the powerful, etc.), and it's fun—when plain little Mack burps, he shakes the bad king Yertle from his throne built on turtles.

10   But which layer is more important—the surface or beneath? Deep thinkers specialize in hidden meanings (building demand, of course, for their interpretive expertise). An Oxford English professor, Lewis himself explored the depths in his scholarly books. But he also defended the literal, lamenting in his essay "On Stories" how modern criticism denigrates the pleasures of a good yarn—and that was 50 years ago.

11   While critics today call it "fallacy" to interpret a work by citing the author's intentions, Lewis left a road map for us marked with special instructions for not annoying children. In his essay "Sometimes Fairy Stories May Say Best What's to Be Said," he denounced as "moonshine" the idea that he wrote the Narnia chronicles to proselytize the young. The lion Aslan, he wrote, bounded into his imagination from his experience as a Christian, coming to him naturally as should all good writing.

12   "Let the pictures tell you their own moral," he advised in "On Three Ways of Writing for Children." "If they don't show you a moral, don't put one in."

13   In keeping with that advice, the Narnia chronicles don't beat you on the head—nor does the faithful movie adaptation. If everyone stays on his own level—the surface for adventurers, and the depths for believers—we can all enjoy, so long as the advertisers stay out of the way.

Reading for Better Writing

1. Identify the two conflicting groups (or viewpoints) in this article, and describe characteristics of each.

2. Summarize Seigel's thesis, and explain why you do or do not agree.

3. In the final paragraph, Seigel differentiates the two categories as "adventurers" and "believers." Are her subgroups **consistent**, **exclusive**, and **distinct**? For example, could a reader be both an adventurer and a believer? How might a third (or fourth) category affect Seigel's argument?

11-5 ILLUSTRATE DISTINCTIVE AND SHARED TRAITS OF CATEGORIES

Many classification essays separate a topic into categories for the purpose of pointing out the distinctive and shared traits of each category. Though the essay does not appear in this chapter, professor John Van Rys's "Four Ways to Talk About Literature" illustrates this purpose. In his essay, Van Rys groups forms of literary criticism into four categories. Then, to illustrate how the categories are similar and different, he explains how a critic representing each category might analyze Robert Browning's poem "My Last Duchess." Read and respond to the essay on pages 168–170 of chapter 15, "Writing About Literature: A Case Study in Analysis."

11-6 WRITE, REVISE, AND EDIT A CLASSIFICATION ESSAY

Writing Guidelines

Planning

1 Select a topic. Start by writing a few general headings like the academic headings below; then list two or three related topics under each heading. Finally, pick a topic that is characterized by a larger set of items or members that can best be explained by ordering them into categories.

Engineering	Biology	Social Work
Machines	Whales	Child welfare
Bridges	Fruits	Organizations

2 Look at the big picture. Do preliminary research to get an overview of your topic. Review your purpose (to explain, persuade, inform, and so on), and consider which classification criteria will help you divide the subject's content into distinct, understandable categories.

3 Choose and test your criteria. Choose a criterion for creating categories. Make sure it produces groups that are consistent (the same criterion is used throughout the sorting process), exclusive (groups are distinct—no member fits into more than one group), and complete (each member fits into a category with no member left over).

4 Gather and organize information. Gather information from reliable sources. To organize your information, take notes, possibly using a classification grid like the one shown below or the one on page 47. Set up the grid by listing the classification criteria down the left column and listing the groups in the top row of the columns. Then fill in the grid with appropriate details. (The grid at the bottom of this page lists the classification criterion and groups discussed in "Latin American Music: A Diverse and Unifying Force," pages 124–125.)

TIP If you do not use a grid, consider using an outline to organize your thoughts.

5 Draft a thesis. Draft a working thesis (you can revise it later as needed) that states your topic and identifies your classification scheme. Include language introducing your criteria for classifying groups.

Drafting

6 Draft the essay. Write your first draft, using organization planned earlier.

- **Opening:** Get the readers' attention, introduce the subject and thesis, and give your criteria for dividing the subject into categories.
- **Middle:** Develop the thesis by discussing each category, explaining its traits, and showing how it is distinct from the other groups. For example, in the middle section of "Latin American Music: A Diverse and Unifying Force," Kathleen Kropp examines each type of music in separate paragraphs. Within each paragraph, she describes the qualities that make that type of music distinct from the others.
- **Closing:** Reflect on and tie together the classification scheme. While the opening and middle of the essay separate the subject into distinct categories, the closing may bring the groups back together. Kropp closes her essay by identifying how all types of Latin American music share a passion that is characteristic of Latin American culture and people.

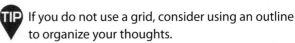

George Dolgikh, 2014 / Used under license from Shutterstock.com

Classification Criteria	Group #1 Indigenous music	Group #2 Iberian and Mestizo	Group #3 Afro-American music	Group #4 Urban popular music
Historical qualities/functions	• Trait #1 • Trait #2 • Trait #3	• Trait #1 • Trait #2 • Trait #3	• Trait #1 • Trait #2 • Trait #3	• Trait #1 • Trait #2 • Trait #3

Revising

7 **Improve the ideas, organization, and voice.** Ask a classmate or someone from the writing center to read your essay, looking for a clear thesis, an engaging introduction, a middle with clearly developed classification categories, and a conclusion that ties the ideas together. The following questions can help you revise your work:

- **Ideas:** Are the classification criteria logical and clear, resulting in categories that are consistent, exclusive, and complete? Is each category clearly defined? Does the discussion include appropriate examples that clarify the nature and function of each group?
- **Organization:** Does the essay include (1) an engaging opening that introduces the subject, thesis, and criteria for classification; (2) a well-organized middle that distinguishes groups, shows why each group is unique, and supports these claims with evidence; and (3) a unifying conclusion that restates the main idea and its relevance?
- **Voice:** Is the tone informed and rational? Does the tone project an authority on the topic?

Editing

8 **Edit the essay.** Polish your writing by addressing these issues:

- **Words:** The words distinguishing classifications are used uniformly. In general, the words are precise, clear, and defined as needed.
- **Sentences:** The sentences and paragraphs are complete, varied, and clear.
- **Correctness:** The usage, grammar, and mechanics are correct.
- **Page Design:** The design follows the assigned formatting rules.

Publishing

9 **Publish the essay** by sharing it with your instructor and classmates, publishing it on your Web site, or submitting it to a print or online journal.

Critical-Thinking and Writing Activities

1. In "Why We Lift," Hillary Gammons classifies weight lifters, who may appear to be one homogeneous group, into four distinct subgroups. Choose a group in your community who are misunderstood to be one homogeneous unit. Then write a classification essay to show how the people may be similar but also distinct.

2. In "Latin American Music: A Diverse and Unifying Force," Kathleen Kropp uses classification to analyze the nature and impact of an art form. Choose an art form that interests you, research the topic, and write an essay that uses classification to explain the art form's historical development and social impact.

3. In "Four Ways to Talk About Literature" from Chapter 15 (pages 168–170), the author examines four approaches to reading and understanding literature. Identify a group of approaches to analysis or problem solving in your program or major. Write an essay in which you break your topic into categories, sort the groups, and explain the topic to the reader.

4. Find an article in a newspaper or an academic journal that uses classification to develop a thesis. Note the writer's criteria for sorting elements of the topic into categories. Then write a brief essay explaining why the criteria do or do not lead to groups that are consistent, exclusive, and complete.

STUDY TOOLS 11

LOCATED AT BACK OF THE TEXTBOOK
☐ Tear-Out Chapter Review Card

LOCATED AT WWW.CENGAGE.COM/LOGIN
☐ Chapter eBook

☐ Graded quizzes and a practice quiz generator

☐ Videos: Writer Interviews

☐ Tutorials

☐ Flashcards

☐ Cengage Learning Write Experience

☐ Interactive activities

12 | Process

"I WAS BROUGHT UP TO BELIEVE THAT THE ONLY THING WORTH DOING WAS TO ADD TO THE SUM OF ACCURATE INFORMATION IN THE WORLD."

MARGARET MEAD

Delpixel, 2014 / Used under license from Shutterstock.com

LEARNING OBJECTIVES

12-1 Understand how to read process essays and instructions.

12-2 Understand and use signal terms.

12-3 Study and use chronological structure.

12-4 Describe and analyze steps in a process.

12-5 Write, revise, and edit a process essay.

After you finish
this chapter
go to
PAGE 143 for STUDY TOOLS

Process writing helps us understand ourselves and the world around us by answering questions such as these: How does cancer spread? How have relations between the Canadian government and Native Canadians changed? Why did Cesar Chavez's reputation as a labor leader rise and decline?

Writing that answers questions like these analyzes a process by breaking it down into steps, often grouped into stages or phases. Sometimes, the analysis also explains the process's causes and effects.

The two basic forms of process writing are a process essay and instructions. This chapter includes guidelines and writing samples that will help you read and write process essays. For a sample of written instructions, see the following Web site: www.cengage.com/login.

 ## 12-1 UNDERSTAND HOW TO READ PROCESS ESSAYS AND INSTRUCTIONS

Process writing is analytical prose in which authors break a process into a clear series of steps (often organized into phases or stages) and then explain how and why those steps lead to a specific outcome. As you read process analyses, note how writers both describe and analyze the process, often using cause-effect reasoning.

12-1a Consider the Rhetorical Situation for Process Writing

Depending on the writer's purpose, audience, and topic, process writing usually takes one of two forms: an essay that describes and analyzes the nature and function of a process, or a set of instructions that tells readers precisely how to do the process.

▶ **Purpose:** If the writer intends to explain the topic, he or she writes an essay. The essay first offers an overview of the process and then explains how each step leads logically to the next and how all the steps together complete the process. If the writer wants to help readers work through a process themselves, he or she writes instructions. These documents begin with a list of materials, and then follow with a detailed list of directives, often including precise signal terms such as "Note:" "Warning!" "CAUTION!" or "DANGER!"

▶ **Audience:** The text should meet the needs of all readers, including those who know little about the topic. To do this, writers should (1) include all the information that readers need, (2) use language that readers will understand, and (3) define unfamiliar or technical terms.

▶ **Topic:** Topics addressed in academic process writing are usually course-related phenomena that interest the writer and offer readers insight into their discipline. For an example, see Kerry Mertz's essay, "Wayward Cells" (pages 132–133). Topics addressed in professional publications should interest and educate their readers.

 ## 12-2 UNDERSTAND AND USE SIGNAL TERMS

In instructions, writers use signal terms (like those cited previously) to help users complete a process safely and successfully. Three organizations—the American National Standards Institute (ANSI), the International Organization for Standardization (ISO), and the U.S. military (MILSPEC)—set the standards for how signal terms must be used in instructions for these and other businesses. To learn more about how these organizations define, design, and use signal terms and related icons, check their Web sites.

 ### Reading Guide:
Process Writing

✔ Does the essay clearly identify the process, outline its stages, explain individual steps, and (if appropriate) discuss causes and effects?

✔ Do the instructions clearly and accurately explain the process, the materials needed, the steps required, and the necessary precautions?

✔ Does the document use clear, precise language and define unfamiliar terms?

STUDY AND USE CHRONOLOGICAL STRUCTURE

Student writer Kerri Mertz wrote the following essay to explain how cancer cells affect the body. Note how she uses chronological order and transitions to distinguish steps in the process.

Essay Outline

Introduction: analogy of workers in room as cells in body

1. First step of cancer development: cell undifferentiating
2. Second step: reproduction of cancer cells, "autonomy"
3. Third step: varieties of damage to the body
4. The development of promising treatments

Closing: restate analogy—wayward cells as wayward workers

(A) # Wayward Cells

SQ3R Survey · Question · Read · Recite · Review

1 Imagine a room containing a large group of people **(B)** all working hard toward the same goal. Each person knows his or her job, does it carefully, and cooperates with other group members. Together, they function smoothly—like a well-oiled machine.

2 Then something goes wrong. One guy suddenly drops his task, steps into another person's workstation, grabs the material that she's working with, and begins something very different—he uses the material to make little reproductions of himself, thousands of them. These look-alikes imitate him—grabbing material and making reproductions of themselves. Soon the bunch gets so big that they spill into other people's workstations, getting in their way, and interrupting their work. As the number of look-alikes grows, the work group's activity slows, stutters, and finally stops.

3 A human body is like this room, and the body's cells are like these workers. If the body is healthy, each cell has a necessary job and does it correctly. For example, right now red blood cells are running throughout your body carrying oxygen to each body part. Other cells are digesting that steak sandwich that you had for lunch, and others are patching up that cut on your left hand. Each cell knows what to do because its genetic code—or DNA—tells it what to do. When a cell begins to function abnormally, it can initiate a process that results in cancer.

4 The problem starts when one cell "forgets" what **(C)** it should do. Scientists call this "undifferentiating"— meaning that the cell loses its identity within the body (Pierce 75). Just like the guy in the group who decided to do his own thing, the cell forgets its job. Why this happens is somewhat unclear.

5 The problem could be caused by a defect in the cell's DNA code or by something in the environment, such as cigarette smoke or asbestos (German 21). Causes from inside the body are called genetic, whereas causes from outside the body are called carcinogens, meaning "any substance that causes cancer" (Neufeldt and Sparks 90). In either case, an undifferentiated cell can disrupt the function of healthy cells in two ways: by not doing its job as specified in its DNA and by not reproducing at the rate noted in its DNA.

6 Most healthy cells reproduce rather quickly, but their **(D)** reproduction rate is controlled. For example, your blood cells completely die off and replace themselves within a matter of weeks, but existing cells make only as many new cells as the body needs. The DNA codes in healthy cells tell them how many new cells to produce. However, cancer cells don't have this control, so they reproduce quickly with no stopping point, a characteristic called

(A) Title: metaphor for process
(B) Introduction: cells-workers analogy

(C) 1 Cancer starts with cell undifferentiating.
(D) 2 Cancer cells reproduce autonomously.

"autonomy" (Braun 3). What's more, all their "offspring" have the same qualities as their messed-up parent, and the resulting overpopulation produces growths called tumors.

7 Tumor cells can hurt the body in a number of
(E) ways. First, a tumor can grow so big that it takes up space needed by other organs. Second, some cells may detach from the original tumor and spread throughout the body, creating new tumors elsewhere. This happens with lymphatic cancer—a cancer that's hard to control because it spreads so quickly. A third way that tumor cells can hurt the body is by doing work not called for in their DNA. For example, a gland cell's DNA code may tell the cell to produce a necessary hormone in the endocrine system. However, if cancer damages or distorts that code, sick cells may produce more of the hormone than the body can use—or even tolerate (Braun 4). Cancer cells seem to have minds of their own, and this is why cancer is such a serious disease.

8 Fortunately, there is hope. Scientific research is
(F) already helping doctors do amazing things for people suffering with cancer. One treatment that has been used for some time is chemotherapy, or the use of chemicals to kill off all fast-growing cells, including cancer cells. (Unfortunately, chemotherapy can't distinguish between healthy and unhealthy cells, so it may cause negative side effects such as damaging fast-growing hair follicles, resulting in hair loss.) Another common treatment is radiation, or the use of light rays to kill cancer cells. One of the newest and most promising treatments is gene therapy—an effort to identify and treat chromosomes that carry a "wrong code" in their DNA. A treatment like gene therapy is promising because it treats the cause of cancer, not just the effect. Year by year, research is helping doctors better understand what cancer is and how to treat it.

9 Much of life involves dealing with problems like
(G) wayward workers, broken machines, or dysfunctional

(E) 3 Tumors damage the body.
(F) 4 Promising treatments offer hope.
(G) Conclusion: wayward cells as wayward workers

organizations. Dealing with wayward cells is just another problem. While the problem is painful and deadly, there is hope. Medical specialists and other scientists are making progress, and some day they will help us win our battle against wayward cells.

Note: The Works Cited page is not shown. For sample pages, see MLA (page 286) and APA (page 320).

Reading for Better Writing

1. Review the opening four-paragraph analogy used to introduce and describe the process. Then review the closing paragraph to see how the writer refers back to the same analogy. Explain why this analogy is or is not effective for describing the main process.
2. Review the three steps cited by the writer. Explain how transitions are used to lead into and out of each step.
3. Explain how the essay both describes and analyzes the process.

12-4 DESCRIBE AND ANALYZE STEPS IN A PROCESS

Daniel Francis is a historian and writer who has written extensively on Canadian history. In the following essay, excerpted from *The Imaginary Indian: The Image of the Indian in Canadian Culture,* Francis analyzes the process through which the Canadian government has attempted to "civilize" Native peoples, an effort that he asserts has disenfranchised and diminished the Aboriginal population.

The Bureaucrat's Indian

SQ3R Survey · Question · Read · Recite · Review

1 The broad outline of Canadian Indian policy in the early twentieth century was an inheritance from the past. In the eighteenth and early nineteenth centuries, Britain needed Native people in its armed struggle for

(A) control of the continent. Accordingly, they received all the respect due to military allies. Following the War of 1812, however, when conflict with the United States ended and settlers began encroaching on the wilderness, British colonial officials who minded Canadian affairs recognized that a new relationship had to be worked out with Native people. No longer needed as military allies, the aboriginals had lost their value to the White intruders—and were now perceived to be a social and economic problem rather than a diplomatic one. Officials began to think in terms of civilizing the Indians so that they might assume a role in mainstream Canadian society. To this end, reserves were created as places where Indians would be taught to behave like Whites. Subsequent legislation codified the policy of civilization in a tangle of laws and regulations that would have the effect of erecting a prison wall of red tape around Canada's Native population.

2   The fundamental expression of the Official Indian became the Indian Act. First promulgated in 1876, amended often since then, the Indian Act consolidated and strengthened the control the federal government (B) exercised over its aboriginal citizens. The aim of the Act, as of all Indian legislation, was to assimilate Native people to the Canadian mainstream. Assimilation as a solution to the "Indian problem" was considered preferable to its only perceived alternative: wholesale extermination. There is nothing to indicate that extermination was ever acceptable to Canadians. Not only was it morally repugnant, it was also impractical. The American example showed how costly it was, in terms of money and lives, to wage war against the aboriginals. The last thing the Canadian government

wanted to do was initiate a full-scale Indian conflict. It chose instead to go about the elimination of the Indian problem by eliminating the Indian way of life: through education and training, the Red Man would attain civilization. Most White Canadians believed that Indians were doomed to disappear anyway. Assimilation was a policy intended to preserve Indians as individuals by destroying them as a people.

The Indian Act defined an Indian as "any male   3 person of Indian blood reputed to belong to a particular band," his wife and children. The Act excluded certain (C) individuals from Indian status. The most notorious exclusion was Native women who married non-Native men. These women were considered no longer to be Indians and lost any privileges under the terms of the Act, a situation which remained unchanged until 1985. Indian became a legislated concept as well as a racial one, maintained solely through political institutions to which Native people, who had no vote until 1960, had no access.

Special status—Indian status—was conceived as   4 a stopgap measure by White legislators who expected Indians gradually to abandon their Native identity in order to enjoy the privilege of full Canadian citizenship—a process formally known as enfranchisement. As soon as Natives met certain basic requirements of literacy, education and moral character, they would be expected to apply for enfranchisement. In return for giving up legal and treaty rights, the enfranchisement would receive a portion of reserve lands and funds and cease to be an Indian, at least in law. The government expected that in time most Indians would opt for enfranchisement, which was conceived as a reward for good behavior. In fact, the vast majority of Native people chose not to be rewarded in this way: in the sixty-three years between 1857, when enfranchisement was legislated, and 1920, only 250 individuals took advantage of the opportunity to shed their Native identity.

(A) The writer begins by outlining the major historical change in government—Native relations—and offering a potent thesis about the outcomes.
(B) The body of the analysis begins with an explanation of the 1876 Indian Act.

(C) Key terms from the Indian Act (e.g., Indian status, enfranchisement) are defined and explained, including their relevance over time.

5 The Indian Act treated Native people as minors incapable of looking after their own interests and in need of the protection of the state. "'The Indian is a ward of the Government still," Arthur Meighen, then minister of the interior, told Parliament in 1918. "The presumption of the law is that he has not the capacity to decide what is for his ultimate benefit in the same degree as his guardian, the Government of Canada." Indians did not possess the rights and privileges of citizenship; they couldn't vote, they couldn't buy liquor, and they couldn't obtain land under the homestead system. The government expected that Indians would abuse these rights if they had them, that they had to be protected from themselves and from predatory Whites who would take advantage of them. By the same token, status Indians did not have to pay federal taxes (if they were able to find employment) and were "protected from debt" (a condition that usually meant they could not secure loans from financial institutions). They were people apart from mainstream Canadian society. But the ultimate aim of Indian policy was not a system of apartheid. Segregationist, apartheid-like laws were sometimes imposed, but their purpose was tactical: they were intended to serve the long-term policy of assimilation.

6 If the government wanted to civilize the Indian, what
(D) constituted civilization in the official mind? There were several qualities which bureaucrats sought to impress on their Native charges. One was a respect for private property. The fact that Native people seemed to lack a sense of private ownership was widely regarded as a sign of their backwardness. Tribalism, or tribal communism as some people called it, was blamed for stifling the development of initiative and personal responsibility. In the hope of eradicating tribalism, the 1876 Act divided reserves into lots. Band members could qualify for location tickets which, after they proved themselves as farmers, gave them title (but not necessarily ownership) to their own piece of land.

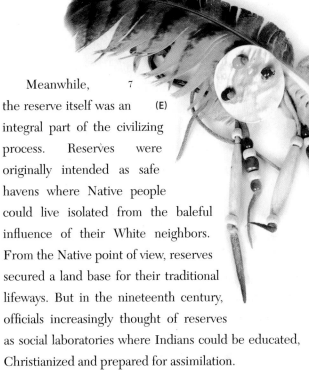

7 Meanwhile, the reserve itself was an (E) integral part of the civilizing process. Reserves were originally intended as safe havens where Native people could live isolated from the baleful influence of their White neighbors. From the Native point of view, reserves secured a land base for their traditional lifeways. But in the nineteenth century, officials increasingly thought of reserves as social laboratories where Indians could be educated, Christianized and prepared for assimilation.

8 Agriculture was an important weapon in the war on
(F) Native culture. As game resources disappeared, farming seemed to be the only alternative way for Natives to make a living, More than that, at a time when industrialism was in its infancy, farming was seen as the profession best suited to a virtuous, civilized person: tilling the soil was an ennobling activity which fostered an orderly home life, industrious work habits and a healthy respect for private property. Farming would cause Natives to settle in one place and end the roving ways so typical of a hunting lifestyle and so detrimental to the sober, reliable routines on which White society prided itself.

9 Another component of civilization was Christianity. Few Whites had any sympathy for or understanding of Native religious ideas, which were dismissed as pagan superstitions. Religious training was left to missionaries, but the government did its part by banning Native traditional religious and ceremonial practices—for example, the potlatch on the West Coast and the sun dance on the Prairies.

(D) With a question, the writer turns to a central issue: the meaning of "civilize" adopted by government bureaucrats.

(E) A transition paragraph outlines the government's shifting attitude to the reserve system.
(F) The writer describes what government policy attempted to do with Natives.

Redkaya, 2014 / Used under license from Shutterstock.com

10 Democratic self-government was also imposed on Native people. The ability to manage elected institutions was believed to be another hallmark of civilized society. Band members were required to elect chiefs and councillors who exercised limited authority over local matters. Indian Department officials retained the power to interfere in the political affairs of the band. The attempt to teach the Indians democracy was part and parcel of the assimilationist agenda. The elected councils were intended to replace traditional forms of Native government over which federal officials lacked control.

11 A property-owning, voting, hard-working, Christian farmer, abstemious in his habits and respectful of his public duties—that was the end product of government Indian policy. "Instead of having a horde of savages in the North-West, as we had a few years ago," Clifford Sifton, the minister of the interior, told Parliament in 1902, "we shall soon have an orderly, fairly educated population, capable of sustaining themselves." The message the minister intended to deliver was that the Indian had gone from painted savage to yeoman farmer in one generation.

12 In reality it was not that simple. As time passed,
(G) officials grew impatient at the slow pace of assimilation. Native people seemed reluctant to embrace the benefits of White civilization. They resisted many of the measures the government imposed on them. As the American historian Brian Dippie put it, civilization seemed to be a gift more appreciated by the donor than the recipient. Officials concluded that Indians were by nature lazy, intellectually backward and resistant to change. It seemed to be the only explanation: to blame the Indian for not becoming a White man fast enough. As a result, the government passed a series of amendments to the Indian Act in an attempt to speed up the process of assimilation. Regulations became increasingly coercive. Officials received authority to spend money belonging to an Indian band without the members' permission. They could impose the elected system of government on

bands, and depose elected leaders of whom they did not approve. At the end of the century, a series of industrial and residential schools removed Native children from their families so that they could be acculturated more easily. A draconian pass system was enacted by which individual Natives could not leave their reserves without the permission of an agent. A system of permits made it difficult for Native people to sell their produce on the open market. While the government said it wanted Natives to become self-sufficient farmers, it erected a series of legal obstacles which made it very difficult for aboriginal farmers to compete with their White neighbors. Frustration at the slow pace of assimilation reached its peak in 1920, when the government took upon itself the legal power to enfranchise an Indian against his or her will; in other words, Indians could be involuntarily stripped of their status. This legislation raised such opposition that it was rescinded two years later, but it was re-enacted in the 1930s. It was a sign of (H) just how desperate the government was to rid itself of the Indian problem by ridding itself of the Indian.

Note: The bibliography is not shown. For sample pages, see MLA (page 286) and APA (page 320).

(H) The final sentence potently captures the essence of assimilation policies and procedures.

Reading for Better Writing

1. While this excerpt from Daniel Francis's book does not discuss current government-Native relations and policies, what is your sense of how the history he describes is still felt today? Conversely, how have things changed?

2. What does the first paragraph of this essay accomplish? How does the opening characterize the process on which the essay focuses?

3. Paragraphs 2–7 focus on the nature and aims of the 1876 Indian Act. What key ideas does Francis present in this section? How do they deepen your understanding of the history?

4. The second half of this essay explores what government policies aimed to accomplish, how

---

(G) The writer traces the government's response over time to Native resistance to assimilation.

Natives resisted, and how the government reacted in turn—all over several decades. What strategies does the writer use to present the history of this relationship?

5. How would you characterize Francis's style and tone? Point to specific sentences and phrases as examples. What does this style contribute to the essay?

Richard Rodriguez is an accomplished writer who has written successfully as a journalist, essayist, and novelist. In the essay that follows, he analyzes the process through which Cesar Chavez's reputation as a successful labor leader developed and also declined.

Saint Cesar of Delano

SQ3R Survey · Question · Read · Recite · Review

1   The funeral for Cesar Chavez took place in an open field near Delano, a small agricultural town at the southern end of California's Central Valley. I remember an amiable Mexican disorder, the crowd listening and not listening to speeches and prayers delivered from a raised platform beneath a canvas tent. I do not remember a crowd numbering 30,000 or 50,000, as some estimates have it—but then I do not remember. Perhaps a cool, perhaps a warm spring sun. Men in white shirts carried forward a pine box. The ease of their movement suggested the lightness of their burden.

2   When Cesar Chavez died in his sleep in 1993, not yet a very old man at 66, he died—as he had so often portrayed himself in life—as a loser. The United Farm Workers (UFW) union he had cofounded was in decline; the union had 5,000 members, equivalent to the population of one very small Central Valley town. The

labor in California's agricultural fields was largely taken up by Mexican migrant workers—the very workers Chavez had been unable to reconcile to his American union; the workers he had branded "scabs."

3   I went to the funeral because I was writing a piece on Chavez for the *Los Angeles Times*. It now occurs to me that I was present at a number of events involving Cesar Chavez. I was at the edge of the crowd in 1966, when Chavez led UFW marchers to the steps of the capitol in Sacramento to rally for a strike against grape growers. I went to hear him speak at Stanford University. I can recall everything about the occasion except why I was there. I remember a light of late afternoon among the oaks beyond the plate-glass windows of Tresidder Union; I remember the Reverend Robert McAfee Brown introducing Cesar Chavez. Something about Chavez embarrassed me—embarrassed me in a way I would be embarrassed if someone from my family had turned up at Stanford to lecture undergraduates on the hardness of a Mexican's life. I did not join in the standing ovation. Well, I was already standing. I wouldn't give him anything. And yet, of course, there was something compelling about his homeliness.

4   In her thoroughly researched and thoroughly unsentimental book *The Union of Their Dreams: Power, Hope, and Struggle in Cesar Chavez's Farm Worker Movement*, journalist Miriam Pawel chronicles the lives of a collection of people—farm workers, idealistic college students, young lawyers from the East Coast, a Presbyterian minister, and others—who gave years of their lives at subsistence pay to work for the UFW. Every person Pawel profiles has left the union—has been fired or has quit in disgust or frustration. Nevertheless, it is not beside the point to notice that Cesar Chavez inspired such a disparate, devoted company.

5   We forget that the era we call "the Sixties" was not only a time of vast civic disaffection; it was also a time of religious idealism. At the forefront of what amounted to the religious revival of America in those years were the black Protestant ministers of the civil rights movement, ministers who insisted upon a moral dimension to the

rituals of everyday American life—eating at a lunch counter, riding a bus, going to school.

6   Cesar Chavez similarly cast his campaign for better wages and living conditions for farm workers as a religious movement. He became for many Americans, especially Mexican Americans (my parents among them), a figure of spiritual authority. I remember a small brown man with an Indian aspect leading labor protests that were also medieval religious processions of women, children, nuns, students, burnt old men—under the banner of Our Lady of Guadalupe.

7   By the time he had become the most famous Mexican American anyone could name—his face on the cover of *Time*—the majority of Mexican Americans lived in cities, far from the tragic fields of California's Central Valley that John Steinbeck had made famous a generation before. Mexican Americans were more likely to work in construction or in service sector jobs than in the fields.

8   Cesar Chavez was born in Yuma, Arizona, in 1927. During the years of his hardscrabble youth, he put away his ambitions for college. He gave his body to the fields in order to keep his mother from having to work in the fields. The young farm worker accumulated an autodidact's library—books on economics, philosophy, history. (Years later, Chavez was apt to quote Winston Churchill at UFW staff meetings.) He studied the black civil rights movement, particularly the writings of Martin Luther King Jr. He studied most intently the lives and precepts of St. Francis of Assisi and Mohandas Gandhi.

9   It is heartening to learn about private acts of goodness in notorious lives. It is discouraging to learn of the moral failures of famously good people. The former console. But to learn that the Reverend Martin Luther King Jr. was a womanizer is to be confronted with the knowledge that flesh is a complicated medium for grace. To learn that there were flaws in the character of Cesar Chavez is again to wonder at the meaning of a good life. During his lifetime, Chavez was considered by many to be a saint. Pawel is writing outside the hagiography, but while reading her book, I could not avoid thinking about the nature of sanctity.

10   Saints? Holiness? I apologize for introducing radiant nouns.

11   Cesar Chavez modeled his life on the lives of saints—an uncommon ambition in a celebrated American life. In America, influence is the point of prominence; power over history is the point. I think Cesar Chavez would have said striving to lead a holy life is the point—a life lived in imitation of Jesus Christ, the most famous loser on a planet spilling over with losers. The question is whether the Mexican saint survives the tale of the compromised American hero.

12   The first portrait in *The Union of Their Dreams* is of Eliseo Medina. At the advent of the UFW, Eliseo was a shy teenager, educated only through the eighth grade. Though he was not confident in English, Medina loved to read El Malcriado, the feisty bilingual weekly published by the UFW. Eliseo Medina remembered how his life changed on a Thursday evening when he went to hear Chavez in the social hall of Our Lady of Guadalupe Church in Delano. Medina was initially "disappointed by the leader's unimpressive appearance." But by the end of the meeting, he had determined to join the union.

13   No Chavez speech I have read or heard approaches the rhetorical brilliance of the Protestant ministers of the black civil rights movement. Chavez was, however, brilliantly theatrical. He seemed to understand, the way Charlie Chaplin understood, how to make an embarrassment of himself—his mulishness, his silence, his witness. His presence at the edge of a field was a blight of beatitude.

14   Chavez studied the power of abstinence. He internalized his resistance to injustice by refusing to eat. What else can a poor man do? Though Chavez had little success encouraging UFW volunteers to follow his example of fasting, he was able to convince millions of Americans (as many as 20 million, by some estimates) not to buy grapes or lettuce.

15   Farmers in the Central Valley were bewildered to find themselves roped into a religious parable. Indeed, Valley growers, many of them Catholics, were dismayed when their children came home from parochial schools and reported that Chavez was upheld as a moral exemplum in religion class.

16   At a time in the history of American business when Avis saw the advantage of advertising itself as "Number Two" and Volkswagen sold itself as "the Bug," Chavez made the smallness of his union, even the haphazardness, a kind of boast. In 1968, during his most publicized fast to support the strike of grape pickers, Chavez issued this statement (he was too weak to read aloud): "Those who oppose our cause are rich and powerful and they have many allies in high places. We are poor. Our allies are few."

17   Chavez broke his 1968 fast with a public relations tableau that was rich with symbol and irony. Physically diminished (in photographs his body seems unable of sustaining an erect, seated position), Chavez was handed bread (sacramental ministration after his trial in the desert) by Chris Hartmire, the Presbyterian minister who gave so much of his life to serving Chavez and his union. Alongside Chavez sat Robert F. Kennedy, then a U.S. senator from New York. The poor and the meek also have allies in high places.

18   Here began a conflict between deprivation and success that would bedevil Chavez through three decades. In a way, this was a struggle between the Mexican Cesar Chavez and the American Cesar Chavez. For it was Mexico that taught Chavez to value a life of suffering. It was America that taught him to fight the causes of suffering.

19   The speech Chavez had written during his hunger strike of 1968 (wherein he likened the UFW to David fighting the Goliath of agribusiness) announced the Mexican theme: "I am convinced that the truest act of courage, the strongest act of manliness is to sacrifice ourselves for others in a totally nonviolent struggle for justice. To be a man is to suffer for others. God help us to be men." (Nearly three decades later, in the program for Chavez's funeral, the wording of his psalm would be revised—"humanity" substituted for "manliness": To be human is to suffer for others. God help me to be human.)

20   Nothing else Chavez would write during his life had such haunting power for me as this public prayer for a life of suffering; no utterance would sound so Mexican. Other cultures in the world assume the reality of suffering as something to be overcome. Mexico assumes the inevitability of suffering. That knowledge informs the folk music of Mexico, the bitter humor of Mexican proverb. To be a man is to suffer for others—you're going to suffer anyway. The code of machismo (which in American English has translated too crudely to sexual bravado) in Mexico derives from a medieval chivalry whereby a man uses his strength or his resolve or even his foolishness (as did Don Quixote) to protect those less powerful. God help us to be men.

21   Mexicans believe that in 1531 the Virgin Mary appeared in brown skin, in royal Aztec raiment, to a converted Indian peasant named Juan Diego. The Virgin asked that a church be erected on the site of her four apparitions in order that Mexican Indians could come to her and tell her of their suffering. The image of Our Lady of Guadalupe was an aspect of witness at every

UFW demonstration.

22   Though he grew up during the American Depression, Chavez breathed American optimism and American activism. In the early 1950s, while still a farm worker, he met Fred Ross of the Community Service Organization, a group inspired by the principles of the radical organizer Saul Alinsky. Chavez later became an official in the CSO, and eventually its president. He persuaded notoriously apathetic Mexican Americans to register to vote by encouraging them to believe they could change their lives in America.

23   If you would understand the tension between Mexico and the United States that is playing out along our mutual border, you must understand the psychic tension between Mexican stoicism—if that is a rich enough word for it—and American optimism. On the one side, Mexican peasants are tantalized by the American possibility of change. On the other side, the tyranny of American optimism has driven Americans to neurosis and depression—when the dream is elusive or less meaningful than the myth promised. This constitutes the great irony of the Mexican-American border: American sadness has transformed the drug lords of Mexico into billionaires, even as the peasants of Mexico scramble through the darkness to find the American dream.

24   By the late 1960s, as the first UFW contracts were being signed, Chavez began to brood. Had he spent his poor life only to create a middle class? Lionel Steinberg, the first grape grower to sign with the UFW, was drawn by Chavez's charisma but chagrined at the union's disordered operations. He wondered: "Is it a social movement or a trade union?" He urged Chavez to use experienced negotiators from the AFL-CIO.

25   Chavez paid himself a subsistence annual wage of $5,000. "You can't change anything if you want to hold

onto a good job, a good way of life, and avoid suffering." The world-famous labor leader would regularly complain to his poorly paid staff about the phone bills they ran up and about what he saw as the misuse of a fleet of second-hand UFW cars. He held the union hostage to the purity of his intent. Eliseo Medina, who had become one of the union's most effective organizers, could barely support his young family; he asked Chavez about setting up a trust fund for his infant son. Chavez promised to get back to him but never did. Eventually, thoroughly discouraged by the mismanagement of the union, Medina resigned.

26   In 1975, Chavez helped to pass legislation prohibiting the use of the short-handled hoe in the fields—its two-foot-long shaft forced farm workers to stoop all day. That achievement would outlast the decline of his union. By the early 1970s, California vegetable growers began signing sweetheart contracts with the rival Teamsters Union. The UFW became mired in scraps with unfriendly politicians in Sacramento. Chavez's attention wandered. He imagined a "Poor Peoples Union" that would reach out to senior citizens and people on welfare. He contacted church officials within the Vatican about the possibility of establishing a lay religious society devoted to service to the poor. Chavez became interested in the Hutterite communities of North America and the Israeli kibbutzim as possible models for such a society.

27   Chavez visited Synanon, the drug rehabilitation commune headed by Charles Dederich, shortly before some Synanon members were implicated in a series of sexual scandals and criminal assaults. Chavez borrowed from Synanon a version of a disciplinary practice called the Game, whereby UFW staff members were obliged to stand in the middle of a circle of peers and submit to fierce criticism. Someone sympathetic to Chavez might argue that the Game was an inversion of an ancient monastic discipline meant to teach humility. Someone less sympathetic might conclude that Chavez was turning

into a petty tyrant. I think both estimations are true.

28 From his reading, Chavez would have known that St. Francis of Assisi desired to imitate the life of Jesus. The followers of Francis desired to imitate the life of Francis. Within 10 years of undertaking his mendicant life, Francis had more than 1,000 followers. Francis realized he could not administer a growing religious order by personal example. He relinquished the administration of the Franciscans to men who had some talent for organization. Cesar Chavez never gave up his position as head of the UFW.

29 In 1977 Chavez traveled to Manila as a guest of President Ferdinand Marcos. He ended up praising the old dictator. There were darker problems within the UFW. There were rumors that some within the inner circle were responsible for a car crash that left Cleofas Guzman, an apostate union member, with permanent brain damage.

30 Chavez spent his last years protesting the use of pesticides in the fields. In April of 1993, he died.

31 After his death, as Cesar Chavez became an American hero, his quarreling family—in the mode of the children of Dr. Martin Luther King Jr.—seemed to want to profit from the public esteem for their father. The year after his death, Chavez was awarded the National Medal of Freedom by President Bill Clinton. In 2002, the U.S. Postal Service unveiled a 37-cent stamp bearing the image of Cesar Chavez. Politicians throughout the West and the Southwest attached Chavez's name to parks and schools and streets and civic buildings of every sort. And there began an effort of mixed success to declare March 31, his birthday, a legal holiday. During the presidential campaign of 2012, President Barack Obama designated the home and burial place of Cesar Chavez in Keene, California, a national monument within the National Park System.

32 The American hero was also a Mexican saint. In 1997 American painter Robert Lentz, a Franciscan brother, painted an icon of Cesar Chavez of California. Chavez is depicted with a golden halo. He holds in his hand a scrolled broadsheet of the U.S. Constitution. He wears a pink sweatshirt bearing the UFW insignia.

33 That same year, executives at the advertising agency TBWA/Chiat/Day came up with a campaign for Apple computers that featured images of some famous dead— John Lennon, Albert Einstein, Frank Sinatra—alongside a grammar-crunching motto: Think different.

34 I remember sitting in bad traffic on the San Diego Freeway one day and looking up to see a photograph of Cesar Chavez on a billboard. His eyes were downcast. He balanced a rake and a shovel over his right shoulder. In the upper-left-hand corner was the corporate logo of a bitten apple.

Reading for Better Writing

1. This essay describes the process through which Cesar Chavez's reputation as a labor leader developed. Summarize that process.

2. Richard Rodriguez opens the essay with three paragraphs that describe Chavez's funeral. What do these paragraphs tell you about (a) Chavez, (b) Rodriguez's purpose for writing, and (c) his assessment of Chavez?

3. Rodriguez claims Chavez's reputation as the co-founder and leader of a labor union increased over time. Cite evidence that Rodriguez uses to support this claim.

4. What personal qualities does Rodriguez suggest helped Chavez succeed?

5. What evidence appears to mark the peak of Chavez's popularity?

6. Which of Chavez's personal traits or actions diminished his success and tainted his reputation?

7. What point about the life of Cesar Chavez is the author trying to make by sharing the personal anecdote in the closing paragraph?

8. What is your personal opinion of Cesar Chavez after reading the essay?

WRITE, REVISE, AND EDIT A PROCESS ESSAY

Writing Guidelines

Planning

1 Select a topic. Use prompts like those below to generate a list of topics.

- A course-related process
- A process in nature
- A process in the news
- A process that helps you get a job

2 Review the process. Use your knowledge of the topic to fill out an organizer like the one on the right. List the subject at the top, each of the steps in chronological order, and the outcome at the bottom. For a complex process, break it down into stages or phases first; then outline the steps within each phase.

> **Process Analysis**
>
> **Subject:**
> - **Step #1**
> - **Step #2**
> - **Step #3**
>
> **Outcome:**

3 Research as needed. Find information that helps you explain the process: what it is, what steps are required, what order the steps follow, how the steps are done, what outcome the process produces, and what safety precautions are needed. If possible, observe the process or perform it yourself. Carefully record correct names, materials, tools, and safety or legal issues.

4 Organize information. Revise the organizer as needed. Then develop an outline, including steps listed in the organizer, as well as supporting details from your research.

Drafting

5 Draft the document. Write the document using the guidelines below.

Describing and Explaining a Process

- **Opening:** Introduce the topic; give an overview of the process, possibly forecasting its main stages; and explain why the process is important.
- **Middle:** Order the process into phases if necessary, clearly describe each step in the process, and link steps with transitions such as *first, second, next, finally,* and *while.* Explain the importance of each step and how it is linked to other steps in the process. Describe the overall outcome of the process and explain its relevance.
- **Closing:** Summarize the process and restate key points as needed; if appropriate, explain follow-up activity.

Writing Instructions

- **Opening:** Name the process in the title, summarize the process's goal, and list any materials and tools needed.
- **Middle:** Present each step in a separate—usually one- or two-sentence—paragraph. Number the steps and state each clearly, using firm commands directed to the reader. Where appropriate, include signal terms indicating **Caution! WARNING!** or **DANGER!**
- **Closing:** In a short paragraph, explain how and when follow-up action should be completed.

TIP To state instructions as direct commands, use action verbs in the imperative mood. (The mood of a verb indicates the tone or attitude it conveys.)

Revising

6 Improve the ideas, organization, and voice. Ask a classmate or someone from the writing center to evaluate the following:

- **Ideas:** Is the process presented as a unified phenomenon that includes a logical series of stages and steps? If causes and effects are addressed, are the claims clear and supported with well-researched details?
- **Organization:** Does the *process essay* include an opening that introduces the process and

thesis, a middle that describes stages and steps clearly and correctly, and a closing that unifies the essay by accenting key points? Do the *instructions* include an opening that correctly names the process and lists materials needed, a middle that states each step (or directive) correctly and in the required order, and a closing that specifies follow-up action?

- **Voice:** Is the tone informed, concerned, and objective? Are sensitive issues well researched, addressed respectfully, and shown to be relevant? Are instructions stated as firm, direct commands using action verbs in the imperative mood?

 TIP Test instructions by using them to perform the process.

Editing

7 Edit the essay. Polish your writing by addressing the following:

- **Words:** The words are precise, clear, and correct.
  - Technical terms are correct, used uniformly, and defined.
  - Transitions link steps, and a consistent verb tense is used.
- **Sentences:** The sentences are smooth, varied in structure, and engaging. In instructions, sentences are shaped as clear, brief commands formatted in accordance with standards set by regulatory agencies such as the American National Standards Institute (ANSI).
- **Correctness:** The finished copy includes correct usage, grammar, punctuation, and spelling.
- **Page Design:** The design features steps in the process. In instructions, signal terms and symbols conform to regulatory standards. If the essay follows MLA or APA style, correct formatting and documentation styles are used.

Publishing

8 Publish the essay by offering it to instructors, students, and nonprofit agencies working with the process. Also consider posting the writing on a suitable Web site.

Critical-Thinking and Writing Activities

1. Reread the topics that you listed under "Select a Topic" on page 142. Choose a topic and write about it as an essay or as a set of instructions.
2. Review "Wayward Cells," the essay that analyzes what cancer is and how it progresses. Then choose another natural- or social-science process that interests you, and write an essay describing and analyzing that process. Conversely, think of a process within the arts and humanities (e.g., a historical or cultural movement, a plot pattern in fiction or film).
3. "The Bureaucrat's Indian" focuses on a cultural development that shaped the present—the legacy of the Indian Act for Canada's Aboriginal peoples. Consider other cultural practices, situations, or developments. How did they come to be? Choose one such topic and explore this question.
4. Review Richard Rodriguez's "Saint Cesar of Delano," in which he analyzes how and why Cesar Chavez's reputation as a labor leader changed over time. Then research a prominent person in your discipline, focusing on how his or her reputation changed. Based on your research, write a process essay in which you explain the causes and effects of this change.

STUDY TOOLS 12

LOCATED AT BACK OF THE TEXTBOOK
- ☐ Tear-Out Chapter Review Card

LOCATED AT WWW.CENGAGEBRAIN.COM/LOGIN
- ☐ Chapter eBook
- ☐ Graded quizzes and a practice quiz generator
- ☐ Videos: Writer Interviews
- ☐ Tutorials
- ☐ Flashcards
- ☐ Cengage Learning Write Experience
- ☐ Interactive activities

13 | Comparison-Contrast

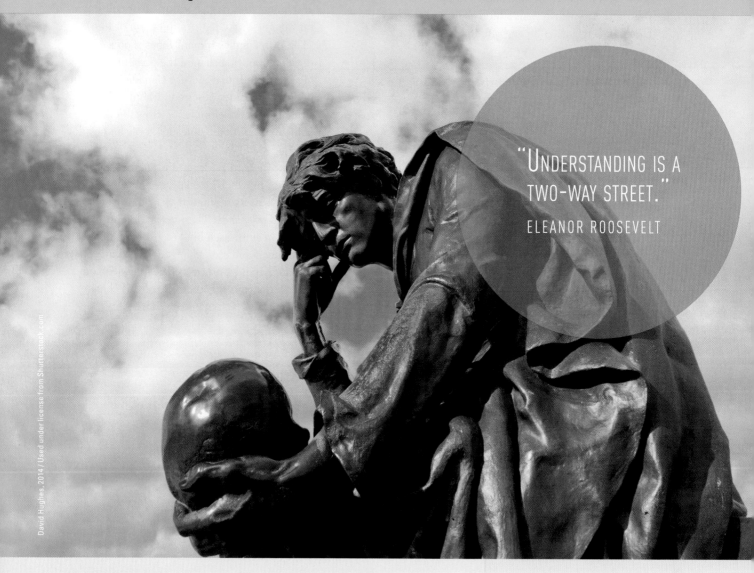

"UNDERSTANDING IS A TWO-WAY STREET."
ELEANOR ROOSEVELT

David Hughes, 2014 / Used under license from Shutterstock.com

LEARNING OBJECTIVES

13-1 Understand how to read comparison-contrast writing.

13-2 Use subject-by-subject or trait-by-trait organization.

13-3 Cite details to support and clarify compare-contrast claims.

13-4 Use comparison-contrast strategies to analyze, illustrate, or define concepts.

13-5 Write, revise, and edit a compare-contrast essay.

After you finish
this chapter
go to
PAGE 153 for STUDY TOOLS

In his plays, William Shakespeare creates characters, families, and even plot lines that mirror each other. As a result, we see Hamlet in relation to Laertes and the Montagues in relation to the Capulets. In the process, we do precisely what the writer wants us to do—we compare and contrast the subjects. The result is clarity and insight: By thinking about both subjects in relation to each other, we understand each one more clearly.

But writers in college and in the workplace also use comparison-contrast as an analytical strategy. To help you read and write such documents, follow the guidelines in this chapter.

13-1 UNDERSTAND HOW TO READ COMPARISON-CONTRAST WRITING

When writers use compare-contrast, what should you as a reader look for? The instruction below will help you read essays like those that follow.

13-1a Consider the Rhetorical Situation for Comparison-Contrast Writing

Think about how a writer might use comparison-contrast to achieve her or his purpose, address an audience, and analyze a topic.

▸ **Purpose:** Writers compare and contrast subjects in order to understand their similarities and differences. Their purpose may be to stress the similarities between seemingly dissimilar things or the differences between things that seem quite similar.

▸ **Audience:** A writer using this strategy may have virtually any reader in mind—the instructor for a student essay or potential clients for a marketing document. Whatever the situation, the writer sees readers as people whose understanding of a topic,

an issue, or a phenomenon can be deepened with comparative analysis.

▸ **Topics:** Writers address a wide range of topics through compare-contrast: people, events, phenomena, technologies, problems, products, stories, and so on. The writer simply thinks through what aspects of the topic may be illuminated through comparison and/or contrast.

13-1b Consider the Compare-Contrast Practices Used

As you read an essay using compare-contrast, look for the following:

▸ **Criteria Used for Comparison:** Writers anchor their analyses in specific points of comparison. For example, a comparison of two characters in a play might focus on their backgrounds, their actions in the play, their psychology, their fate, and so on. As you read, trace the features compared, thinking through the writer's choices.

▸ **Organization of the Comparison:** Such writing is generally structured either subject by subject (first dealing with one topic fully and then the other) or trait by trait (holding up the topics side by side, feature by feature).

▸ **The Point of the Comparison:** Writers use comparison to illuminate topics through a key idea about connections and distinctions. Identify the essential insight of the comparison, whether the writer states it at the beginning or leaves it to the end.

Reading Guide: Comparison-Contrast

✔ Why is the writer comparing these topics? Is the goal to stress similarities, differences, or both? How does the comparison speak to specific readers?

✔ What features or traits of the topics are compared? Why?

✔ How does the writer present the topics and the criteria for comparison?

✔ What conclusion does the writer develop through analysis?

USE SUBJECT-BY-SUBJECT OR TRAIT-BY-TRAIT ORGANIZATION

In the essay that follows, student writer Rachel De Smith uses trait-by-trait organization to analyze characters from two novels. Note how she introduces her characters and then compares and contrasts their isolation, haunting experiences, and escape.

Essay Outline

Introduction: Sethe and Orleanna as surprisingly similar characters

1. Living and isolation and loneliness
2. Haunted by the past
3. Grueling journeys of escape

Conclusion: Sethe and Orleanna as suffering but strong women

(A) ## Sethe in *Beloved* and Orleanna in *Poisonwood Bible*: Isolation, Children, and Getting Out

SQ3R Survey · Question · Read · Recite · Review

1 Toni Morrison's Sethe and Barbara Kingsolver's
(B) Orleanna Price seem to be vastly different women, living in different times and cultures, descended from different races. One has had a faithful spouse forced away from her by circumstances; the other lives in a devastating marriage. One is a former slave, while the other is a comparatively well-off minister's wife. However, these two women are more alike than they first appear. Both live in isolation and loneliness, both are haunted by the past, both risk everything to get their children out of devastating circumstances—and both reap the consequences of such risks.

2 Sethe lives in house number 124, a house generally believed to be haunted, "full of a baby's venom" (Morrison

3). The child's ghost inhabiting the house throws things (C) around, makes spots of colored light appear, shakes floors, (D) and stomps up the stairs. The people of the surrounding community—remembering Sethe's past, fearing ghostly retribution, and resenting the long-ago extravagance of Sethe's mother-in-law, Baby Suggs—diligently avoid the house and its residents. Sethe's one remaining daughter, Denver, will not leave the yard (Morrison 205). The two of them live with the ghost, ostracized.

Orleanna lives in a less malignant but equally 3
isolated situation. When she and her daughters follow (E)
her husband on his zealous missionary trip to the Congo, she is the only white woman in a village of people with whom she shares nothing, not even a word of their language. Preoccupied with the troubles in her own house, she remains separated from the villagers by a gulf of cultural misunderstanding—from how to behave in the marketplace to where to get her drinking water (Kingsolver 89, 172). Even when she returns to the United States, Orleanna lives in isolation, hidden among her flower gardens, set apart by the stigma of her past (Kingsolver 407).

The cause of all this isolation, for both women, is the 4
past. When Sethe saw a slave catcher coming for her, she (F)
attempted to kill all four of her young children in order (G)
to prevent them from becoming slaves (Morrison 149, 163). She succeeded in killing only her second-youngest, known as Beloved. No one went back to the plantation; Sethe went to jail instead. Years later, her two oldest children (sons) run off, unable to face the specter of their dead sister knocking over jars and leaving handprints in cakes. Beloved's death is thus the defining moment not only for Sethe's haunted life but also for Denver's, Baby Suggs', and, in many ways, the entire community's.

Orleanna, like Sethe, has lost a child, though not 5
by her own hand. Her youngest daughter, Ruth May, (H)

(C) 1 Both women live in isolation and loneliness.
(D) (a) Sethe
(E) (b) Orleanna
(F) 2 Isolation for both women is rooted in a haunting past.
(G) (a) Sethe
(H) (b) Orleanna

(A) The title identifies the topics compared and the traits examined.
(B) Introduction: two seemingly different characters share similar lives.

died of snakebite after an ugly disagreement (involving much shouting and plenty of voodoo) between the Price family and the rest of the village. Orleanna is not immediately responsible for Ruth May's death—in fact, she has recently brought the girl miraculously through a bout with malaria (Kingsolver 276). However, Orleanna still feels tremendous guilt about Ruth May's death and even about being in Africa at all. In much of Orleanna's narration, she attempts to move past this guilt, periodically asking her absent daughter's forgiveness. Sethe, also hoping for reconciliation, explains herself in a similar way to Beloved. But Beloved seems to feed off Sethe's remorse, whereas Ruth May, as portrayed in the final chapter of the novel, bears no such ill will. Ruth May says, "Mother, you can still hold on but forgive, forgive . . . I forgive you, Mother" (Kingsolver 537, 543). Beloved continually punishes Sethe for leaving her behind, but Ruth May is willing to forgive.

6 (I) (J)   Both Sethe and Orleanna endure grueling journeys of escape, though the journeys begin very differently. Sethe has spent a long time planning an escape with her fellow slaves. When the opportunity finally comes, Sethe sends her children on ahead and then follows, pausing on the way to give birth to Denver. Oddly enough, the final stage of her journey to "freedom" seems to be her time in jail, an episode that kept her from going back to the Sweet Home plantation. However, even after Sethe leaves jail and begins a life free from the degradations of the plantation, she cannot escape the stigma of her past, particularly Beloved's violent death.

7 (K)   Orleanna's journey, though also long anticipated or at least long desired, is a spontaneous event. Following Ruth May's tragic death (the impetus for her journey), Orleanna simply walks away: Her daughter

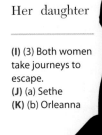

(I) (3) Both women take journeys to escape.
(J) (a) Sethe
(K) (b) Orleanna

Leah recalls that "Mother never once turned around to look over her shoulder" (Kingsolver 389). Their unplanned journey ends up as a fiasco, culminating in malaria during the rainy season somewhere in the depths of the Congo, but all of Orleanna's remaining daughters survive. Though obvious differences exist between the deaths of Ruth May and Beloved, both deaths allow their families some form of escape. In addition, Orleanna, like Sethe, is willing to give up her children in order for them to escape; she sends Rachel with Eeben Axelroot and leaves Leah with Anatole when she and Adah leave the country for good. Orleanna's actions parallel Sethe's, as Sethe sends her children ahead of her (in escape or death) in order for them to leave the plantation. Orleanna sees very little of Rachel and Leah for the rest of her life, but they have escaped the devastation of their lives in the Congo, or at least their lives under Nathan Price, and that is—or must be—enough for her.

8 (L)   Sethe and Orleanna are both haunted women. The deaths of their daughters and estrangement from their remaining children prevent these women from finding peace. Both are haunted by guilt—Sethe for her own actions in the murder of Beloved, and Orleanna for her complicity both in Ruth May's death and in the chaos that enveloped the Congo at the same time. Both women are also isolated and lonely, distanced by distrust and misunderstanding from the people around them. And both women, in the long run, risk everything to gain freedom for their children. Distrust, rage, fear, and bad dreams accompany that risk, but both women keep their children from the evil awaiting them—a plantation, a father's oppression. Paul D. questions Sethe on this point, wondering if other circumstances might be even worse than the plantation. Sethe responds, "It ain't my job to know what's worse. It's my job to know what is and to keep them away from what I know is terrible" (Morrison 165). Sethe is never able to achieve true reconciliation with Beloved, but her relationships

(L) Conclusion: These two haunted characters are strong women who eventually move beyond guilt.

with Denver and Paul D. help to make up for this loss, while Orleanna is forgiven by Ruth May and eventually reunited (albeit briefly) with her other children. Despite the attendant circumstances, both Sethe and Orleanna are revealed to be strong women, and both eventually move past their paralyzing guilt in their efforts to "walk forward into the light" (Kingsolver 543).

Note: The Works Cited page is not shown. For sample pages, see MLA (page 286 and APA (page 320).

Reading for Better Writing

1. Review the title and opening paragraph, describe how the writer focuses her essay, and explain why you do or do not find that introduction well written.

2. A thesis is a type of contract in which the writers states what he or she will do in the essay. Review the writer's thesis and explain whether she does what she promises.

3. Cite passages in the essay that illustrate trait-by-trait organization. Then explain why you think this approach is or is not an effective strategy for analyzing literature.

4. Explain why you think that compare-contrast reasoning is or is not an effective strategy for analyzing literature.

5. Explain why the writer's voice is or is not appropriate for this essay. For example, is the voice informed or uninformed, objective or manipulative, respectful or disrespectful?

13-3 CITE DETAILS TO SUPPORT AND CLARIFY COMPARE-CONTRAST CLAIMS

In the following essay, writer Gelareh Asayesh analyzes how the traditional Islamic clothing that she must wear in Iran affects her sense of self. To that end, she compares and contrasts its advantages and disadvantages and supports her claims with details, anecdotes, and keen observations.

Shrouded in Contradiction

SQ3R   Survey • Question • Read • Recite • Review

I grew up wearing the miniskirt to school, the veil to the mosque. In the Tehran of my childhood, women in bright sundresses shared the sidewalk with women swathed in black. The tension between the two ways of life was palpable. As a schoolgirl, I often cringed when my bare legs got leering or contemptuous glances. Yet, at times, I long for the days when I could walk the streets of my country with the wind in my hair. When clothes were clothes. In today's Iran, whatever I wear sends a message. If it's a chador, it embarrasses my Westernized relatives. If it's a skimpy scarf, I risk being accused of stepping on the blood of the martyrs who died in the war with Iraq. Each time I return to Tehran, I wait until the last possible moment, when my plane lands on the tarmac, to don the scarf and long jacket that many Iranian women wear in lieu of a veil. To wear *hijab*— Islamic covering—is to invite contradiction. Sometimes I hate it. Sometimes I value it.

Most of the time, I don't even notice it. It's annoying, but so is wearing panty hose to work. It ruins my hair, but so does the humidity in Florida, where I live. For many women, the veil is neither a symbol nor a statement. It's simply what they wear, as their mothers did before them. Something to dry your face with after your ablutions before prayer. A place for a toddler to hide when he's feeling shy. Even for a woman like me, who wears it with a hint of rebellion, *hijab* is just not that big a deal.

Except when it is.

"Sister, what kind of get-up is this?" a woman in black, one of a pair, asks me one summer day on the Caspian shore. I am standing in line to ride a gondola up a mountain, where I'll savor some ice cream along with vistas of sea and forest. Women in chadors stand wilting in the heat, faces gleaming with sweat. Women in makeup and clunky heels wear knee-length jackets with pants, their hair daringly exposed beneath sheer scarves.

(A) Two contrasting scenes appear in the first sentence.
(B) Italics distinguish *hijab* as a non-English word.

5 None have been more daring than I. I've wound my scarf into a turban, leaving my neck bare to the breeze. The woman in black is a government employee paid to police public morals. "Fix your scarf at once!" she snaps.

6 "But I'm hot," I say.

7 "You're hot?" she exclaims. "Don't you think we all are?"

8 I start unwinding my makeshift turban. "The men aren't hot," I mutter.

9 Her companion looks at me in shocked reproach. "Sister, this isn't about men and women," she says, shaking her head. "This is about Islam."

10 I want to argue. I feel like a child. Defiant, but
(C) powerless. Burning with injustice, but also with a hint of shame. I do as I am told, feeling acutely conscious of the bare skin I am covering. In policing my sexuality, these women have made me more aware of it.

11 The veil masks erotic freedom, but its advocates
(D) believe *hijab* transcends the erotic—or expands it. In the West, we think of passion as a fever of the body, not the soul. In the East, Sufi poets used earthly passion as a metaphor; the beloved they celebrated was God. Where I come from, people are more likely to find delirious passion in the mosque than in the bedroom.

12 There are times when I feel a hint of this passion. A few years after my encounter on the Caspian, I go to the wake of a family friend. Sitting in a mosque in Mashhad, I grip a slippery black veil with one hand and a prayer book with the other. In the center of the hall, there's a stack of Koranic texts decorated with green-and-black calligraphy, a vase of white gladioluses and a large photograph of the dearly departed. Along the walls, women wait quietly.

13 From the men's side of the mosque, the mullah's voice rises in lament. His voice is deep and plaintive, oddly compelling. I bow my head, sequestered in my veil while at my side a community of women pray and weep with increasing abandon. I remember from girlhood this sense of being exquisitely alone in the company of others. Sometimes I have cried as well, free to weep without having to offer (E) an explanation. Perhaps they are right, those mystics who believe that physical love is an obstacle to spiritual love; those architects of mosques who abstained from images of earthly life, decorating their work with geometric shapes that they believed freed the soul to slip from its worldly moorings. I do not aspire to such lofty sentiments. All I know is that such moments of passionate abandon, within the circle of invisibility created by the veil, offer an emotional catharsis every bit as potent as any sexual release.

14 Outside, the rain pours from a sullen sky. I make my farewells and walk toward the car, where my driver waits. My veil is wicking muddy water from the sidewalk. I gather up the wet and grimy folds with distaste, longing to be home, where I can cast off this curtain of cloth that (F) gives with one hand, takes away with the other.

(E) The writer uses terms of limited certainty, such as *perhaps* and *all I know*.

(F) The final line summarizes the contradictions.

(C) Contradictory feelings are pushed together in a compact list.

(D) The writer offers definitions of passion reflecting three different perspectives.

Reading for Better Writing

1. Sometimes writers use comparison-contrast organization to take a position on an issue—to show that one side is better than the other or to show the difficulty of choosing one side over the other. What do you think is Asayesh's position on *hijab*, and why?

2. What contrasts are listed in paragraph 4? How does the writer use sentence structure and punctuation to mark the contrasts?

3. In paragraph 13, Asayesh uses terms of limited certainty, such as *perhaps* and *all I know*. How do these phrases temper her claims?

4. In what ways are the opening and closing sentences alike? How are these similarities significant for readers?

Shahrul Azman, 2014 / Used under license from Shutterstock.com

iofoto, 2014 / Used under license from Shutterstock.com

13-4 USE COMPARISON-CONTRAST STRATEGIES TO ANALYZE, ILLUSTRATE, OR DEFINE CONCEPTS

Shankar Vedantam, a Nieman Fellow at Harvard University and science reporter for the *Washington Post*, wrote the following essay to define and analyze colorism. Note how he introduces his topic with an anecdote, supports his claims by citing academic studies, and uses comparison-contrast to analyze, illustrate, or define concepts.

Shades of Prejudice

SQ3R Survey · Question · Read · Recite · Review

1
(A) In 2010, the Senate majority leader, Harry Reid, found himself in trouble for once suggesting that Barack Obama had a political edge over other African-American candidates because he was "light-skinned" and had "no Negro dialect, unless he wanted to have one." Mr. Reid was not expressing sadness but a gleeful opportunism that Americans were still judging one another by the color of their skin, rather than—as the Rev. Dr. Martin Luther King Jr., whose legacy we commemorated on Monday, dreamed—by the content of their character.

2
(B) The Senate leader's choice of words was flawed, but positing that black candidates who look "less black" have a leg up is hardly more controversial than saying wealthy people have an advantage in elections. Dozens of research studies have shown that skin tone and other racial features play powerful roles in who gets ahead and who does not. These factors regularly determine who gets hired, who gets convicted and who gets elected.

3
(C) Consider: Lighter-skinned Latinos in the United States make $5,000 more on average than darker-skinned Latinos. The education test-score gap between light-skinned and dark-skinned African-Americans is nearly as large as the gap between whites and blacks.

4
(D) The Harvard neuroscientist Allen Counter has found that in Arizona, California and Texas, hundreds of Mexican-American women have suffered mercury poisoning as a result of the use of skin-whitening creams. In India, where I was born, a best-selling line of women's cosmetics called Fair and Lovely has recently been supplemented by a product aimed at men called Fair and Handsome.

5
(E) This isn't racism, per se: it's colorism, an unconscious prejudice that isn't focused on a single group like blacks so much as on blackness itself. Our brains, shaped by culture and history, create intricate caste hierarchies that privilege those who are physically and culturally whiter and punish those who are darker.

6
Colorism is an intraracial problem as well as an interracial problem. Racial minorities who are alert to white-black or white-brown issues often remain silent about a colorism that asks "how black" or "how brown" someone is within their own communities.

7
(F) If colorism lives underground, its effects are very real. Darker-skinned African-American defendants are more than twice as likely to receive the death penalty as lighter-skinned African-American defendants for crimes of equivalent seriousness involving white victims. This was proven in rigorous, peer-reviewed research into hundreds of capital punishment-worthy cases by the Stanford psychologist Jennifer Eberhardt.

8
Take, for instance, two of Dr. Eberhardt's murder cases, in Philadelphia, involving black defendants—one light-skinned, the other dark. The lighter-skinned defendant, Arthur Hawthorne, ransacked a drug store for money and narcotics. The pharmacist had complied

---

(A) The writer uses an anecdote to introduce and illustrate his thesis.
(B) He asserts that research supports his thesis, but he cites no sources.

(C) He offers examples.
(D) He supports his point by referring to his colleague's research.
(E) The writer distinguishes racism and colorism by comparing and contrasting the nature and effects of each.
(F) To support his claim, he gives an example and cites a study.

(G)

with every demand, yet Mr. Hawthorne shot him when he was lying face down. Mr. Hawthorne was independently identified as the killer by multiple witnesses, a family member and an accomplice.

9   The darker-skinned defendant, Ernest Porter, pleaded not guilty to the murder of a beautician, a crime that he was linked to only through a circuitous chain of evidence. A central witness later said that prosecutors forced him to finger Mr. Porter even though he was sure that he was the wrong man. Two people who provided an alibi for Mr. Porter were mysteriously never called to testify. During his trial, Mr. Porter revealed that the police had even gotten his name wrong—his real name was Theodore Wilson—but the court stuck to the wrong name in the interest of convenience.

10   Both men were convicted. But the lighter-skinned
(H) Mr. Hawthorne was given a life sentence, while the dark-skinned Mr. Porter has spent more than a quarter-century on Pennsylvania's death row.

11   Colorism also influenced the 2008 presidential race.
(I) In an experiment that fall, Drew Westen, a psychologist at Emory, and other researchers shot different versions of a political advertisement in support of Mr. Obama. One version showed a light-skinned black family. Another version had the same script, but used a darker-skinned black family. Voters, at an unconscious level, were less inclined to support Mr. Obama after watching the ad featuring the darker-skinned family than were those who watched the ad with the lighter-skinned family.

12   Political operatives are certainly aware of this dynamic. During the campaign, a conservative group created attack ads linking Mr. Obama with Kwame Kilpatrick, the disgraced former mayor of Detroit, which darkened Mr. Kilpatrick's skin to have a more persuasive effect. Though there can be little doubt (J) that as a candidate Mr. Obama faced voters' conscious and unconscious prejudices, it is simultaneously true that unconscious colorism subtly advantaged him over darker-skinned politicians.

13   In highlighting how Mr. Obama benefited from his links to whiteness, Harry Reid punctured the myth that (K) Mr. Obama's election signaled the completion of the Rev. King's dream. Americans may like to believe that we are now color-blind, that we can consciously choose not to use race when making judgments about other people. It remains a worthy aspiration. But this belief rests on a profound misunderstanding about how our minds work and perversely limits our ability to discuss prejudice honestly.

(J) To support his claim, he offers an example.
(K) To restate his thesis and unify his essay, the writer refers to the anecdote used in the opening.

(G) The writer compares and contrasts how people are treated by the legal system.
(H) He cites a similarity and a difference.
(I) He compares colorism in the legal system with colorism in politics.

Reading for Better Writing

1. Describe how Shankar Vedantam uses an anecdote to open and close his essay. Then explain why you do or do not find that strategy effective.

2. The writer asserts that (a) colorism and racism are different and that (b) colorism is both an intraracial problem and an interracial problem. Explain what he means by each assertion and why you do or do not agree.

3. Review paragraphs 7–10, in which the writer compares and contrasts penalties meted out by the legal system. Then explain why this strategy does or does not help develop his thesis.

4. Note how the writer uses dashes in paragraphs 8 and 9, and then explain why that use is or is not correct.

5. On January 18, 2010, the writer published this essay in *The New York Times*. Cite words or sentences showing that his voice is or is not appropriate for his subject and audience.

WRITE, REVISE, AND EDIT A COMPARE-CONTRAST ESSAY

Writing Guidelines

Planning

1 Select a topic. List subjects that are similar and/ or different in ways that you find interesting, perplexing, disgusting, infuriating, charming, or informing. Then choose two subjects whose comparison and/or contrast gives the reader some insight into who or what they are. *Note:* Make sure that the items have a solid basis for comparison. Comparable items are types of the same thing (e.g., two rivers, two characters, two films, two mental illnesses, two banking regulations, two search engines, two theories).

2 Get the big picture. Using a computer or a paper and pen, create three columns as shown below. Brainstorm a list of traits under each heading. (Also see the Venn diagram on page 46.)

Features Peculiar to Subject #1	Shared Features	Features Peculiar to Subject #2

3 Gather information. Review your list of features, highlighting those that could provide insight into one or both subjects. Research the subjects, using hands-on analysis when possible. Consider writing your research notes in the three-column format shown above.

4 Draft a working thesis. Review your expanded list of features and eliminate those that now seem unimportant. Write a sentence stating the core of what you learned about the subjects: What essential insight have you reached about

the similarities and/or differences between the topics? If you're stuck, try completing the sentence below. (Switch around the terms "similar" and "different" if you wish to stress similarities.)

> Whereas _____ and _____ seem similar, they are different in several ways, and the differences are important because _____ .

5 Get organized. Decide how to organize your essay. Generally, subject by subject works better for short, simple comparisons. Trait by trait works better for longer, more complex comparisons, in that you hold up the topics side by side, trait by trait. Consider, as well, the order in which you will discuss the topics and arrange the traits, choices that depend on what you want to feature and how you want to build and deepen the comparison.

Subject by Subject:	Trait by Trait:
Introduction	Introduction
Subject #1	Trait A
• Trait A	• Subject #1
• Trait B	• Subject #2
Subject #2	Trait B
• Trait A	• Subject #1
• Trait B	• Subject #2

Drafting

6 Write your first draft. Review your outline and draft the paper.

Subject-by-subject pattern:
- **Opening:** Get readers' attention, introduce the subjects, and offer a thesis.
- **Middle:** Discuss the first subject; then analyze the second subject, discussing traits parallel to those you addressed with the first subject.
  - **Conclusion:** Summarize similarities, differences, and implications.

Trait-by-trait pattern:
- **Opening:** Get readers' attention, introduce the subjects, and offer a thesis.
  - **Middle:** Compare and/or contrast the two subjects trait by trait;

include transitions that help readers look back and forth between the two subjects.

- **Conclusion:** Summarize the key relationships and note their significance.

Revising

7 Get feedback. Ask someone to read your paper, looking for a clear thesis, an engaging introduction, a middle that compares and/or contrasts parallel traits in a logical order, and a unifying closing.

8 Rework your draft. Based on feedback, revise for the following issues:

- **Ideas:** The points made and conclusions drawn from comparing and contrasting provide insight into both subjects.
- **Organization:** The structure, whether subject by subject or trait by trait, helps readers grasp the similarities and differences between the subjects.
- **Voice:** The tone is informed, involved, and genuine.

Editing and Proofreading

9 Carefully edit your essay. Look for the following issues:

- **Words are precise**, clear, and defined as needed.
- **Sentences are clear**, well reasoned, varied in structure, and smooth.
- **The copy is correct**, clean, and properly formatted. Graphics are well placed.
- **Page design is attractive** and follows MLA or APA guidelines.

Publishing

10 Publish the essay. Share your writing by submitting it to your instructor, posting it on a Web site, sharing it with friends and family who might be interested in the topic, crafting a presentation or demonstration, or reshaping your comparison writing as a blog.

⚙ Critical-Thinking and Writing Activities

1. Review Rachel De Smith's analysis of Toni Morrison's Sethe and Barbara Kingsolver's Orleanna Price. Then choose two characters from other literary works and write an analysis

of them using compare and/or contrast organization.

2. Review Gelareh Asayesh's article "Shrouded in Contradiction," noting how she uses comparison-contrast strategies in order to take a position. Draft or revise an essay in which you use comparison-contrast to develop or support your thesis.

3. Re-examine how Shankar Vedantam opens and closes "Shades of Prejudice" with an anecdote (or a news story) that was current when he wrote the essay. Revise one of your recent essays by selecting a recent news story that you can use to develop your thesis. For example, you might use the story to get readers' attention or to compare the story with a parallel situation addressed in your paper.

4. Write an essay in which you compare and contrast two people, using subject-by-subject organization. Then revise the essay using trait-by-trait organization. Finally, discuss the essays with a classmate to determine which strategy works better.

STUDY TOOLS 13

LOCATED AT BACK OF THE TEXTBOOK
- ☐ Tear-Out Chapter Review Card

LOCATED AT WWW.CENGAGEBRAIN.COM/LOGIN
- ☐ Chapter eBook
- ☐ Graded quizzes and a practice quiz generator
- ☐ Videos: Writer Interviews
- ☐ Tutorials
- ☐ Flashcards
- ☐ Cengage Learning Write Experience
- ☐ Interactive activities

14 | Cause-Effect

"Shallow men believe in luck. Strong men believe in cause and effect."

RALPH WALDO EMERSON

elwynn, 2014 / Used under license from Shutterstock.com

LEARNING OBJECTIVES

14-1 Understand how to read cause-effect writing.

14-2 Make limited and logical cause-effect claims.

14-3 Support cause-effect reasoning with relevant, reliable evidence.

14-4 Avoid logical fallacies.

14-5 Write, revise, and edit a cause-effect essay.

After you finish
this chapter
go to
PAGE 164 for STUDY TOOLS

Now, why did that happen? We ask this question every day at home, in college, and on the job in order to understand and cope with things that happen in our lives. For example, knowing why a computer crashed will help us avoid that problem, and knowing the causes and effects of a disease such as diabetes can help us control the condition. In other words, cause-and-effect reasoning helps us deal with everyday issues, whether large or small.

In a cause-and-effect essay, the writer develops the thesis through cause-and-effect reasoning. That is, she or he analyzes and explains the causes, the effects, or both the causes and the effects of a phenomenon. The guidelines and samples in this chapter will help you read and write cause-effect analyses.

14-1 UNDERSTAND HOW TO READ CAUSE-EFFECT WRITING

When reading cause-effect writing, note the writer's rhetorical situation and study his or her logic.

14-1a Consider the Rhetorical Situation for Cause-Effect Writing

Assess how the writer's purpose, audience, and topic affect his or her writing strategies.

▶ **Purpose.** Writers use cause-effect analysis to deepen understanding about how specific forces work to bring about particular results. In academia and the workplace, cause-effect logic operates in many forms of writing—from persuasive essays and lab reports to project proposals and market analyses. In each situation, writers use cause-effect thinking to explain a phenomenon or to prove a point.

▶ **Audience.** The audience for cause-effect writing typically have a basic understanding of the topic but

want or need a deeper understanding of the forces operating within it—understanding that may help them make decisions about or take positions on the issue.

▶ **Topic.** Cause-effect topics are phenomena—events, occurrences, developments, processes, problems, conditions, and so on—that need to be more fully explained in terms of their operating forces.

14-1b Consider the Analytical Logic

As you read essays using cause-effect reasoning, identify the problem or phenomenon addressed and look for the following elements of strong cause-effect logic.

▶ **Clear Reasoning:** The thesis clearly identifies a cause-effect idea, and the essay's body carefully and systematically explores and supports this idea. The writer also distinguishes between primary and secondary causes and effects.

▶ **Supporting Details:** Claims identifying causes, effects, and the links between causes and effects are fully supported with reliable, detailed evidence. When appropriate, the writer uses visuals, tables, or multimedia elements effectively. Conversely, the writer avoids relying extensively on circumstantial evidence.

▶ **Logical Analyses:** The reasoning is transparent, unified, and free of logical fallacies such as Bare Assertion (see 188), False Cause (see 189), Slippery Slope (see 189), and False Analogy (see 190).

Reading Guide: Cause-Effect Writing

- ✔ Is the writer's rationale for writing informed, reasonable, and convincing?
- ✔ Who is the intended audience, and does the essay present all the information that they need to understand and respond to the analysis?
- ✔ Is the topic clearly identified and explored as a phenomenon?
- ✔ Is the thesis clear, and is the argument free of logical fallacies?
- ✔ What claims does the writer make regarding causes and effects, and are the statements sufficiently limited, focused, and logical?
- ✔ Are supporting details well researched, relevant, and strong?

MAKE LIMITED AND LOGICAL CAUSE-EFFECT CLAIMS

To build a convincing cause-effect analysis, writers need to start with reasonable, measured claims about cause-effect links. Trina Rys (a student who attended Humber College and the University of Guelph) analyzes the causes and effects of anorexia nervosa. As you read the essay, assess whether her claims are reasonable and measured.

Essay Outline

Introduction: Why do young women practice starvation as a method of weight control?

    1. Cause 1: the psychological pressures of adolescence

    2. Cause 2: expectations of family and peers

    3. Cause 3: potential influence of media

Closing: Cultural values regarding the female body need to change in order for eating disorders to decline.

The Slender Trap

SQ3R   Survey · Question · Read · Recite · Review

1   *Starvation is not a pleasant way to expire. In*
(A) *advanced stages of famine, as the body begins to consume itself, the victim suffers muscle pain, heart disturbances, loss of hair, dizziness, shortness of breath, extreme sensitivity to cold, [and] physical and mental exhaustion. The skin becomes discolored. In the absence of key nutrients, a severe chemical imbalance develops in the brain, inducing convulsions and hallucinations.* (Krakauer, 1996, p. 198)

2   Every day, millions die of hunger. The symptoms of starvation are so horrific that it seems unthinkable anyone would choose this way of death. How is it possible that in the Western world, one in two hundred young women from upper- and middle-class families practices starvation as a method of weight control? How do young women become so obsessed with being thin that they develop anorexia nervosa? To cause such a fearsome and potentially fatal condition, the influencing factors must be powerful indeed. And they are powerful: the psychological pressures of adolescence, the inescapable expectations of family and peers, and the potent influence of the media.

3   A tendency to perfectionism, lack of identity, and feelings of helplessness are three aspects of a young woman's psychology that can contribute to the development of anorexia nervosa. Young women who exhibit perfectionism are particularly susceptible to the (B) disease because they often have unrealistic expectations about their physical appearance. These expectations can lead to feelings of helplessness and powerlessness, and some young women with these feelings see starving themselves as a means to empowerment. Their diet is often the only thing they can control, and they control it with a singlemindedness that astonishes and horrifies their families and friends. As well as the need for control, anorexia in young women can be caused by a weak or unformed identity. Confused about who they are, many young women define themselves by how closely they approximate our society's notion of the ideal woman. Unfortunately, for the past half-century, Western society's ideal female image has been that of an unrealistically thin young woman. When women focus on this impossible image as the ideal and strive to starve their bodies into submission, they suffer emotional and physical damage.

4   In addition to an unstable psychological state, family and peer pressure can contribute to a fragile (C) young woman's development of anorexia nervosa. By emphasizing physical appearance, by criticizing physical features, and even by restricting junk food, family members can push a young woman over the cliff edge that separates health from illness. A home environment in which physical appearance is overvalued can be destructive for young women. Surrounded by

---

(A) Rys begins with a vivid quotation, powerful questions, and a clear cause-effect thesis.

(B) She analyzes the weight of psychological forces on body image.
(C) With a clear transition, the writer turns to the effects of home environment on the desire to be thin.

family members and friends who seem to be concerned primarily about appearance, a young woman can begin to feel insecure about how she looks. This uncertainty can produce the desire—and then the need—to look better. And "better" means thinner. This flawed logic underlies the disease in many young women. A family or peer group that overvalues physical appearance is often also critical of physical flaws. Critical comments about weight and general appearance, even when spoken jokingly, can be instrumental in a young woman's desire to be thin. Ironically, food restrictions imposed by parents can also contribute to anorexia in young women. Restricting the consumption of junk food, for example, has been known to cause bingeing and purging, a condition associated with anorexia.

5   While a young woman's developing psyche and the
(D) pressures of those close to her can exert tremendous influence, the root cause of the "thin is beautiful" trap is a media-inspired body image. Television, fashion magazines, and stereotypical Hollywood images of popular stars provide young women with an unrealistic image of the ideal female body. While only 5 percent of North American females are actually underweight, 32 percent of female television and movie personalities are unhealthily thin (ANRED, 2004). The media's unrealistic portrayal of a woman's ideal body can cause a young woman to develop a sense of inadequacy. To be considered attractive, she feels she must be ultra-thin. Television's unrealistic portrayal of the way young women should look is reinforced in the pages of fashion

(D) She argues that media influence is the root cause of an obsession with thinness.

magazines. Magazine ads feature tall, beautiful, thin women. Media images also perpetuate the stereotype that a woman must be thin in order to be successful. Thanks to television and movies, when we think of a successful woman, the image that comes to mind is that of a tall, well-dressed, thin woman. This stereotypical image leads impressionable young women to associate success with body weight and image. When internalized by young women, these artificial standards can result in the development of anorexia nervosa.

6   If the media do not begin to provide young women with a positive and healthy image of femininity, we will see no lessening in the numbers of anorexia victims. If our cultural ideal of female beauty does not change to reflect a range of healthy body types, the pressures to **(E)** realize idealized and unhealthy physical standards will continue, and young women's feelings of helplessness and inadequacy will persist. In order for anorexia to become less prominent among young women, healthier associations must replace the existing connections among beauty, success, and thinness. Young women must realize that self-inflicted starvation is not a means to empowerment, but a process of self-destruction.

Note: The Works Cited page is not shown. For examples, see MLA (page 286) and APA (page 320).

(E) Rys's conclusion calls for the positive changes needed to prevent eating disorders.

Reading for Better Writing

1. Trina Rys's essay follows a careful, traditional structure: an introduction containing a clear thesis, three points that support the thesis, and a conclusion that pulls together the analysis while deepening it. Examine the strategies that she uses in the introduction, middle, and conclusion of her writing (e.g., the opening quotation, the thesis statement, paragraph topic sentences, closing sentences). Does this structure work for her topic and for the cause-effect analysis she is doing? Explain.

2. Rys analyzes three causes behind eating disorders. Why do you think that she ordered them as she did? How convincing do you find her cause-effect claims and the reasoning in support of those claims? Are there other causes she should have considered?

3. How would you characterize the tone and approach of Rys's conclusion? Does it follow logically from her analysis?

14-3 SUPPORT CAUSE-EFFECT REASONING WITH RELEVANT, RELIABLE EVIDENCE

In "Dutch Discord," student writer Brittany Korver analyzes how the increasing number of Muslim residents in the Netherlands is impacting Dutch culture and raising tension within a society known for its diversity and tolerance. As you read the paper, note how she supports her cause-effect claims with documented evidence.

(A) # Dutch Discord

SQ3R Survey · Question · Read · Recite · Review

1 When people outside the Netherlands think of the
(B) Dutch, what do they envision? Some may picture stoic windmills, grass-covered dikes, and tidy row houses. Others may see barge-filled canals, gay parades, and red-light districts. Still others may envision the Free University in Amsterdam, the harbor in Rotterdam, and the International Court of Justice in The Hague. But when people inside the Netherlands think of common sites in their country, they likely also picture the growing number of domed mosques in Dutch city skylines, veiled faces in the streets, or scarf-covered heads in the

(A) The title identifies the phenomenon.
(B) Introduction: Dutch symbols and ethnic tensions

classrooms. The fact is, these images are increasingly common in the Netherlands as its Muslim population continues to grow and spread ("One Million Muslims"). More importantly, however, this diffusion appears to have increased tension between the progressive ethnic Dutch—long known for tolerating cultural differences—and their new neighbors.

2 The first, most notable influx of Muslims was
(C) drawn to the Netherlands after World War II by job offers (Shadid 10). The Dutch, looking for cheap labor, recruited large numbers of unskilled laborers from poorer countries (10). These immigrants were typically guest workers who expected to stay temporarily and then return to their homelands, as many of them did (Sunier 318).

3 By 1973, an economic crisis hit Europe, and the Netherlands no longer needed extra workers (Van Amersfoort 179). Many Muslims, however, decided to stay because the economic conditions in their home countries were even less desirable than conditions in the Netherlands (Ketner 146). Numerous immigrants became permanent residents and were joined by their families. When the Dutch finally tightened restrictions by lowering quotas and raising standards for refugees, marriages continued between Dutch-Muslim citizens and Muslim foreigners. Since family reunification is a Dutch migration priority, these spouses continued to flow into the Netherlands (Van Amersfoort 179). In addition, the Netherlands experienced increased illegal immigration (179).

4 However, while legal and illegal immigrants increased the Netherlands' Muslim population significantly, the population swelled even more because of Muslims' relatively high fertility rates (Kent). For example, as of 2004, CBS (the Netherlands' statistics bureau) reported 945,000 Muslims living in the country, a jump of more than 339,000 from 10 years earlier ("One Million Muslims"). They currently account for at least 5.8 percent of the population, which makes Muslims the fourth largest religious group in the Netherlands,

(C) 1 Social changes brought about by immigration: history

trailing just behind Dutch Calvinists ("As many Muslims as Calvinists"). While Muslims are distributed quite sparsely in some provinces (e.g., less than 3 percent in Friesland), they make up as much as one-third of the population in cities such as Amsterdam (Rawstome 30).

5
(D) Not surprisingly, this growing minority is both affecting and being affected by Dutch culture. Ethnic foods are increasingly available in stores and restaurants (Wagensveld). New shops and market stands accommodate the demand for folk clothing (Wagensveld). Private Islamic schools are available, and mosques dot the landscape (Landman 1125). Coverage of Turk and Moroccan culture, including their religious festivals, fills many pages in the Netherlands' souvenir books (DeRooi 107). In addition, businesses cater to their new consumers by including dark-haired people in their ads and abandoning potentially offensive practices, such as distributing piggy banks (Charter 40).

6
Dutch culture also leaves its mark on this new community. For example, many Muslims find themselves forgetting Islamic holidays because they are too busy or do not know the Arabic calendar ("Time and Migration" 387). Many have adjusted to the Dutch view of time, making their lives faster paced. Some save religious prayers for after work, disrupting the normal prayer schedule (390). In fact, even some mosques encourage change by offering immigrants Dutch language classes, computer courses, and bicycle lessons (Van Amersfoort 185–186).

7
(E) Though assimilation between most cultural groups in the Netherlands is common, the ethnic Dutch and those who trace their roots to Muslim countries retain conspicuous differences, sometimes leading to tensions between them. For example, fertility runs higher among these immigrants, prompting some ethnic Dutch to fear that they will eventually become a minority (Kent). Muslims still have lower education levels, higher levels of unemployment, and poorer housing than most other residents. And among second-generation Muslims, dropout rates and delinquencies run high (Mamadouh 198).

8
(F) However, the chief challenges that ethnic Dutch have in relating to their Muslim neighbors have little to do with demographic characteristics or economic standing and more to do with cultural practices and worldviews. For example, ethnic Dutch have difficulty accepting or respecting traditional Muslim views regarding women's roles in society and homosexual lifestyles, as well as resident Muslims' high crime rate and violent Islamic extremism ("Veils and Wooden Clogs" 230). The ethnic Dutch are repulsed by stories of wife beating, arranged marriages, women forbidden to hold jobs, homosexuals put to death in the immigrants' home countries, terrorist attacks in Western countries, and violent crimes committed by immigrants in the Netherlands (230). This cultural clash has led the Netherlands to re-evaluate and in some ways redirect its pursuit of a multi-cultural state and return to the nation-state model as the ideal (198 Mamadouh).

9
(G) In some cases, tensions have evolved into an "us vs. them" mentality that includes covert and overt racism and hostility (Shadid 16). In the journal *European Education*, Wasif A. Shadid makes this point by comparing some attitudes in Holland with what appear to be parallel attitudes in South Africa's apartheid system. Examples of these tensions or attitudes include increasing differentiation between the native Dutch and immigrant groups, politicians speaking negatively

---

(D) 2 Impact of Dutch and Muslim cultures on each other
(E) 3 Secondary differences between Dutch and Muslim cultures

(F) 4 Major differences: cultural practices and world view
(G) (a) us vs. them mentality

of Muslim residents (11-16), and sometimes violent acts between Muslims and non-Muslims (Esman 12).

10 Since the turn of the millennium, the ethnic Dutch
(H) fear of Islamic extremism has also increased, brought on in part by international events such as the September 11, 2001, attacks in the United States and the subsequent strikes in Madrid and London. This fear was further intensified when two well-known anti-Islam Dutch politicians were assassinated inside the Netherlands. The first was Pim Fortuyn, who was shot in 2002 (Shadid 17). Fortuyn had his own political party, which called for "stopping all immigration" and a "cold war against Islam" (Esman 12). His assassination created a stir because the Dutch suddenly found their freedom of speech jeopardized, thereby widening the rift between the Dutch and Muslim cultures (Wagensveld).

11 The second Dutch politician assassinated was Theo Van Gogh in 2004, and this event is often referred to as the September 11 of the Netherlands (Esman 12). Like Fortuyn, Van Gogh was very outspoken. He also used offensive language, gained many young followers (Margaronis 6), and, with ex-Muslim and screenwriter Ayaan Hirsi Ali, went on to make the movie *Submission*, a film that exposed Dutch-Muslim domestic abuse (6). Van Gogh was shot and stabbed to death, resulting in a martyr-like legacy for his cause (Rawstome 30).

12 The most recent tension-building event was the March 2008 release of the controversial movie *Fitna* (Arabic for *strife*), directed by Dutch MP Geert Wilders (Rawstome 30). The short movie displays graphic and disturbing images of terrorism and abuse, and it uses quotes from the Koran and Islamic leaders, suggesting that both sources support these violent actions (*Fitna*). The movie is so controversial that fear of violent repercussions is widespread, and many Netherlanders think that Wilders was irresponsible for releasing it (Rawstome 30). Wilders received 600 death threats by late March, has six body guards, and at times he and his wife live in prison cells for safety (30).

(H) (b) fear of extremism, terrorism, and assassinations

As events like these suggest, the growth of the 13
Muslim community in the Netherlands appears to (I)
have increased the tension between the ethnic Dutch and Muslims. As a result, many ethnic Dutch feel disconcerted, and many Dutch Muslims feel alienated (Shadid 20). Whether those who built windmills and those who build mosques will ever live together in unity remains unclear. But what is clear is that such unity never will happen until the two groups learn to live with the differences that now separate them.

(I) Conclusion: Tensions lead to fear and alienation.

Reading for Better Writing

1. Do the title and opening paragraph effectively get your attention and introduce the topic? Explain. How do the opening and closing paragraphs unite the essay?

2. Brittany Korver wrote this essay expecting that it would be read by other college students and her professor. Review her topic, thesis, and core argument; then explain why they are or are not fitting choices for her audience.

3. In paragraphs 2–4, Korver uses chronological order to explain how the Muslim population in the Netherlands increased. Review those paragraphs and explain whether her organization and details adequately describe the increase.

4. Note how the writer builds paragraphs 7–9 by opening each with a topic sentence and following with documented supporting details. Then explain why these choices do or do not strengthen her argument.

5. In paragraphs 10–12, the writer describes three violent events that transpired since 2002. Explain why she might cite these events and whether she uses them effectively to develop her thesis.

6. If Korver's essay were a magazine article, what visuals might deepen readers' understanding of the causes and effects she analyzes? What visuals would be counterproductive?

14-4 AVOID LOGICAL FALLACIES

Steven Pinker teaches in the Department of Psychology at Harvard University, where he also conducts research on language and cognition. He writes regularly for publications such as *Time* and *The New Republic*, and he is the author of seven books, including *How the Mind Works*.

In the essay below, published as an op-ed piece in *The New York Times* on January 10, 2010, Pinker analyzes how our current use of electronic technologies affects our ability to think deeply and process information. Before you read his essay, review common logical fallacies such as bare assertion (page 188), false cause (page 189), slippery slope (page 189), and false analogy (page 190). As you read, record your thoughts and questions tracking the cause-effect thinking Pinker uses.

Mind Over Mass Media

SQ3R Survey · Question · Read · Recite · Review

1   New forms of media have always caused moral panics: the printing press, newspapers, paperbacks and television were all once denounced as threats to their consumers' brainpower and moral fiber.

2   So too with electronic technologies. PowerPoint, we're told, is reducing discourse to bullet points. Search engines lower our intelligence, encouraging us to skim on the surface of knowledge rather than dive to its depths. Twitter is shrinking our attention spans.

3   But such panics often fail basic reality checks. When comic books were accused of turning juveniles into delinquents in the 1950s, crime was falling to record lows, just as the denunciations of video games in the 1990s coincided with the great American crime decline. The decades of television, transistor radios and rock videos were also decades in which I.Q. scores rose continuously.

4   For a reality check today, take the state of science, which demands high levels of brainwork and is measured by clear benchmarks of discovery. These days scientists are never far from their email, rarely touch paper and cannot lecture without PowerPoint. If electronic media were hazardous to intelligence, the quality of science would be plummeting. Yet discoveries are multiplying like fruit flies, and progress is dizzying. Other activities in the life of the mind, like philosophy, history and cultural criticism, are likewise flourishing, as anyone who has lost a morning of work to the Web site *Arts & Letters Daily* can attest.

5   Critics of new media sometimes use science itself to press their case, citing research that shows how "experience can change the brain." But cognitive neuroscientists roll their eyes at such talk. Yes, every time we learn a fact or skill the wiring of the brain changes; it's not as if the information is stored in the pancreas. But the existence of neural plasticity does not mean the brain is a blob of clay pounded into shape by experience.

6   Experience does not revamp the basic information-processing capacities of the brain. Speed-reading programs have long claimed to do just that, but the verdict was rendered by Woody Allen after he read *War and Peace* in one sitting: "It was about Russia." Genuine multitasking, too, has been exposed as a myth, not just by laboratory studies but by the familiar sight of an S.U.V. undulating between lanes as the driver cuts deals on his cellphone.

7   Moreover, as the psychologists Christopher Chabris and Daniel Simons show in their new book *The Invisible Gorilla: And Other Ways Our Intuitions Deceive Us*, the effects of experience are highly specific to the experiences themselves. If you train people to do one thing (recognize shapes, solve math puzzles, find hidden words), they get better at doing that thing, but almost nothing else. Music doesn't make you better at math, conjugating Latin doesn't make you more logical, brain-training games don't make you smarter.

Angela Waye, 2014 / Used under license from Shutterstock.com

Accomplished people don't bulk up their brains with intellectual calisthenics; they immerse themselves in their fields. Novelists read lots of novels, scientists read lots of science.

8 The effects of consuming electronic media are also likely to be far more limited than the panic implies. Media critics write as if the brain takes on the qualities of whatever it consumes, the informational equivalent of "you are what you eat." As with primitive peoples who believe that eating fierce animals will make them fierce, they assume that watching quick cuts in rock videos turns your mental life into quick cuts or that reading bullet points and Twitter postings turns your thoughts into bullet points and Twitter postings.

9 Yes, the constant arrival of information packets can be distracting or addictive, especially to people with attention deficit disorder. But distraction is not a new phenomenon. The solution is not to bemoan technology but to develop strategies of self-control, as we do with every other temptation in life. Turn off email or Twitter when you work, put away your Blackberry at dinner time, ask your spouse to call you to bed at a designated hour.

10 And to encourage intellectual depth, don't rail at PowerPoint or Google. It's not as if habits of deep reflection, thorough research and rigorous reasoning ever came naturally to people. They must be acquired in special institutions, which we call universities, and maintained with constant upkeep, which we call analysis, criticism and debate. They are not granted by propping a heavy encyclopedia on your lap, nor are they taken away by efficient access to information on the Internet.

11 The new media have caught on for a reason. Knowledge is increasing exponentially; human

brainpower and waking hours are not. Fortunately, the Internet and information technologies are helping us manage, search and retrieve our collective intellectual output at different scales, from Twitter and previews to e-books and online encyclopedias. Far from making us stupid, these technologies are the only things that will keep us smart.

Reading for Better Writing

1. Review Pinker's opening paragraph in which he introduces his topic by suggesting that current allegations regarding the negative impact of electronic technologies are similar to past allegations regarding the impact of the printing press, newspapers, paperbacks, and television. Paraphrase his claim, explain why you do or do not agree, and explain whether the opening is or is not effective.

2. The essay is organized as a series of critics' arguments asserting the negative impact of new media, followed by Pinker's counterarguments. Identify three of these exchanges and explain how the point-counterpoint format clarifies both sides of the argument while also making Pinker's position more convincing.

3. Note that Pinker uses cause-effect logic to identify weaknesses in others' claims and to assert the value of his own claims. Identify an example of each that you find persuasive and explain why.

4. Pinker is a scholar aiming to analyze an academic topic with thoughtful, well-researched arguments in an informed, academic tone. Cite passages that illustrate this voice.

5. Pinker is also a writer aiming to engage and inform readers who have likely not studied the topic themselves. Identify passages in which the examples and word choice illustrate his effort to connect with these readers.

6. Study the image on the page 161. How does the image relate to Pinker's analysis? Does the visual content effectively reinforce his claims?

WRITE, REVISE, AND EDIT A CAUSE-EFFECT ESSAY

Writing Guidelines

Planning

❶ Select a topic. Begin by thinking about categories such as those listed below and listing phenomena related to each category. From this list, choose a topic and analyze its causes, its effects, or both.

- **Family Life:** adult children living with parents, more stay-at-home dads, families simplifying their lifestyles, adults squeezed by needs of children and parents
- **Politics:** fewer student voters, increasing support for green-energy production, increased interest in third-party politics, tension between political-action groups
- **Society:** nursing shortage, doctor shortage, terrorist threats, increasing immigrant-advocacy efforts, shifting ethnic ratios, decreasing number of newspapers
- **Environment:** common water pollutants, new water-purification technology, decreasing U.S. space exploration, increasing number of wind turbines

❷ Narrow and research the topic. State your topic, and below it list related causes and effects in two columns. Next, do preliminary research to expand the list and distinguish primary causes and effects from secondary ones. Revise your topic as needed to address only primary causes and/or effects that research links to a specific phenomenon.

Cause/Effect Topic: _____

Causes (Because of)	Effects (the results)
1. _____	1. _____
2. _____	2. _____
3. _____	3. _____

❸ Draft and test your thesis. Based on your preliminary research, draft a working thesis (you may revise it later) that introduces the topic, along with the causes and/or effects you intend to discuss. Limit your argument to only those points you can prove.

❹ Gather and analyze information. Research your topic, looking for clear evidence that links specific causes to specific effects. As you study the phenomenon, distinguish between primary and secondary causes (main and contributing), direct and indirect results, short-term and long-term effects, and so on. At the same time, test your analysis to avoid mistaking a coincidence for a cause-effect relationship. Use the list of logical fallacies (see pages 188–191) to weed out common errors in logic. For example, finding chemical pollutants in a stream running beside a chemical plant does not "prove" that the plant caused the pollutants. In addition, carefully study any tables, diagrams, graphs, images, or videos that clarify the topic's causes and/or effects.

❺ Get organized. Develop an outline that lays out your thesis and argument in a clear pattern. Under each main point asserting a cause-effect connection, list details from your research that support the connection.

Point #1	Point #2	Point #3
• Supporting details	• Supporting details	• Supporting details
• Supporting details	• Supporting details	• Supporting details

Nejc Vesel, 2014 / Used under license from Shutterstock.com

Drafting

❻ Use your outline to draft the essay. Try to rough out the essay's overall argument before you attempt to revise it. As you write, show how specific causes led to specific effects, citing examples as needed.

To show those cause-effect relationships, use transitional words like the following:

accordingly	hence	therefore
as a result	just as	thus
because	since	to illustrate
consequently	so	whereas
for this purpose	such as	
for this reason	thereby	

Revising

7 **Get feedback.** Ask a peer reviewer or someone from the college's writing center to read your essay for an engaging opening, a thoughtful cause-effect thesis, clear and convincing reasoning that links specific causes to specific effects, and a closing that deepens and extends the cause-effect analysis of the phenomenon.

8 **Revise the essay.** Whether your essay presents causes, effects, or both, use the checklist below to trace and refine your argument.

- **Ideas:** The essay explains the causes and/or effects of the topic in a clear, well-reasoned analysis. The analysis is supported by credible information and is free of logical fallacies.
- **Organization:** The structure helps clarify the cause-effect relationships through a well-traced line of thinking; and the links between the main points, supporting points, and evidence are clear.
- **Voice:** The tone is informed, polite, and logical.

Editing and Proofreading

9 **Edit the essay for clarity and correctness.** Check for the following:

- **Words:** The diction is precise and clear, and technical or scientific terms are defined. Causes are linked to effects with transitional words and phrases.
- **Sentences:** Structures are clear, varied, and smooth.
- **Correctness:** The writing is correct in terms of grammar, punctuation, mechanics, usage, and spelling.
- **Design:** The format, layout, and typography adhere to expectation; any visuals used enhance the written analysis and clarify the paper's cause-effect reasoning.

Publishing

10 **Publish your essay.** Share your writing by submitting it to your instructor, posting it on the class's or department's Web site, or turning it into a presentation.

Critical-Thinking and Writing Activities

1. In "The Slender Trap," Trina Rys analyzes the causes and effects of an illness that concerns her. Select a health-related topic that interests you, research it, and write an essay in which you analyze the topic's causes and effects.

2. In "Dutch Discord," Brittany Korver analyzes the causes and effects of a shift in the Netherlands' immigration practices. Identify a similar shift in the policies or practices of a city, state, or country that interests you. Then write an essay in which you analyze the causes and effects of this shift.

3. "Mind Over Mass Media" analyzes changes brought by technology. Identify a technological change that has impacted your life; then analyze the causes or effects of that change.

4. Scan editorials in two or three newspapers, looking for arguments based on cause-effect reasoning. Then examine the arguments for logical fallacies such as false-cause or slippery-slope claims (for help, see page 189). Present your findings to the class.

STUDY TOOLS 14

LOCATED AT BACK OF THE TEXTBOOK
- ☐ Tear-Out Chapter Review Card

LOCATED AT WWW.CENGAGEBRAIN.COM/LOGIN
- ☐ Chapter eBook
- ☐ Graded quizzes and a practice quiz generator
- ☐ Videos: Writer Interviews
- ☐ Tutorials
- ☐ Flashcards
- ☐ Cengage Learning Write Experience
- ☐ Interactive activities

ONE APPROACH.
70 UNIQUE SOLUTIONS.

CENGAGE
Learning

www.cengage.com/4ltrpress

15 | Reading Literature:
A Case Study in Analysis

"THE ONLY IMPECCABLE
WRITERS ARE THOSE
WHO NEVER WROTE."
WILLIAM HAZLITT

michaeljung, 2014 / Used under license from Shutterstock.com

LEARNING OBJECTIVES

15-1 Understand how to read literary analyses.

15-2 Identify approaches to literary analysis.

15-3 Analyze a short story.

15-4 Analyze a poem.

15-5 Understand and use literary terms.

15-6 Write a literary analysis.

After you finish
this chapter
go to
PAGE 181 for STUDY TOOLS

In college, analyzing a literary text is a critical, interpretive process. For that reason, the process must begin with a deep reading of a poem, short story, play, or other literary work. When you research and write the essay, you assume that your readers have also read the text, and your aim is to illuminate some dimension of the work that is not fully understood: the motivations of a particular character, the image patterns of a lyric, the historical context of a Renaissance play, and so on.

In this way, literary analysis is a special form of the analytical writing explained in chapters 10–14. In this application of analysis, your primary research is reading, rereading, and thinking through the literary text itself in order to develop a sound, insightful interpretation; secondary research supplements your primary reading by providing a range of support from historical background to scholarly criticism.

15-1 UNDERSTAND HOW TO READ LITERARY ANALYSES

The instructions below will help you read various essays about literature.

15-1a Consider the Rhetorical Situation for Literary Analyses

To understand literary analyses, think about the writer's purpose, audience, and topic.

▸ **Purpose:** Most writers aim to analyze a literary text: to describe its features, to explain how it impacts readers, and to understand its essential qualities. However, writers reviewing a book focus more on its strengths and weaknesses.

▸ **Audience:** In college, the primary audience for writing about literature is students and instructors; off campus, stories and reviews are written for any community members interested in art events, art-related issues, or reading books.

▸ **Topic:** The topic might be one work (e.g., a novel or a film), multiple works created by the same writer (e.g., a series of poems), a group performance (e.g., a play), an individual performance (e.g., an actor), or critical approaches to literature.

15-1b Understand Terms Used to Write About the Arts

As you read, note the terms used to address specific works of literature:

▸ **Plays and Films:** To describe characters, writers use terms such as *antagonist*, *protagonist*, or *tragic hero*; to discuss plots, they use words like *exposition*, *rising action*, and *denouement*; or to describe a setting, they might use *stage picture*, *proscenium arch*, or *thrust stage*.

▸ **Stories and Novels:** Writers might describe diction with terms such as *archaic* or *slang*; narrative method with phrases such as *first person* and *third person*; or genre with terms such as *satire* or *melodrama*.

▸ **Poetry:** Writers might describe word sounds with terms such as *assonance*, *consonance*, and *alliteration*; rhythmic effects with words such as *iambic* or *trochaic meter*; and figurative language with words such as *metaphor* and *simile*.

Zastolskiy Victor, 2014 / Used under license from Shutterstock.com

15-1c Understand Approaches to Literary Analysis

Literary texts can be interpreted through different critical approaches or schools. Each school, with its specific foci and questions, offers a way of "conversing" about a text. What follows are the four basic approaches, which are outlined more fully in the essay "Four Ways to Talk About Literature" on pages 168–170.

1. **Formalist criticism** focuses on the literary text itself, especially its structure and **genre**.
2. **Rhetorical criticism** is audience-centered, focused on the "transaction" between text and reader.
3. **Historical criticism** focuses on the historical context of the literary text, including its author.
4. **Ideological criticism** applies ideas outside of literature (e.g., psychology, mythology, feminism) to literary texts.

15-1d Understand Primary and Secondary Research

Writers' reading of a literary text—primary research—is usually the focus of their analyses. However, secondary research can serve many purposes, such as these:

▸ **Biographical research:** Learning about the author's life may enrich a writer's analysis by helping the person to explore sources of inspiration, personal and literary influences, and modes of thought.

▸ **Research into historical and cultural context:** Such research illuminates the text by clarifying important contextual issues and historical details.

▸ **Research into literary concepts:** This type of research deepens the writer's understanding of literary issues and techniques (e.g., the nature of tragedy).

▸ **Research into theory:** Such research examines philosophies and ideologies that might illuminate a specific text (e.g., feminism, reader-response).

▸ **Research into scholarly interpretations:** In this research, writers review articles and books that offer interpretations of the text in question—lending scholarly insight and debate to the literary analysis.

Reading Guide: Analyzing Literature

✔ Does the writer understand the elements of the genre, what distinguishes a quality work, and how to assess those qualities?

✔ Does the essay explore nuances such as ironies, motifs, symbols, or allusions?

✔ Does the essay have a clear thesis and logical claims supported by relevant evidence?

✔ Is the tone informed, respectful, and honest?

genre a category or type of literature based on its style, form, and content

15-2 IDENTIFY APPROACHES TO LITERARY ANALYSIS

In this essay, John Van Rys, a college professor, classifies four approaches to literary criticism. To illustrate similarities and differences, he shows how a critic using each approach might analyze Robert Browning's "My Last Duchess." For reference, Browning's poem follows the essay.

Four Ways to Talk About Literature

SQ3R Survey · Question · Read · Recite · Review

Have you ever been in a conversation in which you suddenly felt lost—out of the loop? Perhaps you feel that way in your literature class. You may think a poem or short story means one thing, and then your instructor suddenly pulls out the "hidden meaning." Joining the conversation about literature—in class or in an essay—may indeed seem daunting, but you can do it if you know what to look for and what to talk about. There are four main perspectives, or approaches, that you can use to converse about literature.   1 (A)

Text-centered approaches focus on the literary piece itself. Often called *formalist criticism,* such approaches claim that the structure of a work and the rules of its genre are crucial to its meaning. The formalist critic determines how various elements (plot, character, language, and so on) reinforce the meaning and unify the work. For example, the formalist may ask the following questions concerning Robert Browning's poem "My Last Duchess": How do the main elements in the poem—irony, symbolism, and verse form—help develop the main theme (deception)? How does Browning use the dramatic monologue genre in this poem?   2 (B) (C)

(A) The writer introduces the topic and criterion for creating four subgroups.
(B) He describes the first subgroup and gives an example.
(C) Genre means a class or category of something.

3 Audience-centered approaches focus on (D) the "transaction" between text and reader—the dynamic way the reader interacts with the text. Often called rhetorical or reader-response criticism, these approaches see the text not as an object to be analyzed, but as an activity that is different for each reader. A reader-response critic might ask these questions of "My Last Duchess": How does the reader become aware of the duke's true nature if it's never actually stated? Do men and women read the poem differently? Who were Browning's original readers?

4 Author-centered approaches focus on the origins (E) of a text (the writer and the historical background). For example, an author-centered study examines the writer's life—showing connections, contrasts, and conflicts between his or her life and the writing. Broader historical studies explore social and intellectual currents, showing links between an author's work and the ideas, events, and institutions of that period. Finally, the literary historian may make connections between the text in question and earlier and later literary works. The author-centered critic might ask these questions of "My Last Duchess": What were Browning's views of marriage, men and women, art, class, and wealth? As an institution, what was marriage like in Victorian England (Browning's era) or Renaissance Italy (the duke's era)? Who was the historical Duke of Ferrara?

5 The fourth approach to criticism applies ideas (F) outside literature to literary works. Because literature mirrors life, argue these critics, disciplines that explore human life can help us understand literature. Some critics, for example, apply psychological theories to literary works by exploring dreams, symbolic meanings, and motivation. Myth or archetype criticism uses insights from psychology, cultural anthropology, and classical studies to explore a text's universal appeal. Moral

criticism, rooted in religious studies and ethics, explores the moral dilemmas literary works raise. Ecocriticism, connecting literature and environmental studies, examines the nature–culture relationship expressed by literary texts. Marxist, feminist, minority, and postcolonial criticisms are, broadly speaking, sociological approaches to interpretation. While the Marxist critic examines the themes of class struggle, economic power, and social justice in texts, the feminist critic explores the just and unjust treatment of women as well as the effect of gender on language, reading, and the literary canon. The critic interested in race and ethnic identity explores similar issues, with the focus shifted to a specific cultural group, while postcolonial criticism focuses specifically on the literature of former colonies in terms of the effects of colonialism.

6 Such ideological criticism might ask a wide variety (G) of questions about "My Last Duchess": What does the poem reveal about the duke's psychological state and his (H) personality? How does the reference to Neptune deepen the poem? What does the poem suggest about the nature of evil and injustice? In what ways are the duke's motives class-based and economic? How does the poem present the duke's power and the duchess's weakness? What is the status of women in this society?

7 If you look at the variety of questions critics (I) might ask about "My Last Duchess," you see both the diversity of critical approaches and the common ground

(D) He describes the second subgroup and gives an example.
(E) He describes the third subgroup and gives examples.
(F) He describes the fourth approach and gives examples of each subgroup in it.

(G) He cites sample questions.
(H) Neptune is an ancient Roman god of the sea.
(I) The closing presents qualities shared by all four approaches.

between them. In fact, interpretive methods actually share important characteristics: (1) a close attention to literary elements such as character, plot, symbolism, and metaphor; (2) a desire not to distort the work; and (3) a sincere concern for increasing interest and understanding in a text. In actual practice, critics may develop a hybrid approach to criticism, one that matches their individual questions and concerns about a text. Now that you're familiar with some of the questions defining literary criticism, exercise your own curiosity (and join the ongoing literary dialogue) by discussing a text that genuinely interests you.

(J) A hybrid is a fusion of two or more sources.

Reading for Better Writing

1. Explain how the writer introduces the subject and attempts to engage the reader. Is this strategy effective? Why or why not?

2. The writer uses one poem to illustrate how each of the four critical approaches works. Explain why this strategy is or is not effective.

3. Review the last paragraph and explain why it does or does not unify the essay.

4. How might this classification of critical approaches apply to other forms of art or narrative? Modify this scheme for viewing films or listening to music.

Follow Up

To help you understand "Four Ways to Talk About Literature" more fully, here is the poem "My Last Duchess," referenced throughout the essay. Robert Browning, a British Victorian poet, first published "My Last Duchess" in 1842. The poem is a dramatic monologue, meaning that the speaker (here the Duke of Ferrara, indicated below the poem's title) is imagined as speaking to a silent listener (an agent for a count with whom the duke is attempting to negotiate another marriage after the death of his first wife). The duke speaking in the poem is believed to be the historical Alfonso Il d'Este (1533-1598), who at the age of 25 married 14-year-old Lucrezia di Cosimo de Medici, the figure in the portrait being

Lucrezia de' Medici, Duchess of Ferrara

described by the duke. It is suspected that when Lucrezia died at the age of 17, she had been poisoned by her husband, the duke. With this background in mind, engage "My Last Duchess" by doing the following:

1. Read the poem aloud (more than once, if helpful), paying attention to the rhythms and sounds at work.

2. Work through the poem slowly, line by line, to sort out what the duke is saying to the agent and why he would be saying it.

3. Through freewriting, explore your response to the poem—the story that it tells, the voice and personality of the duke, the ethical puzzle that it presents, or anything else that strikes you about this dramatic monologue.

4. Develop an interpretation of the poem using "Four Ways to Talk About Literature" and other resources within this chapter.

"My Last Duchess"

Ferrara

That's my last Duchess painted on the wall,
Looking as if she were alive. I call
That piece a wonder, now: Frà Pandolf's hands
Worked busily a day, and there she stands.
Will't please you sit and look at her? I said
"Frà Pandolf" by design, for never read
Strangers like you that pictured countenance,
The depth and passion of its earnest glance,
But to myself they turned (since none puts by
The curtain I have drawn for you, but I)
And seemed as they would ask me, if they durst,
How such a glance came there; so, not the first
Are you to turn and ask thus. Sir, 'twas not
Her husband's presence only, called that spot
Of joy into the Duchess' cheek: perhaps
Frà Pandolf chanced to say "Her mantle laps

Over my Lady's wrist too much," or "Paint
Must never hope to reproduce the faint
Half-flush that dies along her throat": such stuff
Was courtesy, she thought, and cause enough
For calling up that spot of joy. She had
A heart—how shall I say?—too soon made glad,
Too easily impressed; she liked whate'er
She looked on, and her looks went everywhere.
Sir, 'twas all one! My favour at her breast,
The dropping of the daylight in the West,
The bough of cherries some officious fool
Broke in the orchard for her, the white mule
She rode with round the terrace—all and each
Would draw from her alike the approving speech,
Or blush, at least. She thanked men,—good! but thanked
Somehow—I know not how—as if she ranked
My gift of a nine-hundred-years-old name
With anybody's gift. Who'd stoop to blame
This sort of trifling? Even had you skill
In speech—(which I have not)—to make your will
Quite clear to such an one, and say, "Just this
Or that in you disgusts me; here you miss,
Or there exceed the mark"—and if she let
Herself be lessoned so, nor plainly set
Her wits to yours, forsooth, and made excuse,
—E'en then would be some stooping, and I choose
Never to stoop. Oh sir, she smiled, no doubt,
Whene'er I passed her; but who passed without
Much the same smile? This grew; I gave commands;
Then all smiles stopped together. There she stands
As if alive. Will't please you rise? We'll meet
The company below, then. I repeat,
The Count your master's known munificence
Is ample warrant that no just pretence
Of mine for dowry will be disallowed;
Though his fair daughter's self, as I avowed
At starting, is my object. Nay, we'll go
Together down, sir. Notice Neptune, though,
Taming a sea-horse, thought a rarity,
Which Claus of Innsbruck cast in bronze for me!

15-3 ANALYZE A SHORT STORY

In the essay below, student writer Anya Terekhina analyzes Flannery O'Connor's short story "Good Country People." Note how Terekhina focuses on the story's characters, plot, symbols, and diction.

"Good Country People": Broken Body, Broken Soul

SQ3R Survey · Question · Read · Recite · Review

1 Flannery O'Connor's short stories are filled with characters who are bizarre, freakish, devious, and (A) sometimes even murderous. Every short story, according to O'Connor in *Mystery and Manners: Occasional Prose*, should be "long in depth" and meaning (94). To achieve this, O'Connor develops characters with heavily symbolic attributes and flaws, and "it is clearly evident that boldly outlined inner compulsions are reinforced dramatically by a mutilated exterior self" (Muller 22). In "Good Country People," Joy-Hulga is a typical O'Connor character—grotesque yet real. Her realness comes from her many flaws, and ironically, her flaws are a self-constructed set of illusions. Throughout the story, O'Connor carefully links Joy-Hulga's physical impairments with deeper handicaps of the soul; then, at the closing, she strips Hulga of these physical flaws while helping her realize that her corresponding beliefs are flawed as well.

2 O'Connor first introduces her character as Joy Hopewell, a name of optimism. However, we soon understand that her chosen name, Hulga, is more fitting.

(A) The writer provides background for understanding the characters in O'Connor's stories.

The new name distresses her mother, Mrs. Hopewell, who is "certain that she [Joy] had thought and thought until she had hit upon the ugliest name in any language" (O'Connor 1943). Hulga has connotations of "hull = hulk = huge = ugly" (Grimshaw 51), and all of these are accurate descriptions of her. Far from having a sweet temperament, Hulga stomps and sulks around the farm, "constant outrage . . . [purging] every expression from her face" (1942).

3
(B) Although Hulga's demeanor could be blamed on her physical impairments, she devises her own rationalizations for behaving as she does. Ironically, each rationale is symbolized by one of her physical disabilities, yet she doesn't recognize the handicaps for what they imply.

4 One of Hulga's many ailments is her weak heart, which will likely limit her life span. Hulga blames this affliction for keeping her on the Hopewell farm, making it plain that "if it had not been for this condition, she would be far from these red hills and good country people" (1944). Having a Ph.D. in philosophy, Hulga claims to want work as a university professor, lecturing to people at her intellectual level. Hulga's weak heart functions as more than a dream-crusher; it "symbolizes her emotional detachment—and inability to love anyone or anything" (Oliver 233). She exhibits no compassion or love for anything, not even "dogs or cats or birds or flowers or nature or nice young men" (1944–45).

5 Hulga also suffers from poor vision. Without her eyeglasses, she is helpless. Strangely though, her icy blue eyes have a "look of someone who has achieved blindness by an act of will and means to keep it" (1942). Her self-induced blindness symbolizes her blindness to reality. She is indeed intelligent, but she has packed her brain full of ideas and thoughts that only obscure common sense, let alone truth. Because of Hulga's extensive

education and her focus on philosophical reasoning, she considers herself superior to everyone around her. For example, she yells at her mother, "Woman! . . . Do you ever look inside and see what you are not? God!" (1944).

6 Hulga's last and most noticeable physical impairment is her missing leg, which was "literally blasted off" (1944) in a hunting accident when she was 10 years old. In *Mystery and Manners*, O'Connor stresses that the wooden leg operates interdependently at a literal and a symbolic level, which means "the wooden leg continues to accumulate meaning" throughout the story (99). Hulga's biggest physical handicap symbolizes her deepest affliction: her belief in nothing.

7
(C) Hulga's philosophical studies did focus on the study of nothing, particularly on the arguments of the French philosopher Nicolas Malebranche. O'Connor describes Hulga as believing "in nothing but her own belief in nothing" (Mystery 99). Over time, Hulga's belief in nothing develops into more than just academic study. Her nihilism becomes her religion—suitable for a woman who considers herself superior and despises platitudes. As she explains to Manley Pointer, "We are all damned . . . but some of us have taken off our blindfolds and see that there's nothing to see. It's a kind of salvation" (1952). Hulga's religious terms suggest that she uses faith in nothingness to find the meaning that she can't find elsewhere.

8
(D) Hulga's nihilism is symbolized by her wooden leg, which is the only thing she tends to with care: "She took care of it as someone else would his soul, in private and almost with her own eyes turned away" (1953). This limb is wooden and corresponds to Hulga's wooden soul. Whereas she believes she worships nothing, what she actually worships is an "artificial leg and an artificial belief" (Oliver 235).

9 Not realizing that her false leg and false religion cripple her both physically and spiritually,

(B) The writer begins listing the protagonist's physical disabilities and explains how each one symbolizes a deeper problem in her soul.

(C) She points out the root of the protagonist's problems: her lack of belief in anything.
(D) The writer demonstrates how the protagonist's flaws lead her to make distorted judgments.

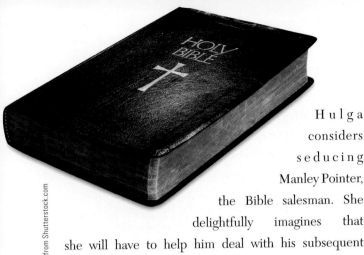

Hulga considers seducing Manley Pointer, the Bible salesman. She delightfully imagines that she will have to help him deal with his subsequent remorse, and then she will instruct him into a "deeper understanding of life" (1950). Of course, her intellectual blindness keeps her from realizing that her superiority is only an illusion. Instead, she views Manley as "a vulnerable innocent, a naïve Fundamentalist, and she wishes to seduce him to prove that her sophisticated textbook nihilism is superior to his simpleminded faith" (Di Renzo 76).

10   In classic O'Connor fashion, the characters and situation reverse dramatically at the end of the story. Hulga and Manley are alone in a hayloft and begin embracing. At first, Hulga is pleased with her reaction to kissing, as it aligns well with Malebranche's teachings: "It was an unexceptional experience and all a matter of the mind's control" (1951). Soon, however, she realizes that she is enjoying the first human connection of her life. At this point, the innocent Bible salesman has already stripped Hulga of her first physical impairment: her weak heart.

11   Hulga hardly notices when Manley takes advantage
(E) of her next impairment: "when her glasses got in his way, he took them off of her and slipped them into his pocket" (1952). With her heart opened and her intellectual perspective fuzzy, Hulga swiftly descends into what she despises—platitudes. Hulga and Manley exchange cliched mumblings of love, and this leads Manley to ask if he can remove her artificial leg. After brief hesitation, Hulga agrees because she feels he has touched and understood a central truth inside her. She considers it a complete surrender, "like losing her own life and finding it again, miraculously, in his" (1953).

12   As soon as the artificial leg is off, Manley whips out one of his Bibles, which is hollow. Inside are whiskey, obscene playing cards, and contraceptives. In only moments, Hulga loses control: As each of her physical handicaps is exploited, pieces of her world view crumble, leaving her confused and weak.

13   In an ironic reversal, Hulga becomes the naïf and Manley becomes the cynic. Hulga pleads in disbelief, **(F)** "Aren't you . . . just good country people?" (1954). She knows that she has reverted to her mother's platitudes: "If the language is more sophisticated than any at Mrs. Hopewell's command, it is no less trite, and the smug self-deception underlying it . . . is, if anything, greater" (Asals 105). Manley assumes a startling, haughty air, exclaiming, "'I hope you don't think . . . that I believe in that crap! I may sell Bibles but I know which end is up and I wasn't born yesterday and I know where I'm going!'" (1954). Although they exchange roles, both characters use cliches to express their immature, yet authentic, worldviews.

14   Manley runs off with Hulga's wooden leg, leaving her vulnerable and dependent, two things she previously despised. But "Hulga's artificial self—her mental fantasy of her own perfection—has gone out the door with her artificial limb. She is stuck in the hayloft with her actual self, her body, her physical and emotional incompleteness" (Di Renzo 79).

15   In one brief morning of delusional seduction, Hulga learns more about herself and her world than she learned **(G)** in all her years of university. Forced to acknowledge her physical, emotional, and spiritual disabilities, Hulga begins to realize what she is not—neither a wise intellectual for whom there is hope, nor "good country people" who merely hope well.

Note: The Works Cited page is not shown. For sample pages, see MLA (page 286) and APA (page 320).

(E) She revisits the protagonist's physical disabilities, showing how the Bible salesman exploits each one.

(F) The writer reflects on the change in both characters.
(G) She explains how the protagonist finally acknowledges the truth about herself.

Reading for Better Writing

1. In her opening paragraph, Terekhina cites Flannery O'Connor's view that every short story should be "long in depth" and meaning. How does Terekhina explore that depth and meaning?

2. In her second paragraph, Terekhina analyzes Hulga Hopewell's first name; in the last paragraph, she comments on the last name. Does Terekhina's attention to names help you understand Hulga's character and the story's themes? How?

3. A writer's thesis is a type of "contract" that he or she makes with readers, spelling out what the essay will do. Review Terekhina's thesis (last sentence, first paragraph) and assess how effectively she fulfills that contract. Cite supporting details.

4. Flannery O'Connor has received strong acclaim for her clearly developed, complex characters. Does Terekhina adequately explore that complexity? Explain.

5. Many praise O'Connor for the challenging philosophical or ethical questions raised in her fiction. What questions does Terekhina identify in "Good Country People," and does she effectively discuss them?

6. What does Terekhina say about the story's plot, symbols, and diction? Does she effectively analyze these elements? How so?

canadastock, 2014 / Used under license from Shutterstock.com

 15-4 ANALYZE A POEM

In the essay that follows, student writer Sherry Van Egdom analyzes the form and meaning of the following poem, "Let Evening Come," by American poet Jane Kenyon. Born in 1947 and raised on a farm near Ann Arbor, Michigan, Kenyon settled in New Hampshire at Eagle Pond Farm after she married fellow poet Donald Hall. During her life, Kenyon struggled with her faith, with depression, and with cancer. At the time of her death in 1995 from leukemia, she was the poet laureate of New Hampshire.

Before you read the student writer's analysis, read the poem aloud to enjoy its sounds, rhythm, images, diction, and comparisons. Then read the piece again to grasp more fully how the poem is structured, what it expresses, and how its ideas might relate to your life. Finally, read Van Egdom's analysis and answer the questions that follow it.

Let Evening Come

Let the light of late afternoon
shine through chinks in the barn, moving
up the bales as the sun moves down.

Let the crickets take up chafing
as a woman takes up her needles
and her yarn. Let evening come.

Let dew collect on the hoe abandoned
in long grass. Let the stars appear
and the moon disclose her silver horn.

Let the fox go back to its sandy den.
Let the wind die down. Let the shed
go black inside. Let evening come.

To the bottle in the ditch, to the scoop
in the oats, to air in the lung
let evening come.

Let it come, as it will, and don't
be afraid. God does not leave us
comfortless, so let evening come.

"Let Evening Come": An Invitation to the Inevitable

1
(A) The work of American poet Jane Kenyon is influenced primarily by the circumstances and experiences of her own life. She writes carefully crafted, deceptively simple poems that connect both to her own life and to the lives of her readers. Growing out of her rural roots and her
(B) struggles with illness, Kenyon's poetry speaks in a still voice of the ordinary things in life in order to wrestle with issues of faith and mortality (Timmerman 163). One of these poems is "Let Evening Come." In this poem, the poet takes the reader on a journey into the night, but she points to hope in the face of that darkness.

2
That movement toward darkness is captured in the stanza form and in the progression of stanzas. Each three-line stanza offers a self-contained moment in the progress of transition from day to night. The first stanza positions the reader in a simple farm setting. Late afternoon fades
(C) into evening without the rumble of highways or the gleam of city lights to distract one's senses from nature, the peace emphasized by the alliteration of "l" in "Let the light of late afternoon." As the sun sinks lower on the horizon, light seeps through cracks in the barn wall, moving up the bales of hay. In the second stanza, the crickets get busy with their nighttime noises. Next, a forgotten farm hoe becomes covered with dew drops, and the silvery stars and moon appear in the sky. In the fourth stanza, complete blackness arrives as a fox returns to its empty den and the silent wind rests at close of day. The alliteration of "d" in "den" and "die down" gives a
(D) sinking, settling feeling (Timmerman 176). In the fifth stanza, a bottle and scoop keep still, untouched in their respective places, while sleep comes upon the human body. In the final stanza, Kenyon encourages readers to

meet this emerging world of darkness without fear.

3
Within this stanza progression, the journey into the night is intensified by strong images, figures of speech, and symbols. The natural rhythm of work and rest on the farm is symbolized by the light that rises and falls in the first stanza (Timmerman 175). The simile comparing the crickets taking up their song to a woman picking up (E) her knitting suggests a homespun energy and conviction. The moon revealing her "silver horn" implies that the moon does not instantly appear with brightness and beauty but rather reveals her majesty slowly as the night comes on. The den, the wind, and the shed in stanza four stress a kind of internal, hidden darkness. Then stanza five focuses on connected objects: the thoughtlessly discarded bottle resting in the ditch, oats and the scoop for feeding, human lungs and the air that fills them. Kenyon mentions the air in the lung after the bottle, ditch, scoop, and oats in order to picture humanity taking its position among the established natural rhythm of the farm (Harris 31).

4
The refrain, "let evening come," is a powerful part of the poem's journey toward darkness, though critics interpret the line differently. Judith Harris suggests that it symbolizes an acceptance of the inevitable: (F) Darkness will envelop the world, and night will surely come, just as mortality will certainly take its toll in time. This acceptance, in turn, acts as a release from the confinement of one's pain and trials in life. Rather than wrestle with something that cannot be beaten or worry about things that must be left undone, Kenyon advises herself and her readers to let go (31). Night intrudes upon the work and events of the day, perhaps leaving them undone just as death might cut a life short and leave it seemingly unfinished.

5
By contrast, John Timmerman argues that "let" is used 12 times in a supplicatory, prayer-like manner (176). The final two lines, in turn, act as a benediction upon the supplications. The comfort of God is as inevitable as

---

(A) The writer introduces the poet and her poetry.
(B) Narrowing her focus to the specific poem, the writer states her thesis.
(C) She begins her analysis by explaining the stanza structure and progression.
(D) The writer shows attention to the poem's fine details and to secondary sources on the poem.

(E) She advances her reading of the poem by exploring images, comparisons, and symbols: the poem's "imaginative logic."
(F) The writer compares possible interpretations of a central, repeated statement in the poem.

the evening, so cling to faith and hope, and let evening come. Although the Comforter is mentioned only in the last two lines, that statement of faith encourages readers to find a spiritual comfort in spite of the coming of the night.

6   When asked how she came to write "Let Evening
(G) Come," Jane Kenyon replied that it was a redemptive poem given to her by the Holy Ghost. When there could be *nothing*—a great darkness and despair, there is a great *mystery* of love, kindness, and beauty (Moyers 238). In the poem's calm journey into the night, Kenyon confronts darkness and suffering with a certain enduring beauty and hope (Timmerman 161). Death will come, but there remains divine comfort. "Let Evening Come" encourages readers to release their grip on the temporary and pay attention to the Comforter, who reveals Himself both day and night.

Note: The Works Cited page is not shown. For sample pages, see MLA (page 286) and APA (page 320).

(G) In her conclusion, the writer offers the poet's explanation of the poem's origin and then expands on the thesis.

Reading for Better Writing

1. Review the opening and closing paragraphs of the essay. How do they create a framework for the writer's analysis of the poem?

2. On which elements of the poem does the writer focus? Does this approach make sense for her analysis? Explain.

3. In her essay, the writer refers to the poet's life and to ideas from secondary sources. Do these references work well with her analysis? Why or why not?

4. Read the essay "Four Ways to Talk About Literature" on pages 168–170. Which approach does the student writer use to analyze Kenyon's poem? Does this approach make sense? How might another approach interpret the poem differently?

 15-5 UNDERSTAND AND USE LITERARY TERMS

Your analysis of novels, poems, plays, and films will be deeper and more sophisticated if you understand the most common literary terms.

Allusion is a reference to a person, a place, or an event in history, literature, or popular culture.

Analogy is a comparison of two or more similar objects, suggesting that if they are alike in certain respects, they will probably be alike in other ways, too.

Anecdote is a short summary of an interesting or humorous, often biographical incident or event.

Antagonist is the person or thing actively working against the protagonist, or hero.

Climax is the turning point, an intense moment characterized by a key event, discovery, or decision.

Conflict is the problem or struggle in a story that triggers the action. There are five basic types of conflict:

- **Person versus person:** One character in a story is in conflict with one or more of the other characters.
- **Person versus society:** A character is in conflict with some element of society: the school, the law, the accepted way of doing things, and so on.
- **Person versus self:** A character faces conflicting inner choices.
- **Person versus nature:** A character is in conflict with some natural happening: a snowstorm, an avalanche, the bitter cold, or any other element of nature.
- **Person versus fate:** A character must battle what seems to be an uncontrollable problem. Whenever the conflict is a strange or unbelievable coincidence, the conflict can be attributed to fate.

Denouement is the outcome of a play or story. See *Resolution.*

Diction is an author's choice of words based on their correctness or effectiveness.

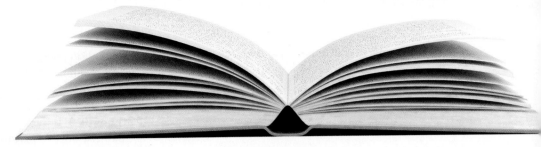

- **Archaic** words are old-fashioned and no longer sound natural when used, such as "I believe thee not" for "I don't believe you."
- **Colloquialism** is an expression that is usually accepted in informal situations and certain locations, as in "He really grinds my beans."
- **Heightened** language uses vocabulary and sentence constructions that produce a stylized effect unlike that of standard speech or writing, as in much poetry and poetic prose.
- **Profanity** is language that shows disrespect for someone or something regarded as sacred.
- **Slang** is the everyday language used by group members among themselves.
- **Trite** expressions lack depth or originality, or are overworked or not worth mentioning.
- **Vulgarity** is language that is generally considered common, crude, gross, and, at times, offensive. It is sometimes used in fiction, plays, and films to add realism.

Exposition is the introductory section of a story or play. Typically, the setting, main characters, and themes are introduced, and the action is initiated.

Falling action is the action of a play or story that follows the climax and shows the characters dealing with the climactic event or decision.

Figure of speech is a literary device used to create a special effect or to describe something in a fresh way. The box that follows describes common figures of speech.

- **Antithesis** is an opposition, or contrast, of ideas.

  "It was the best of times, it was the worst of times, it was the age of wisdom, it was the age of foolishness . . ."
  — Charles Dickens, *A Tale of Two Cities*

- **Hyperbole** (hi-pur´ ba-lee) is an extreme exaggeration or overstatement.

  "I have seen this river so wide it had only one bank."
  —Mark Twain, *Life on the Mississippi*

- **Metaphor** is a comparison of two unlike things in which no word of comparison (*as* or *like*) is used: "Life is a banquet."
- **Metonymy** (ma-ton´a-mee) is the substituting of one term for another that is closely related to it, but not a literal restatement.

  "Friends, Romans, countrymen, lend me your ears." (The request is for the attention of those assembled, not literally their ears.)

- **Personification** is a device in which the author speaks of or describes an animal, object, or idea as if it were a person: "The rock stubbornly refused to move."
- **Simile** is a comparison of two unlike things in which *like* or *as* is used.

  "She stood in front of the altar, shaking like a freshly caught trout."
  —Maya Angelou,
  I Know Why the Caged Bird Sings

- **Understatement** is stating an idea with restraint, often for humorous effect. Mark Twain described Aunt Polly as being "prejudiced against snakes." (Because she hated snakes, this way of saying so is understatement.)

Genre refers to a category or type of literature based on its style, form, and content. The mystery novel is a literary genre.

Imagery refers to words or phrases that a writer uses to appeal to the reader's senses.

  "The sky was dark and gloomy, the air was damp and raw, the streets were wet and sloppy."
  —Charles Dickens, *The Pickwick Paper*

Irony is a deliberate discrepancy in meaning or in the way something is understood. There are three kinds of irony:

- **Dramatic irony**, in which the reader or the audience sees a character's mistakes or misunderstandings, but the character does not

- **Verbal irony,** in which the writer says one thing and means another
- **Irony of situation,** in which there is a great difference between the purpose of a particular action and the result

Mood is the feeling that a piece of literature arouses in the reader: *happiness, sadness, peacefulness, anxiety,* and so forth.

Paradox is a statement that seems contrary to common sense yet may, in fact, be true: "The coach considered this a good loss."

Plot is the action or sequence of events in a story. It is usually a series of related incidents that build upon one another as the story develops. There are five basic elements in a plot line: *exposition, rising action, climax, falling action,* and *resolution.*

resolution comes after the climax and falling action and is intended to bring the story to a satisfactory end.

Rising action is the series of conflicts or struggles that builds a story or play to a fulfilling climax.

Satire is a literary tone used to ridicule or make fun of human vice or weakness, often with the intent of correcting, or changing, the subject of the satiric attack.

Setting is the time and place in which the action of a literary work occurs.

Structure is the form or organization a writer uses for her or his literary work. A great number of possible forms are used regularly in literature: parable, fable, romance, satire, and so on.

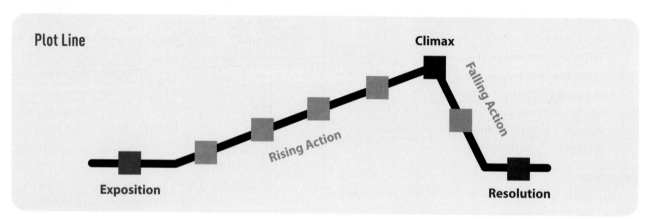

Plot Line

Climax

Rising Action

Falling Action

Exposition

Resolution

Point of view is the vantage point from which the story unfolds.
- In the **first-person** point of view, the story is told by one of the characters: "I stepped into the darkened room and felt myself go cold."
- In the **third-person** point of view, the story is told by someone outside the story: "He stepped into the darkened room and felt himself go cold."
- **Third-person** narrations can be *omniscient,* meaning that the narrator has access to the thoughts of all the characters, or *limited,* meaning that the narrator focuses on the inner life of one central character.

Protagonist is the main character of the story.

Resolution (or *denouement*) is the portion of the play or story in which the problem is solved. The

Style refers to how the author uses words, phrases, and sentences to form his or her ideas. Style is also thought of as the qualities that distinguish one writer's work from the work of others.

Symbol is a person, a place, a thing, or an event used to represent something else. For example, the dove is a symbol of peace.

Theme is the statement about life that a particular work shares with readers. In stories written for children, the theme is often spelled out clearly at the end. In more complex literature, the theme will be implied, not stated.

Tone is the overall feeling, or effect, created by a writer's use of words. This feeling may be serious, mock-serious, humorous, satiric, and so on.

Poetry Terms

Alliteration is the repetition of initial consonant sounds in words, such as "rough and ready."

Assonance is the repetition of vowel sounds without the repetition of consonants.

Blank verse is an unrhymed form of poetry. Each line normally consists of 10 syllables in which every other syllable, beginning with the second, is stressed (iambic pentameter).

Consonance is the repetition of consonant sounds.

> "...and high school girls with clear-skin smiles..."
>
> —Janis Ian, "At Seventeen"

Foot is the smallest repeated pattern of stressed and unstressed syllables in a poetic line. (See *Verse*.)

- **Iambic** an unstressed followed by a stressed syllable (re-peat´)
- **Anapestic:** two unstressed followed by a stressed syllable (in-ter-rupt´)
- **Trochaic:** a stressed followed by an unstressed syllable (old´-er)
- **Dactylic:** a stressed followed by two unstressed syllables (o´-pen-ly)
- **Spondaic:** two stressed syllables (heart´-break´)
- **Pyrrhic:** two unstressed syllables (Pyrrhic seldom appears by itself.)

Onomatopoeia is the use of a word whose sound suggests its meaning, as in *clang* and *buzz*.

Refrain is the repetition of a line or phrase of a poem at regular intervals, especially at the end of each stanza. A song's refrain may be called the *chorus*.

Rhythm is the ordered or free occurrences of stressed syllables in poetry. Ordered or regular rhythm is called *meter*. Irregularly patterned rhythm is called *free verse*.

Stanza is a division of poetry named for the number of lines it contains:

- **Couplet:** two-line stanza
- **Triplet:** three-line stanza
- **Quatrain:** four-line stanza
- **Quintet:** five-line stanza
- **Sestet:** six-line stanza
- **Septet:** seven-line stanza
- **Octave:** eight-line stanza

Verse is a metric line of poetry. It is named according to the kind and number of feet composing it. (See *Foot*.)

- **Monometer:** one foot
- **Dimeter:** two feet
- **Trimeter:** three feet
- **Tetrameter:** four feet
- **Pentameter:** five feet
- **Hexameter:** six feet
- **Heptameter:** seven feet
- **Octometer:** eight feet

WRITE A LITERARY ANALYSIS

Writing Guidelines

Pressmaster, 2014 / Used under license from Shutterstock.com

Planning

1 Select a topic. Choose a literary work with which you are familiar or that you are willing to learn about.

2 Understand the work. Experience it thoughtfully (two or three times, if possible), looking carefully at its content, form, and overall effect.

- For plays and films, examine the plot, props, setting, characters, dialogue, lighting, costumes, sound effects, music, acting, and directing.
- For novels and short stories, focus on point of view, plot, setting, characters, style, diction, symbols, and theme. (See pages 176–178.)
- For poems, examine diction, tone, sound patterns, figures of speech (e.g., metaphors), symbolism, irony, structure, genre, and theme. (See page 179.)

3 Develop a focus and approach. Take notes on what you experience, using the list above to guide you. Seek to understand the whole work before you analyze the parts, exploring your ideas and digging deeply through freewriting and annotating. Select a dimension of the work as a focus, considering what approach to analyzing that element might work. (See "Four Ways to Talk About Literature" on pages 168–170.) In addition, consider what interpretive questions you want to answer in your analysis, and then consider how specific modes of analysis (definition, classification, process, comparison-contrast,

cause-effect) might help you answer these questions. Refer to the instruction in chapters 10–14 as needed.

4 Organize your thoughts. Review the notes that you took as you analyzed the work. What key insights has your analysis led you to see? Make a key insight your thesis, and then organize supporting points logically in an outline.

Drafting

5 Write the first draft.

- **Opening:** Use ideas like the following to gain your readers' attention, identify your topic, narrow the focus, and state your thesis:
  - Summarize your subject briefly. Include the title, the writer's name, and the literary form or performance.

    > **Example:** In her poem "Let Evening Come," Jane Kenyon points to hope in the face of death.

  - Start with a quotation from the work and then comment on its importance.
  - Explain the writer's purpose and how well she or he achieves it.
  - Open with a general statement about the writer's style or aesthetic process.

    > **Example:** The work of American poet Jane Kenyon is influenced primarily by the circumstances and experiences of her own life.

  - Begin with a general statement about the plot or performance.

    > **Example:** In Stephen Spielberg's movie *War of the Worlds*, Ray Ferrier and his two children flee from their New Jersey home in a stolen minivan.

  - Assert your thesis. State the key insight about the work that your analysis has revealed—the insight your essay will seek to support.

- **Middle:** Develop or support your focus by following this pattern:
  - State the main points, relating them clearly to the focus of your essay.
  - Support each main point with specific details or direct quotations.
  - Explain how these details prove your point.

- **Conclusion:** Tie key points together and assert your thesis or evaluation in a fresh way, leaving readers with a sense of the larger significance of your analysis.

Revising

6 Improve the ideas, organization, and voice.
Review your draft for its overall content and tone. Ask a classmate or writing-center tutor for help, if appropriate.

- **Ideas:** Does the essay show clear and deep insight into specific elements of the text or performance? Is that insight effectively developed with specific references to the work itself?
- **Organization:** Does the opening effectively engage the reader, introduce the text, and focus attention on an element or issue? Does the middle carefully work through a "reading" of the work? Does the conclusion reaffirm the insight into the work and expand the reader's understanding?
- **Voice:** Does the tone convey a controlled, measured interest in the text? Is the analytical attitude confident but reasonable?

Editing

7 Edit and proofread the essay by checking issues like these:

- **Words:** Language, especially the terminology, is precise and clear.
- **Sentences:** Constructions flow smoothly and are varied in length and structure; quotations are effectively integrated into sentence syntax.
- **Correctness:** The copy includes no errors in spelling, usage, punctuation, grammar, or mechanics.
- **Design:** The page design is correctly formatted and attractive; references are properly documented according to the required system (e.g., MLA).

Publishing

8 Publish your essay. Submit your essay to your instructor, but consider other ways of sharing your insights about this work or writer—blogging, submitting a review to a periodical (print or online), or leading classmates in a discussion (e.g., book club, post-performance meeting).

Cross-Curricular Connections

- Obviously, literary analyses happen most often in literature courses; however, instructors in a number of disciplines (e.g., history, psychology, health sciences, social work, and environmental studies) may turn to poetry, fiction, plays, and films as a means of deepening course content. Doing so often gets at the human dimension and ethical complexity of the subject matter in question. As you progress in your field of study, look for connections between literature and your courses.

- The principles in this chapter focus on literature, but they might be expanded to include analyses of music, painting, sculpture, and so on. Depending on your interests and your field of study, consider ways that you can transfer the principles here to other art forms.

Critical-Thinking and Writing Activities

1. Get a copy of "Good Country People," read the story, write your own analysis, and share the essay with your class.
2. Review "Let Evening Come" and write your own analysis of the poem. Read your essay to the class and discuss how its style and content compare with that of the essay on pages 175–176.
3. Choose a film and watch it critically, preferably twice. Then find two reviews of the film, note their theses and supporting evidence, and write an essay in which you evaluate why the reviews are (or are not) informed, insightful, and fair.

STUDY TOOLS 15

LOCATED AT BACK OF THE TEXTBOOK
- ☐ Tear-Out Chapter Review Card

LOCATED AT WWW.CENGAGEBRAIN.COM/LOGIN
- ☐ Chapter eBook
- ☐ Graded quizzes and a practice quiz generator
- ☐ Videos: Writer Interviews
- ☐ Tutorials
- ☐ Flashcards
- ☐ Cengage Learning Write Experience
- ☐ Interactive activities

16 | Strategies for Argumentation and Persuasion

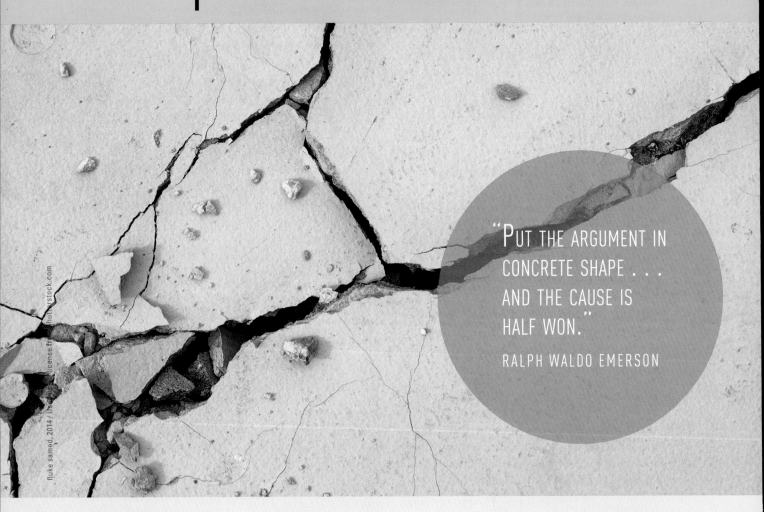

"PUT THE ARGUMENT IN CONCRETE SHAPE . . . AND THE CAUSE IS HALF WON."

RALPH WALDO EMERSON

fluke samed, 2014 / Used under license from Shutterstock.com

LEARNING OBJECTIVES

16-1 Understand how to build an argument.

16-2 Prepare your argument.

16-3 Make and qualify your claims.

16-4 Support your claims.

16-5 Identify and avoid logical fallacies.

16-6 Engage the opposition.

16-7 Use appropriate appeals.

After you finish
this chapter
go to
PAGE 193 for STUDY TOOLS

"I wasn't convinced." "I just didn't buy it." Maybe you've said something similar while watching a political debate, viewing a TV ad, or discussing an issue in class or at work. You simply didn't find the argument logical or convincing.

College is a place where big issues get argued out—in class and out. To participate in that dialogue, you must be able to read and listen to others' arguments, analyze them, and build your own.

This chapter will help you do that. It explains what argumentation is, how to identify weak arguments, and how to construct strong ones. The three ensuing chapters then explain and model three forms of written argumentation: taking a position, persuading readers to act, and proposing a solution.

16-1 UNDERSTAND HOW TO BUILD AN ARGUMENT

What is an argument?
Formally, an *argument* is a series of statements arranged in a logical sequence, supported with sound evidence, and expressed powerfully so as to sway your reader or listener. Arguments appear in a variety of places:

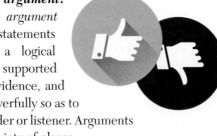

- A research paper about email surveillance by the FBI.
- An analysis of "Good Country People" (short story) or *The Poisonwood Bible* (novel).
- A debate about the ethics of transferring copyrighted music over the Internet.

16-1a Follow a Process

Step 1: Consider your audience, purpose, and topic.

▶ **Identify your audience and purpose.** Who is your audience and what is your goal? Do you want to take a position, persuade readers to act, or offer a solution?

▶ **Generate ideas and gather solid evidence.** You can't base an argument on opinions. Find accurate, pertinent information about the issue and uncover all viewpoints on it.

▶ **Develop a line of reasoning.** To be effective, you need to link your ideas in a clear, logical sequence.

Step 2: Make and qualify your claim.

▶ **Draw reasonable conclusions from the evidence.** State your claim (a debatable idea) as the central point for which you will argue. For example, you might assert that something is true, has value, or should be done.

▶ **Add qualifiers.** Words such as "typically" and "sometimes" soften your claim, making it more reasonable and acceptable.

Step 3: Support your claim.

▶ **Support each point in your claim** with solid evidence.

▶ **Identify logical fallacies.** Test your thinking for errors in logic (see pages 188–191).

Step 4: Engage the opposition.

▶ **Make concessions,** if needed, by granting points to the opposition.

▶ **Develop rebuttals** that expose the weaknesses of the opposition's position, whenever possible.

▶ **Use appropriate appeals**—emotional "tugs" that ethically and logically help readers see your argument as convincing.

16-2 PREPARE YOUR ARGUMENT

An argument is a reason or chain of reasons used to support a claim. To use argumentation well, you need to know how to draw logical conclusions from sound evidence. Preparing an effective argument involves a number of specific steps, starting with those discussed below.

16-2a Consider the Situation

- **Clearly identify your purpose and audience.** This step is essential for all writing but especially true when building an argument. (See pages 30–31.)
- **Consider a range of ideas** to broaden your understanding of the issue and to help focus your thinking on a particular viewpoint. (See pages 184–185.)
- **Gather sound evidence** to support your viewpoint. (See pages 186–188.)

16-2b Develop a Line of Reasoning

Argumentative writing requires a clear line of reasoning with each point logically supporting your argument. Develop the line of reasoning as you study the issue, or use either of the following outlines as a guide.

Sample Argumentative Outlines

Outline 1:

Present your supporting arguments, then address counterarguments, and conclude with the strongest argument.

Introduction: question, concern, or claim
1. Strong argument-supporting claim
   - Discussion and support
2. Other argument-supporting claims
   - Discussion of and support for each argument
3. Objections, concerns, and counterarguments
   - Discussion, concessions, answers, and rebuttals
4. Strongest argument-supporting claim
   - Discussion and support

Conclusion: argument consolidated—claim reinforced

Outline 2:

Address the arguments and counterarguments point by point.

Introduction: question, concern, or claim
1. Strong argument-supporting claim
   - Discussion and support
   - Counterarguments, concessions, and rebuttals
2. Other argument-supporting claims
   - For each argument, discussion and support
   - For each argument, counterarguments, concessions, and rebuttals
3. Strongest argument-supporting claim
   - Discussion and support
   - Counterarguments, concessions, and rebuttals

Conclusion: argument consolidated—claim reinforced

16-3 MAKE AND QUALIFY YOUR CLAIMS

An argument centers on a claim—a debatable statement. That claim is the thesis, or key point you wish to explain and defend so well that readers agree with it. A strong claim has the following traits:

- **It's clearly arguable**—it can be vigorously debated.
- **It's defendable**—it can be supported with sufficient arguments and evidence.
- **It's responsible**—it takes an ethically sound position.
- **It's understandable**—it uses clear terms and defines key words.
- **It's interesting**—it is challenging and worth discussing, not bland and easily accepted.

16-3a Distinguish Claims from Facts and Opinions

A claim is a conclusion drawn from logical thought and reliable evidence. A fact, in contrast, is a statement that can be checked for accuracy. An opinion is a personally held taste or attitude. A claim can be debated, but a fact or an opinion cannot While the fact's accuracy can easily be checked, the opinion statement simply offers a personal feeling. Conversely, the claim states an idea that can be supported with reasoning and evidence.

> **Fact:** *The Fault in Our Stars* is a 2014 film directed by Josh Boone and based on the 2012 novel by John Green.
>
> **Opinion:** I liked the movie almost as much as the book.
>
> **Claim:** While the film version of *The Fault in Our Stars* does not completely follow the novel's plot, the film does faithfully capture the spirit of Green's novel.

16-3b Distinguish Three Types of Claims

Truth, value, and policy—these types of claims are made in an argument. The differences among them are important because each type has a distinct goal.

Claims of truth state that something is or is not the case. As a writer, you want readers to accept your claim as trustworthy.

> The Arctic ice cap will begin to disappear as early as 2050.
>
> The cholesterol in eggs is not as dangerous as previously feared.

Comment: Avoid statements that are (1) obviously true or (2) impossible to prove. Also, truth claims must be argued carefully because accepting them (or not) can have serious consequences.

> **Sample Essay:** "Nuclear Is Not the Answer" by Alyssa Woudstra, pages 196–198.

Claims of value state that something does or does not have worth. As a writer, you want readers to accept your judgment.

> Volunteer reading tutors provide a valuable service.
>
> Many music videos fail to present positive images of women.

Comment: Claims of value must be supported by referring to a known standard or by establishing an agreed-upon standard. To avoid making biased claims, base your judgments on the known standard, not on your feelings.

> **Sample Essay:** "Our Wealth: Where Is It Taking Us?" pages 208–210

Claims of policy state that something ought or ought not to be done. As a writer, you want readers to approve your course of action.

> Special taxes should be placed on gas-guzzling SUVs.
>
> The developer should not be allowed to fill in the pond where the endangered tiger salamander lives.

Comment: Policy claims focus on action. To arrive at them, you must often first establish certain truths and values; thus an argument over policy may include both truth and value claims.

> **Sample Essay:** "In Africa, AIDS Has a Woman's Face," pages 214–215

16-3c Develop Supportable Claims

An effective claim balances confidence with common sense. Follow these tips:

Avoid all-or-nothing, extreme claims. Propositions using words that are overly positive or negative—such as *all, best, never,* and *worst*—may be difficult to support. Statements that leave no room for exceptions are easy to attack.

> **Extreme:** All people charged even once for DUI should never be allowed to drive again.

Make a truly meaningful claim. Avoid claims that are obvious, trivial, or unsupportable. None is worth the energy needed to argue the point.

> **Obvious:** College athletes sometimes receive special treatment.
>
> **Trivial:** The College Rec Center is a good place to get fit.
>
> **Unsupportable:** Athletics are irrelevant to college life.

Use qualifiers to temper your claims. Qualifiers are words or phrases that make claims more reasonable. Notice the difference between these two claims:

Unqualified: Star athletes take far too many academic shortcuts.

Qualified: Some star athletes take improper academic shortcuts.

 TIP The "qualified" claim is easier to defend because it narrows the focus and leaves room for exceptions. Use qualifier words like these:

almost	maybe	some
frequently	might	tends to
likely	often	typically
many	probably	usually

16-4 SUPPORT YOUR CLAIMS

A claim stands or falls on its support. It's not the popular strength of your claim that matters, but rather the strength of your reasoning and evidence. To develop strong support, consider how to select and use evidence.

16-4a Gather Evidence

Several types of evidence can support claims. To make good choices, review each type, as well as its strengths and weaknesses.

Observations and anecdotes share what people (including you) have seen, heard, smelled, touched, tasted, and experienced. Such evidence offers an "eyewitness" perspective shaped by the observer's viewpoint, which can be powerful but may also prove narrow and subjective.

Most of us have closets full of clothes: jeans, sweaters, khakis, T-shirts, and shoes for every occasion.

Statistics offer concrete numbers about a topic. Numbers don't "speak for themselves," however. They need to be interpreted and compared properly—not slanted or taken out of context. They also need to be up-to-date, relevant, and accurate.

Pennsylvania spends $30 million annually in deer-related costs.

Wisconsin has an estimated annual loss of $37 million for crop damage alone.

Tests and experiments provide hard data developed through the scientific method, data that must nevertheless be carefully studied and properly interpreted.

According to the two scientists, the rats with unlimited access to the functional running wheel ran each day and gradually increased the amount of running; in addition, they started to eat less.

Graphics provide information in visual form—from simple tables to more complex charts, maps, drawings, and photographs. When poorly done, however, graphics can distort the truth.

Analogies compare two things, creating clarity by drawing parallels. However, every analogy breaks down if pushed too far.

It is obvious today that America has defaulted on this promissory note insofar as her citizens of color are concerned. Instead of honoring this sacred obligation, America has given the Negro people a bad check; a check which has come back marked "insufficient funds." But we refuse to believe that the bank of justice is bankrupt.
—Martin Luther King, Jr. (See page 210.)

Expert testimony offers insights from an authority on the topic. Such testimony always has limits: Experts don't know it all, and they work from distinct perspectives, which means that they can disagree.

One specialist opposed to drilling is David Klein, a professor at the Institute of Arctic Biology at the University of Alaska–Fairbanks. Klein argues that if the oil industry opens up the ANWR for drilling, the number of caribou will likely decrease because the calving locations will change.

Illustrations, examples, and demonstrations support general claims with specific instances, making such statements seem concrete and observable. Of course, an example may not be your best support if it isn't familiar.

Think about how differently one can frame Rosa Parks' historic action. In prevailing myth, Parks—a holy innocent—acts almost on whim. . . . The real story is more empowering: It suggests that change is the product of deliberate, incremental action.

Analyses examine parts of a topic through thought patterns—cause/effect, compare/contrast, classification, process, or definition. Such analysis helps make sense of a topic's complexity but muddles the topic when poorly done.

> If colorism lives underground, its effects are very real. Darker-skinned African-American defendants are more than twice as likely to receive the death penalty as lighter-skinned African-American defendants for crimes of equivalent seriousness. . . . (See page 150.)

Predictions offer insights into possible outcomes or consequences by forecasting what might happen under certain conditions. Like weather forecasting, predicting can be tricky. To be plausible, a prediction must be rooted in a logical analysis of present facts.

> While agroterrorist diseases would have little direct effect on people's health, they would be devastating to the agricultural economy, in part because of the many different diseases that could be used in an attack.

16-4b Use Evidence

Finding evidence is one thing; using it well is another. To marshal evidence in support of your claim, follow three guidelines:

1. Go for quality and variety, not just quantity.

More evidence is not necessarily better. Instead, support your points with sound evidence in different forms. Quality evidence is . . .

- *accurate:* correct and verifiable in each detail.
- *complete:* filled with pertinent facts.
- *concrete:* filled with specifics.
- *relevant:* clearly related to the claim.
- *current:* reliably up-to-date.
- *authoritative:* backed by expertise, training, and knowledge.
- *appealing:* able to influence readers.

2. Use inductive and deductive patterns of logic.

Depending on your purpose, use inductive or deductive reasoning. (See pages 10–11.)

Induction: Inductive reasoning works from the particular toward general conclusions. In a persuasive essay using induction, look at facts first, find a pattern in them, and then lead the reader to your conclusion.

> For example, in "Nuclear Is Not the Answer," Alyssa Woudstra first examines the benefits and liabilities of nuclear energy versus fossil fuels before asserting her claim that using the latter is a better choice. (See pages 196–198.)

Deduction: Deductive reasoning—the opposite of inductive reasoning—starts from accepted truths and applies them to a new situation so as to reach a conclusion about it. For deduction to be sound, be sure the starting principles or facts are true, the new situation is accurately described, and the application is logical.

> For example, Martin Luther King opened his 1963 "I Have a Dream" speech by noting that more than 100 years earlier, the Emancipation Proclamation promised African Americans justice and freedom. He then described the continuing unjust treatment of African Americans, deducing that the promises in the Proclamation remained unfulfilled. (See pages 210–213.)

3. Reason using valid warrants.

To make sense, claims and their supporting reasons must have a logical connection. That connection is called the warrant—the often unspoken thinking used to relate the reasoning to the claim. If warrants are good, arguments hold water; if warrants are faulty, then arguments break down. In other words, beware of faulty assumptions.

Check the short argument outlined below. Which of the warrants seem reasonable and strong, and which seem weak? Where does the argument fail?

> **Reasoning:** If current trends in water usage continue, the reservoir will be empty in two years.
>
> **Claim:** Therefore, Emeryville should immediately shut down its public swimming pools.

Unstated Warrants or Assumptions:

> It is not good for the reservoir to be empty.
>
> The swimming pools draw significant amounts of water from the reservoir.
>
> Emptying the pools would help raise the level of the reservoir.
>
> No other action would better prevent the reservoir from emptying.
>
> It is worse to have an empty reservoir than an empty swimming pool.

Insight: Because an argument is no stronger than its warrants, you must make sure that your reasoning clearly and logically supports your claims.

16-5 IDENTIFY AND AVOID LOGICAL FALLACIES

Fallacies are false arguments—that is, bits of fuzzy, dishonest, or incomplete thinking. They may crop up in your own thinking, in your opposition's thinking, or in such public "arguments" as ads, political appeals, and talk shows. Because fallacies may sway an unsuspecting audience, they are dangerously persuasive. By learning to recognize fallacies, however, you may identify them in opposing arguments and eliminate them from your own writing. In this section, logical fallacies are grouped according to how they falsify an argument.

16-5a Distorting the Issue

The following fallacies falsify an argument by twisting the logical framework.

Bare Assertion The most basic way to distort an issue is to deny that it exists. This fallacy claims, "That's just how it is."

> The private ownership of handguns is a constitutional right. (Objection: The claim shuts off discussion of the U.S. Constitution or the reasons for regulation.)

Begging the Question Also known as circular reasoning, this fallacy arises from assuming in the basis of your argument the very point you need to prove.

> We don't need a useless film series when every third student owns a DVD player or VCR. (Objection: There may be uses for a public film series that private

video viewing can't provide. The word "useless" begs the question.)

Oversimplification This fallacy reduces complexity to simplicity. Beware of phrases like "It's a simple question of." Serious issues are rarely simple.

> Capital punishment is a simple question of protecting society.

Either/Or Thinking Also known as black-and-white thinking, this fallacy reduces all options to two extremes. Frequently, it derives from a clear bias.

> Either this community develops light-rail transportation, or the community will not grow in the future. (Objection: The claim ignores the possibility that growth may occur through other means.)

Complex Question Sometimes by phrasing a question a certain way, a person ignores or covers up a more basic question.

> Why can't we bring down the prices that corrupt gas stations are charging? (Objection: This question ignores a more basic question—"Are gas stations really corrupt?")

Straw Man In this fallacy, the writer argues against a claim that is easily refuted. Typically, such a claim exaggerates or misrepresents the opponents' position.

> Those who oppose euthanasia must believe that the terminally ill deserve to suffer.

16-5b Sabotaging the Argument

These fallacies falsify the argument by twisting it. They destroy reason and replace it with something hollow or misleading.

Red Herring This strange term comes from the practice of dragging a stinky fish across a trail to throw tracking dogs off the scent. When a person puts forth a volatile idea that pulls readers away from the real issue, readers become distracted. Suppose the argument addresses drilling for oil in the Arctic National Wildlife Refuge (ANWR) of

Alaska, and the writer begins with this statement:

> In 1989, the infamous oil spill of the Exxon Valdez led to massive animal deaths and enormous environmental degradation of the coastline. (Objection: Introducing this notorious oil spill distracts from the real issue—how oil drilling will affect the ANWR.)

Misuse of Humor Jokes, satire, and irony can lighten the mood and highlight a truth; when humor distracts or mocks, however, it undercuts the argument. What effect would the mocking tone of this statement have in an argument about tanning beds in health clubs?

> People who use tanning beds will just turn into wrinkled old prunes or leathery sun-dried tomatoes!

Appeal to Pity This fallacy engages in a misleading tug on the heartstrings. Instead of using a measured emotional appeal, an appeal to pity seeks to manipulate the audience into agreement.

> Affirmative action policies ruined this young man's life. Because of them, he was denied admission to Centerville College.

Use of Threats A simple but unethical way of sabotaging an argument is to threaten opponents. More often than not, a threat is merely implied: "If you don't accept my argument, you'll regret it."

> If we don't immediately start drilling for oil in the ANWR, you will soon face hour-long lines at gas stations from New York to California.

Bandwagon Mentality Someone implies that a claim cannot be true because a majority of people are opposed to it, or it must be true because a majority support it. (History shows that people in the minority have often had the better argument.) At its worst, such an appeal manipulates people's desire to belong or be accepted.

> It's obvious to intelligent people that cockroaches live only in the apartments of dirty people. (Objection: Based on popular opinion, the claim appeals to a kind of prejudice and ignores scientific evidence about cockroaches.)

Appeal to Popular Sentiment This fallacy consists of associating your position with something popularly loved: the American flag, baseball, apple pie. Appeals to popular sentiment sidestep thought to play on feelings.

> Anyone who has seen *Bambi* could never condone hunting deer.

16-5c Drawing Faulty Conclusions from the Evidence

This group of fallacies falsifies the argument by short-circuiting proper logic in favor of assumptions or faulty thinking.

Appeal to Ignorance
This fallacy suggests that because no one has proven a particular claim, it must be false; or, because no one has disproven a claim, it must be true. Appeals to ignorance unfairly shift the burden of proof onto someone else.

> Flying saucers are real. No scientific explanation has ruled them out.

Hasty or Broad Generalization Such a claim is based on too little evidence or allows no exceptions. In jumping to a conclusion, the writer may use intensifiers such as *all*, *every*, or *never*.

> Today's voters spend too little time reading and too much time being taken in by 30-second sound bites. (Objection: Quite a few voters may, in fact, spend too little time reading about the issues, but it is unfair to suggest that this is true of everyone.)

False Cause This well-known fallacy confuses sequence with causation: If A comes before B, A must have caused B. However, A may be one of several causes, or A and B may be only loosely related, or the connection between A and B may be entirely coincidental.

> Since that new school opened, drug use among young people has skyrocketed. Better that the school had never been built.

Slippery Slope This fallacy argues that a single step will start an unstoppable chain of events. While such a slide may occur, the prediction lacks evidence.

> If we legalize marijuana, it's only a matter of time before hard drugs follow and America becomes a nation of junkies and addicts.

16-5d Misusing Evidence

These fallacies falsify the argument by abusing or distorting the evidence.

Impressing with Numbers In this case, the writer drowns readers in statistics and numbers that overwhelm the readers into agreement. In addition, the numbers haven't been properly interpreted.

> At 35 ppm, CO levels factory-wide are only 10 ppm above the OSHA recommendation, which is 25 ppm. Clearly, that 10 ppm is insignificant in the big picture, and the occasional readings in some areas of between 40 and 80 ppm are aberrations that can safely be ignored. (Objection: The 10 ppm may be significant, and higher readings may indicate real danger.)

Half-Truths A half-truth contains part of but not the whole truth. Because a half-truth leaves out "the rest of the story," the assertion is both true and false simultaneously.

> The new welfare bill is good because it will get people off the public dole. (Objection: This may be true, but the bill may also cause undue suffering for some truly needy individuals.)

Unreliable Testimonial An appeal to authority has force only if the authority is qualified in the proper field. If he or she is not, the testimony is irrelevant. Note that fame is not the same thing as authority.

> On her talk show, Alberta Magnus recently claimed that most pork sold in the United States is tainted. (Objection: Although Magnus may be an articulate talk show host, she is not an expert on food safety.)

Attack Against the Person This fallacy directs attention to a person's character, lifestyle, or beliefs rather than to the issue.

> Would you accept the opinion of a candidate who experimented with drugs in college?

Hypothesis Contrary to Fact This fallacy relies on "if only" thinking. It bases the claim on an assumption of what would have happened if something else had, or had not, happened. Being pure speculation, such a claim cannot be tested.

> If only multiculturalists hadn't pushed through affirmative action, the United States would be a united nation.

False Analogy Sometimes a person will argue that X is good (or bad) because it is like Y. Such an analogy may be valid, but it weakens the argument if the grounds for the comparison are vague or unrelated.

> Don't bother voting in this election; it's a stinking quagmire. (Objection: Comparing the election to a "stinking quagmire" is unclear and exaggerated.)

16-5e Misusing Language

Essentially, all logical fallacies misuse language. However, three fallacies falsify the argument, especially by the misleading use of words.

Obfuscation This fallacy involves using fuzzy terms like *throughput* and *downlink* to muddy the issue. These words may make simple ideas sound more profound than they really are, or they may make false ideas sound true.

> Through the fully functional developmental process of a streamlined target-refractory system, the U.S. military will successfully reprioritize its data throughputs. (Objection: What does this sentence mean?)

Ambiguity Ambiguous statements can be interpreted in two or more opposite ways. Although ambiguity can result from unintentional careless thinking, writers sometimes use ambiguity to obscure a position.

> Many women need to work to support their children through school, but they would be better off at home. (Objection: Does *they* refer to *children* or *women*? What does *better off* mean? These words and phrases can be interpreted in opposite ways.)

Slanted Language By choosing words with strong positive or negative connotations, a writer can draw readers away from the true logic of the argument. Here

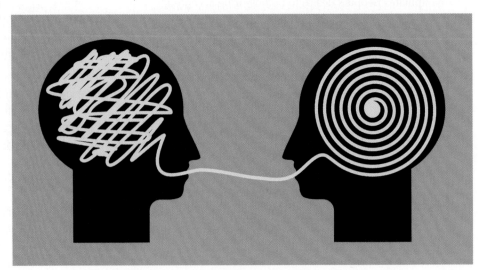

is an example of three synonyms for the word *stubborn* that the philosopher Bertrand Russell once used to illustrate the bias in slanted language:

> I am *firm*. You are *obstinate*. He is *pigheaded*.

16-6 ENGAGE THE OPPOSITION

Think of an argument as an intelligent, lively dialogue with readers. Anticipate their questions, concerns, objections, and counterarguments. Then follow these guidelines.

16-6a Make Concessions

By offering concessions—recognizing points scored by the other side—you acknowledge your argument's limits and the truth of other positions. Paradoxically, such concessions strengthen your overall argument by making it seem more credible. Concede your points graciously, using words such as the following:

Admittedly	I accept
Granted	No doubt
I agree that	Of course
I cannot argue with	Certainly it's the case
It is true that	I concede that
You're right	Perhaps

> While foot-and-mouth disease is not dangerous to humans, other animal diseases are.

16-6b Develop Rebuttals

Even when you concede a point, you can often answer that objection by rebutting it. A good rebuttal is a small, tactful argument aimed at a weak spot in the opposing argument. Try these strategies:

1. **Point out the counterargument's** limits by putting the opposing point in a larger context. Show that the counterargument leaves something important out of the picture.

2. **Tell the other side of the story.** Offer an opposing interpretation of the evidence, or counter with stronger, more reliable, more convincing evidence.

3. **Address logical fallacies in the counterargument.** Check for faulty reasoning or emotional manipulation. For example, if the

counterargument presents a half-truth, offer information that presents "the rest of the story."

> It is true that the Chernobyl accident occurred more than 20 years ago, so safety measures for nuclear reactors have been greatly improved. However, that single accident is still affecting millions of people who were exposed to the radiation. (See pages 196–198.)

16-6c Consolidate Your Claim

After making concessions and rebutting objections, you may need to regroup. Restate your claim so carefully that the weight of your whole argument can rest on it.

> One of these is bovine spongiform encephalopathy, better known as mad-cow disease.

16-7 USE APPROPRIATE APPEALS

For your argument to be persuasive, it must not only be logical, but also "feel right." It must treat readers as real people by appealing to their common sense, hopes, pride, and notion of right and wrong. How do you appeal to all these concerns? Do the following: (1) build credibility, (2) make logical appeals, and (3) focus on readers' needs.

Mike Flippo, 2014 / Used under license from Shutterstock.com

16-7a Build Credibility

A persuasive argument is credible—so trustworthy that readers can change their minds painlessly. To build credibility, observe these rules:

- **Be thoroughly honest.** Demonstrate integrity toward the topic—don't falsify data, spin evidence, or ignore facts. Document your sources and cite them wherever appropriate.
- **Make realistic claims, projections, and**

promises. Avoid emotionally charged statements, pie-in-the-sky forecasts, and undeliverable deals.

- **Develop and maintain trust.** From your first word to your last, develop trust—in your attitude toward the topic, your treatment of readers, and your respect for opposing viewpoints.

16-7b Make Logical Appeals

Arguments stand or fall on their logical strength, but your readers' acceptance of those arguments is often affected more by the emotional appeal of your ideas and evidence. To avoid overly emotional appeals, follow these guidelines:

- **Engage readers positively.** Appeal to their better natures—to their sense of honor, justice, social commitment, altruism, and enlightened self-interest. Avoid appeals geared toward ignorance, prejudice, selfishness, or fear.
- **Use a fitting tone.** Use a tone that is appropriate for the topic, purpose, situation, and audience.
- **Aim to motivate, not manipulate, readers.** While you do want them to accept your viewpoint, it's not a win-at-all-costs situation. Avoid bullying, guilt-tripping, and exaggerated tugs on heartstrings.
- **Don't trash-talk the opposition.** Show tact, respect, and understanding. Focus on issues, not personalities.
- **Use arguments and evidence that readers can understand and appreciate.** If readers find your thinking too complex, too simple, or too strange, you've lost them.

16-7c Focus On Readers' Needs

Instead of playing on readers' emotions, connect your argument with readers'

needs and values. Follow these guidelines:

- **Know your real readers.** Who are they—peers, professors, or fellow citizens? What are their allegiances, their worries, their dreams?
- **Picture readers as resistant.** Accept that your readers, including those inclined to agree with you, need convincing.
- **Use appeals that match needs and values.** Your argument may support or challenge readers' needs and values. To understand those needs, study the pyramid below, which is based on the thinking of psychologist Abraham Maslow. Maslow's hierarchy ranks people's needs on a scale from the most basic to the most complex. The bottom level of the pyramid identifies the most basic needs. The needs progress in complexity as you move up the pyramid. This information can help you connect your argument to your audience's specific needs. For example, if you're writing to argue for more affordable housing for the elderly, you'd argue differently to legislators (whose focus is on helping others) than to the elderly who need the housing (whose focus is on having necessities). Follow these tips and the information in the table on the next page:
  - Use appeals that match the foremost needs and values of your readers.
    - If appropriate, constructively challenge those needs and values.

Self-actualization

Esteem

Love/Belonging

Safety

Physiological

- Phrase your appeals in positive terms.
- After analyzing your readers' needs, choose a persuasive theme for your argument—a positive benefit, advantage, or outcome that readers can expect if they accept your claim.

Reader needs . . .	Use persuasive appeals to . . .
To make the world better by helping others	values and social obligations
To achieve by being good at something, getting recognition	self-fulfillment, status appreciation
To belong by being part of a group	group identity, acceptance
To survive by avoiding threats, having necessities	safety, security, physical needs

⚙ Critical-Thinking and Writing Activities

1. Select an essay from chapters 17–19, "Taking a Position," "Persuading Readers to Act," or "Proposing a Solution." Read the essay carefully. Then describe and evaluate the essay's argumentative strategies by answering the questions below:
   - What is the main claim the writer makes? Is it a claim of truth, value, or policy?
   - Is the claim arguable—that is, is it supportable, qualified, and effectively phrased?
   - What arguments does the writer develop in support of the claim? Are these arguments logical?
   - What types of evidence does the writer provide to support her or his discussion?
   - Is the evidence valid, sufficient, and accurate?
   - Does the writer effectively address questions, alternatives, objections, and counterarguments?

2. Review the essay that you read for the first activity, and then answer the following questions:
   - Describe the writer's tone. Is it engaging?
   - Does the argument seem credible and authoritative? Explain.

3. Find a quality article in a respected journal in your major. Read the article and then answer these questions: What forms of reasoning, appeals, and evidence does the author use? What forms does she or he avoid? Is the reasoning convincing? Why?

4. Browse respected online or print news sources for an opinion column or editorial on a current controversial issue. Examine the strengths and weaknesses of the writer's argument: Does the argument seem credible and authoritative? What forms of reasoning, appeals, and evidence does the author use? What forms does she or he avoid? Does the writing address all major counterclaims?

STUDY TOOLS 16

LOCATED AT BACK OF THE TEXTBOOK
- ☐ Tear-Out Chapter Review Card

LOCATED AT WWW.CENGAGEBRAIN.COM/LOGIN
- ☐ Chapter eBook
- ☐ Graded quizzes and a practice quiz generator
- ☐ Videos: Writer Interviews
- ☐ Tutorials
- ☐ Flashcards
- ☐ Cengage Learning Write Experience
- ☐ Interactive activities

17 | Taking a Position

"THE ULTIMATE MEASURE OF MAN IS NOT WHERE HE STANDS IN MOMENTS OF COMFORT AND CONVENIENCE, BUT WHERE HE STANDS AT TIMES OF CHALLENGE AND CONTROVERSY."

MARTIN LUTHER KING JR.

LEARNING OBJECTIVES

17-1 Understand how to read position papers.

17-2 Develop sound claims with reliable evidence.

17-3 Make concessions and rebut opposing arguments.

17-4 Make effective appeals.

17-5 Write, revise, and edit a logical position paper.

After you finish
this chapter
go to
PAGE 205 for STUDY TOOLS

Sometimes you just have to take a stand. An issue comes up that upsets you or challenges your thinking, and in response, you say, "Okay, this is what I believe, and this is why I believe it."

Learning to read and write position papers enables you to do this. The reading skills help you analyze others' positions, recognize their strengths, and identify their weaknesses. The writing skills help you probe a topic, refine your own perspective on the issues, educate others about the topic, and convince them that your position has value.

This chapter will help you hone both skills. Learning this chapter's writing skills and strategies will help you succeed in the classroom today and in the workplace throughout your career.

17-1 UNDERSTAND HOW TO READ POSITION PAPERS

How should you read a position paper? The instructions below will guide you.

17-1a Consider the Rhetorical Situation for Position Papers

Think first about how the writer uses persuasion to achieve a specific purpose, affect a particular audience, and address a given topic.

- **Purpose:** In most cases, writers produce position papers in order to educate and to persuade: They want (1) to inform you about the nature and relevance of a topic and (2) to persuade you that their position on the topic is the best, most reasonable option.

- **Audience:** A writer may address a variety of readers: people opposed to the writer's position, people uncertain of what position to take, people unaware

that an issue exists, or even people who agree with the writer's position but are looking for sensible reasons. Good writers shape the content, organization, and tone of position essays to effectively address such intended readers.

- **Topic:** The topics addressed in meaningful position papers are debatable issues about which informed people can reasonably disagree. Therefore, as a reader, you will learn more about a paper's topic by focusing not only on the writer's position, but also on the reasoning that she or he uses to develop that position, including her or his attention to alternative positions.

17-1b Consider Qualities of Strong Arguments

When reading a position paper, look for the following:

- **Informed Writing:** The writer has researched the topic thoroughly and understands it fully, including positions other than his or her own.

- **Logical Writing:** The writer presents the topic objectively, describes alternative positions fairly, and takes the position supported by the best evidence and strongest logic. The writing avoids logical fallacies such as oversimplification, either/or thinking, straw-man claims, red-herring assertions, appeals to pity, or attacks against opponents. (For information on these and other fallacies, see pages 188–191.) If the writer uses visuals, they should fairly represent the issue.

- **Engaging Writing:** Rather than quarreling or pontificating, the writer converses with readers by making reasonable concessions, rebutting opposing arguments, and consolidating or refocusing claims. (For details on these strategies, see pages 191–193.)

 Reading Guide: Taking a Position

✔ What is the topic, and is it debatable, stated fairly, and addressed fully?

✔ What are the writer's claims, and are they supported by reliable evidence?

✔ Is the overall argument clear, unified, and free of logical fallacies and manipulative visuals?

✔ Is the tone measured, reasonable, and free of manipulative language?

DEVELOP SOUND CLAIMS WITH RELIABLE EVIDENCE

Student writer Alyssa Woudstra wrote the following essay to take a position on an environmental issue—energy production. A convincing position is built on sound, measured claims supported by clear, reliable evidence. As you read Alyssa's essay, assess whether her claims are sound and her evidence is reliable.

(A) Nuclear Is Not the Answer

SQ3R Survey · Question · Read · Recite · Review

1   In the last decade, it has become popular to be "green" in all areas of life. Celebrities and corporations **(B)** constantly advertise natural cleaning products, fuel-efficient cars, and energy-efficient light bulbs. Governments offer home-improvement grants to people who renovate their homes to include low-flush toilets, weather-proof windows, and additional insulation. Due to climate change and pollution, concern for the environment is rising. One major issue centers on which type of energy production is best for the environment. Nuclear power and fossil fuels are two major methods for energy production, and nuclear power could be seen as the "greener" option. However, the risks of nuclear power far outweigh its benefits, making fossil fuels the safer and more environmentally responsible option.

2   As a significant method of energy production, nuclear power does offer distinct advantages. The Nuclear Energy **(C)** Institute's statistics show that nuclear energy accounted for 11.5 percent of the world's electricity production in 2012, and that as of May 2014, 31 countries were using nuclear power ("Around the World"). This popularity speaks to nuclear power's advantages over fossil fuels. First, nuclear power plants do not release the harmful emissions that coal-burning plants do, so nuclear power does not contribute greatly to global warming (Evans 115). Second, a single nuclear power plant can produce a large amount of energy, making nuclear an efficient source ("Pros and Cons"). In fact, according to Robert Evans, "The amount of thermal energy released from just one kilogram of U235 undergoing fission is equivalent to that obtained by burning some 2.5 million kilograms, or 2,500 tonnes, of coal" (116).

3   Nevertheless, these advantages of nuclear power are outweighed by its disadvantages. Nuclear power plants produce radioactive waste, which is an enormous **(D)** health and safety concern. The waste cannot simply be disposed of but must be carefully stored for hundreds of generations. The isotopes used in nuclear reactions have half-lives of thousands of years. For example, plutonium-239 has a half-life of around 24,000 years (American Assembly 24). This radioactive waste must be stored safely to prevent radiation poisoning, but it would be nearly impossible to do so for that long.

4   A further danger of nuclear power is that while every safety precaution might be in place, it is possible for terrible accidents to happen. The most famous nuclear **(E)** accident took place on April 26, 1986, when reactor number four at the Chernobyl Nuclear Power Plant in the Ukraine, which was then part of the Soviet Union, exploded after a power excursion. That explosion then caused the rest of the plant to explode (Hawks et. al. 98-102). This accident released 100 times more radiation than the bombings of Hiroshima and Nagasaki combined

argus, 2014 / Used under license from Shutterstock.com

(A) The title partly declares the position.
(B) Alyssa starts with common ground and narrows to her position on energy production.
(C) She examines the positives of what she actually opposes.

(D) She turns to the disadvantages of nuclear energy: its risks and dangers.
(E) The writer reminds readers of a historical illustration.

("No More Chernobyls"). Chernobyl's radiation spread all over Europe, affecting people as far away as Romania and Bulgaria, exposing more than 600,000 to the effects of radiation poisoning (Medvedev 194-216). More than 20 years after Chernobyl, people are still dying from cancer that was likely caused by the disaster.

5

(F) It is true that Chernobyl occurred more than 25 years ago, so safety measures for nuclear reactors have since been greatly improved. However, that single accident is still affecting millions of people who were exposed to the radiation. Moreover, the accident had a devastating impact on the environment: Even now, vegetation in the area around Chernobyl is practically non-existent. If more nuclear power plants are built, the risk of similar accidents will rise.

6

Beyond accidents, however, is the possibility of deliberate sabotage in the form of terrorism ("Pros and Cons"). If terrorists wanted to cause mass devastation, they could attack a nuclear power plant or become employees who purposely cause errors to create an explosion. On September 11, 2001, millions of people were affected at once. If a power plant were attacked, it would also affect millions, since it would cause the loss of not only many jobs but also many lives. Moreover, the risk of terrorism also surrounds the nuclear waste left behind after the reactions. Easier to obtain than pure uranium, such waste could be used to build "dirty bombs" (Evans 133).

(F) Alyssa concedes and rebuts a concern.

temiropix, 2014 / Used under license from Shutterstock.com

7

Beyond the risks and dangers of nuclear power, still another argument against it is that it is nonrenewable. Fossil fuels are also nonrenewable, but nuclear power is not an alternative in this way. In their reactors, nuclear power plants use uranium, a rare element. It is estimated that the Earth's supply of uranium will last only 30 to 60 years, depending on how much is actually used in reactors ("Pros and Cons").

8

(G) But is energy from fossil fuels really better than nuclear power? The burning of fossil fuels (including coal, oil, and natural gas) is the most common method of energy production. Like nuclear fuel, fossil fuels are nonrenewable. However, burning fossil fuels, for the time being, is a better option than using nuclear energy. It is true that using fossil fuels has a negative effect on the environment. In order to obtain fossil fuels, much damage is caused to the environment by drilling for oil or mining for coal. Also, burning fossil fuels produces gases that can aggravate respiratory conditions like asthma and emits greenhouse gases that damage the atmosphere. Moreover, particles emitted from smokestacks collect in clouds, causing acid rain (Sweet 25). With oil, spills can contaminate groundwater and surface water, creating risks to animals, plants, and humans.

9

(H) Despite the fact that using fossil fuels involves many risks, it has some advantages over nuclear energy. Significantly, fossil fuels are much less expensive than uranium. Although it is still expensive to access fossil fuels, it is drastically cheaper than the cost of nuclear energy. In addition, if large deposits of coal or oil are found, it will not be necessary to excavate in as many places to retrieve them. Although a larger area would be disturbed, fewer sites would be affected. Also, while fossil fuels are nonrenewable, they may be used wisely, conserving them until a better energy source can be established (Heron).

10

However, perhaps the biggest advantage of fossil fuel energy over nuclear energy lies in the possibility of

---

(G) Alyssa concedes and rebuts a concern.
(H) Alyssa supports her position on fossil fuels by stressing its advantages and calling for improvements.

progress to make current methods more environmentally friendly. At this time, burning coal for power uses only one-third of its potential energy (Heron). If scientists study more efficient uses of the coal, this waste, as well as many health and environmental concerns, could be prevented. For example, burning coal can be made cleaner through electrostatic precipitators. Also known as "smokestack scrubbers," these filters can be used in smokestacks to prevent soot particles from getting into the air. As the soot-filled air passes through the smokestack, it goes through a set of wires that negatively charge the soot particles. As the air continues through the pipe, it passes through positively charged metal plates. The negatively charged soot particles, which are made up mostly of unburned carbon, "stick" to the positively charged plates, and the particle-free air continues out the smokestack. The stuck particles are then either manually scraped or automatically shaken off by the machine itself ("Static Electricity"). If more factories used electrostatic precipitators, a large amount of air pollution would be prevented.

11   Although it is not ideal, burning fossil fuels is still a better option than nuclear power until renewable energy

(I)   sources such as wind, solar, and geothermal power become more available. Clearly, society must continue to work toward greater conservation and use of renewable energy. As stewards of the Earth, all humans should be concerned about the environment. If people continue to use nuclear power, the risks related to accidents, sabotage, and radioactive waste will not only be their responsibility but will also impact their descendants for many generations.

Note: The Works Cited page is not shown. For examples, see MLA (page 286) and APA (page 320).

(I) She restates her position and places it within a larger context of environmental changes.

Reading for Better Writing

1. Woudstra begins her essay by examining extensively an opposing position—support for nuclear energy. How effective is this strategy? How reliable is the evidence?

2. Review how Woudstra supports her position on energy from fossil fuels. How complete and compelling is this support?

3. Two other major energy-related disasters are the BP oil spill in the Gulf of Mexico and the Fukushima Daiichi power-plant meltdown. How might acknowledging these environmental disasters change her essay?

17-3   MAKE CONCESSIONS AND REBUT OPPOSING ARGUMENTS

Eric Foner is a professor of history at Columbia University and the author of numerous publications, including *The Fiery Trial: Abraham Lincoln and American Slavery* and the essay that follows. He published the essay on December 31, 2012, one day before the 150th anniversary of Lincoln's signing of the "Emancipation Proclamation." Note how Foner states his claims, supports them, and rebuts opposing arguments.

The Emancipation of Abe Lincoln

SQ3R   Survey · Question · Read · Recite · Review

One hundred and fifty years ago, on January 1, 1863,   1
Abraham Lincoln presided over the annual White House   **(A)**
New Year's reception. Late that afternoon, he retired to his study to sign the "Emancipation Proclamation." When he took up his pen, his hand was shaking from exhaustion. Briefly, he paused—"I do not want it to appear as if I hesitated," he remarked. Then Lincoln affixed a firm signature to the document.

Like all great historical transformations,   2

(A) The opening introduces the topic: Lincoln's signing of the "Emancipation Proclamation."

(B) emancipation was a process, not a single event. It arose from many causes and was the work of many individuals. It began at the outset of the Civil War, when slaves sought refuge behind Union lines. It did not end until December 1865, with the ratification of the 13th Amendment, which irrevocably abolished slavery throughout the nation.

3 But the Emancipation Proclamation was the crucial
(C) turning point in this story. In a sense, it embodied a double emancipation: for the slaves, since it ensured that if the Union emerged victorious, slavery would perish, and for Lincoln himself, for whom it marked the abandonment of his previous assumptions about how to abolish slavery and the role blacks would play in post-emancipation American life.

4 There is no reason to doubt the sincerity of
(D) Lincoln's statement in 1864 that he had always believed slavery to be wrong. During the first two years of the Civil War, despite insisting that the conflict's aim was preservation of the Union, he devoted considerable energy to a plan for ending slavery inherited from prewar years. Emancipation would be undertaken by state governments, with national financing. It would be gradual, owners would receive monetary compensation and emancipated slaves would be encouraged to find a homeland outside the United States—this last idea known as "colonization."

Lincoln's plan sought to win the cooperation 5
of slave holders in ending slavery. As early as (E)
November 1861, he proposed it to political leaders in Delaware, one of the four border states (along with Kentucky, Maryland and Missouri) that remained in the Union. Delaware had only 1,800 slaves; the institution was peripheral to the state's economy. But Lincoln found that even there, slave holders did not wish to surrender their human property. Nonetheless, for most of 1862, he avidly promoted his plan to the border states and any Confederates who might be interested.

Lincoln also took his proposal to black Americans. 6
In August 1862, he met with a group of black leaders (F)
from Washington. He seemed to blame the presence of blacks in America for the conflict: "but for your race among us there could not be war." He issued a powerful indictment of slavery—"the greatest wrong inflicted on any people"—but added that, because of racism, blacks would never achieve equality in America. "It is better for us both, therefore, to be separated," he said. But most blacks refused to contemplate emigration from the land of their birth.

In the summer of 1862, a combination of events 7
propelled Lincoln in a new direction. Slavery was disintegrating in parts of the South as thousands of (G)
slaves ran away to Union lines. With the war a stalemate, more Northerners found themselves agreeing with the abolitionists, who had insisted from the outset that slavery must become a target. Enthusiasm for enlistment was waning in the North. The Army had long refused to accept black volunteers, but the reservoir of black manpower could no longer be ignored. In response, Congress moved ahead of Lincoln, abolishing slavery in the District of Columbia, authorizing the president to enroll blacks in the Army and freeing the slaves of pro-Confederate owners in areas under military control.

(B) The writer claims that emancipation was a process.
(C) He explains how the document was a "double emancipation."
(D) The first stage in the process is introduced.

(E) Events in this stage are listed.
(F) Related events are cited.
(G) The phrase "In the summer" signals the second stage in Lincoln's thought process.

Lincoln signed all these measures that summer.

8 **(H)** The hallmark of Lincoln's greatness was his combination of bedrock principle with open-mindedness and capacity for growth. That summer, with his preferred approach going nowhere, he moved in the direction of immediate emancipation. He first proposed this to his cabinet on July 22, but Secretary of State William H. Seward persuaded him to wait for a military victory, lest it seem an act of desperation.

9 **(I)** Soon after the Union victory at Antietam in September, Lincoln issued the Preliminary Emancipation Proclamation, a warning to the Confederacy that if it did not lay down its arms by January 1, he would declare the slaves "forever free."

10 **(J)** Lincoln did not immediately abandon his earlier plan. His annual message to Congress, released on Dec. 1, 1862, devoted a long passage to gradual, compensated abolition and colonization. But in the same document, without mentioning the impending proclamation, he indicated that a new approach was imperative: "The dogmas of the quiet past, are inadequate to the stormy present," he wrote. "We must disenthrall our selves, and then we shall save our country." Lincoln included himself in that "we." On Jan. 1, he proclaimed the freedom of the vast majority of the nation's slaves.

11 The Emancipation Proclamation is perhaps the most misunderstood of the documents that have shaped American history. Contrary to legend, Lincoln did not free the nearly four million slaves with a stroke of his pen. It had no bearing on slaves in the four border states, since they were not in rebellion. It also exempted certain parts of the Confederacy occupied by the Union. All told, it left perhaps 750,000 slaves in bondage. But the remaining 3.1 million, it declared, "are, and henceforward shall be free."

12 The proclamation did not end slavery in the United States on the day it was issued. Indeed, it could not even be enforced in most of the areas where it applied, which were under Confederate control. But it ensured the eventual death of slavery—assuming the Union won the war. Were the Confederacy to emerge victorious, slavery, in one form or another, would undoubtedly have lasted a long time.

13 A military order, whose constitutional legitimacy rested on the president's war powers, the proclamation often disappoints those who read it. It is dull and legalistic; it contains no soaring language enunciating the rights of man. Only at the last minute, at the urging of Treasury Secretary Salmon P. Chase, an abolitionist, did **(K)** Lincoln add a conclusion declaring the proclamation an "act of justice."

14 Nonetheless, the proclamation marked a dramatic transformation in the nature of the Civil War and in Lincoln's own approach to the problem of slavery. No longer did he seek the consent of slave holders. The proclamation was immediate, not gradual, contained no mention of compensation for owners, and made no reference to colonization.

15 In it, Lincoln addressed blacks directly, not as property subject to the will of others but as men and women whose loyalty the Union must earn. For the first time, he welcomed black soldiers into the Union Army; over the next two years some 200,000 black men would serve in the Army and Navy, playing a critical role in achieving Union victory. And Lincoln urged freed slaves to go to work for "reasonable wages"—in the United States. He never again mentioned colonization in public.

16 Having made the decision, Lincoln did not look back. In 1864, with casualties mounting, there was talk of **(L)**

(H) The writer suggests what Lincoln's transition might imply about his character.
(I) The writer reflects on the implications of stage 1 events.
(J) He describes the document's limited effects and offers evidence supporting his claim.

(K) He contrasts the document's unexceptional diction with the document's exceptional claims and effects.
(L) The phrase "Having made" signals a transition into the final stage of Lincoln's thought process.

a compromise peace. Some urged Lincoln to rescind the proclamation, in which case, they believed, the South could be persuaded to return to the Union. Lincoln refused. Were he to do so, he told one visitor, "I should be damned in time and eternity."

17   Wartime emancipation may have settled the fate of slavery, but it opened another vexing question: the role of former slaves in American life. Colonization had allowed its proponents to talk about abolition without having to confront this issue; after all, the black population would be gone. After January 1, 1863, Lincoln for the first time began to think seriously of the United States as a biracial society.

18   While not burdened with the visceral racism of many of his white contemporaries, Lincoln shared some of their prejudices. He had long seen blacks as an alien people who had been unjustly uprooted from their homeland and were entitled to freedom, but were not **(M)** an intrinsic part of American society. During his Senate campaign in Illinois, in 1858, he had insisted that blacks should enjoy the same natural rights as whites (life, liberty and the pursuit of happiness), but he opposed granting them legal equality or the right to vote.

19   By the end of his life, Lincoln's outlook had changed **(N)** dramatically. In his last public address, delivered in April 1865, he said that in reconstructing Louisiana, and by implication other Southern states, he would "prefer" that limited black suffrage be implemented. He singled out the "very intelligent" (educated free blacks) and "those who serve our cause as soldiers" as most worthy. Though

hardly an unambiguous embrace of equality, this was the first time an American president had endorsed any political rights for blacks.

20   And then there was his magnificent second inaugural address of March 4, 1865, in which Lincoln ruminated on the deep meaning of the war. He now identified the institution of slavery—not the presence of blacks, as in 1862—as its fundamental cause. The war, he said, might well be a divine punishment for the evil of slavery. And God might will it to continue until all the wealth the slaves had created had been destroyed, and "until every drop of blood drawn with the lash, shall be paid by another drawn by the sword." Lincoln was reminding Americans that violence did not begin with the firing on Fort Sumter, S.C., in April 1861. What he called "this terrible war" had been preceded by 250 years of the terrible violence of slavery.

21   In essence, Lincoln asked the nation to confront unblinkingly the legacy of slavery. What were the requirements of justice in the face of this reality? What **(O)** would be necessary to enable former slaves and their descendants to enjoy fully the pursuit of happiness? Lincoln did not live to provide an answer. A century and a half later, we have yet to do so.

(O) The writer suggests that in his death, Lincoln left the country to work out its own emancipation.

(M) The writer reflects on the events distinguishing Lincoln's earlier thinking.
(N) The writer claims—and cites evidence—that Lincoln's thinking changed.

Reading for Better Writing

1. Describe how the writer introduces his topic and thesis.
2. Review his claim (in paragraph two) that emancipation was a process, not a single event. What does he mean, and how does he support this claim?
3. Cite examples showing how the writer builds transitions that (1) link stages in the process and (2) link specific events within a stage.
4. Identify a passage in which the writer analyzes how specific events caused a shift in Lincoln's thinking. What does this passage contribute to the essay?

17-4 MAKE EFFECTIVE APPEALS

In this op-ed, Natalie Angier demonstrates the position-taking strategies addressed earlier in this chapter: developing sound claims with reliable evidence, while also making concessions but rebutting opposing arguments. However, as discussed in the previous chapter on pages 182–193, a sound argument also involves using appropriate appeals to credibility, logic, and emotion, while avoiding a wide range of logical fallacies. As you read the essays, study and evaluate these appeals and check the arguments for logical fallacies such as oversimplifying, either-or thinking, appeals to pity, and attacks against opponents.

(A) ## Sorry, Vegans: Brussels Sprouts Like to Live, Too

SQ3R Survey · Question · Read · Recite · Review

1   I stopped eating pork about eight years ago, after a scientist happened to mention that the animal whose teeth most closely resemble our own is the pig. Unable
(B) to shake the image of a perky little pig flashing me a brilliant George Clooney smile, I decided it was easier to forgo the Christmas ham. A couple of years later, I gave up on all mammalian meat, period. I still eat fish and poultry, however, and pour eggnog in my coffee. My dietary decisions are arbitrary and inconsistent, and when friends ask why I'm willing to try the duck but not the lamb, I don't have a good answer. Food choices are often like that: difficult to articulate yet strongly held. And lately, debates over food choices have flared with particular vehemence.

2   In his book, *Eating Animals*, the novelist Jonathan Safran Foer describes his gradual transformation from
(C) omnivorous, oblivious slacker who "waffled among any number of diets" to "committed vegetarian." Last month, Gary Steiner, a philosopher at Bucknell University, argued on the Op-Ed page of *The New York Times* that people should strive to be "strict ethical vegans" like

himself, avoiding all products derived from animals, including wool and silk. Killing animals for human food and finery is nothing less than "outright murder," he said, Isaac Bashevis Singer's "eternal Treblinka."

But before we cede the entire moral penthouse to   3
"committed vegetarians" and "strong ethical vegans," we
might consider that plants no more aspire to being stir-   (D)
fried in a wok than a hog aspires to being peppercorn-studded in my Christmas clay pot. This is not meant as a trite argument or a chuckled aside. Plants are lively and seek to keep it that way. The more that scientists learn about the complexity of plants—their keen sensitivity to the environment, the speed with which they react to changes in the environment, and the extraordinary number of tricks that plants will rally to fight off attackers and solicit help from afar—the more impressed researchers become, and the less easily we can dismiss plants as so much fiberfill backdrop, passive sunlight collectors on which deer, antelope and vegans can conveniently graze. It's time for a green revolution, a reseeding of our stubborn animal minds.

When plant biologists speak of their subjects, they   4
use active verbs and vivid images. Plants "forage" for   (E)
resources like light and soil nutrients and "anticipate" rough spots and opportunities. By analyzing the ratio of red light and far red light falling on their leaves, for example, they can sense the presence of other chlorophyllated competitors nearby and try to grow the other way. Their roots ride the underground "rhizosphere" and engage in cross-cultural and microbial trade.

"Plants are not static or silly," said Monika Hilker of   5
the Institute of Biology at the Free University of Berlin. "They respond to tactile cues, they recognize different wavelengths of light, they listen to chemical signals, they can even talk" through chemical signals. Touch, sight, hearing, speech. "These are sensory modalities and abilities we normally think of as only being in animals," Dr. Hilker said.

(A) The title introduces the topic and sets a playful tone.
(B) Angier describes her position on meat eating as personal and arbitrary versus strict and ideological.
(C) She describes two opposing positions.

(D) She suggests a position that approves eating plants but disapproves eating meat is logically inconsistent.
(E) Angier explains animal-plant parallels.

6   Plants can't run away from a threat but they can stand their ground. "They are very good at avoiding getting eaten," said Linda Walling of the University of California, Riverside. "It's an unusual situation where insects can overcome those defenses." At the smallest nip to its leaves, specialized cells on the plant's surface release chemicals to irritate the predator or sticky goo to entrap it. Genes in the plant's DNA are activated to wage system-wide chemical warfare, the plant's version of an immune response. We need terpenes, alkaloids, phenolics—let's move.

7   "I'm amazed at how fast some of these things
(F) happen," said Consuelo M. De Moraes of Pennsylvania State University. Dr. De Moraes and her colleagues did labeling experiments to clock a plant's systemic response time and found that, in less than 20 minutes from the moment the caterpillar had begun feeding on its leaves, the plant had plucked carbon from the air and forged defensive compounds from scratch.

8   Just because we humans can't hear them doesn't mean plants don't howl. Some of the compounds that plants generate in response to insect mastication—their feedback, you might say—are volatile chemicals that
(G) serve as cries for help. Such airborne alarm calls have been shown to attract both large predatory insects like dragon flies, which delight in caterpillar meat, and tiny parasitic insects, which can infect a caterpillar and destroy it from within.

9   Enemies of the plant's enemies are not the only ones
(H) to tune into the emergency broadcast. "Some of these cues, some of these volatiles that are released when a focal plant is damaged," said Richard Karban of the University of California, Davis, "cause other plants of the same species, or even of another species, to likewise become more resistant to herbivores."

10 Yes, it's best to nip trouble in the bud.

11 Dr. Hilker and her colleagues, as well as other
(I) research teams, have found that certain plants can

(F) She supports her assertions by quoting several experts.
(G) She compares plants and humans.
(H) Angier quotes an expert and playfully supports his opinion.
(I) She describes how plants communicate with insects.

KIM NGUYEN, 2014 / Used under license from Shutterstock.com

sense when insect eggs have been deposited on their leaves and will act immediately to rid themselves of the incubating menace. They may sprout carpets of tumorlike neoplasms to knock the eggs off, or secrete ovicides to kill them, or sound the S O S. Reporting in *The Proceedings of the National Academy of Sciences*, Dr. Hilker and her coworkers determined that when a female cabbage butterfly lays her eggs on a brussels sprout plant and attaches her treasures to the leaves with tiny dabs of glue, the vigilant vegetable detects the presence of a simple additive in the glue, benzyl cyanide. Cued by the additive, the plant swiftly alters the chemistry of its leaf surface to beckon female parasitic wasps. Spying the anchored bounty, the female wasps in turn inject their eggs inside, the gestating wasps feed on the gestating butterflies, and the plant's problem is solved.

12 Here's the lurid Edgar Allan Poetry of it: that benzyl cyanide tip-off had been donated to the female butterfly by the male during mating. "It's an anti-aphrodisiac
(J) pheromone, so that the female wouldn't mate anymore," Dr. Hilker said. "The male is trying to ensure his paternity, but he ends up endangering his own offspring."

13 Plants eavesdrop on one another benignly and malignly. As they described in *Science* and other journals, Dr. De Moraes and her colleagues have discovered that seedlings of the dodder plant, a parasitic weed related to morning glory, can detect volatile chemicals released by potential host plants like the tomato. The young dodder then grows inexorably toward the host, until it can encircle the victim's stem and begin sucking the life phloem right out of it. The parasite can even distinguish

(J) She playfully labels and describes the process.

between the scents of healthier and weaker tomato plants and then head for the hale one.

14 "Even if you have quite a bit of knowledge about plants," Dr. De Moraes said, "it's still surprising to see how sophisticated they can be."

15 It's a small daily tragedy that we animals must kill to stay alive. Plants are the ethical autotrophs here, the ones that wrest their meals from the sun. Don't expect them to boast: they're too busy fighting to survive.

Reading for Better Writing

1. Paraphrase Natalie Angier's core argument and list her supporting claims. Assess the strength of her reasoning, taking into account the supporting claims and the evidence offered.

2. Describe Angier's voice and cite words or phrases exemplifying that voice. Then explain how her writing voice colors her argument.

3. Examine the argument for logical fallacies such as either/or thinking (page 188), appeal to pity (page 189), and attack against the person (page 190). If you find examples, explain how they affect Angier's argument.

 17-5 ## WRITE, REVISE, AND EDIT A LOGICAL POSITION PAPER

Writing Guidelines

Planning

❶ **Select a debatable topic.** Review the list below and add topics as needed.

- **Current Affairs:** Explore recent trends, new laws, and emerging controversies discussed in the news media, blogs, or social media.
- **Burning Issues:** What issues related to family, work, education, technology, the environment, or popular culture do you care about?
- **Dividing Lines:** What issues divide your communities? Religion, gender, politics, regionalism, nationalism? Choose a topic and freewrite to clarify your position.

❷ **Take stock.** Before you dig into your topic, assess your starting point. What is your current position on the topic? Why? What evidence do you have?

❸ **Get inside the issue.** To take a defensible position, study the issue carefully:

- Investigate all possible positions on the issue and research as needed.
- Do firsthand research that produces current, relevant information.
- Write your position at the top of a page. Below it, set up "Pro" and "Con" columns. List arguments in each column.
- Develop reasoning that supports your position and test it for the following: (a) no logical fallacies, such as slanted language, oversimplification, either/or thinking, straw-man and red-herring claims, appeals to pity, and personal attacks (see pages 188–191); and (b) an effective range of support: statistics, observations, expert testimony, comparisons, experiences, and analysis (see pages 186–188).

❹ **Refine your position.** By now, you may have sharpened or radically changed your initial position on the topic. Before you organize and draft your essay, reflect on those changes. If it helps, use this formula:

❙ I believe this to be true about _____ .

❺ **Organize your argument and support.** Now you've committed yourself to a position. Before drafting, review these organizational options:

- **Traditional Pattern:** Introduce the issue, state your position, support it, address and refute opposition, and restate your position.
- **Blatant Confession:** Place your position statement in the first sentence.
- **Delayed Gratification:** Describe various positions on the topic, compare and contrast them, and then take and defend your position.
- **Changed Mind:** If your research changed your mind, explain how and why.
- **Winning Over:** If readers oppose your position, address their concerns by anticipating and answering each objection or question.

Drafting

❻ **Write your first draft.** Using freewriting and/or your notes, draft the paper.

- **Opening:** Seize the reader's attention, possibly with a bold title—or raise concern for the issue with a dramatic story, a pointed example, a thought-provoking question, or a personal confession. Supply background information that readers need to understand the issue.

- **Development:** Deepen, clarify, and support your position statement, using solid logic and reliable support. Address opposing views fairly as part of a clear, well-reasoned argument that helps readers understand and accept your position. If appropriate, use graphs or visual elements to advance your position.
- **Closing:** End on a thoughtful note that stresses your commitment. If appropriate, make a direct or indirect plea to readers to adopt your position.

Revising

7 **Improve the ideas, organization, and voice.**
Ask a peer to read your position paper for the following:

- **Ideas:** Does the writing effectively establish and defend a stand on a debatable issue? Is the position clearly stated and effectively qualified and refined? Do the reasoning and support help the reader understand and appreciate the position? If visuals are used, do they effectively deepen the thinking?
- **Organization:** Does the opening effectively raise the issue? Does the middle offer a carefully sequenced development and defense of the position? Does the closing magnify the position?
- **Voice:** Is the voice thoughtful, measured, committed, and convincing?

Editing

8 **Edit and proofread** by addressing these issues:

- **Words:** Language is precise, concrete, and lively—no jargon, clichés, or insults.
- **Sentences:** Constructions flow smoothly.
- **Correctness:** The copy is free of errors in spelling, usage, punctuation, and grammar.
- **Design:** The page design is correctly formatted; information is properly documented according to the required system (e.g., MLA, APA).

Publishing

9 **Publish your essay.** Submit your essay according to your instructor's requirements. In addition, seek a forum for your position—with peers or online.

Critical-Thinking and Writing Activities

1. Reflect on hot topics in your major—check textbooks, talk to professors or other experts, and review journals in the field. Then write a position paper on a controversial issue.
2. Review Alyssa Woudstra's essay, "Nuclear Is Not the Answer." Then research this or another energy-related topic and write an essay in which you take a clear, well-reasoned position on one or more key issues.
3. Review Natalie Angier's essay on what we should or should not eat. Then research the topic and develop your own argument in which you address relevant issues that she raises, as well as other issues that you think are relevant. Seek to state your position clearly and support your claims with reliable evidence.
4. Draft or revise a position paper that addresses a controversial issue that exists within a community to which you belong (e.g., city, neighborhood, generation, race or ethnic group, consumer group, gender, online network) by respectfully describing opposing ideas and showing how each view is reasonable and acceptable.

18 | Persuading Readers to Act

"PASSION IS OFTEN MORE EFFECTUAL THAN FORCE."

AESOP

a katz, 2014 / Used under license from Shutterstock.com

LEARNING OBJECTIVES

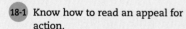

18-1 Know how to read an appeal for action.

18-2 Describe a debatable issue.

18-3 Make clear and rational claims, supported with reliable evidence.

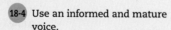

18-4 Use an informed and mature voice.

18-5 Write, revise, and edit an essay persuading readers to act.

After you finish
this chapter
go to
PAGE 217 for STUDY TOOLS

Persuading people to do something is challenging, requiring that you convince them to believe you, to rethink their own perspectives, and to take a concrete step. In the end, you need to change people's minds in order to change their actions.

Writers achieve this goal with sound logic, reliable support, and fitting appeals. Every day, persuasive writing like this appears in newsletters, editorials, marketing documents, business proposals, academic journals, white papers, and traditional essays.

Because the form is so common, you can expect to read and write versions of it in college and in the workplace. As you read the essays in this chapter, carefully analyze how writers develop convincing appeals for action. Then when you write your own essay, try these same strategies.

18-1 KNOW HOW TO READ AN APPEAL FOR ACTION

How should you read an argument that urges you to act on an issue? The instructions below offer helpful tips.

18-1a Consider the Rhetorical Situation for Persuasive Writing

When reading an appeal to act, anticipate what the writer wants people to do, what audience he or she has in mind, and how the topic is treated.

▶ **Purpose:** Whether in academics, the workplace, or public life, writers call for action because they believe change is needed. Something is not right. Something needs to be improved or fixed. The writer's goal is to convince readers to care about the issue strongly enough to take a concrete step.

▶ **Audience:** The intended readers are people who the writer believes need to be pressed to act. Readers may be unaware of the issue, may feel overwhelmed by it, may have an interest in not acting, or may not care enough about the issue to actually act. The writer thus educates and urges such readers.

▶ **Topic:** In academics, the topics addressed might be related to a specific discipline (e.g., educational mentoring campaign, expanding an arts program), a political or social issue (e.g., shelter for abused women, Special Olympics program), or a general humanitarian concern (e.g., help for victims of an epidemic, a flood, or a war).

18-1b Look for Convincing Qualities

When reading an appeal to act, look for the following:

▶ **Compelling Argument:** The writer accurately describes the issue, convinces readers of its importance, and calls for a doable and effective action. The writer's claims are fact based and reasonable, not extreme, trivial, or unqualified (see pages 184–186).

▶ **Logical Argument:** The argument is based on reliable evidence such as appropriate anecdotes, tests, experiments, analogies, and expert testimony (see pages 186–188); and the argument avoids logical fallacies such as half-truths (page 190), unreliable testimonials, attacks against a person (page 190), and false analogies (page 190).

▶ **Mature Voice:** The writing sounds informed and genuine; it includes no manipulative appeals, quarrelsome language, or demeaning accusations.

> ### Reading Guide:
> ### Persuasive Essays
>
> ✔ What is the issue, and what action is requested to address it?
> ✔ Who are the intended readers, and what capacity do they have to act?
> ✔ Are the writer's claims accurate, compelling, and logical?
> ✔ Is the argument's tone informed, genuine, and respectful?
> ✔ Is the writing convincing—does it move readers to do what the writer requests?

DESCRIBE A DEBATABLE ISSUE

Student writer Henry Veldboom, a mature student with children of his own, wrote this essay to call North American readers to reconsider what they value.

(A) Our Wealth: Where Is It Taking Us?

SQ3R Survey • Question • Read • Recite • Review

1   North America's wealth and the lifestyle it affords are known throughout the world. This knowledge has created (B) a belief that wealth and happiness are synonymous, which in turn has perpetuated the dreams of people around the globe who hope to achieve the same successes witnessed here in the West. Is there truth to the idea that wealth and happiness coexist? Ask North Americans if they would willingly trade life here for that in a struggling country, and they would likely say "No." Their wealth has made their lives quite comfortable. Most would admit to enjoying the lifestyle such wealth allows; few would want to give it up. But what is this wealth really costing North Americans—especially children?

2   While North American wealth grew out of the capitalism that culminated in the nineteenth-century (C) Industrial Revolution, today's capitalism is a system largely based on consumerism—an attitude that values

---

(A) Title: issue and central question
(B) Introduction: North American wealth and its real cost
(C) Modern capitalism is based on harmful consumerism.

---

the incessant acquisition of goods in the belief that it is necessary and beneficial. The goal, then, of a modern capitalist economy is to produce many goods as cheaply as possible and have these goods purchased on a continual basis. The forces behind capitalism—business owners at the demand of stockholders—employ an ever-expanding array of marketing techniques to accomplish the goal of selling products. Expert on marketing George Barna defines marketing as the process of directing "goods and services from the producer to the consumer, to satisfy the needs and desires of the consumer and the goals of the producer" (41). On the receiving end of today's capitalism are consumers whose needs are, in general, self-serving and based on self-actualization. Corporations promote this way of thinking and capitalize on it through marketing techniques. Social commentator Benjamin Barber describes this modern interaction in the following way: "[This thinking] serves capitalist consumerism directly by nurturing a culture of impetuous consumption necessary to selling puerile goods in a developed world that has few genuine needs" (81).

3   Admittedly, deciphering genuine needs from superfluous wants is not an easy task. However, putting debates about materialism aside, people must consider (D) the results of their consumption. The 2008-2009 economic upheaval still lingers in people's minds despite the recent upward trend in the North American economy. When such financial turmoil happens, the typical response is to lay blame. Some people are quick to accuse corporations of causing the turmoil and governments of allowing corporations to operate as they do. Noted journalist and anti-establishment advocate Linda McQuaig comments on the shift in the 1970s that gave individuals more freedoms; in turn, corporations accommodated the lax attitudes of government to themselves and were "ensured freedom from their restraints on their profit-making" (22).

(D) Consumers must consider the results of their consumption.

Do North American corporations and governments share the responsibility to properly use wealth and direct the economy? Yes, they most certainly do. However, individuals must also examine their own fiscal responsibility. McQuaig addresses this issue as well, highlighting "the power and centrality of greed in our culture" (23). She uses a word that no one wants to be labeled with—greed. When people begin discussing their financial woes in relation to individual greed, the blame rests squarely on each member of society.

4
(E) The behavior that has led to the current financial crisis is not only impacting adults but also putting children at risk. Deceptive marketing tactics make use of psychological knowledge and social patterning research to convince consumers to purchase particular products.

(F) Adults who possess the mental capacity to discern motives and detect subversion are being effectively manipulated by cunning advertising techniques, resulting in massive debt loads, addiction, and bankruptcy. However, the greater concern with these marketing practices is that they are being aimed at children who have less ability to defend themselves. Psychiatrist Susan Linn describes the marketing aimed at children as "precisely targeted, refined by scientific method, and honed by child psychologists . . ." (5). It isn't the case that children are getting caught in marketing traps set for adults; rather, kids are being targeted. Linn remarks that developmental psychology, which was once used solely for treating children's mental health, is now used to determine "weaknesses" in children's thinking in order to exploit these weaknesses (24). The weaknesses are due to children's brains not having reached full cognitive development, resulting in unstable patterns of thinking in areas such as reasoning, memory, and problem solving (Weiten 47). At such a disadvantage, children are unable to withstand the marketing ploys aimed at them.

5
Knowing that children are the targets of aggressive mass marketing is all the more serious when the scope of the situation is considered. Much research has been done on purchasing patterns, and while the fact that North Americans spend large amounts of money on goods may not be surprising, when children are added to the equation, the picture changes. Expert on consumerism, economics, and family studies Juliet Schor has done a considerable amount of convincing research in this area. She comments on the purchasing influence of children and notes that children aged four to twelve influenced an estimated $670 billion of adult purchasing in 2004 (23). Children having influence on such large amounts of money being spent catches the attention of producers who consequently aim their marketing at kids in order to sell adult products. Schor also notes the results of a Nickelodeon (an entertainment company) study that states when it comes to recognizing brands, "the average 10 year old has memorized 300 to 400 brands" (25). Kids know the products and they know what they want; the dollar amount parents are spending in response to their children reflects this.

(G)

6
(H) The effects of aggressive marketing and consumerism on North American children are exhibited in a wide range of health problems. At first glance, the relationship between consumerism and children's health may appear to be coincidental. However, much research shows a direct link between marketing to children and their health. Having done her own research and examined other studies, Juliet Schor concludes that "the more [children] buy into the commercial and materialist messages, the worse they feel about themselves, the more depressed they are, and the more they are beset by anxiety, headaches, stomach-aches, and boredom" (173). (On a related note, the time spent by children sitting in front of televisions

---

(E) People must examine how consumerism harms children.
(F) Marketing manipulation

(G) Influence on parental spending
(H) Physical and mental health problems

and computers is an important factor in this outcome. These media are the prime vehicles for advertising and are contributing to sedentary lifestyles, which in turn cause health problems.) Materialism is having an effect not only on adults but also on youth. When children are asked what they aspire to be, the top answer is "to be rich" (37). The health of the minds and bodies of North American children is deteriorating as a result of consumerism and the new capitalism.

7   Having examined the current state of North American society in terms of the economic and personal

(I)   health related to the new capitalism, one begins to see that society is in a situation that is neither beneficial nor sustainable. Changes must be made. If the response is to look for someone or something to blame, everyone must stop and take a look in the mirror. Changing habits and attitudes must start with the individual. While adopting a particular economic ideology is not the point, North Americans must take a hard look at their society and decide if this is how they want to live. If this society carries on unchanged, what future will its children have? North America has an abundance of wealth; the decision of where to go with it must be made: Time is running out.

Note: The Works Cited pages is not shown. For sample pages, see MLA (page 286) and APA (page 320).

(I) Conclusion: Individual consumers must change if society is to change.

Reading for Better Writing

1. In his title, Veldboom identifies the issue as wealth. How does he clarify and deepen the issue in the essay's opening paragraphs?

2. While acknowledging economic and social systems, Veldboom stresses individual values and responsibilities. How effective is this emphasis?

3. What action does the essay call for? Do you find the action practical and compelling? Why or why not?

4. Select three claims that Veldboom makes and explain why they are or are not (a) rational and (b) adequately supported.

18-3 MAKE CLEAR AND RATIONAL CLAIMS, SUPPORTED WITH RELIABLE EVIDENCE

Dr. Martin Luther King, Jr., was a leader in the Civil Rights Movement during the 1950s and 1960s. On August 28, 1963, he delivered this persuasive speech to a crowd of 250,000 people gathered at the Lincoln Memorial in Washington, D.C. To appreciate its strong images and rhythmical language, read the speech aloud. Then assess the clarity and logic of its claims, looking specifically for half-truths (190), unreliable testimonials (190), attacks against the person (190), and false analogies (190).

I Have a Dream

SQ3R Survey • Question • Read • Recite • Review

1   Five score years ago, a great American, in whose symbolic shadow we stand, signed the Emancipation Proclamation. This momentous decree came as a great **(A)** beacon light of hope to millions of Negro slaves who had been seared in the flames of withering injustice. It came as a joyous daybreak to end the long night of captivity.

2   But one hundred years later, we must face the tragic fact that the Negro is still not free. One hundred years later, the life of the Negro is still sadly crippled by the manacles of segregation and the chains of discrimination. **(B)** One hundred years later, the Negro lives on a lonely island of poverty in the midst of a vast ocean of material prosperity. One hundred years later, the Negro is still languishing in the corners of American society and finds

---

(A) King starts with a tragic contrast.
(B) He uses figurative language to describe the present situation.

himself an exile in his own land. So we have come here today to dramatize an appalling condition.

3   In a sense we have come to our nation's Capitol to cash a check. When the architects of our republic
(C) wrote the magnificent words of the Constitution and the Declaration of Independence, they were signing a promissory note to which every American was to fall heir. This note was a promise that all men would be guaranteed the unalienable rights of life, liberty, and the pursuit of happiness.

4   It is obvious today that America has defaulted on this promissory note insofar as her citizens of color are
(D) concerned. Instead of honoring this sacred obligation, America has given the Negro people a bad check; a check which has come back marked "insufficient funds." But we refuse to believe that the bank of justice is bankrupt. We refuse to believe that there are insufficient funds in the great vaults of opportunity of this nation. So we have come to cash this check—a check that will give us

upon demand the riches of freedom and the security of justice. We have also come to this hallowed spot to remind America of the fierce urgency of now. This is no time to engage in the luxury of cooling off or to take the tranquilizing drug of gradualism. Now is the time to make real the promises of Democracy. Now is the time to rise from the dark and desolate valley of segregation to the sunlit path of racial justice. Now is the time to open the doors of opportunity to all of God's children. Now is the time to lift our nation from the quicksands of racial injustice to the solid rock of brotherhood.

5   It would be fatal for the nation to overlook the urgency of the moment and to underestimate the determination of the Negro. This sweltering summer of the Negro's legitimate discontent will not pass until there is an invigorating autumn of freedom and equality. 1963 is not an end, but a beginning. Those who hope that the Negro needed to blow off steam and will now be content will have a rude awakening if the nation returns to business as usual. There will be neither rest nor tranquility in America until the Negro is granted his citizenship rights. The whirlwinds of revolt will continue to shake the foundations of our nation until the bright day of justice emerges.

6   But there is something I must say to my people who
(E) stand on the warm threshold which leads into the palace of justice. In the process of gaining our rightful place we must not be guilty of wrongful deeds. Let us not seek to satisfy our thirst for freedom by drinking from the cup of bitterness and hatred. We must forever conduct our struggle on the high plane of dignity and discipline. We must not allow our creative protest to degenerate into physical violence. Again and again we must rise to the majestic heights of meeting physical force with soul force. The marvelous new militancy which has engulfed the Negro community must not lead us to a distrust of all white people, for many of our white brothers, as evidenced by their presence here today, have come to

(C) An analogy clarifies the problem.
(D) Repeated words and phrases create urgency.

(E) King addresses specific audiences in turn.

realize that their destiny is tied up with our destiny and their freedom is inextricably bound to our freedom. We cannot walk alone.

7 (F) And as we talk, we must make the pledge that we shall march ahead. We cannot turn back. There are those who are asking the devotees of civil rights, "When will you be satisfied?" We can never be satisfied as long as the Negro is the victim of the unspeakable horrors of police brutality. We can never be satisfied as long as our bodies, heaving with the fatigue of travel, cannot gain lodging in the motels of the highways and the hotels of the cities. We cannot be satisfied as long as the Negro's basic mobility is from a smaller ghetto to a larger one. We can never be satisfied as long as a Negro in Mississippi cannot vote and a Negro in New York believes he has nothing for which to vote. No, no, we are not satisfied, and we will not be satisfied until justice rolls down like waters and righteousness like a mighty stream.

8 (G) I am not unmindful that some of you have come here out of great trials and tribulations. Some of you have come fresh from narrow jail cells. Some of you have come from areas where your quest for freedom left you battered by the storms of persecution and staggered by the winds of police brutality. You have been the veterans of creative suffering. Continue to work with the faith that unearned suffering is redemptive.

9 Go back to Mississippi, go back to Alabama, go back to South Carolina, go back to Georgia, go back to Louisiana, go back to the slums and ghettos of our northern cities, knowing that somehow this situation can and will be changed. Let us not wallow in the valley of despair.

10 I say to you today, my friends, that in spite of the difficulties and frustrations of the moment I still have a dream. It is a dream deeply rooted in the American dream.

11 I have a dream that one day this nation will rise up and live out the true meaning of its creed: "We hold these truths to be self-evident; that all men are created equal."

12 I have a dream that one day on the red hills of Georgia the sons of former slaves and the sons of former slave owners will be able to sit down together at the table of brotherhood.

13 (H) I have a dream that the state of Mississippi, a desert state sweltering with the heat of injustice and oppression, will be transformed into an oasis of freedom and justice.

14 I have a dream that my four little children will one day live in a nation where they will not be judged by the color of their skin but by the content of their character.

15 I have a dream today.

16 I have a dream that the state of Alabama, whose governor's lips are presently dripping with the words of interposition and nullification, will be transformed into a situation where little black boys and black girls will be able to join hands with little white boys and girls and walk together as sisters and brothers.

17 I have a dream today.

18 (I) I have a dream that one day every valley shall be exalted, every hill and mountain shall be made low, the rough places will be made plain, and the crooked places will be made straight, and the glory of the Lord shall be revealed, and all flesh shall see it together.

19 This is our hope. This is the faith with which I return to the South. With this faith we will be able to hew out of the mountain of despair a stone of hope. With this faith we will be able to transform the jangling discords of our nation into a beautiful symphony of brotherhood. With this faith we will be able to work together, to pray together, to struggle together, to go to jail together, to stand up for freedom together, knowing that we will be free one day.

20 This will be the day when all God's children will be able to sing with new meaning.

(F) He responds to the arguments of opponents.
(G) Appropriate emotional appeals are used in the context of suffering.

(H) The repetition of key phrases becomes a persuasive refrain.
(I) King's vision offers hope and motivates readers to change society.

> *My country 'tis of thee*
> *Sweet land of liberty,*
> *Of thee I sing,*
> *Land where my fathers died,*
> *Land of the pilgrims' pride,*
> *From every mountainside*
> *Let freedom ring.*

21 And if America is to be a great nation this must become true. So let freedom ring from the prodigious hilltops of New Hampshire. Let freedom ring from the mighty mountains of New York. Let freedom ring from the heightening Alleghenies of Pennsylvania!

22 Let freedom ring from the snow-capped Rockies of Colorado!

23 Let freedom ring from the curvaceous peaks of California!

24 But not only that; let freedom ring from Stone Mountain of Georgia!

25 Let freedom ring from Lookout Mountain of Tennessee!

26 Let freedom ring from every hill and molehill of Mississippi! From every mountainside, let freedom ring.

27 When we let freedom ring, when we let it ring from every village and every hamlet, from every state and every city, we will be able to speed up that day when all of God's children, black men and white men, Jews and **(K)** Gentiles, Protestants and Catholics, will be able to join hands and sing in the words of the old Negro spiritual, "Free at last! Free at last! Thank God almighty, we are free at last!"

(J) He appeals to ideals and to humanity's better nature, ending with a vision of a just society.

(K) The closing urges readers to work for a better future.

Reading for Better Writing

1. King is actually speaking to several audiences at the same time. Who are these different audiences? How does King address each?

2. For what specific changes does King call? What does he want his listeners to do?

3. Explore the writer's style. How does he use religious imagery, comparisons, and analogies? How does repetition function as a persuasive technique?

4. In a sense, King's speech addresses a gap between reality and an ideal. How does he present this gap?

5. For five decades, critics have judged this speech to be an exceptionally effective appeal for action. Explain why you do or do not agree.

kropic1, 2014 / Used under license from Shutterstock.com

USE AN INFORMED AND MATURE VOICE

Kofi Annan, the former Secretary General of the United Nations, wrote the essay below in order to urge readers worldwide to help address AIDS and famine in Africa. Read the essay carefully, noting the logic and tone of his claims. Then assess whether Annan's voice illustrates an informed and mature voice.

In Africa, AIDS Has a Woman's Face

SQ3R Survey · Question · Read · Recite · Review

1
(A) A combination of famine and AIDS is threatening the backbone of Africa—the women who keep African societies going and whose work makes up the economic foundation of rural communities. For decades, we have known that the best way for Africa to thrive is to ensure that its women have the freedom, power, and knowledge to make decisions affecting their own lives and those of their families and communities. At the United Nations, we have always understood that our work for development depends on building a successful partnership with the African farmer and her husband.

2 Study after study has shown that there is no effective development strategy in which women do not play a central role. When women are fully involved, the benefits can be seen immediately: families are healthier; they are
(B) better fed; their income, savings and reinvestment go up. And, what is true of families is true of communities and, eventually, of whole countries.

3 But today, millions of African women are threatened by two simultaneous catastrophes: famine and AIDS. More than 30 million people are now at risk of starvation in southern Africa and the Horn of Africa. All of these

---

(A) The title and introduction aim to create urgency about the issue.
(B) Stressing the importance of women in African societies, Annan outlines the double catastrophe happening.

predominantly agricultural societies are also battling serious AIDS epidemics. This is no coincidence: AIDS and famine are directly linked.

4 Because of AIDS, farming skills are being lost, agricultural development efforts are declining, rural livelihoods are disintegrating, productive capacity to work the land is dropping, and household earnings are shrinking—all while the cost of caring for the ill is rising exponentially. At the same time, H.I.V. infection and AIDS are spreading dramatically and disproportionately among women. A United Nations report released last month shows that women now make up 50 percent of those infected with H.I.V. worldwide—and in Africa that figure is now 59 percent. Today, AIDS has a woman's face.

5 AIDS has already caused immense suffering by killing almost 2.5 million Africans this year alone. It has left 11 million African children orphaned since the epidemic began. Now it is attacking the capacity of these countries to resist famine by eroding those mechanisms that enable populations to fight back—the coping abilities provided by women.

6 In famines before the AIDS crisis, women proved more resilient than men. Their survival rate was higher, and their coping skills were stronger. Women were the ones who found alternative foods that could sustain their children in time of drought. Because droughts happened once a decade or so, women who had experienced previous droughts were able to pass on survival techniques to younger women. Women are the ones who

nurture social networks that can help spread the burden in times of famine.

7

(C) But today, as AIDS is eroding the health of Africa's women, it is eroding the skills, experience and networks that keep their families and communities going. Even before falling ill, a woman will often have to care for a sick husband, thereby reducing the time she can devote to planting, harvesting and marketing crops. When her husband dies, she is often deprived of credit, distribution networks or land rights. When she dies, the household will risk collapsing completely, leaving children to fend for themselves. The older ones, especially girls, will be taken out of school to work in the home or the farm. These girls, deprived of education and opportunities, will be even less able to protect themselves against AIDS.

8

(D) Because this crisis is different from past famines, we must look beyond relief measures of the past. Merely shipping in food is not enough. Our effort will have to combine food assistance and new approaches to farming with treatment and prevention of H.I.V. and AIDS. It will require creating early-warning and analysis systems that monitor both H.I.V. infection rates and famine indicators. It will require new agricultural techniques, appropriate to a depleted work force. It will require a renewed effort to wipe out H.I.V.-related stigma and silence.

9

It will require innovative, large-scale ways to care for orphans, with specific measures that enable children in AIDS-affected communities to stay in school. Education and prevention are still the most powerful weapons against the spread of H.I.V. Above all, this new international effort must put women at the center of our strategy to fight AIDS.

10

Experience suggests that there is reason to hope.

(C) Annan contrasts women's situation before and after the arrival of AIDS.
(D) He presses for a new combination of necessary, related actions.

The recent United Nations report shows that H.I.V. (E) infection rates in Uganda continue to decline. In South Africa, infection rates for women under 20 have started to decrease. In Zambia, H.I.V. rates show signs of dropping among women in urban areas and younger women in rural areas. In Ethiopia, infection levels have fallen among young women in the center of Addis Ababa.

We can and must build on those successes and 11 replicate them elsewhere. For that, we need leadership, partnership, and imagination from the international community and African governments. If we want to save Africa from two catastrophes, we would do well to focus on saving Africa's women.

(E) He points to hopeful signs and cases as a way of convincing readers that change can happen.

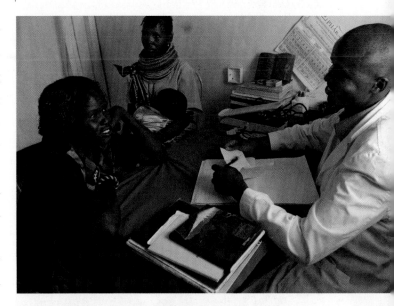

American Spirit, 2014 / Used under license from Shutterstock.com

Reading for Better Writing

1. How does the writer introduce the topic and focus the essay? Explain.

2. What does Annan ask readers to do? Is his request clear and convincing? Why?

3. Choose a paragraph that you find particularly convincing, and explain why.

East, 2014 / Used under license from Shutterstock.com

WRITE, REVISE, AND EDIT AN ESSAY PERSUADING READERS TO ACT

18-5

Writing Guidelines

Planning

① Select a topic. List issues about which you feel passionately, such as community problems, international issues, disaster-relief efforts, educational outreach programs, environmental clean-up efforts, or social or political campaigns. Then choose a related topic that is debatable, significant, current, and manageable.

Not Debatable

- Statistics on spending practices
- The existence of racism
- Recyclables are dumped in landfills

Debatable

- The injustice of consumerism
- Solutions to racism
- Tax on paper/plastic grocery bags

② Choose and analyze your audience. Think about who your readers are and why they might resist the change that you advocate.

③ Narrow your focus and determine your purpose. Should you focus on one aspect of the issue or all of it? What should you and can you try to change? How might you best organize your argument?

④ Generate ideas and support. Use prewriting strategies like those below to develop your thinking and gather support:

- Set up "opposing viewpoints" columns in which you list arguments accepted by advocates of each position.
- Research the issue to find current, reliable sources from multiple perspectives.
- Research other calls to action on this issue, noting their appeals, supporting evidence, and success.
- Brainstorm the range of actions that might be taken in response to the issue. For each action, explore how attractive and doable it might be for your readers.
- Consider what outcomes or results you want.

⑤ Organize your thinking. Consider using the following strategies:

- Make a sharp claim (like those below) that points toward action:

  > On the issue of _____ , I believe _____ .
  > Therefore, we must change _____ .

- Review the evidence, and develop your line of reasoning by generating an outline or using a graphic organizer. (See pages 46–47.)

Simple Outline:

Introduction: the issue and initial claim

> *Describing the issue and its importance:* point 1, 2, and so on
>
> *Explaining possible actions and benefits:* point 1, 2, and so on

Conclusion: call to specific action

Drafting

⑥ Write your first draft. As you write, remember your goal and specific readers:

- **Opening:** Gain the readers' attention, raise the issue, help the readers care about it, and state your claim.
- **Development:** Decide where to place your most persuasive supporting argument: first or last. Anticipate readers' questions and objections, and use appropriate logical and emotional appeals to overcome their resistance to change.
- **Closing:** Restate your claim, summarize your support, and call your readers to act.

- **Title:** Develop a thoughtful, energetic working title that stresses a vision or change. (For ideas, scan the titles of the sample essays in this chapter.)

Revising

7 **Improve the ideas, organization, and voice.** Ask a classmate or someone from the college's writing center to read your call-to-action paper for the following:

Ideas: Does the writing prompt readers to change their thinking and behavior? Does the essay show effective reasoning, good support, and a clear call to action—without logical fallacies such as half-truths, unreliable testimonials, attacks against a person, and false analogies (see pages 188–191)?

Organization: Does the opening engagingly raise the issue? Does the middle carefully press the issue and the need for action through logical reasoning and appeals? Does the closing successfully call for specific changes and actions?

Voice: Is the tone energetic but controlled, confident but reasonable? Does the writing inspire readers to join your cause and act?

Editing

8 **Edit and proofread the essay by checking issues like these:**

Words: Language is precise, concrete, and easily understood—no jargon, clichés, doublespeak, or loaded terms.

Sentences: Constructions flow smoothly and are varied in structure.

Correctness: The copy includes no errors in grammar, punctuation, usage, mechanics, or spelling.

Design: The page design is correctly formatted and attractive; information is properly documented according to the required system (e.g., MLA, APA).

Publishing

9 **Prepare and publish your final essay.** Submit the essay to your instructor. If appropriate, solicit feedback from another audience—perhaps on a Web site, in the school newspaper, at a campus club, or from a community organization.

Critical-Thinking and Writing Activities

1. The three essays in this chapter address significant social and ethical issues: wealth and poverty, health and famine, racial equality. List topics like these, choose one, narrow the focus to a specific issue, and then write an essay that persuades readers to do something related to the issue.

2. Choose an issue that is related to your major and requires change. Then write an essay in which you describe the issue and persuade readers to take the action that you recommend.

3. As a service project, visit an administrator at a local nonprofit agency (e.g., school, hospital, church, employment office, YMCA) and offer to write an editorial, news article, or letter in which you describe one of the agency's needs and persuade readers to offer their help.

4. What issues have come up in your job? Contemplate issues such as pay equity, equal opportunity, management policies, and unsafe work conditions. Then write a persuasive report to a decision maker or to fellow employees.

STUDY TOOLS 18

LOCATED AT BACK OF THE TEXTBOOK
☐ Tear-Out Chapter Review Card

LOCATED AT WWW.CENGAGEBRAIN.COM/LOGIN
☐ Chapter eBook
☐ Graded quizzes and a practice quiz generator
☐ Videos: Writer Interviews
☐ Tutorials
☐ Flashcards
☐ Cengage Learning Write Experience
☐ Interactive activities

19 | Proposing a Solution

"I BELIEVE THAT IF YOU SHOW PEOPLE THE PROBLEMS AND YOU SHOW THEM SOLUTIONS, THEY WILL BE MOVED TO ACT."

BILL GATES

Ruslan Grumble, 2014 / Used under license from Shutterstock.com

LEARNING OBJECTIVES

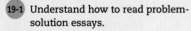 **19-1** Understand how to read problem-solution essays.

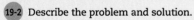 **19-2** Describe the problem and solution.

19-3 Analyze the problem.

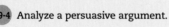 **19-4** Analyze a persuasive argument.

19-5 Write, revise, and edit a problem-solution essay.

After you finish
this chapter
go to
PAGE 229 for STUDY TOOLS

Proposals are prescriptions for change. As such, they challenge readers to care about a problem, accept a solution, and act on it. A strong proposal offers a logical, practical, and creative argument that leads toward positive change.

Proposal writers argue for such remedies in all areas of life. In your college courses, you'll be challenged to generate solutions to many difficult problems. In your community, you may participate in policy making and civic development. In the workplace, you may write proposals that justify expenditures, sell products, or troubleshoot problems. In each situation, you'll have to clearly explain the problem, offer a solution, argue for adopting it, and possibly also explain how to implement it.

19-1 UNDERSTAND HOW TO READ PROBLEM-SOLUTION ESSAYS

The instructions below will help you understand and use problem-solution logic.

19-1a Consider the Rhetorical Situation for Problem-Solution Writing

When reading problem-solution writing, think about its purpose, audience, and topic.

▶ **Purpose:** Problem-solution writing aims to inform: to describe a problem accurately, to present workable solutions, and to explain the strengths and weaknesses of each. However, such writing also aims to persuade: to convince readers that a problem is urgent, that one solution is better than others, or that readers should implement it.

▶ **Audience:** Potentially, writers could have four audiences: people responsible for the problem, de-

cision makers with the power to adopt a solution, people affected by the problem, and a public who just wants information about the problem. When reading the document, note whether it (1) offers all of its readers the information that they need and (2) communicates in language that they can understand and trust.

▶ **Topic:** Clearly, problem-solution writing focuses on a problem, but it can be a problem broadly conceived—perhaps as a challenge or an opportunity. Across the college curriculum, such problems are typically discipline related (e.g., dyslexia in Education, oil spills in Environmental Studies, agoraphobia in Psychology). In the workplace, problem-solution reasoning is used in proposals.

19-1b Consider the Reasoning

When reading problem-solution writing, look for the following:

▶ **Accurate Description:** The writer correctly describes the problem, including relevant details regarding its history, causes, effects, dangers, costs, and direct or indirect impact on readers. The writing also describes all reasonable solutions, including details about their history, side effects, costs, successes, and failures.

▶ **Thorough Analysis:** The writer carefully analyzes the problem, each solution, and why the recommended solution is the best choice. The writer supports all claims with reliable data and logical reasoning.

▶ **Rational Argument:** The writer's claims and appeals for action are thoughtful; stated in objective terms; and presented in a measured, informed voice.

 Reading Guide: Problem-Solution

✔ What is the problem, what is its history, and why should the problem be resolved?

✔ What is the solution, and how does it resolve the problem and with what side effects?

✔ What action does the writer call for, and is it effective, realistic, and cost effective?

✔ Are persuasive statements reasonable, well documented, and free of fallacies?

DESCRIBE THE PROBLEM AND SOLUTION

Journalism major Renee Wielenga wrote and published "Dream Act . . ." as a newspaper article. She then revised the piece as an essay but retained the problem-solution reasoning used in her original article. As you read the essay, assess whether her description of the problem and solution is accurate and free of fallacies.

Essay Outline

Introduction: (Problem) Students' dreams foiled by immigration laws; (Solution) Dream Act offers route to legal residency.

1. Bill's requirements for residency and citizenship
2. Bill's origin and increasing support
3. Bill's remaining impediments

Conclusion: The Dream Act warrants readers' support.

(A)
Dream Act May Help Local Student Fight for Residency

SQ3R Survey · Question · Read · Recite · Review

1 Attending college, joining the military, creating a
(B) career path: These are dreams for most U.S. high school graduates. But for Maria Lopez, a senior at San Marshall High School who has lived in the U.S for seven years, there is only one legal option: return to Mexico. She is one of nearly 65,000 high school students each year who do not have the opportunity to pursue their dreams because they arrived in the U.S. illegally. Like many of these students, Maria is highly motivated, hard working, and excited to be involved in her high school. However, Maria's parents brought her to this country without going through the legal immigration process. As a

result, by law she is an undocumented alien who has no method to achieve legal residency while living in the U.S.

Currently, children like Maria have only one route 2 to legal residency: go back to their country of birth, (C) file the proper paperwork, and then return to the U.S. Unfortunately, attempts to return legally are often difficult, with roadblocks such as a 10-year restriction on re-entering the U.S. However, one piece of proposed federal legislation could help these young people pursue their dreams: The Development, Relief, and Education for Alien Minors Act (S. 729), better known as the Dream Act, is an amendment to the Illegal Immigration Reform and Immigrant Responsibility Act of 1996.

The current version of this bill would grant eligible 3 immigrant students six years of conditional residency (D) during which they could earn full citizenship. To be eligible for conditional residency, a student must: (1) graduate from a U.S. high school or obtain a GED, (2) be of good moral character, (3) have arrived in the U.S. under the age of 16, (4) have proof of residence in the U.S. for at least five consecutive years since the arrival date, and (5) be between the ages of 12 and 35 at the time of the bill's enactment. To gain full citizenship, the student must do one of the following during his or her residency: (1) complete at least two years of work toward a four-year college degree, (2) earn a two-year college degree, or (3) serve in the military for two years. If, within the six-year period, a student does not complete either the college requirement or the military-service requirement, the person would lose his or her temporary residency and be subject to deportation.

(C) (Solution) Dream Act offers route to legal residency.
(D) Bill's requirements for residency and citizenship

Konstantin L. 2014 / Used under license from Shutterstock.com

(A) Title: the problem and solution
(B) Introduction: (Problem) Students' dreams foiled by immigration laws

4 (E) While the Dream Act was first introduced in 2001, and its progress toward approval has been slow, the bill's popularity has grown each year since then. For example, in March 2009, the bill was re-introduced in the U.S. Senate by Richard Durbin (D-IL) and Richard Lugar (R-IN). Also at that time, Howard Berman (D-CA), Lincoln Diaz-Balart (R-FL), Lucille Roybal-Allard (D-CA), and a number of other legislators introduced the bill in the House of Representatives, where the document is called the American Dream Act (H.R. 1751). In addition to these officials, many citizens such as Maria's guidance counselor, Ben Barry, favor the bill, believing that it would give immigrant students a chance to give back to the country that has given so much to them, and the bill would offer those students an opportunity to utilize their hard-earned education and talents.

5 (F) However, as of January 2010, the bill remains in the first step in the legislative process—a process in which bills go to committees or "mini congresses" that deliberate, investigate, and revise the bill before it is brought up for general debate in either the Senate or the House of Representatives. The disheartening fact, though, is that the majority of bills never make it out of these committees. Furthermore, supporters of Comprehensive Immigration Reform (CIR) are in favor of including the Dream Act as part of CIR, which could make the Dream Act subject to change yet again.

6 (G) Given such debates, it might be a long time before the bill becomes law, thereby dashing the dreams of nearly 65,000 high school students like Maria who can't wait another year because they may already be in deportation proceedings. We need to step up and educate our representatives and senators about the importance of passing the Dream Act on its own instead of including the bill along with CIR. We need to urge them to debate and approve the Dream Act now, thereby making Maria's dreams—and the dreams of thousands of students like her—a reality!

(E) Bill's origin and increasing support
(F) Bill's remaining impediments
(G) Conclusion: The Dream Act warrants our support.

Reading for Better Writing

1. What problem does Wielenga address, and how does she get readers to care about it?
2. What solution does she propose, and how does she explain or assert its value?
3. In paragraph 6, Wielenga urges readers to promote her solution. Explain why you do or do not find her rationale for action convincing.

19-3 ANALYZE THE PROBLEM

In the essay that follows, David Blankenhorn argues that America is losing its understanding of and appreciation for fatherhood. To help readers understand that the problem does exist and must be resolved, he analyzes its history, causes, and effects.

Fatherless America

SQ3R Survey · Question · Read · Recite · Review

1   The United States is becoming an increasingly fatherless society. A generation ago, an American child could reasonably expect to grow up with his or her father. Today, an American child can reasonably expect not to. Fatherlessness is now approaching a rough parity with fatherhood as a defining feature of American childhood.

2   This astonishing fact is reflected in many statistics, but here are the two most important. Tonight, about 40 percent of American children will go to sleep in homes in which their fathers do not live. Before they reach the age of 18, more than half of our nation's children are likely to spend at least a significant portion of their childhoods living apart from their fathers. Never before in this country have so many children been voluntarily abandoned by their fathers. Never before have so many children grown up without knowing what it means to have a father.

3   Fatherlessness is the most harmful demographic trend of this generation. It is the leading cause of declining child well-being in our society. It is also the engine driving our most urgent social problems, from crime to

adolescent pregnancy to child abuse to domestic violence against women. Yet, despite its scale and social consequences, fatherlessness is a problem that is frequently ignored or denied. Especially within our elite discourse, it remains largely a problem with no name.

4   If this trend continues, fatherlessness is likely to change the shape of our society. Consider this prediction. After the year 2000, as people born after 1970 emerge as a large proportion of our working-age adult population, the United States will be a nation divided into two groups, separate and unequal. The two groups will work in the same economy, speak a common language, and remember the same national history. But they will live fundamentally divergent lives. One group will receive basic benefits—psychological, social, economic, educational, and moral—that are denied to the other group.

5   The primary fault line dividing the two groups will not be race, religion, class, education, or gender. It will be patrimony. One group will consist of those adults who grew up with the daily presence and provision of fathers. The other group will consist of those who did not. By the early years of the next [twenty-first] century, these two groups will be roughly the same size.

6   Surely a crisis of this scale merits a response. At a minimum, it requires a serious debate. Why is fatherhood declining? What can be done about it? Can our society find ways to invigorate effective fatherhood as a norm of male behavior? Yet, to date, the public discussion on this topic has been remarkably weak and defeatist. There is a prevailing belief that not much can—or even should—be done to reverse the trend.

7   When the crime rate jumps, politicians promise to do something about it. When the unemployment rate rises, task forces assemble to address the problem. As random shootings increase, public health officials worry about the preponderance of guns. But when it comes to the mass defection of men from family life, not much happens.

8   There is debate, even alarm, about specific social problems. Divorce. Out-of-wedlock childbearing. Children growing up in poverty. Youth violence. Unsafe neighborhoods. Domestic violence. The weakening of parental authority. But in these discussions, we seldom acknowledge the underlying phenomenon that binds together these otherwise disparate issues: the flight of males from their children's lives. In fact, we seem to go out of our way to avoid the connection between our most pressing social problems and the trend of fatherlessness.

9   We avoid this connection because, as a society, we are changing our minds about the role of men in family life. As a cultural idea, our inherited understanding of fatherhood is under siege. Men in general, and fathers in particular, are increasingly viewed as superfluous to family life: either as expendable or as part of the problem. Masculinity itself, understood as anything other than a rejection of what it has traditionally meant to be male, is typically treated with suspicion and even hostility in our cultural discourse. Consequently, our society is now manifestly unable to sustain, or even find reason to believe in, fatherhood as a distinctive domain of male activity.

10   The core question is simple: Does every child need a father? Increasingly, our society's answer is "no" or at least "not necessarily." Few idea shifts in this century are as consequential as this one. At stake is nothing less than what it means to be a man, who our children will be, and what kind of society we will become.

11   This [essay] is a criticism not simply of fatherlessness but of a culture of fatherlessness. For, in addition to losing fathers, we are losing something larger: our idea

of fatherhood. Unlike earlier periods of father absence in our history, we now face more than a physical loss affecting some homes. We face a cultural loss affecting every home. For this reason, the most important absence our society must confront is not the absence of fathers but the absence of our belief in fathers.

12   In a larger sense, this [essay] is a cultural criticism because fatherhood, much more than motherhood, is a cultural invention. Its meaning for the individual man is shaped less by biology than by cultural script or story—a societal code that guides, and at times pressures, him into certain ways of acting and of understanding himself as a man.

13   Like motherhood, fatherhood is made up of both a biological and a social dimension. Yet in societies across the world, mothers are far more successful than fathers at fusing these two dimensions into a coherent parental identity. Is the nursing mother playing a biological or social role? Is she feeding or bonding? We can hardly separate the two, so seamlessly are they woven together.

14   But fatherhood is a different matter. A father makes his sole biological contribution at the moment of conception—nine months before the infant enters the world. Because social paternity is only indirectly linked to biological paternity, the connection between the two cannot be assumed. The phrase "to father a child" usually refers only to the act of insemination, not to the responsibility for raising a child. What fathers contribute to their offspring after conception is largely a matter of cultural devising.

15   Moreover, despite their other virtues, men are not ideally suited to responsible fatherhood. Although they certainly have the capacity for fathering, men are inclined to sexual promiscuity and paternal waywardness. Anthropologically, human fatherhood constitutes what might be termed a necessary problem. It is necessary because, in all societies, child well-being and societal success hinge largely upon a high level of paternal investment: the willingness of adult males to devote energy and resources to the care of their offspring. It is a problem because adult males are frequently—indeed, increasingly—unwilling or unable to make that vital investment.

16   Because fatherhood is universally problematic in human societies, cultures must mobilize to devise and enforce the father role for men, coaxing and guiding them into fatherhood through a set of legal and extralegal pressures that require them to maintain a close alliance with their children's mother and to invest in their children. Because men do not volunteer for fatherhood as much as they are conscripted into it by the surrounding culture, only an authoritative cultural story of fatherhood can fuse biological and social paternity into a coherent male identity.

17   For exactly this reason, Margaret Mead and others have observed that the supreme test of any civilization is whether it can socialize men by teaching them to be fathers—creating a culture in which men acknowledge their paternity and willingly nurture their offspring. Indeed, if we can equate the essence of the antisocial male with violence, we can equate the essence of the socialized male with being a good father. Thus, at the center of our most important cultural imperative, we find the fatherhood script: the story that describes what it ought to mean for a man to have a child.

18   Just as the fatherhood script advances the social goal of harnessing male behavior to collective needs, it also reflects an individual purpose. That purpose, in a word, is happiness. Anthropologists have long understood that the genius of an effective culture is its capacity to reconcile individual happiness with collective well-being. By situating individual lives within a social narrative, culture endows private behavior with larger meaning. By linking the self to moral purposes larger than the self, an effective culture tells us a story in which individual fulfillment transcends selfishness, and personal satisfaction transcends narcissism.

19   In this respect, our cultural script is not simply a set of imported moralisms, exterior to the individual and designed only to compel self-sacrifice. It is also a pathway—indeed, our only pathway—to what the founders of the American experiment called the pursuit of happiness.

20   The stakes on this issue could hardly be higher. Our society's conspicuous failure to sustain or create compelling norms of fatherhood amounts to a social and personal disaster. Today's story of fatherhood features one-dimensional characters, an unbelievable plot, and an unhappy ending. It reveals in our society both a failure of collective memory and a collapse of moral imagination. It undermines families, neglects children, causes or aggravates our worst social problems, and makes individual adult happiness—both male and female—harder to achieve.

21   Ultimately, this failure reflects nothing less than a culture gone awry: a culture increasingly unable to establish the boundaries, erect the sign-posts, and fashion the stories that can harmonize individual happiness with collective well-being. In short, it reflects a culture that increasingly fails to "enculture" individual men and women, mothers and fathers.

22   In personal terms, the end result of this process, the final residue from what David Gutmann calls the "deculturation" of paternity, is narcissism: a me-first egotism that is hostile not only to any societal goal or larger moral purpose but also to any save the most puerile understanding of personal happiness. In social terms, the primary results of decultured paternity are a decline in children's well-being and a rise in male violence, especially against women. In a larger sense, the most significant result is our society's steady fragmentation into atomized individuals, isolated from one another and estranged from the aspirations and realities of common membership in a family, a community, a nation, bound by mutual commitment and shared memory.

23   [A good father] is a cultural model, or what Max Weber calls an ideal social type—an anthropomorphized composite of cultural ideas about the meaning of paternity. I call him the Good Family Man. As described by one of the fathers [I] interviewed [...], a Good Family Man "puts his family first."

24   A good society celebrates the ideal of the man who puts his family first. Because our society is now lurching in the opposite direction, I see the Good Family Man as the principal casualty of today's weakening fatherhood script. And because I cannot imagine a good society without him, I offer him as the protagonist in the stronger script that I believe is both necessary and possible.

Reading for Better Writing

1. In your own words, state the problem that Blankenhorn identifies and his proposed solution.

2. Choose five paragraphs and analyze their structure (e.g., topic sentence, supporting details, sentence structure, and transitions linking paragraphs). Then explain how these elements do or do not help present a clear message.

3. Working with a classmate, choose seven logical fallacies explained on pages 188–191. Then discuss why you believe that Blankenhorn's argument does or does not include these fallacies. Share your ideas with the class.

4. In paragraph 9, Blankenhorn makes the following claim: "Masculinity itself, understood as anything other than a rejection of what it has traditionally meant to be male, is typically treated with suspicion and even hostility in our cultural discourse." Explain what he means and why you find it a strong or weak claim.

19-4 ANALYZE A PERSUASIVE ARGUMENT

In the following essay, published in August 2009, Barbara Ehrenreich argues that whereas America's poor citizens sometimes loiter, trespass, or panhandle, most do these things because they're poor—not because they're criminals. In response to such behavior, she urges readers to show compassion and to act on behalf of the poor. Note how she supports her argument with logical appeals (192) linked to readers' needs and values (192).

Is It Now a Crime to Be Poor?

SQ3R Survey · Question · Read · Recite · Review

1   It's too bad so many people are falling into poverty at a time when it's almost illegal to be poor. You won't

(A) be arrested for shopping in a Dollar Store, but if you are truly, deeply, in-the-streets poor, you're well advised not to engage in any of the biological necessities of life—like sitting, sleeping, lying down, or loitering. City officials boast that there is nothing discriminatory about the ordinances that afflict the destitute, most of which go back to the dawn of gentrification in the '80s and '90s. "If you're lying on a sidewalk, whether you're homeless or a millionaire, you're in violation of the ordinance," a city attorney in St. Petersburg, Fla., said in June, echoing Anatole France's immortal observation that "the law, in its majestic equality, forbids the rich as well as the poor to sleep under bridges."

2   In defiance of all reason and compassion, the criminalization of poverty has actually been intensifying as the recession generates ever more poverty. So concludes a new study from the National Law Center on Homelessness and Poverty, which found that the number of ordinances against the publicly poor has been rising since 2006, along with ticketing and arrests for more "neutral" infractions like jaywalking, littering or carrying an open container of alcohol. [See *Homes Not Handcuffs: The Criminalization of Homelessness in U.S. Cities.*]

(A) As you read, highlight strategies and take marginal notes exploring how Ehrenreich raises the issue and calls for action.

3   The report lists America's 10 "meanest" cities—the largest of which are Honolulu, Los Angeles and San Francisco—but new contestants are springing up every day. The City Council in Grand Junction, Colo., has been considering a ban on begging, and at the end of June, Tempe, Ariz., carried out a four-day crackdown on the indigent. How do you know when someone is indigent? As a Las Vegas statute puts it, "An indigent person is a person whom a reasonable ordinary person would believe to be entitled to apply for or receive" public assistance.

4   That could be me before the blow-drying and eyeliner, and it's definitely Al Szekely at any time of day. A grizzled 62-year-old, he inhabits a wheelchair and is often found on G Street in Washington—the city that is ultimately responsible for the bullet he took in the spine in Fu Bai, Vietnam, in 1972. He had been enjoying the luxury of an indoor bed until last December, when the police swept through the shelter in the middle of the night looking for men with outstanding warrants.

5   It turned out that Mr. Szekely, who is an ordained minister and does not drink, do drugs or curse in front of ladies, did indeed have a warrant—for not appearing in court to face a charge of "criminal trespassing" (for sleeping on a sidewalk in a Washington suburb). So he was dragged out of the shelter and put in jail. "Can you imagine?" asked Eric Sheptock, the homeless advocate (himself a shelter resident) who introduced me to Mr. Szekely. "They arrested a homeless man in a shelter for being homeless."

6   The viciousness of the official animus toward the indigent can be breathtaking. A few years ago, a group called Food Not Bombs started handing out free vegan food to hungry people in public parks around the nation.

A number of cities, led by Las Vegas, passed ordinances forbidding the sharing of food with the indigent in public places, and several members of the group were arrested. A federal judge just overturned the anti-sharing law in Orlando, Fla., but the city is appealing. And now Middletown, Conn., is cracking down on food sharing.

7   If poverty tends to criminalize people, it is also true that criminalization inexorably impoverishes them. Scott Lovell, another homeless man I interviewed in Washington, earned his record by committing a significant crime—by participating in the armed robbery of a steak house when he was 15. Although Mr. Lovell dresses and speaks more like a summer tourist from Ohio than a felon, his criminal record has made it extremely difficult for him to find a job.

8   For Al Szekely, the arrest for trespassing meant a further descent down the circles of hell. While in jail, he lost his slot in the shelter and now sleeps outside the Verizon Center sports arena, where the big problem, in addition to the security guards, is mosquitoes. His stick thin arms are covered with pink crusty sores, which he treats with a regimen of frantic scratching.

9   For the not-yet homeless, there are two main paths to criminalization—one involving debt, and the other skin color. Anyone of any color or pre-recession financial status can fall into debt, and although we pride ourselves on the abolition of debtors' prison, in at least one state, Texas, people who can't afford to pay their traffic fines may be made to "sit out their tickets" in jail.

10   Often the path to legal trouble begins when one of your creditors has a court issue a summons for you, which you fail to honor for one reason or another. (Maybe your address has changed or you never received it.) Now you're in contempt of court. Or suppose you miss a payment and, before you realize it, your car insurance lapses; then you're stopped for something like a broken headlight. Depending on the state, you may have your car impounded or face a steep fine—again, exposing you to a possible summons. "There's just no end to it once the cycle starts," said Robert Solomon of Yale Law School. "It just keeps accelerating."

11   By far the most reliable way to be criminalized by poverty is to have the wrong-color skin. Indignation runs high when a celebrity professor encounters racial profiling, but for decades whole communities have been effectively "profiled" for the suspicious combination of being both dark-skinned and poor, thanks to the "broken windows" or "zero tolerance" theory of policing popularized by Rudy Giuliani, when he was mayor of New York City, and his police chief William Bratton.

12   Flick a cigarette in a heavily patrolled community of color and you're littering; wear the wrong color T-shirt and you're displaying gang allegiance. Just strolling around in a dodgy neighborhood can mark you as a potential suspect, according to *Let's Get Free: A Hip-Hop Theory of Justice*, an eye-opening new book by Paul Butler, a former federal prosecutor in Washington. If you seem at all evasive, which I suppose is like looking "overly anxious" in an airport, Mr. Butler writes, the police "can force you to stop just to investigate why you don't want to talk to them." And don't get grumpy about it or you could be "resisting arrest."

13   There's no minimum age for being sucked into what the Children's Defense Fund calls "the cradle-to-prison pipeline." In New York City, a teenager caught in public housing without an ID—say, while visiting a friend or relative—can be charged with criminal trespassing and wind up in juvenile detention, Mishi Faruqee, the director of youth justice programs for the Children's Defense Fund of New York, told me. In just the past few months, a growing number of cities have taken to ticketing and sometimes handcuffing teenagers found on the streets during school hours.

14   In Los Angeles, the fine for truancy is $250; in Dallas, it can be as much as $500—crushing amounts for people living near the poverty level. According to

the Los Angeles Bus Riders Union, an advocacy group, 12,000 students were ticketed for truancy in 2008.

15   Why does the Bus Riders Union care? Because it estimates that 80 percent of the "truants," especially those who are black or Latino, are merely late for school, thanks to the way that over-filled buses whiz by them without stopping. I met people in Los Angeles who told me they keep their children home if there's the slightest chance of their being late. It's an ingenious anti-truancy policy that discourages parents from sending their youngsters to school.

16   The pattern is to curtail financing for services that might help the poor while ramping up law enforcement: starve school and public transportation budgets, then make truancy illegal. Shut down public housing, then make it a crime to be homeless. Be sure to harass street vendors when there are few other opportunities for employment. The experience of the poor, and especially poor minorities, comes to resemble that of a rat in a cage scrambling to avoid erratically administered electric shocks.

17   And if you should make the mistake of trying to escape via a brief marijuana-induced high, it's "gotcha" all over again, because that of course is illegal too. One result is our staggering level of incarceration, the highest in the world. Today the same number of Americans—2.3 million—reside in prison as in public housing.

18   Meanwhile, the public housing that remains has become ever more prisonlike, with residents subjected to drug testing and random police sweeps. The safety net, or what's left of it, has been transformed into a dragnet.

19   Some of the community organizers I've talked to around the country think they know why "zero tolerance" policing has ratcheted up since the recession began. Leonardo Vilchis of the Union de Vecinos, a community organization in Los Angeles, suspects that "poor people have become a source of revenue" for recession-starved cities, and that the police can always find a violation leading to a fine. If so, this is a singularly demented fund-raising strategy. At a Congressional hearing in June, the president of the National Association of Criminal Defense Lawyers testified about the pervasive "overcriminalization of crimes that are not a risk to public safety," like sleeping in a cardboard box or jumping turnstiles, which leads to expensively clogged courts and prisons.

20   A Pew Center study released in March found states spending a record $51.7 billion on corrections, an amount that the center judged, with an excess of moderation, to be "too much."

21   But will it be enough—the collision of rising prison populations that we can't afford and the criminalization of poverty—to force us to break the mad cycle of poverty and punishment? With the number of people in poverty increasing (some estimates suggest it's up to 45 million to 50 million, from 37 million in 2007) several states are beginning to ease up on the criminalization of poverty—for example, by sending drug offenders to treatment rather than jail, shortening probation and reducing the number of people locked up for technical violations like missed court appointments. But others are tightening the screws: not only increasing the number of "crimes" but also charging prisoners for their room and board—assuring that they'll be released with potentially criminalizing levels of debt.

22   Maybe we can't afford the measures that would begin to alleviate America's growing poverty—affordable housing, good schools, reliable public transportation and so forth. I would argue otherwise, but for now I'd be content with a consensus that, if we can't afford to truly help the poor, neither can we afford to go on tormenting them.

Reading for Better Writing

1. Note how Ehrenreich uses the title, opening sentence, and opening paragraph to introduce her topic and focus her argument. Are these strategies effective?
2. Identify two passages in which the writer makes a claim and then supports it by citing a study or an academic authority. Is this strategy convincing?
3. Cite two passages in which the writer uses an anecdote or illustration to support a claim. Do these strategies strengthen her argument?
4. Precisely what problem does the writer identify, and what solution does she advocate?

WRITE, REVISE, AND EDIT A PROBLEM-SOLUTION ESSAY

Writing Guidelines

Planning

❶ Select and narrow a topic. Brainstorm possibilities from this list:

- **People Problems:** Consider generations—your own or a relative's. What problems face this generation? Why, and how can they be solved?
- **College Problems:** List problems faced by college students. In your major, what problems are experts trying to solve?
- **Social Problems:** What problems do our communities and country face? Where do you see suffering, injustice, inequity, waste, or harm?
- **Workplace Problems:** What job-related problems have you experienced or might you experience?
- **Then test your topic:**
  - Is the problem real, serious, and currently—or potentially—harmful?
  - Do you care about this problem and believe that it must be solved? Why?
  - Can you offer a workable solution—or should you focus on part of the problem?

❷ Identify and analyze your audience. You could have four audiences: people responsible for the problem, decision makers with the power to deliver change, people affected by the problem, and a public that wants to learn about it.

- What do readers know about the problem? What are their questions or concerns?
- Why might they accept or resist change? What solution might they prefer?
- What arguments and evidence would convince them to acknowledge the problem, to care about it, and to take action?

❸ Probe the problem. If helpful, use the graphic organizers on pages 46–47.

- **Define the problem.** What is it, exactly? What are its parts or dimensions?
- **Determine the problem's seriousness.** Why should it be fixed? Who is affected and how?

What are its immediate, long-term, and potential effects?

- **Analyze causes.** What are its root causes and contributing factors?
- **Explore context.** What is the problem's background, history, and connection to other problems? What solutions have been tried in the past? Who, if anyone, benefits from the problem's existence?
- **Think creatively.** Look at the problem from other perspectives—other states and countries, both genders, different races and ethnic groups, and so on.

❹ Choose the best solution. List all imaginable solutions—both modest and radical fixes. Then evaluate the alternatives:

- List criteria that any solution should meet.
- List solutions and analyze their strengths, weaknesses, costs, and so on.
- Choose the best solution and gather evidence supporting your choice.

Drafting

❺ Outline your proposal and complete a first draft. Describe the problem, offer a solution, and defend it using strategies that fit your purpose and audience.

- **The problem:** Inform and/or persuade readers about the problem by using appropriate background information, cause-effect analysis, examples, analogies, parallel cases, visuals, and expert testimony.
- **The solution:** If necessary, first argue against alternative solutions. Then present your solution,

stating what should happen, who should be involved, and why.

- **The support:** Show how the solution solves the problem. Use facts, analysis, and expert testimony to argue that your solution is feasible and to address objections. If appropriate, use visuals such as photographs, drawings, or graphics to help readers grasp the nature and impact of the problem.

Revising

6 Improve the ideas, organization, and voice. Ask a classmate or someone from the college's writing center to read your paper for the following:

- **Ideas:** Does the solution fit the problem? Is the proposal precise, well researched, and well reasoned—free from oversimplification and obfuscation?
- **Organization:** Does the writing move convincingly from problem to solution, using fitting compare/contrast, cause/effect, and process structures?
- **Voice:** Is the tone positive, confident, objective, and sensitive to opposing viewpoints—and appropriate to the problem's seriousness?

Editing

7 Edit and proofread the essay. Look for these issues:

- **Words:** Words are precise, effectively defined, and clear.
- **Sentences:** Sentences are smooth, energetic, and varied in structure.
- **Correctness:** The copy includes no errors in spelling, usage, punctuation, grammar, or mechanics.
- **Design:** The page design is correctly formatted and attractive; information is properly documented according to the required system (e.g., MLA, APA). Any graphics and visuals used are effectively integrated with written text.

Publishing

8 Prepare and share your final essay. Submit your proposal to your instructor, but also consider sharing it with audiences who have a stake in solving the problem.

Critical-Thinking and Writing Activities

1. Think about current conditions and trends, forecast a problem, and write a proposal explaining how to prepare for or prevent it.

2. Review the section in chapter 16 about engaging the opposition (pages 191–192). Also review how David Blankenhorn engages his opposition in "Fatherless America." Then consider a persuasive piece that you are drafting or revising. How might you engage the opposition in a dialogue about your arguments? Revise your writing as needed.

3. Review the section in chapter 16 about "Identifying Logical Fallacies" (pages 188–191). Write a humorous problem/solution essay in which you make an argument that includes a number of obvious logical fallacies. Share your writing with the class.

4. What are some challenges facing the planet Earth and the human race in the foreseeable future? Find a focused challenge and write a proposal that addresses it.

STUDY TOOLS 19

LOCATED AT BACK OF THE TEXTBOOK
- ☐ Tear-Out Chapter Review Card

LOCATED AT WWW.CENGAGEBRAIN.COM/LOGIN
- ☐ Chapter eBook
- ☐ Graded quizzes and a practice quiz generator
- ☐ Videos: Writer Interviews
- ☐ Tutorials
- ☐ Flashcards
- ☐ Cengage Learning Write Experience
- ☐ Interactive activities

20 | Planning Your Research Project

"LIFE IS EITHER A DARING ADVENTURE OR NOTHING AT ALL."

HELEN KELLER

kuznetcov_konstantin_2014 / Used under license from Shutterstock.com

LEARNING OBJECTIVES

20-1 Understand academic research.

20-2 Initiate the process.

20-3 Develop a research plan.

20-4 Consider possible resources and sites.

20-5 Distinguish types of sources.

After you finish
this chapter
go to
PAGE 237 for STUDY TOOLS

In 1978, Ben Cohen and Jerry Greenfield pooled $8,000 of their own money and borrowed another $4,000 to open a small ice cream shop in Burlington, Vermont. From that small start, Ben and Jerry's Ice Cream has grown into a highly profitable, multinational business known for its innovations and social conscience. (In 2000, Unilever, an Anglo-Dutch corporation, bought Ben and Jerry's for $326 million dollars.)

From a distance, it would seem that Cohen and Greenfield have approached this "project" with a *joie de vivre* that should be the envy of everyone. They've developed an irresistible line of ice cream, created a wonderful work environment, committed millions to good causes, and on and on. What's not to like about Ben and Jerry's?

So what does this story have to tell you about your own research projects? (1) Start with topics that truly interest you; this is the only way you can do meaningful work. (2) Learn as much as you can about each topic. You can't guess in a research paper; you have to know what you're talking about. (3) Take a few risks by approaching each topic in a new or unusual way. (4) And give yourself plenty of time to research a variety of sources. Quality research can't be rushed.

This chapter will help you initiate such meaningful research projects, beginning with understanding the nature of college-level research.

 # 20-1 UNDERSTAND ACADEMIC RESEARCH

When you work on a research project, you ask important questions, look systematically for answers, and share your conclusions with readers.

20-1a Consider the Rhetorical Situation for Research Projects

Examine the rhetorical elements to better understand the key parts of academic research projects.

- ▶ **Topic:** Take ownership of each research project by exploring a topic or an angle that truly interests you and compels you to get started.

- ▶ **Purpose:** Your main goal is to become thoroughly knowledgeable about your topic and share your findings in a thoughtful way.

- ▶ **Form:** The traditional research paper is a fairly long essay (5 to 15 pages), complete with a thesis statement, supporting evidence, integrated sources, and documentation. Research can also be presented in a field report, on a Web site, or in a multimedia presentation.

- ▶ **Audience:** Your instructors, peers, and the academic community in general will be your main audience. However, you may also have a more specific audience in mind—smokers, Floridians, key political constituents, fellow immigrants, and so on.

- ▶ **Voice:** The expected voice in most research projects is formal or semiformal. Always try to maintain a thoughtful, confident tone throughout your writing. Generally, you should avoid the pronouns "I" and "you" in an effort to remain objective and academic. Unfortunately though, avoiding "I" and "you" can result in the overuse of the pronoun "one," so watch for that problem as well.

 TIP Some instructors encourage students to connect research with personal experience, meaning that you can, at times, use the pronouns "I" and "you." But be careful to keep the focus where it belongs—on the topic. The best research writing always centers on compelling ideas and information about the topic.

20-1b Research Involves Many Steps

The research process involves getting started, planning, conducting research, and developing the results. While research generally follows these steps, you should understand that the process is dynamic and recursive, meaning that it can be full of twists and turns, detours and side trips. For example, during your research, you may discover information that will change your mind about the topic or about the thesis statement you developed earlier. The flowchart below shows you the different tasks related to research.

A Research Flowchart

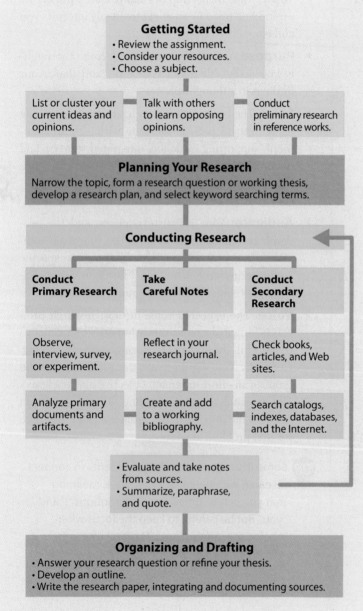

20-2 INITIATE THE PROCESS

To get started, you need to do four things: (1) understand the assignment, (2) select a topic, (3) build research questions, and (4) develop a working thesis. Your research project will only be as good as the planning that you put into it, so attend to each step with care.

20-2a Understand the Assignment

The first important step in a research project is to thoroughly review the assignment. Take some initial notes about it; record key words, options, restrictions, and requirements. Finally, write down any questions you still have about the project, find answers, and proceed.

20-2b Select a Topic

Author Joyce Carol Oates says, "As soon as you connect with your true subject, you will write." Your goal at the outset of a research project is to find your "true subject," an appropriate topic you sincerely want to explore and write about.

Making It Manageable

In most cases, your instructor will establish a general subject area to get you started. Your job is to select a specific, manageable topic related to that subject. A topic is "manageable" when you can learn about it in a reasonable amount of time. (You may have to carry out some cursory research in order to select a topic.)

General Subject	Area of Interest	Manageable Topic
urban social problems	the homeless	increase in homeless families
World War II legislation & initiatives	the Marshall Plan	the Plan's impact on the new world order
alternative energy	new generation of vehicles	hybrid-electric vehicles

20-2c Building Research Questions

Generating research questions helps you find meaningful information and ideas about your topic. These questions sharpen your research goal, and the answers become the focus of your writing. Create questions by following the guidelines below.

wavebreakmedia, 2014 / Used under license from Shutterstock.com

Needing to Know

List questions about your topic—both simple and complex—to discover what you need to know about it. Keep listing until you land on the **main question** you want to answer—the **main issue** you need to address. Then brainstorm supporting questions that you must research in order to adequately answer the main question.

Main Question:

Should consumers embrace hybrid-electric vehicles?

Supporting Questions

(Who? What? When? Where? Why? How?):

- *Who* has developed hybrid-electric cars?
- *What* is a hybrid-electric car?
- *When* were they developed?
- *Where* are they currently in use?
- *Why* are hybrids in use?
- *How* do they work?

✓ CHECKLIST: MAIN QUESTION

____ Is the question too narrow, too broad, or just about right for a research paper?

____ Is the question too easy or too hard to answer?

____ Am I committed to answering this question? Does it interest me?

____ Will I be able to find enough information about it within a reasonable amount of time?

____ Will the question and answers interest the reader?

20-2d Developing a Working Thesis

A **working thesis** offers a preliminary answer to your main research question. An effective working thesis keeps you focused during your research, helping you decide whether to read a particular book or just skim it, fully explore a Web site or quickly surf through it. When forming your working thesis, don't settle for a simple statement of fact about your topic; instead, form a statement that demands to be proved or that requires thoughtful explanation. The quick guide that follows includes a formula for writing this statement.

Formula:

a limited topic + a tentative claim, statement, or hypothesis = a working thesis

Samples:

Hybrid-electric cars offer consumers a reasonable alternative to gas-only cars.

The sharp increase in homeless families will force city planners to rethink their social service policies.

The Marshall Plan benefited Europe and the United States in three significant ways.

Use the following checklist to evaluate your working thesis.

✓ CHECKLIST: WORKING THESIS

____ Does my working thesis focus on a single, limited topic?

____ Is it stated clearly and directly?

____ Does it provide a preliminary answer to my main research question?

____ Do I have access to information that supports it?

____ Does my working thesis meet the requirements of the assignment?

Remember that your working thesis is set in sand, not stone. Your thinking on it might change as you research the topic because different sources may push you in new directions. Such changes show that you are truly engaged in your research. For more help with developing and refining a thesis, see pages 41–43.

> **working thesis** a preliminary answer to your main research question, the focus of your research

20-3 DEVELOP A RESEARCH PLAN

As you develop your research plan, consider what you already know about your topic. You can find this out by freewriting, clustering, or talking about your topic. (See pages 33–35.) Push yourself to gather as many of your own thoughts and feelings about the topic as you can before you conduct any "outside" research. Once you determine what you already know, then you can decide what you still need to find out. You should also figure out what resources can help you develop your research questions and working thesis.

20-3a Choose Research Methods

Do you need more background information? Is primary research a possibility? What other types of research are you interested in? The following information will answer your questions about planning your research.

Background Research

Take these steps to find information about central concepts and key terms related to your topic.

- Use the **Library of Congress** subject headings to find keywords for searching the library catalog, periodical databases, and the Internet (page 239).
- Conduct a preliminary search of the library catalog, journal databases, and the Internet to confirm that strong resources on your topic exist.
- Use specialized reference works to find background information, definitions, facts, and statistics (pages 245–246).

Library of Congress classification a system of classification used in most academic and research libraries

artifact any object made or modified by a human culture and later discovered

Primary Research

If at all possible, conduct primary research about your topic. Primary research is firsthand research in which you carry out interviews, observe the topic in action, and so on in order to develop your distinctive approach to the topic.

- Use interviews and surveys (pages 241–242) to get key information from experts and others.
- Conduct observations or experiments to obtain hard data.
- Analyze original documents or **artifacts**.

Library Research

With the help of a librarian or research specialist, search for important library resources. As you probably know, the library contains a wide variety of useful materials.

- Use scholarly books to get in-depth, reliable material (pages 245–246).
- Refer to periodical articles (print or electronic) to get current, reliable information (pages 246–247). Select from news sources, popular magazines, scholarly journals, and trade journals.
- Consider other resources, such as recorded interviews, pamphlets, marketing studies, or various government publications.

Internet Research

The Internet serves as an incredible resource that you can access at your fingertips. Use the following information to help you plan effective Internet searches.

- Use tools, such as search engines and subject guides, that will lead you to quality resources (pages 249–252).
- Select reputable Web sites that librarians, instructors, or other experts recommend (pages 254–257).
- Test Web sites for reliability (pages 259–261).

Sketch out tentative deadlines for completing each phase of your work: getting started, conducting research, drafting, and so on. Generally, you should spend about half your time on research and planning and half on writing. For some projects, you may have to formalize your planning in the form of a proposal, which shows your instructor that your plan is workable within the constraints of the assignment.

20-4 CONSIDER POSSIBLE RESOURCES AND SITES

When researching your topic, be sure to use a wide range of quality resources, as opposed to relying exclusively on information, substantial or not, from a few Web sites. (Your instructor may establish guidelines for the number and type of resources you should consult.) As you review your researching options, consider which resources will give you the best information about your topic. A sociology paper on airport behavior may require personal, direct research; a business paper on the evolution of subprime mortgage loans may best be researched in business publications, government reports, journals, newspapers, and so on.

20-4a Consider Information Resources

The sources of information available to you are almost unlimited, from interviewing someone to referring to bibliographies, from reviewing journal articles to studying graphics. Listed here are the common sources of information.

Type of Resource	Examples
Personal, primary resources	Memories, diaries, journals, logs, experiments, tests, observations, interviews, surveys
Reference works (print and electronic)	Dictionaries, thesauruses, encyclopedias, almanacs, yearbooks, atlases, directories, guides, handbooks, indexes, abstracts, catalogs, bibliographies
Books (print and electronic)	Nonfiction, how-to, biographies, fiction, trade books, scholarly and scientific studies
Periodicals and news sources	Print newspapers, magazines, and journals; broadcast news and news magazines; online magazines, news sources, and discussion groups
Audiovisual, digital, and multimedia resources	Graphics (tables, graphs, charts, maps, drawings, photos), audiotapes, CDs, videos, DVDs, Web pages, online databases
Government publications	Guides, programs, forms, legislation, regulations, reports, records, statistics
Business and nonprofit publications	Correspondence, reports, newsletters, pamphlets, brochures, ads, catalogs, instructions, handbooks, manuals, policies and procedures, seminar and training materials

20-4b Consider Information Sites

Where do you go to find the resources that you need? Consider the information sites listed below, remembering that many resources may be available in different forms in different locations. For example, a journal article may be available in a library or in an electronic database.

Information Location	Specific Sites
People	Experts (knowledge area, skill, occupation) Population segments or individuals (with representative or unusual experiences)
Libraries	General: public, college, online Specialized: legal, medical, government, business
Computer resources	Computers: software, CDs Networks: Internet and other online services (email, limited-access databases, discussion groups, MUDs, chat rooms, Web sites, blogs, YouTube, image banks, wikis); intranets
Mass media	Radio (AM and FM), television (network, public, cable, satellite), print (newspapers, magazines, journals)
Testing, training, meeting, and observation sites	Plants, facilities, field sites, laboratories, research centers, universities, think tanks, conventions, conferences, seminars, museums, galleries, historical sites
Municipal, state, and federal government offices	Elected officials, representatives, offices and agencies, Government Printing Office (GPO, www.gpoaccess.gov), and Web sites
Business and nonprofit publications	Computer databases, company files, desktop reference materials, bulletin boards (physical and electronic), company and department Web sites, departments and offices, associations, professional organizations, consulting, training, and business information services

DISTINGUISH TYPES OF SOURCES

Information sources can be **primary**, **secondary**, or **tertiary**. Depending on your assignment, you may be required to use primary and/or secondary sources, but rarely tertiary.

▶ **Primary sources** are original sources, which means they give firsthand information on a topic. These sources (such as diaries, people, or events) inform you directly about the topic, rather than through other people's explanations or interpretations. The most common forms of primary research are observations, interviews, surveys, experiments, and analyses of original documents and artifacts.

Upside of Primary Research: Primary sources produce information precisely tailored to your research needs, giving you direct, hands-on access to your topic. If, for example, you were researching the impact of hurricanes on Gulf Coast communities, interviews with survivors would provide information directly tailored to your project.

Downside of Primary Research: Primary research can take a lot of time and many resources, as well as specialized skills (e.g., designing surveys and analyzing statistics).

▶ **Secondary sources** present secondhand information on your topic—information at least once removed from the original. This information has been compiled, summarized, analyzed, synthesized, interpreted, or evaluated by someone studying primary sources. Journal articles, documentaries, and nonfiction books are typical examples of such secondary sources.

Upside of Secondary Research: Good secondary sources—especially scholarly ones that have gone through a peer review process—offer quality information in the form of expert perspectives on and analysis of your topic. As such, secondary sources can save you plenty of research labor while providing you with extensive data. In addition, secondary sources can help you see your topic from multiple angles through multiple perspectives; they can tell you the story of research done on your topic.

Downside of Secondary Research: Because secondary research isn't written solely with you and your project in mind, you may need to do some digging to find relevant data. Moreover, the information that you find may be filtered through the researcher's bias. In fact, the original research related through the secondary source may be faulty, a point suggesting that the quality of secondary sources can vary greatly. Finally, because knowledge about your topic can grow or radically change over time, secondary sources can become dated.

▶ **Tertiary sources** present thirdhand information on your topic. They are essentially reports of reports of research and, therefore, are distant from the original information. Examples of tertiary sources would include some articles in popular magazines and entries in Wikipedia. Aside from giving you ideas for focusing your topic and for conducting further research, tertiary sources should generally not be used in college research projects and should not appear in works-cited or reference lists.

primary sources original sources that give firsthand information about a topic
secondary sources sources that are at least once removed from the original; sources that provide secondhand information
tertiary sources sources that provide thirdhand information, such as wikis; discouraged for college research projects

Upside of Tertiary Research: Tertiary sources are typically easy to find, easy to access, and easy to read. Used cautiously, tertiary sources can serve as one starting point for your research—to find basic facts that you'll likely have to verify elsewhere, some ideas for narrowing your topic, or some leads and links to further research.

Downside of Tertiary Research: The main weakness of tertiary sources is their distance from the original research and information. Because the information and ideas have been passed along in this way, the possibility of error, distortion, gaps, and oversimplification of complex issues is greater than with primary and secondary sources. Generally, tertiary sources lack the reliability and depth necessary for college-level research projects.

The following information lists possible primary and secondary sources for a research project exploring hybrid car technology and its viability. Note: Whether a source is primary or secondary depends on what you are studying. For example, if you were studying U.S. attitudes toward hybrid cars, a newspaper editorial or a TV roundtable discussion would be a primary source. However, if you were studying hybrid technology itself, the same newspaper editorial or TV roundtable would be a secondary source.

Hybrid Car Technology

Primary Sources

- Email interview with automotive engineer
- Fuel-efficiency legislation
- Test-drive of a car at a dealership
- Published statistics about hybrid car sales

Secondary Sources

- Journal article discussing the development of hybrid car technology
- Newspaper editorial on fossil fuels
- Magazine article on innovations in hybrid car technology
- TV news roundtable discussion of hybrid car advantages and disadvantages
- Promotional literature for a specific hybrid car

Critical-Thinking and Writing Activities

1. Examine a research paper that you wrote in the past (e.g., in high school). What features of that paper are consistent with a college-level approach to research writing? What would you have to change to improve the thinking, level, and approach of the paper?

2. From the broad list of research subjects below, select one and (a) brainstorm a list of related topics, (b) select and refine a topic, (c) list key research questions, (d) formulate a working thesis, and (e) develop a list of possible resources (primary, secondary, and tertiary) for the topic.

   Subjects: museums, organic foods, department stores, the entertainment industry, third-world struggles, communication technology, comedy, wealth, mental illness, forests

3. Using what you have learned in this chapter, develop a research plan that identifies a topic of interest to you, clarifies the value of the research, zeros in on specific research questions and a working thesis, maps out research methods, and establishes a workable schedule.

STUDY TOOLS 20

LOCATED AT BACK OF THE TEXTBOOK
- ☐ Tear-Out Chapter Review Card

LOCATED AT WWW.CENGAGEBRAIN.COM/LOGIN
- ☐ Chapter eBook
- ☐ Graded quizzes and a practice quiz generator
- ☐ Videos: Writer Interviews
- ☐ Tutorials
- ☐ Flashcards
- ☐ Cengage Learning Write Experience
- ☐ Interactive activities

21 | Doing Your Research

"BASIC RESEARCH IS WHAT I AM DOING WHEN I DON'T KNOW WHAT I AM DOING."

WERNHER VON BRAUN

wavebreakmedia, 2014 / Used under license from Shutterstock.com

LEARNING OBJECTIVES

21-1 Learn keyword searching.

21-2 Conduct primary research.

21-3 Do library research.

21-4 Use books.

21-5 Find periodical articles.

21-6 Understand the Internet.

21-7 Find reliable free-Web information.

21-8 Evaluate online sources.

After you finish
this chapter
go to
PAGE 257 for STUDY TOOLS

Merriam-Webster's Collegiate Dictionary thinks it's pretty clever. A person who consults it to find the origin of the word **research** learns that it comes from the Middle French *recercher*, which means "to go about seeking"—after which *Webster's* promises "more at SEARCH."

In looking up *search*, one learns that the word comes from the Late Latin *circare*, which means "to go about" and which comes from the Latin *circum*, which means "round about." Then *Webster's* indicates there is "more at CIRCUM-."

Circum-, it turns out, comes from the Latin *circus*, which means "circle," and, yes, there's "more at CIRCLE." *Circle* comes from *circus,* of course, but it is also from (or akin to) the Greek *krikos*, which means "ring" and which is akin to the Old English *hring*, and—you guessed it—there's "more at RING."

So, you see, the clever editors of *Merriam-Webster's Collegiate Dictionary* are not content simply to provide you the etymology of *research*. They want you to research *research*. They want you "to go about seeking," to go "round about" in "circles" that feel like "circuses" and are all about "rings." They don't just define *research* for you—they give you a quick sampler of doing it.

In this chapter, you'll learn how research is about searching and re-searching and going about in circles—circles that will nevertheless lead you, through whatever tangents and side trips, to the knowledge you are seeking.

21-1 LEARN KEYWORD SEARCHING

Keyword searching can help you find solid information in electronic library catalogs, online databases that index periodical articles (e.g., Gale's Academic OneFile), print indexes to periodical publications, Internet resources, print books, and e-books. If you need additional help, consult with an information specialist in your library.

21-1a Choose Keywords

Keywords give you compass points for navigating the vast sea of information ahead of you. To plot the best course, choose the best keywords.

▸ **Begin brainstorming a list of possible keywords**—topics, titles, and names—based on your current knowledge and background reading.

▸ **Then consult the Library of Congress subject headings** to find the keywords librarians use when classifying materials. Topic entries like the one in the next column contain keywords to use, along with narrower, related, and/or broader terms. When you are conducting subject searches of catalogs and databases, these are the terms that will get the best results.

Topic	**Immigrants** (*May Subd Geog*)
	Here are entered works on foreign-born persons who enter a country intending to become permanent residents or citizens. This heading may be locally subdivided by names of places where immigrants settle. For works discussing emigrants from a particular place, an additional heading is assigned to designate the nationality of origin of the emigrant group and the place to which they have immigrated, e.g., Chinese—United States; American—Foreign countries.
Tips	
"Used for"	UF Emigrants
	Foreign-born population
	Foreign population
"Broader term"	BT Persons
"Related term"	RT Aliens
"Narrower term"	NT Children of immigrants
	Social work with immigrants
	Teenage immigrants
	Women immigrants
Subtopic	— Employment
	USE Alien labor
Recommended keywords	— Housing (*May Subd Geog*)
	— — Great Britain
	— Legal status, laws, etc.
	USE Emigration and immigration law

21-1b Employ Keyword Search Strategies

The goal of a keyword search is to find quality sources of information. To realize the best sources, employ these strategies:

▸ **Get to know the database.** Look for answers to these questions: What material does the database contain? What time frames? What are you searching—authors, titles, subjects, full text? What are the search rules? How can you narrow the search?

▸ **Use a shotgun approach.** Start with the most likely keyword. If you have no "hits," choose a related term. Once you get some hits, check the citations for clues regarding which words to use as you continue searching.

▸ **Use Boolean operators to refine your search.** When you combine keywords with **Boolean operators**—such as those in the box below—you will obtain better results.

21-2 CONDUCT PRIMARY RESEARCH

When published sources can't give you all the information that you need, consider conducting primary research. Primary research gives you direct, hands-on access to your topic, providing information precisely tailored to your needs. Such research takes time, however. It also requires special skills like designing surveys or analyzing statistics and original documents. The following quick guide is an overview of research methods. Choose those that best suit your project.

Quick Guide:
Boolean Operators

Narrowing a Search ▸ and, +, not, –

Use when one term gives you too many hits, especially irrelevant ones.

buffalo **and** bison *or* buffalo + bison	Searches for citations containing both keywords
buffalo **not** water *or* buffalo -water	Searches for "buffalo" but not "water," so you eliminate material on water buffalo

Expanding a Search ▸ or

Combine a term providing few hits with a related word.

buffalo **or** bison	Searches for citations containing either term

Specifying a Phrase ▸ quotation marks

Indicate that you wish to search for the exact phrase enclosed in quotation marks.

"reclamation project"	Searches for the exact phrase "reclamation project"

Sequencing Operations ▸ parentheses

Indicate that the operation should be performed before other operations in the search string.

(buffalo or bison) and ranching	Searches first for citations containing either "buffalo" or "bison" before checking the resulting citations for "ranching"

Finding Variations ▸ wild-card symbols

Depending on the database, symbols such as $, ?, or # can find variations of a word.

ethic# ethic$	Searches for terms like *ethics* and *ethical*

boolean operators words or symbols used when searching research databases and that describe the relationship between various words or phrases in a search

21-2a Primary Research Methods

▶ **Surveys:** Surveys and **questionnaires** gather written responses you can review, tabulate, and analyze. These research tools pull together varied information—from simple facts to personal opinions and attitudes.

▶ **Interviews:** Interviews involve consulting two types of people. First, you can interview experts for their insights on your topic. Second, you can interview people whose direct experiences with the topic give you their personal insights. (See bonus online chapter A for more about interviews.)

▶ **Observations:** **Observations**, **inspections**, and **field research** require you to examine and analyze people, places, events, and so on. Whether you rely simply on your five senses or use scientific techniques, observing provides insights into the present state of your subject.

▶ **Experiments:** Experiments test hypotheses—predictions about why things do what they do—to arrive at conclusions that can be accepted and acted upon. Such testing often explores cause-effect relationships.

▶ **Analysis:** Analysis of documents and artifacts involves studying original reports, statistics, legislation, literature, artwork, and historical records. Such analysis provides unique, close-up interpretations of your topic.

21-2b Conducting Surveys

Writing Guidelines

Your goal is to create a survey or questionnaire that collects facts and opinions from a target audience about your topic. To get valid information, follow these guidelines:

❶ **Find a focus.** Define the writing situation. What is your specific topic? What is the purpose of your survey (what do you want to find out)? Who is the audience for your survey?

❷ **Create effective questions.** Phrase questions so that they can be easily understood. Use neutral language to avoid skewing results. Use **closed questions** (e.g., rating, multiple choice, yes/no) to generate data that can be charted and quantified. Use **open-ended questions** (e.g., fill-in-the-blank, write-in answers) to bring in a wider variety of complex data.

❸ **Draft your survey.** Whether you present your survey on paper or online, organize it so that it's easy to complete.

- **Opening:** State who you are and why you need the information. Explain how to complete the survey and when and where to return it.
- **Middle:** Provide the questions. Guide the reader with numbers, instructions, and headings. Begin with basic, closed questions and progress to complex, open-ended questions. Move in a logical order from topic to topic.
  - **Ending:** Thank the respondent for taking the survey and remind the person when and where to return it.

survey/questionnaire a set of questions created for the purpose of gathering information from respondents about a specific topic

observation noting information received in person through the senses

inspection the purposeful analysis of a site or situation in order to understand it

field research an on-site scientific study conducted for the purpose of attaining raw data

closed questions questions that can be answered with a simple fact or with a yes or a no

open-ended questions questions that require elaborate answers

4 Revise your survey. Ask a friend or classmate to take your survey and help you revise it, if necessary, before publishing it. Take the survey yourself. Note questions that should be added or reworded or removed, parts that should be reorganized, places in which the voice should be more neutral, and instructions that should be clearer. After revising, try out your survey with a small test group, and revise again.

5 Edit your survey. Check sentences, words, letters, and each punctuation mark. Make certain your survey is error free before publishing it.

6 Conduct your survey. Distribute the survey to a clearly defined group that won't prejudice the sample (random or cross-section). Encourage the target group to respond, aiming for 10 percent response if at all possible. Tabulate responses carefully and objectively. To develop statistically valid results, you may need expert help. Check with your instructor.

Student Model

Student writer Cho Lang created the following paper survey to determine how many athletes at her college used training supplements, how, and why. She also created a Web-based version of the survey, asking athletes to sign on anonymously to complete it.

Confidential Survey

(A) My name is Cho Lang, and I'm conducting research about the use of training supplements. I'd like to hear from you, Alfred University's athletes. Please answer the questions below by circling or writing out your responses. Return your survey to me, care of the Dept. of Psychology, through campus mail by Friday, April 5. Your responses will remain confidential.

(B)
1. Circle your gender.
    Male   Female

2. Circle your year.
    Freshman   Sophomore   Junior   Senior

(C)
3. List the sports that you play.

4. Are you presently using a training supplement?
    Yes   No
    Note: If you circled "no," you may turn in your survey at this point.

5. Describe your supplement use (type, amount, and frequency).

6. Who supervises your use of this training supplement?
    Coach   Trainer   Self   Others

7. How long have you used it?
    Less than 1 month   1–12 months   12+ months

8. How many pounds have you gained while using this supplement?   (D)

9. How much has your athletic performance improved?
    None   1   2   3   4   5   Greatly

10. Circle any side effects you've experienced.
    Dehydration   Nausea   Diarrhea

Thank you for taking the time to complete this confidential survey. Please return it by Friday, April 5, to Cho Lang, care of the Dept. of Psychology, through campus mail.

(A) The introduction includes the essential information about the survey.
(B) The survey begins with clear, basic questions.
(C) The survey asks an open-ended question.
(D) The survey covers the topic thoroughly.

21-3 DO LIBRARY RESEARCH

The library door is your gateway to information. Inside, the college library holds a wide range of research resources, from books to periodicals, from reference librarians to electronic databases.

21-3a Making the Library Work

To improve your ability to succeed at all of your research assignments, become familiar with your college library system. Take advantage of tours and orientation sessions to learn its physical layout, resources, and services. Check your library's Web site for policies, tutorials, and research tools.

Knowing Where to Go

The college library offers four basic resources for your research projects.

- **Librarians** are information experts who manage the library's materials and guide you to resources. They also can help you perform online searches.
- **Collections** are the materials housed within the library, including books and electronic materials, periodicals, reference materials, and special collections.
- **Research tools** are the systems and services to help you find what you need. They include online catalogs, print indexes and **subscription databases**, and Internet access to other libraries and online references.
- **Special services** are additional options to help you complete research, including interlibrary loan, "hold" and "reserve" services, the reference desk, photocopies, CD burners, scanners, and presentation software.

21-3b Catalog Searches

Library materials are cataloged so that they are easy to find. In most college libraries, books, videos, and other holdings are cataloged in an electronic database. To find material, use book titles, author names, and related keyword searching. (See pages 239–240.)

When you find a citation for a book or other resource, the result will likely provide the author or editor's name, the title and subtitle, publisher and copyright date,

descriptive information, subject headings (crucial list of topics), call number, and location. Use that information to determine whether the resource is worth exploring further and to figure out other avenues of research. *Note:* A number of items appearing in blue underlined type provide links to related books and other resources in the catalog.

Cudworth, Erika, 1966–

Title: Environment and Society

Publisher: London; New York: Routledge, 2003.

Physical descript.: xii, 232 p.: ill.; 24 cm.

Subjects: Human ecology [65 rec.]
Nature—Effect of human being on [15 rec.]
Environmental protection [25 rec.]

Call number: GF 41 .C83 2003

---

collections the materials housed within a library

subscription databases online services that, for a fee, provide access to hundreds of thousands of articles

---

[Computer screen illustration]

● Keyword ○ Browse ○ Exact

[search box]

SEARCH EVERYTHING | AUTHOR | TITLE | SUBJECT | SERIES | PERIODICAL TITLE

1. Enter the word(s) you want to find.
   Keyword returns records containing the word(s) entered.
   Browse returns catalog headings beginning with the first word entered.
   Exact returns records that exactly match the word(s) entered.
2. Choose a target search field.
   Search everything targets all indexed fields within a record.
   All other choices target specified fields within a record.

yanugkelid, 2014 / Used under license from Shutterstock.com

Locating by Call Numbers

Library of Congress (LC) **call numbers** combine letters and numbers to specify a resource's broad subject area, topic, and authorship or title. Finding a book, DVD, or other item involves combining both the alphabetical and the numerical order.

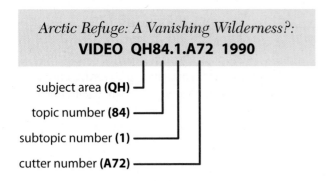

Arctic Refuge: A Vanishing Wilderness?:
VIDEO QH84.1.A72 1990

subject area **(QH)**

topic number **(84)**

subtopic number **(1)**

cutter number **(A72)**

To find the example resource in the library, first note the tab VIDEO. Although not part of the call number, this locator will send you to a specific area of the library. Once there, follow the parts of the call number one at a time:

1. Find the section on natural history containing videos with the "QH" designation.
2. Follow the numbers until you reach "84."
3. Within the "84" items, find those with the subtopic "1."
4. Use the cutter number "A72" to locate the resource alphabetically with "A" and numerically with "72."

 TIP In the LC system, pay careful attention to the arrangement of subject area letters, topic numbers, and subtopic numbers: Q98 comes before QH84; QH84 before QH8245; QH84.A72 before QH84.1.A72.

Library of Congress call numbers a set of numbers and letters specifying the subject area, topic, and authorship or title of a book

Classification Systems

The **LC classification system** combines letters and numbers. **The Dewey decimal system**, which is used in some libraries, uses numbers only. Here is a list of the subject classes for both the LC and Dewey systems.

Category	LC	Dewey Decimal
General Works	A	000–999
Philosophy Psychology Religion	B	100–199 150–159 200–299
History: Auxiliary Sciences	C	910–929
History: General and Old World	D	930–999
History of the Americas	E–F	970–979
Geography Anthropology Recreation	G	910–919 571–573 700–799
Social Sciences	H	300–399
Political Science	J	320–329
Law	K	340–349
Education	L	370–379
Music	M	780–789
Fine Arts	N	700–799
Language Literature	P	800–899 400–499
Science	Q	500–599
Medicine	R	610–619
Agriculture	S	630–639
Technology	T	600–699
Military Science	U	355–359, 623
Naval Science	V	359, 623
Bibliography and Library Science	Z	010–019 020–029

Quick Guide: Reference Works

Reference works, whether print or digital, are information-rich resources that can give you an overview of your topic, supply basic facts, share common knowledge about your topic, and offer ideas for focusing and furthering your research. While some reference resources are available on the free Web (see, for example, the discussion of Wikipedia on pages 254–255), your library offers you excellent access to both print and digital works (e.g., the Gale Virtual Reference Library). Consider these options:

Informational Reference Resources

- **Encyclopedias** supply facts and overviews for topics arranged alphabetically. General encyclopedias, such as *Encyclopedia Britannica* or *Collier's Encyclopedia*, cover many fields of knowledge. Specialized encyclopedias, such as the *Encyclopedia of American Film Comedy*, focus on a single topic.
- **Almanacs, yearbooks, and statistical resources,** normally published annually, contain diverse facts. *The World Almanac and Book of Facts* presents information on politics, history, religion, business, social programs, education, and sports. *Statistical Abstract of the United States* provides data on population, geography, politics, employment, business, science, and industry.
- **Vocabulary resources** supply information on languages. General dictionaries, such as *The American Heritage College Dictionary* and *Newbury House Dictionary*, supply definitions and histories for a whole range of words. Specialized dictionaries, such as the *Dictionary of Engineering* or *The New Harvard Dictionary of Music*, define words common to a field, topic, or group. Bilingual dictionaries translate words from one language to another.

- **Biographical resources** supply information about people. General biographies, such as *Who's Who in America*, cover a broad range of people. Other biographies, such as the *Dictionary of Scientific Biography* or *World Artists 1980-1990*, focus on people from a specific group.
- **Directories** supply contact information for people, groups, and organizations: *The National Directory of Addresses and Telephone Numbers*, *USPS ZIP Code Lookup and Address Information* (online), *Official Congressional Directory*.

Reference Works as Research Tools

- **Guides and handbooks** help readers explore specific topics: *The Handbook of North American Indians*, *A Guide to Prairie Fauna*.
- **Indexes** point you to useful resources. Some indexes are general, such as *Readers' Guide to Periodical Literature*; others are more specific, such as *Environment Index* or *Business Periodicals Index*. (Many are now available online in databases your library subscribes to.)
- **Bibliographies** list resources on a specific topic. A good current bibliography can be used as an example when you compile your own bibliography on a topic.
- **Abstracts**, like indexes, direct you to articles on a particular topic. But abstracts also summarize those materials so you learn whether a resource is relevant before you invest time in locating and reading it. Abstracts are usually organized into subject areas: Computer Abstracts, Environmental Abstracts, Social Work Abstracts. They are incorporated in many online subscription databases.

---

encyclopedias reference works filled with articles written about a variety of topics

almanacs/yearbooks regularly published references that chronicle the major events of a specific time period

directories references that provide contact information for people, groups, and organizations

indexes searchable lists of resources on various topics

abstracts summaries of resources; a collection of summaries in a specific subject area

---

21-4 USE BOOKS

Your college library contains a range of books, from scholarly studies and reference works to trade books and biographies.

When you find a helpful book, browse nearby shelves for more books. If your library subscribes to an e-book service such as NetLibrary, you can conduct electronic searches, browse or check out promising books, and read them online.

Unfortunately, for most research projects, you simply don't have time to read an entire book, and rarely do the entire contents relate to your topic. Instead, use the strategy that follows to refine your research effort.

Research Strategy

▶ **Check out front and back information.** The title and copyright pages give the book's full title and subtitle; the author's name; and publication information, including publication date and Library of Congress subject headings. The back may contain a note on the author's credentials and other publications.

▶ **Scan the table of contents.** Examine the contents page to see what the book covers and how it is organized. Ask yourself which chapters are relevant to your project.

▶ **Using key words, search the index.** Check the index for coverage and page locations of the topics most closely related to your project. Are there plenty of pages or just a few? Are these pages concentrated or scattered throughout the book?

▶ **Skim the foreword, preface, or introduction.** Skimming the opening materials will often indicate the book's perspective, explain its origin, and preview its contents.

▶ **Check appendixes, glossaries, or bibliographies.** These special sections may be good sources of tables, graphics, definitions, statistics, and clues for further research.

▶ **Carefully read appropriate chapters and sections.** Think through the material you've read, and take good notes. (See pages 262–264.) Follow references to authors and other works to do further research on the topic. Study footnotes and endnotes for insights and leads.

appendixes sections (in a book) that provide additional or background information

glossaries lists of important terms and their definitions

bibliographies lists of works that cover a particular subject

---

21-5 FIND PERIODICAL ARTICLES

Periodicals are publications or broadcasts produced at regular intervals (daily, weekly, monthly, quarterly). Although some periodicals are broad in their subject matter and audience, as a rule they focus on a narrow range of topics geared toward a particular audience.

There are basically three forms of periodical publications. **Daily newspapers and newscasts** provide up-to-date information on current events, opinions, and trends—from politics to natural disasters (*Wall Street Journal, USA Today, The NewsHour*). **Weekly and monthly** magazines **and newscasts** generally provide more in-depth information on a wide range of topics (*Time, Newsweek, 60 Minutes*). Finally, **journals**, generally published quarterly, provide specialized scholarly information for a narrowly focused audience (*English Journal*).

21-5a Online Databases

If your library subscribes to Gale Databases or another database service, use keyword searching (see pages 239–240) to find citations on your topic. You might start with the general version of such databases, such as Gale's Academic OneFile, which provides access to more than 9,000 scholarly publications covering all disciplines.

Basic Search

The example (**Sample 1 on next page**) shows an Academic OneFile search screen for a search on hybrid electric cars. Notice how limiters, expanders, and other advanced features help you find the highest-quality materials.

21-5b Making the Advanced Search

A more focused research strategy involves turning to specialized databases, which are available for virtually every discipline and are often an option within search services such as Gale Databases.

Citation Lists

Your database search should generate lists of citations, brief descriptions of articles that were flagged through keywords in titles, subject terms, abstracts, and so on. For example, a search focused on hybrid vehicles leads to the results shown (**Sample 2 below**). At this point, study the results and do the following:

- Refine the search by narrowing or expanding it.
- Mark specific citations for "capture" or further study.
- Re-sort the results.
- Follow links in a specific citation to further information.

Identifying Information

By studying citations (especially abstracts), you can determine if the article is relevant to your research, is available in an electronic version, and is available as a periodical. To develop your working bibliography (see pages 262–262), you should also "capture" the article's identifying details by using the save, print, or email function; or by recording the periodical's title, the issue and date, and the article's title and page numbers.

Full-Text Articles

When citations indicate that you have promising articles, access those articles efficiently, preferably through a direct link in the citation to an electronic copy. From there you can print, save, or email the article. If the article is not available electronically, track down a print version.

Check the online citation to see if your library has the article. If necessary, check your library's inventory of periodicals held; this list should be available online and/or in print. Examine especially closely the issues and dates available, the form (print or microfilm), and the location (bound or current shelves).

To get the article, follow your library's procedure. You may have to submit a request slip so that a librarian can get the periodical, or you may be able to get it yourself in the current, bound, or microfilm collection. If the article is not available online or in your library, use interlibrary loan.

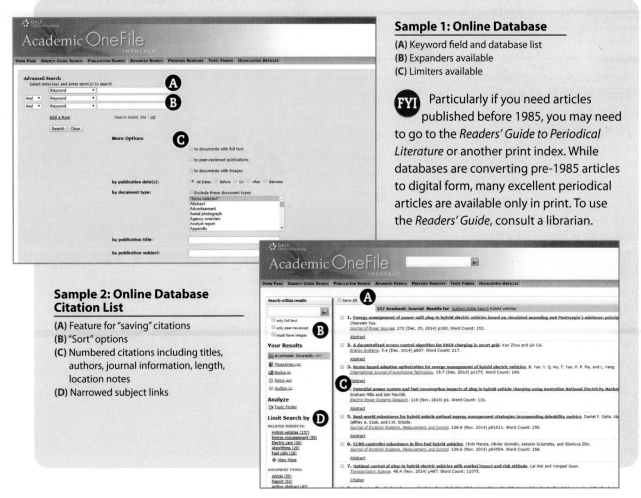

Sample 1: Online Database

(A) Keyword field and database list
(B) Expanders available
(C) Limiters available

FYI Particularly if you need articles published before 1985, you may need to go to the *Readers' Guide to Periodical Literature* or another print index. While databases are converting pre-1985 articles to digital form, many excellent periodical articles are available only in print. To use the *Readers' Guide*, consult a librarian.

Sample 2: Online Database Citation List

(A) Feature for "saving" citations
(B) "Sort" options
(C) Numbered citations including titles, authors, journal information, length, location notes
(D) Narrowed subject links

UNDERSTAND THE INTERNET

You're probably familiar with the Internet and may already understand the basics of searching this medium. However, the following information may help you do quality research on the Net.

The **Internet** is a worldwide network of connected local computers and computer networks that allows computers to share information with one another. Your college's network likely gives you access to the library, local resources, and the Internet.

21-6a How the Network Works

The **World Wide Web** provides access to much of the material on the Internet. Millions of Web pages are available because of **hypertext links** that connect them. These links appear as clickable icons or highlighted Web addresses. A **Web site** is a group of related **Web pages** posted by the same sponsor or organization. A **home page** is a Web site's "entry" page. A **Web browser** such as Safari, Internet Explorer, or Firefox gives you access to Web resources through a variety of tools, such as directories and search engines. (Directories and **search engines** are special Web sites that provide a searchable listing of many services on the Web.)

Distinguish between the **deep Web** and the free Web. The deep Web includes material not generally accessible with popular search engines, such as all the scholarly research available through your library's subscription databases. The free Web offers less reliable information.

Understanding Internet Addresses

An Internet address is called a uniform resource locator (**URL**). The address includes the protocol indicating how the computer file should be accessed—often *http:* or *ftp:* (followed by a double slash); a domain name—often beginning with *www;* and additional path information (following a single slash) to access other pages within a site.

http://www.nrcs.usda.gov/news/

Internet a worldwide network of connected computers that allows sharing of information

World Wide Web the collection of Web sites on the Internet accessible to Web browsers and search engines

hypertext link a clickable bit of text that connects the user to another location on the Web

Web site a group of related Web pages posted by the same sponsor or organization

Web page a page viewable as a single unit on a Web site

Web browser a program that provides access to Web resources through a variety of tools

deep Web Internet materials not accessible via popular search engines but available through a library's subscription databases

URL the uniform resource locator; the Web address telling the browser how to access a certain file

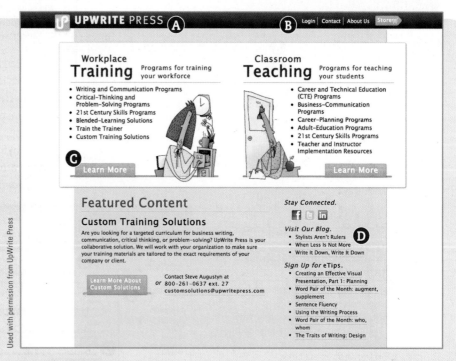

Used with permission from UpWrite Press

Sample Web Page

(A) Title bar   (C) Graphic link
(B) Navigation bar   (D) Text links

The **domain name** is a key part of the address because it indicates what type of organization created the site and gives you clues about its goal or purpose—to educate, inform, persuade, sell, and/or entertain. Most sites combine a primary purpose with secondary ones.

Sample Domain Names

.com	a commercial organization or business
.gov	a government organization—federal, state, or local
.edu	an educational institution
.org	a nonprofit organization
.net	an organization that is part of the Internet's infrastructure
.mil	a military site
.biz	a business site
.info	any site primarily providing information

International addresses generally include national abbreviations (for example, Canada = .ca). This clue helps you determine the origin of the information and communicate more sensitively on the Internet.

Saving Internet Information

Accurately saving Internet addresses and material is an essential part of good research. Moreover, you may want to revisit sites and embed URLs in your research writing. Save Internet information through these methods:

- **Bookmark:** Your browser can save a site's address through a "bookmark" or "favorites" function on your menu bar. In addition, many bookmarking applications, such as Evernote, can help you save and organize useful Web sources.
- **Printout:** If a document looks promising, print a hard copy of it. Remember to write down all details needed for citing the source. (Although many details will automatically print with the document, some could be missing.)
- **Save or download:** To keep an electronic copy of material, save the document to a specific drive on your computer. Beware of large files with many graphics: They take up a lot of space. To save just the text, highlight it, copy it, and then paste it into a word-processing program.
- **Email:** If you're not at your own computer, you can email the document's URL to your email address through copy and paste.

21-7 FIND RELIABLE FREE-WEB INFORMATION

Because the Internet contains so much information of varying reliability, you need to become familiar with search tools that locate information you can trust. The key is knowing which search tool to use in which research situation. It's also important to proceed with caution.

Adhere to your assignment's restrictions on using Web sites (number and type). In fact, some instructors may not allow Web resources for specific projects, limiting you to print sources and scholarly articles available in subscription databases.

When you are using Web resources, make sure the sites are sponsored by legitimate, recognizable organizations: government agencies, nonprofit groups, and educational institutions. For most projects, avoid relying on personal, commercial, and special-interest sites, as well as chat rooms, blogs, and news groups. Test the quality and reliability of online information by using the benchmarks outlined on pages 259–261.

Avoid developing your paper by simply copying and pasting together chunks of Web pages. By doing so, you not only fail to engage your sources meaningfully, but you also commit plagiarism. For more on plagiarism, see pages 269–272.

> **domain name** the name of a site, including the extension after the dot (.), which indicates what type of organization created the site

21-7a Reliable Web Sites

Your library may sponsor a Web site that gives you access to quality Internet resources. For example, it may provide tutorials on using the Internet, guides to Internet resources in different disciplines, links to online document collections (Project Gutenberg, Etext Archives, New Bartleby Digital Library, and so on), or connections to other virtual resources (virtual libraries, subscription databases, search engines, directories, government documents, and online reference works).

Finding other useful Web sites can be as easy as typing in a URL. If you don't have the exact URL, sometimes you can guess it, especially for an organization (company, government agency, or nonprofit group). Of course, you can also search for the Web site, checking the URLs that are presented to make sure you select the actual site you seek, not a copycat.

You can also find useful sites by following links provided on other useful sites. If you come across a helpful link (often highlighted in blue), click on the link to visit that new page. Note that the link may take you to another site.

Your browser keeps a record of the pages you visit. Click the back arrow to go back one page or the forward arrow to move ahead again. Clicking the right mouse button on these arrows shows a list of recently visited pages.

21-7b Subject Trees

A **subject tree**, sometimes called a subject guide or directory, lists Web sites that have been organized into categories by experts who have reviewed those sites. Use subject trees or directories if you need to narrow a broad topic or if you want sites that have been evaluated (quality over quantity).

How does a subject tree work? Essentially, it allows you to select from a broad range of subjects or "branches." With each topic choice, you narrow your selection until you arrive at a list of Web sites, or you can keyword-search a limited number of Web sites.

Check whether your library subscribes to subject tree resources, such as databases in which subject experts catalogue Internet resources by topic or academic discipline. Here are some other common subject directories that you can likely access at your library:

Gale's Academic OneFile · http://www.gale.cengage.com/PeriodicalSolutions/academicOnefile.htm

Open Directory Project · http://www.dmoz.org/

WWW Virtual Library · http://vlib.org/Overview.html

Yahoo Directory · https://dir.yahoo.com/

EBSCOhost · http://www.ebscohost.com/academic

LexisNexis Academic · http://www.lexisnexis.com/hottopics/lnacademic/

Linkopedia · http://www.linkopedia.com/

Galaxy · http://www.galaxy.com/

TIP To get the best results from your search, avoid these problems: misspelling keywords; using vague or broad keywords (e.g., *education* or *business*); incorrectly combining Boolean operators; or shortening keywords too much.

Examine the subject-tree search that follows. Afterward, conduct your own search using a subject tree available through your library.

venimo, 2014 / Used under license from Shutterstock.com

subject tree a listing of Web sites, arranged by experts

Subject-Tree Search (Invasive Plant Species)

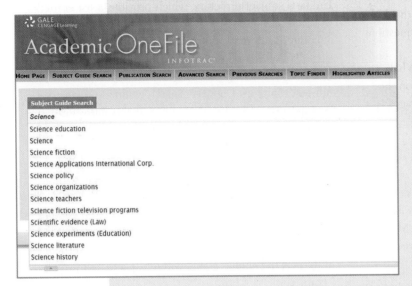

Step 1: Select an appropriate broad category. Study the subject-tree search to the left provided by Gale's Academic OneFile. To find reviewed Web sites containing information on invasive plant species, you could select from various categories of science, depending on the angle you want to explore: science education, science, science policy, science organizations, science history, and so on.

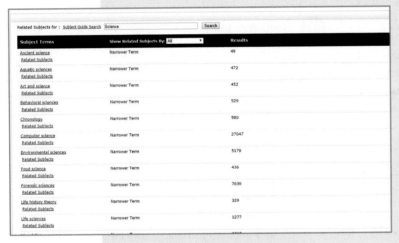

Step 2: Choose a fitting subcategory. If you simply chose "Science," more specific subcategories (shown to the left) would appear. At this point, you would again have several choices: ancient science, environmental sciences, life sciences, and so on. Each choice might lead to a distinct set of Web sites.

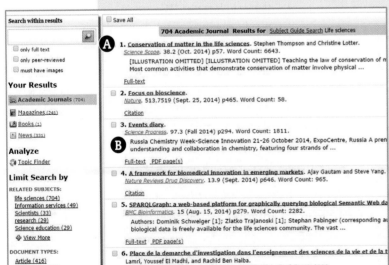

Courtesy of Cengage Learning.

Step 3: Work toward a listing of Web sites. As you work your way through more specific subcategories, you will see listings of relevant Web sites. Such sites, remember, have all been reviewed in terms of quality, though you still need to evaluate what you find. In the citation for a site, study the site title and the description of information available. Visit the site and notice its Web address (particularly the domain name). Use that information to determine the site's relevance to your research.

(A) Site title and link
(B) Site description and types of content

Visiting, Exploring, and Evaluating

Look through the listing of recommended sites. Once you have identified a promising site, follow the links provided. Study and evaluate the site by asking questions such as these:

1. Who authored or sponsored the site? What is the author's or sponsor's perspective on the topic? Why did the author post these pages? What can you find out about the author through a broader Internet search?

2. What content does the site offer? What depth of information is available?

3. Does the Web site function as a primary, secondary, or tertiary source? (See page 236.)

4. What external links does the site offer? Might these links take you to additional resources that are relevant and reliable?

Careful investigation and evaluation of Web sites is even more important when you use search engines like those discussed on the next page. Use the resource evaluation guidelines on page 255 for Web pages that you find through either subject directories or search engines. Always proceed with caution, making sure that your research writing does not rely on unstable, shallow Web pages.

21-7c Search and Metasearch

Unlike a subject directory, which provides a list crafted with human input, a search engine provides a list generated automatically by scouring millions of Web sites. Not all search engines are the same. Some search citations of Internet materials, whereas others conduct full-text searches. Choose a search engine that covers a large portion of the Internet, offers quality indexing, and provides high-powered search capabilities.

Basic **search engines** search millions of Web pages, and they include engines such as Google and Yahoo. (The URL for each of these is the engine name, without spaces, followed by ".com.")

Metasearch tools search several basic search engines at once, and they include sites such as Ask, Dog Pile, Ixquick, and Northern Light. (The URL for each of these is the engine name, without spaces, followed by ".com.")

FYI Deep-Web tools check Internet databases and other sources not accessible to basic search engines.

Basic Web Search (Wisconsin "invasive plant" –genetics)

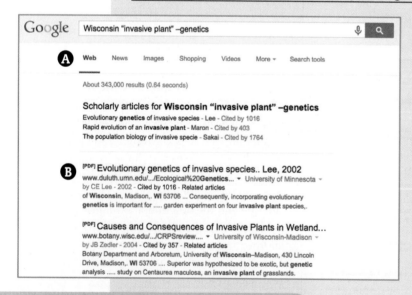

Step 1: Begin the search with precise terms. Using Boolean operators and quotation marks, you might begin with the search terms "Wisconsin" and "invasive plant–genetics." The more precise your terms are, the better your results will be.

Step 2: Study the results and refine your search. The results of the initial search appear here. At this point, you can click one of the resulting Web links, click a sponsored link, follow links on the right to related topics, or narrow or broaden your search.

(A) Results: sponsored sites (primarily advertising)
(B) Results: other Web pages

search engines sites that search other Web sites using keywords

metasearch tools sites that search other search engines

21-7d Understanding the Uses and Limits of Wikipedia

You likely recognize the screen below—an article from Wikipedia. From its beginning in 2001 to today, a large population of volunteer writers and editors has made Wikipedia a top-ten Internet-traffic site. But is Wikipedia acceptable for college-level research? Put simply, Wikipedia is a controversial resource for academic research.

Knowing Wikipedia's Strengths

Because of its wiki nature, Wikipedia offers researchers a number of advantages.

- **Consensus Model of Knowledge:** Articles represent a collaborative agreement about a topic—a topical knowledge base that is fair and fairly comprehensive. Generally, articles improve over time, offering "open-source" knowledge.
- **Currency of Information:** Because they are Web based, articles are regularly monitored and updated—a distinct advantage over print encyclopedias.
- **Breadth of Information:** With its size and global community, Wikipedia offers articles on a wide range of topics—especially strong in pop culture, current events, computer, and science topics.
- **Links:** Articles are linked throughout so that readers can pursue associated topics, sources, recommended reading, and related categories.

Understanding Wikipedia's Standards for Truth

Wikipedia applies a different standard of truth than more traditional sources of information do. Information does not necessarily have to be true or accurate to appear on Wikipedia, as long as the information can be traced back to some other source, often through a hyperlink.

Screen Features

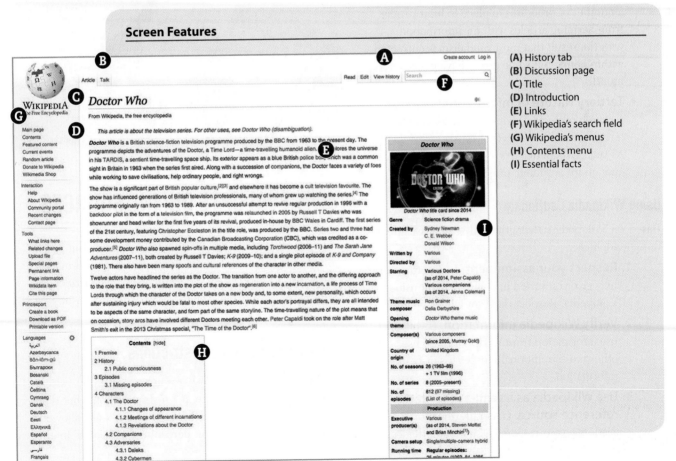

(A) History tab
(B) Discussion page
(C) Title
(D) Introduction
(E) Links
(F) Wikipedia's search field
(G) Wikipedia's menus
(H) Contents menu
(I) Essential facts

Knowing Wikipedia's Weaknesses

In some ways, Wikipedia's strengths are closely related to its weaknesses for college-level research. Consider these issues:

- **Popularity Model of Knowledge:** The dynamics of popularity can lead to bias, imbalance, and errors. In some ways, this approach minimizes the value of training, education, and expertise while promoting a kind of democracy of knowledge.

- **Anonymity of Authorship:** Wikipedia allows contributors to remain anonymous. Researchers thus have little way of checking credentials and credibility.

- **Variable Quality of Content:** While many well-established articles are quite stable, balanced, and comprehensive, other articles can be partial, driven by a biased perspective, erroneous, and poorly sourced.

- **Variable Coverage:** Wikipedia's strength in some content areas is matched by gaps and incompleteness in other content areas.

- **Vulnerability to Vandalism:** Wikipedia has a number of processes in place to limit people from harming articles with misinformation, with the result that most vandalism is corrected within hours, but some errors have persisted for months.

- **Tertiary Nature of Information:** For most research projects, Wikipedia articles function as tertiary sources—reports of reports of research. As such, Wikipedia articles are not substantial enough for academic projects.

Using Wikipedia Cautiously

Based on Wikipedia's strengths and weaknesses, follow these guidelines:

1. **Respect your assignment.** Instructors may give you varied instruction about using Wikipedia. Respect their guidelines.

2. **Verify Wikipedia information.** If you use information from Wikipedia, also use other more traditional sources to verify that information.

3. **Use Wikipedia as a semi-authoritative reference source.** Generally, the more academic your research assignment, the less

you should rely on Wikipedia articles, which are essentially sources of basic and background information.

4. **Use Wikipedia as one starting point.** From a Wikipedia article, you can learn what is considered "open-source" knowledge on your topic, gather ideas for developing a topic, find links to related topics and other resources, and begin to build a bibliography.

5. **Study individual articles to get a sense of their reliability.** When you find a Wikipedia article relevant to your research project, check the article for quality and stability. Use the evaluation criteria on the following pages, but also check the article's history, its discussion page, any tags or icons indicating the article's state, and the "what links here" link in the toolbox at the left of the screen.

21-8 EVALUATE ONLINE SOURCES

The Internet contains a wealth of information, but much of it is not suitable for a research report. The information may be incorrect, biased, outdated, plagiarized, or otherwise unreliable. These pages discuss issues to watch for.

21-8a Assignment Restrictions

Before engaging any Web resources, carefully review your assignment and note any restrictions on what type of sources may be used. If Web resources are allowed, abide by the number or percentage indicated in the assignment.

21-8b Author/Organization

When using Web resources, make sure the sites are sponsored by legitimate, recognizable organizations: government agencies, nonprofit groups, and educational institutions. For most projects, avoid relying on personal or special-interest sites, as well as chat rooms, blogs, news groups, or wikis. (These sources may help you explore a topic, but they do not provide scholarly material suitable for most research reports.)

21-8c Balance or Bias

Be aware of the purpose of a site or an article. Editorials and reviews, for example, express the point of view of a given author but are not sources for unbiased information. Unless your purpose is to show the author's point of view or point out two sides of an argument, avoid sources that show a bias toward or against a specific region, country, political party, industry, gender, race, ethnic group, or religion. Also, avoid sites that promote a specific cause, product, service, or belief.

21-8d Quality of Information

Test the quality of information on a site. Note whether the information is current (when was it posted/updated last), and check it against other sources for corroboration. Also, favor sites with a depth of information and those that show they truly engage their topic rather than treat it superficially.

21-8e Quality of Writing and Design

Avoid sites that show sloppy editing and poor design. These surface flaws can reveal a lack of scholarly rigor or serious commitment on the part of the site's creators.

sergign, 2014 / Used under license from Shutterstock.com

Checklist: Evaluation

Use this checklist to assess the reliability of Web sources. The more items you check off, the more reliable the source is.

Assignment Restrictions

___ Does the source fit with the type and number allowed in the assignment?

Author/Organization

___ Is the person or organization behind the site reliable?

___ Is contact information for the person or organization provided?

___ Is the site well known and well connected in the field?

___ Does the site have a clear "About Us" page and mission statement?

Balance or Bias

___ Is the material on the site balanced and unbiased?

___ Does the site avoid unfair and inflammatory language?

___ Does the site avoid pushing a particular product, cause, service, or belief?

___ Does the site provide ample support for its claims?

___ Does the site avoid logical fallacies and twisted statistics? (See pages 188–191.)

Quality of Information

___ Is the material current?

___ Is the Web site often updated?

___ Is the Web site information rich?

___ Is the information backed up by other reputable print and online sources?

Quality of Writing and Design

___ Is the text free of errors in punctuation, spelling, and grammar?

___ Is the site effectively and clearly designed?

Reliable

▶ **Assignment Restrictions** The site below would be appropriate for most assignments about the life and work of William Faulkner, as long as free-Web sources are allowed.

▶ **Author/Organization** This site is sponsored by the University of Mississippi, a scholarly source of information, and the article's author, Dr. John B. Padgett, is an authority on Faulkner.

▶ **Balance or Bias** The site clearly extols Faulkner as a great writer but does not shy from showing his

shortcomings. The claims are fair and amply supported, without logical fallacies.

▶ **Quality of Information** The Web site is current, often updated, and information rich. It is also connected to many other Faulkner resources available on the Web.

▶ **Quality of Writing and Design** The site is well designed, with easy navigation, readable text, informative headings, helpful photos, and strong links. The text is well written and well edited.

▶ Publications
▶ Other Features
▶ Writer Listings

Go to
▶ Gallery
▶ Publications
▶ Bibliography
▶ Media Adaptations
▶ Internet Resources

See also:
▶ Book Info:
Faulkner in the Twenty-first Century (February 2003)
William Faulkner: Six Decades of Criticism (October 2002)
Absalom, Absalom! (September 2002)
Faulkner and the Politics of Reading, by Karl Zender

© The Cofield Collection
William Faulkner

William Faulkner

The man himself never stood taller than five feet, six inches tall, but in the realm of American literature, William Faulkner is a giant. More than simply a renowned Mississippi writer, the Nobel Prize-winning novelist and short story writer is acclaimed throughout the world as one of the twentieth century's greatest writers, one who transformed his "postage stamp" of native soil into an apocryphal setting in which he explored, articulated, and challenged "the old verities and truths of the heart." During what is generally considered his period of greatest artistic achievement, from *The Sound and the Fury* in 1929 to *Go Down, Moses* in 1942, Faulkner accomplished in a little over a decade more artistically than most writers accomplish over a lifetime of writing. It is one of the more remarkable feats of American literature, how a young man who never graduated from high school, never received a college degree, living in a small town in the poorest state in the nation, all the while balancing a growing family of dependents and impending financial ruin, could during the Great Depression write a series of novels all set in the same small Southern county — novels that include *As I Lay Dying*, *Light in August*, and above all, *Absalom, Absalom!* — that would one day be recognized as among the greatest novels ever written by an American.

The Early Years

William Cuthbert Falkner (as his name was then spelled) was born on September 25, 1897, in New Albany, Mississippi, the first of four sons born to Murry and Maud Butler

Related Links & Info

Authored by John Padgett / http://www.olemiss.edu/mwp/dir/faulkner_william/

⚙ Critical-Thinking and Writing Activities

1. Focus on a research project that you are doing now. How might primary research and library research (scholarly books and journal articles) strengthen your writing? Why not do all your research on the free Web using Google and resources like Wikipedia? What blend of primary research, library research, and/or free-Web research might this project require?

2. By working with your library's Web site and its orientation tools, identify where you can physically and/or electronically locate books, reference resources, and journals. Similarly, explore your library's handouts and Web site for information about Internet research. What

services, support, and access does the library provide? Now use what you have discovered to conduct research for your current project.

3. Indicate which section of the library would house the following items: (a) *JAMA, the Journal of the American Medical Association*, (b) *Places Rated Almanac*, and (c) *Principles of Corporate Finance* (a book).

4. Using the variety of Internet search methods outlined in this chapter, work with some classmates to search the free Web for information on a controversial topic, event, person, or place. Carefully analyze and evaluate the range of Web information you find—the quality, perspective, depth, and reliability. Create a report on your findings.

Unreliable

▸ **Assignment Restrictions** As a blog, the made-up Web site below would not be appropriate for an assignment about the life and work of William Faulkner. A site such as this should be recognized as reflective only of the writer's opinion, not of reliable information or fact.

▸ **Author/Organization** There is no author or organization listed for this Web site. The domain name—myviewsonliterature.wordpress.com—shows that this is a personal opinion blog. Its lack of connection to other Web sites shows it represents an isolated opinion.

▸ **Balance or Bias** This blog post shows a strong bias against William Faulkner. The few facts cited inad-equately support the writer's main point, and logical fallacies are apparent. The tone of the post is un-scholarly, with inflammatory language.

▸ **Quality of Information** Though this Web site is frequently updated, the blog post does not represent current scholarship about William Faulkner. The Web site is information poor and is not backed up by any reputable print or online sources.

▸ **Quality of Writing and Design** The site has an amateurish design and numerous errors, including the persistent misspelling of William Faulkner's name. The writing is slipshod and the editing is poor.

Home	Pages	Archives	Recently	Topics	RSS

Recently

As I Lie Dying (seriously)

Tortilla Flat Like a Bad Taco

Death Comes for the Reader

A Farewell to Hemmingway

The (Not So) Great Gatsby

Gee, Tennessee Williams

The Bonfire of the Bad Novels

William Falkner

Some people consider William Falkner to be one of the greatest writers in American History. They say that fact is amazing since he did not complete high school, let alone college. They consider his lack of apostrophes and his ellipsises that go on for miles to be a sign of genius. Yes, Falkner knew how to write compound-complex sentences that never seemed to end, but again, is this a sign of genius or of someone with series problems? Anybody who wants to understand why Falkner wrote the way he wrote has to remember that her was an alcoholic.

Falkner is garulous and intense, overly emotional, and trying too hard to convince you of something he strongly believes but can't quite remember right now. The fact was that when Falkner worked in Hollywood, they had to have a clause in his contract that he couldn't drink while he was writing scripts. And when they got the scripts he worked on they pretty much rewrote them all. He got screen credit for only one movie he worked on.

STUDY TOOLS 21

LOCATED AT BACK OF THE TEXTBOOK
☐ Tear-Out Chapter Review Card

LOCATED AT WWW.CENGAGEBRAIN.COM/LOGIN
☐ Chapter eBook

☐ Graded quizzes and a practice quiz generator

☐ Videos: Writer Interviews

☐ Tutorials

☐ Flashcards

☐ Cengage Learning Write Experience

☐ Interactive activities

22 | Working with Your Sources

"THE OUTCOME OF ANY SERIOUS RESEARCH CAN ONLY BE TO MAKE TWO QUESTIONS GROW WHERE ONLY ONE GREW BEFORE."

THORSTEIN VEBLEN

Thomas Bethge, 2014 / Used under license from Shutterstock.com

LEARNING OBJECTIVES

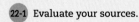 Evaluate your sources.

 Create a working bibliography.

22-3 Take notes effectively.

22-4 Summarize, paraphrase, and quote.

After you finish
this chapter
go to
PAGE 266 for STUDY TOOLS

What does it mean to speak from authority? It doesn't come from a mere title. Titles can be withdrawn as easily as awarded. Instead, authority comes from familiarity with a topic. You probably know someone you trust to advise about family issues, someone you consult for mechanical problems, someone who can help with a difficult subject in your coursework. Each of these people is an authority based on knowledge of a subject.

When you do research-based writing, you need to become an authority on your chosen topic. You must gain a broad knowledge of the information available, evaluate it for trustworthiness and applicability, and effectively incorporate it into your writing—with proper credit. This chapter will help you with those things so that your reader will recognize your authority.

22-1 EVALUATE YOUR SOURCES

Sources of information can be rated for depth and reliability based on their authorship, length, topic treatment, documentation, method of publication, distance from primary sources, and so on. Remember that credible sources boost your own credibility; sources that are not credible destroy it.

22-1a Rate Sources

Don't automatically use sources simply because they support your opinion; conversely, don't reject sources simply because they disagree with your perspective. Instead, base your selection of information on reliable, thoughtful criteria.

From Good to Bad

Use this rating scale to target sources that fit your project's goals, to assess the quality of the sources, and to build a strong bibliography. The scale is organized according to the depth and reliability of different sources, with "10" being the deepest and most reliable, and "0" being the thinnest, most unreliable.

10 Scholarly Books and Articles: largely based on careful research; written by experts for experts; address topics in depth; involve peer review and careful editing; offer stable discussion of topic

9 Trade Books and Journal Articles: largely based on careful research; written by experts for educated general audience; sample periodicals: *The Atlantic, Scientific American, Nature, Orion*

8 Government Resources: books, reports, Web pages, guides, statistics developed by experts at government agencies; provided as service to citizens; relatively objective; sample source: *Statistical Abstract of the United States*

7 Reviewed Official Online Documents: Internet resources posted by legitimate institutions—colleges and universities, research institutes, service organizations; although offering a particular perspective, sources tend to be balanced

6 Reference Works and Textbooks: provide general and specialized information; carefully researched, reviewed, and edited; lack depth for focused research (e.g., general encyclopedia entry)

5 News and Topical Stories from Quality Sources: provide current-affairs coverage (print and online), introduction-level articles of interest to general public; may lack depth and length;

sample sources: the *Washington Post, The New York Times; Time, Psychology Today;* NPR's *All Things Considered*

4 **Popular Magazine Stories:** short, introductory articles often distant from primary sources and without documentation; heavy advertising; sample sources: *Glamour, Seventeen, Reader's Digest*

3 **Business and Nonprofit Publications:** pamphlets, reports, news releases, brochures, manuals; range from informative to sales-focused

2 **List Server Discussions, Usenet Postings, Blog Articles, Talk Radio Discussions:** highly open, fluid, undocumented, untested exchanges and publications; unstable resource

1 **Unregulated Web Material:** personal sites, joke sites, chat rooms, special-interest sites, advertising and junk email (spam); no review process, little accountability, biased presentation

0 **Tabloid Articles (print and Web):** contain exaggerated and untrue stories written to titillate and exploit; sample source: the *National Enquirer,* the *Weekly World News*

22-1b Test Print and Online Source Reliability

When assessing the credibility of a source, consider the author and his or her perspective (or bias), and consider the source's timeliness and accuracy. The benchmarks in the following quick guide apply to both print and online sources; note, however, the additional tests concerning sources on the Web, as well as the discussion on pages 254–256 concerning how to evaluate Web sites.

Quick Guide:
Reliability Test

Credible Author

Is the author an expert on this topic? What are her or his credentials, and can you confirm them? For example, an automotive engineer would be an expert on hybrid-vehicle technology, whereas a celebrity in a commercial would not.

> **Web test:** Is an author indicated? If so, are the author's credentials noted and contact information offered (for example, an email address)?

Reliable Publication

Has the source been published by a scholarly press, a peer-reviewed professional journal, a quality trade-book publisher, or a trusted news source? Did you find this resource through a reliable search tool?

> **Web test:** Which individual or group posted this page? Is the site rated by a subject directory or library organization? How stable is the site—has it been around for a while, and is the material current, well-documented, and readily accessible? Check the site's home page, and read "About Us" pages and mission statements.

Unbiased Discussion

While all sources come from a specific perspective and represent specific commitments, a biased source may be pushing an agenda in an unfair, unbalanced, incomplete manner. Watch for bias toward a certain region, country, political party, industry, gender, race, ethnic group, or religion. Be alert to connections among authors, financial backers, and the points of view shared. For example, if an author has functioned as a consultant to or a lobbyist for a particular industry or group (oil, animal rights), his or her allegiances may lead to a biased presentation of an issue.

> **Web test:** Is the online document one-sided? Is the site nonprofit (.org), government (.gov), commercial (.com), educational (.edu), business (.biz), informational (.info), network-related (.net), or military (.mil)? Is the site produced in the U.S. or internationally? Is this organization pushing a cause, product, service, or belief? How do advertising or special interests affect the site?

Current Information

A five-year-old book on computers may be outdated, but a forty-year-old book on Abraham Lincoln could still be the best source. Given what you need, is this source's discussion up-to-date?

Web test: When was the material originally posted and last updated? Are links live or dead?

Accurate Information

Bad research design, poor reporting, and sloppy documentation can lead to inaccurate information. Check the source for factual errors, statistical flaws, and conclusions that don't add up.

Web test: Is the site information-rich or -poor—filled with helpful, factual materials or fluffy with thin, unsubstantiated opinions? Can you trace and confirm sources by following links or conducting your own search?

Full, Logical Support

Is the discussion of the topic reasonable, balanced, and complete? Are claims backed up with quality evidence? Does the source avoid faulty assumptions, twisted statistical analysis, logical fallacies, and unfair persuasion tactics? (See pages 188–191 for help.)

Web test: Does the page offer well-supported claims and helpful links to more information?

Quality Writing

Is the source well written? Is it free of sarcasm, derogatory terms, clichés, catch phrases, mindless slogans, grammar slips, and spelling errors?

Web test: Are words neutral ("conservative perspective") or emotionally charged ("fascist agenda")?

Positive Relationship with Other Sources

Does the source disagree with other sources? If yes, is the disagreement about the facts themselves or about how to interpret the facts? Which source seems more credible?

Web test: Is the site's information logically consistent with print sources? Do other reputable sites offer links to this site?

Design and Visual Resources

Is the graphic informative or merely decorative?

Are graphics manipulative in any way? What do they include or exclude? Are they well designed? And are they the product of a reliable source?

Web test: Are pages well designed—with clear rather than flashy, distracting multimedia elements? Is the site easy to navigate?

22-2 CREATE A WORKING BIBLIOGRAPHY

A **working bibliography** lists sources that you have used and/or intend to use. Compiling this list helps you track your research, develop your final bibliography, and avoid plagiarism.

22-2a Building a Bibliography

Use note cards (see below), a small notebook, or a computer for your work. Research software such as EasyBib, iSource, or Quick Cite may prove helpful.

Include Identifying Information

The explanations that follow tell you which details to include for each type of source you use. You may find it helpful later to record bibliographic details in the format of the documentation system you are expected to use—MLA or APA (pages 288–321). Also give each source a code number or letter.

Sample Working Bibliography Entries

▸ **Books:** author, title and subtitle, publication details (place, publisher, date), call number

#2

Howells, Coral Ann.

Alice Munro. Contemporary World Writers. Manchester and New York: Manchester UP, 1998.

PS 8576.U57 Z7 1998

Book provides good introduction to Alice Munro's fiction, chapters arranged by Munro's works; contains intro, conclusion, and bibliography; 1998 date means author doesn't cover Munro's recent fiction.

working bibliography a list of sources that you have read and/or intend to use in your research

- **Periodicals:** author, article title, journal name, publication information (volume, number, date), page numbers, method of access (stacks, current periodical, database)

#5

Valdes, Marcela. "Some Stories Have to Be Told by Me: A Literary History of Alice Munro." *Virginia Quarterly Review* 82.3 (Summer 2006): 82-90.

Gale's Academic OneFile

http://www.gale.cengage.com/PeriodicalSolutions/academicOnefile.htm

Article offers good introduction to Munro's life, her roots in Ontario, her writing career, and the key features of her stories.

- **Online sources:** author (if available), document title, site sponsor, database name, publication or posting date, access date, other publication information, URL

#3

"Alice Munro." Athabasca University Centre for Language and Literature: Canadian Writers. Updated 31 January 2015. Accessed 17 April 2015.

http://www.athabascau.ca/writers/munro.html

Site offers good introduction to Munro's writing, along with links to bibliography and other resources.

- **Primary or field research:** date conducted, name and/or descriptive title of person interviewed, place observed, survey conducted, document analyzed

#4

Thacker, Robert. Email interview. 7 March 2015.

rthacker@mdu.edu

Author of critical biography on Munro, *Alice Munro: Writing Her Lives,* offered really helpful insights into her creative process, especially useful for story "Carried Away."

22-3 TAKE NOTES EFFECTIVELY

Accurate, thoughtful notes serve as the foundation for your research writing. A good note-taking system should help you (1) work efficiently, (2) glean key information from sources, (3) engage sources critically and reflectively, and (4) record summaries, quotations, and paraphrases. Effective notes separate source material from your own ideas, which, in turn, helps you to avoid unintentional plagiarism.

22-3a Select a System

When taking notes, think carefully about the information that you record. Each idea should clearly relate to or enhance your understanding of the topic. What you shouldn't do is simply collect quotations to plunk in your paper, gather a lot of disconnected facts and details, or create extensive notes for every source.

Four note-taking systems are outlined in this section. Choose the system that works best for your project, or combine elements to develop your own system. Be aware that one note-taking style may work better than another, depending on the discipline. For example, in a literature class, the copy-and-annotating method works especially well.

System 1: Paper or Electronic Note Cards

Using paper note cards is the traditional method of note taking; however, note-taking software is now available with most word-processing programs and with applications like iSource and EndNote. Here's how a note-card system works:

1. Establish one set of cards (3 × 5 inches, if paper) for your bibliography.

2. On a second set of cards (4 × 6 inches, if paper), take notes on sources:
   - Record one point from one source per card.
     - Clarify the source: List the author's last name, a shortened title, or a code from the matching bibliography card. Include a page number.
       - Provide a topic or heading: Called a slug, the topic helps you categorize and order information.
         - Label the note as a summary, paraphrase, or quotation of the original.
         - Distinguish between the source's information and your own thoughts.

Slug	**PROBLEMS WITH INTERNAL-COMBUSTION CARS**
Quotation	"In one year, the average gas-powered car produces five tons of carbon dioxide, which, as it slowly builds up in the atmosphere, causes global
Page Number	warming." (p. 43)
	— helpful fact about the extent of pollution caused by the traditional i-c engine
Comments	— How does this number compare with what a hybrid produces?
Source	#7

Pros & Cons: Although note cards can be initially tedious and time consuming, they are very helpful for categorizing and organizing material for an outline and a first draft.

System 2: Copy (or Save) and Annotate

The copy-and-**annotate** method involves working with photocopies, print versions, or digital texts of sources:

1. Selectively photocopy, print, or save important sources. Copy carefully, making sure you have full pages, including the page numbers.

2. As needed, add identifying information on the copy—author, publication details, and date. Each page should be easy to identify and trace. When working with books, simply copy the title and copyright pages and keep them with the rest of your notes.

3. As you read, mark up the copy and highlight key statements. In the margins or digital file, record your ideas:

   - Ask questions. Insert a "?" in the margin, or write out the question.
   - Make connections. Draw arrows to link ideas, or make notes like "see page 36."
   - Add asides. Record what you think and feel while reading.
   - Define terms. Note important words that you need to understand.
   - Create a marginal index. Write key words to identify themes and main parts.

Pros & Cons: Even though organizing the various pages for drafting can be inconvenient, copying, printing, or saving gives you an accurate record of your sources. And annotating, when approached with more care than mere skimming and highlighting, encourages critical thinking.

System 3: The Computer Notebook or Research Log

The computer notebook or research log method involves taking notes on a computer or on sheets of paper. Here's how it works:

1. Establish a central location for your notes—a notebook, a binder, or an electronic folder.

2. Take notes one source at a time, making sure to identify the source fully. Number your note pages.

3. Using your initials or some other symbol, distinguish your own thoughts from source material.

4. Use codes in your notes to identify which information in the notes relates to which topic in your outline. Then, under each topic in the outline, write the page number in your notes where that information is recorded. With a notebook or log, you may be able to rearrange your notes into an outline by using copy and paste—but don't lose source information in the process!

Pros & Cons: Taking notes in this way feels natural, although using them to outline and draft may require some time-consuming paper shuffling.

System 4: The Double-Entry Notebook

The double-entry notebook involves parallel note taking—notes from sources beside your own brainstorming, reaction, and reflection. Using a notebook or the columns feature of your word-processing program, do the following:

annotate underline or highlight important passages in a text and make notes in the margins

wavebreakmedia, 2014 / Used under license from Shutterstock.com

1. Divide pages vertically.

2. In the left column, record bibliographic information and take notes on sources.

3. In the right column, write your responses. Think about what the source is saying, why the point is important, whether you agree with it, and how the point relates to other ideas and other sources.

Pros & Cons: Although organizing the double-entry notes for drafting may be challenging, this method creates accurate source records and directly engages the researcher with the material.

Bibliographic Info and Notes	Responses
Cudworth, Erika. *Environment and Society*. Routledge Introductions to Environment Series. London and New York: Routledge, 2003.	I've actually had a fair bit of personal experience with animals—the horses, ducks, dogs, and cats on our hobby farm. Will this chapter make trouble for my thinking?
Ch. 6 "Society, Culture and Nature—Human Relations with Animals"	
Chapter looks at how social scientists have understood, historically, the relationship between people and animals (158).	Yes, what really are the connections and differences between people and animals? Is it a different level of intelligence? Is there something more basic or fundamental? Are we afraid to see ourselves as animals, as creatures?
The word "animal" is itself a problem when we remember that people too are animals, but the distinction is often sharply made by people themselves (159).	
"In everyday life, people interact with animals continually" (159). Author gives many common examples.	Many examples—pets, food, TV programs, zoos—apply to me. Hadn't thought about how much my life is integrated with animal life! What does that integration look like? What does it mean for me, for the animals?

summarize to condense in your own words the main points in a passage

paraphrase to put a whole passage in your own words

quotation a word-for-word statement or passage from an original source

22-4 SUMMARIZE, PARAPHRASE, AND QUOTE

As you work with sources, decide what to put in your notes and how to record it—as a summary, a paraphrase, or a quotation. The passage below comes from an article on GM's development of fuel-cell technology. On the following pages, note how the researchers **summarize**, **paraphrase**, and **quote** material. Then practice the same strategies in your own source notes.

22-4a Source Passage

From Burns, L. D., McCormick, J. B., and Borroni-Bird, C. E. "Vehicle of Change." *Scientific American* 287:4 (October 2002): 10 pp.

When Karl Benz rolled his Patent Motorcar out of the barn in 1886, he literally set the wheels of change in motion. The advent of the automobile led to dramatic alterations in people's way of life as well as the global economy—transformations that no one expected at the time. The ever increasing availability of economical personal transportation remade the world into a more accessible place while spawning a complex industrial infrastructure that shaped modern society.

Now another revolution could be sparked by automotive technology: one fueled by hydrogen rather than petroleum. Fuel cells—which cleave hydrogen atoms into protons and electrons that drive electric motors while emitting nothing worse than water vapor—could make the automobile much more environmentally friendly. Not only could cars become cleaner, they could also become safer, more comfortable, more personalized—and even perhaps less expensive. Further, these fuel-cell vehicles could be instrumental in motivating a shift toward a "greener" energy economy based on hydrogen. As that occurs, energy use and production could change significantly. Thus, hydrogen fuel-cell cars and trucks could help ensure a future in which personal mobility—the freedom to travel independently—could be sustained indefinitely, without compromising the environment or depleting the earth's natural resources.

A confluence of factors makes the big change seem increasingly likely. For one, the petroleum-fueled internal-combustion engine (ICE), as highly refined, reliable, and economical as it is, is finally reaching its limits. Despite steady improvements, today's ICE vehicles are only 20 to 25 percent efficient in converting the energy content of fuels into drive-wheel power. And although the U.S. auto industry has cut exhaust emissions substantially since the unregulated 1960s—hydrocarbons dropped by 99 percent, carbon monoxide by 96 percent, and nitrogen oxides by 95 percent—the continued production of carbon dioxide causes concern because of its potential to change the planet's climate.

22-4b Summarize

Summarizing condenses in your own words the main points in a passage. Summarize when the source provides relevant ideas and information on your topic.

1. Reread the passage, jotting down a few key words.
2. State the main point in your own words. Add key supporting points, leaving out examples, details, and long explanations. Be objective: Don't mix your reactions with the summary.
3. Check your summary against the original, making sure that you use quotation marks around any exact phrases you borrow.

Sample Summary:

While the introduction of the car in the late nineteenth century led to dramatic changes in society and world economics, another dramatic change is now taking place in the shift from gas engines to hydrogen technologies. Fuel cells may make the car "greener," and perhaps even safer, cheaper, and more comfortable. These automotive changes will affect the energy industry by making it more environmentally friendly; as a result, people will continue to enjoy mobility while transportation moves to renewable energy. One factor leading to this technological shift is that the internal-

combustion engine has reached the limits of its efficiency, potential, and development—while remaining problematic with respect to emissions, climate change, and health.

FYI For instruction on effectively integrating quotations, paraphrases, and summaries into your writing, see pages 272–274.

22-4c Paraphrase

Paraphrasing puts a whole passage in your own words. Paraphrase passages that present key points, explanations, or arguments that are useful to your project. Follow these steps:

1. Quickly review the entire passage for a sense of the whole, and then reread it sentence by sentence.
   - State the ideas in your own words.
   - Edit for clarity, but don't change the meaning.
   - Put directly borrowed phrases in quotation marks.
2. Check your paraphrase against the original for accurate tone and meaning.

Sample Paraphrase:

The passage below paraphrases the second paragraph in the source passage beginning on page 264.

Automobile technology may be delivering another radical economic and social change through the shift from gasoline to hydrogen fuel. By breaking hydrogen into protons and electrons so that the electrons run an electric motor with water vapor as the only the by-product, fuel cells could make the car a "green" machine. But this technology could also increase the automobile's safety, comfort, personal tailoring, and affordability. Moreover, this shift to fuel-cell engines in automobiles could lead to dramatic, environmentally friendly changes in the broader energy industry, an industry that will be tied to hydrogen rather than to fossil fuels. The result of this shift will be radical changes in the way we use and produce energy. In other words, the shift to clean technology and hydrogen-powered vehicles could maintain society's valued mobility while preserving the environment and earth's natural resources.

22-4d Quote

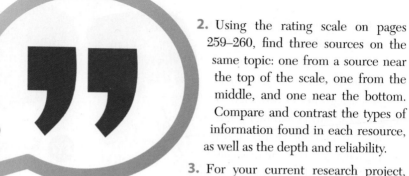

Quoting records statements or phrases from an original source word for word. Quote nuggets only—statements that are well phrased or authoritative:

1. Note the quotation's context—how it fits in the author's discussion.
2. Copy the passage word for word, enclosing it in quotation marks and checking its accuracy.
3. If you omit words, note that omission with an ellipsis. If you change any word for grammatical reasons, enclose it in brackets. (See page 361).

Careful note taking helps prevent unintentional plagiarism. Plagiarism—using source material without giving credit—is treated more fully elsewhere (pages 269–272). But at the planning stage, you can prevent this problem by (1) maintaining an accurate working bibliography, (2) distinguishing source material from your own ideas in your notes, (3) paraphrasing, summarizing, and quoting source material selectively and accurately, and (4) clearly identifying the source of the information, including material gleaned from the Internet.

Sample Quotations:

This sentence captures the authors' main claim about the benefits and future of fuel-cell technology.

"[H]ydrogen fuel-cell cars and trucks could help ensure a future in which personal mobility . . . could be sustained indefinitely, without compromising the environment or depleting the earth's natural resources."

This quotation offers a well-phrased statement about the essential problem.

"[T]he petroleum-fueled internal-combustion engine (ICE), as highly refined, reliable, and economical as it is, is finally reaching its limits."

⚙ Critical-Thinking and Writing Activities

1. What note-taking practices have you used for research projects in the past? Compare and contrast your practices with the guidelines outlined in this chapter; what do you plan to change?

2. Using the rating scale on pages 259–260, find three sources on the same topic: one from a source near the top of the scale, one from the middle, and one near the bottom. Compare and contrast the types of information found in each resource, as well as the depth and reliability.

3. For your current research project, carry out the following tasks based on the results of your primary, library, and free-Web research:

- Shape your list of resources into a working bibliography. Then add a commentary to the bibliography explaining why you believe this list to represent good, balanced research.
- Using the instructions on evaluating sources (pages 260–261), assess the quality and reliability of three of your sources. Summarize your comparative assessment in a paragraph.
- Summarize a passage from one of your key sources. Then choose a portion of the passage and paraphrase it. Finally, record a significant statement in the passage as a direct quotation.

STUDY TOOLS 22

LOCATED AT BACK OF THE TEXTBOOK
☐ Tear-Out Chapter Review Card

LOCATED AT WWW.CENGAGEBRAIN.COM/LOGIN
☐ Chapter eBook

☐ Graded quizzes and a practice quiz generator

☐ Videos: Writer Interviews

☐ Tutorials

☐ Flashcards

☐ Cengage Learning Write Experience

☐ Interactive activities

WHY CHOOSE?

Every 4LTR Press solution comes complete with a visually engaging textbook in addition to an interactive eBook. Go to CourseMate for **COMP3** to begin using the eBook. Access at www.cengagebrain.com

23 | Writing a Research Paper

> "FACTS ARE STUBBORN THINGS; AND WHATEVER MAY BE OUR WISHES, OUR INCLINATIONS, OR THE DICTATES OF OUR PASSION, THEY CANNOT ALTER THE STATE OF FACTS AND EVIDENCE."
>
> JOHN ADAMS

LEARNING OBJECTIVES

23-1 Avoid plagiarism.

23-2 Avoid other source abuses.

23-3 Use sources well.

23-4 Write a research paper.

23-5 Follow a model.

After you finish
this chapter
go to
PAGE 287 for STUDY TOOLS

In 1960, the famed paleontologist Louis Leakey sent his young secretary on a four-month expedition to Tanzania to observe chimpanzees in the wild. Jane Goodall was not a trained scientist, but she was a keen observer, patient and meticulous and gentle. She did something naturalists had never thought of doing. She sat still and let the animals come to her. The first chimpanzee who approached she named David Greybeard—not Specimen TZ196001. And she took extensive notes, created detailed drawings, and learned more about wild chimpanzees in four months than humanity had learned since the dawn of time.

Then Jane came back to civilization. She had so much to report, but no one would listen to a twenty-something woman with no scientific degree who lived with chimps in the wild. At Leakey's request, Jane enrolled at Cambridge and by 1965 received her Ph.D. She did her paper chase and became Dr. Jane Goodall and wrote up her findings and changed the world.

The point is this: You can do all the research you want, but until you put it into a documented form that others in your field can read and respond to, your discoveries make no impact. You have to do the paper chase. You have to document.

Writing your research paper is the culmination of your discovery process. It's the chance for you to share your discoveries and change minds. This chapter will guide you through the process.

23-1 AVOID PLAGIARISM

The road to **plagiarism** may be paved with the best intentions—or the worst. Either way, the result is a serious academic offense. As you write your research paper, do everything you can to stay off that road! Start by studying your school's and your instructor's guidelines on plagiarism and other academic offenses. Then study the following pages.

23-1a Plagiarism Defined

Plagiarism is using someone else's words, ideas, or images (what's called intellectual property) so that they appear to be your own. When you plagiarize, you use source material—whether published in print or online—without acknowledging the source. In this sense, plagiarism refers to a range of thefts: submitting a paper you didn't write (even if you bought it), pasting source material into your paper and passing off that content as your own, using exact quotations without quotation marks and **documentation**, and summarizing and paraphrasing material without documentation. And plagiarism is more than "word theft." The rules also apply to images, tables, graphs, charts, maps, music, videos, and so on.

What makes it wrong?

Plagiarism is stealing, and colleges punish it as such. It may result in a failing grade for the assignment or course, a note on your **academic transcript** (often seen by potential employers), and possibly even expulsion.

Aside from the punitive aspects, plagiarism short-circuits dialogue within a discipline. It discounts the work of other thinkers, disrespects writers and readers, insults instructors, and damages the reputation of colleges.

Also consider what plagiarism does to you. It prevents you from learning the skills you need to have as a scholar. It also demonstrates to others around you that you are not a serious thinker, that you aren't to be trusted, relied upon, or listened to. In short, it damages your reputation, a key component to your success academically and professionally.

---

documentation crediting sources of information through in-text citations or references and a list of works cited or references

academic transcript the permanent record of educational achievement and activity

What does it look like?

Plagiarism can take on a number of forms. Read the passage below and then review the four types of plagiarism that follow, noting how each misuses the source.

> What makes Munro's characters so enthralling is their inconsistency; like real people, at one moment they declare they will cover the house in new siding, at the next, they vomit on their way to the hospital. They fight against and seek refuge in the people they love. The technique that Munro has forged to get at such contradictions is a sort of pointillism, the setting of one bright scene against another, with little regard for chronology.

Excerpt taken from page 87 of "Some Stories Have to Be Told by Me: A Literary History of Alice Munro," by Marcela Valdes, published in the *Virginia Quarterly Review* 82.3 (Summer 2006).

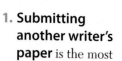

1. **Submitting another writer's paper** is the most blatant form of plagiarism. Whether the paper was written by another student, was downloaded and reformatted from the Internet, or was purchased from a "paper mill," the result is still plagiarism. Remember that though it may seem easy to plagiarize material from the Internet, it's equally easy for professors to use Internet tools to discover plagiarism.

2. **Pasting material into your paper and passing it off as your own** is another form of plagiarism. In the example below, the red material is plagiarized from the original article, masquerading as the writer's own idea.

> Life typically unfolds mysteriously for Munro's characters, with unexplained events and choices. Like real people, at one moment they declare they will cover the house in new siding, at the next, they vomit on their way to the hospital.

working bibliography list of the sources that you have used and/or intend to use in your research

3. **Using material without quotation marks and citation** is another form of plagiarism. Whether you use a paragraph or a phrase, if you use the exact wording of a source, you must enclose the material in quotation marks and provide a source citation. The lack of quotation marks makes the red material plagiarized.

> What makes Munro's characters so typically human is that they fight against and seek refuge in the people they love (Valdes 87).

4. **Failing to cite a source for summarized or paraphrased ideas** is another form of plagiarism. Even if borrowed information has been reworded, the source must be acknowledged. In the following example, the writer correctly summarizes the passage's ideas but offers no citation.

> For the reader, the characters in Munro's stories are interesting because they are so changeable. Munro shows these changes by using a method of placing scenes side by side for contrast, without worrying about the chronological connections.

How do I avoid it?

Of course, some types of plagiarism may happen by accident, perhaps through sloppy note taking or inexpert use of punctuation. Plagiarism is like speeding—regardless of whether the infraction was purposeful or accidental, it carries the same consequences.

Preventing plagiarism begins the moment you get an assignment. Essentially, prevention requires commitment and diligence throughout the process. Begin, of course, by pledging never to plagiarize, no matter how easy the Internet may make it. Also follow the rules established by your college and your professor, as well as these strategies:

- **As you research,** take orderly notes and maintain an accurate **working bibliography**. Make sure to carefully summarize, paraphrase, and quote material. (See pages 264–266.)

- **As you write,** carefully credit all material that is quoted, summarized, or paraphrased from another source. For quoted material, use quotation marks. For summaries and paraphrases, signal where borrowed material begins by using a phrase like "As Valdes notes, many of Munro's characters exhibit . . ."; then signal where the material ends by providing the source citation.

- **After you write,** compile a complete, accurate works-cited or reference list with full source information for all borrowed material in your writing.

AVOID OTHER SOURCE ABUSES

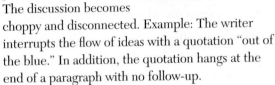

Plagiarism, though the most serious offense, is not the only source abuse to avoid when writing a paper with documented research. The information that follows covers source abuses that are subtly deceptive or make for poor research writing. The examples reference the excerpt on the previous page.

1. **Using sources inaccurately:** When you get a quotation wrong, botch a summary, paraphrase poorly, or misstate a statistic, you misrepresent the original. Example: In this quotation, the writer carelessly uses several wrong words that change the meaning, and also adds two words that are not in the original.

   > As Marcela Valdes explains, "[w]hat makes Munro's characters so appalling is their consistency. . . . They fight against and seek refuse in the people they say they love" (87).

2. **Using source material out of context:** By ripping a statement out of its **context** and forcing it into yours, you can make a source seem to say something that it didn't really say. Example: This writer uses part of a statement to say the opposite of the original.

   > According to Marcela Valdes, while Munro's characters are interesting, Munro's weakness as a fiction writer is that she shows "little regard for chronology" (87).

3. **Overusing source material:** When your paper reads like a string of references, especially quotations, your own thinking disappears. Example: The writer takes the source passage, chops it up, and splices it together.

   > Anyone who has read her stories knows that "[w]hat makes Munro's characters so enthralling is their inconsistency." That is to say, "like real people, at one moment they declare they will cover the house in new siding, at the next, they vomit on their way to the hospital." Moreover, "[t]hey fight against and seek refuge in the people they love." This method "that Munro has forged to get at such contradictions is a sort of pointillism," meaning "the setting of one bright scene against another, with little regard for chronology" (Valdes 87).

4. **"Plunking" quotations:** You "plunk" or "drop" quotations into your paper by failing both to introduce them to the reader and to provide a follow-up. The discussion becomes choppy and disconnected. Example: The writer interrupts the flow of ideas with a quotation "out of the blue." In addition, the quotation hangs at the end of a paragraph with no follow-up.

   > Typically, characters such as Del Jordan, Louisa Doud, and Almeda Roth experience a crisis through contact with particular men. "They fight against and seek refuge in the people they love" (Valdes 87).

5. **Using "blanket" citations:** Blanket citations make the reader guess where borrowed material begins and ends. For example, if you place a parenthetical citation at the end of a paragraph, does that citation cover the whole paragraph or just the final sentence?

6. **Relying heavily on one source:** If your writing is dominated by one source, the reader may doubt the depth and integrity of your research. Instead, your writing should show your reliance on a balanced diversity of sources.

7. **Failing to match in-text citations to bibliographic entries:** All in-text citations must clearly refer to accurate entries in the works-cited, reference, or endnote pages. Mismatching occurs when (a) an in-text citation refers to a source not listed in the bibliography or (b) a bibliographic entry is never referenced in the paper itself.

8. **Violating copyrights:** When you copy, distribute, and/or post in whole or in part any intellectual property without permission from or payment to the copyright holder, you commit a copyright infringement, especially when you profit from this use. To avoid copyright violations in your research projects, follow the strategies on the next page.

> **context** the set of circumstances in which a statement is made; the text and other factors that surround a specific statement and are crucial to understanding it

- **Observe fair use guidelines:** Quote small portions of a document for limited purposes, such as education or research. Avoid copying large portions for your own gain.

- **Understand what's in the public domain:** You need not obtain permission to copy and use public domain materials—primarily documents created by the government, but also some material posted on the Internet as part of the "copy left" movement.

- **Observe intellectual property and copyright laws:** First, know your college's policies on copying documents. Second, realize that copyright protects the expression of ideas in a range of materials— writings, videos, songs, photographs, drawings, computer software, and so on. Always obtain permission to copy and distribute copyrighted materials.

- **Avoid changing a source** (e.g., a photo) without permission of the creator or copyright holder.

23-3 USE SOURCES WELL

After you've found good sources and taken good notes on them, you want to use that research effectively in your writing. Specifically, you want to show (1) what information you are borrowing and (2) where you got it. By doing so, you create credibility. This section shows you how to develop credibility by integrating and documenting sources so as to avoid plagiarism and other abuses. (Note: For a full treatment of documentation, see pages 288–307.)

23-3a Integrate Sources

Source material—whether summary, paraphrase, or quotation—should be integrated smoothly into your discussion. To do so, you should focus on what you want to say, not on all the sources you've collected. Use sources to deepen and develop your point, provide evidence for your argument, give authority to your position, illustrate your point, or address a counterargument.

Managing Your Sources

Failure to manage your sources will result in those sources determining the course and character of your work. Here's a pattern you can follow to make sure you control your sources, rather than letting them control you:

Source Management Pattern

1. State and explain your idea, creating context for the source.
2. Identify and introduce the source, linking it to your discussion.
3. Summarize, paraphrase, or quote the source.
4. Provide a citation in an appropriate spot.
5. Comment on the source by explaining, expanding on, or refuting it.
6. When appropriate, refer again to a source to further develop the ideas it contains. (Review the keyed model that follows.)

The motivation and urgency to create and improve hybrid-electric technology comes from a range of complex forces. Some of these forces are economic, others environmental, and still others social. In "Societal Lifestyle Costs of Cars with Alternative Fuels/Engines," Joan Ogden, Robert Williams, and Eric Larson argue that "[c]ontinued reliance on current transportation fuels and technologies poses serious oil supply insecurity, climate change, and urban air pollution risks" (7). Because of the nonrenewable nature of fossil fuels as well as their negative side effects, the transportation industry is confronted with making the most radical changes since the introduction of the internal-combustion automobile more than 100 years ago. Hybrid-electric vehicles are one response to this pressure.

Incorporating Quotations

Be especially careful with quotations, which can overwhelm your own thinking and create a choppy flow. Use restraint. Include only quotations that are key statements by authorities, well-phrased claims and conclusions, or passages that require word-by-word analysis and interpretation. Quotations—especially long ones—need to pull their weight, so generally paraphrase or summarize source material instead.

When you do use quotations, work them into your writing as smoothly as possible, paying attention to style, punctuation, and syntax. Use enough of the quotation to make your point without changing the meaning of the original. Place quotation marks around key phrases taken from the source.

> Ogden, Williams, and Larson also conclude that the hydrogen fuel-cell vehicle is "a strong candidate for becoming the Car of the Future," given the trend toward "tighter environmental constraints" and the "intense efforts underway" by automakers to develop commercially viable versions of such vehicles (25).

23-3b Document Sources

Just as you need to integrate source material carefully into your writing, so you must also carefully document where that source material comes from. The reader should recognize which material is yours and which is not.

Identifying the Start

Sources need to be introduced. It's the introduction that signals an encounter with ideas and facts from someone other than you, the writer.

▶ **First Reference:** For the first reference to a source, use an attributive statement that indicates some of the following: author's name and credentials, title of the source, nature of the study or research, and helpful background.

> Joan Ogden, Robert Williams, and Eric Larson, members of the Princeton Environmental Institute, explain that modest improvements in energy efficiency and emissions reductions will not be enough over the next century because of anticipated transportation increases (7).

▶ **Subsequent References:** For subsequent references to a source, use a simplified **attributive phrase**, such as the author's last name or a shortened version of the title.

> Ogden, Williams, and Larson go on to argue that "effectively addressing environmental and oil supply concerns will probably require radical changes in automotive engine/fuel technologies" (7).

▶ **Other References:** In some situations, such as quoting straightforward facts, simply skip the attributive phrase. The parenthetical citation supplies sufficient attribution.

> Various types of transportation are by far the main consumers of oil (three-fourths of world oil imports); moreover, these same technologies are responsible for one-fourth of all greenhouse gas sources (Ogden, Williams, and Larson 7).

The verb you use to introduce source material is key. Use fitting verbs, such as those in the table below. Normally, use the present tense. (Use the past tense only to stress the previous time frame of a source.)

> In their 2004 study, "Societal Lifecycle Costs of Cars with Alternative Fuels/Engines," Ogden, Williams, and Larson present a method for comparing and contrasting alternatives to internal-combustion engines. Earlier, these authors made preliminary steps . . .

Quick Guide: Introductory Verbs

accepts	declares	points out
acknowledges	defends	praises
adds	denies	proposes
affirms	describes	refutes
argues	disagrees	rejects
asserts	discusses	reminds
believes	emphasizes	responds
cautions	enumerates	shares
claims	explains	shows
compares	highlights	states
concludes	identifies	stresses
confirms	insists	suggests
considers	interprets	supports
contradicts	lists	urges
contrasts	maintains	verifies
criticizes	outlines	warns

attributive phrase a group of words that indicates the source of an idea or a quotation

Identifying the End

▶ **Quotations and Ideas:** Closing quotation marks and a citation, as shown in the following example, indicate the end of a source quotation. Generally, place the citation immediately after any quotation, paraphrase, or summary. However, you may also place the citation early in the sentence or at the end if the parenthetical note is obviously obtrusive. When you discuss several details from a page in a source, use an attributive phrase at the beginning of your discussion and a single citation at the end.

> As the "Lifestyle Costs" study concludes, when greenhouse gases, air pollution, and oil insecurity are factored into the analysis, alternative-fuel vehicles "offer lower LCCs than typical new cars" (Ogden, Williams, and Larson 25).

▶ **Longer Quotations:** If a quotation is longer than four typed lines, set it off from the main text. Generally, introduce the quotation with a complete sentence and a colon. Indent the quotation one inch (10 spaces) and double-space it, but don't put quotation marks around it. Put the citation outside the final punctuation mark.

> Toward the end of the study, Ogden, Williams, and Larson argue that changes to the fuel delivery system must be factored into planning:
>
> > In charting a course to the Car of the Future, societal LCC comparisons should be complemented by considerations of fuel infrastructure requirements. Because fuel infrastructure changes are costly, the number of major changes made over time should be minimized. The bifurcated strategy advanced here—of focusing on the H2FCV for the long term and advanced liquid hydrocarbon-fueled ICEVs and ICE/HEVs for the near term—would reduce the number of such infrastructure changes to one (an eventual shift to H2). (25)

▶ **Changing Quotations:** You may shorten or change a quotation so that it fits more smoothly into your

> **ellipsis** a set of three periods with one space preceding and following each; a punctuation mark that indicates deletion of material

sentence—but don't alter the original meaning. Use an **ellipsis** within square brackets [. . .] to indicate that you have omitted words from the original. An ellipsis is three periods with spaces between them.

> In their projections of where fuel-cell vehicles are heading, Ogden, Williams, and Larson discuss GM's AUTOnomy vehicle, with its "radical redesign of the entire car. [. . .] In these cars, steering, braking, and other vehicle systems are controlled electronically rather than mechanically" (24).

▶ **Using Brackets:** Use square brackets to indicate a clarification, to change a pronoun or verb tense, or to switch around uppercase and lowercase.

> As Ogden, Williams, and Larson explain, "[e]ven if such barriers [the high cost of fuel cells and the lack of an H2 fuel infrastructure] can be overcome, decades would be required before this embryonic technology could make major contributions in reducing the major externalities that characterize today's cars" (25).

 ## 23-4 WRITE A RESEARCH PAPER

Writing Guidelines

Your research may generate a mass of notes, printouts, photocopies, electronic files, and more. Your goal is to move from this mass to a coherent structure for the paper you need to write. If you have systematically taken good notes, you are well on the way. Review the guidelines that follow to move toward order.

❶ Review your research materials. Is the information complete or at least sufficient for the project? Is the information reliable and accurate? How do different pieces of evidence connect to each other? What patterns do you see? By reviewing your research once, twice, and even three times, you'll begin to see your research paper taking shape before you.

❷ Revisit your research questions and deepen your thesis. Given the research that you have completed, does your working thesis stand up? It is possible, of course, that your research has led you to a conclusion quite different from your original working thesis. If so, rewrite your thesis accordingly. However, you might also retain your original thesis but strengthen it by using these strategies.

- **Use richer, clearer terms.** Test your working thesis for vague, broad, or inappropriate terms or concepts. Replace them with terms that have rich meanings, are respected in discussions about your topic, and refine your original thinking.

- **Introduce qualifying terms where needed.** With qualifying terms such as "normally," "often," and "usually," as well as with phrases that limit the reach of your thesis, you are paradoxically strengthening your thesis by making it more manageable.

- **Stress your idea through opposition.** You can deepen your working thesis by adding an opposing thought (usually phrased in a dependent clause). Note this revision:

  > **Original Working Thesis:** In Alice Munro's "An Ounce of Cure," infatuation messes with the narrator's head so her life gets turned upside down.

  > **Revised Working Thesis:** While Alice Munro's "An Ounce of Cure" tells a simple story of infatuation leading to confusion and trouble, the story is more importantly about the "plots of life"—the ways in which the narrator experiences life as a competing set of stories (romance, fairy tale, farce), none of which does justice to the complexity of real life.

❸ Organize your work effectively. Reread the assignment, which may suggest a pattern of organization, such as comparison-contrast. If not, use a pattern of organization suggested by your thesis and support. Turn key ideas into main headings and arrange support and evidence under each. After categorizing information, decide on the best sequence for your ideas. The following quick guide explains some common organizational patterns available to you.

Quick Guide: Organizational Patterns

- **Argumentation** asserts and supports a claim, counters opposition, and reasserts the claim.
- **Cause-effect** explores the factors that lead to an event and the consequences that result from it.
- **Chronological order** puts items in a time sequence.
- **Classification** groups details into categories based on common traits or qualities.
- **Comparison-contrast** shows similarities and differences between two subjects.
- **Description** orders details in terms of spatial relationships.
- **Explanation** clarifies how something works by breaking the object or phenomenon into parts or phases and showing how they work together.
- **Order of importance** arranges items from most to least or least to most important.
- **Problem-solution** states a problem, explores its causes and effects, and presents solutions.
- **Question-answer** moves back and forth from questions to answers in a sequence that logically clarifies a topic.

❹ Develop your first draft. As you write your paper, your main goal is to develop and support your ideas, referring to sources but not being dominated by them. Your second goal is to respect sources by integrating them naturally and accurately, with correct documentation. Review pages 272–274 to understand how to use source material. Also follow these tips for respecting your sources while drafting.

- **Avoid strings of references and chunks of source material** without your discussion, explanation, or interpretation in between.
- **Don't offer entire paragraphs of material from a source** (whether paraphrased or quoted) with a single in-text citation at the end; when you do so, your thinking disappears.
- **Be careful not to overload your draft with complex information** and dense data lacking explanation.

- **Resist the urge to copy-and-paste big chunks from sources.** Even if you document the sources, your paper will quickly become a patchwork of source material with a few stitches (your contribution) holding the paper together.

With those tips in mind, develop the following parts:

- **Opening.** Start by saying something interesting or surprising to gain your reader's attention. Then establish common ground with your reader and the topic, and identify a specific issue or challenge. Finally, offer your thesis.
- **Middle.** Develop your thesis by presenting each main point, expanding upon the points logically, and including evidence such as facts and examples and other source material to analyze each issue. Think of each main point as a conversation you are having with your reader, in which you share the most interesting, amazing, and salient aspects of each point. Don't try to cram everything you have learned into the draft.
- **Closing.** Review or tie together important points in your paper, reinforce your thesis, and draw a conclusion. In closing, expand the scope of your text by connecting the topic of the paper to the reader's experience or to life in general.

5 **Revise your first draft.** Ask a peer to read your first draft and indicate any parts that could be improved. Reread your draft as well, and use the following checklist questions to help you revise it.

Checklist: Revising

____ Is my thesis clear?

____ Do I support the thesis with strong main points?

____ Do I support the main points with evidence and analysis?

____ Have I used an organizational plan that fits the assignment, my topic, and purpose?

____ Do the main points appear in the best order?

____ Are the paragraphs (and the sentences within them) in the best order?

____ Is my writing voice objective and scholarly, focused on the topic?

____ Is my writing voice knowledgeable and engaging?

____ Have I selected strong words and correctly used topic-specific terms?

____ Do my sentences read smoothly?

6 **Edit your paper.** Once you have finished making large-scale improvements to your paper, it's time to edit your work and create a works-cited or reference section. Your paper should adhere to the conventions of Standard English as well as specific documentation guidelines. Use the following checklist questions to help you edit your work.

Checklist: Editing

____ Have I replaced general nouns and verbs with more specific nouns and verbs?

____ Have I correctly punctuated sentences and abbreviations?

____ Have I used correct capitalization with proper nouns?

____ Have I avoided sentence problems?

____ Do all subjects and verbs agree in number?

____ Do all pronouns and antecedents agree in number?

____ Are quotation marks correctly placed in quoted information, titles, or dialogue?

____ Have I double-checked the spelling of all specialized words, authors' names, and titles?

____ Have I watched for easily confused words *(there, their, they're)*?

____ Have I carefully checked the format of each in-text citation or reference? (See pages 290–297.)

____ Have I carefully checked the format of each entry in my works-cited or reference section? (See pages 297–307.)

7 **Design your paper.** The two major documentation styles (MLA and APA) have strict requirements for the final presentation of a research report, including headings, pagination, spacing, and margin size. Make certain that your paper follows the appropriate style and abides by any guidelines your instructor may have provided.

FYI The paper on the following pages shows MLA format and documentation. For more on both MLA and APA systems, see the following chapter, pages 288–321.)

FOLLOW A MODEL

Paige Louter wrote the following argumentative research paper for an expository writing course. The paper examines the fair trade movement, asking whether it achieves its goal of global justice. As you read Paige's paper, study her reasoning, her use of sources, and her MLA documentation practices.

Louter 1

Paige Louter **(A)**

Dr. Van Rys

English 302

15 February 2012

Why the World Deserves Better than Fair Trade **(B)**

The 2004 book *Fair Trade: Market-Driven Ethical Consumption* opens with **(C)** the following account of what fair trade can do for the "world's poor": "I used to live in a thatch hut with a mud floor," says fair trade farmer Jeronimo Tush. "Now I have two concrete houses. And [. . .] my children now only go to school. We don't need them to work" (qtd. in Nicholls and Opal 3). Why would anyone argue against a system of trade that provides improved housing and eliminates the need for child labor? Fair trade is admirable in its effort to address injustice, to promote human rights all over the world, to fight poverty, and to promote ethical food-production and consumption practices. However, there is a darker side **(D)** to the fair trade movement: This seemingly just-trade model is in reality falling short of its idealistic claims and is in fact creating new problems. Though the fair trade movement is perhaps not beyond saving, it must undergo radical change to survive. Additionally, in order to demand change and perhaps even offer solutions themselves, consumers—especially those who wish to call themselves socially conscious—must educate themselves as to the harmful effects for which fair trade is responsible.

To begin with, the term "fair trade" itself is a source of confusion among many **(E)** consumers. "Fair trade," not capitalized and written as two words, is the general term for the concept. However, "fairtrade" written as one word is the official name of products labeled by the Fairtrade Labelling Organizations International (FLO)—thereby making the products eligible for the Fairtrade International certification mark (see Figure 1). Here's where it gets more confusing: The American branch of fair trade product certification is called Fair Trade USA— two words, both capitalized (Figure 2 below). Anyone can claim that his or her

---

(A) The heading (in MLA format) supplies identifying details.
(B) The title (centered) indicates the paper's topic and theme.
(C) The writer opens with a quotation that gives the topic a real voice.

(D) The introduction turns to the problem that the paper will address and calls for change.
(E) The writer begins her argument by clarifying a point of confusion.

product is fair trade, but without one of the logos below, a product cannot be Fairtrade (or Fair Trade); however, companies themselves may not fully realize this. As Amarjit Sahota, the director of Organic Monitor puts it, "Companies do not always distinguish between Fairtrade and fair trade. Only the first concept is independently audited and internationally recognized. [. . .] Firms that use the latter term aren't necessarily trying to deceive consumers. It's simply hard to distinguish [between the two]" (qtd. in Hodge 17-18). This essay will consistently use the terms "fair trade" and "Fairtrade."

(F)

Fig. 1. This yin-yang-esque image is the official certification label of Fairtrade International (Hussey 16).

(G)

Fig. 2. Fair Trade USA's label suggests a racially based dichotomy between producer and consumer (Hussey 16).

Considering this difference in terminology, then, what guidelines are necessary for a product to achieve Fairtrade status? "Fair trade" as a general term could potentially be applied to any product that appears to empower disadvantaged producers. "Fairtrade" as a label, however, indicates certain guarantees for those supplying the products. These guarantees are, according to the Fairtrade International Web site, "Stable prices [. . .] a Fairtrade Premium [. . .] partnership [. . . and] empowerment of farmers and workers" ("What is [sic] Fairtrade?"). Further unpacked, this means that Fairtrade producers have guaranteed minimum prices for their goods, an extra amount, or Premium, paid to the management of the producers, and a say in how their own goods are to be produced and sold. The Premium is a concept that consumers are often unfamiliar with, and in concept, it could indeed do much good for the communities of Fairtrade producers; the Premium is intended for investment in beneficial projects such as schools and healthcare facilities. None of these guarantees appear to be objectively wrong, and perhaps in a perfect world Fairtrade could operate

(H)

(F) A direct quotation is introduced with an attributive phrase, smoothly integrated into sentence syntax, and properly punctuated. In the parenthetical citation, "qtd. in" indicates that the source was quoted in another source (an indirect quotation). Brackets and ellipses indicate omissions from and changes to the quotation.

(G) Visuals are properly referenced in the essay, labeled, and documented.
(H) A reliable Web site is clearly identified; since Web sites usually have no pagination, no parenthetical citation is needed.

under these principles in an entirely beneficial way. There is a shocking gap, however, between Fairtrade ideals and reality—a concept that will be more fully addressed later in the essay.

Before criticizing the fair trade movement, one should pay attention to (I) the benefits that the movement provides. Paul Chandler, the chief executive of Traidcraft (a fair trade organization in the UK), offers a succinct summary of the positive effects of purchasing fair trade products:

> Fair trade activity has a positive impact on the livelihoods and welfare of those producers directly involved in fair trade supply chains. [. . .] Second, fair trade gives consumers an opportunity to exercise a moral choice in their own purchasing practices. [. . .] Third, fair trade offers an effective (J) critique of business practices, showing there are practical alternative ways of trading that can be more beneficial for the poor. (Chandler 256)

Chandler is obviously not bias free in his analysis of the fair trade industry, yet his points have merit. There are indeed many success stories generated by fair trade practices: families lifted out of poverty, farmers supported when they would have otherwise faced ruin, children freed from daily labor and allowed to go to school. In addition, fair trade does provide consumers with at least the awareness that their dollars can make a difference when it comes to social justice. Finally, the fair trade movement does deserve credit for demonstrating that the current global system of trade, which does not always have the concerns of the poor at heart, is not the only option.

After taking all these benefits into account, it seems that ethically minded (K) consumers should choose fair trade products whenever possible. These pros, however, are only a small piece of the bigger picture. In fact, each of Chandler's claims is only partially true: Each declaration needs to be modified and qualified before it can accurately speak to the reality of fair trade. First, not every producer "directly involved in fair trade supply chains" benefits from the guaranteed minimum price that is a key tenent of Fairtrade products (Chandler 256). Next, as Philip Booth and Linda Whetstone argue, "Those promoting fair trade should have the humility to accept that their way of doing business is not objectively better for the poor than other ways of doing business" (29). In other words, fair

(I) In her argument, Louter acknowledges the benefits of fair trade before continuing her argument about its weaknesses.
(J) A quotation longer than four typed lines is inset—indented 10 spaces (about 1 inch) and double-spaced throughout; ellipses in brackets indicate material left out of the quotation; end punctuation is placed before the parenthetical citation.

(K) The writer transitions to arguments critiquing fair trade; she quotes from and debates a source.

trade is not necessary for consumers to "exercise a moral choice" with their money (Chandler 256). Chandler's final claim is that fair trade shows that alternative ways of trading, ones that better address the needs of the poor around the world, can and do exist. Yet while most consumers would immediately agree that poverty must be addressed head-on, Chandler offers no objective reasons as to why fair trade practice is the best avenue through which to do this. Still, the fair trade movement has demonstrated that many consumers are willing to spend more in response to the promise that their dollars are helping those in need. In addition, perhaps future ethical consumption initiatives will gain more immediate legitimacy as a result.

Later in this essay, each of these responses to Chandler's claims will be unpacked in further detail and with more support. This initial set of responses is valuable, however, because it demonstrates a key problem with the claims of many who support fair trade: The claims are often only partially true, based on feel-good rhetoric and fair trade ideals rather than on hard evidence. Further, evidence, when cited, is often very selective. Nevertheless, many fair trade proponents have legitimate, well-supported arguments that will be addressed later in this paper.

Considering that the livelihoods (and lives) of many are at stake in the failure **(L)** of the fair trade movement, perhaps a less dramatic—yet serious—problem is that the quality of certified Fairtrade coffee is often significantly poorer than coffee that is not Fairtrade. However, this problem is significant when one considers that some consumers will forgo Fairtrade coffee based on its inferior taste. If the World Fair Trade Organization (WFTO) wishes to avoid charges of providing charity rather than actual trade opportunities to its producers, the organization must have some way of ensuring that its products are purchased for their quality as well as for the economic aid they offer farmers. One critic of the Fairtrade industry asserted that it is "stuck in a charity-driven, charity-supported model [. . .] that smacks of colonialism" (Hutchens 458). In order to address this issue, one must ask why Fairtrade coffee would taste consistently poorer than other coffee. The answer essentially comes down to a lack of quality control. There are, shockingly, no Fairtrade standards regarding the quality of the product. Because quality control is lacking, and because there is a maximum amount of

---

(L) Louter develops her critique by addressing issues of coffee quality and (in the next paragraph) of gender inequity.

coffee beans that the Fairtrade buyers will accept from any one cooperative, the farmers can sell only part of their produce at the Fairtrade price, and they sell the remainder on the open market. In other words, because the Fairtrade market does not monitor the quality of the beans that they receive, farmers consistently sell their higher quality beans on the open market. In addition, the coffee co-ops do not keep track of which beans come from which farmers. In fact, co-ops regularly mix all purchased beans together, thereby removing any incentive for farmers to sell only their best beans as fair trade produce. David Henderson calls this a "free-ride problem" (63). In contrast to the "Organic Specialty" label that assures a consumer that a product is healthier, grown with less harmful chemicals, and so on, the "Fairtrade" label offers no similar assurance of quality. Therefore, Fairtrade consumers are often purchasing products out of charity, a practice that is not a sustainable business model. Furthermore, when quality standards are not enforced, the implication is that the Fairtrade system believes that the producers are incapable of creating excellent product.

Unfortunately, Fairtrade has even bigger problems than quality control, one of which is its failure to promote women's rights, a principle ostensibly championed by the WFTO. However, as Anna Hutchens puts it, there is an "absence of a policy framework and institutional mechanisms that promote women's empowerment as a rights-based rather than a culture-based issue" (449). In other words, the WFTO does not intentionally seek to universalize human rights when it comes to women. Consumers are told that women in the Fairtrade system are empowered and uplifted, but in practice, the WFTO does not seek to actively include them. The best that can be said is that they are not actively excluded. In order to achieve FLO certification, producer organizations are not required to meet any standards when it comes to working to empower women, and when it came to one coffee cooperative, "only seven of the 116 [. . .] members [. . .] were female and no women had served on the cooperative board or its managerial positions" (Hutchens 452). Sadly, this particular cooperative appears **(M)** to be the rule rather than the exception. A further problem, stemming from the lack of universally applied empowerment of women, is that "women are not made exempt from their existing household duties" despite their increased workload

(M) Quotations from one source begin with a complete in-text citation but then follow with page numbers only, as quotes are clearly from the same source. The last quotation is introduced with a complete sentence ending in a colon; words in quotation marks within the quotation are put in single quotation marks, not double.

of producing Fairtrade goods (452). And even those women who manage to find time to balance their domestic and fair trade producing roles may not benefit as they should: "Fairtrade payments typically go to the assumed male head of the household and cannot be assumed to 'trickle down' to benefit all the household members" (452).

Though gender-based disparity is bad enough, women are not the only ones who do not reap the full reward that the WFTO would like consumers to believe exists. Others denied these rewards are the farmers barred from entering the Fairtrade coffee business, as well as those workers who are employed under the Fairtrade label yet work in substandard conditions and receive substandard pay. Many agree that "there are [. . .] significant opportunities for corruption within the fair trade co-operatives [sic]" (Booth and Whetstone 33). In other words, the idea that the payment for a cup of coffee purchased in Europe or North America goes directly to the hand of an impoverished coffee bean farmer is a myth.

Beyond all these problems, many economists, such as those who work at **(N)** the Adam Smith Institute, say that fair trade simply does not make sense in terms of the market system by which it operates. These economic arguments are potentially devastating if it is found that fair trade ultimately increases, rather than alleviates, the economic hardships in which the producers work. Fair trade operates on the principle of guaranteeing a minimum price for a product, regardless of how low the real market value for that product drops. This minimum price is called a price floor, which, when set above the market price, creates a surplus, which in turn creates a price drop in the market price. "If there were a free market," writes Jeremy Weber, "new entrants would increase supply and decrease price. The minimum price [. . .] by definition prevents that outcome" (113). The result? There is just too much Fairtrade coffee being produced. Farmers are often unable to sell more than a small percentage of their coffee beans to Fairtrade buyers, and new producers who wish to enter the Fairtrade business are finding it nearly impossible: "The increased difficulty of entering the Fair Trade market threatens to exclude the marginalized coffee growers who Fair Trade supposedly supports" (Weber 113). For example, starting in 2004, Fair Trade certification cost $3,200. In fact, dual-certification of Fairtrade and

(N) The writer transitions to a critique based upon economic theory, summarizing and quoting from a source.

Organic is often now required, and the latter costs anywhere between $300 and $2,000. But the difficulty doesn't end there—renewal fees too can cost thousands of dollars. As a result, even if a coffee cooperative desiring the Fairtrade mark can raise the necessary money, the waiting list is seemingly endless; thousands of co-ops await certification, hoping to get a chance to sell their products at artificially high Fairtrade prices. Essentially, the economic principles on which Fairtrade operates are inevitably leading toward increased difficulties for any coffee farmer who did not achieve Fairtrade certification in the early days of the movement. "Fair trade may be fashionable and give people a nice warm feeling," say Paul Booth and Linda Whetstone, "but only free trade backed up by the rule of law and the protection of private property have actually lifted entire populations out **(O)** of poverty for the long term" (35). **(P)**

Perhaps of less concern to the world at large, but of more concern to the university and college community (and indeed most North American and European consumers), is the illusion evoked by purchasing fair trade products. First, the purchase can lull consumers into a false sense of accomplishment, leaving them less likely to investigate the idealistic claims of the movement or to seek out alternate forms of spending ethically. "The fair trade movement [. . .] suggests that the production and purchase of fair trade produce somehow lies on a higher moral plane than other business activity," say Booth and Whetstone (30). However, consumers do have other options, such as simply purchasing cheaper coffee and donating the difference in price between the regular and the fair trade product to a charity. Booth and Whetstone continue: "The fair trade movement may have found a successful marketing device for increasing philanthropy but that does not make their products ethical" (31).

But Fairtrade customers are also subject to a second illusion: that their purchases make them more ethical than other consumers who do not actively pursue Fairtrade purchases. There are countless alternatives to certified Fairtrade in terms of ethical consumption, many of which are more sustainable in the long term and not as rife with complications and downsides. Fairtrade purchases, though, tend to have a public component; people can see and hear other consumers requesting Fairtrade coffee or chocolate at cafés or grocery stores, and

---

(O) After discussing economic theory and providing some statistics, the writer concludes her point with an authoritative and well-phrased quotation.

(P) In a series of paragraphs, the writer enumerates judgment traps created by fair trade, culminating in neo-colonialism.

these same militantly moral consumers can publicly call attention to those who do not make the same choice.

Finally, Fairtrade consumers can misjudge producers. Whereas Fairtrade has been rightly criticized for inadvertently spreading a sort of neo-colonial attitude, consider, for instance, the problem of quality control that was explored earlier: that Fairtrade does not press producers to develop high quality products. "Companies such as Green & Black's," on the other hand, "say they aid farmers more by helping them to improve quality and go organic rather than just guaranteeing a price" (Beattie 34). The Fairtrade model ensures that producers will never be able to grow beyond the need for a fixed minimum, while alternate models seek to empower producers. It is not hard to see which paradigm is rife with paternalistic, colonialist implications. Getting consumers in the right frame of mind is not an irrelevant need. As Ian Hussey puts it, "decolonization is not just a material process, but also a mental one" (17). Fair trade, he says, "serves to reinforce racist and colonial distinctions between the poor Global South farmer and the benevolent Global North consumer" (15). In the long run, this mindset is destructive in that it denigrates Fairtrade producers as charity cases rather than potential partners.

It may at this point appear that fair trade and its proponents have not been given a fair voice. After all, as thinkers such as Andrew Walton have pointed out, fair trade needs to be understood as being an interim measure for seeking justice. The world is "non-ideal," and fair trade is only a second-best measure— not "global market justice" in and of itself (Walton 435). Indeed, critics of the movement do fair trade an injustice when they argue that it should be rejected simply because it is not a perfect and complete alternative to the current global economy. Ignoring for a moment all practical considerations, fair trade and movements such as the "Make Poverty History" campaign do the entire world a service in bringing issues of poverty and injustice to the forefront of the continuing global conversation. How consumers spend their money can make a serious difference. It is a shame that fair trade has not proven to be the solution that it originally aspired to be.

In this light, the future of fair trade, of ethical consuming at all, seems bleak.

(Q)

(Q) In her closing paragraphs, the writer consolidates her critique while offering some balance, and then points forward to possible solutions.

The claims of Fairtrade organizations do not match up with reality, and the best intentions of countless activists and socially concerned consumers appear to have ultimately done more damage than good. But it is not enough to tear down an existing structure such as fair trade. Alternatives or changes to fair trade must be sought; consumers and producers alike have a right and a responsibility to demand better. In the future, strong claims such as those of the fair trade movement must "be subject to strong tests" (Booth and Whetstone 29). Consumers must no longer praise a solution such as fair trade without being educated as to its implications and consequences. Luckily, the burden for change does not rest on the "Global North consumer" alone. By transcending the colonial mindset, North can work with South, and a united global force can share the challenges of addressing injustices from the personal to the economic. Fair trade may not have all the answers, but it has certainly taught us to ask the right questions.

Works Cited (A)

Beattie, Alan. "The Price of Being Fair." *New Statesman* 136.4833 (2007): 34-35.
    Literary Reference Center. Web. 18 Jan. 2012.

Booth, Philip, and Linda Whetstone. "Half a Cheer for Fair Trade." *Economic* (B)
    Affairs 27.2 (2007): 29-36. *Business Source Elite.* Web. 19 Jan. 2012.

Chandler, Paul. "Fair Trade and Global Justice." Globalizations 3.2 (2006): 255-57.
    Academic Search Premier. Web. 19 Jan. 2012.

Henderson, David R. "Fair Trade Is Counterproductive—And Unfair." *Economic*
    Affairs 28.3 (2008): 62-64. *Business Source Elite.* Web. 19 Jan. 2012.

Hodge, Neil. "Chocs Away." *Financial Management* (2010): 14-21. *Business* (C)
    Source Elite. Web. 18 Jan. 2012.

Hussey, Ian. "Fair Trade and Empire: An Anti-Capitalist Critique of the Fair
    Trade Movement." *Briarpatch* 40.5 (2011): 15-18. *Canadian Reference*
    Centre. Web. 18 Jan. 2012.

Hutchens, Anna. "Empowering Women Through Fair Trade? Lessons from Asia."
    Third World Quarterly 31.3 (2010): 449-67. *Academic Search Premier.* Web.
    18 Jan. 2012.

Nichols, Alex, and Charlotte Opal. *Fair Trade: Market-Driven Ethical*
    Consumption. London: Sage, 2004. Print.

Walton, Andrew. "What Is Fair Trade?" *Third World Quarterly* 31.3 (2010): 431- (D)
    47. *Academic Search Premier.* Web. 19 Jan. 2012.

"What is [sic] Fairtrade?" *Fairtrade International.* Fairtrade Labelling (E)
    Organizations International, n.d. Web. 10 Feb. 2012.

Weber, Jeremy. "Fair Trade Coffee Enthusiasts Should Confront Reality." *CATO* (F)
    Journal 27.1 (2007): 109-17. *Academic Search Premier.* Web. 19 Jan. 2012.

(A) The list of works cited begins on a separate page and includes the title, header, and page number.

(B) The paper's bibliography lists a range of scholarly books, trade books, scholarly articles, popular articles, and Web sites on the topic.

(C) Sources are listed in alphabetical order by author (or by title if no author is given) and identified by medium.

(D) Quotation marks and italics are properly used with titles, as are punctuation and abbreviations.

(E) Items are double-spaced throughout. Second and subsequent lines are indented (hanging indent).

(F) Each entry provides complete identifying information, properly formatted.

Reading for Better Writing

1. How did Paige Louter's research paper impact your understanding of fair trade and global justice?

2. Identify Louter's thesis in the first paragraph. Then review the tips for deepening a thesis on page 275. Does Louter's thesis include rich, clear terms? Are any qualifiers used? If so, name them. Does she stress her main idea through opposition? Overall, is Louter's thesis strong? Could any improvements be made?

3. By reviewing topic sentences and skimming the paper, outline Louter's argument. How would you characterize her logic? How does her reasoning unfold?

4. What types of evidence does Louter use? Where has she gotten her evidence? Are her sources reliable? Does she have a balanced range of sources?

5. How does Louter distinguish her own thinking from source material? Why are these strategies necessary?

⚙ Critical-Thinking and Writing Activities

1. With some classmates, debate the seriousness of plagiarism and the use of tools such as Turnitin.com. Specifically, discuss these questions: Why is it necessary to credit the sources of ideas or words that you use in your research reports? Why are the consequences of plagiarism so serious?

2. Research your school's academic integrity policies. How does your school define plagiarism, and how does it address it in its policies and procedures?

3. Review the list of source abuses on pages 269–271. Which of these abuses is most common in research writing? Which abuse is most serious? Write a paragraph focusing on the type of source abuse and explaining its effect on scholarship.

4. Reflect on the consequences of unethical research. In the wider world, what happens when research is shoddy or deceptive? Research a story of unethical research that happened in the past decade. Share what you discover with your classmates.

5. Reflect on the dangers of relying too heavily on the information from one source in a research paper. What type of pitfalls may occur from this? Develop a research plan to avoid this source abuse in your own research writing.

6. Closely examine one of your most recent research papers. Have you followed this chapter's guidelines for treating sources in a research paper?

STUDY TOOLS 23

LOCATED AT BACK OF THE TEXTBOOK
- ☐ Tear-Out Chapter Review Card

LOCATED AT WWW.CENGAGEBRAIN.COM/LOGIN
- ☐ Chapter eBook
- ☐ Graded quizzes and a practice quiz generator
- ☐ Videos: Writer Interviews
- ☐ Tutorials
- ☐ Flashcards
- ☐ Cengage Learning Write Experience
- ☐ Interactive activities

24 | MLA and APA Styles

"THE PALEST INK IS BETTER THAN THE BEST MEMORY."

CHINESE PROVERB

LEARNING OBJECTIVES

24-1 Learn the basics of MLA and APA documentation.

24-2 Identify source material through in-text citations.

24-3 Develop bibliographic entries.

24-4 List books and other nonperiodical documents.

24-5 List print periodical articles.

24-6 List online sources.

24-7 List other sources.

24-8 Follow format guidelines for MLA and APA.

After you finish
this chapter
go to
PAGE 321 for STUDY TOOLS

In research papers, it is commonly said, "You are commanded to borrow but forbidden to steal." To borrow ideas while avoiding plagiarism (see pages 269–272), you must not only mention the sources you borrow from but also document them completely and accurately. You must follow to the last dot the format and documentation conventions required for your paper.

The two styles most frequently used in college have been developed by the Modern Language Association (MLA) and the American Psychological Association (APA). Whereas MLA is used most frequently in the Humanities, APA is typically used in the Social Sciences—with each system reflecting the specific concerns of the disciplines involved. The systems are similar, however, in that both require (1) parenthetical citations within the body of the paper and (2) a final listing of all resources cited in the paper.

In this chapter, we provide you with instructions for using those two styles to format your research paper pages and to document your sources within the text of your paper and at its end. To best illuminate the rationale of each style, we compare them side by side throughout the chapter. In those few cases where one style calls for an item not covered by the other (as in MLA's standard for short

Stokkete, 2014 / Used under license from Shutterstock.com

verse citations, a source not likely to be used in APA), we have called out that information in a separate box.

As anyone who has studied a foreign tongue can attest, one's native language is revealed in a brand-new way by comparison. Contrast makes things clear. That is our goal in presenting MLA and APA styles side by side in this chapter.

LEARN THE BASICS OF MLA AND APA DOCUMENTATION

Both the MLA and APA documentation systems involve two parts: (1) an in-text citation within your paper when you refer to a source and (2) a matching bibliographic entry at the end of your paper. While each system involves specific conventions and practices (as outlined in the rest of this chapter), let's start with an overview of the basics.

MLA

In the body of your paper, you use signal phrases and parenthetical references to set off source material from your own thinking and discussion. By doing so, you direct readers to alphabetized sources in the bibliography at the end of your paper, called a works-cited list. In the example below, the signal phrase "As Anna Hutchens puts it" and the parenthetical reference "(449)" tell the reader the following things:

- The borrowed material came from a source written by Anna Hutchens.
- The specific material can be found on page 449 of the source.
- Full source details are in the works-cited list under the author's last name.

1. In-Text Citation in Body of Paper

As Anna Hutchens puts it, there is an "absence of a policy framework and institutional mechanisms that promote women's empowerment as a rights-based rather than a culture-based issue" (449).

2. Matching Works-Cited Entry at End of Paper

Hutchens, Anna. "Empowering Women Through Fair Trade? Lessons from Asia." *Third World Quarterly* 31.3 (2010): 449-67. *Academic Search Premier.* Web. 18 Jan. 2012.

APA

Often called an author-date system, APA uses signal phrases and parenthetical references to set off source material from your own thinking, directing readers to an alphabetized list of sources in what is called a references page. Because publication dates are especially important in social science research, the publication year is emphasized in APA, as shown in the following example. The parenthetical material "Pascopella, 2011, p. 32" tells the reader these things:

- The borrowed material came from a source authored by Pascopella.
- The source was published in 2011.
- The specific material can be found on page 32 of the source.
- Full source details are in the reference list under the surname Pascopella.

1. In-Text Citation in Body of Paper

In newcomer programs, "separate, relatively self-contained educational interventions" (Pascopella, 2011, p. 32) are implemented to meet the academic and transitional needs of recent immigrants before they enter a mainstream English Language Development.

2. Matching Reference Entry at End of Paper

Pascopella, A. (2011). Successful strategies for English language learners. *District Administration, 47*(2), 29-44.

Modella, 2014 / Used under license from Shutterstock.com

IDENTIFY SOURCE MATERIAL THROUGH IN-TEXT CITATIONS

In-text citation identifies borrowed material within your paper. Whether you are following MLA or APA style, present in-text citations according to these guidelines:

▸ **Keep citations brief and integrate them smoothly into your writing.**

▸ **When paraphrasing or summarizing, make it clear where your borrowing begins and ends.** Use stylistic cues to distinguish the source's thoughts ("Kalmbach points out . . . ," "Some critics argue . . .") from your own ("I believe . . . ," "It seems obvious, however . . ."). See pages 272–273 for more on integrating sources.

▸ **Make sure each in-text citation clearly points to an entry in your list of sources.** The identifying information (usually the author's last name) must be the word or words by which the entry is alphabetized in that list.

▸ **When using a shortened title of a work, begin with the word by which the work is alphabetized in your list of sources** (e.g., "Egyptian, Classical," for "Egyptian, Classical, and Middle Eastern Art").

▸ **When including a parenthetical citation at the end of a sentence, place it before the end punctuation.**

24-2a In-Text Citations: The Basics

The material that follows offers detailed guidelines on using in-text citations in MLA and APA.

MLA

In MLA, in-text citations typically follow these guidelines:

1. Refer to the author (plus the work's title, if helpful) and a page number by using one of these methods:

   Last name and page number in parentheses:

   Fair trade is not necessary for consumers to "exercise a moral choice" with their money
   ┌─ (Chandler 256). ── no "p." for "page"
   last name only in citation └── no comma between name and page number

   Name cited in sentence, page number in parentheses: ┌── full name in first reference

   As Paul Chandler admits, fair trade is not necessary for consumers to "exercise a moral choice" with their money (256). ── page number only in citation

2. Present and punctuate citations using these rules:
   - Place the parenthetical reference after the source material.
   - Within the parentheses, normally give the author's last name only.
   - Do not put a comma between the author's last name and the page reference.
   - Cite the page number as a numeral, not a word.
   - Don't use *p.*, *pp.*, or *page(s)* before the page number(s).
   - When citing inclusive page numbers larger than 99, give only two digits of the second number (e.g., 346–48).
   - Place any sentence punctuation after the closed parenthesis.

APA

Both the author and the date of publication must be indicated in the text when citing a source. Both details may be integrated into the flow of the sentence, or they may be cited according to the guidelines below.

1. Refer to the author(s) and date of publication by using one of these methods:

   Last name(s), publication date in parentheses:

   ELLs normally spend just three years in 30-minute "pull-out" English language development programs (Calderón et al., 2011).

   Last name(s) cited in text with publication date in parentheses:

   In "Key Issues for Teaching English Learners in Academic Classrooms," Carrier (2005) explained that it takes an average of one to three years to reach conversational proficiency in a second language but five to seven years to reach academic proficiency.

2. Present and punctuate citations according to these rules:
   - Keep authors and publication dates as close together as possible in the sentence.
   - Separate the author's last name, the date, and any locating detail with commas.
   - If referencing part of a source, use an appropriate abbreviation: p. (page), para. (paragraph)—but do not abbreviate *chapter*.

One Author: A Complete Work

MLA

You do not need an in-text citation if you identify the author in your text. (This is the preferred way of citing a complete work.) Do not offer page numbers when citing complete works, articles in alphabetized encyclopedias, one-page articles, and unpaginated sources.

> In *No Need for Hunger,* Robert Spitzer recommends that the U.S. government develop a new foreign policy to help Third World countries overcome poverty and hunger.

However, you must give the author's last name in an in-text citation if it is not mentioned in the text.

> *No Need for Hunger* recommends that the U.S. government develop a new foreign policy to help Third World countries overcome poverty and hunger (Spitzer).

When a source is listed in your works-cited page with an editor, a translator, a speaker, or an artist, instead of the author, use that person's name in your citation.

APA

The correct form for a parenthetical reference to a single source by a single author is parenthesis, last name, comma, space, year of publication, parenthesis.

> … in this way, the public began to connect certain childhood vaccinations with an autism epidemic (Baker, 2008).

If the author is identified in your text, include the year in parentheses immediately after.

> Dohman (2009) argues that parents of affected children . . .

One Author: Part of a Work

MLA

List the necessary page numbers in parentheses if you borrow words or ideas from a particular source. Leave a space between the author's last name and the page reference. No abbreviation or punctuation is needed. (The first example below identifies the author in text, the second in parentheses.)

> Bullough writes that genetic engineering was dubbed "eugenics" by a cousin of Darwin's, Sir Francis Galton, in 1885 (5).
>
> Genetic engineering was dubbed "eugenics" by a cousin of Darwin's, Sir Francis Galton, in 1885 (Bullough 5).

APA

When you cite a specific part of a source, give the page, paragraph, or chapter, using the appropriate abbreviation (*p.* or *pp., para.*) or word (*chapter*). Always give the page number for a direct quotation.

> … while a variety of political and scientific forces were at work in the developing crisis, it was parents who pressed the case "that autism had become epidemic and that vaccines were its cause" (Baker, 2008, p. 251).

Two or More Works by the Same Author(s)

MLA

In addition to the author's last name(s) and page number(s), include a shortened version of the work's title when you cite two or more works by the same author(s).

APA

If the same author has published two or more articles in the same year, avoid confusion by placing a small letter *a* after the year for the first work listed in the reference list, *b* after the year for the next one, and so on. Alphabetize by title.

Wallerstein and Blakeslee claim that divorce creates an enduring identity for children of the marriage (*Unexpected Legacy* 62).

They are intensely lonely despite active social lives (Wallerstein and Blakeslee, *Second Chances* 51).

Volodymyr Krasyuk, 2014 / Used under license from Shutterstock.com

Parenthetical Citation:

Reefs harbor life forms heretofore unknown (Milius, 2001a, 2001b).

References:

Milius, D. (2001a). Another world hides inside coral reefs. *Science News,* 160(16), 244.

Milius, D. (2001b). Unknown squids—with elbows—tease science. *Science News,* 160(24), 390.

Works by Authors with the Same Last Name

MLA

When citing different sources by authors with the same last name, it is best to use the authors' full names in the text to avoid confusion. If circumstances call for parenthetical references, add each author's first initial. If first initials are the same, use each author's full name.

> Some critics think *Titus Andronicus* too abysmally melodramatic to be a work of Shakespeare (A. Parker 73). Others suggest that Shakespeare meant it as black comedy (D. Parker 486).

APA

When citing different sources by authors with the same last name, add the authors' initials to avoid confusion, even if the publication dates are different.

> While J. D. Wallace (2005) argued that privatizing social security would benefit only the wealthiest citizens, others such as E. S. Wallace (2006) supported greater control for individuals.

Works by Multiple Authors

MLA

When citing a work **by two or three authors**, give the last names of every author in the same order that they appear in the works-cited section. (The correct order of the authors' names can be found on the title page of the book.)

> Students learned more than a full year's Spanish in 10 days using the complete supermemory method (Ostrander and Schroeder 51).

When citing a work **by four or more authors**, give the first author's last name as it appears in the works-cited section, followed by "et al." (meaning "and others").

> Communication on the job is more than talking; it is "inseparable from your total behavior" (Culligan et al. 111).

APA

When citing **from two to five authors**, all must be mentioned in the first text citation. The last two authors' names are always separated by a comma and an ampersand (&) when enclosed in parentheses.

> Love changes not just who we are, but who we can become, as well (Lewis, Amini, & Lannon, 2000).

Subsequently, for works with **two authors**, *list both in every citation*. For works with **three to five authors**, *list all only the first time*; after that, use only the name of the first author followed by "et al.," like this:

> These discoveries lead to the hypothesis that love actually alters the brain's structure (Lewis et al., 2000).

If your source has **six or more authors**, refer to the work by the first author's name followed by "et al.," both for the first reference in the text and all references after that. However, be sure to list all the authors (up to seven) in your references list.

> According to a recent study, post-traumatic stress disorder (PTSD) continues to dominate the lives of Vietnam veterans, though in modified forms (Trembley et al., 2014).

A Work Authored by an Agency, a Committee, or an Organization

MLA

If a book or other work was written by an organization such as an agency, a committee, or a task force, it is said to have a corporate author. If the corporate name is long, include it in the text (rather than in parentheses) to avoid disrupting the flow of your writing. After the full name has been used at least once, use a shortened form of the name (common abbreviations are acceptable) in subsequent references. For example, *Task Force* may be used for *Task Force on Education for Economic Growth*.

> The thesis of the Task Force's report is that economic success depends on our ability to improve large-scale education and training as quickly as possible (113–14).

APA

Treat the name of the group as if it were the last name of the author. If the name is long and easily abbreviated, provide the abbreviation in square brackets.

> A problem for many veterans continues to be heightened sensitivity to noise (National Institute of Mental Health [NIMH], 2014).

Use the abbreviation without brackets in subsequent references.

> In addition, veterans suffering from PTSD continue to have difficulty discussing their experiences (NIMH, 2014).

A Work with No Author Indicated

MLA

When there is no author listed, give the title or a shortened version of the title as it appears in the works-cited section.

> Statistics indicate that drinking water can make up 20 percent of a person's total exposure to lead (*Information* 572).

APA

If your source lists no author, treat the first few words of the title (capitalized normally) as you would an author's last name. A title of an article or a chapter belongs in quotation marks; the titles of books or reports should be italicized.

> …including a guide to low-stress postures ("How to Do It," 2014).

Two or More Works Included in One Citation

To cite multiple works within a single parenthetical reference, separate the references with a semicolon.

MLA

The following example refers to a work by Albala and another by Lewis.

> In Medieval Europe, Latin translations of the works of Rhazes, a Persian scholar, were a primary source of medical knowledge (Albala 22; Lewis 266).

APA

Remember to include the year of publication. Place the citations in alphabetical order, just as they would be ordered in the reference list:

> Others report near-death experiences (Rommer, 2008; Sabom, 2013).

MLA: A Series of Citations from a Single Work

If no confusion is possible, it is not necessary to name a source repeatedly when making multiple parenthetical references to that source in a single paragraph. If all references are to the same page, identify that page in a parenthetical note after the last reference. If the references are to different pages within the same work, you need identify the work only once, and then use a parenthetical note with page number alone for the subsequent references.

> Domesticating science meant not only spreading scientific knowledge, but also promoting it as a topic of public conversation (Heilbron 2). One way to enhance its charm was by depicting cherubic putti as "angelic research assistants" in book illustrations (5).

A Work Referred to in Another Work

MLA

If you must cite an indirect source—that is, information from a source that is quoted from another source—use the abbreviation *qtd. in* (quoted in) before the indirect source in your reference.

> Paton improved the conditions in Diepkloof (a prison) by "removing all the more obvious aids to detention. The dormitories [were] open at night: the great barred gate [was] gone" (qtd. in Callan xviii).

APA

If you need to cite a source that you have found referred to in another source (a "secondary" source), mention the original source in your text. Then, in your parenthetical citation, cite the secondary source, using the words "as cited in."

> …theorem given by Ullman (as cited in Hoffman, 2013).

A Work in an Anthology or a Collection

MLA

When citing an entire work that is part of an anthology or a collection, a work identified by author in your list of works cited, treat the citation as you would for any other complete work.

> In "The Canadian Postmodern," Linda Hutcheon offers a clear analysis of the self-reflexive nature of contemporary Canadian fiction.

Similarly, if you are citing particular pages of such a work, follow the directions for citing part of a work.

> According to Hutcheon, "postmodernism seems to designate cultural practices that are fundamentally self-reflexive, in other words, art that is self-consciously artifice" (18).

An entry from a **reference work** such as an encyclopedia or a dictionary should be cited similarly to a work from an anthology or a collection. For a dictionary definition, include the abbreviation *def.* followed by the particular entry designation.

> This message becomes a juggernaut in the truest sense, a belief that "elicits blind devotion or sacrifice" ("Juggernaut," def. 1).

While many such entries are identified only by title (as above), some reference works include an author's name for each entry (as below). Others may identify the entry author by initials, with a list of full names elsewhere in the work.

> The decisions of the International Court of Justice are "based on principles of international law and cannot be appealed" (Pranger).

See pages 297–298 for guidelines on formatting these entries in your works-cited list.

APA

When citing an article or a chapter in an anthology or a collection, use the authors' names for the specific article, not the names of the anthology's editors. (Similarly, the article should be listed by its authors' names in the reference section.)

> Phonological changes can be understood from a variationist perspective (Guy, 2005).

A Sacred Text or Famous Literary Work

Sacred texts and famous literary works are published in many different editions. For that reason, when you are referring to specific sections of the work, it is best to identify parts, chapters, or other divisions instead of (or in addition to) your version's page numbers. Note that books of the Bible and other well-known literary works may be abbreviated, if no confusion is possible.

MLA: Quoting Verse

Do not use page numbers when referencing classic verse plays and poems. Instead, cite them by division (act, scene, canto, book, part) and line, using Arabic numerals for the various divisions unless your instructor prefers Roman numerals. Use periods to separate the various numbers.

> In the first act, Hamlet comments, "How weary, stale, flat and unprofitable, / Seem to me all the uses of this world" (1.2.133-34).

A slash, with a space on each side, shows where each new line of verse begins. If you are citing lines only, use the word *line* or *lines* in your first reference and numbers only in additional references.

> At the beginning of the sestet in Robert Frost's "Design," the speaker asks this pointed question: "What had that flower to do with being white, / The wayside blue and innocent heal-all?" (lines 9–10).

MLA

If using page numbers, list them first, followed by an abbreviation for the type of division and the division number.

> The more important a person's role in society—the more apparent power an individual has—the more that person is a slave to the forces of history (Tolstoy 690; bk. 9, ch. 1).

> As Shakespeare's famous Danish prince observes, "One may smile, and smile, and be a villain" (*Ham.* 1.5.104).

APA

The original date of publication may be unavailable or not pertinent. In such cases, use your edition's year of translation (for example, *trans. 2003*) or indicate your edition's year of publication (*2003 version*).

> An interesting literary case of such dysfunctional family behavior can be found in Franz Kafka's *The Metamorphosis,* where it becomes the commandment of family duty for Gregor's parents and sister to swallow their disgust and endure him (trans. 1972, part 3).

> "Generations come and generations go, but the earth remains forever" (*The New International Version Study Bible,* 1985 version, Eccles. 1.4).

Citing Internet Sources

MLA

The seventh edition of the *MLA Handbook* discourages use of Internet addresses, or URLs, as they can so easily change with time. Ideally, you should refer to an entire Web site by its title, or to a specific article on a site by its author; then, include full reference information in your works-cited list. A URL should be listed in your document or in your works-cited list only when the reader probably cannot locate the source without it or

APA

As with print sources, cite an electronic source by the author (or by shortened title if the author is unknown) and the publication date (not the date you accessed the source). If citing a specific part of the source, use an appropriate abbreviation: *p.* for page and *para.* for paragraph.

> One study compared and contrasted the use of Web and touch screen transaction log files in a hospital setting (Nicholas, Huntington, & Williams, 2001).

if your instructor requires it. If that is the case, enclose the address in angle brackets:

<www.gale.cengage.com/
PeriodicalSolutions/
academicOnefile.htm>

Whenever possible, cite a Web site by its author and posting date. In addition, refer to a specific page or document rather than to a home page or a menu page. If you are referring to a specific part of a Web page that does not have page numbers, direct your reader, if possible, with a section heading and a paragraph number.

> According to the National Multiple Sclerosis Society (2011, "Complexities" section, para. 2), understanding of MS could not begin until scientists began to research nerve transmission in the 1920s.

APA: Personal Communications

If for APA papers you do the kind of personal research recommended elsewhere in *COMP*, you may have to cite personal communications that have provided you with some of your knowledge. Personal communications may include personal letters, phone calls, memos, and so forth. Because they are not published in a permanent form, APA style does not place them among the citations in your reference list. Instead, cite them only in the text of your paper in parentheses, like this:

> … according to M. T. Cann (personal communication, April 1, 2015).
>
> … by today (M. T. Cann, personal communication, April 1, 2015).

 24-3 # DEVELOP BIBLIOGRAPHIC ENTRIES

In both MLA and APA styles, in-text citations refer to sources listed in a bibliography at the end of your paper—called works cited in MLA and references in APA. What follows are guidelines for each style, along with instruction for specific types of sources.

MLA Works Cited

The works-cited section lists only the sources you have cited in your text. Begin your list on the page after the text and continue numbering each page. Format your works-cited pages using these guidelines and page 286.

1. Type the page number in the upper right corner, one-half inch from the top of the page, with your last name before it.

2. Center the title *Works Cited* (not in italics or underlined) one inch from the top; then double-space before the first entry.

3. Begin each entry flush with the left margin. If the entry runs more than one line, indent additional lines one-half inch (five spaces) or use the hanging indent function on your computer.

4. End each element of the entry with a period. (Elements are separated by periods in most cases unless only a space is sufficient.) Use a single space after all punctuation.

5. Double-space lines within each entry and between entries.

6. List each entry alphabetically by the author's last name. If there is no author, use the first word of the title (disregard *A*, *An*, or *The* as the first word). If there are multiple authors, alphabetize them according to which author is listed first in the publication.

7. The *MLA Handbook*, Seventh Edition, requires that each source be identified as *Print*, *Web*, or other (such as *Television* or *DVD*). For print sources, this information is included after the publisher and date. For Web publications, include *Web.* after the date of publication or updating of the site, and before the date you accessed the site.

8. Publishers' names should be shortened by omitting articles (*A, An, The*), business abbreviations (*Co., Inc.*), and descriptive words (*Books, Press*). For publishing houses that consist of the names of more than one person, cite only the first of the surnames. Abbreviate University Press as UP. Also use standard abbreviations whenever possible (*Assn., Acad.*). In addition, use the following abbreviations in place of any information you cannot supply:

n.p.	No place of publication given	*n.d.*	No date of publication given
n.p.	No publisher given	*n. pag.*	No pagination given

9. Use these templates for the most common entries:

- **Template for Book:**

  Author's Last Name, First Name. *Title of Book*. Publication City: Publisher, year of publication. Medium. (Other publication details are integrated as needed.)

  Nichols, Alex. *Fair Trade: Market-Driven Ethical Consumption*. London: Sage, 2004. Print.

- **Template for Periodical Article in an Online Database:**

  Author's Last Name, First Name. "Title of Article." *Journal Title* volume, issue, and/or date details: page numbers. *Title of Database*. Medium. Date of Access.

  Chandler, Paul. "Fair Trade and Global Justice." *Globalization* 3.2 (2006): 255-57. *Academic Search Premier*. Web. 19 Jan. 2014.

- **Template for a Web Document:**

  Author or Editor's Last Name, First Name (if available). "Title of Page, Posting, or Document." *Title of Web site* (if different from document title). Version or edition used. Publisher or sponsor of site (if known; if not, use *N.p.*). Date of publication, last update, or posting (if known; if not, use *n.d.*). Medium. Date of access.

  "What is Fairtrade?" *Fairtrade International*. Fairtrade Labelling Organizations Intl., n.d. Web. 10 February 2014.

APA References

The reference section lists all of the sources you have cited in your text (with the exception of personal communications such as phone calls and emails). Begin your reference list on a new page after the last page of your paper. Number each reference page, continuing the numbering from the text. Then format your reference list by following the guidelines below.

1. Type the running head in the upper left corner and the page number in the upper right corner, approximately one-half inch from the top.

2. Center the title, *References*, approximately one inch from the top; then double-space before the first entry.

3. Begin each entry flush with the left margin. If the entry runs more than one line, indent additional lines approximately one-half inch (five to seven spaces), using a hanging indent.

4. Adhere to the following conventions about spacing, capitalization, and italics:
   - Double-space between all lines on the reference page.
   - Use one space following each word and punctuation mark.
   - With book and article titles, capitalize only the first letter of the title (and subtitle) and proper nouns.

        Example: The impact of the cold war on Asia.

     (Note that this capitalization practice differs from the presentation of titles in the body of the essay.)
   - Use italics for titles of books and periodicals, not underlining.

5. List each entry alphabetically by the last name of the author, or, if no author is given, by the title (disregarding *A*, *An*, or *The*). For works with multiple authors, use the first author listed in the publication.

6. Follow these conventions with respect to abbreviations:
   - With authors' names, generally shorten first and middle names to initials, leaving a space after the period. For a work with more than one author, use an ampersand (&) before the last author's name.
   - For publisher locations, use the full city name plus the two-letter U.S. Postal Service abbreviation for the state. For international publishers, include a spelled-out province and country name.
   - Spell out "Press" or "Books" in full, but omit unnecessary terms like "Publishers," "Company," or "Inc."

7. Use these templates for the most common entries:

   - **Template for Book:**

        Author's Last Name, Initials. (Publication Year). *Title of Book*. Publication City, State or Country: Publisher. (Other publication details are integrated as needed.)

        Pandya, J.Z. (2011) *Overtested: How high-stakes accountability fails English Language Learners*. New York, NY: Teachers College Press.

   - **Template for Periodical Article:**

        Author's Last Name, Initials. (Publication Year). Title of article. *Journal Title, volume*(issue), page numbers. [Other publication details are integrated as needed. For online periodical articles, add the digital object identifier.]

        Slama, R.B. (2012) A longitudinal analysis of academic English proficiency outcomes for adolescent English Language Learners in the United States. *Journal of Educational Psychology, 104*(2), 265-285. doi: 10.1037/z0025861

   - **Template for a Web Document:**

        Author's Last Name, Initials. (Publication Date). *Title of work* OR Title of entry. DOI (digital object identifier) OR Retrieval statement including URL

        U.S. Department of Education. (2013, January) *Projection of education statistics to 2021*. Retrieved from http://nces.gov/programs/projections/projections2021/

24-4 # LIST BOOKS AND OTHER NONPERIODICAL DOCUMENTS

A Book by One Author

MLA

The example below demonstrates the most basic book entry.

> Richardson, Catherine. *Shakespeare and Material Culture*. New York: Oxford UP, 2011. Print.

APA

Capitalize only the first word of the title and the first word of any subtitle, along with proper nouns and initialisms.

> Quinlan, J. P. (2011). *The last economic superpower: The retreat of globalization, the end of American dominance, and what we can do about it.* New York: McGraw-Hill.

Two or More Books by the Same Author

MLA

List the books alphabetically according to title. After the first entry, substitute three hyphens for the author's name.

> Dershowitz, Alan M. *Rights from Wrongs*. New York: Basic, 2005. Print.
>
> - - - . *Supreme Injustice: How the High Court Hijacked Election 2000*. Oxford: Oxford UP, 2001. Print.

APA

Arrange multiple works by the same author in chronological order, earliest first.

> Sacks, O. (1995). *An anthropologist on Mars: Seven paradoxical tales.* New York, NY: Alfred A. Knopf.
>
> Sacks, O. (2007). *Musicophilia: Tales of music and the brain.* New York, NY: Alfred A. Knopf.

A Work by Two or More Authors

MLA

For **two or three authors**, list them all, in title-page order, reversing only the first author's name.

> Naifeh, Steven, and Gregory White Smith. *Van Gogh: The Life*. New York: Random, 2011. Print.

For **four or more authors**, list only the first, followed by "et al."

> Schulte-Peevers, Andrea, et al. *Germany*. Victoria: Lonely Planet, 2000. Print.

APA

List **up to seven authors** by last name and first initial, separating them by commas, with an ampersand (&) before the last.

> Hooyman, N., & Kramer, B. (2006). *Living through loss: Interventions across the life span.* New York, NY: Columbia University Press.

For **eight or more authors**, list the first six followed by an ellipsis, and then the last.

An Anonymous Book

MLA

If no author or editor is listed, begin the entry with the title.

> *Chase's Calendar of Events 2002*. Chicago: Contemporary, 2002. Print.

Note: For a work authored by an agency, a committee, or an organization, treat the organization as the author.

APA

If an author is listed as "Anonymous," treat it as the author's name. Otherwise, put the title in the author's spot.

> *Publication manual of the American Psychological Association* (6th ed.). (2010). Washington, DC: American Psychological Association.

Note: For a work authored by an agency, a committee, or an organization, treat the organization as the author.

A Single Work from an Anthology

MLA

Place the title of the single work in quotation marks before the title of the complete work. (Note: Some large single works, such as complete plays, may call for italics instead.)

> Mitchell, Joseph. "The Bottom of the Harbor." *American Sea Writing*. Ed. Peter Neill. New York: Lib. of America, 2000. 584-608. Print.

APA

Start with information about the individual work, followed by details about the collection in which it appears, including the page span. When editors' names come in the middle of an entry, follow the usual order: initial first, surname last. Note the placement of Eds. in parentheses in the following example.

> Guy, G. R. (2005). Variationist approaches to phonological change. In B. D. Joseph & R. D. Janda (Eds.), *The handbook of historical linguistics* (pp. 369-400). Malden, MA: Blackwell.

MLA: Citing Multiple Works or a Complete Anthology

To avoid unnecessary repetition when citing two or more entries from a larger collection, you may cite the collection once with complete publication information (see Rothfield, below). The individual entries (see Becker and Cuno, below) can then be cross-referenced by listing the author, title of the piece, editor of the collection, and page numbers.

> Becker, Carol. "The Brooklyn Controversy: A View from the Bridge." Rothfield 15-21.
>
> Cuno, James. "Sensation and the Ethics of Funding Exhibitions." Rothfield 162-170.
>
> Rothfield, Lawrence, ed. *Unsettling Sensation: Arts-Policy Lessons from the Brooklyn Museum of Art Controversy*. New Brunswick: Rutgers UP, 2001. Print. Rutgers Series on the Public Life of the Arts.

If you cite a **complete anthology**, begin the entry with the editor(s).

> Neill, Peter, ed. *American Sea Writing*. New York: Lib. of America, 2000. Print.
>
> Smith, Rochelle, and Sharon L. Jones, eds. *The Prentice Hall Anthology of African American Literature*. Upper Saddle River: Prentice, 2000. Print.

One Volume of a Multivolume Work

MLA

Include the volume number after the title of the complete work.

> Cooke, Jacob Ernest, and Milton M. Klein, eds. *North America in Colonial Times*. Vol. 2. New York: Scribner's, 1998. Print.

If you cite two or more volumes of a multivolume work, give the total number of volumes in the work. Offer specific references to volume and page numbers in the parenthetical reference in your text, like this: (8: 112–114).

> Salzman, Jack, David Lionel Smith, and Cornel West. *Encyclopedia of African-American Culture and History*. 5 vols. New York: Simon, 1996. Print.

APA

Indicate the volume in parentheses after the work's title.

> Salzman, J., Smith, D. L., & West, C. (Eds.). (1996). *Encyclopedia of African-American culture and history* (Vol. 4). New York, NY: Simon & Schuster Macmillan.

When a work is part of a larger series or collection, make a two-part title with the series and the particular volume you are citing.

> The Associated Press. (1995). *Twentieth-century America: Vol. 8. The crisis of national confidence: 1974-1980*. Danbury, CT: Grolier Educational Corp.

A Chapter, an Introduction, a Preface, a Foreword, or an Afterword

MLA

To cite a chapter from a book, list the chapter title in quotation marks after the author's name. For an introduction, preface, foreword, or afterword, identify the part by type, with no quotation marks or underlining. Next, identify the author of the work, using the word "by." (If the book's author and the part's author are the same person, give just the last name after "by.") For a book that gives cover credit to an editor instead of an author, identify the editor as usual. Finally, list any page numbers for the part cited.

> Proulx, Annie. Introduction. *Dance of the Happy Shades.* By Alice Munro. Toronto: Penguin Canada, 2005. ix–xvi. Print.

APA

List the chapter title after the date of publication, followed by a period or appropriate end punctuation. Use "In" before the book title, and follow the book title with the inclusive page numbers of the chapter.

> Tattersall, I. (2002). How did we achieve humanity? In *The monkey in the mirror* (pp. 138-168). New York, NY: Harcourt.

A Group Author as Publisher

MLA

List the unabbreviated group name as author, omitting any initial article (*A, An, The*), then again as publisher, abbreviated as usual.

> Amnesty International. *Maze of Injustice: The Failure to Protect Indigenous Women from Sexual Violence in the USA.* London: Amnesty Intl., 2007. Print.

APA

When the author is also the publisher, simply put *Author* in the spot where you would list the publisher's name.

> Amnesty International. (2007). *Maze of injustice: The failure to protect indigenous women from sexual violence in the USA.* London England: Author.

If the publication is a brochure, identify it as such in brackets after the title.

24-5 LIST PRINT PERIODICAL ARTICLES

MLA

The general form for a periodical entry in MLA format follows.

> Author's last name, first name. "Article Title." *Periodical Title Series* number or name. Volume. issue. [separated by period but no space]. (Publication date): page numbers. Medium (Print).

APA

The general form for a periodical entry in APA format follows. If the periodical does not use volume and issue numbers, include some other designation with the year, such as the month and day, the month, or a season.

> Author, A. (year). Article title. *Periodical Title, volume number* (issue number if paginated by issue), page numbers.

An Article in a Magazine or Scholarly Journal

Africa Studio, 2014 / Used under license from Shutterstock.com

MLA

For a scholarly journal, list the volume number immediately after the journal title, followed by a period and the issue number, and then the date of publication (in parentheses). For a magazine, do not include volume and issue number. End with the page numbers of the article followed by the medium of publication (Print).

> Go, Kenji. "Montaigne's 'Cannibals' and *The Tempest* Revisited." *Studies in Philology* 109.4 (2012): 455-73. Print.
>
> Slater, Dan. "A Million First Dates: How Online Dating Is Threatening Monogamy." *Atlantic Monthly* Apr. 2013: 40-46. Print.

Note: For a scholarly journal, if no volume number exists, list the issue number alone.

APA

List author and year as for a book reference. (For a magazine, also include other date elements, as the month and day or the season.) In the article's title, lowercase all but the first word, proper nouns, acronyms, initialisms, and the first word of any subtitle. Capitalize the journal's title normally and italicize it. Italicize the volume number and place the issue number in parentheses, without italics. Provide inclusive page numbers.

> Weintraub, B. (2007, October). Unusual suspects. *Psychology Today, 40*(5), 80-87.
>
> Tomatoes target toughest cancer. (2002, February). *Prevention, 54*(2), 53.
>
> Benson, P., Karlof, K. L., & Siperstein, G. N. (2008). Maternal involvement in the education of young children with autism spectrum disorders. *Autism: The International Journal of Research & Practice, 12*(1), 47-63.

> **Note:** Do not include an issue number for a journal that continues pagination from issue to issue.

A Newspaper Article

MLA

Cite the edition of a major daily newspaper (if given) after the date (1 May 1995, Midwest ed.: 1). If a local paper's name does not include the city of publication, add it in brackets (not italicized) after the name.

> Segal, Jeff, and Lauren Silva. "Case of Art Imitating Life?" *Wall Street Journal* 3 March 2008, Eastern ed.: C9. Print.
>
> Swiech, Paul. "Human Service Agencies: 'It's Going to Take a Miracle.'" *Pantagraph* [Bloomington, IL] 30 June 2009: B7. Print.

To cite an article in a lettered section of the newspaper, list the section and the page number. (For example, A4 would refer to page 4 in section A of the newspaper.) If the sections are numbered, however, use a comma after the year (or the edition); then indicate the section and follow it with a colon, the page number (sec. 1:20), and the medium of publication you used. An unsigned newspaper article follows the same format:

> "Bombs—Real and Threatened—Keep Northern Ireland Edgy." *Chicago Tribune* 6 Dec. 2001, sec. 1: 20. Print.

If an article is an unsigned editorial, put *Editorial* (no italics) and a period after the title.

> "Hospital Power." Editorial. *Bangor Daily News* 14 Sept. 2004: A6. Print.

To identify a letter to the editor, put *Letter* (no italics) and a period after the author's name.

> Sory, Forrest. Letter. *Discover* July 2001: 10. Print.

APA

For newspaper articles, include the full publication date, year first followed by a comma, the month (spelled out) and the day. Identify the article's location in the newspaper using page numbers and section letters, as appropriate. If the article is a letter to the editor, identify it as such in brackets following the title. For newspapers, use *p.* or *pp.* before the page numbers; if the article is not on continuous pages, give all the page numbers, separated by commas.

> Schmitt, E., & Shanker, T. (2008, March 18). U.S. adapts cold-war idea to fight terrorists. *The New York Times*, pp. 1A, 14A-15A.

An Abstract

An abstract is a summary of a work.

MLA

To cite an abstract, first give the publication information for the original work (if any); then list the publication information for the abstract itself. Add the term *Abstract* and a period between these if the journal title does not include that word. If the journal identifies abstracts by item number, include the word *item* followed by the number. (Add the section identifier [A, B, or C] for those volumes of *Dissertation Abstracts [DA]* and *Dissertation Abstracts International [DAI]* that have one.) If no item number exists, list the page number(s).

> Faber, A. J. "Examining Remarried Couples Through a Bowenian Family System Lens." *Journal of Divorce and Remarriage* 40.4 (2004): 121-33. *Social Work Abstracts* 40 (2004): item 1298. Print.

APA

When referencing an abstract published separately from an article, provide publication details of the article followed by information about where the abstract was published.

> Shlipak, M. G., Simon, J. A., Grady, O., Lin, F., Wenger, N. K., & Furberg, C. D. (2001, September). Renal insufficiency and cardiovascular events in postmenopausal women with coronary heart disease. *Journal of the American College of Cardiology, 38*, 705-711. Abstract retrieved from *Geriatrics*, 2001, *56*(12), Abstract No. 5645351.

24-6 LIST ONLINE SOURCES

MLA

Start with the same elements given for a print source.

> Author's last name, first name. Title of Work (in italics or quotation marks). *Web Site Title* (if different from title of work). Version or edition used. Publisher or sponsor (or n.p. if none identified). Publication date (or n.d.). Medium (Web). Date of access.

Include a URL only if your reader needs it to locate the source (or if your instructor requires it). See "Using URLs" on the next page for instructions.

APA

Whenever possible, use the final, archival version of an electronic resource (often called the version of record), as opposed to a prepublished version. In the reference entry for an electronic source, start with the same elements in the same order given for a print or other fixed-media resource (author, title, and so on). Then add the most reliable electronic retrieval information that will (a) clarify what version of the source you used and (b) help your reader find the source.

DOI: If possible, use the electronic document's digital object identifier (DOI). The DOI will usually be published at the beginning of the article or be available in the article's citation.

> Author, A. A. (year). Title of article. *Title of Periodical*, volume number (issue number), pages. doi: code

URL: If a DOI is not available, give the URL (without a period at the end). Use the home or menu-page URL for subscription-only databases and online reference works.

> Author, A. A. (year). Title of article. *Title of Periodical*, volume number (issue number), pages. Retrieved from URL

Retrieval Date: If the content of the document is stable (e.g., archival copy or copy of record with DOI), do not include a retrieval date in your reference entry. However, if the content is likely to change or be updated, then offer a retrieval date.

> Author, A. A. (year). *Title of document*. Retrieved date from website: URL

Using URLs

MLA and APA documentation styles differ slightly in how they treat URLs (Internet addresses).

MLA

If you need to include a URL, place it immediately following the date of access, a period, and a space. The URL should be enclosed in angle brackets and end with a period. Give the complete address, including *http*, for the work you are citing.

> MacLeod, Donald. "Shake-Up for Academic Publishing." *Guardian Unlimited*. Guardian News and Media Ltd., 10 Nov. 2008. Web. 6 Jan. 2015. <http://www.guardian.co.uk/Archive/>.

> "Fort Frederica." *National Parks Service*. U.S. Department of the Interior, n.d. Web. 27 Feb. 2015. <http://home.nps.gov/fofr/forteachers/curriculummaterials.htm>.

If the URL must be divided between two lines, break it only *after* a **single** or **double slash**. Do not add a hyphen.

APA

When necessary, break a URL *before* a **slash** or **other punctuation mark**. Do not underline or italicize the URL, place it in angle brackets, or end it with a period.

An Undated Online Item

MLA

List "n.d." in place of the missing date.

> Booth, Philip. "Robert Frost's Prime Directive." *Poets. org*. Academy of American Poets, n.d. Web. 1 Oct. 2014.

APA

List "(n.d.)" in place of the missing date.

> National Institute of Allergy and Infectious Diseases. (n.d.). *Antimicrobial (drug) resistance*. Retrieved June 19, 2015, from http://www3.niaid.nih.gov /topics/AntimicrobialResistance/default.htm

A Home Page

MLA

If a nonperiodical publication has no title, identify it with a descriptor such as *Home page, Introduction,* or *Online posting* (using no italics or quotation marks). You may add the name of the publication's creator or editor after the overall site title, if appropriate.

> Wheaton, Wil. Home page. *Wil Wheaton dot Net*. n.p., 31 May 2006. Web. 19 Mar. 2015.

APA

Whenever possible, cite a Web site by its author and posting date. In addition, refer to a specific page or document rather than to a home page or a menu page.

An Entry in an Online Reference Work

Unless the author of the entry is identified, begin with the entry name.

MLA

Place the entry name in quotation marks.

> "Eakins, Thomas." *Britannica Online Encyclopedia*. Encyclopedia Britannica, 2008. Web. 26 Sept. 2015.

APA

Use the word "In" to identify the larger source.

> Agonism. (2008). In *Encyclopaedia Britannica*. Retrieved March 18, 2015, from http://search .eb.com

An Electronic Book

MLA

Include publication information for the original print version if available. Follow the date of publication with the electronic information.

> Simon, Julian L. *The Ultimate Resource II: People, Materials, and Environment.* College Park: U of Maryland, 1996. U of Maryland Libraries. Web. 9 Apr. 2015.

APA

Provide the DOI (see page 304) if one exists. Otherwise, use the phrase "Retrieved from" to introduce the URL.

> Bittlestone, R. (2005). *Odysseus unbound.* doi: 10.2277/0521853575

> Kafka, F. (2002). *Metamorphosis.* D. Wylie (Trans.). Retrieved from http://www.gutenberg.org /etext/5200

MLA: Online Multimedia

For online postings of photographs, videos, sound recordings, works of art, and so on, follow the examples on pages 304–305. In place of the original medium of publication, however, include the title of the database or Web site (italicized), followed by the medium (Web) and the date of access, as for other online entries.

> Brumfield, William Craft. *Church of Saint Nicholas Mokryi.* 1996. Prints and Photographs Div., Lib. of Cong. *Brumfield Photograph Collection.* Web. 9 May 2015.

> Sita Sings the Blues. Prod. Nina Paley. 2008. *Internet Archive.* Web. 5 June 2015.

24-7 LIST OTHER SOURCES

A Television or Radio Program

MLA

Include the medium (Television or Radio) at the end of the citation, followed by a period.

> "Florence and the Machine; Lykke Li." *Austin City Limits.* PBS. KDIN, Iowa, 24 Apr. 2013. Television.

APA

Indicate the episode by writers and directors, if possible. Then follow with the airing date, the episode title, and the type of series in brackets. Add the producer(s) as you would the editors(s) of a print medium, and complete the entry with details about the series itself.

> Benioff, D, & Weiss, D.B. (Writers), & Nutter, D, (Director). (2013, June 2). The Rains of Castamere [Television series episode]. In D. Benioff & D.B. Weiss (Producers). *Game of Thrones* New York, NY: HBO.

> Berger, C. (Writer). (2001, December 19). Feederwatch [Radio series program]. In D. Byrd & J. Block (Producers). *Earth & Sky.* Austin, TX: The Production Block.

A Motion Picture or Performance

MLA

The director, distributor, and year of release follow the title. Other information may be included if pertinent. End with the medium, in this case *Film*, followed by a period.

> *Lincoln.* Dir. Steven Spielberg. Perf. Daniel Day-Lewis, Sally Field. DreamWorks, 2012. Film.

Treat a **performance** as you would a film, but add its location and date.

> *Clybourne Park.* McGuire Proscenium, Guthrie Theater, Minneapolis. 4 Aug. 2013. Performance.

A Video Recording or an Audio Recording

MLA

Cite a filmstrip, slide program, videocassette, or DVD as you do a film; include the medium of publication last, followed by a period.

> *Monet: Shadow & Light.* Devine Productions, 1999. Videocassette.

If you are citing a specific song on a musical recording, place its title in quotation marks before the title of the recording.

> Bernstein, Leonard. "Maria." *West Side Story.* Columbia, 1995. CD.

A Lecture, Speech, Reading, or Dissertation

MLA

Provide the speaker's name, the title of the presentation (if known) in quotation marks, the meeting and the sponsoring organization, the location, and the date. End with an appropriate descriptive label such as *Address, Lecture,* or *Reading.*

> Gopnik, Adam. "Radical Winter." CBC Massey Lectures. Dalhousie Arts Centre, Halifax, Nova Scotia. 12 Oct. 2011. Lecture.

APA

Give the name and function of the director, producer, or both.

> Lee, A. (Director). (2012). *Life of Pi* [Motion picture]. United States: Twentieth-Century Fox.

APA

Begin the entry with the speaker's or writer's name, not the producer. Indicate the type of recording in brackets.

> Kim, E. (Author, speaker). (2000). *Ten thousand sorrows* [CD]. New York, NY: Random House.

For a music recording, give the name and function of the originators or primary contributors. Indicate the recording medium in brackets following the title.

> ARS Femina Ensemble. (1998). *Musica de la puebla de Los Angeles: Music by women of baroque Mexico, Cuba, & Europe* [CD]. Louisville, KY: Nannerl Recordings.

APA

For an unpublished paper presented at a meeting, indicate when the paper was presented, at what meeting, in what location.

> Sifferd, K., & Hirstein, W. (2012, June). *On the criminal culpability of successful and unsuccessful psychopaths.* Paper presented at the meeting of the Society for Philosophy and Psychology, Boulder, CO.

For an unpublished doctoral dissertation, place the dissertation's title in italics. Indicate the school at which the writer completed the dissertation.

> Roberts, W. (2001). *Crime amidst suburban wealth* (Unpublished doctoral dissertation). Bowling Green State University, Bowling Green, OH.

24-8 FOLLOW FORMAT GUIDELINES FOR MLA AND APA

Both MLA and APA offer guidelines not only for documentation but also for the paper's format—its parts and their presentation. These guidelines are outlined and modeled for each system in the pages that follow.

24-8a Guidelines for MLA Format

Whole-Paper Format and Printing Issues

The instructions below and on the next pages explain how to set up the parts of your paper and print it for submission.

▶ **Running Head and Pagination**

- Number pages consecutively in the upper-right corner, one-half inch from the top and flush with the right margin (1 inch from the edge of the page).
- Use numerals only—without *p., page, #,* or any other symbol.
- Include your last name on each page typed one space before the page number. (Your name identifies the page if it's misplaced.)

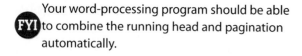 Your word-processing program should be able to combine the running head and pagination automatically.

▶ **Heading on First Page**

MLA does not require a separate title page. On the first page of your paper, include the following details flush left and double spaced, one inch from the top:

- Your name, both first and last in regular order
- Your professor's or instructor's name (presented as he or she prefers)
- The course name and number, plus the section number if appropriate (e.g., History 100-05); follow your instructor's directions.
- The date that you are submitting the paper: use the international format (e.g., 11 November 2013)

▶ **Paper Title**

- Double-spaced below the heading, center your paper's title.
- Do not italicize, underline, or boldface the title; put it in quotation marks or all caps; or

use a period (though a question mark may be acceptable if warranted).
- Follow standard capitalization practices for titles.

▶ **Works-Cited List**

- Start the list on a new page immediately after your paper's conclusion.
- Continue the running head and pagination.
- Center the heading "Works Cited" one inch from the top of the page; don't use quotation marks, underlining, boldface, or any other typographical markers.
- Begin your list two spaces below the heading. Arrange all entries alphabetically by the authors' last names; for sources without identified authors, alphabetize using the work's title, ignoring *a, an,* or *the.*
- If you are listing two or more works by the same author, alphabetize them by the titles of the works. Use the author's name for the first entry; in later entries, replace the name with three hyphens.
- Start each entry flush left; indent second and subsequent lines for specific entries one-half inch. Use your word-processing program's hanging indent feature.
- Double-space within and between all entries, and follow standard rules for capitalization, italics, quotation marks, and punctuation.
- Do not repeat the "Works Cited" heading if your list runs longer than one page.
- Print on standard 8.5-by 11-inch paper.

Page-Layout Issues

▶ **Spacing**

- **Margins:** Set margins top and bottom, left and right at one inch, with the exception of the running head (one-half inch from top).
- **Line Spacing:** Double-space the entire paper—including the heading and works-cited entries, as well as tables, captions, and inset quotations.
- **Line Justification:** Use left justified throughout, except for the running head (right justified) and the title and works-cited heading (both centered). Leave the right margin ragged.

- **Word Hyphenation:** Avoid hyphenating words at the end of lines; in your word processor, turn off this tool.
- **Spacing after Punctuation:** Use one space after most forms of punctuation, including end punctuation—but not before or after a dash or a hyphen.
- **Paragraph Indenting:** Indent all paragraphs one-half inch.

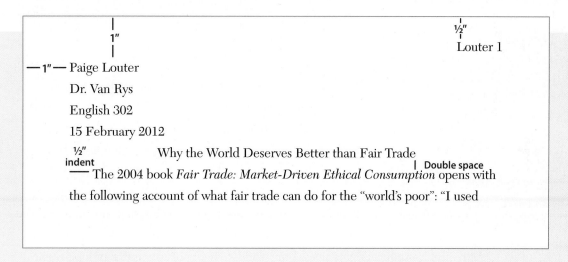

▶ **Longer (Inset) Quotations**

- Indent one inch verse quotations longer than three lines and prose quotations longer than four typed lines.
- Use no quotation marks, and place the parenthetical citation after the closing punctuation.
- With a verse quotation, make each line of the poem or play a new line; do not run the lines together. Follow the indenting and spacing in the verse itself.
- To quote two or more paragraphs, indent the first line of each paragraph one-quarter inch in addition to the one inch for the whole passage. However, if the first sentence quoted does not begin a paragraph in the source, do not make the additional indent. Indent only the first lines of subsequent paragraphs.

▶ **Tables and Illustrations**

Position tables, illustrations, and other visuals near your discussion of them—ideally, immediately after your first reference to the graphic, whether pasted in after a paragraph or positioned on a separate following page. Observe these rules:

- **Tables:** Identify all tables using "Table," an Arabic numeral, and a caption (descriptive title). Both the identifying headings and captions should be flush left, appropriately capitalized. Provide source information and explanatory notes below the table. Identify notes with superscript lowercase letters, not numerals. Double-space throughout the table.
- **Illustrations:** Number and label other visuals (graphs, charts, drawings, photos, maps, etc.) using "Figure" or "Fig.," an Arabic numeral (followed by a period), and a title or caption one space after the period—all flush left below the illustration, along with source information and notes.

24-8b MLA Format at a Glance

You can find a complete model in MLA style, Paige Louter's "Why the World Deserves Better than Fair Trade," at the end of chapter 23 (pages 277–286). The full paper explores the limited success of the fair trade movement, documenting sources using MLA style. What follows, however, are excerpts showing basic rules for MLA formatting. The side notes give information about the excerpt's running head and pagination, first-page heading, title, and works-cited list. Use this information as a guide to formatting your own research paper using MLA style.

MLA Paper (Excerpt)

The typeface is a traditional serif type, Times New Roman.

The writer's last name and page number are placed in the upper right corner of every page.

The heading identifies the writer, the professor, the course, and the date—in the order and format shown, flush left.

The title is centered, in regular typeface and type size—no special effects such as boldface.

The text is double-spaced throughout.

One-inch margins are used left and right, top and bottom, with the exception of the header, which is one-half inch from the top.

Louter 1

Paige Louter

Dr. Van Rys

English 302

15 February 2012

Why the World Deserves Better than Fair Trade

The 2004 book *Fair Trade: Market-Driven Ethical Consumption* opens with the following account of what fair trade can do for the "world's poor": "I used to live in a thatch hut with a mud floor," says fair trade farmer Jeronimo Tush. "Now I have two concrete houses. And [. . .] my children now only go to school. We don't need them to work" (qtd. in Nicholls and Opal 3). Why would anyone argue against a system of trade that provides improved housing and eliminates the need for child labor? Fair trade is admirable in its effort to address injustice, to promote human rights all over the world, to fight poverty, and to promote ethical food-production and consumption practices. However, there is a darker side to the fair trade movement: This seemingly just-trade model is in reality falling short of its idealistic claims and is in fact creating new problems. Though the fair trade movement is perhaps not beyond saving, it must undergo radical change to survive. Additionally, in order to demand change and perhaps even offer solutions themselves, consumers—especially those who wish to call themselves socially conscious—must educate themselves as to the harmful effects for which fair trade is responsible.

To begin with, the term "fair trade" itself is a source of confusion among many consumers. "Fair trade," not capitalized and written as two words, is the general term for the concept. However, "fairtrade" written as one word is the official name of products labeled by the Fairtrade Labelling Organizations International (FLO)—thereby making the products eligible for the Fairtrade International certification mark (see Figure 1). Here's where it gets more confusing: The . . .

MLA Works-Cited List

The list of works cited begins on a separate page and includes the title, header, and page number.

The paper's bibliography lists a range of scholarly books, scholarly articles, and Web sites on the topic.

Sources are listed in alphabetical order by author (or by title if no author is given) and identified by medium.

Quotation marks and italics are properly used with titles, as are punctuation and abbreviations.

Items are double-spaced throughout. Second and subsequent lines are indented half an inch (hanging indent).

Works Cited

Beattie, Alan. "The Price of Being Fair." *New Statesman* 136.4833 (2007): 34-35. *Literary Reference Center*. Web. 18 Jan. 2012.

Booth, Philip, and Linda Whetstone. "Half a Cheer for Fair Trade." *Economic Affairs* 27.2 (2007): 29-36. *Business Source Elite*. Web. 19 Jan. 2012.

Chandler, Paul. "Fair Trade and Global Justice." *Globalizations* 3.2 (2006): 255-57. *Academic Search Premier*. Web. 19 Jan. 2012.

Henderson, David R. "Fair Trade Is Counterproductive—And Unfair." *Economic Affairs* 28.3 (2008): 62-64. *Business Source Elite*. Web. 19 Jan. 2012.

Hodge, Neil. "Chocs Away." *Financial Management* (2010): 14-21. *Business Source Elite*. Web. 18 Jan. 2012.

Hussey, Ian. "Fair Trade and Empire: An Anti-Capitalist Critique of the Fair Trade Movement." *Briarpatch* 40.5 (2011): 15-18. *Canadian Reference Centre*. Web. 18 Jan. 2012.

Hutchens, Anna. "Empowering Women Through Fair Trade? Lessons from Asia." *Third World Quarterly* 31.3 (2010): 449-67. *Academic Search Premier*. Web. 18 Jan. 2012.

Nichols, Alex, and Charlotte Opal. *Fair Trade: Market-Driven Ethical Consumption*. London: Sage, 2004. Print.

Walton, Andrew. "What Is Fair Trade?" *Third World Quarterly* 31.3 (2010): 431-47. *Academic Search Premier*. Web. 19 Jan. 2012.

"What is [sic] Fairtrade?" *Fairtrade International*. Fairtrade Labelling Organizations International, n.d. Web. 10 Feb. 2012.

Weber, Jeremy. "Fair Trade Coffee Enthusiasts Should Confront Reality." *CATO Journal* 27.1 (2007): 109-17. *Academic Search Premier*. Web. 19 Jan. 2012.

24-8c Guidelines for APA Format

The instructions below explain how to set up the parts of your paper and print it for submission in APA format.

▶ **Title Page:** On the first page, include your paper's title, your name, and your institution's name on three separate lines, double-spaced, centered, and positioned in the top half of the page. Flush left at the top, type *Running head:* (no italics) followed by your abbreviated title in all uppercase letters; and flush right at the top, type the page number 1.

▶ **Abstract:** On the second page, include an abstract—a 150- to 250-word paragraph summarizing your paper. Place the title *Abstract* (no italics) approximately one inch from the top of the page and center it. Place the running head and page number 2 at the top of the page.

▶ **Body:** Format the body (which begins on the third page) as follows:

▶ **Margins:** Leave a one-inch margin on all four sides of each page (one and one-half inches on the left if the paper will be bound). Do not justify lines, but rather leave a ragged right margin; and do not break words at the ends of lines.

▶ **Line Spacing:** Double-space your entire paper, unless your instructor allows single spacing for tables and figures.

▶ **Page Numbers:** Place your running head and the page number flush left and flush right respectively, at the top of each page, beginning with the title page.

▶ **Headings:** Like an outline, headings show the organization of your paper and the importance of each topic. All topics of equal importance should have headings of the same level, or style. Below are the various levels of headings used in APA papers. ***Important note:*** The first heading should come after the title of the paper; do not treat the paper title as a level-1 heading.

▶ **Appendix:** Tables and figures (graphs, charts, maps, etc.) already appear on separate pages following the reference list. If necessary, one or more appendices may also supplement your text, following any tables or figures.

Level 1:	**Centered, Boldface, Uppercase and Lowercase Heading**
Level 2:	**Flush Left, Boldface, Uppercase and Lowercase Side Heading**
Level 3:	**Indented, boldface, lowercase paragraph heading ending with a period.**
Level 4:	***Indented, boldface, italicized, lowercase paragraph heading with a period.***
Level 5:	*Indented, italicized, lowercase paragraph heading with a period.*

Example:

> **The English Learner Landscape**
>
> **Myths and Misconceptions**
>
> **Myth 1: Exposure will lead to learning.**
>
> ***The need for explicit morphological instruction.***
>
> *Reductive approaches.*

24-8d APA Research Report: Format and Documentation

Amanda Khoe wrote the following paper in her Writing in Education course as a survey of articles (called a literature review) on teaching English Language Learners (ELL—students for whom English is not their first language). Her paper serves as an introduction to an anthology of these articles. You can use Amanda's paper to study how a social-science literature review synthesizes published research and how format and documentation practices work in APA style.

APA Title Page

Place manuscript page headers one-half inch from the top. Put five spaces between the page header and the page number.

Full title, authors, and school name are centered on the page, typed in uppercase and lowercase.

Running head: TEACHING K–12 ENGLISH LANGUAGE LEARNERS   1

Teaching K-12 English Language Learners
in the Mainstream Classroom
Amanda Khoe
University of California-Davis

APA Abstract

The abstract summarizes the paper's central issue, its main conclusion, the key reasoning and evidence presented, and the study's significance.

TEACHING K–12 ENGLISH LANGUAGE LEARNERS   2

Abstract

While ELLs are the fastest-growing student subpopulation in K–12, they are more likely than other students to perform poorly on standardized tests and to drop out of school. One explanation is that teachers in the mainstream classroom are underprepared for teaching ELLs and thus need additional training. Recent studies have shown that the best approach to ELL instruction is to use an array of teaching strategies that fit varied ELL contexts. While diverse programs exist (e.g., dual language, newcomer, English Language Development), so do myths and misconceptions about ELL pedagogy: that ELLs will learn English simply through exposure, that second-language acquisition follows a universal pattern, that what works with non-ELL students will work with ELLs, and that nonverbal methods work best with ELL students. Given that ELLs need 1–3 years to gain conversational proficiency and 5–7 years to gain academic proficiency in English, teachers in the mainstream classroom need to do more than follow just good teaching (JGT) practices. They need to use (in ways that fit their classroom context) interactive teaching techniques, comprehensive vocabulary instruction, scaffolding strategies, varied modes of assessment, and cultural sensitivity to ensure greater success for ELLs.

Keywords: ELL, K–12, ELD, SIOP, JGT, scaffolding

Teaching K–12 English Language Learners in the Mainstream Classroom

English Language Learners (ELLs) are the fastest-growing student subpopulation in the United States. From 1979 to 1999, overall enrollment in America's K–12 public schools increased by 6 percent while the ELL population soared by 138 percent (Harper & de Jong, 2004). By the 2007–2008 school year, 5.3 million ELLs constituted 10.6 percent of K–12 public school enrollment (Calderón, Slavin, & Sánchez, 2011). Even as their population burgeons, ELL students remain more likely to perform poorly on standardized tests and to drop out of school than their non-ELL peers (Verdugo & Flores, 2007). ELLs' low academic achievement can be attributed in large part to the shortage of prepared classroom teachers. Though 42 percent of K–12 public school teachers have ELLs in their class, only 12.5 percent have received more than eight hours of professional development in ELL teaching practices (de Jong & Harper, 2005). English Language Learners require well-trained teachers and tailored instruction; unfortunately, mainstream K–12 teachers with ELL students are too often ill equipped to educate these unique students.

The size of the ELL population coupled with its disturbingly low academic achievement has spawned many studies and much heated debate on how to improve ELL pedagogy. To avoid "succumb[ing] to the allure of strategy books" (Carrier, 2005, p. 5), teachers must first understand peripheral issues affecting the ELL population. Presently, no federal guidelines exist for states regarding how to identify, assess, place, or instruct ELLs (Calderón et al., 2011). The best strategies for serving ELLs are informed by distinct, in some cases even opposing, schools of thought. As the following studies have demonstrated, effective ELL education is kaleidoscopic, with various strategies to match the array of possible contexts.

This anthology introduction begins with a report on the demographic composition and needs of ELL students, follows with basic theoretical frameworks that currently guide ELL education, and ends with a synthesis of the ELL literature that yields concrete strategies for teaching in a mainstream classroom with English Language Learners.

The English Language Learner Landscape

Though ELL students bring myriad languages, cultures, and personal histories to the classroom, they are typically classified as a single group. In "Effective Instruction for English Learners," Calderón et al. (2011) have cataloged four discrete subcategories within the ELL population: special education ELLs, ELLs inappropriately reclassified as general education after passing a district language test, migrant ELLs whose education is interrupted as their family follows the crops from one location to another, and transnational ELLs who

Center the title one inch from the top. Double-space throughout.

Using properly referenced statistics, Amanda raises the challenges of ELL students in the mainstream classroom.

Citing issues that teachers face, she offers her thesis about ELL education, a thesis rooted in her survey of the literature.

A brief paragraph forecasts the content of her research paper.

A heading identifies a new section.

return to their native country and attend school only to re-emigrate to the United States. Over 20 percent of ELLs are recent immigrants, and 80 percent of second-generation children (U.S.-born children whose parents were born outside the U.S.) are ELLs. Evidently, ELLs are as diverse as they are prevalent.

In contrast to Calderón et al. (2011), Pascopella (2011) has explained in "Successful Strategies for English Language Learners" that there are various ELL program types to match the various types of ELL students. In dual language programs, bilingual students receive instruction in English and another language (e.g., Spanish). In newcomer programs, "separate, relatively self-contained educational interventions" (p. 32) are implemented to meet the academic and transitional needs of recent immigrants before they enter a mainstream English Language Development (ELD) program. In structured English immersion programs, students are taught entirely in English. Today, sheltered English programs are the dominant trend. The prototypical sheltered English program— Sheltered Instruction Observation Protocol (SIOP)—uses nonconventional methods to teach academic content to English Language Learners.

Myths and Misconceptions

In "Misconceptions about Teaching English-Language Learners," Harper and de Jong (2004) have called attention to the negative effects of ELL teaching practices based on misinformation. First, some teachers assume that mere exposure to English and interaction with English speakers will result in English-language learning. Conversely, the authors have asserted that ELLs require deliberate instruction in the grammatical, morphological, and phonological aspects of English if they are to communicate successfully in an academic context. Second, today's reductive approaches to ELL education are based on the premise that second-language acquisition follows a universal pattern. Unfortunately, such methods fail to meet ELLs' idiosyncratic language needs. Third, it is a common misconception that if a teaching practice is good for native English speakers, it is also good for ELLs. De Jong and Harper (2005) have argued that teaching strategies in a classroom with non-native and native English speakers often emphasize that students must "talk to learn" but fail to address how students will "learn to talk" (p. 102). Fourth, ELL teachers tend to believe that presenting concepts using purely nonverbal techniques is most effective. While nonverbal methods can support ELLs' English acquisition, Harper and de Jong (2004) have warned that overdependence on nonlinguistic instruction can impede students' ability to integrate language and content.

In "Effective Instruction for English-Language Learners" (2011), Protheroe has attempted to dispel myths about young ELLs. Contrary to the notion that English-only instruction produces the best second-language acquisition results, Protheroe found that high literacy in a student's first language (L1) presages

---

When authors are identified in the sentence, only the date is required in the in-text citation.

In her topic sentence, the writer sets up a contrast between two sources. A direct quotation is cited with a page number.

A subheading further divides this section of the essay.

The writer enumerates misconceptions using clear transition words and references to multiple sources.

Summarizing a source, Amanda identifies myths about ELLs.

high levels of reading achievement in his/her second language (L2). Accordingly, teachers should supplement their English instruction with instruction in the native language(s) of their students as much as possible. Unlike Harper and de Jong, Protheroe has asserted that instruction that works well for non-ELLs is equally effective for ELLs, so long as modifications are made to accommodate students' language "capacities, needs, and limitations" (p.28).

Linguistic Needs

English Language Learners undertake the challenge of simultaneously learning a new language and new academic content. In "Key Issues for Teaching English Learners in Academic Classrooms," Carrier (2005) has explained that it takes an average of one to three years to reach conversational proficiency in a second language, but five to seven years to reach academic proficiency. In spite of this, ELLs normally spend just three years in 30-minute "pull-out" English Language Development programs (Calderón et al., 2011). Calderón et al. have argued that this is but one example of how ELL teaching practices are unsympathetic to the considerably greater linguistic needs of English Language Learners.

Researchers in educational linguistics have found that second language learners often possess more knowledge than they can express. Nonstandard accents help illustrate this point. Underestimating their ELL students' intellectual capacity, teachers often emphasize pronunciation over other language dimensions and academic content. But ELLs are likely to be as cognitively mature as their non-ELL peers. Typically, ELLs acquire content at a faster rate than second language skills. Thus, English Language Learners often understand more than they can articulate through spoken or written language (de Jong & Harper, 2005). Educators must recognize that an ELL's accent or imprecise grammar does not necessarily indicate academic incompetence. Accordingly, second-language instruction should provide non-linguistic means for students to demonstrate their learning.

Best Practices for ELL Education

The current educational climate prizes inclusive instruction. While this emphasis is not inherently detrimental, it is driven by the "just good teaching (JGT), native-speaker perspective" (de Jong & Harper, 2005, p. 102), which assumes that all students possess at least rudimentary oral and literacy skills in English and that ELLs learn at the same pace and in the same manner as non-ELLs. JGT practices include "activating knowledge, using cooperative learning, process writing, and graphic organizers" (p. 102). In "Preparing Mainstream Teachers for English-Language Learners: Is Being a Good Teacher Good Enough?" de Jong and Harper (2005) insisted that ELLs require more than generic JGT practices to fully acquire academic content and build language skills.

Moving beyond JGT involves activating and strengthening background knowledge in order to prime students for new content (Coleman and Goldenberg, 2011; Short & Echevarria, 2004; Verdugo & Flores, 2007). In "Promoting Literacy Development," Coleman and Goldenberg (2011) have suggested interactive and direct teaching techniques for extracting students' existing knowledge. Interactive teaching, defined as "verbal interaction that gives students opportunities to converse with the teacher and with peers" (p. 16), combined with "extended academic talk" (Short & Echevarria, 2004, p. 12) challenge ELLs both linguistically and in other cognitive domains. Calderón et al. (2011) have maintained that the consort to background content knowledge is background vocabulary knowledge. Students need long-term, explicit, and comprehensive vocabulary instruction in all subject areas to foster both word-level skills (e.g., decoding) and text-level skills (e.g., fluency). Through exposure to words in multiple forms and contexts, students develop phonological awareness and better reading comprehension. Moreover, repetition prompts students to operate on their own vocabulary (and content) background in novel ways.

Researchers have also found that stressing academic language can help both ELLs and struggling non-ELLs retain specific subject material (Carrier, 2005; de Jong & Harper, 2005; Harper & de Jong, 2004; Protheroe, 2011). To avoid diluting the curriculum, teachers should concentrate on introducing vocabulary terms that are key to understanding the subject matter (de Jong & Harper, 2005). The Sheltered Instruction Observation Protocol Model (SIOP) recommends "emphasizing academic vocabulary development" (Short & Echevarria, 2004, p. 12). For example, academic language in a unit on earthquakes might include the words *plate tectonics, magnitude*, and *seismoscope*. Spotlighting academic vocabulary serves the dual goals of facilitating content and language acquisition.

Multiple Modes, Scaffolding, and L1 Development

Needless to say, English Language Learners benefit from extensive scaffolding strategies. When a teacher scaffolds, he or she shifts the difficulty and pace to meet the needs of the student. One way to scaffold learning is to use "multiple modes of input and output" that are not dependent on language (Carrier, 2005, p. 4; de Jong & Harper, 2005). Manipulatives, drama/role play, and graphics can be used by educators to "input" content and by ELL students to "output" their own knowledge when they cannot adequately express themselves through language (Coleman & Goldenberg, 2011). Likewise, various modes of assessment can be used to capture the full scope of learning. For instance, asking a student to draw instead of write the answer to a test question can reveal learning that goes beyond rote memorization (de Jong & Harper, 2005). In a related vein, teaching strategies such as question-generating, summarizing, and predicting can foster metacognitive skill-building and help ELLs take ownership of their own learning (Verdugo & Flores, 2007). Multiple modes of instruction and assessment should be used regularly in ELL education.

In addition, a community orientation has proven effective in ELL instruction. In "English-Language Learners: Key Issues," Verdugo and Flores found higher ELL retention rates in "supportive school environments" (2007, p. 177) where ELL families were involved in students' learning and small group instruction was a common practice. In peer groups, students gain confidence and build social skills (Mays, 2008). Additionally, students can scaffold each others' learning by offering translations between English and an ELL's primary language.

ELLs' development in their primary languages can predict and facilitate their development in English. Thus, classroom teachers with ELL students must avoid the temptation to implement English-only policies. Such policies can actually hinder rather than help ELLs' English acquisition (Coleman & Goldenberg, 2011; Mays, 2008). Teachers should use students' primary language as much as possible to "support [students…] and to make content more accessible" (Coleman & Goldenberg, 2011, p. 16). A teacher might draw a Spanish-speaking student's attention to the cognates found in English and Spanish (e.g., "activity" and "actividad"). If the teacher cannot speak the student's primary language, he or she can opt for the scaffolding strategies mentioned earlier.

Cultural Considerations

English Language Learners straddle the border between the world of their heritage (native/primary) language and the English-speaking world. Mays (2008) has emphasized the importance of cultural sensitivity in the ELL classroom in "The Cultural Divide of Discourse: Understanding How English-Language Learners' Primary Discourse Influences Acquisition of Literacy." While the American classroom values active questioning and collaboration, many ELLs are accustomed to classroom etiquette that is radically hierarchical. ELL students may be uncomfortable expressing their own opinions and questioning the authority of the teacher or the textbook. Some ELLs may, in fact, consciously reject the "host [American] culture and [English] language" (de Jong & Harper, 2005, p. 117) because acquiring English would signal assimilation and cost them social capital. Moreover, multicultural sensitivity doesn't account for all the issues that arise in a multilingual classroom.

Cultural incongruence between mainstream teachers and their ELL students can obstruct teaching and learning. In California public schools, where 61 percent of students are from minority backgrounds, just 21 percent of teachers identify as minorities (Verdugo & Flores, 2007). Consciously or not, non-minority teachers might hold lower expectations for their minority students. Thus, teachers must be self-critical about their own attitudes toward multilingualism and vigilant about the implicit messages sent by "English-only" classroom policies (de Jong & Harper,

---

Backed up by two sources, Amanda cautions against English-only policies for ELL students.

With a new subheading, Amanda turns to cultural issues that impact ELLs in the mainstream classroom.

Changes to a direct quotation are signalled by brackets.

2005). To reconcile cultural differences, teachers are responsible for familiarizing themselves with students' cultures and primary discourses (Mays, 2008).

Teachers can support the diverse cultures and languages of their students through assignments, assessments, and classroom materials. For example, assigning personal narratives for homework and facilitating multilingual book clubs mitigate the collision of students' primary discourses and the academic discourse. In addition to assigning tasks that encourage students to share their family and community experiences, teachers should maintain a classroom library that is representative of students' diversity. Indeed, embedding instruction and materials from different cultures forges an atmosphere of tolerance for ELL and non-ELL students alike. Finally, Mays (2008) has advocated "culturally responsive management styles and unbiased assessments" (p. 416). Teachers should vary question types and media, and they should discuss the process of arriving at an answer (whether correct or incorrect). Taking the time to "value the ELL voice" (p. 418) builds student-teacher relationships based on mutual trust and respect; in turn, these genuine bonds nurture learning.

Closing Remarks

In 1972, the Supreme Court ruling in Lau v. Nichols mandated that school districts help students overcome language barriers so that they can participate in and benefit from mainstream schooling. Nearly 40 years later, the severe disparities in academic achievement between ELLs and non-ELLs continue to hinder the nation's overall educational attainment. While policymakers, researchers, and educators have yet to reach a consensus on how to best instruct this growing subpopulation, competing theories on ELL teaching share several themes. The model for future ELL education is naturally multifaceted, refined by trial and error, and ultimately based on contextual features.

Collectively, the research articles cited in this introduction detail ELL teaching practices that are effective in most circumstances. A concerted training program is needed to prepare teachers for the multilingual classroom. Broadly speaking, effective ELL teaching begins with an understanding of the second-language acquisition process and an embracing of the diversity within the ELL population. In the classroom, mainstream teachers should strive to tap into students' existing knowledge and relate academic content to students' cultural backgrounds. By identifying the distinct linguistic demands inherent in different subjects, teachers can provide explicit vocabulary instruction—an essential foundation for literacy development. To encourage long-term academic literacy, teachers should capitalize on innovative scaffolding strategies, including multiple modes of instruction and assessment, as well as using students' primary language. Given these frameworks, K–12 classroom teachers can tailor effective strategies to promote their English Language Learners' academic achievement.

A final main heading signals the conclusion.

Amanda puts issues surrounding ELL education in historical and political context.

The last paragraph summarizes the findings of the research surveyed and synthesizes the advice on best ELL teaching practices for the mainstream classroom.

References

All works referred to in the paper appear on the reference page, listed alphabetically by author (or title).

Carrier, K. A. (2005). Key issues for teaching English Language Learners in academic classrooms. *Middle School Journal 37*(2), 4–9. Retrieved from www.firstsearch.org

Calderón, M., Slavin, R., & Sánchez, M. (2011). Effective instruction for English learners. *The Future of Children 21*(1), 103–127.

Coleman, R., & Goldenberg, C. (2011). Promoting literacy development. *Education Digest 76*(6), 14–18.

de Jong, E. J., & Harper, C. A. (2005). Preparing mainstream teachers for English Language Learners: Is being a good teacher good enough? *Teacher Education Quarterly 32*(2), 101–118. Retrieved from www.firstsearch.org

Harper, C., & de Jong, E. (2004). Misconceptions about teaching English Language Learners. *Journal of Adolescent & Adults Literacy 48*(2), 152–162.

Mays, L. (2008). The cultural divide of discourse: Understanding how English Language Learners' primary discourse influences acquisition of literacy. *The Reading Teacher 61*(5), 415–418.

Pascopella, A. (2011). Successful strategies for English Language Learners. *District Administration 47*(2), 29–44.

Protheroe, N. (2011). Effective instruction for English Language Learners. *Principal 90*(3), 26–29.

Short, D., & Echevarria, J. (2004). Teacher skills to support English Language Learners. *Educational Leadership 62*(4), 8–13.

Verdugo, R. R., & Flores, R. (2007). English-Language Learners: Key issues. *Education and Urban Society 39*: 167–194. doi: 10.1177/00131245062948

Each entry follows APA guidelines for listing authors, dates, titles, and publishing information.

Capitalization, punctuation, and hanging indentation are consistent with APA format.

Critical-Thinking and Writing Activities

1. The MLA and APA systems involve many rules about format and documentation. To make sense of these rules, compare and contrast the essential logic of each system.

2. Create MLA works-cited entries for the following publications:
   - An article in the summer 2009 issue (volume 34, no. 2) of the periodical *MELUS*, by Joni Adamson and Scott Slovic: "The Shoulders We Stand On: An Introduction to Ethnicity and Ecocriticism" (pages 5-24)
   - Ernest Hemingway's novel *A Farewell to Arms*, published in 1986 by Collier Books, located in New York City
   - The Web page "Vaccines for Children Program (VCP)," part of the Vaccines and Immunizations section of the Centers for Disease Control and Prevention (CDC) Web site, sponsored by the U.S. government's Department of Health and Human Services. No author or publication date is listed. The site was last accessed January 26, 2015, at http://www.cdc.gov/vaccines/programs/vfc/index.html.

3. Create reference list entries in correct APA style for the following sources:
   - An article in the summer 2009 issue (volume 34, no. 2) of the periodical *MELUS*, by Joni Adamson and Scott Slovic: "The Shoulders We Stand On: An Introduction to Ethnicity and Ecocriticism" (pages 5-24)
   - The book *The Playful World: How Technology Is Transforming Our Imagination*, by Mark Pesce, published in 2000 by Ballantine Books, located in New York City
   - The Web page "Vaccines for Children Program (VCP)," part of the Vaccines and Immunizations section of the Centers for Disease Control and Prevention (CDC) Web site, sponsored by the U.S. government's Department of Health and Human Services. No author or publication date is listed. The site was last accessed January 26, 2015, at http://www.cdc.gov/vaccines/programs/vfc/index.html.

4. Compare and contrast the sample MLA paper at the end of chapter 23 (pages 277–286) with the sample APA paper in this chapter (pages 313–320). Aside from issues of format and documentation, how do the research essay (MLA model) and the research report (APA model) compare in terms of focus, organization, voice, and treatment of sources?

STUDY TOOLS 24

LOCATED AT BACK OF THE TEXTBOOK
☐ Tear-Out Chapter Review Card

LOCATED AT WWW.CENGAGEBRAIN.COM/LOGIN
☐ Chapter eBook

☐ Graded quizzes and a practice quiz generator

☐ Videos: Writer Interviews

☐ Tutorials

☐ Flashcards

☐ Cengage Learning Write Experience

☐ Interactive activities

25 | Grammar

"GRAMMAR IS THE FOUNDATION FOR COMMUNICATION—THE BETTER THE GRAMMAR, THE CLEARER THE MESSAGE."

WILLIAM B. BRADSHAW

Alex Yeung, 2014 / Used under license from Shutterstock.com

LEARNING OBJECTIVES

25-1 Noun

25-2 Pronoun

25-3 Verb

25-4 Adjective

25-5 Adverb

25-6 Preposition

25-7 Conjunction

25-8 Interjection

Grammar is the study of the structure and features of the language, consisting of rules and standards that are to be followed to produce acceptable writing and speaking. Understanding grammar rules will help you communicate more clearly and ensure that your writing ideas will be understood. But let's be clear: Even seasoned writers struggle to keep track of all the rules and standards of the English language. This chapter and the rest of the chapters in the Handbook section offer a handy reference to all the rules.

This chapter focuses on the parts of speech, the eight different categories that indicate how words are used in the English language—as nouns, pronouns, verbs, adjectives, adverbs, prepositions, conjunctions, or interjections.

25-1 NOUN

A **noun** is a word that names something: a person, a place, a thing, or an idea.

Malcolm Gladwell/author	*Frozen*/film
Renaissance/era	UC-Davis/university
A Congress of Wonders/book	

25-1a Classes of Nouns

All nouns are either **proper nouns** or **common nouns**. Nouns may also be classified as *individual* or *collective*, or *concrete* or *abstract*.

▶ **Proper Nouns** — A proper noun, which is always capitalized, names a specific person, place, thing, or idea.

Rembrandt, Bertrand Russell............person
Stratford-upon-Avon, Tower of London... places
The Night Watch, Rosetta stone.......... things
New Deal, Christianity .... ideas

▶ **Common Nouns** — A common noun is a general name for a person, a place, a thing, or an idea. Common nouns are not capitalized.

optimist, instructor.....................person
cafeteria, park.......................... places
computer, chair .... things
freedom, love .... ideas

▶ **Collective Nouns** — A collective noun names a group or a unit.

family • audience • crowd • committee
team • class

▶ **Concrete Nouns** — A concrete noun names a thing that is tangible (can be seen, touched, heard, smelled, or tasted).

child • the Black Keys • gym • village • microwave oven • pizza

▶ **Abstract Nouns** — An abstract noun names an idea, a condition, or a feeling—in other words, something that cannot be seen, touched, heard, smelled, or tasted.

beauty • Jungian psychology • anxiety agoraphobia • trust

25-1b Forms of Nouns

Nouns are grouped according to their *number*, *gender*, and *case*.

▶ **Number of Nouns** — Number indicates whether a noun is singular or plural. A singular noun refers to one person, place, thing, or idea. A plural noun refers to more than one person, place, thing, or idea.

Singular:
apple • laboratory
lecture • note
grade • result

Plural:
apples • laboratories • lectures
notes • grade • results

▶ **Gender of Nouns** — Gender indicates whether a noun is masculine, feminine, neuter, or indefinite.

> **Masculine:**
> father • king • brother • men
> colt • rooster
>
> **Feminine:**
> mother • queen • sister • women
> filly • hen
>
> **Neuter** (without gender)**:**
> notebook • monitor • car • printer
>
> **Indefinite** (masculine or feminine)**:**
> professor • customer • children
> doctor • people

▶ **Case of Nouns** — The case of a noun tells what role the noun plays in a sentence. There are three cases: *nominative, possessive,* and *objective.*

Nominative: A noun in the nominative case is used as a subject. The subject of a sentence tells who or what the sentence is about.

> **Dean Henning** manages the College of Arts and Communication.

Note: A noun is also in the nominative case when it is used as a predicate noun (or predicate nominative). A predicate noun follows a linking verb, usually a form of the *be* verb (such as *am, is, are, was, were, be, being, been*), and repeats or renames the subject.

> Ms. Yokum is the **person** to talk to about the college's impact in our community.

Possessive: A noun in the possessive case shows possession or ownership. In this form, it acts as an adjective.

> Our **president's** willingness to discuss concerns with students has boosted campus morale.

Objective: A noun in the objective case serves as an object of the preposition, a direct object, an indirect object, or an object complement.

> To survive, institutions of higher **learning** sometimes cut **budgets** in spite of **protests** from **students** and **instructors**.

(*Learning* is the object of the preposition *of, protests* is the object of the preposition *in spite of, budgets* is the direct object of the verb *cut,* and *students* and *instructors* are the objects of the preposition *from.*)

➕ **A Closer Look:**
Direct and Indirect Objects

A **direct object** is a noun (or pronoun) that identifies what or who receives the action of the verb.

> Budget cutbacks reduced class **choices**. (*Choices* is the direct object of the active verb *reduced.*)

An **indirect object** is a noun (or pronoun) that identifies the person *to whom* or *for whom* something is done, or the thing *to which* or *for which* something is done. An indirect object is always accompanied by a direct object.

> Recent budget cuts have given **students** fewer class choices. (*Choices* is the direct object of *have given; students* is the indirect object.)

ELL Note: Not every transitive verb is followed by both a direct object and an indirect object. Both can, however, follow *give, send, show, tell, teach, find, sell, ask, offer, pay, pass,* and *hand.*

25-2 PRONOUN

A pronoun is a word that is used in place of a noun. Most pronouns have an antecedent. An antecedent is the noun or pronoun that the pronoun refers to or replaces. Most pronouns have antecedents, but not all do. (See "Indefinite Pronouns" on page 325.)

> **Sample Pronouns:**
>
> Roger was the most interesting 10-year-old **I** ever taught. **He** was a good thinker and thus a good writer. **I** remember **his** paragraph about the cowboy hat **he** received from **his** grandparents. **It** was "too new looking." The brim was not rolled properly. But the hat's imperfections were not the main idea in Roger's writing. No, the main idea was how **he** was fixing the hat **himself** by wearing **it** when **he** showered.

Sample Antecedents:

As the wellness **counselor** checked *her* chart, several **students** *who* were waiting *their* turns shifted uncomfortably.

(*Counselor* is the antecedent of *her*; *students* is the antecedent of *who* and *their*.)

Note: Each pronoun must agree with its antecedent in number, person, and gender. (See page 345.)

25-2a Classes of Pronouns

There are several classes of pronouns: *personal, reflexive and intensive, relative, indefinite, interrogative, demonstrative,* and *reciprocal.*

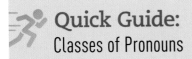

Quick Guide:
Classes of Pronouns

Personal

I, me, my, mine / we, us, our, ours / you, your, yours / they, them, their, theirs / he, him, his, she, her, hers / it, its

Reflexive and Intensive

myself, yourself, himself, herself, itself, ourselves, yourselves, themselves

Relative

who, whose, whom, which, that

Indefinite

all, another, any, anybody, anyone, anything, both, each, each one, either, everybody, everyone, everything, few, many, most, much, neither, nobody, none, no one, nothing, one, other, several, some, somebody, someone, something, such

Interrogative

who, whose, whom, which, what

Demonstrative

this, that, these, those

Reciprocal

each other, one another

▶ **Personal Pronouns** — A **personal pronoun** refers to a specific person or thing.

> *Marge* started her car; **she** drove the antique convertible to *Monterey*, where **she** hoped to sell *it* at an auction.

▶ **Reflexive Pronouns** — A **reflexive pronoun** is formed by adding *-self* or *-selves* to a personal pronoun. A reflexive pronoun can act as a direct object or an indirect object of a verb, an object of a preposition, or a predicate nominative.

> Charles loves **himself**. (direct object of *loves*)
>
> Charles gives **himself** A's for fashion sense (indirect object of *gives*)
>
> Charles smiles at **himself** in store windows. (object of preposition *at*)
>
> Charles can be **himself** anywhere. (predicate nominative)

▶ **Intensive Pronouns** — An **intensive pronoun** intensifies, or emphasizes, the noun or pronoun it refers to.

> Leo **himself** taught his children to invest their lives in others.
>
> The lesson was sometimes painful—but they learned it **themselves**.

▶ **Relative Pronouns** — A **relative pronoun** relates an adjective dependent (relative) clause to the noun or pronoun it modifies. (The noun is italicized in each example below; the relative pronoun is in bold.)

> *Freshmen* **who** believe they have a lot to learn are absolutely right.
>
> Just navigating this *campus*, **which** is huge, can be challenging.

▶ **Indefinite Pronouns** — An **indefinite pronoun** refers to unnamed or unknown people, places, or things.

> **Everyone** seemed amused when I was searching for my classroom in the student center. (The antecedent of *everyone* is unnamed.)
>
> **Nothing** is more unnerving than rushing at the last minute into the wrong room for the wrong class. (The antecedent of *nothing* is unknown.)

Most indefinite pronouns are singular, so when they are used as subjects, they should have singular verbs. (See pages 345–346.)

▶ **Interrogative Pronouns** — An **interrogative pronoun** asks a question.

> So **which** will it be—highlighting and attaching a campus map to the inside of your backpack, or being lost and late for the first two weeks?

Note: When an interrogative pronoun modifies a noun, it functions as an adjective.

▶ **Demonstrative Pronouns** — A **demonstrative pronoun** points out people, places, or things.

> We advise **this**: Bring along as many maps and schedules as you need.

> **Those** are useful tools. **That** is the solution.

Note: When a demonstrative pronoun modifies a noun, it functions as an adjective.

25-2b Forms of Personal Pronouns

The **form** of a personal pronoun indicates its *number* (singular or plural), its *person* (first, second, or third), its *case* (nominative, possessive, or objective), and its *gender* (masculine, feminine, neuter, or indefinite).

▶ **Number of Pronouns** — A personal pronoun is either singular (I, you, he, she, it) or plural (we, you, they).

> **He** should have a budget and stick to it. (singular)

> **We** can help new students learn about budgeting. (plural)

▶ **Person of Pronouns** — The person of a pronoun indicates whether the person is speaking (first person), is spoken to (second person), or is spoken about (third person).

First person is used to name the speaker(s).

first-person point of view

> **I** love the open road. All that is ahead of **me** is gray pavement and beautiful countryside. For this reason, whenever **I** feel **my** stress levels rising, **I** hop on **my** bike and ride. (singular)

> **We** all decided to drive to **our** favorite lake resort. (plural)

Second person is used to name the person(s) spoken to.

second-person point of view

> Maria, did **you** receive the email? (singular)

> John and Tanya, can **you** incorporate the changes? (plural)

Andrey Armyagov, 2014 / Used under license from Shutterstock.com

wavebreakmedia, 2014 / Used under license from Shutterstock.com

Quick Guide: Number, Person, and Case of Personal Pronouns

	Nominative Case	Possessive Case	Objective Case
First Person Singular	I	my, mine	me
Second Person Singular	you	your, yours	you
Third Person Singular	he, she, it	his, her, hers, its	him, her, it
First Person Plural	we	our, ours	us
Second Person Plural	you	your, yours	you
Third Person Plural	they	their, theirs	them

Third person is used to name the person(s) or thing(s) spoken about.

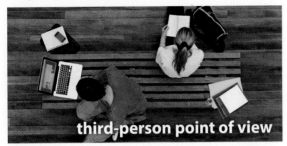

third-person point of view

Today's students are almost always connected to technology. **They** are concerned with **their** online image and reputation. (plural)

Todd updates **his** LinkedIn profile with new work experience. (singular)

One of the advantages of communicating online is that **it** is easy to keep a record of the conversation. (singular)

▶ **Case of Pronouns** — The case of each pronoun tells what role it plays in a sentence. There are three cases: *nominative*, *possessive*, and *objective*.

Nominative: A pronoun in the nominative case is used as a subject. The following are nominative forms: *I, you, he, she, it, we, they*.

He found an old map in the trunk.

My friend and **I** went biking. (not *me*)

A pronoun is also in the nominative case when it is used as a predicate nominative, following a linking verb (*am, is, are, was, were, seems*) and renaming the subject.

It was **he** who discovered electricity. (not *him*)

Possessive: A pronoun in the possessive case shows possession or ownership: *my, mine, our, ours, his, her, hers, their, theirs, its, your, yours*. A possessive pronoun before a noun acts as an adjective: *your coat*.

That coat is **hers**.

This coat is **mine**.

Your coat is lost.

Objective: A pronoun in the objective case can be used as the direct object, indirect object, object of a preposition, or object complement: *me, you, him, her, it, us, them*.

Professor Adler hired **her**. (*Her* is the direct object of the verb *hired*.)

He showed Mary and **me** the language lab. (*Me* is the indirect object of the verb *showed*.)

He introduced the three of **us**—Mary, Shavonn, and **me**—to the faculty. (*Us* is the object of the preposition *of*; *me* is part of the appositive renaming *us*.)

▶ **Gender of Pronouns** — The gender of a pronoun indicates whether the pronoun is masculine, feminine, neuter, or indefinite.

Masculine:
he • him • his

Feminine:
she • her • hers

Neuter (without gender)**:**
it • its

Indefinite (masculine or feminine)**:**
they • them • their

25-3 VERB

A verb shows action (*pondered, grins*), links words (*is, seemed*), or accompanies another action verb as an auxiliary or helping verb (*can, does*).

Harry **honked** the horn. (shows action)

Harry **is** impatient. (links words)

Harry **was** honking the truck's horn. (accompanies the verb *honking*)

25-3a Classes of Verbs

Verbs are classified as action, auxiliary (helping), or linking (state of being).

▶ **Action Verbs: Transitive and Intransitive** — As its name implies, an action verb shows action. Some action verbs are *transitive*; others are *intransitive*. (The term *action* does not always refer to a physical activity.)

Rain **splashed** the windshield. (transitive verb)

Josie **drove** off the road. (intransitive verb)

bikeriderlondon, 2014 / Used under license from Shutterstock.com

Transitive: Transitive verbs have direct objects that receive the action.

> The health-care industry **employs** more than 7 million **workers** in the United States. (*Workers* is the direct object of the action verb *employs*.)

Intransitive: Intransitive verbs communicate action that is complete in itself. They do not need an object to receive the action.

> My new college roommate **smiles** and **laughs** a lot.

Note: Some verbs can be either transitive or intransitive.

> Ms. Hull **teaches** physiology and microbiology. (transitive)

> She **teaches** well. (intransitive)

▶ **Auxiliary (Helping) Verbs** — Auxiliary verbs (helping verbs) help to form some of the *tenses*, the *mood*, and the *voice* of the main verb. (See pages 329–330.)

Auxiliary Verbs

is	will
am	would
are	shall
was	should
were	may
be	might
being	must
been	have
can	has
could	did

ELL Note: "Be" auxiliary verbs are always followed by either a verb ending in *ing* or a past participle.

▶ **Linking (State of Being) Verbs** — A linking verb is a special form of intransitive verb that links the subject of a sentence to a noun, a pronoun, or an adjective in the predicate.

> The streets **are** flooded. (adjective)

> The streets **are** rivers! (noun)

Common Linking Verbs

am	become	is
are	been	was
be	being	were

Additional Linking Verbs

appear	seem	remain
feel	sound	smell
look	grow	taste

Note: The verbs listed as "additional linking verbs" above function as linking verbs when they do not show actual action. An adjective usually follows these linking verbs.

> The sky **looked** ominous. (adjective)

> My little brother **grew** frightened. (adjective)

Note: When these same words are used as action verbs, an adverb, a prepositional phrase, or a direct object may follow them.

> I **looked** carefully at him. (adverb)

> My little brother **grew** corn for a science project. (direct object)

25-3b Forms of Verbs

A verb's form differs depending on its *number* (singular, plural), *person* (first, second, third), tense (present, past, future, present perfect, past perfect, future perfect), *voice* (active, passive), and *mood* (indicative, imperative, subjunctive).

▶ **Number of a Verb** — Number indicates whether a verb is singular or plural. The verb and its subject both must be singular, or they both must be plural. (See "Subject-Verb Agreement," pages 343–345.)

> My college **enrolls** high schoolers in summer programs. (singular)

> Many colleges **enroll** high schoolers in summer courses. (plural)

▶ **Person of a Verb** — Person indicates whether the subject of the verb is *first*, *second*, or *third person*. The verb and its subject must be in the same person. Verbs usually have a different form only in **third person singular of the present tense**.

	1st Person	2nd Person	3rd Person
Singular	I think	you think	he/she/it thinks
Plural	we think	you think	they think

▶ **Tense of a Verb** — Tense indicates the time of an action or state of being. There are three basic *tenses* (past, present, and future) and three verbal *aspects* (progressive, perfect, and perfect progressive).

Present tense: This tense expresses action happening at the present time or regularly.

> In the United States, more than 75 percent of workers **hold** service jobs.

Present progressive tense: This tense also expresses action that is happening continually, in an ongoing fashion at the present time, but it is formed by combining *am, are,* or *is* and the present participle (ending in *ing*) of the main verb.

> More women than ever before **are working** outside the home.

Present perfect tense: This tense expresses action that began in the past and has recently been completed or that continues up to the present time.

> My sister **has taken** four years of swimming lessons.

Present perfect progressive tense: This tense also expresses an action that began in the past but stresses the continuing nature of the action. Like the present progressive tense, it is formed by combining auxiliary verbs (*have been* or *has been*) and present participles.

> She **has been taking** them since she was six years old.

Past tense: This tense expresses action that was completed at a particular time in the past.

> A hundred years ago, more than 75 percent of laborers **worked** in agriculture.

Past progressive tense: This tense expresses past action that continued over time. It is formed by combining *was* or *were* with the present participle of the main verb.

> In 1900, my great-grandparents **were farming**.

Past perfect tense: This tense expresses an action in the past that was completed at a specific time before another past action occurred.

> By the time we sat down for dinner, my cousins **had eaten** all the olives.

Past perfect progressive tense: This tense expresses a past action but stresses the continuing nature of the action. It is formed by using *had been* along with the present participle.

> They **had been eating** the olives all afternoon.

Future tense: This tense expresses action that will take place in the future.

> Next summer I **will work** as a lifeguard.

Future progressive tense: This tense expresses an action that will be continuous in the future.

> I **will be working** for the park district at North Beach.

Future perfect tense: This tense expresses future action that will be completed by a specific time.

> By 10:00 p.m., I **will have completed** my research project.

Future perfect progressive tense: This tense also expresses future action that will be completed by a specific time but (as with other perfect progressive tenses) stresses the action's continuous nature. It is formed using *will have been* along with the present participle.

> I **will have been researching** the project for three weeks by the time it's due.

▶ **Voice of a Verb** — Voice indicates whether the subject is acting or being acted upon.

Active voice: This voice indicates that the subject of the verb is performing the action.

> People **update** their résumés on a regular basis. (The subject, *people*, is acting; *résumés* is the direct object.)

Quick Guide:
Using Active Voice

Generally, use active voice rather than passive voice for more direct, energetic writing. To change your passive sentences to active ones, do the following:

1. First, find the noun that is doing the action, and make it the subject.

2. Then find the word that had been the subject, and use it as the direct object.

Passive

The winning goal **was scored** by Eva. (The subject, *goal*, is not acting.)

Active

Eva **scored** the winning goal. (The subject, *Eva*, is acting.)

Note: When you want to emphasize the receiver more than the doer—or when the doer is unknown—use the passive voice. (Much technical and scientific writing regularly uses the passive voice.)

Passive voice: This voice indicates that the subject of the verb is being acted upon or is receiving the action. A passive verb is formed by combining a *be* verb with a past participle.

> Your résumé **should be updated** on a regular basis. (The subject, *résumé*, is receiving the action.)

▶ **Mood of a Verb** — The mood of a verb indicates the tone or attitude with which a statement is made.

Indicative mood: This mood, the most common, is used to state a fact or to ask a question.

> **Can** any theme **capture** the essence of the complex 1960s culture? President John F. Kennedy's directive [in the next column] **represents** one ideal popular during that decade.

Imperative mood: This mood is used to give a command. (The subject of an imperative sentence is *you*, which is usually understood and not stated in the sentence.)

> **Ask** not what your country can do for you—**ask** what you can do for your country.
> —John F. Kennedy

Subjunctive mood: This mood is used to express a wish, an impossibility or unlikely condition, or a necessity. The subjunctive mood is often used with *if* or *that*. The verb forms below create an atypical subject-verb agreement, forming the subjunctive mood.

> If I **were** rich, I would travel for the rest of my life. (a wish)

> If each of your brain cells **were** one person, there would be enough people to populate 25 planets. (an impossibility)

> The English Department requires that every student **pass** a proficiency test. (a necessity)

▶ **Verbals** — A verbal is a word that is made from a verb, but it functions as a noun, an adjective, or an adverb. There are three types of verbals: *gerunds, infinitives,* and *participles*.

Gerund: A **gerund** ends in *ing* and is used as a noun.

> **Waking** each morning is the first challenge. (subject)

> I start **moving** at about seven o'clock. (direct object)

> I work at **jump-starting** my weary system. (object of the preposition)

> As Woody Allen once said, "Eighty percent of life is **showing up**." (predicate nominative)

Infinitive: An **infinitive** is *to* and the base form of the verb. The infinitive may be used as a noun, an adjective, or an adverb.

> **To succeed** is not easy. (noun)

> That is the most important thing **to remember**. (adjective)

> Students are wise **to work** hard. (adverb)

ELL Note: It can be difficult to know whether a gerund or an infinitive should follow a verb. It's helpful to become familiar with lists of specific verbs that can be followed by one but not the other.

Participle: A **present participle** ends in *ing* and functions as an adjective. A **past participle** ends in *ed* (or another past tense form) and also functions as an adjective.

> The **studying** students were annoyed by the **partying** ones.

> The students **playing** loud music were **annoying**.

(These participles function as adjectives: *studying*, *partying*, *playing*, and *annoying* students. Notice, however, that *playing* has a direct object: *music*. All three types of verbals may have direct objects. See "Verbal Phrase" on page 339.)

studying student

Quick Guide: Using Verbals

Make sure that you use verbals correctly; look carefully at the examples below.

Verbal

Diving is a popular Olympic sport. (*Diving* is a gerund used as a subject.)

Diving gracefully, the Olympian hoped to get high marks. (*Diving* is a participle modifying *Olympian*.)

Active

The next competitor was **diving** in the practice pool. (Here, *diving* is a verb, not a verbal.)

25-3c Irregular Verbs

Irregular verbs can often be confusing. That's because the past tense and past participle of irregular verbs are formed by changing the word itself, not merely by adding *d* or *ed*. The following list contains the most troublesome irregular verbs.

Present Tense	Past Tense	Past Participle
am, be	was, were	been
arise	arose	arisen
awake	awoke, awaked	awoken, awaked
beat	beat	beaten
become	became	become
begin	began	begun
bite	bit	bitten, bit
blow	blew	blown
break	broke	broken
bring	brought	brought
build	built	built
burn	burnt, burned	burnt, burned
burst	burst	burst
buy	bought	bought
catch	caught	caught
choose	chose	chosen
come	came	come
cost	cost	cost
cut	cut	cut
dig	dug	dug
dive	dived, dove	dived
do	did	done
draw	drew	drawn
dream	dreamed, dreamt	dreamed, dreamt
drink	drank	drunk
drive	drove	driven
eat	ate	eaten
fall	fell	fallen
feel	felt	felt
fight	fought	fought
find	found	found
flee	fled	fled
fly	flew	flown
forget	forgot	forgotten, forgot
freeze	froze	frozen
get	got	gotten
give	gave	given
go	went	gone
grow	grew	grown
hang (execute)	hanged	hanged
hang (suspend)	hung	hung
have	had	had

Irregular Verbs Continued

Present Tense	Past Tense	Past Participle
hear	heard	heard
hide	hid	hidden
hit	hit	hit
keep	kept	kept
know	knew	known
lay	laid	laid
lead	led	led
leave	left	left
lend	lent	lent
let	let	let
lie (deceive)	lied	lied
lie (recline)	lay	lain
make	made	made
mean	meant	meant
meet	met	met
pay	paid	paid
prove	proved	proved, proven
put	put	put
read	read	read
ride	rode	ridden
ring	rang	rung
rise	rose	risen
run	ran	run
see	saw	seen
set	set	set
shake	shook	shaken
shine (light)	shone	shone
shine (polish)	shined	shined
show	showed	shown
shrink	shrank	shrunk
sing	sang	sung
sink	sank	sunk
sit	sat	sat
sleep	slept	slept
speak	spoke	spoken
spend	spent	spent
spring	sprang	sprung
stand	stood	stood
steal	stole	stolen
strike	struck	struck, stricken
strive	strove	striven
swear	swore	sworn
swim	swam	swum
swing	swung	swung
take	took	taken
teach	taught	taught
tear	tore	torn
tell	told	told
think	thought	thought

25-4 ADJECTIVE

An adjective describes or modifies a noun or pronoun. The articles *a, an,* and *the* are adjectives.

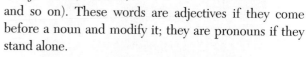

> Advertising is a **big** and **powerful** industry. (*A, big,* and *powerful* modify the noun *industry.*)

N o t e : Many demonstrative, indefinite, and interrogative forms may be used as either adjectives or pronouns (*that, these, many, some, whose,* and so on). These words are adjectives if they come before a noun and modify it; they are pronouns if they stand alone.

> **Some** advertisements are less than truthful. (*Some* modifies *advertisements* and is an adjective.)

> **Many** cause us to chuckle at their outrageous claims. (*Many* stands alone; it is a pronoun and replaces the noun *advertisements.*)

▸ **Proper Adjectives** — Proper adjectives are created from proper nouns and are capitalized.

> **English** has been influenced by advertising slogans. (proper noun)

> The **English** language is constantly changing. (proper adjective)

▸ **Predicate Adjectives** — A predicate adjective follows a form of the *be* verb (or other linking verb) and describes the subject. (See "Linking (State of Being) Verbs" on page 328.)

> At its best, advertising is **useful**; at its worst, **deceptive**. (*Useful* and *deceptive* modify the noun *advertising.*)

▸ **Forms of Adjectives** — Adjectives have three forms: *positive, comparative,* and *superlative.*

The **positive form** is the adjective in its regular form. It describes a noun or a pronoun without comparing it to anyone or anything else.

Joysport walking shoes are **strong** and **comfortable**.

The **comparative form** (*-er, more,* or *less*) compares two things. (*More* and *less* are used generally with adjectives of two or more syllables.)

Air soles make Mile Eaters **stronger** and **more comfortable** than Joysports.

The **superlative form** (*-est, most,* or *least*) compares three or more things. (*Most* and *least* are used most often with adjectives of two or more syllables.)

My old Canvas Wonders are the **strongest, most comfortable** shoes of all!

25-5 ADVERB

An adverb describes or modifies a verb, an adjective, another adverb, or a whole sentence. An adverb answers questions such as *how, when, where, why, how often,* or *how much.* (*Not* and *never* are adverbs.)

Adverbs can be placed in different positions in a sentence.

The temperature fell **sharply**. (*Sharply* modifies the verb *fell*.)

The temperature was **quite** low. (*Quite* modifies the adjective *low.*)

The temperature dropped **very quickly**. (*Very* modifies the adverb *quickly*, which modifies the verb *dropped.*)

Unfortunately, the temperature stayed cool. (*Unfortunately* modifies the whole sentence.)

▶ **Types of Adverbs** — Adverbs can be grouped in four ways: *time, place, manner,* and *degree.*

Time: These adverbs tell *when, how often,* and *how long.*

today • yesterday • daily • weekly • briefly • eternally

Place: These adverbs tell *where, to where,* and *from where.*

here • there • nearby • beyond • backward • forward

Manner: These adverbs often end in *ly* and tell *how* something is done.

precisely • regularly • regally • well

Degree: These adverbs tell *how much* or *how little.*

substantially • greatly • entirely

▶ **Forms of Adverbs** — Adverbs have three forms: *positive, comparative,* and *superlative.*

The **positive form** is the adverb in its regular form. It describes a verb, an adjective, or another adverb without comparing it to anyone or anything else.

With Joysport shoes, you'll walk **fast**. They support your feet **well**.

The **comparative form** (*-er, more,* or *less*) compares two things. (*More* and *less* are used generally with adverbs of two or more syllables.)

Wear Jockos instead of Joysports, and you'll walk **faster**. Jockos' special soles support your feet **better** than the Joysports do.

The **superlative form** (*-est, most,* or *least*) compares three or more things. (*Most* and *least* are used most often with adverbs of two or more syllables.)

Really, I walk **fastest** wearing my old Canvas Wonders. They seem to support my feet, my knees, and my pocketbook **best** of all.

Quick Guide:
Regular and Irregular Adverbs

	Regular	Irregular
Positive	fast	well
	effectively	badly
Comparative	faster	better
	more effectively	worse
Superlative	fastest	best
	most effectively	worst

25-6 PREPOSITION

A preposition is a word (or group of words) that shows the relationship between its object (a noun or pronoun following the preposition) and another word in the sentence.

> **Regarding** your reasons **for** going **to** college, do they all hinge **on** getting a good job **after** graduation? (In this sentence, *reasons, going, college, getting,* and *graduation* are objects of their preceding prepositions *regarding, for, to, on,* and *after.*)

Prepositions

aboard	concerning	onto
about	considering	on top of
above	despite	opposite
according to	down	out
across	down from	out of
across from	during	outside
after	except	outside of
against	except for	over
along	excepting	over to
alongside	for	owing to
alongside of	from	past
along with	from among	prior to
amid	from between	regarding
among	from under	round
apart from	in	save
around	in addition to	since
as far as	in behalf of	subsequent to
aside from	in front of	through
at	in place of	throughout
away from	in regard to	till
back of	inside	to
because of	inside of	together with
before	in spite of	toward
behind	instead of	under
below	into	underneath
beneath	like	until
beside	near	unto
besides	near to	up
between	of	upon
beyond	off	up to
but	on	with
by	on account of	within
by means of	on behalf of	without

ELL Note: Prepositions often pair up with a verb and become part of an idiom, a slang expression, or a two-word verb.

▶ **Prepositional Phrases** — A prepositional phrase includes the preposition, the object of the preposition, and the modifiers of the object. A prepositional phrase may function as an adverb or an adjective.

> A broader knowledge **of the world** is one benefit of **higher education**. (The two phrases function as adjectives modifying the nouns *knowledge* and *benefit* respectively.)

> He placed the flower **in the window**. (The phrase functions as an adverb modifying the verb *placed*.)

25-7 CONJUNCTION

A conjunction connects individual words or groups of words.

> **When** we came back to Paris, it was clear **and** cold **and** lovely.
> —Ernest Hemingway

▶ **Coordinating Conjunctions** — Coordinating conjunctions usually connect a word to a word, a phrase to a phrase, or a clause to a clause. The words, phrases, or clauses joined by a coordinating conjunction are equal in importance or are of the same type.

> Civilization is a race between education **and** catastrophe.
> —H. G. Wells

▶ **Correlative Conjunctions** — Correlative conjunctions are a type of coordinating conjunction used in pairs.

> There are two inadvisable ways to think: **either** believe everything **or** doubt everything.

▶ **Subordinating Conjunctions** — Subordinating conjunctions connect two clauses that are not equally important. A subordinating conjunction connects a dependent clause to an independent clause. The conjunction is part of the dependent clause.

> Experience is the worst teacher; it gives the test **before** it presents the lesson. (The clause *before it presents the lesson* is dependent. It connects to the independent clause *it gives the test.*)

Note: Relative pronouns can also connect clauses. (See "Relative Pronouns" on page 344.)

Conjunctions

Coordinating:
and • but • or • nor • for • so • yet

Correlative:
either • or; neither • nor; not only • but (but also); both • and; whether • or

Subordinating:
after • although • as • as if • as long as • because • before • even though • if • in order that • provided that • since • so that • than • that • though • unless • until • when • whenever • where • while

25-8 INTERJECTION

An interjection is a word or phrase that communicates strong emotion or surprise (*oh, ouch, hey, help,* and so on). Punctuation (often a comma or an exclamation point) is used to set off an interjection.

> **Hey! Wait! Well,** so much for catching the bus.

Note: Do not overuse interjections, especially in academic writing. Like shouting, too many interjections can distract from rather than enhance your writing.

➕ A Closer Look: Parts of Speech

Noun: A noun is a word that names something: a person, a place, a thing, or an idea.

Malcolm Gladwell/author	*Frozen*/film
UC–Davis/university	Renaissance/era
A Congress of Wonders/book	

Pronoun: A pronoun is a word used in place of a noun.

I	which	everybody
my	it	you
that	ours	
themselves	they	

Verb: A verb is a word that expresses action, links words, or acts as an auxiliary verb to the main verb.

are	run	catch	tear
break	sit	eat	were
drag	was	is	
fly	bite	see	

Adjective: An adjective describes or modifies a noun or pronoun. (The articles *a, an,* and *the* are adjectives.)

> **The carbonated drink** went down easy on **that hot, dry** day. (*The* and *carbonated* modify *drink; that, hot,* and *dry* modify *day.*)

Adverb: An adverb describes or modifies a verb, an adjective, another adverb, or a whole sentence. An adverb generally answers questions such as *how, when, where, how often,* or *how much.*

greatly	here	slowly
precisely	today	yesterday
regularly	partly	nearly
there	quickly	loudly

Preposition: A preposition is a word (or group of words) that shows the relationship between its object (a noun or pronoun that follows the preposition) and another word in the sentence. Prepositions introduce prepositional phrases, which are modifiers.

across	with	to
for	out	of

Conjunction: A conjunction connects individual words or groups of words.

and	for	so
because	or	yet
but	since	

Interjection: An interjection is a word that communicates strong emotion or surprise. Punctuation (often a comma or an exclamation point) is used to set off an interjection from the rest of the sentence.

> **Stop! No! What,** am I invisible?

26 | Sentences

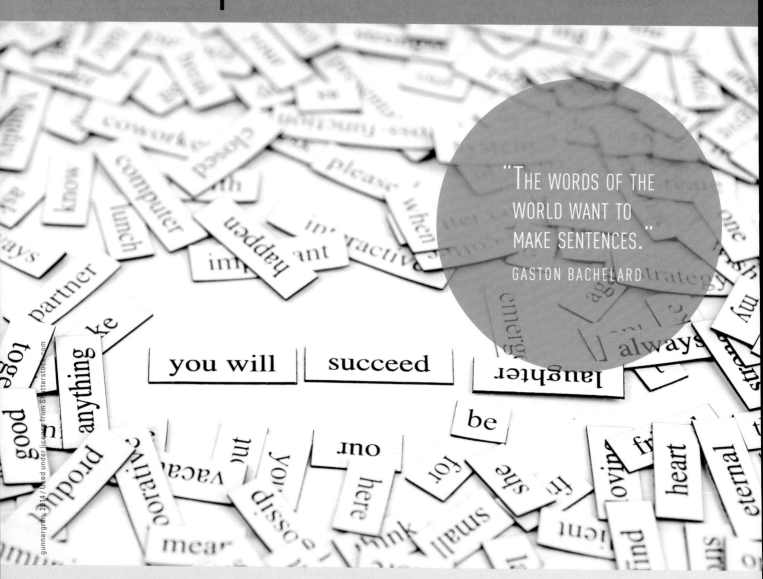

"THE WORDS OF THE WORLD WANT TO MAKE SENTENCES."
GASTON BACHELARD

you will   succeed

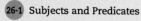

LEARNING OBJECTIVES

26-1 Subjects and Predicates

26-2 Phrases

26-3 Clauses

26-4 Sentence Variety

A sentence is made up of at least a subject (sometimes one that is understood) and a verb and expresses a complete thought. Sentences can make statements, ask questions, give commands, or express feelings.

> The Web delivers the universe in a box.

 26-1 # SUBJECTS AND PREDICATES

Sentences have two main parts: a **subject** and a **predicate**.

| Technology frustrates many people.

Note: In the sentence above, *technology* is the subject—the sentence talks about technology. *Frustrates many people* is the complete predicate—it tells what the subject is doing.

26-1a The Subject

The subject names the person or thing either performing the action, receiving the action, or being described or renamed. The subject is most often a noun or a pronoun.

| **Technology** is an integral part of almost every business.

| **Manufacturers** need technology to compete in the world market.

| **They** could not go far without it.

A verbal phrase or a noun dependent clause may also function as a subject.

| **To survive without technology** is difficult. (infinitive phrase)

| **Downloading information from the Web** is easy. (gerund phrase)

| **That the information age would arrive** was inevitable. (noun dependent clause)

Note: To determine the subject of a sentence, ask yourself *who* or *what* performs or receives the action or is described. In most sentences, the subject comes before the verb; however, in many questions and some other instances, that order is reversed.

ESL Note: Some languages permit the omission of a subject in a sentence; English does not. A subject must be included in every sentence. (The only exception is an "understood subject," which is discussed below.)

▶ **Simple Subject** — A **simple subject** is the subject without the words that describe or modify it.

| Thirty years ago, reasonably well-trained **mechanics** could fix any car on the road.

▶ **Complete Subject** — A **complete subject** is the simple subject and the words that describe or modify it.

| Thirty years ago, **reasonably well-trained mechanics** could fix any car on the road.

▶ **Compound Subject** — A **compound subject** is composed of two or more simple subjects joined by a conjunction and sharing the same predicate(s).

| Today, **mechanics** and **technicians** would need to master a half million manual pages to fix every car on the road.

| **Dealerships** and their service **departments** must sometimes explain that situation to the customers.

▶ **Understood Subject** — Sometimes a subject is **understood**. This means it is not stated in the sentence, but a reader clearly understands what the subject is. An understood subject occurs in a command (imperative sentence).

| **(You)** Park on this side of the street. (The subject *you* is understood.)

| Make a playlist of those songs.

▶ **Delayed Subject** — In sentences that begin with *There is, There was,* or *Here is,* the subject follows the verb.

| There are 70,000 **fans** in the stadium. (The subject is *fans; are* is the verb. *There* is an expletive, an empty word.)

| Here is a **problem** for stadium security. (*Problem* is the subject. *Here* is an adverb.)

The subject is also delayed in questions.

| Where was the **event**? (*Event* is the subject.)

| Was **Beyonce** performing? (*Beyonce* is the subject.)

26-1b The Predicate (Verb)

The **predicate**, which contains the verb, is the part of the sentence that either tells what the subject is doing, tells what is being done to the subject, or describes or renames the subject.

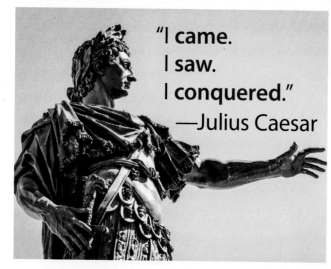

"I came.
I saw.
I conquered."
—Julius Caesar

FooTToo, 2014 / Used under license from Shutterstock.com

▶ **Simple Predicate** — A **simple predicate** is the complete verb without the words that describe or modify it. (The complete verb can consist of more than one word.)

| Today's workplace **requires** employees to have a range of skills.

▶ **Complete Predicate** — A **complete predicate** is the verb, all the words that modify or explain it, and any objects or complements.

| Today's workplace **requires employees to have a range of skills**.

▶ **Compound Predicate** — A **compound predicate** is composed of two or more verbs, all the words that modify or explain them, and any objects or complements.

| Engineers **analyze problems** and **calculate solutions**.

▶ **Direct Object** — A **direct object** is the part of the predicate that receives the action of an active transitive verb. A direct object makes the meaning of the verb complete.

| Marcos visited several **campuses**. (The direct object *campuses* receives the action of the verb *visited* by answering the question "Marcos visited what?")

Note: A direct object may be compound.

| A counselor explained the academic **programs** and the application **process**.

▶ **Indirect Object** — An **indirect object** is the word(s) that tells *to whom/to what* or *for whom/for what* something is done. A sentence must have a direct object before it can have an indirect object.

| I wrote **them** a note.

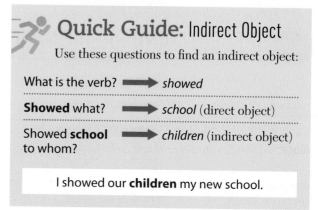

Quick Guide: Indirect Object

Use these questions to find an indirect object:

What is the verb?	➡	*showed*
Showed what?	➡	*school* (direct object)
Showed school to whom?	➡	*children* (indirect object)

| I showed our **children** my new school.

Note: An indirect object may be compound.

| I gave the **instructor** and a few **classmates** my email address.

26-2 PHRASES

A **phrase** is a group of related words that functions as a single part of speech. A phrase lacks a subject, a predicate, or both. There are three phrases in the following sentence:

Examples **of technology can be found in ancient civilizations**.

of technology
(prepositional phrase that functions as an adjective; no subject or predicate)

can be found
(verb phrase—all of the words of the verb; no subject)

in ancient civilizations
(prepositional phrase that functions as an adverb; no subject or predicate)

26-2a Types of Phrases

There are several types of phrases: *verb, verbal, prepositional, appositive,* and *absolute.*

▶ **Verb Phrase** — A **verb phrase** consists of a main verb and its helping verbs.

> Students, worried about exams, **have camped** at the library all week.

▶ **Verbal Phrase** — A **verbal phrase** is a phrase that expands on one of the three types of verbals: *gerund, infinitive,* or *participle.*

• **Gerund Phrase:** A gerund phrase consists of a gerund and its modifiers and objects. The whole phrase functions as a noun.

> **Becoming a marine biologist** is Rashanda's dream. (The gerund phrase is used as the subject of the sentence.)

> She has acquainted herself with the various methods for **collecting sea-life samples**. (The gerund phrase is the object of the preposition *for.*)

Note: Some sentences may contain a phrase that resembles a gerund phrase but is actually a present-participle phrase. A present-participle phrase functions as an adjective. If a comma is included directly after the phrase in a sentence, the phrase is likely a present participle. For example, the sentence "Working in a retail pharmacy for the summer, I learned how to manage many different personalities" contains a present participle phrase, not a gerund phrase. (See more on page 331.)

• **Infinitive Phrase:** An infinitive phrase consists of an infinitive and its modifiers and objects. The whole phrase functions as a noun, an adjective, or an adverb.

> **To dream** is the first step in any endeavor. (The infinitive phrase functions as a noun used as the subject.)

> Remember **to make a plan to realize your dream**. (The infinitive phrase *to make a plan* functions as a noun used as a direct object; *to realize your dream* functions as an adjective modifying *plan.*)

> Finally, apply all of your talents and skills **to achieve your goals**. (The infinitive phrase functions as an adverb modifying *apply.*)

• **Participial Phrase:** A participial phrase consists of a present or past participle (a verb form ending in *ing* or *ed*) and its modifiers. The phrase functions as an adjective.

> **Doing poorly in biology,** Theo signed up for a tutor. (The participial phrase modifies the noun *Theo.*)

> Some students **frustrated by difficult course work** don't seek help. (The participial phrase modifies the noun *students.*)

A Closer Look:
Functions of Verbal Phrases

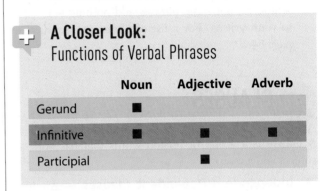

	Noun	Adjective	Adverb
Gerund	■		
Infinitive	■	■	■
Participial		■	

▶ **Prepositional Phrase** — A **prepositional phrase** is a group of words beginning with a preposition and ending with its object, a noun or a pronoun. Prepositional phrases are used mainly as adjectives and adverbs. See page 334 for a list of prepositions.

> Denying the existence **of exam week** hasn't worked **for anyone** yet. (The prepositional phrase *of exam week* is used as an adjective modifying the noun *existence; for anyone* is used as an adverb modifying the verb *has worked.*)

> Test days still dawn and GPAs still plummet **for the unprepared student**. (The prepositional phrase *for the unprepared student* is used as an adverb modifying the verbs *dawn* and *plummet.*)

ESL Note: Do not mistake the following adverbs for nouns and incorrectly use them as objects of prepositions: *here, there, everywhere.*

▶ **Appositive Phrase** — An **appositive phrase**, which follows a noun or a pronoun and renames it, consists of a noun and its modifiers. An appositive adds new information about the noun or pronoun it follows.

> The Olympic-size pool, **a prized addition to the physical education building,** gets plenty of use. (The appositive phrase renames *pool.*)

> **Absolute Phrase** — An **absolute phrase** consists of a noun and a participle (plus the participle's object, if there is one, and any modifiers). It usually modifies the entire sentence.

| **Their enthusiasm sometimes waning,** the students who cannot swim are required to take lessons. (The noun *enthusiasm* is modified by the present participle *waning;* the entire phrase modifies *students*.)

Note: Phrases can add valuable information to sentences, but some phrases add nothing but "fat" to your writing. For a list of phrases to avoid, see page 84.

26-3 CLAUSES

A **clause** is a group of related words that has both a subject and a verb.

> **Independent/Dependent Clauses** — An **independent clause** contains at least one subject and one verb, presents a complete thought, and can stand alone as a sentence; a **dependent clause** (also called a subordinate clause) does not present a complete thought and cannot stand alone (make sense) as a sentence.

| Though airplanes are twentieth-century inventions (dependent clause), people have always dreamed of flying (independent clause).

26-3a Types of Clauses

There are three basic types of dependent, or subordinate, clauses: *adverb, adjective,* and *noun.* These dependent clauses are combined with independent clauses to form complex and compound-complex sentences.

> **Adverb Clause** — An **adverb clause** is used like an adverb to modify a verb, an adjective, or an adverb. All adverb clauses begin with subordinating conjunctions.

| **Because Orville won a coin toss,** he got to fly the power-driven air machine first. (The adverb clause modifies the verb *got.*)

> **Adjective Clause** — An **adjective clause** is used like an adjective to modify a noun or a pronoun. Adjective clauses begin with relative pronouns (*which, that, who*).

The men **who invented the first airplane** were brothers, Orville and Wilbur Wright. (The adjective clause modifies the noun *men. Who* is the subject of the adjective clause.)

The first flight, **which took place December 17, 1903,** was made by Orville. (The adjective clause modifies the noun *flight. Which* is the subject of the adjective clause.)

> **Noun Clause** — A **noun clause** is used in place of a noun. Noun clauses can appear as subjects, as direct or indirect objects, as predicate nominatives, or as objects of prepositions. Noun clauses can also play a role in the independent clause. They are introduced by subordinating words such as *what, that, when, why, how, whatever, who, whom, whoever,* and *whomever.*

| He wants to know **what made modern aviation possible.** (The noun clause functions as the object of the infinitive.)

| **Whoever invents an airplane with vertical takeoff ability** will be a hero. (The noun clause functions as the subject.)

Note: If you can replace a whole clause with the pronoun *something* or *someone*, it is a noun clause.

26-4 SENTENCE VARIETY

A sentence can be classified according to the kind of statement it makes and according to the way it is constructed.

26-4a Kinds of Sentences

Sentences can make five basic kinds of statements: *declarative, interrogative, imperative, exclamatory,* or *conditional.*

> **Declarative Sentence** — **Declarative sentences** make statements. They tell us something about a person, a place, a thing, or an idea.

alvie_alive, 2014 / Used under license from Shutterstock.com

In 1955, Rosa Parks refused to follow segregation rules on a bus in Montgomery, Alabama.

▸ **Interrogative Sentence** — **Interrogative sentences** ask questions.

> Do you think Ms. Parks knew she was making history?

> Would you have had the courage to do what she did?

▸ **Imperative Sentence** — **Imperative sentences** give commands. They often contain an understood subject *(you)*.

> Read chapters 6 through 10 for tomorrow.

ESL Note: Imperative sentences with an understood subject are the only sentences in which it is acceptable to have no subjects stated.

▸ **Exclamatory Sentence** — **Exclamatory sentences** communicate strong emotion or surprise. They are punctuated with exclamation points.

> I simply can't keep up with these long reading assignments!

> Oh my gosh, you scared me!

▸ **Conditional Sentence** — **Conditional sentences** express two circumstances. One of the circumstances depends on the other circumstance. The words *if, when,* or *unless* are often used in the dependent clause in conditional sentences.

> **If** you practice a few study-reading techniques, college reading loads will be manageable.

> **When** I manage my time, it seems I have more of it.

> Don't ask me to help you **unless** you are willing to do the reading first.

26-4b Structure of Sentences

A sentence may be *simple, compound, complex,* or *compound-complex,* depending on how the independent and dependent clauses are combined.

▸ **Simple Sentence** — A **simple sentence** contains one independent clause. The independent clause

may have compound subjects and verbs, and it may also contain phrases.

> My **back aches**. (single subject: *back;* single verb: *aches*)

> My **teeth** and my **eyes hurt**. (compound subject: *teeth* and *eyes;* single verb: *hurt*)

> My **memory** and my **logic come** and **go**. (compound subject: *memory* and *logic;* compound verb: *come* and *go*)

> **I must need** a **vacation**. (single subject: *I;* single verb: *must need;* direct object: *vacation*)

▸ **Compound Sentence** — A **compound sentence** consists of two independent clauses. The clauses must be joined by a semicolon, by a comma and a coordinating conjunction (*and, but, or, nor, so, for, yet*), or by a semicolon followed by a conjunctive adverb (*besides, however, instead, meanwhile, then, therefore*) and a comma.

> I take good care of myself**;** I get enough sleep.

> I had eight hours of sleep, **so** why am I so exhausted?

> I still feel fatigued**; therefore,** I must need more exercise.

▸ **Complex Sentence** — A **complex sentence** contains one independent clause (in bold) and one or more dependent clauses (underlined).

> When I can, **I get eight hours of sleep**. (dependent clause; independent clause)

> When I get up on time, and if someone hasn't used up all the milk, **I eat breakfast**. (two dependent clauses; independent clause)

When the dependent clause comes before the independent clause, use a comma.

▸ **Compound-Complex Sentence** — A **compound-complex sentence** contains two or more independent clauses (in bold type) and one or more dependent clauses (underlined).

> If I'm not in a hurry, **I take leisurely walks,** and **I try to spot some wildlife**. (dependent clause; two independent clauses)

> **I saw a hawk** when I was walking, and **other smaller birds were chasing it**. (independent clause, dependent clause; independent clause)

27 | Sentence Errors

"OBSTACLES DON'T HAVE TO STOP YOU. IF YOU RUN INTO A WALL, DON'T TURN AROUND. FIGURE OUT HOW TO CLIMB IT, GO THROUGH IT, OR WORK AROUND IT."

MICHAEL JORDAN

LEARNING OBJECTIVES

27-1 Subject-Verb Agreement

27-2 Pronoun-Antecedent Agreement

27-3 Shifts in Sentence Construction

27-4 Fragments, Comma Splices, and Run-Ons

27-5 Misplaced and Dangling Modifiers

27-6 Ambiguous Wording

27-7 Nonstandard Language

This chapter will help you familiarize yourself with common sentence errors so that you will know what to watch for when editing your writing. Remember, sentence errors can derail the meaning of your writing, so be careful to avoid them.

 27-1 SUBJECT-VERB AGREEMENT

The subject and verb of any clause must agree in both *person* and *number*. *Person* indicates whether the subject of the verb is *first*, *second*, or *third* person. *Number* indicates whether the subject and verb are *singular* or *plural*.

	Singular	Plural
First Person	I think	we think
Second Person	you think	you think
Third Person	he/she/it thinks	they think

▶ **Agreement in Number** — A verb must agree in number (singular or plural) with its subject.

> The **student was** rewarded for her hard work. (Both the subject *student* and the verb *was* are singular; they agree in number.)

Note: Do not be confused by phrases that come between the subject and the verb. Such phrases may begin with words like *in addition to, as well as,* or *together with.*

> The **instructor**, as well as the students, is expected to attend the orientation. (*Instructor*, not *students*, is the subject.)

▶ **Compound Subjects** — **Compound subjects** connected with *and* usually require a plural verb.

> **Dedication and creativity are** trademarks of successful students.

Note: If a compound subject joined by *and* is thought of as a unit, use a singular verb.

> **Macaroni and cheese is** always available in the cafeteria.

▶ **Delayed Subjects** — **Delayed subjects** occur when the verb comes *before* the subject in a sen-

tence. In these inverted sentences, the true (delayed) subject must still agree with the verb.

> There **are** many nontraditional **students** on our campus. Here **is** the **syllabus** you need. (*Students* and *syllabus* are the subjects of these sentences, not the expletives *there* and *here*.)

Note: Using an inverted sentence, on occasion, will lend variety to your writing style. Simply remember to make the delayed subjects agree with the verbs.

> However, included among the list's topmost items **was "revise research paper."** (Because the true subject here is singular—one item— the singular verb *was* is correct.)

▶ **Titles as Subjects** — When the subject of a sentence is the title of a work of art, literature, or music, the verb should be singular. This is also true of a word (or phrase) being used as a word (or phrase).

> *Lyrical Ballads* **was published** in 1798 by two of England's greatest poets, Wordsworth and Coleridge. (Even though the title of the book, *Lyrical Ballads*, is plural in form, it is still a single title being used as the subject, correctly taking the singular verb *was*.)

> **"Over-the-counter drugs" is** a phrase that means nonprescription medications. (Even though the phrase is plural in form, it is still a single phrase being used as the subject, correctly taking the singular verb *is*.)

▶ **Singular Subjects with *Or* or *Nor*** — **Singular subjects** joined by *or* or *nor* take a singular verb.

> Neither a **textbook** nor a **notebook is required** for this class.

Note: When the subject nearer a present-tense verb is the singular pronoun *I* or *you*, the correct singular verb does not end in *s*.

> Neither **Marcus** nor **I feel** (not *feels*) right about this.

> Either **Rosa** or **you have** (not *has*) to take notes for me.

> Either **you** or **Rosa has** to take notes for me.

▶ **Singular/Plural Subjects** — When one of the subjects joined by *or* or *nor* is singular and one is plural, the verb must agree with the subject nearer the verb.

Neither the **professor** nor her **students were** in the lab. (The plural subject *students* is nearer the verb; therefore, the plural verb *were* agrees with *students*.)

Neither the **students** nor the **professor was** in the lab. (The singular subject *professor* is nearer the verb; therefore, the singular verb *was* is used to agree with *professor*.)

▸ **Collective Nouns** — Generally, **collective nouns** (*faculty, pair, crew, assembly, congress, species, crowd, army, team, committee,* and so on) take a singular verb. However, if you want to emphasize differences among individuals in the group or are referring to the group as individuals, you can use a plural verb.

My lab **team takes** its work very seriously. (*Team* refers to the group as a unit; it requires a singular verb, *takes*.)

The **team assume** separate responsibilities for each study they undertake. (In this example, *team* refers to individuals within the group; it requires a plural verb, *assume*.)

Note: Collective nouns such as (the) *police, poor, elderly,* and *young* use plural verbs.

The police direct traffic here between 7:00 and 9:00 a.m.

▸ **Plural Nouns with Singular Meaning** — Some nouns that are plural in form but singular in meaning take a singular verb: *mumps, measles, news, mathematics, economics, robotics,* and so on.

Economics is sometimes called "the dismal science."

The economic **news is** not very good.

Note: The most common exceptions are *scissors, trousers, tidings,* and *pliers.*

The **scissors are** missing again.

Are these **trousers** prewashed?

▸ **With Linking Verbs** — When a sentence contains a linking verb (usually a form of *be*)—and a noun or pronoun comes before and after that verb—the verb must agree with the subject, not the predicate nominative (the noun or pronoun coming after the verb).

The cause of his problem **was** poor study habits. (*Cause* requires a singular verb, even though the predicate nominative, *habits*, is plural.)

His poor study habits **were** the cause of his problem. (*Habits* requires a plural verb, even though the predicate nominative, *cause*, is singular.)

▸ **Nouns Showing Measurement, Time, and Money** — Mathematical phrases and phrases that name a period of time, a unit of measurement, or an amount of money take a singular verb.

Three and three **is** six.

Eight pages **is** a long paper on this topic.

In my opinion, two dollars **is** a high price for a cup of coffee.

▸ **Relative Pronouns** — When a **relative pronoun** (*who, which, that*) is used as the subject of a dependent clause, the number of the verb is determined by that pronoun's antecedent. (The *antecedent* is the word to which the pronoun refers.)

This is one of the **books that are** required for English class. (The relative pronoun *that* requires the plural verb *are* because its antecedent is *books*, not the word *one*. To test this type of sentence for agreement, read the *of* phrase first: *Of the books that are . . .*)

Note: Generally, the antecedent is the nearest noun or pronoun to the relative pronoun and is often the object of a preposition. Sometimes, however, the antecedent is not the nearest noun or pronoun, especially in sentences with the phrase "the only one of."

Dr. Graciosa wondered why Claire was the only **one** of her students **who was** not attending lectures regularly. (In this case, the addition of the modifiers *the only* changes the meaning of the sentence. The antecedent of *who* is *one*, not *students*. Only one student was not attending.)

▸ **Indefinites Pronoun with Singular Verbs** — Many indefinite pronouns (*someone, somebody, something; anyone, anybody, anything; no one,* *nobody, nothing; everyone, everybody, everything; each, either, neither, one, this*) serving as subjects require a singular verb.

| **Everybody is** welcome to attend the chancellor's reception.

| **No one was** sent an invitation.

Note: Although it may seem to indicate more than one, *each* is a singular pronoun and requires a singular verb. Do not be confused by words or phrases that come between the indefinite pronoun and the verb.

| **Each** of the new students **is** (not *are*) **encouraged** to attend the reception.

▸ **Indefinite Pronouns with Plural Verbs** — Some indefinite pronouns (*both, few, many, most,* and *several*) are plural; they require a plural verb.

| **Few are** offered the opportunity to study abroad.

| **Most take** advantage of opportunities closer to home.

▸ **Indefinite Pronouns or Quantity Words with Singular/Plural Verbs** — Some indefinite pronouns or quantity words (*all, any, most, part, half, none,* and *some*) may be either singular or plural, depending on the nouns they refer to. Look inside the prepositional phrase to see what the antecedent is.

| **Some** of the students **were** missing. (*Students*, the noun that *some* refers to, is plural; therefore, the pronoun *some* is considered plural, and the plural verb *were* is used to agree with it.)

| **Most** of the lecture **was** over by the time we arrived. (Because *lecture* is singular, *most* is also singular, requiring the singular verb *was*.)

27-2 PRONOUN–ANTECEDENT AGREEMENT

A pronoun must agree in number, person, and gender (sex) with its *antecedent*. The antecedent is the word to which the pronoun refers.

| **Yoshi** brought **his** laptop and iPad to school. (The pronoun *his* refers to the antecedent *Yoshi*. Both the pronoun and

its antecedent are singular, third person, and masculine; therefore, the pronoun is said to agree with its antecedent.)

▸ **Singular Pronoun** — Use a singular pronoun to refer to such antecedents as *each, either, neither, one, anyone, anybody, everyone, everybody, somebody, another, nobody,* and *a person*.

| **Each** of the maintenance vehicles has **their** doors locked at night. (Incorrect)

| **Each** of the maintenance vehicles has **its** doors locked at night. (Correct: Both *Each* and *its* are singular.)

| **Somebody** left **his or her** (not *their*) vehicle unlocked. (Correct)

▸ **Plural Pronoun** — When a plural pronoun (*they, their*) is mistakenly used with a singular indefinite pronoun (such as *everyone* or *everybody*), you may correct the sentence by replacing *their* or *they* with optional pronouns (*her* or *his* or *he* or *she*) or by making the antecedent plural.

| **Everyone** must learn to wait **their** turn. (Incorrect)

| **Everyone** must learn to wait **her or his** turn. (Correct: Optional pronouns *her* or *his* are used.)

| **People** must learn to wait **their** turns. (Correct: The singular antecedent, *Everyone*, is changed to the plural antecedent, *People*.)

▸ **Two or More Antecedents** — When two or more antecedents are joined by *and,* they are considered plural.

| **Tomas** and **Jamal** are finishing **their** assignments.

When two or more singular antecedents are joined by *or* or *nor,* they are considered singular.

| **Connie** or **Shavonn** left **her** headset in the library.

Note: If one of the antecedents is masculine and one feminine, the pronouns should likewise be masculine and feminine.

| Is **Ahmad** or **Phyllis** bringing **his or her** laptop?

Note: If one of the antecedents joined by *or* or *nor* is singular and one is plural, the pronoun is made to agree with the nearer antecedent.

> Neither **Ravi** nor **his friends** want to spend **their** time studying.
>
> Neither **his friends** nor **Ravi** wants to spend his time studying.

27-3 SHIFTS IN SENTENCE CONSTRUCTION

A shift is an improper change in structure midway through a sentence. The following examples will help you identify and fix several different kinds of shifts.

▶ **Shift in Person** — **Shift in person** is mixing first, second, or third person within a sentence.

> *Shift:* **One** may get spring fever unless **you** live in California or Florida. (The sentence shifts from third person, *one*, to second person, *you*.)
>
> *Corrected:* **You** may get spring fever unless **you** live in California or Florida. (Stays in second person)
>
> *Corrected:* **People** may get spring fever unless **they** live in California or Florida. (*People*, a third person plural noun, requires a third person plural pronoun, *they*.)

▶ **Shift in Tense** — **Shift in tense** is using more than one tense in a sentence when only one is needed.

> *Shift:* Sheila **looked** at nine apartments in one weekend before she **had chosen** one. (Tense shifts from past to past perfect for no reason.)
>
> *Corrected:* Sheila **looked** at nine apartments in one weekend before she **chose** one. (Tense stays in past.)

▶ **Shift in Voice** — **Shift in voice** is mixing active with passive voice. Usually, a sentence beginning in active voice should remain so to the end.

> *Shift:* As you look (active voice) for just the right place, many interesting apartments **will probably be seen**. (passive voice)
>
> *Corrected:* As you look (active voice) for just the right place, **you will probably see** (active voice) many interesting apartments.

▶ **Unparallel Construction** — **Unparallel construction** occurs when the kind of words or phrases being used shifts or changes in the middle of a sentence.

> *Shift:* In my hometown, people pass the time shooting pool, fishing, and at softball games. (Sentence shifts from a series of gerund phrases, *shooting pool* and *fishing*, to the prepositional phrase *at softball games*.)
>
> *Parallel:* In my hometown, people pass the time **shooting pool, fishing, and playing softball**. (Now all three activities are gerund phrases—they are consistent, or parallel.)

27-4 FRAGMENTS, COMMA SPLICES, AND RUN-ONS

Except in a few special situations, you should use complete sentences when you write. By definition, a complete sentence expresses a complete thought. However, a sentence may actually contain several ideas, not just one. The trick is getting those ideas to work together to form a clear, interesting sentence that expresses your exact meaning. Among the most common sentence errors that writers make are fragments, comma splices, and run-ons.

▶ **Fragments** — A **fragment** is a phrase or dependent clause used as a sentence. It is not a sentence, however, because a phrase lacks a subject, a verb, or some other essential part, and a dependent clause must be connected to an independent clause to complete its meaning.

> *Fragment:* Pete gunned the engine. Forgetting that the boat was hooked to the truck. (This is a sentence followed by a fragment. This error can be corrected by combining the fragment with the sentence.)

Corrected: Pete gunned the engine, forgetting that the boat was hooked to the truck.

Fragment: Even though my best friend had a little boy last year. (This clause does not convey a complete thought. We need to know what is happening despite the birth of the little boy.)

Corrected: Even though my best friend had a little boy last year, I do not comprehend the full meaning of "motherhood."

▶ **Comma Splices** — A **comma splice** is a mistake made when two independent clauses are connected ("spliced") with only a comma. The comma is not enough: A period, semicolon, or conjunction is needed.

Splice: People say that being a stay-at-home mom or dad is an important job, their actions tell a different story.

Corrected: People say that being a stay-at-home mom or dad is an important job, **but** their actions tell a different story. (The coordinating conjunction *but*, added after the comma, corrects the splice.)

Corrected: People say that being a stay-at-home mom or dad is an important job**;** their actions tell a different story. (A semicolon—rather than just a comma—makes the sentence correct.)

Corrected: People say that being a stay-at-home mom or dad is an important job. **Their** actions tell a different story. (A period creates two sentences and corrects the splice.)

▶ **Run-Ons** — A **run-on sentence** is actually two sentences (two independent clauses) joined without adequate punctuation or a connecting word.

Run-on: The Alamo holds a special place in American history it was the site of an important battle between the United States and Mexico.

Corrected: The Alamo holds a special place in American history **because** it was the site of an important battle between the United States and Mexico. (A subordinating conjunction is added to fix the run-on by making the second clause dependent.)

Run-on: Antonio de Santa Anna, the president of Mexico who once held a funeral for his amputated leg, is the same Santa Anna who stormed the Alamo he led his troops to victory over the Texan rebels defending that fort. Two famous American frontiersmen died they were James Bowie and Davy Crockett. Santa Anna enjoyed fame, power, and respect among his followers. He died in 1876 he was poor, blind, and ignored.

Corrected: Antonio de Santa Anna, the president of Mexico who once held a funeral for his amputated leg, is the same Santa Anna who stormed the Alamo. He led his troops to victory over the Texan rebels defending that fort. Two famous American frontiersmen were killed in the battle; they were James Bowie and Davy Crockett. Santa Anna enjoyed fame, power, and respect among his followers. When he died in 1876, he was poor, blind, and ignored.

The writer corrected the run-on sentences in the paragraph above by adding punctuation and making one sentence a dependent clause. The writer makes further improvements in the paragraph below by revising one sentence and by combining two sets of short sentences into one stronger sentence.

Improved

Antonio de Santa Anna, the president of Mexico who once held a funeral for his amputated leg, is the same Santa Anna who stormed the Alamo. He led his troops to victory over Texan rebels defending that fort. Two famous American frontiersmen, **James Bowie and Davy Crockett, were killed in the battle**. Santa Anna enjoyed fame, power, and respect among his followers; **but when** he died in 1876, he was poor, blind, and ignored.

Palto, 2014 / Used under license from Shutterstock.com

MISPLACED AND DANGLING MODIFIERS

Writing is thinking. Before you can write clearly, you must think clearly. Nothing is more frustrating for the reader than having to reread writing just to understand its basic meaning. Look carefully at the common errors that follow. Then use this section as a checklist when you revise. Always avoid leaving misplaced or dangling modifiers in your finished work.

▶ **Misplaced Modifiers** — **Misplaced modifiers** are descriptive words or phrases so separated from what they are describing that the reader is confused.

> *Misplaced:* The neighbor's dog has nearly been barking nonstop for two hours. (*Nearly* been barking?)
>
> *Corrected:* The neighbor's dog has been barking nonstop **for nearly two hours.** (Watch your placement of *only, just, nearly, barely,* and so on.)

> *Misplaced:* The commercial advertised an assortment of combs for active people with unbreakable teeth. (*People* with unbreakable teeth?)
>
> *Corrected:* The commercial advertised an assortment of **combs with unbreakable teeth** for active people. (*Combs* with unbreakable teeth)

> *Misplaced:* The pool staff gave large beach towels to the students marked with chlorine-resistant ID numbers. (*Students* marked with chlorine-resistant ID numbers?)
>
> *Corrected:* The pool staff gave **large beach towels marked with chlorine-resistant ID numbers** to the students. (*Towels* marked with chlorine-resistant ID numbers)

▶ **Dangling Modifiers** — **Dangling modifiers** are descriptive phrases that tell about a subject that isn't stated in the sentence. These often occur as participial phrases containing *ing* or *ed* words.

> *Dangling:* After standing in line all afternoon, the manager informed us that all the tickets had been sold. (It sounds as if the manager has been *standing in line all afternoon.*)
>
> *Corrected:* **After we had stood in line all afternoon,** the manager informed us that all the tickets had been sold.

> *Dangling:* After living in the house for one month, the electrician recommended we update all the wiring. (It sounds as if the electrician has been *living in the house.*)
>
> *Corrected:* After living in the house for one month, **we hired an electrician, who recommended we update all the wiring.**

AMBIGUOUS WORDING

Sloppy sentences confuse readers. No one should have to wonder, "What does this writer mean?" When you revise and edit, check for indefinite pronoun references, incomplete comparisons, and unclear wording.

▶ **Indefinite Pronoun References** — An **indefinite reference** is a problem caused by careless use of pronouns. There must always be a word or phrase nearby (its antecedent) that a pronoun clearly replaces.

> *Indefinite:* When Tonya put her dictionary on the shelf, it fell to the floor. (The pronoun *it* could refer to either the dictionary or the shelf since both are singular nouns.)
>
> *Corrected:* When Tonya put her dictionary on the shelf, **the shelf** fell to the floor.

> *Indefinite:* Juanita reminded Kerri that she needed to photocopy her résumé before going to her interview. (Who *needed to photocopy her résumé*—Juanita or Kerri?)
>
> *Corrected:* Juanita reminded Kerri **to photocopy her résumé before going to her interview.**

▶ **Incomplete Comparisons** — **Incomplete comparisons**—leaving out words that show exactly what is being compared to what—can confuse readers.

> *Incomplete:* After completing our lab experiment, we concluded that helium is lighter. (*Lighter* than what?)

> **Corrected:** After completing our lab experiment, we concluded that helium is lighter **than oxygen**.

▶ **Unclear Wording** — Avoid wording that has two or more possible meanings due to an unclear reference to something elsewhere in the sentence.

> *Unclear:* Dao intended to wash the car when he finished his homework, but he never did. (It is unclear which he never did—wash the car or finish his homework.)

> **Corrected:** Dao intended to wash the car when he finished his homework, **but he never did manage to wash the car.**

27-7 NONSTANDARD LANGUAGE

Nonstandard language is language that does not conform to the standards set by schools, media, and public institutions. It is often acceptable in everyday conversation and in fictional writing but seldom is used in formal speech or other forms of writing.

▶ **Colloquial Language** — **Colloquial language** is wording used in informal conversation that is unacceptable in formal writing.

> *Colloquial:* Hey, wait up! Cal wants to go with.
> Standard: **Hey, wait!** Cal wants to go with us.

▶ **Double Preposition** — The use of certain **double prepositions**—*off of, off to, from off*—is unacceptable.

> *Double Preposition:* Pick up the dirty clothes from off the floor.
> Standard: Pick up the dirty clothes **from the floor**.

▶ **Substitution** — Avoid substituting *and* for *to*.

> *Substitution:* Try and get to class on time.
> Standard: **Try to** get to class on time.

Avoid substituting *of* for *have* when combining with *could, would, should,* or *might*.

> *Substitution:* I should of studied for that exam.
> Standard: **I should have** studied for that exam.

▶ **Double Negative** — A double negative is a sentence that contains two negative words used to express a single negative idea. Double negatives are unacceptable in academic writing.

> *Double Negative:* After paying for essentials, I haven't got no money left.
> Standard: I **haven't got any** money left. / I **have no** money left.

▶ **Slang** — Avoid the use of slang or any "in" words in formal writing.

> *Slang:* The way the stadium roof opened was way cool.
> Standard: The way the stadium roof opened was **remarkable**.

Quick Guide:
Avoiding Sentence Problems

Does every subject agree with its verb?

- In person and number?
- When a word or phrase comes between the subject and the verb?
- When the subject is delayed?
- When the subject is a title?
- When a compound subject is connected with *or*?
- When the subject is a collective noun?
- When the subject is a relative pronoun?
- When the subject is an indefinite pronoun?

Does every pronoun agree with its antecedent?

- When the pronoun is a singular indefinite pronoun, such as *each, either,* or *another*?
- When two antecedents are joined with *and* or *or*?

Are any inappropriate shifts present?

- In person?
- In tense?
- From active voice to passive voice?
- In another unparallel construction?

Are all of your sentences complete?

- Have you used sentence fragments?
- Are some sentences "spliced" or run together?

Did you avoid any misplaced modifiers, ambiguous wording, or nonstandard language?

- Have you used misplaced or dangling modifiers?
- Have you used incomplete comparisons or indefinite references?
- Have you used slang or colloquial language?
- Have you used double negatives or double prepositions?

28 | Punctuation

"A PERIOD IS A STOP SIGN. A SEMICOLON IS A ROLLING STOP SIGN; A COMMA IS MERELY AN AMBER LIGHT."

ANDREW OFFUTT

marekuliasz, 2014 / Used under license from Shutterstock.com

LEARNING OBJECTIVES

This chapter will help you use correct punctuation. Applying these rules will make your writing clearer and easier to follow.

28-1 PERIOD

▶ **After Sentences** — Use a **period** to end a sentence that makes a statement, requests something, or gives a mild command.

> Statement: By 2014, women made up 56 percent of undergraduate students and 59 percent of graduate students**.**
>
> Request: Please read the instructions carefully**.**
>
> Mild command: If your topic sentence isn't clear, rewrite it**.**
>
> Indirect question: The professor asked if we had completed the test**.**

Note: It is not necessary to place a period after a statement that has parentheses around it and is part of another sentence.

> Think about joining a club (**the student affairs office has a list of organizations**) for fun and for leadership experience.

▶ **After Initials and Abbreviations** — Use a period after an initial and some abbreviations.

Mr.	Mrs.	B.C.E.	Ph.D.	Sen. John McCain
Jr.	Sr.	D.D.S.	U.S.	Booker T. Washington
Dr.	M.A.	p.m.	B.A.	A. A. Milne

Some abbreviations (such as *pm*) also can be written without periods. Use no spacing in abbreviations except when providing a person's initials. When an abbreviation is the last word in a sentence, use only one period at the end of the sentence.

> Mikhail eyed each door until he found the name Rosa Lopez, **Ph.D.**

▶ **As Decimal Points** — Use a period as a decimal point.

> The government spends approximately **$15.5** million each year just to process student loan forms.

28-2 ELLIPSIS

▶ **To Show Omitted Words** — Use an **ellipsis** (three periods) to show that one or more words have been omitted in a quotation. When typing, leave one space before and after each period.

> (Original) We the people **of the United States**, in order to form a more perfect Union, **establish justice, insure domestic tranquility, provide for the common defense, promote the general welfare, and secure the blessings of liberty to ourselves and our posterity, do ordain and** establish this Constitution for the United States of America.
> —Preamble, U.S. Constitution

> (Quotation) "We the people . . . in order to form a more perfect Union . . . establish this Constitution for the United States of America."

Note: Omit internal punctuation (a comma, a semicolon, a colon, or a dash) on either side of the ellipsis marks unless it is needed for clarity.

▶ **To Use After Sentences** — If words from a quotation are omitted at the end of a sentence, place the ellipsis after the period or other end punctuation.

> (Quotation) "Five score years ago, a great American, in whose symbolic shadow we stand, signed the Emancipation Proclamation. . . . But one hundred years later, we must face the tragic fact that the Negro is still not free."
> —Martin Luther King, Jr., "I Have a Dream"

The first word of a sentence following a period and an ellipsis may be capitalized, even though it was not capitalized in the original.

> (Quotation) "Five score years ago, a great American . . . signed the Emancipation Proclamation. . . . **O**ne hundred years later . . . the Negro is still not free."

Note: If the quoted material forms a complete sentence (even if it was not in the original), use a period, then an ellipsis.

> (Original) I am tired; my heart is sick and sad. From where the sun now stands I will fight no more forever. —Chief Joseph of the Nez Percé

> (Quotation) "I am tired. . . . I will fight no more forever."

▶ **To Show Pauses** — Use an ellipsis to indicate a pause or to show unfinished thoughts.

> Listen . . . did you hear that?
>
> I can't figure out . . . this number doesn't . . . just how do I apply the equation in this case?

28-3 QUESTION MARK

▶ **After Direct Questions** — Use a **question mark** at the end of a direct question.

> What can I know? What ought I to do? What may I hope? —Immanuel Kant
>
> Since when do you have to agree with people to defend them from injustice? —Lillian Hellman

▶ **Not After Indirect Questions** — No question mark is used after an indirect question.

> After listening to Edgar sing, Mr. Noteworthy asked him if he had ever had formal voice training.

Note: When a single-word question like *how, when,* or *why* is woven into the flow of a sentence, capitalization and special punctuation are not usually required.

> The questions we need to address at our next board meeting are not *why* or *whether,* but *how* and *when.*

▶ **After Quotations That Are Questions** — When a question ends with a quotation that is also a question, use only one question mark, and place it within the quotation marks. (Also see page 359.)

> Do you often ask yourself, "What should I be?"

▶ **To Show Uncertainty** — Use a question mark within parentheses to show uncertainty about a word or phrase within a sentence.

> This July will be the 34th (?) anniversary of the first moon walk.

Note: Do *not* use a question mark in this manner for formal writing.

▶ **For Questions in Parentheses or Dashes** — A question within parentheses—or a question set off by dashes—is punctuated with a question mark unless the entire sentence ends with a question mark.

> You must consult your handbook (**what choice do you have?**) when you need to know a punctuation rule.
>
> Should I use your charge card (you have one, don't you), or should I pay cash?
>
> Maybe somewhere in the pasts of these humbled people, there were cases of bad mothering or absent fathering or emotional neglect—**what family surviving the '50s was exempt?**—but I couldn't believe these human errors brought the physical changes in Frank.
> —Mary Kay Blakely, *Wake Me When It's Over*

28-4 COMMA

▶ **Between Independent Clauses** — Use a **comma** between independent clauses that are joined by a coordinating conjunction (*and, but, or, nor, for, yet, so*).

> The television show *Game of Thrones* is closely adapted from George R.R. Martin's series of fantasy novels, **but** the show and books do have some differing plot points.

Note: Do not confuse a compound verb with a compound sentence.

> Martin is an executive producer for *Game of Thrones* and scripts one episode per season. (compound verb)
>
> The first book in Martin's series of novels is called *A Game of Thrones,* but the book series itself is titled *A Song of Fire and Ice.* (compound sentence)

▶ **Between Items in a Series** — Use commas to separate individual words, phrases, or clauses in a series. (A series contains at least three items.)

> Many college students must balance studying with **taking care of a family, working a job, getting exercise, and finding time to relax.**

Note: Do *not* use commas when all the items in a series are connected with *or, nor,* or *and.*

> Hmm . . . should I study **or** do laundry **or** go out?

To Separate Adjectives — Use commas to separate adjectives that *equally* modify the same noun. Notice in the examples below that no comma separates the last adjective from the noun.

> You should exercise regularly and follow a **sensible, healthful** diet.

> A good diet is one that includes lots of **high-protein, low-fat** foods.

Quick Guide:
To Determine Equal Modifiers

To determine whether the adjectives in a sentence modify a noun *equally*, use these two tests.

1. Reverse the order of the adjectives; if the sentence is clear, the adjectives modify equally. (In the example below, *hot* and *crowded* can be reversed, and the sentence is still clear; *short* and *coffee* cannot.)

> Matt was tired of working in the **hot, crowded** lab and decided to take a **short coffee** break.

2. Insert *and* between the adjectives; if the sentence reads well, use a comma when *and* is omitted. (The word *and* can be inserted between *hot* and *crowded*, but *and* does not make sense between *short* and *coffee*.)

To Set Off Nonrestrictive Appositives — A specific kind of explanatory word or phrase called an appositive identifies or renames a preceding noun or pronoun.

> Albert Einstein, **the famous mathematician and physicist,** developed the theory of relativity.

Note: Do **not** use commas with restrictive appositives. A *restrictive appositive* is essential to the basic meaning of the sentence.

> The famous mathematician and physicist **Albert Einstein** developed the theory of relativity.

To Set Off Adverb Dependent Clauses — Use a comma after most introductory dependent clauses functioning as adverbs.

> **Although Charlemagne was a great patron of learning,** he never learned to write properly. (adverb dependent clause)

You may use a comma if the adverb dependent clause following the independent clause is not essential. Adverb clauses beginning with *even though*, *although*, *while*, or *another* conjunction expressing a contrast are usually not needed to complete the meaning of a sentence.

> Charlemagne never learned to write properly, **even though he continued to practice**. (adverb dependent clause)

Note: A comma is *not* used if the dependent clause following the independent clause is needed to complete the meaning of the sentence.

> Maybe Charlemagne didn't learn **because he had an empire to run**.

After Introductory Phrases — Use a comma after introductory phrases.

> **In spite of his practicing,** Charlemagne's handwriting remained poor.

Note: A comma is usually omitted if the phrase follows an independent clause.

> Charlemagne's handwriting remained poor **in spite of his practicing**.

Also Note: You may omit the comma after a short (four or fewer words) introductory phrase unless it is needed to ensure clarity.

> **At 6:00 a.m.** he would rise and practice his penmanship.

To Set Off Transitional Expressions — Use a comma to set off conjunctive adverbs and transitional phrases. (See page 356.)

> Handwriting is not, **as a matter of fact,** easy to improve upon later in life; **however,** it can be done if you are determined enough.

Note: If a transitional expression blends smoothly with the rest of the sentence, it does not need to be set off. **Example:** If you are in fact coming, I'll see you there.

► **To Set Off Items in Addresses and Dates** — Use commas to set off items in an address and the year in a date.

> Send your letter to **1600 Pennsylvania Avenue, Washington, DC 20006, before January 1, 2014,** or send an email to president@ whitehouse.gov.

Note: No comma is placed between the state and ZIP code. Also, no comma separates the items if only the month and year are given: January 2014.

► **To Set Off Dialogue** — Use commas to set off the words of the speaker from the rest of the sentence.

> **"Never be afraid to ask for help,"** advised Ms. Kane.

> **"With the evidence that we now have,"** Professor Thom said, **"many scientists believe there is life on Mars."**

► **To Separate Nouns of Direct Address** — Use a comma to separate a noun of direct address from the rest of the sentence.

> **Jamie,** would you please stop whistling while I'm trying to work?

Let's eat grandma.
Let's eat, grandma.

Punctuation Saves Lives

Tomacco, 2014 / Used under license from Shutterstock.com

A Closer Look:
Nonrestrictive and Restrictive Clauses and Phrases

Use Commas with Nonrestrictive Clauses and Phrases

Use commas to enclose **nonrestrictive** (unnecessary) phrases or dependent (adjective) clauses. A nonrestrictive phrase or dependent clause adds information that is not necessary to the basic meaning of the sentence. For example, if the clause or phrase (in **boldface**) were left out of the two examples below, the meaning of the sentences would remain clear. Therefore, commas are used to set off the nonrestrictive information.

> The locker rooms in Swain Hall, **which were painted and updated last summer,** give professors a place to shower. (nonrestrictive clause)

> Work-study programs, **offered on many campuses,** give students the opportunity to earn tuition money. (nonrestrictive phrase)

Don't Use Commas with Restrictive Clauses and Phrases

Do *not* use commas to set off **restrictive** (necessary) adjective clauses and phrases. A restrictive clause or phrase adds information that the reader needs to understand the sentence. For example, if the adjective

clause and phrase (in **boldface**) were dropped from the examples that follow, the meaning would be unclear.

> Only the professors **who run at noon** use the locker rooms in Swain Hall to shower. (restrictive clause)

> Using tuition money **earned through work-study programs** is the only way some students can afford to go to college. (restrictive phrase)

Using "That" or "Which"

Use *that* to introduce restrictive (necessary) adjective clauses; use *which* to introduce nonrestrictive (unnecessary) adjective clauses. When the two words are used in this way, the reader can quickly distinguish the necessary information from the unnecessary.

> Campus jobs **that are funded by the university** are awarded to students only. (restrictive)

> The cafeteria, **which is run by an independent contractor,** can hire nonstudents. (nonrestrictive)

Note: Clauses beginning with *who* can be either restrictive or nonrestrictive.

> Students **who pay for their own education** are highly motivated. (restrictive)

> The admissions counselor, **who has studied student records,** said that many returning students earn high GPAs in spite of demanding family obligations. (nonrestrictive)

354   PART Three: Handbook

▶ **To Separate Interjections** — Use a comma to separate a mild interjection from the rest of the sentence.

▌ **Okay,** so now what do I do?

Note: Exclamation points are used after strong interjections: Wow! You're kidding!

▶ **To Set Off Interruptions** — Use commas to set off a word, phrase, or clause that interrupts the movement of a sentence. Such expressions usually can be identified through the following tests: (1) They may be omitted without changing the meaning of a sentence; and (2) they may be placed nearly anywhere in the sentence without changing its meaning.

▌ For me, **well,** it was just a good job gone!
▌ —Langston Hughes, "A Good Job Gone"

▌ Lela, **as a general rule,** always comes to class ready for a pop quiz.

▶ **To Separate Numbers** — Use commas to separate a series of numbers to distinguish hundreds, thousands, millions, and so on.

▌ Do you know how to write the amount **$2,025** on a check?
▌ **25,000**   **973,240**   **18,620,197**

▶ **To Enclose Explanatory Words** — Use commas to enclose an explanatory word or phrase.

▌ Time management, **according to many professionals,** is such an important skill that it should be taught in college.

▶ **To Separate Contrasted Elements** — Use commas to separate contrasted elements within a sentence.

▌ We work to become, **not to acquire**.
▌ —Eugene Delacroix

▌ Where all think alike, **no one thinks very much**.
▌ —Walter Lippmann

▶ **Before Tags** — Use commas before tags, which are short statements or questions at the ends of sentences.

▌ You studied for the test, **right**?

▶ **To Enclose Titles or Initials** — Use commas to enclose a title or initials and given names that follow a surname.

▌ Until Martin, **Sr.,** was 15, he never had more than three months of schooling in any one year.
▌ —Ed Clayton

▌ The genealogical files included the names Sanders, **L. H.,** and Sanders, **Lucy Hale**.

Note: Some style manuals no longer require commas around titles.

▶ **For Clarity or Emphasis** — Use a comma for clarity or for emphasis. There will be times when none of the traditional rules call for a comma, but one will be needed to prevent misreading or to emphasize an important idea.

▌ What she does, does matter to us. (clarity)

▌ It may be those who do most, dream most. (emphasis)
▌ —Stephen Leacock

Quick Guide:
Avoid Overusing Commas

The commas (in **red**) below are used incorrectly. Do *not* use a comma between the subject and its verb or the verb and its object.

> Current periodicals on the subject of psychology, are available at nearly all bookstores.
>
> I think she should read, *Psychology Today*.

Do *not* use a comma before an indirect quotation.

> My roommate said, that she doesn't understand the notes I took.

28-5 SEMICOLON

▶ **To Join Two Independent Clauses** — Use a **semicolon** to join two or more closely related independent clauses that are not connected with a coordinating conjunction. In other words, each of the clauses could stand alone as a separate sentence.

▌ I was thrown out of college for cheating on the metaphysics exam**;** I looked into the soul of the boy next to me. —Woody Allen

- **Before Conjunctive Adverbs** — Use a semicolon before a conjunctive adverb when the word clarifies the relationship between two independent clauses in a compound sentence. A comma often follows the conjunctive adverb. Common conjunctive adverbs include *also, besides, however, instead, meanwhile, then,* and *therefore.*

  > Many college freshmen are on their own for the first time**; however,** others are already independent and even have families.

- **Before Transitional Phrases** — Use a semicolon before a transitional phrase when the phrase clarifies the relationship between two independent clauses in a compound sentence. A comma usually follows the transitional phrase.

  > Pablo was born in the Andes**; as a result,** he loves mountains.

Transitional Phrases

after all	in addition
as a matter of fact	in conclusion
as a result	in fact
at any rate	in other words
at the same time	in the first place
even so	on the contrary
for example	on the other hand
for instance	

- **To Separate Independent Clauses Containing Commas** — Use a semicolon to separate independent clauses that contain internal commas, even when the independent clauses are connected by a coordinating conjunction.

  > Your tablet computer, bike, and other valuables are expensive to replace**;** so include these items in your homeowner's insurance policy, and remember to use the locks on your door, bike, and storage area.

- **To Separate Items in a Series That Contains Commas** — Use a semicolon to separate items in a series that already contain commas.

  > My favorite foods are pizza with pepperoni, onions, and olives**;** peanut butter and banana sandwiches**;** and liver with bacon, peppers, and onions.

28-6 COLON

- **After Salutations** — Use a **colon** after the salutation of a business letter.

  > Dear Mr. Spielberg**:**   Dear Professor Higgins**:**
  > Dear Members**:**

- **Between Numbers Indicating Time or Ratios** — Use a colon between the hours, minutes, and seconds of a number indicating time.

  > 8:30 p.m.   9:45 a.m.   10:24:55

  Use a colon between two numbers in a ratio.

  > The ratio of computers to students is 1:20. (one to twenty)

- **For Emphasis** — Use a colon to emphasize a word, a phrase, a clause, or a sentence that explains or adds impact to the main clause.

  > I have one goal for myself**:** to become the first person in my family to graduate from college.

- **To Distinguish Parts of Publications** — Use a colon between a title and a subtitle, volume and page, and chapter and verse.

  > *Ron Brown: An Uncommon Life*
  > *Britannica* 4**:** 211   Psalm 23**:**1–6

- **To Introduce Quotations** — Use a colon to introduce a quotation following a complete sentence.

  > **John Locke is credited with this prescription for a good life:** "A sound mind in a sound body."

  > **Lou Gottlieb, however, offered this version:** "A sound mind or a sound body—take your pick."

- **To Introduce a List** — Use a colon to introduce a list following a complete sentence.

  > **A college student needs a number of things to succeed:** basic skills, creativity, and determination.

28-7 HYPHEN

▶ **In Compound Words** — Use a **hyphen** to make some compound words.

> mother-in-law (noun)
> three-year-old (noun or adjective)

Writers sometimes combine words in new and unexpected ways. Such combinations are usually hyphenated.

> And they pried pieces of **baked-too-fast** sunshine cake from the roofs of their mouths and looked once more into the boy's eyes.
> —Toni Morrison, *Song of Solomon*

Note: Consult a dictionary to find how it lists a particular compound word. Some compound words (*living room*) do not use a hyphen and are written separately. Some are written solid (*bedroom*). Some do not use a hyphen when the word is a noun (*ice cream*) but do use a hyphen when it is a verb or an adjective (*ice-cream sundae*).

▶ **To Join Letters and Words** — Use a hyphen to join a capital letter or a lowercase letter to a noun or a participle.

> T-shirt   U-turn   V-shaped   x-ray

▶ **To Join Words in Compound Numbers** — Use a hyphen to join the words in compound numbers from twenty-one to ninety-nine when it is necessary to write them out. (See page 382.)

> **Forty-two** people found seats in the cramped classroom.

▶ **Between Numbers in Fractions** — Use a hyphen between the numerator and the denominator of a fraction, but not when one or both of these elements are already hyphenated.

> four-tenths   five-sixteenths
> seven thirty-seconds (7/32)

▶ **In a Special Series** — Use a hyphen when two or more words have a common element that is omitted in all but the last term.

> We have cedar posts in **four-, six-,** and **eight-inch** widths.

▶ **To Create New Words** — Use a hyphen to form new words beginning with the prefixes *self, ex, all,* and *half.* Also use a hyphen to join any prefix to a proper noun, a proper adjective, or the official name of an office.

> post-Depression   mid-May   ex-mayor

▶ **To Prevent Confusion** — Use a hyphen with prefixes or suffixes to avoid confusion or awkward spelling.

> **re-cover** (not *recover*) the sofa
> **shell-like** (not *shelllike*) shape

▶ **To Join Numbers** — Use a hyphen to join numbers indicating a range, a score, or a vote.

> Students study **30-40** hours a week.
> The final score was **84-82.**

▶ **To Divide Words** — Use a hyphen to divide a word between syllables at the end of a line of print.

Guidelines for Word Division

1. Leave enough of the word at the end of the line to identify the word.
2. Never divide a one-syllable word: **rained, skills, through.**
3. Avoid dividing a word of five or fewer letters: **paper, study, July.**
4. Never divide a one-letter syllable from the rest of the word: **omit-ted,** not **o-mitted.**
5. Always divide a compound word between its basic units: **sister-in-law,** not **sis-ter-in-law.**
6. Never divide abbreviations or contractions: **shouldn't,** not **should-n't.**
7. When a vowel is a syllable by itself, divide the word after the vowel: **epi-sode,** not **ep-isode.**
8. Avoid dividing a numeral: **1,000,000,** not **1,000,-000.**
9. Avoid dividing the last word in a paragraph.
10. Never divide the last word in more than two lines in a row.
11. Check a dictionary for acceptable word divisions.

▶ **To Form Adjectives** — Use a hyphen to join two or more words that serve as a single-thought adjective before a noun.

> In real life I am a large, **big-boned** woman with rough, **man-working** hands.
> —Alice Walker, "Everyday Use"

Most single-thought adjectives are not hyphenated when they come after the noun. (Check the dictionary to be sure.)

> In real life, I am large and **big boned.**

Note: When the first of these words is an adverb ending in *ly*, do not use a hyphen. Also, do not use a hyphen when a number or a letter is the final element in a single-thought adjective.

fresh**ly** painted barn

grade **A** milk (letter is the final element)

28-8 DASH

▶ **To Set Off Nonessential Elements** — Use a **dash** to set off nonessential elements—explanations, examples, or definitions—when you want to emphasize them.

Near the semester's end—**and this is not always due to poor planning**—some students may find themselves in academic trouble.

The term *caveat emptor*—**let the buyer beware**—is especially appropriate to Internet shopping.

Note: Don't use a single hyphen when a dash (two hyphens) is required.

▶ **To Set Off an Introductory Series** — Use a dash to set off an introductory series from the clause that explains the series.

Cereal, coffee, and Twitter—without these I can't get going in the morning.

▶ **To Show Missing Text** — Use a dash to show that words or letters are missing.

Mr. — won't let us marry. —Alice Walker, *The Color Purple*

▶ **To Show Interrupted Speech** — Use a dash (or an ellipsis) to show interrupted or faltering speech in dialogue. (Also see pages 351–352.)

Well, I—**ah**—had this terrible case of the flu, **and—then—ah—the** library closed because of that flash flood, **and—well—the** high humidity jammed my printer.
—Excuse No. 101

"If you *think* you can—"
"Oh, I *know*—"
"Don't interrupt!"

▶ **For Emphasis** — Use a dash in place of a colon to introduce or to emphasize a word, a series, a phrase, or a clause.

Jogging—that's what he lives for.

Life is like a grindstone—whether it grinds you down or polishes you up depends on what you're made of.

This is how the world moves—not like an arrow, but a boomerang.
—Ralph Ellison

28-9 QUOTATION MARKS

▶ **To Punctuate Titles** — Use **quotation marks** to punctuate some titles. (Also see page 360.)

"Two Friends" (short story)
"New Car Designs" (newspaper article)
"Let It Go" (song)
"Multiculturalism and the Language Battle" (lecture title)
"The New Admissions Game" (magazine article)
"Reflections on Advertising" (chapter in a book)
"Blink" (television episode from *Doctor Who*)
"Annabel Lee" (short poem)

▶ **For Special Words** — Use quotation marks (1) to show that a word is being discussed as a word, (2) to indicate that a word or phrase is directly quoted, (3) to indicate that a word is slang, or (4) to point out that a word is being used in a humorous or ironic way.

A commentary on the times is that the word **"honesty"** is now preceded by **"old-fashioned."**

She said she was **"incensed."**

I drank a Dixie and ate bar peanuts and asked the bartender where I could hear **"chanky-chank,"** as Cajuns call their music.
—William Least Heat-Moon, *Blue Highways*

In an attempt to be popular, he works very hard at being **"cute."**

Note: A word used as a word can be italicized instead of using quotation marks.

▶ **Placement of Periods or Commas** — Always place periods and commas inside quotation marks.

"Dr. Slaughter wants you to have liquids, Will**,**" Mama said anxiously. "He said not to give you any solid food tonight**.**"
—Olive Ann Burns, *Cold Sassy Tree*

▶ **Placement of Exclamation Points or Question Marks** — Place an exclamation point or a question mark inside quotation marks when it punctuates both the main sentence and the quotation or just the quotation; place it outside when it punctuates the main sentence.

> Do you often ask yourself, "What should I be**?**"

> I almost croaked when he asked, "That won't be a problem, will it**?**"

> Did he really say, "Finish this by tomorrow"**?**

▶ **Placement of Semicolons or Colons** — Always place semicolons or colons outside quotation marks.

> I just read "Computers and Creativity"**;** I now have some different ideas about the role of computers in the arts.

A Closer Look:
Marking Quoted Material

For Direct Quotations

Use quotation marks before and after a direct quotation—a person's exact words.

> Sitting in my one-room apartment, I remember Mom saying, **"Don't go to the party with him."**

Note: Do *not* use quotation marks for *indirect* quotations.

> I remember Mom saying **that I should not date him**. (These are not the speaker's exact words.)

For Quoted Passages

Use quotation marks before and after a quoted passage. Any word that is not part of the original quotation must be placed inside brackets.

> (Original) First of all, it must accept responsibility for providing shelter for the homeless.

> (Quotation) "First of all, it **[the federal government]** must accept responsibility for providing shelter for the homeless."

Note: If you quote only part of the original passage, be sure to construct a sentence that is both accurate and grammatically correct.

> The report goes on to say that the federal government **"must accept responsibility for providing shelter for the homeless."**

For Long Quotations

If more than one paragraph is quoted, quotation marks are placed before each paragraph and at the end of the last paragraph (**Example A**). Quotations that are five or more lines (MLA style) or forty words or more (APA style) are usually set off from the text by indenting ten spaces from the left margin (a style called "block form"). Do not use quotation marks before or after a block-form quotation (**Example B**), except in cases where quotation marks appear in the original passage (**Example C**).

Example A

Example B

Example C

For Quoting Quotations

Use single quotation marks to punctuate quoted material within a quotation.

> "I was lucky," said Jane. "The proctor announced, **'Put your pencils down,'** just as I was filling in the last answer."

28-10 ITALICS (UNDERLINING)

▶ **In Handwritten and Printed Material — Italics** is a printer's term for a style of type that is slightly slanted. In this sentence, the word *happiness* is printed in italics. In material that is handwritten or typed on a machine that cannot print in italics, underline each word or letter that should be in italics.

> In <u>The Road to Memphis</u>, racism is a contagious disease. (typed or handwritten)

> Mildred Taylor's *The Road to Memphis* exposes racism. (printed)

▶ **In Titles** — Use italics to indicate the titles of magazines, newspapers, books, pamphlets, full-length plays, films, videos, radio and television programs, book-length poems, ballets, operas, lengthy musical compositions, CDs, paintings and sculptures, legal cases, Web sites, and the names of ships and aircraft. (Also see page 358.)

> *The Week* (magazine)
>
> *To Kill a Mockingbird* (book)
>
> *Enola Gay* (airplane)
>
> *ACLU v. State of Ohio* (legal case)
>
> *The Wolf of Wall Street* (film)
>
> *The Big Bang Theory* (television program)
>
> *College Loans* (pamphlet)
>
> *Sacramento Bee* (newspaper)
>
> *Yankee Tavern* (play)
>
> *Abbey Road* (album)
>
> *Billy the Kid* (ballet)
>
> *The Thinker* (sculpture)
>
> *Slate* (Web site)

When one title appears within another title, punctuate as follows:

> **I read an article entitled "The Making of *Up*."** (title of movie in an article title)

> **He wants to watch *Inside* The New York Times on PBS tonight.** (title of newspaper in title of TV program)

▶ **For Key Terms** — Italics are often used for a key term in a discussion or for a technical term, especially when it is accompanied by its definition. Italicize the term the first time it is used. Thereafter, put the term in roman type.

> This flower has a ***zygomorphic*** (bilateral symmetry) structure.

▶ **For Foreign Words and Scientific Names** — Use italics for foreign words that have not been adopted into the English language; italics are also used to denote scientific names.

> Say ***arrivederci*** to your fears, and try new activities. (foreign word)

> The voyageurs discovered the shy ***Castor canadensis***, or North American beaver. (scientific name)

28-11 PARENTHESES

▶ **To Enclose Explanatory or Supplementary Material** — Use **parentheses** to enclose explanatory or supplementary material that interrupts the normal sentence structure.

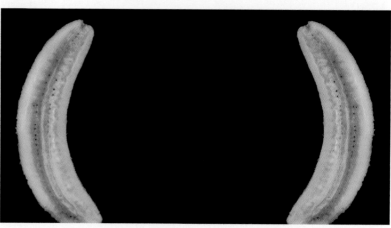

> The RA **(resident assistant)** became my best friend.

▶ **To Set Off Numbers in a List** — Use parentheses to set off numbers used with a series of words or phrases.

> Dr. Beck told us **(1)** plan ahead, **(2)** stay flexible, and **(3)** follow through.

▶ **For Parenthetical Sentences** — When using a full sentence within another sentence, do not capitalize it or use a period inside the parentheses.

> Your friend doesn't have the assignment **(he was just thinking about calling you)**, so you'll have to make a few more calls.

When the parenthetical sentence comes after the main sentence, capitalize and punctuate it the same way you would any other complete sentence.

> But Mom doesn't say boo to Dad; she's always sweet to him. **(Actually she's sort of sweet to everybody.)**
> —Norma Fox Mazer, *Up on Fong Mountain*

▶ **To Set Off References** — Use parentheses to set off references to authors, titles, pages, and years.

> The statistics are alarming **(see page 9)** and demand action.

Note: For unavoidable parentheses within parentheses use brackets, (. . . [. . .] . . .). Avoid overuse of parentheses by using commas instead.

28-12 DIAGONAL

▶ **To Form Fractions or Show Choices** — Use a **diagonal** (also called a *slash*) to form a fraction. Also place a diagonal between two words to indicate that either is acceptable.

> My **walking/running** shoe size is **5 1/2**; my dress shoes are **6 1/2**.

> Jill was promoted to **senior vice president/ director of sales** at her company.

▶ **When Quoting Poetry** — When quoting poetry, use a diagonal (with one space before and after) to show where each line ends in the actual poem.

> A dryness is upon the house **/** My father loved and tended. **/** Beyond his firm and sculptured door **/** His light and lease have ended.
> —Gwendolyn Brooks, "In Honor of David Anderson Brooks, My Father"

28-13 BRACKETS

▶ **With Words That Clarify** — Use **brackets** before and after words that are added to clarify what another person has said or written.

> "They'd **[the sweat bees]** get into your mouth, ears, eyes, nose. You'd feel them all over you."
> —Marilyn Johnson and Sasha Nyary, "Roosevelts in the Amazon"

Note: The brackets indicate that the words *the sweat bees* are not part of the original quotation but were added for clarification. (See page 358.)

▶ **Around Comments by Someone Other Than the Author** — Place brackets around comments that have been added by someone other than the author or speaker.

> "In conclusion, *docendo discimus*. Let the school year begin!" **[Huh?]**

▶ **Around Editorial Corrections** — Place brackets around an editorial correction or addition.

> "Brooklyn alone has 8 percent of lead poisoning **[victims]** nationwide," said Marjorie Moore.
> —Donna Actie, student writer

▶ **Around the Word *Sic*** — Brackets should be placed around the word *sic* (Latin for "so" or "thus") in quoted material; the word indicates that an error appearing in the quoted material was made by the original speaker or writer.

> "There is a higher principal **[sic]** at stake here: Is the school administration aware of the situation?"

28-14 EXCLAMATION POINT

▶ **To Express Strong Feeling** — Use an **exclamation point** to express strong feeling. It may be placed at the end of a sentence (or an elliptical expression that stands for a sentence). Use exclamation points sparingly.

> Did you hear? I did it! I passed my exam to become a Certified Public Accountant. I'm officially a CPA**!**

> "That's not the point," said Wangero. "These are all pieces of dresses Grandma used to wear. She did all this stitching by hand. **Imagine!**"
> —Alice Walker, "Everyday Use"

> Su-su-something's crawling up the back of my neck**!**
> —Mark Twain, *Roughing It*

> She was on tiptoe, stretching for an orange, when they heard, "**HEY YOU!**"
> —Beverley Naidoo, *Journey to Jo'burg*

28-15 APOSTROPHE

▶ **In Contractions** — Use an **apostrophe** to show that one or more letters have been left out of two words joined to form a contraction.

can't	. . . . **no** is left out
don't	. . . . **o** is left out
she'd	. . . . **woul** is left out
I'm	. . . .**a** is left out
it's	. . . . **i** is left out
we're	. . . .**a** is left out
we've	. . . .**ha** is left out

Note: An apostrophe is also used to show that one or more numerals or letters have been left out of numbers or words.

class of '**14**	. . . . **20** is left out
good **mornin'**	. . . . **g** is left out

▶ **To Form Plurals** — Use an apostrophe and an s to form the plural of a letter, a number, a sign, or a word discussed as a word.

A. . . . . A**'s**	8. . . . . 8**'s**	+. . . . . +**'s**

| You use too many **and's** in your writing.

Note: If two apostrophes are called for in the same word, omit the second one.

| Follow closely the do's and **don'ts** (not *don't's*) on the checklist.

▶ **To Form Singular Possessives** — The possessive form of singular nouns is usually made by adding an apostrophe and an *s*.

| **Spock's** ears   my **computer's** memory

Note: When a singular noun of more than one syllable ends with an *s* or a *z* sound, the possessive may be formed by adding just an apostrophe—or an apostrophe and an *s*.

When the singular noun is a one-syllable word, however, the possessive is usually formed by adding both an apostrophe and an *s*.

| **Dallas'** sports teams *or* **Dallas's** sports teams (two-syllable word)

| **Kiss's** last concert *or* my **boss's** generosity (one-syllable words)

▶ **To Form Plural Possessives** — The possessive form of plural nouns ending in *s* is made by adding just an apostrophe.

| the **Joneses'** great-grandfather

| **bosses'** offices

Note: For plural nouns not ending in *s*, add an apostrophe and *s*.

| **women's** health issues

| **children's** program

▶ **To Determine Ownership** — You will punctuate possessives correctly if you remember that the word that comes immediately before the apostrophe is the owner.

| **girl's** guitar (*girl* is the owner)
| **girls'** guitar (*girls* are the owners)

| **boss's** office (*boss* is the owner)
| **bosses'** office (*bosses* are the owners)

▶ **To Show Shared Possession** — When possession is shared by more than one noun, use the possessive form for the last noun in the series.

| Jason, Kamil, and **Elana's** sound system (All three own the same system.)

| **Jason's, Kamil's, and Elana's** sound systems (Each owns a separate system.)

▶ **In Compound Nouns** — The possessive of a compound noun is formed by placing the possessive ending after the last word.

> his **mother-in-law's** name (singular)
>
> the **songbird's** tweet (singular)
>
> the **secretary of state's** career (singular)
>
> their **mothers-in-law's** names (plural)
>
> the **songbirds'** tweets (plural)
>
> the **secretaries of state's** careers (plural)

▶ **With Indefinite Pronouns** — The possessive form of an indefinite pronoun is made by adding an apostrophe and an *s* to the pronoun. (See page 325.)

> **everybody's** grades
>
> **no one's** mistake
>
> **another's** basket
>
> **one's** choice
>
> **Nothing's** for certain.
>
> **Anything's** possible.

In expressions using *else*, add the apostrophe and *s* after the last word.

> **anyone else's**
>
> **somebody else's**
>
> **everybody else's**

▶ **To Show Time or Amount** — Use an apostrophe and an *s* with an adjective that is part of an expression indicating time or amount.

> **yesterday's** news
>
> **tomorrow's** schedule
>
> a **day's** wage
>
> a **month's** pay

 Quick Guide:
Punctuation Marks

´ (é)	Accent, acute	(ä)	Dieresis
` (è)	Accent, grave	. . .	Ellipsis
< >	Angle brackets	!	Exclamation point
'	Apostrophe	-	Hyphen
*	Asterisk	.....	Leaders
{ }	Braces	¶	Paragraph
[ ]	Brackets	( )	Parentheses
^	Caret	.	Period
ç	Cedilla	?	Question mark
^ (â)	Circumflex	" "	Quotation marks
:	Colon	§	Section
,	Comma	;	Semicolon
†	Dagger	˜ (ñ)	Tilde
—	Dash	___	Underscore
/	Diagonal/slash		

29 | Mechanics

"CONVENTIONS ARE SUBJECT TO THE VAGARIES OF TIME AND FASHION. THE WRITERS OF THE CONSTITUTION CAPITALIZED WORDS IN THE MIDDLE OF SENTENCES."

MITCHELL IVERS

Vadim Ivanov, 2014 / Used under license from Shutterstock.com

LEARNING OBJECTIVES

29-1 Capitalization

29-2 Plurals

29-3 Numbers

29-4 Abbreviations

29-5 Acronyms and Initialisms

29-6 Basic Spelling Rules

This chapter focuses on the mechanical part of the English language. Learning and applying these rules will help you tune up your writing and keep it running smoothly.

29-1 CAPITALIZATION

▸ **Proper Nouns and Adjectives** — Capitalize all proper nouns and all proper adjectives (adjectives derived from proper nouns). The chart below provides a quick overview of capitalization rules. The following categories explain specific or special uses of capitalization.

▸ **First Words** — Capitalize the first word in every sentence and the first word in a full-sentence direct quotation. (Also see page 359.)

> **Attending** the orientation for new students is a good idea.
>
> Max suggested, "**Let's** take the guided tour of the campus first."

▸ **Sentences in Parentheses** — Capitalize the first word in a sentence that is enclosed in parentheses if that sentence is not contained within another complete sentence.

> The bookstore has the software. (**Now** all I need is the computer.)

Note: Do *not* capitalize a sentence that is enclosed in parentheses and is located in the middle of another sentence. (Also see page 360.)

> Your college will probably offer everything (**this** includes general access to a computer) that you'll need for a successful year.

▸ **Sentences Following Colons** — Capitalize a complete sentence that follows a colon when that sentence is a formal statement, a quotation, or a sentence that you want to emphasize. (Also see page 356.)

> Sydney Harris had this to say about computers: "**The** real danger is not that computers will begin to think like people, but that people will begin to think like computers."

▸ **Salutation and Complimentary Closing** — In a letter, capitalize the first and all major words of the salutation. Capitalize only the first word of the complimentary closing.

> **Dear Personnel Director:**   **Sincerely** yours,

Quick Guide:
Capitalization at a Glance

Days of the week	Sunday, Monday, Tuesday
Months	June, July, August
Holidays, holy days	Thanksgiving, Easter, Hanukkah
Periods, events in history	Middle Ages, World War I
Special events	Tate Memorial Dedication Ceremony
Political parties	Republican Party, Socialist Party
Official documents	the Declaration of Independence
Trade names	Oscar Mayer hot dogs, Pontiac Firebird
Formal epithets	Alexander the Great
Official titles	Mayor John Spitzer, Senator Feinstein
Official state nicknames	the Badger State, the Aloha State

Geographical names

Planets, heavenly bodies	Jupiter, the Milky Way
Continents	Australia, South America
Countries	Ireland, Grenada, Sri Lanka
States, provinces	Ohio, Utah, Nova Scotia
Cities, towns, villages	El Paso, Burlington, Wonewoc
Streets, roads, highways	Park Avenue, Route 66, Interstate 90
Sections of the United States and the world	the Southwest, the Far East
Landforms	the Rocky Mountains, the Kalahari Desert
Bodies of water	the Nile River, Lake Superior, Bee Creek
Public areas	Central Park, Yellowstone National Park

▶ **Sections of the Country** — Words that indicate sections of the country are proper nouns and should be capitalized; words that simply indicate direction are not proper nouns.

> Many businesses move to the **South**. (section of the country)

> They move **south** to cut fuel costs and other expenses. (direction)

▶ **Languages, Ethnic Groups, Nationalities, and Religions** — Capitalize languages, ethnic groups, nationalities, and religions.

> African   American   Latino
> Navajo   French   Islam

Nouns that refer to the Supreme Being and holy books are capitalized.

> God   Allah   Jehovah
> the **Koran**   Exodus   the **Bible**

▶ **Titles** — Capitalize the first word of a title, the last word, and every word in between except articles (*a, an, the*), short prepositions, *to* in an infinitive, and coordinating conjunctions. Follow this rule for titles of books, newspapers, magazines, poems, plays, songs, articles, films, works of art, and stories.

> *Going to Meet the Man*   *Chicago Tribune*
> "Nothing Gold Can Stay"   "Jobs in the Cyber Arena"
> *A Midsummer Night's Dream*   *The War of the Roses*

Note: When citing titles in a bibliography, check the style manual you've been asked to follow. For example, in APA style, only the first word of a title is capitalized.

▶ **Organizations** — Capitalize the name of an organization or a team and its members.

> American Indian Movement
> Democratic Party
> Tampa Bay Buccaneers
> Tucson Drama Club

▶ **Abbreviations** — Capitalize abbreviations of titles and organizations. (Some other abbreviations are also capitalized. See page 370.)

> M.D.   NAACP   B.C.E.
> Ph.D.   C.E.   GPA

▶ **Letters** — Capitalize letters used to indicate a form or shape.

> **U**-turn   **S**-curve   **T**-shirt
> **I**-beam   **V**-shaped

▶ **Words Used as Names** — Capitalize words like *father, mother, uncle, senator,* and *professor* when they are parts of titles that include a personal name or when they are substituted for proper nouns (especially in direct address). (Also see page 354.)

> Hello, **Senator** McCain. (*Senator* is part of the name.)
> Our **senator** is an environmentalist.

> Who was your chemistry **professor** last quarter?
> I had **Professor** Williams for Chemistry 101.

Note: To test whether a word is being substituted for a proper noun, simply read the sentence with a proper noun in place of the word. If the proper noun fits in the sentence, the word being tested should be capitalized. Usually the word is not capitalized if it follows a possessive—*my, his, our, your,* and so on.

> Did **Dad (Brad)** pack the stereo in the trailer? (*Brad* works in this sentence.)

> Did your **dad (Brad)** pack the stereo in the trailer? (*Brad* does not work in this sentence; the word *dad* follows the possessive *your*.)

▶ **Titles of Courses** — Words such as *technology, history,* and *science* are proper nouns when they are included in the titles of specific courses; they are common nouns when they name a field of study.

> Who teaches **Art History 202**? (title of a specific course)

> Professor Bunker loves teaching **history**. (a field of study)

Note: The words *freshman, sophomore, junior,* and *senior* are not capitalized unless they are part of an official title.

The **seniors** who maintained high GPAs were honored at the **Mount Mary Senior Honors Banquet**.

▸ **Internet and Email** — The words *Internet* and *World Wide Web* are always capitalized because they are considered proper nouns. When your writing includes a Web address (URL), capitalize any letters that the site's owner does (on printed materials or on the site itself). Not only is it respectful to reprint a Web address exactly as it appears elsewhere, but, in fact, some Web addresses are case sensitive and must be entered into a browser's address bar exactly as presented.

When doing research on the **Internet**, be sure to record each site's **Web** address (**URL**) and each contact's **email** address.

Note: Some people include capital letters in their email addresses to make certain features evident. Although email addresses are not case sensitive, repeat each letter in print just as its owner uses it.

➕ A Closer Look:
Avoid Capitalization Errors

Do not capitalize any of the following:
- A prefix attached to a proper noun
- Seasons of the year
- Words used to indicate direction or position
- Common nouns and titles that appear near, but are not part of, a proper noun

Capitalize	Do Not Capitalize
American	un-American
January, February	winter, spring
The South is quite conservative.	Turn south at the stop sign.
Duluth City College	a Duluth college
Chancellor John Bohm	John Bohm, our chancellor
President Obama	the president of the United States
Earth (the planet)	earthmover
Internet	email

29-2 PLURALS

▸ **Nouns Ending in a Consonant** — Some nouns remain unchanged when used as plurals (*species, moose, halibut,* and so on), but the plurals of most nouns are formed by adding an *s* to the singular form.

dorm—dorm**s**	credit—credit**s**
midterm—midterm**s**	

The plurals of nouns ending in *sh, ch, x, s,* and *z* are made by adding *es* to the singular form.

lunch—lun**ches**	wish—wi**shes**
class—clas**ses**	

▸ **Nouns Ending in** *y* — The plurals of common nouns that end in *y* (preceded by a consonant) are formed by changing the *y* to *i* and adding *es*.

duty—dut**ies**	sorority—sororit**ies**
dormitory—dormitor**ies**	

The plurals of common nouns that end in *y* (preceded by a vowel) are formed by adding only an *s*.

attorn**ey**—attorn**eys**	monk**ey**—monk**eys**
to**y**—to**ys**	

The plurals of all proper nouns ending in *y* (whether preceded by a consonant or a vowel) are formed by adding an *s*.

the three Kath**ys**	the five Fahe**ys**

▸ **Nouns Ending in** *o* — The plurals of words ending in *o* preceded by a vowel are formed by adding an *s*.

radi**o**—radi**os**	cam**eo**—cam**eos**
stud**io**—stud**ios**	

The plurals of most nouns ending in *o* preceded by a consonant are formed by adding *es*.

echo—ech**oes**	hero—her**oes**
toma**to**—toma**toes**	

Musical terms always form plurals by adding an *s*; check a dictionary for other words of this type.

alto—alto**s**	banjo—banjo**s**
solo—solo**s**	piano—piano**s**

▸ **Nouns Ending in** *f* **or** *fe* — The plurals of nouns that end in *f* or *fe* are formed in one of two ways: If the final *f* sound is still heard in the plural form of the word, simply add *s*; if the final sound is a *v* sound, change the *f* to *ve* and add an *s*.

Plural ends with *f* sound:

roof—roo**fs**   chief—chie**fs**

Plural ends with *v* sound:

wife—wi**ves**   loaf—loa**ves**

Note: The plurals of some nouns that end in *f* or *fe* can be formed by either adding *s* or changing the *f* to *ve* and adding an *s*.

Plural ends with either sound:

hoof—hoo**fs**, hoo**ves**

▶ **Irregular Spelling** — Many foreign words (as well as some of English origin) form a plural by taking on an irregular spelling; others are now acceptable with the commonly used *s* or *es* ending. Take time to check a dictionary.

child—chil**dren**   datum—da**ta**

ra**di**us—ra**dii**,   alum**nus**—alum**ni**
ra**di**uses
                            sylla**bus**—sylla**bi**,
goose—g**ee**se   sylla**buses**

▶ **Words Discussed as Words** — The plurals of symbols, letters, figures, and words discussed as words are formed by adding an apostrophe and an *s*.

Many colleges have now added **A/B's** and **B/C's** as standard grades.

Note: You can choose to omit the apostrophe when the omission does not cause confusion.

YMCA's *or* **YMCAs**   **CD's** *or* **CDs**

▶ **Nouns Ending in *ful*** — The plurals of nouns that end with *ful* are formed by adding an *s* at the end of the word.

three teaspoon**fuls**   two tank**fuls**

▶ **Compound Nouns** — The plurals of compound nouns are usually formed by adding an *s* or an *es* to the important word in the compound. (Also see page 363.)

brothers-in-law   **maid**s of honor
secretaries of state

▶ **Collective Nouns** — Collective nouns do not change in form when they are used as plurals.

class (a unit—singular form)

class (individual members—plural form)

Because the spelling of the collective noun does not change, it is often the pronoun used in place of the collective noun that indicates whether the noun is singular or plural. Use a singular pronoun (*its*) to show that the collective noun is singular. Use a plural pronoun (*their*) to show that the collective noun is plural.

The class needs to change **its** motto. (The writer is thinking of the group as a unit.)

The class brainstormed with **their** professor. (The writer is thinking of the group as individuals.)

ESL Note: To determine whether a plural requires the article *the*, you must first determine whether it is definite or indefinite. Definite plurals use *the*, whereas indefinite plurals do not require any article. (See page 374.)

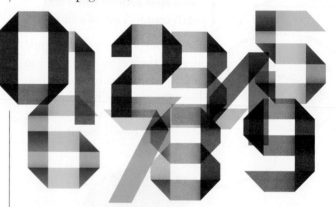

29-3 NUMBERS

▶ **Numerals or Words** — **Numbers** from one to one hundred are usually written as words; numbers 101 and greater are usually written as numerals. (APA style uses numerals for numbers 10 and higher.) Hyphenate numbers written as two words if less than 100.

two	ten	106
seven	fifty-one	1,079

The same rule applies to the use of ordinal numbers.

second	ninety-eighth
tenth	106th
twenty-fifth	333rd

If numbers greater than 101 are used infrequently in a piece of writing, you may spell out those that can be written in one or two words.

two hundred	six billion
fifty thousand	

You may use a combination of numerals and words for very large numbers.

| 1.5 million | 6 trillion |

3 billion to 3.2 billion

Numbers being compared or contrasted should be kept in the same style.

8 to **11** years old *or* **eight** to **eleven** years old

Particular decades may be spelled out or written as numerals.

the **'80s** and **'90s** *or* the **eighties** and **nineties**

▸ **Numerals Only** — Use numerals for the following forms: decimals, percentages, pages, chapters (and other parts of a book), addresses, dates, telephone numbers, identification numbers, and statistics.

26.2	a vote of **23** to **4**
pages **287–289**	chapter **7**
398-55-0000	**(212) 555–1234**
8 percent	May **8, 2007**
Highway **36**	

Note: Abbreviations and symbols are often used in charts, graphs, footnotes, and so forth, but typically they are not used in texts.

He is **five feet one** inch tall and **ten years old**.

She walked **three and one-half miles** to work through **twelve inches** of snow.

However, abbreviations and symbols may be used in scientific, mathematical, statistical, and technical texts (APA style).

Between **20%** and **23%** of the cultures yielded positive results.

Your **245B** model requires **220V**.

Always use numerals with abbreviations and symbols.

| **5'4"** | **10** in. | **6** lb. **8** oz. |
| **8%** | **3** tbsp. | **90°F** |

Use numerals after the name of local branches of labor unions.

The Office and Professional Employees International Union, Local **8**

▸ **Hyphenated Numbers** — Hyphens are used to form compound modifiers indicating measurement. They are also used for inclusive numbers and written-out fractions.

a **three-mile** trip

the **2001–2005** presidential term

a **2,500-mile** road trip

one-sixth of the pie

a **thirteen-foot** clearance

three-eighths of the book

▸ **Time and Money** — If time is expressed with an abbreviation, use numerals; if it is expressed in words, spell out the number.

4:00 a.m. *or* **four** o'clock (not 4 o'clock)

the **5:15** p.m. train

a **seven** o'clock wake-up call

If money is expressed with a symbol, use numerals; if the currency is expressed in words, spell out the number.

$20 *or* **twenty** dollars (not 20 dollars)

Abbreviations of time and of money may be used in text.

The concert begins at **7:00** p.m., and tickets cost $**30**.

▸ **Words Only** — Use words to express numbers that begin a sentence.

Fourteen students "forgot" their assignments.

Three hundred contest entries were received.

Note: Change the sentence structure if this rule creates a clumsy construction.

Six hundred thirty-nine students are new to the campus this fall. (Clumsy)

This fall, **639** students are new to the campus. (Better)

Use words for numbers that precede a compound modifier that includes a numeral. (If the compound modifier uses a spelled-out number, use numerals in front of it.)

She sold **twenty 35-millimeter** cameras in one day.

The chef prepared **24 eight-ounce** filets.

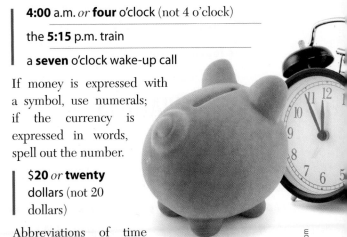

Use words for the names of numbered streets of one hundred or less.

> **Ninth** Avenue
>
> **123 Forty-fourth** Street

Use words for the names of buildings if that name is also its address.

> **One Thousand State Street**
>
> **Two Fifty Park Avenue**

Use words for references to particular centuries.

> **the twenty-first century**
>
> **the fourth century B.C.E.**

29-4 ABBREVIATIONS

An abbreviation is the shortened form of a word or a phrase. These abbreviations are always acceptable in both formal and informal writing:

> **Mr.**   **Mrs.**   **Ms.**   **Dr.**
>
> **a.m. (A.M.)**   **p.m. (P.M.)**

Note: In formal writing, do not abbreviate the names of states, countries, months, days, units of measure, or courses of study. Do ***not*** abbreviate the words *Street, Road, Avenue, Company,* and similar words when they are part of a proper name. Also, do not use signs or symbols (%, &, #, @) in place of words. (The dollar sign, however, is appropriate when numerals are used to express an amount of money. See page 369.)

Also Note: When abbreviations are called for (in charts, lists, bibliographies, notes, and indexes, for example), standard abbreviations are preferred. Reserve the postal abbreviations for ZIP code addresses.

29-5 ACRONYMS AND INITIALISMS

▸ **Acronyms** — An **acronym** is a word formed from the first (or first few) letters of words in a set phrase. Even

though acronyms are abbreviations, they require no periods.

> **radar** **r**adio **d**etecting **a**nd **r**anging
>
> **CARE** **C**ooperative for **A**ssistance and **R**elief Everywhere
>
> **NASA** **N**ational **A**eronautics and **S**pace Administration
>
> **VISTA** **V**olunteers **i**n **S**ervice **t**o **A**merica
>
> **FICA** **F**ederal **I**nsurance **C**ontributions **A**ct

▸ **Initialisms** — An **initialism** is similar to an acronym except that the initials used to form this abbreviation are pronounced individually.

> **CIA** **C**entral **I**ntelligence **A**gency
>
> **FBI** **F**ederal **B**ureau of **I**nvestigation
>
> **FHA** **F**ederal **H**ousing **A**dministration
>
> **IRS** **I**nternal **R**evenue **S**ervice
>
> **VA** **V**eterans **A**dministration

29-6 BASIC SPELLING RULES

▸ **Write *i* Before *e*** — Write *i* before *e* except after *c*, or when sounded like *a* as in *neighbor* and *weigh.*

> **believe**   **receive**
>
> **relief**   **eight**

Note: This sentence contains eight exceptions:

> **Neither sheik** dared **leisurely seize either weird species** of **financiers.**

▸ **Words with Consonant Endings** — When a one-syllable word (*bat*) ends in a consonant (*t*) preceded by one vowel (*a*), double the final consonant before adding a suffix that begins with a vowel (*batting*).

> sum—**summary**
>
> god—**goddess**

Note: When a multisyllable word (*control*) ends in a consonant (*l*) preceded by one vowel (*o*), the accent is on the last syllable (*con trol´*), and the suffix begins with a vowel (*ing*)—the same rule holds true: Double the final consonant (*controlling*).

prefer—**preferred**	begin—**beginning**
forget—**forgettable**	admit—**admittance**

▶ **Words with a Final Silent *e*** — If a word ends with a silent *e*, drop the *e* before adding a suffix that begins with a vowel. Do *not* drop the *e* when the suffix begins with a consonant.

state—**stating**—**statement**

use—**using**—**useful**

nine—**ninety**—**nineteen**

like—**liking**—**likeness**

Note: Exceptions are **judgment**, **truly**, **argument**, **ninth**.

▶ **Words Ending in *y*** — When *y* is the last letter in a word and the *y* is preceded by a consonant, change the *y* to *i* before adding any suffix except those beginning with *i*.

fry—**fries, frying**

hurry—**hurried, hurrying**

lady—**ladies**

ply—**pliable**

happy—**happiness**

beauty—**beautiful**

Note: When forming the plural of a word that ends with a *y* that is preceded by a vowel, add *s*.

toy—**toys**	monkey—**monkeys**
play—**play**	

 Never trust your spelling to even the best spell checker. Carefully proofread and use a dictionary for words you know your spell checker does not cover.

Allways chek for speling erors

Quick Guide:
Steps to Becoming a Better Speller

1. **Be patient.** Becoming a good speller takes time.

2. **Check the correct pronunciation of each word you are attempting to spell.** Knowing the correct pronunciation of each word can help you to remember its spelling.

3. **Note the meaning and history of each word as you are checking the dictionary for the pronunciation.** Knowing the meaning and history of a word provides you with a better notion of how the word is properly used, and it can help you remember the word's spelling.

4. **Before you close the dictionary, practice spelling the word.** You can do so by looking away from the page and trying to "see" the word in your "mind's eye." Write the word on a piece of paper. Check the spelling in the dictionary, and repeat the process until you are able to spell the word correctly.

5. **Learn some spelling rules.** The four rules in this handbook are four of the most useful—although there are others.

6. **Make a list of the words that you misspell.** Select the first 10 words and practice spelling them.
   - **First:** Read each word carefully; then write it on a piece of paper. Look at the written word to see that it's spelled correctly. Repeat the process for those words that you misspelled.
   - **Then:** Ask someone to read the words to you so you can write them again. Then check for misspellings. Repeat both steps with your next 10 words.

7. **Write often.** As noted educator Frank Smith said,

   "There is little point in learning to spell if you have little intention of writing."

30 | Multilingual and ESL Guidelines

"ONE LANGUAGE SETS YOU IN A CORRIDOR FOR LIFE. TWO LANGUAGES OPEN EVERY DOOR ALONG THE WAY."

FRANK SMITH

ivosar, 2014, Used under license from Shutterstock.com

LEARNING OBJECTIVES

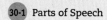 **30-1** Parts of Speech

30-2 Sentence Basics

 30-3 Sentence Problems

 30-4 Numbers, Word Parts, and Idioms

If English is not your native language, you are an English Language Learner (ELL). While chapters 25–29 supply most of the instruction that you will need for mastering English, this chapter will address specific ELL challenges.

PARTS OF SPEECH

30-1a Noun

Nouns are words that name people, places, and things. This information tells how to use nouns correctly.

▶ **Count Nouns** — Count nouns refer to things that can be counted. They can have *a, an, the,* or *one* in front of them. One or more adjectives can come between the articles *a, an, the,* or *one* and the singular count noun.

   an apple, one orange, a plum, a purple plum

Count nouns can be singular, as in the examples above, or plural, as in the examples below.

   plums, apples, oranges

Note: When count nouns are plural, they can have the article *the,* a number, or a demonstrative adjective in front of them. (See page 374.)

   I used **the** plums to make a pie.

   He placed **five** apples on my desk.

   These oranges are so juicy!

The *number* of a noun refers to whether it names a single thing (*book*), in which case its number is *singular,* or whether it names more than one thing (*books*), in which case the number of the noun is *plural.*

Note: There are different ways in which the plural form of nouns is created. For more information, see pages 367–368.

▶ **Noncount Nouns** — Noncount nouns refer to things that cannot be counted. Do not use *a, an,* or *one* in front of them. They have no plural form, so they always take a singular verb. Some nouns that end in *s* are not plural; they are noncount nouns.

   fruit, furniture, rain, thunder, advice, mathematics, news

Abstract nouns name ideas or conditions rather than people, places, or objects. Many abstract nouns are noncount nouns.

   The students had **fun** at the party. Good **health** is a wonderful gift.

Collective nouns name a whole category or group and are often noncount nouns.

   homework, furniture, money

Note: The parts or components of a group or category named by a noncount noun are often count nouns. For example, *report* and *assignment* are count nouns that are parts of the collective, noncount noun *homework.*

▶ **Two-Way Nouns** — Some nouns can be used as either count or noncount nouns, depending on what they refer to.

   I would like a **glass** of water. (count noun)

   Glass is used to make windows. (noncount noun)

Articles and Other Noun Markers

Use articles and other noun markers or modifiers to give more information about nouns.

▶ **Specific Articles** — Use articles and other noun markers or modifiers to give more information about nouns. The **specific** (or **definite**) **article** *the* is used to refer to a specific noun.

   I found **the** book I misplaced yesterday.

▶ **Indefinite Articles and Indefinite Adjectives** — Use the **indefinite article** *a* or *an* to refer to a nonspecific noun. Use *an* before singular nouns beginning with the vowels *a, e, i, o,* and *u.* Use *a* before nouns beginning with all other letters of the alphabet, the consonants. Exceptions do occur: *a* unit; *a* university.

   I always take **an** apple to work.

   It is good to have **a** book with you when you travel.

Indefinite adjectives can also mark nonspecific nouns—*all, any, each, either, every, few, many, more, most, neither, several, some* (for singular and plural count nouns); *all, any, more, most, much, some* (for noncount nouns).

   Every student is encouraged to register early.

   Most classes fill quickly.

Quick Guide:
Determining Whether to Use Articles

Listed below are a number of guidelines to help you determine whether to use an article and which one to use.

Use *a* or *an* with singular count nouns that do not refer to one specific item.	**A zebra** has black and white stripes. **An apple** is good for you.
Do not use *a* or *an* with plural count nouns.	**Zebras** have black and white stripes. **Apples** are good for you.
Do not use *a* or *an* with noncount nouns.	**Homework** needs to be done promptly.
Use *the* with singular count nouns that refer to one specific item.	**The apple** you gave me was delicious.
Use *the* with plural count nouns.	**The zebras** at Brookfield Zoo were healthy.
Use *the* with noncount nouns.	**The money** from my uncle is a gift.
Do not use *the* with most singular proper nouns.	**Mother Teresa** loved the poor and downcast.

Note: There are many exceptions: *the* Sahara Desert, *the* University of Minnesota, *the* Fourth of July.

Use *the* with plural proper nouns.	**the Joneses** (both Mr. and Mrs. Jones), **the Rocky Mountains, the United States**

▶ **Possessive Adjectives** — The possessive case of nouns and pronouns can be used as adjectives to mark nouns.

Possessive Nouns: *Tanya's, father's, store's*

> The car is **Tanya's**, not her **father's**.

Possessive Pronouns: *my, your, his, her, its, our*

> **My** hat is purple.

▶ **Demonstrative Adjectives** — Demonstrative pronouns can be used as adjectives to mark nouns.

trekandshoot, 2014 / Used under license from Shutterstock.com

Demonstrative adjectives: *this, that, these, those* (for singular and plural count nouns); *this, that* (for noncount nouns)

> **Those** chairs are lovely. Where did you buy **that** furniture?

▶ **Quantifiers** — **Expressions of quantity and measure** are often used with nouns. Below are some of these expressions and guidelines for using them. The following expressions of quantity can be used with count nouns: *each, every, both, a couple of, a few, several, many, a number of*.

> We enjoyed **both** concerts we attended. **A couple of** songs performed were familiar to us.

Use a number to indicate a specific quantity of a count noun.

> I saw **fifteen** cardinals in the park.

To indicate a specific quantity of a noncount noun, use *a* + quantity (such as *bag, bottle, bowl, carton, glass,* or *piece*) + *of* + noun.

> I bought **a carton of milk, a head of lettuce, a piece of cheese**, and **a bag of flour** at the grocery store.

The following expressions can be used with noncount nouns: *a little, much, a great deal of*.

> We had **much** wind and **a little** rain as the storm passed through yesterday.

The following expressions of quantity can be used with both count and noncount nouns: *no/not any, some, a lot of, lots of, plenty of, most, all, this, that*.

> I would like **some** apples (*count noun*) and **some** rice (*noncount noun*), please.

30-1b Verb

As the main part of the predicate, a verb conveys much of a sentence's meaning. Using verb tenses and forms correctly ensures that your readers will understand your sentences as you intend them to. For a more thorough review of verbs, see pages 327–332.

▶ **Progressive (Continuous) Tenses** — Progressive or continuous tense verbs express action in progress (see page 329). To form the **present progressive** tense, use the helping verb *am, is,* or *are* with the *ing* form of the main verb.

> He **is washing** the car right now.

> Kent and Chen **are studying** for a test.

To form the **past progressive** tense, use the helping verb *was* or *were* with the *ing* form of the main verb.

> Yesterday he **was working** in the garden all day.

> Julia and Juan **were watching** a movie.

To form the future progressive tense, use *will* or a phrase that indicates the future, the helping verb *be*, and the *ing* form of the main verb.

> Next week he **will be painting** the house.

> He **plans to be painting** the house soon.

Note that some verbs are generally not used in the progressive tenses, such as the following groups of frequently used verbs:

- Verbs that express thoughts, attitudes, and desires: *know, understand, want, prefer*
- Verbs that describe appearances: *seem, resemble*

- Verbs that indicate possession: *belong, have, own, possess*
- Verbs that signify inclusion: *contain, hold*

> **Correct:** Kala **knows** how to ride a motorcycle.
>
> **Incorrect:** Kala is **knowing** how to ride a motorcycle.

30-1c Objects and Complements of Verbs

Active transitive verbs take objects. These can be direct objects, indirect objects, or object complements. Linking verbs take subject complements—predicate nominatives or predicate adjectives—that rename or describe the subject.

▶ **Infinitives as Objects** — Infinitives can follow many verbs, including these: *agree, appear, attempt, consent, decide, demand, deserve, fail, hope, need, offer, plan, prepare, promise, refuse, seem, tend, volunteer, wish*. (See also page 330.)

> He **promised to** bring some samples.

The following verbs are among those that can be followed by a noun or pronoun plus the infinitive: *ask, beg, choose, expect, intend, need, prepare, promise, want*.

> I **expect you to be** there on time.

Note: Except in the passive voice, the following verbs must have a noun or pronoun before the infinitive: *advise, allow, appoint, authorize, cause, challenge, command, convince, encourage, forbid, force, hire, instruct, invite, order, permit, remind, require, select, teach, tell, tempt, trust*.

> I will **authorize Emily to use** my credit card.

Unmarked infinitives (no *to*) can follow these verbs: *have, help, let, make*.

> These glasses **help me see** the board.

▶ **Gerunds as Objects** — Gerunds can follow these verbs: *admit, avoid, consider, deny, discuss, dislike, enjoy, finish, imagine, miss, postpone, quit, recall, recommend, regret*. (Also see page 330.)

> I **recommended hiring** Ian for the job.

Here *hiring* is the direct object of the active verb *recommended*, and *Ian* is the object of the gerund.

▶ **Infinitives or Gerunds as Objects** — Either **gerunds** or **infinitives** can follow these verbs: *be-*

gin, continue, hate, like, love, prefer, remember, start, stop, try.

> I **hate having** cold feet. I **hate to have** cold feet. (In either form, the verbal phrase is the direct object of the verb *hate*.)

Note: Sometimes the meaning of a sentence will change depending on whether you use a gerund or an infinitive.

> I **stopped to smoke**. (I *stopped* weeding the garden to smoke a cigarette.)
>
> I **stopped smoking**. (I no longer smoke.)

▶ **Common Modal Auxiliary Verbs** — **Modal auxiliary verbs** are a kind of auxiliary verb. (See page 328.) They help the main verb express meaning. Modals are sometimes grouped with other helping or auxiliary verbs. Modal verbs must be followed by the base form of a verb without *to* (not by a gerund or an infinitive). Also, modal verbs do not change form; they are always used as they appear in the following chart.

Modal	Expresses	Sample Sentence
can	ability	I **can** program a VCR.
could	ability	I **could** babysit Tuesday.
	possibility	He **could** be sick.
might	possibility	I **might** be early.
may, might	possibility	I **may** sleep late Saturday.
	request	**May** I be excused?
must	strong need	I **must** study more.
have to	strong need	I **have to** (have got to) exercise.
ought to	feeling of duty	I **ought to** (should) help Dad.
should	advisabillity	She **should** retire.
	expectation	I **should** have caught that train.
shall	intent	**Shall** I stay longer?
will	intent	I **will** visit my grandma soon.
would	intent	I **would** live to regret my offer.
	repeated action	He **would** walk in the meadow.
would + you	polite request	**Would you** help me?
could + you	polite request	**Could you** type this letter?
will + you	polite request	**Will you** give me a ride?
can + you	polite request	**Can you** make supper tonight?

▶ **Common Two-Word Verbs** — This chart lists some common verbs in which two words—a verb and a preposition—work together to express a specific action. A noun or pronoun is often inserted between the parts of the two-word verb when it is used in a sentence: *break it down, call it off.*

break down	to take apart or fall apart
call off	cancel
call up	make a phone call
clear out	leave a place quickly
cross out	draw a line through
do over	repeat
figure out	find a solution
fill in/out	complete a form or an application
fill up	fill a container or tank
find out	discover
get in	enter a vehicle or building
get out of	leave a car, a house, or a situation
get over	recover from a sickness or a problem
give back	return something
give in/up	surrender or quit
hand in	give homework to a teacher
hand out	give someone something
hang up	put down a phone receiver
leave out	omit or don't use
let in/out	allow someone or something to enter or go out
look up	find information
mix up	confuse
pay back	return money or a favor
pick out	choose
point out	call attention to
put away	return something to its proper place
put down	place something on a table, the floor, and so on
put off	delay doing something
shut off	turn off a machine or light
take part	participate
talk over	discuss
think over	consider carefully
try on	put on clothing to see if it fits
turn down	lower the volume
turn up	raise the volume
write down	write on a piece of paper

30-1d Spelling Guidelines for Verb Forms

The same spelling rules that apply when adding a suffix to other words apply to verbs as well. Most verbs need a suffix to indicate tense or form. The third-person singular form of a verb, for example, usually ends in *s*, but it can also end in *es*. Formation of *ing* and *ed* forms of verbs and verbals needs careful attention, too. Consult the rules below to determine which spelling is correct for each verb. (For general spelling guidelines, see page 370.)

Note: There may be exceptions to these rules when forming the past tense of irregular verbs because the verbs are formed by changing the word itself, not merely by adding *d* or *ed*. (See the chart of irregular verbs on pages 331–332.)

Past Tense: Adding *ed*

▶ **Add *ed* ...**
   - When a verb ends with two consonants:

     | touch—**touched**   pass—**passed**
     | ask—**asked**

   - When a verb ends with a consonant preceded by two vowels:

     | heal—**healed**   gain—**gained**

   - When a verb ends in *y* preceded by a vowel:

     | annoy—**annoyed**   flay—**flayed**

   - When a multisyllable verb's last syllable is not stressed (even when the last syllable ends with a consonant preceded by a vowel):

     | budget—**budgeted**
     | enter—**entered**
     | interpret—**interpreted**

▶ **Change *y* to *i* and add *ed*** when a verb ends in a consonant followed by *y*:

   | liquefy—**liquefied**   worry—**worried**

▶ **Double the final consonant and add *ed* ...**
   - When a verb has one syllable and ends with a consonant preceded by a vowel:

     | wrap—**wrapped**   drop—**dropped**

   - When a multisyllable verb's last syllable (ending in a consonant preceded by a vowel) is stressed:

     | admit—**admitted**   abut—**abutted**
     | confer—**conferred**

Past Tense: Adding *d*

▶ **Add *d* ...**
   - When a verb ends with *e*:

     | chime—**chimed**   tape—**taped**

   - When a verb ends with *ie*:

     | tie—**tied**   lie—**lied**
     | die—**died**

Present Tense: Adding *s* or *es*

▶ **Add *es* ...**
   - When a verb ends in *ch*, *sh*, *s*, *x*, or *z*:

     | watch—**watches**   fix—**fixes**

   - To *do* and *go*:

     | do—**does**   go—**goes**

▶ **Change *y* to *i* and add *es*** when the verb ends in a consonant followed by *y*:

   | liquefy—**liquefies**
   | quantify—**quantifies**

▶ **Add *s*** to most other verbs, including those already ending in *e* and those that end in a vowel followed by *y*:

   | write—**writes**   buy—**buys**

Present Tense: Adding *ing*

▶ **Drop the *e* and add *ing*** when the verb ends in *e*:

   | drive—**driving**   rise—**rising**

▶ **Double the final consonant and add *ing* ...**
   - When a verb has one syllable and ends with a consonant preceded by a single vowel:

     | wrap—**wrapping**   sit—**sitting**

   - When a multisyllable verb's last syllable (ending

in a consonant preceded by a single vowel) is stressed:

	forget—**forgetting**
	begin—**beginning**
	abut—**abutting**

▶ **Change *ie* to *y* and add *ing*** when a verb ends with *ie*:

tie—**tying**	lie—**lying**
die—**dying**	

▶ **Add *ing* . . .**

- When a verb ends with two consonants:

touch—**touching**	pass—**passing**
ask—**asking**	

- When a verb ends with a consonant preceded by two vowels:

heal—**healing**	gain—**gaining**

- When a verb ends in *y*:

buy—**buying**	cry—**crying**
study—**studying**	

- When a multisyllable verb's last syllable is not stressed (even when the last syllable ends with a consonant preceded by a vowel):

budget—**budgeting**	
enter—**entering**	
interpret—**interpreting**	

Note: Never trust your spelling to even the best computer spell checker. Carefully proofread. Use a dictionary for questionable words your spell checker may miss.

30-1e Adjective

Placing Adjectives

You probably know that an adjective often comes before the noun it modifies. When several adjectives are used in a row to modify a single noun, it is important to arrange the adjectives in the well-established sequence used in English writing and speaking. The following list shows the usual order of adjectives. (Also see page 353.)

First, place . . .

1. articles . . . . a, an, the
   demonstrative adjectives . . . . that, those
   possessives . . . . my, her, Misha's

Then place words that . . .

2. indicate time . . . . first, next, final
3. tell how many . . . . one, few, some
4. evaluate . . . . beautiful, dignified, graceful
5. tell what size . . . . big, small, short, tall
6. tell what shape . . . . round, square
7. describe a condition . . . . messy, clean, dark
8. tell what age . . . . old, young, new, antique
9. tell what color . . . . blue, red, yellow
10. tell what nationality . . . . English, Chinese, Mexican
11. tell what religion . . . . Buddhist, Jewish, Protestant
12. tell what material . . . . satin, velvet, wooden

Finally, place nouns . . .

13. used as adjectives . . . . car [tire], spice [rack]

my second try (1 + 2 + noun)	
gorgeous young white swans (4 + 8 + 9 + noun)	

Present and Past Participles as Adjectives

Both the **present participle** and the **past participle** can be used as adjectives. (Also see page 331.) Exercise care in choosing whether to use the present participle or the past participle. A participle can come either before a noun or after a linking verb.

Present Participle
Continuing Action

Past Participle
Completed Action

▶ **A present participle** used as an adjective should describe a person or thing that is causing a feeling or situation.

His **annoying** comments made me angry.

▶ **A past participle** should describe a person or thing that experiences a feeling or situation.

He was **annoyed** because he had to wait so long.

Note: Within each of the following pairs, the present (*ing* form) and past (*ed* form) participles have different meanings.

annoying/annoyed	exciting/excited
boring/bored	exhausting/exhausted
confusing/confused	fascinating/fascinated
depressing/depressed	surprising/surprised

Nouns as Adjectives

Nouns sometimes function as adjectives by modifying another noun. When a noun is used as an adjective, it is always singular.

> Many European cities have **rose** gardens.

> Marta recently joined a **book** club.

 TIP Try to avoid using more than two nouns as adjectives for another noun. These "noun compounds" can get confusing. Prepositional phrases may get the meaning across better than long noun strings.

> *Correct:* Omar is a **crew** member in the **restaurant** kitchen during second **shift**.

> **Not correct:** Omar is a **second-shift restaurant kitchen crew** member.

30-1f Adverb

Placing Adverbs

Consider the following guidelines for placing adverbs correctly. See page 333 for more information about adverbs.

- **Place adverbs that tell how often** (*frequently, seldom, never, always, sometimes*) after a helping (auxiliary) verb and before the main verb. In a sentence without a helping verb, adverbs that tell how often are placed before an action verb but after a linking verb.

  > The salesclerk will **usually** help me.

- **Place adverbs that tell when** (*yesterday, now, at five o'clock*) at the end of a sentence.

  > Auntie El came home **yesterday**.

- **Adverbs that tell where** (*upside-down, around, downstairs*) usually follow the verb they modify. Many prepositional phrases (*at the beach, under the stairs, below the water*) function as adverbs that tell where.

  > We waited **on the porch**.

- **Adverbs that tell how** (*quickly, slowly, loudly*) can be placed either at the beginning, in the middle, or at the end of a sentence—but not between a verb and its direct object.

  > **Softly** he called my name.

  > He **softly** called my name.

  > He called my name **softly**.

- **Place adverbs that modify adjectives** directly before the adjective.

  > That is a **most** unusual dress.

- **Adverbs that modify clauses** are most often placed in front of the clause, but they can also go inside or at the end of the clause.

  > **Fortunately**, we were not involved in the accident.

  > We were not involved, **fortunately**, in the accident.

  > We were not involved in the accident, **fortunately**.

Note: Adverbs that are used with verbs that have direct objects must **not** be placed between the verb and its object.

> *Correct:* Luis **usually** catches the most fish.

> *Correct:* **Usually**, Luis catches the most fish.

> **Not correct:** Luis catches **usually** the most fish.

30-1g Preposition

A **preposition** combines with a noun to form a prepositional phrase, which acts as a modifier—an adverb or an adjective. See page 334 for a list of common prepositions and for more information about prepositions.

Using *In*, *On*, *At*, and *By*

In, on, at, and *by* are four common prepositions that refer to time and place. Here are some examples of how these prepositions are used in each case.

- **To show time**

  in part of a day: . . . .
        in the afternoon

  in a year or month: . . . .
        in 2008, *in* April

  in a period of time: . . . .
        completed **in** an hour

  by a specific time or date: . . . . .
        by noon, *by* the fifth of May

  at a specific time of day or night:
        at 3:30 this afternoon

▶ **To show place**

    at a meeting place or location: . . . . . . **at** school, **at** the park

    at the edge of something: . . . sitting **at** the bar

    at the corner of something: . . . . . turning **at** the intersection

    at a target: . . . . . . throwing a dart **at** the target

    on a surface: . . . . left **on** the floor

    on an electronic medium: . . . . **on** the Internet, **on** television

    in an enclosed space: . . **in** the box, **in** the room

    in a geographic location: . . . . **in** New York City, **in** Germany

    in a print medium: . . . . **in** a journal

    by a landmark: . . . . **by** the fountain

Do **not** insert a preposition between a transitive verb and its direct object. Intransitive verbs, however, are often followed by a prepositional phrase (a phrase that begins with a preposition).

> I cooked hot dogs on the grill. (transitive verb)

> I ate in the park. (intransitive verb)

Phrasal Prepositions

Some **prepositional phrases** begin with more than one preposition. These phrasal prepositions are commonly used in both written and spoken communication. A list of common phrasal prepositions follows:

according to	in case of
across from	in spite of
along with	instead of
because of	on the side of
by way of	up to
except for	

30-2 SENTENCE BASICS

Simple sentences in the English language follow the five basic patterns shown below. (See pages 336–341 for more information.)

▶ **Subject + Verb**

> $\underline{\text{S}}$ $\underline{\text{V}}$
> Naomie winked.

Some verbs like *winked* are intransitive. Intransitive verbs do not need a direct object to express a complete thought. (See pages 327–328.)

▶ **Subject + Verb + Direct Object**

> $\underline{\text{S}}$ $\underline{\text{V}}$ $\underline{\text{DO}}$
> Harris grinds his teeth.

Some verbs like *grinds* are transitive. Transitive verbs *do* need a direct object to express a complete thought. (See pages 327–328.)

▶ **Subject + Verb + Indirect Object + Direct Object**

> $\underline{\text{S}}$ $\underline{\text{V}}$ $\underline{\text{IO}}$ $\underline{\text{DO}}$
> Elena offered her friend an anchovy.

The direct object names who or what receives the action; the indirect object names to whom or for whom the action was done.

▶ **Subject + Verb + Direct Object + Object Complement**

> $\underline{\text{S}}$ $\underline{\text{V}}$ $\underline{\text{DO}}$ $\underline{\text{OC}}$
> The chancellor named Ravi the outstanding student of 2010.

The object complement renames or describes the direct object.

▶ **Subject + Linking Verb + Predicate Nominative (or Predicate Adjective)**

> $\underline{\text{S}}$ $\underline{\text{LV}}$ $\underline{\text{PN}}$
> Paula is a biologist.
> $\underline{\text{S}}$ $\underline{\text{LV}}$ $\underline{\text{PA}}$
> Paula is very intelligent.

A linking verb connects the subject to the predicate noun or predicate adjective. The predicate noun renames the subject; the predicate adjective describes the subject.

Inverted Order

In the previous sentence patterns, the subject comes before the verb. In a few types of sentences, such as those below, the subject comes after the verb.

$$\overset{LV}{\text{Is}}\ \overset{S}{\text{Larisa}}\ \overset{PN}{\text{a poet?}}\quad \text{(A question)}$$

$$\text{There}\ \overset{LV}{\text{was}}\ \overset{S}{\text{a meeting.}}\quad \text{(A sentence beginning}$$
with "there")

30-3 SENTENCE PROBLEMS

This section looks at potential trouble spots and sentence problems. For more information about English sentences, their parts, and how to construct them, see pages 336–341 in the handbook. Pages 342–349 cover the types of problems and errors found in English writing. The guide to avoiding sentence problems found on page 349 is an excellent editing tool.

Double Negatives

When making a sentence negative, use *not* or another negative adverb (*never, rarely, hardly, seldom,* and so on), but not both. Using both results in a double negative (see page 349).

Subject–Verb Agreement

Be sure the subject and verb in every clause agree in person and number. (See pages 343–345.)

The **student was** rewarded for her hard work.

The **students were** rewarded for their hard work.

The **instructor**, as well as the students, **is** expected to attend the orientation.

The **students**, as well as the instructor, **are** expected to attend the orientation.

Omitted Words

Do not omit subjects or the expletives *there* or *here*. In all English clauses and sentences (except imperatives in which the subject *you* is understood), there must be a subject.

Correct: Your mother was very quiet; **she** seemed to be upset.

Not correct: Your mother was very quiet; seemed to be upset.

Correct: **There** is not much time left.

Not correct: Not much time left.

Repeated Words

Do not repeat the subject of a clause or sentence.

Correct: The doctor prescribed an antibiotic.

Not correct: The doctor, **she** prescribed an antibiotic.

Do not repeat an object in an adjective dependent clause.

Correct: I forgot the flowers that I intended to give to my hosts.

Not correct: I forgot the flowers that I intended to give them to my hosts.

Note: Sometimes the relative pronoun that begins the adjective dependent clause is omitted but understood.

I forgot the flowers I intended to give to my hosts. (The relative pronoun *that* is omitted.)

Conditional Sentences

Conditional sentences express a situation requiring that a condition be met in order to be true. Selecting the correct verb tense for use in the two clauses of a conditional sentence can be problematic. Following, you will find an explanation of the three types of conditional sentences and the verb tenses that are needed to form them.

1. **Factual conditionals** begin with *if, when, whenever,* or a similar expression. Furthermore, the verbs in the conditional clause and the main clause should be in the same tense.

   Whenever we **had** time, we **took** a break and **went** for a swim.

2. **Predictive conditionals** express future conditions and possible results. The conditional clause begins with *if* or *unless* and has a present tense verb. The main clause uses a modal (*will, can, should, may, might*) plus the base form of the verb.

   Unless we **find** a better deal, we **will buy** this sound system.

3. **Hypothetical past conditionals** describe a situation that is unlikely to happen or that is contrary to fact. To describe situations in the past, the verb in the conditional clause is in the past

perfect tense, and the verb in the main clause is formed from *would have, could have,* or *might have* plus the past participle.

> If we **had started out** earlier, we **would have arrived** on time.

Note: If the hypothetical situation is a present or future one, the verb in the conditional clause is in the past tense, and the verb in the main clause is formed from *would, could,* or *might* plus the base form of the verb.

> If we **bought** groceries once a week, we **would** not **have** to go to the store so often.

Quoted and Reported Speech

Sergey Nivens, 2014 / Used under license from Shutterstock.com

Quoted speech is the use of exact words from another source in your own writing; you must enclose these words in quotation marks. It is also possible to report nearly exact words without quotation marks. This is called **reported speech**, or indirect quotation. (See pages 358–359 for a review of the use of quotation marks.)

> **Direct quotation:** Felicia said, "Don't worry about tomorrow."
>
> **Indirect quotation:** Felicia said that you don't have to worry about tomorrow.

In the case of a question, when a direct quotation is changed to an indirect quotation, the question mark is not needed.

> **Direct quotation:** Ahmad asked, "Which of you will give me a hand?"
>
> **Indirect quotation:** Ahmad asked which of us would give him a hand.

Notice how pronouns are often changed in indirect quotations.

> **Direct quotation:** My friends said, "**You're** crazy."
>
> **Indirect quotation:** My friends said that **I** was crazy.

30-4 NUMBERS, WORD PARTS, AND IDIOMS

30-4a Numbers

As a multilingual/ESL learner, you may be accustomed to a way of writing numbers that is different than the way it is done in North America. Become familiar with the North American conventions for writing numbers. Pages 368–370 show you how numbers are written and punctuated in both word and numeral form.

Using Punctuation with Numerals

Note that the period is used to express percentages (5.5%), and the comma is used to organize large numbers into units (7,000; 23,100; 231,990,000). Commas are not used, however, in writing the year (2011).

Cardinal Numbers

Cardinal numbers are used when counting a number of parts or objects. Cardinal numbers can be used as nouns (she counted to **ten**), pronouns (I invited many guests, but only **three** came), or adjectives (there are **ten** boys here).

Write out in words the numbers one through one nine. Numbers 10 and greater are often written as numerals. (See page 369.)

Ordinal Numbers

Ordinal numbers show place or succession in a series: the fourth row, the twenty-first century, the tenth time, and so on. Ordinal numbers are used to talk about the parts into which a whole can be divided, such as a fourth or a tenth, and as the denominator in fractions, such as one-fourth or three-fifths. Written fractions can also be used as nouns (I gave him **four-fifths**) or as adjectives (a **four-fifths** majority).

Note: See the list below for names and symbols of the first 12 ordinal numbers. Consult a college dictionary for a complete list of cardinal and ordinal numbers.

First	1st	Seventh	7th
Second	2nd	Eighth	8th
Third	3rd	Ninth	9th
Fourth	4th	Tenth	10th
Fifth	5th	Eleventh	11th
Sixth	6th	Twelfth	12th

30-4b Prefixes, Suffixes, and Roots

Following is a list of many common word parts and their meanings. Learning them can help you determine the meaning of unfamiliar words as you come across them in your reading. For instance, if you know that *hemi* means "half," you can conclude that *hemisphere* means "half of a sphere."

Quick Guide:
Prefixes, Suffixes, and Roots

Prefixes	Meaning
a, an	not, without
anti, ant	against
co, con, com	together, with
di	two, twice
dis, dif	apart, away
ex, e, ec, ef	out
hemi, semi	half
il, ir, in, im	not
inter	between
intra	within
multi	many
non	not
ob, of, op, oc	toward, against
per	throughout
post	after
super, supr	above, more
trans, tra	across, beyond

Suffixes	Meaning
able, ible	able, can do
age	act of, state of
al	relating to
ate	cause, make
en	made of
ence, ency	action, quality
esis, osis	action, process
ice	condition, quality
ile	relating to
ish	resembling
ment	act of, state of
ology	study, theory
ous	full of, having
sion, tion	act of, state of
some	like, tending to
tude	state of

Roots	Meaning
acu	sharp
am, amor	love, liking
anthrop	man
aster, astr	star
auto	self
biblio	book
bio	life
capit, capt	head
chron	time
cit	to call, start
cred	believe
dem	people
dict	say, speak
erg	work
fid, feder	faith, trust
fract, frag	break
graph, gram	write, written
ject	throw
log, ology	word, study, speech
man	hand
micro	small
mit, miss	send
nom	law, order
onym	name
path, pathy	feeling, suffering
port	carry
rupt	break
scrib, script	write
spec, spect, spic	look
tele	far
tempo	time
tox	poison
vac	empty
ver, veri	true

30-4c Idioms

Idioms are phrases that are used in a special way. An idiom can't be understood just by knowing the meaning of each word in the phrase. It must be learned as a whole. For example, the idiom to *bury the hatchet* means to "settle an argument," even though the individual words in the phrase mean something different. Here are some common idioms in American English.

a bad apple

One troublemaker on a team may be called **a bad apple**. *(a bad influence)*

an axe to grind

Mom has **an axe to grind** with the owners of the dog that dug up her flower garden. *(a problem to settle)*

as the crow flies

She lives only two miles from here **as the crow flies**. *(in a straight line)*

beat around the bush

Dad said, "Where were you? Don't **beat around the bush**." *(avoid getting to the point)*

benefit of the doubt

Ms. Hy gave Henri the **benefit of the doubt** when he explained why he fell asleep in class. *(another chance)*

beyond the shadow of a doubt

Salvatore won the 50-yard dash **beyond the shadow of a doubt**. *(for certain)*

bone to pick

Nick had a **bone to pick** with Adrian when he learned they both liked the same girl. *(problem to settle)*

break the ice

Shanta was the first to **break the ice** in the room full of new students. *(start a conversation)*

when pigs fly

burn the midnight oil

Carmen had to **burn the midnight oil** the day before the big test. *(work late into the night)*

chomping at the bit

Dwayne was **chomping at the bit** when it was his turn to bat. *(eager, excited)*

cold shoulder

Alicia always gives me the **cold shoulder** after our disagreements. *(ignores me)*

cry wolf

If you **cry wolf** too often, no one will come when you really need help. *(say you are in trouble when you aren't)*

drop in the bucket

My donation was a **drop in the bucket**. *(a small amount compared with what's needed)*

face the music

José had to **face the music** when he got caught cheating on the test. *(deal with the consequences)*

flew off the handle

Tramayne **flew off the handle** when he saw his little brother playing with matches. *(became very angry)*

food for thought

The coach gave us some **food for thought** when she said that winning isn't everything. *(something to think about)*

get down to business

In five minutes you need to **get down to business** on this assignment. *(start working)*

get the upper hand

The other team will **get the upper hand** if we don't play better in the second half. *(probably win)*

go overboard

The teacher told us not to **go overboard** with fancy lettering on our posters. *(do too much)*

hit the ceiling

Rosa **hit the ceiling** when she saw her sister painting the television. *(was very angry)*

in a nutshell

In a nutshell, Coach Roby told us to play our best. *(to summarize)*

in the nick of time

Zong grabbed his little brother's hand **in the nick of time** before he touched the hot pan. *(just in time)*

in the same boat

My friend and I are **in the same boat** when it comes to doing Saturday chores. *(have the same problem)*

iron out

Jamil and his sister had to **iron out** their differences about cleaning their room. *(solve, work out)*

knuckle down

Grandpa told me to **knuckle down** at school if I want to be a doctor. *(work hard)*

learn the ropes

Being new in school, it took me some time to **learn the ropes**. *(get to know how things are done)*

let's face it

"**Let's face it**!" said Mr. Sills. "You're a better distance runner than you are a sprinter." *(let's admit it)*

let the cat out of the bag

Tia **let the cat out of the bag** and got her sister in trouble. *(told a secret)*

lose face

If I strike out again, I will **lose face**. *(be embarrassed)*

nose to the grindstone

If I keep my **nose to the grindstone**, I will finish my homework in one hour. *(working hard)*

on cloud nine

Walking home from the party, I was **on cloud nine**. *(feeling very happy)*

on pins and needles

I was **on pins and needles** as I waited to see the doctor. *(feeling nervous)*

put his foot in his mouth

Chivas **put his foot in his mouth** when he called his teacher by the wrong name. *(said something embarrassing)*

put your best foot forward

Grandpa said that whenever you do something, you should **put your best foot forward**. *(do the best that you can do)*

rock the boat

The coach said, "Don't **rock the boat** if you want to stay on the team." *(cause trouble)*

rude awakening

I had a **rude awakening** when I saw the letter F at the top of my quiz. *(sudden, unpleasant surprise)*

save face

Grant tried to **save face** when he said he was sorry for making fun of me in class. *(fix an embarrassing situation)*

see eye to eye

My sister and I finally **see eye to eye** about who gets to use the phone first after school. *(are in agreement)*

sight unseen

Grandma bought the television **sight unseen**. *(without seeing it first)*

take it with a grain of salt

If my sister tells you she has no homework, **take it with a grain of salt**. *(don't believe everything you're told)*

take the bull by the horns

This team needs to t**ake the bull by the horns** to win the game. *(take control)*

through thick and thin

Max and I will be friends **through thick and thin**. *(in good times and in bad times)*

time flies

When you're having fun, **time flies**. *(time passes quickly)*

time to kill

We had **time to kill** before the ballpark gates would open. *(extra time)*

under the weather

I was feeling **under the weather**, so I didn't go to school. *(sick)*

APPENDIX

Common Abbreviations

abr. abridged, abridgment

AC, ac alternating current, air-conditioning

ack. acknowledgment

AM amplitude modulation

A.M., a.m. before noon (Latin *ante meridiem*)

AP advanced placement

ASAP as soon as possible

avg., av. average

B.A. bachelor of arts degree

BBB Better Business Bureau

B.C.E. before common era

bibliog. bibliography

biog. biographer, biographical, biography

B.S. bachelor of science degree

C 1. Celsius 2. centigrade 3. coulomb

c. 1. *circa* (about) 2. cup(s)

cc 1. cubic centimeter 2. carbon copy 3. community college

CDT, C.D.T. central daylight time

C.E. common era

CEEB College Entrance Examination Board

chap. chapter(s)

cm centimeter(s)

c/o care of

COD, c.o.d. 1. cash on delivery 2. collect on delivery

co-op cooperative

CST, C.S.T. central standard time

cu 1. cubic 2. cumulative

D.A. district attorney

d.b.a., d/b/a doing business as

DC, dc direct current

dec. deceased

dept. department

disc. discount

DST, D.S.T. daylight saving time

dup. duplicate

ed. edition, editor

EDT, E.D.T. eastern daylight time

e.g. for example (Latin *exempli gratia*)

EST, E.S.T. eastern standard time

etc. and so forth (Latin *et cetera*)

F Fahrenheit, French, Friday

FM frequency modulation

F.O.B., f.o.b. free on board

FYI for your information

g 1. gravity 2. gram(s)

gal. gallon(s)

gds. goods

gloss. glossary

GNP gross national product

GPA grade point average

hdqrs. headquarters

HIV human immunodeficiency virus

hp horsepower

Hz hertz

ibid. in the same place (Latin *ibidem*)

id. the same (Latin *idem*)

i.e. that is (Latin *id est*)

illus. illustration

inc. incorporated

IQ, I.Q. intelligence quotient

IRS Internal Revenue Service

ISBN International Standard Book Number

JP, J.P. justice of the peace

K 1. kelvin (temperature unit) 2. Kelvin (temperature scale)

kc kilocycle(s)

kg kilogram(s)

km kilometer(s)

kn knot(s)

kw kilowatt(s)

L liter(s), lake

lat. latitude

l.c. lowercase

lit. literary, literature

log logarithm, logic

long. longitude

Ltd., ltd. limited

m meter(s)

M.A. master of arts degree

man. manual

Mc, mc megacycle

MC master of ceremonies

M.D. doctor of medicine (Latin *medicinae doctor*)

mdse. merchandise

MDT, M.D.T. mountain daylight time

mfg. manufacture, manufacturing

mg milligram(s)

mi. 1. mile(s) 2. mill(s) (monetary unit)

misc. miscellaneous

mL milliliter(s)

mm millimeter(s)

mpg, m.p.g. miles per gallon

mph, m.p.h. miles per hour

MS 1. manuscript 2. multiple sclerosis

Ms. title of courtesy for a woman

M.S. master of science degree

MST, M.S.T. mountain standard time

NE northeast

neg. negative

N.S.F., n.s.f. not sufficient funds

NW northwest

oz, oz. ounce(s)

PA public-address system

pct. percent

pd. paid

PDT, P.D.T. Pacific daylight time

PFC, Pfc. private first class

pg., p. page

Ph.D. doctor of philosophy

P.M., p.m. after noon (Latin *post meridiem*)

POW, P.O.W. prisoner of war

pp. pages

ppd. 1. postpaid 2. prepaid

PR, P.R. public relations

PSAT Preliminary Scholastic Aptitude Test

psi, p.s.i. pounds per square inch

PST, P.S.T. Pacific standard time

PTA, P.T.A. Parent-Teacher Association

R.A. residence assistant

RF radio frequency

R.P.M., rpm revolutions per minute

R.S.V.P., r.s.v.p. please reply (French *répondez s'il vous plaît*)

SAT Scholastic Aptitude Test

SE southeast

SOS 1. international distress signal 2. any call for help

Sr. 1. senior (after surname) 2. sister (religious)

SRO, S.R.O. standing room only

std. standard

SW southwest

syn. synonymous, synonym

tbs., tbsp. tablespoon(s)

TM trademark

UHF, uhf ultrahigh frequency

v 1. physics: velocity 2. volume

V electricity: volt

VA Veterans Administration

VHF, vhf very high frequency

VIP informal: very important person

vol. 1. volume 2. volunteer

vs. versus, verse

W 1. electricity: watt(s) 2. physics: (also w) work 3. west

whse., whs. warehouse

whsle. wholesale

wkly. weekly

w/o without

wt. weight

www World Wide Web

Word Parts

Prefixes

Prefixes are word parts that come *before* the root words (*pre* = before). Depending upon its meaning, a prefix changes the intent, or sense, of the base word.

a, an [not, without] amoral (without a sense of moral responsibility), atypical, atom (not cuttable), apathy (without feeling), anesthesia (without sensation)

ab, abs, a [from, away] abnormal, abduct, absent, avert (turn away)

acro [high] acropolis (high city), acrobat, acronym, acrophobia (fear of height)

ambi, amb [both, around] ambidextrous (skilled with both hands), ambiguous, amble

amphi [both] amphibious (living on both land and water), amphitheater

ante [before] antedate, anteroom, antebellum, antecedent (happening before)

anti, ant [against] anticommunist, antidote, anticlimax, antacid

be [on, away] bedeck, belabor, bequest, bestow, beloved

bene, bon [well] benefit, benefactor, benevolent, benediction, bonanza, bonus

bi, bis, bin [both, double, twice] bicycle, biweekly, bilateral, biscuit, binoculars

by [side, close, near] bypass, bystander, by-product, bylaw, byline

cata [down, against] catalog, catapult, catastrophe, cataclysm

cerebro [brain] cerebral, cerebrum, cerebellum

circum, circ [around] circumference, circumnavigate, circumspect, circular

co, con, col, com [together, with] copilot, conspire, collect, compose

coni [dust] coniosis (disease that comes from inhaling dust)

contra, counter [against] controversy, contradict, counterpart

de [from, down] demote, depress, degrade, deject, deprive

deca [ten] decade, decathlon, decapod (10 feet)

di [two, twice] divide, dilemma, dilute, dioxide, dipole, ditto

dia [through, between] diameter, diagonal, diagram, dialogue (speech between people)

dis, dif [apart, away, reverse] dismiss, distort, distinguish, diffuse

dys [badly, ill] dyspepsia (digesting badly), dystrophy, dysentery

em, en [in, into] embrace, enslave

epi [upon] epidermis (upon the skin, outer layer of skin), epitaph, epithet

eu [well] eulogize (speak well of, praise), euphony, euphemism, euphoria

ex, e, ec, ef [out] expel (drive out), ex-mayor, exorcism, eject, eccentric (out of the center position), efflux, effluent

extra, extro [beyond, outside] extraordinary (beyond the ordinary), extrovert, extracurricular

for [away or off] forswear (to renounce an oath)

fore [before in time] forecast, foretell (to tell beforehand), foreshadow

hemi, demi, semi [half] hemisphere, demitasse, semicircle (half of a circle)

hex [six] hexameter, hexagon

homo [man] Homo sapiens, homicide (killing man)

hyper [over, above] hypersensitive (overly sensitive), hyperactive

hypo [under] hypodermic (under the skin), hypothesis

il, ir, in, im [not] illegal, irregular, incorrect, immoral

in, il, im [into] inject, inside, illuminate, illustrate, impose, implant, imprison

infra [beneath] infrared, infrasonic

inter [between] intercollegiate, interfere, intervene, interrupt (break between)

intra [within] intramural, intravenous (within the veins)

intro [into, inward] introduce, introvert (turn inward)

macro [large, excessive] macrodent (having large teeth), macrocosm

mal [badly, poorly] maladjusted, malady, malnutrition, malfunction

meta [beyond, after, with] metaphor, metamorphosis, metaphysical

mis [incorrect, bad] misuse, misprint

miso [hate] misanthrope, misogynist

mono [one] monoplane, monotone, monochrome, monocle

multi [many] multiply, multiform

neo [new] neopaganism, neoclassic, neophyte, neonatal

non [not] nontaxable (not taxed), nontoxic, nonexistent, nonsense

ob, of, op, oc [toward, against] obstruct, offend, oppose, occur

oct [eight] octagon, octameter, octave, octopus

paleo [ancient] paleoanthropology (pertaining to ancient humans), paleontology (study of ancient life-forms)

para [beside, almost] parasite (one who eats beside or at the table of another), paraphrase, paramedic, parallel, paradox

penta [five] pentagon (figure or building having five angles or sides), pentameter, pentathlon

per [throughout, completely] pervert (completely turn wrong, corrupt), perfect, perceive, permanent, persuade

peri [around] perimeter (measurement around an area), periphery, periscope, pericardium, period

poly [many] polygon (figure having many angles or sides), polygamy, polyglot, polychrome

post [after] postpone, postwar, postscript, posterity

pre [before] prewar, preview, precede, prevent, premonition

pro [forward, in favor of] project (throw forward), progress, promote, prohibition

pseudo [false] pseudonym (false or assumed name), pseudopodia

quad [four] quadruple (four times as much), quadriplegic, quadratic, quadrant

quint [five] quintuplet, quintuple, quintet, quintile

re [back, again] reclaim, revive, revoke, rejuvenate, retard, reject, return

retro [backward] retrospective (looking backward), retroactive, retrorocket

se [aside] seduce (lead aside), secede, secrete, segregate

self [by oneself] self-determination, self-employed, self-service, selfish

sesqui [one and a half] sesquicentennial (one and one-half centuries)

sex, sest [six] sexagenarian (sixty years old), sexennial, sextant, sextuplet, sestet

sub [under] submerge (put under), submarine, substitute, subsoil

suf, sug, sup, sus [from under] sufficient, suffer, suggest, support, suspend

super, supr [above, over, more] supervise, superman, supernatural, supreme

syn, sym, sys, syl [with, together] system, synthesis, synchronize (time together), synonym, sympathy, symphony, syllable

trans, tra [across, beyond] transoceanic, transmit (send across), transfusion, tradition

tri [three] tricycle, triangle, tripod, tristate

ultra [beyond, exceedingly] ultramodern, ultraviolet, ultraconservative

un [not, release] unfair, unnatural, unknown

under [beneath] underground, underlying

uni [one] unicycle, uniform, unify, universe, unique (one of a kind)

vice [in place of] vice president, viceroy, vice admiral

Numerical Prefixes

Prefix	Symbol	Multiples and Submultiples	Equivalent
tera	T	10^{12}	trillionfold
giga	G	10^9	billionfold
mega	M	10^6	millionfold
kilo	k	10^3	thousandfold
hecto	h	10^2	hundredfold
deka	da	10	tenfold
deci	d	10^{-1}	tenth part

Prefix	Symbol	Multiples and Submultiples	Equivalent
centi	c	10^{-2}	hundredth part
milli	m	10^{-3}	thousandth part
micro	u	10^{-6}	millionth part
nano	n	10^{-9}	billionth part
pico	p	10^{-12}	trillionth part
femto	f	10^{-15}	quadrillionth part
atto	a	10^{-18}	quintillionth part

Suffixes

Suffixes come at the end of a word. Very often a suffix will tell you what kind of word it is part of (noun, adverb, adjective). For example, words ending in *-ly* are usually adverbs.

able, ible [able, can do] capable, agreeable, edible, visible (can be seen)

ade [result of action] blockade (the result of a blocking action), lemonade

age [act of, state of, collection of] salvage (act of saving), storage, forage

al [relating to] sensual, gradual, manual, natural (relating to nature)

algia [pain] neuralgia (nerve pain)

an, ian [native of, relating to] African, Canadian, Floridian

ance, ancy [action, process, state] assistance, allowance, defiance, truancy

ant [performing, agent] assistant, servant

ary, ery, ory [relating to, quality, place where] dictionary, bravery, dormitory

ate [cause, make] liquidate, segregate (cause a group to be set aside)

cian [having a certain skill or art] musician, beautician, magician, physician

cule, ling [very small] molecule, ridicule, duckling (very small duck), sapling

cy [action, function] hesitancy, prophecy, normalcy (function in a normal way)

dom [quality, realm, office] freedom, kingdom, wisdom (quality of being wise)

ee [one who receives the action] employee, nominee (one who is nominated), refugee

en [made of, make] silken, frozen, oaken (made of oak), wooden, lighten

ence, ency [action, state of, quality] difference, conference, urgency

er, or [one who, that which] baker, miller, teacher, racer, amplifier, doctor

escent [in the process of] adolescent (in the process of becoming an adult), obsolescent, convalescent

ese [a native of, the language of] Japanese, Vietnamese, Portuguese

esis, osis [action, process, condition] genesis, hypnosis, neurosis, osmosis

ess [female] actress, goddess, lioness

et, ette [a small one, group] midget, octet, baronet, majorette

fic [making, causing] scientific, specific

ful [full of] frightful, careful, helpful

fy [make] fortify (make strong), simplify, amplify

hood [order, condition, quality] manhood, womanhood, brotherhood

ic [nature of, like] metallic (of the nature of metal), heroic, poetic, acidic

ice [condition, state, quality] justice, malice

id, ide [a thing connected with or belonging to] fluid, fluoride

ile [relating to, suited for, capable of] missile, juvenile, senile (related to being old)

ine [nature of] feminine, genuine, medicine

ion, sion, tion [act of, state of, result of] contagion, aversion, infection (state of being infected)

ish [origin, nature, resembling] foolish, Irish, clownish (resembling a clown)

ism [system, manner, condition, characteristic] heroism, alcoholism, Communism

ist [one who, that which] artist, dentist

ite [nature of, quality of, mineral product] Israelite, dynamite, graphite, sulfite

ity, ty [state of, quality] captivity, clarity

ive [causing, making] abusive (causing abuse), exhaustive

ize [make] emphasize, publicize, idolize

less [without] baseless, careless (without care), artless, fearless, helpless

ly [like, manner of] carelessly, quickly, forcefully, lovingly

ment [act of, state of, result] contentment, amendment (state of amending)

ness [state of] carelessness, kindness

oid [resembling] asteroid, spheroid, tabloid, anthropoid

ology [study, science, theory] biology, anthropology, geology, neurology

ous [full of, having] gracious, nervous, spacious, vivacious (full of life)

ship [office, state, quality, skill] friendship, authorship, dictatorship

some [like, apt, tending to] lonesome, threesome, gruesome

tude [state of, condition of] gratitude, multitude (condition of being many), aptitude

ure [state of, act, process, rank] culture, literature, rupture (state of being broken)

ward [in the direction of] eastward, forward, backward

y [inclined to, tend to] cheery, crafty, faulty

Roots

A *root* is a base upon which other words are built. Knowing the root of a difficult word can go a long way toward helping you figure out its meaning.

acer, acid, acri [bitter, sour, sharp] acrid, acerbic, acidity (sourness), acrimony

acu [sharp] acute, acupuncture

ag, agi, ig, act [do, move, go] agent (doer), agenda (things to do), agitate, navigate (move by sea), ambiguous (going both ways), action

ali, allo, alter [other] alias (a person's other name), alibi, alien (from another place), alloy, alter (change to another form)

alt [high, deep] altimeter (a device for measuring heights), altitude

am, amor [love, liking] amiable, amorous, enamored

anni, annu, enni [year] anniversary, annually (yearly), centennial (occurring once in 100 years)

anthrop [man] anthropology (study of mankind), philanthropy (love of mankind), misanthrope (hater of mankind)

anti [old] antique, antiquated, antiquity

arch [chief, first, rule] archangel (chief angel), architect (chief worker), archaic (first, very early), monarchy (rule by one person), matriarchy (rule by the mother)

aster, astr [star] aster (star flower), asterisk, asteroid, astronomy (star law), astronaut (star traveler, space traveler)

aud, aus [hear, listen] audible (can be heard), auditorium, audio, audition, auditory, audience, ausculate

aug, auc [increase] augur, augment (add to; increase), auction

auto, aut [self] autograph (self-writing), automobile (self-moving vehicle), author, automatic (self-acting), autobiography

belli [war] rebellion, belligerent (warlike or hostile)

bibl [book] Bible, bibliography (list of books), bibliomania (craze for books), bibliophile (book lover)

bio [life] biology (study of life), biography, biopsy (cut living tissue for examination)

brev [short] abbreviate, brevity, brief

cad, cas [to fall] cadaver, cadence, caducous (falling off), cascade

calor [heat] calorie (a unit of heat), calorify (to make hot), caloric

cap, cip, cept [take] capable, capacity, capture, reciprocate, accept, except, concept

capit, capt [head] decapitate (to remove the head from), capital, captain, caption

carn [flesh] carnivorous (flesh eating), incarnate, reincarnation

caus, caut [burn, heat] caustic, cauterize (to make hot, to burn)

cause, cuse, cus [cause, motive] because, excuse (to attempt to remove the blame or cause), accusation

ced, ceed, cede, cess [move, yield, go, surrender] procedure, secede (move aside from), proceed (move forward), cede (yield), concede, intercede, precede, recede, success

centri [center] concentric, centrifugal, centripetal, eccentric (out of center)

chrom [color] chrome, chromosome (color body in genetics), chromosphere, monochrome (one color), polychrome

chron [time] chronological (in order of time), chronometer (time measured), chronicle (record of events in time), synchronize (make time with, set time together)

cide, cise [cut down, kill] suicide (killing of self), homicide (human killer), pesticide (pest killer), germicide (germ killer), insecticide, precise (cut exactly right), incision, scissors

cit [to call, start] incite, citation, cite

civ [citizen] civic (relating to a citizen), civil, civilian, civilization

clam, claim [cry out] exclamation, clamor, proclamation, reclamation, acclaim

clud, clus, claus [shut] include (to take in), conclude, claustrophobia (abnormal fear of being shut up, confined), recluse (one who shuts himself away from others)

cognosc, gnosi [know] recognize (to know again), incognito (not known), prognosis (forward knowing), diagnosis

cord, cor, cardi [heart] cordial (hearty, heartfelt), concord, discord, courage, encourage (put heart into), discourage (take heart out of), core, coronary, cardiac

corp [body] corporation (a legal body), corpse, corpulent

cosm [universe, world] cosmic, cosmos (the universe), cosmopolitan (world citizen), cosmonaut, microcosm, macrocosm

crat, cracy [rule, strength] democratic, autocracy

crea [create] creature (anything created), recreation, creation, creator

cred [believe] creed (statement of beliefs), credo (a creed), credence (belief), credit (belief, trust), credulous (believing too readily, easily deceived), incredible

cresc, cret, crease, cru [rise, grow] crescendo (growing in loudness or intensity), concrete (grown together, solidified), increase, decrease, accrue (to grow)

crit [separate, choose] critical, criterion (that which is used in choosing), hypocrite

cur, curs [run] concurrent, current (running or flowing), concur (run together, agree), incur (run into), recur, occur, precursor (forerunner), cursive

cura [care] curator, curative, manicure (caring for the hands)

cycl, cyclo [wheel, circular] Cyclops (a mythical giant with one eye in the middle of his forehead), unicycle, bicycle, cyclone (a wind blowing circularly, a tornado)

deca [ten] decade, decalogue, decathlon

dem [people] democracy (people-rule), demography (vital statistics of the people: deaths, births, and so on), epidemic (on or among the people)

dent, dont [tooth] dental (relating to teeth), denture, dentifrice, orthodontist

derm [skin] hypodermic (injected under the skin), dermatology (skin study), epidermis (outer layer of skin), taxidermy (arranging skin; mounting animals)

dict [say, speak] diction (how one speaks, what one says), dictionary, dictate, dictator, dictaphone, dictatorial, edict, predict, verdict, contradict, benediction

doc [teach] indoctrinate, document, doctrine

domin [master] dominate, dominion, predominant, domain

don [give] donate, condone

dorm [sleep] dormant, dormitory

dox [opinion, praise] doxy (belief, creed, or opinion), orthodox (having the correct, commonly accepted opinion), heterodox (differing opinion), paradox (contradictory)

drome [run, step] syndrome (run-together symptoms), hippodrome (a place where horses run)

duc, duct [lead] produce, induce (lead into, persuade), seduce (lead aside), reduce, aqueduct (water leader or channel), viaduct, conduct

dura [hard, lasting] durable, duration, endurance

dynam [power] dynamo (power producer), dynamic, dynamite, hydrodynamics

endo [within] endoral (within the mouth), endocardial (within the heart), endoskeletal

equi [equal] equinox, equilibrium

erg [work] energy, erg (unit of work), allergy, ergophobia (morbid fear of work), ergometer, ergonomic

fac, fact, fic, fect [do, make] factory (place where workers make goods of various kinds), fact (a thing done), manufacture, amplification, confection

fall, fals [deceive] fallacy, falsify

fer [bear, carry] ferry (carry by water), coniferous (bearing cones, as a pine tree), fertile (bearing richly), defer, infer, refer

fid, fide, feder [faith, trust] confidant, Fido, fidelity, confident, infidelity, infidel, federal, confederacy

fila, fili [thread] filament (a single thread or threadlike object), filibuster, filigree

fin [end, ended, finished] final, finite, finish, confine, fine, refine, define, finale

fix [attach] fix, fixation (the state of being attached), fixture, affix, prefix, suffix

flex, flect [bend] flex, reflex (bending back), flexible, flexor (muscle for bending), inflexibility, reflect, deflect

flu, fluc, fluv [flowing] influence (to flow in), fluid, flue, flush, fluently, fluctuate (to wave in an unsteady motion)

form [form, shape] form, uniform, conform, deform, reform, perform, formative, formation, formal, formula

fort, forc [strong] fort, fortress (a strong place), fortify (make strong), forte (one's strong point), fortitude, enforce

fract, frag [break] fracture (a break), infraction, fragile (easy to break), fraction (result of breaking a whole into equal parts), refract (to break or bend)

gam [marriage] bigamy (two marriages), monogamy, polygamy (many spouses or marriages)

gastr(o) [stomach] gastric, gastronomic, gastritis (inflammation of the stomach)

gen [birth, race, produce] genesis (birth, beginning), genetics (study of heredity), eugenics (well born), genealogy (lineage by race, stock), generate, genetic

geo [earth] geometry (earth measurement), geography (earth writing), geocentric (earth centered), geology

germ [vital part] germination (to grow), germ (seed; living substance, as the germ of an idea), germane

gest [carry, bear] congest (bear together, clog), congestive (causing clogging), gestation

gloss, glot [tongue] glossary, polyglot (many tongues), epiglottis

glu, glo [lump, bond, glue] glue, agglutinate (make to hold in a bond), conglomerate (bond together)

grad, gress [step, go] grade (step, degree), gradual (step-by-step), graduate (make all the steps, finish a course), graduated (in steps or degrees), progress

graph, gram [write, written] graph, graphic (written, vivid), autograph (self-writing, signature), graphite (carbon used for writing), photography (light writing), phonograph (sound writing), diagram, bibliography, telegram

grat [pleasing] gratuity (mark of favor, a tip), congratulate (express pleasure over success), grateful, ingrate (not thankful)

grav [heavy, weighty] grave, gravity, aggravate, gravitate

greg [herd, group, crowd] gregarian (belonging to a herd), congregation (a group functioning together), segregate (tending to group aside or apart)

helio [sun] heliograph (an instrument for using the sun's rays to send signals), heliotrope (a plant that turns to the sun)

hema, hemo [blood] hemorrhage (an outpouring or flowing of blood), hemoglobin, hemophilia

here, hes [stick] adhere, cohere, cohesion

hetero [different] heterogeneous (different in birth), heterosexual (with interest in the opposite sex)

homo [same] homogeneous (of same birth or kind), homonym (word with same pronunciation as another), homogenize

hum, human [earth, ground, man] humus, exhume (to take out of the ground), humane (compassion for other humans)

hydr, hydra, hydro [water] dehydrate, hydrant, hydraulic, hydraulics, hydrogen, hydrophobia (fear of water)

hypn [sleep] hypnosis, Hypnos (god of sleep), hypnotherapy (treatment of disease by hypnosis)

ignis [fire] ignite, igneous, ignition

ject [throw] deject, inject, project (throw forward), eject, object

join, junct [join] adjoining, enjoin (to lay an order upon, to command), juncture, conjunction, injunction

juven [young] juvenile, rejuvenate (to make young again)

lau, lav, lot, lut [wash] launder, lavatory, lotion, ablution (a washing away), dilute (to make a liquid thinner and weaker)

leg [law] legal (lawful; according to law), legislate (to enact a law), legislature, legitimize (make legal)

levi [light] alleviate (lighten a load), levitate, levity (light conversation; humor)

liber, liver [free] liberty (freedom), liberal, liberalize (to make more free), deliverance

liter [letters] literary (concerned with books and writing), literature, literal, alliteration, obliterate

loc, loco [place] locality, locale, location, allocate (to assign, to place), relocate (to put back into place), locomotion (act of moving from place to place)

log, logo, ogue, ology [word, study, speech] catalog, prologue, dialogue, logogram (a symbol representing a word), zoology (animal study), psychology (mind study)

loqu, locut [talk, speak] eloquent (speaking well and forcefully), soliloquy, locution, loquacious (talkative), colloquial (talking together; conversational or informal)

luc, lum, lus, lun [light] translucent (letting light come through), lumen (a unit of light), luminary (a heavenly body; someone who shines in his or her profession), luster (sparkle, shine), Luna (the moon goddess)

magn [great] magnify (make great, enlarge), magnificent, magnanimous (great of mind or spirit), magnate, magnitude, magnum

man [hand] manual, manage, manufacture, manacle, manicure, manifest, maneuver, emancipate

mand [command] mandatory (commanded), remand (order back), mandate

mania [madness] mania (insanity, craze), monomania (mania on one idea), kleptomania, pyromania (insane tendency to set fires), maniac

mar, mari, mer [sea, pool] marine (a soldier serving on a ship), marsh (wetland, swamp), maritime (relating to the sea and navigation), mermaid (fabled sea creature: half fish, half woman)

matri [mother] maternal (relating to the mother), matrimony, matriarchate (rulership of women), matron

medi [half, middle, between, halfway] mediate (come between, intervene), medieval (pertaining to the Middle Ages), Mediterranean (lying between lands), mediocre, medium

mega [great, million] megaphone (great sound), megalopolis (great city; an extensive urban area including a number of cities), megacycle (a million cycles), megaton

mem [remember] memo (a reminder), commemoration (the act of remembering by a memorial or ceremony), memento, memoir, memorable

meter [measure] meter (a metric measure), voltameter (instrument to measure volts), barometer, thermometer

micro [small] microscope, microfilm, microcard, microwave, micrometer (device for measuring small distances), omicron, micron (a millionth of a meter), microbe (small living thing)

migra [wander] migrate (to wander), emigrate (one who leaves a country), immigrate (to come into the land)

mit, miss [send] emit (send out, give off), remit (send back, as money due), submit, admit, commit, permit, transmit (send across), omit, intermittent (sending between, at intervals), mission, missile

mob, mot, mov [move] mobile (capable of moving), motionless (without motion), motor, emotional (moved strongly by feelings), motivate, promotion, demote, movement

mon [warn, remind] monument (a reminder or memorial of a person or an event), admonish (warn), monitor, premonition (forewarning)

mor, mort [mortal, death] mortal (causing death or destined for death), immortal (not subject to death), mortality (rate of death), mortician (one who prepares the dead for burial), mortuary (place for the dead, a morgue)

morph [form] amorphous (with no form, shapeless), metamorphosis (a change of form, as a caterpillar into a butterfly), morphology

multi [many, much] multifold (folded many times), multilinguist (one who speaks many languages), multiped (an organism with many feet), multiply

nat, nasc [to be born, to spring forth] innate (inborn), natal, native, nativity, renascence (a rebirth, a revival)

neur [nerve] neuritis (inflammation of a nerve), neurology (study of nervous systems), neurologist (one who practices neurology), neural, neurosis, neurotic

nom [law, order] autonomy (self-law, self-government), astronomy, gastronomy (art or science of good eating), economy

nomen, nomin [name] nomenclature, nominate (name someone for an office)

nov [new] novel (new, strange, not formerly known), renovate (to make like new again), novice, nova, innovate

nox, noc [night] nocturnal, equinox (equal nights), noctilucent (shining by night)

numer [number] numeral (a figure expressing a number), numeration (act of counting), enumerate (count out, one by one), innumerable

omni [all, every] omnipotent (all-powerful), omniscient (all-knowing), omnipresent (present everywhere), omnivorous

onym [name] anonymous (without name), synonym, pseudonym (false name), antonym (name of opposite meaning)

oper [work] operate (to labor, function), cooperate (work together)

ortho [straight, correct] orthodox (of the correct or accepted opinion), orthodontist (tooth straightener), orthopedic (originally pertaining to straightening a child), unorthodox

pac [peace] pacifist (one for peace only; opposed to war), pacify (make peace, quiet), Pacific Ocean (peaceful ocean)

pan [all] panacea (cure-all), pandemonium (place of all the demons, wild disorder), pantheon (place of all the gods in mythology)

pater, patr [father] paternity (fatherhood, responsibility), patriarch (head of the tribe, family), patriot, patron (a wealthy person who supports as would a father)

path, pathy [feeling, suffering] pathos (feeling of pity, sorrow), sympathy, antipathy (feeling against), apathy (without feeling), empathy (feeling or identifying with another), telepathy (far feeling; thought transference)

ped, pod [foot] pedal (lever for a foot), impede (get the feet in a trap, hinder), pedestal (foot or base of a statue), pedestrian (foot traveler), centipede, tripod (three-footed support), podiatry (care of the feet), antipodes (opposite feet)

pedo [child] orthopedic, pedagogue (child leader; teacher), pediatrics (medical care of children)

pel, puls [drive, urge] compel, dispel, expel, repel, propel, pulse, impulse, pulsate, compulsory, expulsion, repulsive

pend, pens, pond [hang, weigh] pendant pendulum, suspend, appendage, pensive (weighing thought), ponderous

phil [love] philosophy (love of wisdom), philanthropy, philharmonic, bibliophile, Philadelphia (city of brotherly love)

phobia [fear] claustrophobia (fear of closed spaces), acrophobia (fear of high places), hydrophobia (fear of water)

phon [sound] phonograph, phonetic (pertaining to sound), symphony (sounds with or together)

photo [light] photograph (light-writing), photoelectric, photogenic (artistically suitable for being photographed), photosynthesis (action of light on chlorophyll to make carbohydrates)

plac [please] placid (calm, peaceful), placebo, placate, complacent

plu, plur, plus [more] plural (more than one), pluralist (a person who holds more than one office), plus (indicating that something more is to be added)

pneuma, pneumon [breath] pneumatic (pertaining to air, wind, or other gases), pneumonia (disease of the lungs)

pod (see ped)

poli [city] metropolis (mother city), police, politics, Indianapolis, Acropolis (high city, upper part of Athens), megalopolis

pon, pos, pound [place, put] postpone (put afterward), component, opponent (one put against), proponent, expose, impose, deposit, posture (how one places oneself), position, expound, impound

pop [people] population, populous (full of people), popular

port [carry] porter (one who carries), portable, transport (carry across), report, export, import, support, transportation

portion [part, share] portion (a part; a share, as a portion of pie), proportion (the relation of one share to others)

prehend [seize] comprehend (seize with the mind), apprehend (seize a criminal), comprehensive (seizing much, extensive)

prim, prime [first] primacy (state of being first in rank), prima donna (the first lady of opera), primitive (from the earliest or first time), primary, primal, primeval

proto [first] prototype (the first model made), protocol, protagonist, protozoan

psych [mind, soul] psyche (soul, mind), psychiatry (healing of the mind), psychology, psychosis (serious mental disorder), psychotherapy (mind treatment), psychic

punct [point, dot] punctual (being exactly on time), punctuation, puncture, acupuncture

reg, recti [straighten] regiment, regular, regulate, rectify (make straight), correct, direction

ri, ridi, risi [laughter] deride (mock, jeer at), ridicule (laughter at the expense of another, mockery), ridiculous, derision

rog, roga [ask] prerogative (privilege; asking before), interrogation (questioning; the act of questioning), derogatory

rupt [break] rupture (break), interrupt (break into), abrupt (broken off), disrupt (break apart), erupt (break out), incorruptible (unable to be broken down)

sacr, sanc, secr [sacred] sacred, sanction, sacrosanct, consecrate, desecrate

salv, salu [safe, healthy] salvation (act of being saved), salvage, salutation

sat, satis [enough] saturate, satisfy (to give as much as is needed)

sci [know] science (knowledge), conscious (knowing, aware), omniscient (knowing everything)

scope [see, watch] telescope, microscope, kaleidoscope (instrument for seeing beautiful forms), periscope, stethoscope

scrib, script [write] scribe (a writer), scribble, manuscript (written by hand), inscribe, describe, subscribe, prescribe

sed, sess, sid [sit] sediment (that which sits or settles out of a liquid), session (a sitting), obsession (an idea that sits stubbornly in the mind), possess, preside (sit before), president, reside, subside

sen [old] senior, senator, senile (old; showing the weakness of old age)

sent, sens [feel] sentiment (feeling), consent, resent, dissent, sentimental (having strong feeling or emotion), sense, sensation, sensitive, sensory, dissension

sequ, secu, sue [follow] sequence (following of one thing after another), sequel, consequence, subsequent, prosecute, consecutive (following in order), second (following "first"), ensue, pursue

serv [save, serve] servant, service, preserve, subservient, servitude, conserve, reservation, deserve, conservation

sign, signi [sign, mark, seal] signal (a gesture or sign to call attention), signature (the mark of a person written in his or her own handwriting), design, insignia (distinguishing marks)

simil, simul [like, resembling] similar (resembling in many respects), assimilate (to make similar to), simile, simulate (pretend; put on an act to make a certain impression)

sist, sta, stit [stand] persist (stand firmly; unyielding; continue), assist (to stand by with help), circumstance, stamina (power to withstand, to endure), status (standing), state, static, stable, stationary, substitute (to stand in for another)

solus [alone] soliloquy, solitaire, solitude, solo

solv, solu [loosen] solvent (a loosener, a dissolver), solve, absolve (loosen from, free from), resolve, soluble, solution, resolution, resolute, dissolute (loosened morally)

somnus [sleep] insomnia (not being able to sleep), somnambulist (a sleepwalker)

soph [wise] sophomore (wise fool), philosophy (love of wisdom), sophisticated

spec, spect, spic [look] specimen (an example to look at, study), specific, aspect, spectator (one who looks), spectacle, speculate, inspect, respect, prospect, retrospective (looking backward), introspective, expect, conspicuous

sphere [ball, sphere] stratosphere (the upper portion of the atmosphere), hemisphere (half of the earth), spheroid

spir [breath] spirit (breath), conspire (breathe together; plot), inspire (breathe into), aspire (breathe toward), expire (breathe out; die), perspire, respiration

string, strict [draw tight] stringent (drawn tight; rigid), strict, restrict, constrict (draw tightly together), boa constrictor (snake that constricts its prey)

stru, struct [build] construe (build in the mind, interpret), structure, construct, instruct, obstruct, destruction, destroy

sume, sump [take, use, waste] consume (to use up), assume (to take; to use), sump pump (a pump that takes up water), presumption (to take or use before knowing all the facts)

tact, tang, tag, tig, ting [touch] contact, tactile, intangible (not able to be touched), intact (untouched, uninjured), tangible, contingency, contagious (able to transmit disease by touching), contiguous

tele [far] telephone (far sound), telegraph (far writing), television (far seeing), telephoto (far photography), telecast

tempo [time] tempo (rate of speed), temporary, extemporaneously, contemporary (those who live at the same time), pro tem (for the time being)

ten, tin, tain [hold] tenacious (holding fast), tenant, tenure, untenable, detention, content, pertinent, continent, obstinate, abstain, pertain, detain

tend, tent, tens [stretch, strain] tendency (a stretching; leaning), extend, intend, contend, pretend, superintend, tender, extent, tension (a stretching, strain), pretense

terra [earth] terrain, terrarium, territory, terrestrial

test [to bear witness] testament (a will; bearing witness to someone's wishes), detest, attest (bear witness to), testimony

the, theo [God, a god] monotheism (belief in one god), polytheism (belief in many gods), atheism, theology

therm [heat] thermometer, therm (heat unit), thermal, thermostat, thermos, hypothermia (subnormal temperature)

thesis, thet [place, put] antithesis (place against), hypothesis (place under), synthesis (put together), epithet

tom [cut] atom (not cuttable; smallest particle of matter), appendectomy (cutting out an appendix), tonsillectomy, dichotomy (cutting in two; a division), anatomy (cutting, dissecting to study structure)

tort, tors [twist] torture (twisting to inflict pain), retort (twist back, reply sharply), extort (twist out), distort (twist out of shape), contort, torsion (act of twisting, as a torsion bar)

tox [poison] toxic (poisonous), intoxicate, antitoxin

tract, tra [draw, pull] tractor, attract, subtract, tractable (can be handled), abstract (to draw away), subtrahend (the number to be drawn away from another)

trib [pay, bestow] tribute (to pay honor to), contribute (to give money to a cause), attribute, retribution, tributary

turbo [disturb] turbulent, disturb, turbid, turmoil

typ [print] type, prototype (first print; model), typical, typography, typewriter, typology (study of types, symbols), typify

ultima [last] ultimate, ultimatum (the final or last offer that can be made)

uni [one] unicorn (a legendary creature with one horn), unify (make into one), university, unanimous, universal

vac [empty] vacate (to make empty), vacuum (a space entirely devoid of matter), evacuate (to remove troops or people), vacation, vacant

vale, vali, valu [strength, worth] valiant, equivalent (of equal worth), validity (truth; legal strength), evaluate (find out the value), value, valor (value; worth)

ven, vent [come] convene (come together, assemble), intervene (come between), venue, convenient, avenue, circumvent (come or go around), invent, prevent

ver, veri [true] very, aver (say to be true, affirm), verdict, verity (truth), verify (show to be true), verisimilitude

vert, vers [turn] avert (turn away), divert (turn aside, amuse), invert (turn over), introvert (turn inward), convertible, reverse (turn back), controversy (a turning against; a dispute), versatile (turning easily from one skill to another)

vic, vicis [change, substitute] vicarious, vicar, vicissitude

vict, vinc [conquer] victor (conqueror, winner), evict (conquer out, expel), convict (prove guilty), convince (conquer mentally, persuade), invincible (not conquerable)

vid, vis [see] video, television, evident, provide, providence, visible, revise, supervise (oversee), vista, visit, vision

viv, vita, vivi [alive, life] revive (make live again), survive (live beyond, outlive), vivid, vivacious (full of life), vitality

voc [call] vocation (a calling), avocation (occupation not one's calling), convocation (a calling together), invocation, vocal

vol [will] malevolent, benevolent (one of goodwill), volunteer, volition

volcan, vulcan [fire] volcano (a mountain erupting fiery lava), volcanize (to undergo volcanic heat), Vulcan (Roman god of fire)

volvo [turn about, roll] revolve, voluminous (winding), voluble (easily turned about or around), convolution (a twisting)

vor [eat greedily] voracious, carnivorous (flesh eating), herbivorous (plant eating), omnivorous (eating everything), devour

zo [animal] zoo (short for zoological garden), zoology (study of animal life), zodiac (circle of animal constellations), zoomorphism (being in the form of an animal), protozoa (one-celled animals)

CREDITS

Professional Samples

Page 5: Dan Heath, Why Change Is So Hard: Self-Control Is Exhaustible, *Fast Company*, June 2, 2010. Copyright 2010 Mansueto Ventures LLC. All rights reserved. Permission conveyed through the Copyright Clearance Center.

Page 100: Mary Seymour. "Call Me Crazy, But I Have to Be Myself." Originally appeared in *Newsweek*, July 29, 2002. Reprinted by permission of the author.

Page 102: "The Muscle Mystique" from HIGH TIDE IN TUCSON: ESSAYS FROM NOW OR NEVER by BARBARA KINGSOLVER. Copyright (c) 1995 by Barbara Kingsolver. Reprinted by permission of HarperCollins Publishers.

Page 114: Essay, "Daft or Deft," by David Schelhaas. Reprinted by permission of the author.

Page 115: ©2014 National Public Radio, Inc. News report titled "Segregated from Its History, How 'Ghetto' Lost Its Meaning" by Camila Domonoske was originally published on NPR.org on April 27, 2014, and is used with the permission of NPR. Any unauthorized duplication is strictly prohibited.

Page 126: Jessica Seigel, "The Lion, the Witch, and the Metaphor." From The New York Times, December 12, 2005. © 2005 The New York Times. All rights reserved. Used by permission and protected by the Copyright Laws of the United States. The printing, copying, redistribution, or retransmission of this Content without express written permission is prohibited.

Page 133: Daniel Francis, "The Bureaucrat's Indian." From *The Imaginary Indian: The Image of the Indian in Canadian Culture*. Reprinted by permission of the author.

Page 137: "Saint Cesar of Delano." From DARLING: A SPIRITUAL AUTOBIOGRAPHY by Richard Rodriguez, copyright (c) 2013 by Richard Rodriguez. Used by permission of Viking Penguin, a division of Penguin Group (USA) LLC.

Page 148: Gelareh Asayesh, "Shrouded in Contradiction." Copyright 2001. Gelareh Asayesh. First appeared in The New York Times Magazine, November 2, 2001. Reprinted by permission of the author.

Page 150: Shankar Vedantam, "Shades of Prejudice." Reprinted by permission of SLL/Sterling Lord Literistic, Inc. Copyright by Shankar Vedantam.

Page 161: Steven Pinker, "Mind Over Mass Media" From The New York Times, June 11, 2010.© 2010 The New York Times. All rights reserved. Used by permission and protected by the Copyright Laws of the United States. The printing, copying, redistribution, or retransmission of this Content without express written permission is prohibited.

Page 168: John Van Rys, "Four Ways to Talk About Literature." Reprinted by permission of the author.

Page 170: Robert Browning, "My Last Duchess" Reprinted under the public domain.

Page 174: Jane Kenyon, "Let Evening Come" from Collected Poems. Copyright © 2005 by The Estate of Jane Kenyon. Reprinted with the permission of The Permissions Company, Inc. on behalf of Graywolf Press, Minneapolis, Minnesota, www.graywolfpress.org.

Page 198: Eric Foner, "The Emancipation of Abe Lincoln." From The New York Times, December 31, 2012. © 2012 The New York Times. All rights reserved. Used by permission and protected by the Copyright Laws of the United States. The printing, copying, redistribution, or retransmission of this Content without express written permission is prohibited.

Page 202: Natalie Angier, "Sorry Vegans: Brussels Sprouts Like to Live, Too" From The New York Times, November 22, 2009. © 2009 The New York Times. All rights reserved. Used by permission and protected by the Copyright Laws of the United States. The printing, copying, redistribution, or retransmission of this Content without express written permission is prohibited.

Page 210 Martin Luther King Jr., "I Have a Dream" Copyright 1963 Dr. Martin Luther King Jr; copyright renewed 1991 Coretta Scott King. Reprinted by arrangement with The Heirs to the Estate of Martin Luther King Jr., c/o Writers House as agent for proprietor New York, NY.

Page 214: Kofi A. Annan, "In Africa, AIDS Has a Woman's Face" From The New York Times, December 29, 2002. © 2002 The New York Times. All rights reserved. Used by permission and protected by the Copyright Laws of the United States. The printing, copying, redistribution, or retransmission of this Content without express written permission is prohibited..

Page 221: David Blankenhorn, "Fatherless America," from FATHERLESS AMERICA: Confronting Our Most Urgent Social Problems, 1995, pp 1-5. Copyright 1996 David Blankenhorn. Reprinted by permission of Basic Books, a member of Perseus BooksGroup. Permission conveyed through the Copyright Clearance Center.

Page 225: The High Cost of Being Poor © 2009 by Barbara Ehrenreich. Used by permission. All rights reserved.

Student Samples

INDEX

E

LEARNING OBJECTIVES

1-1 Use the SQ3R reading strategy.

Using the SQ3R strategy will help you gain the most from your academic reading texts. SQ3R stands for Survey, Question, Read, Recite, and Review. Here is a description of each part:

- **Survey:** Check the text for clues to each part of the rhetorical situation: writer, message, medium, reader, and context. Titles, headings, boldface terms, and author information may reveal this information.
- **Question:** Ask questions that you hope to answer as you read. Consider asking the journalistic questions or turning headings into questions.
- **Read:** Search for answers to your prereading questions. Use annotating, note taking, mapping, and outlining as needed.
- **Recite:** Answer the *Who? What? When? Where? Why?* and *How?* questions.
- **Review:** Look back and answer your reading questions. Use memory techniques to remember key points.

1-2 Read actively.

Active reading is a kind of mental dialogue with the writer. You can read actively by pacing your reading and anticipating what is coming next; reading difficult parts aloud; taking thoughtful notes; and annotating the text. After you finish reading, use mapping or outlining to understand the text.

1-3 Respond to a text.

Write an initial response to the reading. A response can take varied forms, from a journal entry to a blog to a discussion-group posting.

1-4 Summarize a text.

In your own words, write a formal summary of the main points of the reading.

1-5 Effectively analyze images.

When you view an image, analyze through careful viewing and interpreting. The active viewing process involves these steps:

1. **Survey the image.** See it as a whole, but also study the focal point.
2. **Inspect the image.** Examine all the details.
3. **Question the image.** Ask journalistic questions.
4. **Understand the purpose.** Think about the purpose.

1-6 Think critically through writing.

Think critically about topics and issues by analyzing complex processes, synthesizing concepts, weighing the value of opposing perspectives, and applying principles. To think critically through your writing, practice these strategies:

- **Ask probing questions,** including open-ended and rhetorical questions.
- **Use inductive and deductive logic.** Questions invite thinking; reasoning responds to that challenge in an organized way.

KEY TERMS

1-1
SQ3R strategy a step-by-step approach to critical reading; stands for Survey, Question, Read, Recite, and Review)

rhetorical situation refers to the key parts of text: writer, message, medium, reader, and context

1-2
annotating an active reading strategy that involves marking up a text—highlighting and underlining key points and recording notes and observations

mapping an active reading strategy that involves "clustering" key concepts using lines and word bubbles

outlining an active reading strategy that uses parallel structure to record main points and subordinate points

1-3
personal response initial thoughts and reflections about a reading

1-4
summary states the main points of a reading in your own words

1-5
interpreting analyzing an image to discover meaning

1-6
critical thinking deep thinking that involves analyzing, synthesizing, evaluating, and applying

inductive logic reasoning from specific information toward general conclusions

deductive logic reasoning from general principles toward specific applications

LEARNING OBJECTIVES

This chapter shows the process one student writer used to complete a writing assignment.

2-1 Understand the assignment.

Examine the assignment by considering the parts of the rhetorical situation: sender, message, purpose, medium, receiver, and context. Explore the assignment using a cluster. Then freewrite about it to narrow your focus.

2-2 Focus your topic and plan the writing.

Focus your writing topic by answering the journalistic questions (five W's and H). Then research the topic to collect key details and data for your writing. With your topic and research in mind, choose an organizational pattern for your writing. Here is a three-step process for choosing a pattern:

1. Review your assignment and record your response.
2. Decide on your thesis statement and think about your essay's possible content and organization.
3. Choose an overall method and reflect on its potential effectiveness.

2-3 Write a first draft.

Compose opening, middle, and closing paragraphs.

2-4 Revise the draft.

Revise the writing for global issues related to the ideas, organization, and voice.

2-5 Seek a reviewer's response.

Ask a peer to review your work.

2-6 Edit the writing for style.

Review sentences for clarity and smoothness.

2-7 Edit the writing for correctness.

Edit the copy for punctuation, agreement issues, and spelling.

2-8 Check for documentation and page-design problems.

Add documentation and a reference page as needed.

KEY TERMS

2-2

Journalistic questions Five W's and H: *Who? What? Where? When? Why? How?*

LEARNING OBJECTIVES

3-1 Discover your process.

Approaching writing as a process will relieve some of the pressure of completing a writing project by breaking down writing into manageable steps. The writing process involves six steps: (1) getting started, (2) planning, (3) drafting, (4) revising, (5) editing and proofreading, and (6) submitting. Writers can adapt the process to their situation and assignment.

3-2 Understand the rhetorical situation.

The rhetorical situation refers to the important elements a writer should consider when approaching any writing assignment.

- Think of your role as the writer.
- Understand your subject.
- Understand your purpose.
- Understand your audience.
- Understand the medium (form).
- Think about the context.

3-3 Understand the assignment.

Most writing assignments will spell out (1) the objective, (2) the task, (3) the formal requirements, and (4) the suggested approaches and topics. To gain a full understanding of an assignment, do the following:

1. Read the assignment. Search for key words, options, and restrictions.
2. Relate the assignment to the goals of the course.
3. Relate the assignment to other assignments.
4. Relate the assignment to your own interests.
5. Reflect on the assignment.

3-4 Select, limit, and explore your topic.

A writing topic must meet the requirements of the assignment; be limited in scope; seem reasonable (that is, be within your means to research); and genuinely interest you.

3-5 Research your topic.

To develop a thoughtful piece of writing, you must gain a thorough understanding of your topic; to do so, you must carry out the necessary reading, reflecting, and researching. Use the guidelines that follow when you start collecting information.

- Find out what you already know. Consider freewriting, clustering, 5 W's, and directed writing.
- Ask questions.
- Identify possible sources.

When using sources in writing, track them in a working bibliography; use a note-taking system that respects sources; and distinguish summaries, paraphrases, and quotations.

KEY TERMS

3-3

analyze break down a topic into subparts, showing how those parts relate

argue defend a claim with logical arguments

classify divide a large group into well-defined subgroups

compare/contrast point out similarities and/or differences

define give a clear, thoughtful definition or meaning of something

describe show in detail what something is like

evaluate weigh the truth, quality, or usefulness of something

explain give reasons, list steps, or discuss the causes of something

interpret tell in your own words what something means

reflect share your well-considered thoughts about a subject

summarize restate someone else's ideas very briefly in your own words

synthesize connect facts or ideas to create something new

3-4

freewriting spontaneously writing in journal style as a means of generating or identifying ideas

3-5

working bibliography lists sources that you have used or intend to use

summary states the main points of a reading in your own words

paraphrase rewrites a passage point by point in your own words

quotation records a passage from the source word for word

LEARNING OBJECTIVES

4-1 Revisit the rhetorical situation.

Use this checklist to determine whether to move ahead with your planning or to reconsider your writing topic:

Writer
_____ Am I interested in this topic?
_____ How much do I now know about this topic, and is it enough?

Subject
_____ Does the topic I have developed still fit with the subject requirements of the assignment?
_____ Has my research sufficiently deepened my understanding of the topic?

Purpose
_____ Are my goals clear enough for me to proceed with planning my writing?
_____ Am I writing to entertain, inform, explain, analyze, persuade, reflect?

Form
_____ What form should I create: essay, proposal, report, review?

Audience
_____ Will my readers be interested in this topic? How can I interest them, given what I have learned?
_____ What do they know and need to know about it? What opinions do they have?

Context
_____ What weight does this assignment have in terms of my grade?
_____ How will the assignment be assessed?

4-2 Form your thesis statement.

A thesis statement identifies the central idea for your writing. State your thesis in a sentence that effectively expresses what you want to explore or explain in your essay. To discover a focus, examine your writing topic from a particular angle or perspective. Keep in mind the following formula for creating your thesis:

- Limited topic + specific focus = an effective thesis statement.

4-3 Select a method of development.

The next step of planning involves deciding on an overall organizing structure for your essay. An organizing pattern is built right into some assignments. When a pattern is not apparent, examine your thesis statement to see what method of development it suggests.

4-4 Develop a plan or an outline.

Consider the following strategies for organizing your research: quick lists, topic outlines, sentence outlines, writing blueprints, and graphic organizers.

KEY TERMS

4-2

thesis statement the central idea in a piece of writing, usually highlighting a special condition or feature of the topic, expressing a specific claim about it, or taking a stand

working thesis statement a preliminary statement that directs your planning, but may change if your thinking on the topic evolves

4-4

quick list a brief listing of main points

topic outline a parallel list of main points and essential details

sentence outline a parallel list of main points and essential details written as sentences

writing blueprints basic organizational strategies preferred for different forms of writing

graphic organizers an arrangement of main points and essential details in an appropriate chart or diagram

LEARNING OBJECTIVES

5-1 Review your writing situation.

Before you get started drafting, revisit the rhetorical situation and remind yourself of the basic structure of an essay. Then consider the basic structure that your draft will follow.

5-2 Opening: Introduce your topic and line of thinking.

The opening paragraph of an essay should (1) engage the reader; (2) establish your direction, tone, and level of language; and (3) introduce your line of thought. Here are four strategies for engaging readers:

- Mention little-known facts about the topic.
- Pose a challenging question.
- Offer a thought-provoking quotation.
- Tell a brief, illuminating story.

5-3 Middle: Develop and support your main points.

The middle of the essay should develop the main points that support your thesis statement. Design paragraphs as units of thought that develop and advance your thesis clearly and logically. Choose between the following organizational strategies and use transitions to develop coherency.

- **Definition:** provides the denotation (dictionary meaning) and connotation (implied meaning) of a given term
- **Illustration:** supports a general idea with specific reasons, facts, and details
- **Analogy:** offers a comparison that a writer uses to explain a complex or unfamiliar phenomenon in terms of a familiar one
- **Cause and Effect:** shows how events are linked to their results
- **Narration:** orders details in chronological order to share a story
- **Process:** describes the steps in a process
- **Chronological (Time) Order:** presents steps in a process or details of a story in order
- **Classification:** breaks a subject into categories and examines how the categories are alike and different from each other
- **Climax:** presents details and then provides a general climactic statement or conclusion drawn from the details
- **Compare-Contrast:** shows how two or more subjects are similar and different

5-4 Closing: Complete, clarify, and unify your message.

Closing paragraphs clarify loose ends, summarize key points, or sign off with the reader. The closing helps the reader look back over the essay with new understanding and appreciation. Here are some closing strategies:

- Reassert the main point.
- Urge the reader to act, or think a certain way.
- Complete and unify your message.

KEY TERMS

5-3

explain provide important facts, details, and examples

narrate share a brief story or re-create an experience to illustrate an idea

describe tell in detail how someone appears or how something works

define identify or clarify the meaning of a specific term or idea

analyze examine the parts of something to better understand the whole

compare provide examples to show how two things are alike or different

argue use logic and evidence to prove that something is true

reflect express your thoughts or feelings about something

cite authorities add expert analysis or personal commentary

LEARNING OBJECTIVES

6-1 Assess the state of your draft.

When revising, first look at the big picture. Determine whether the content is interesting, informative, and worth sharing. Note any gaps or soft spots in your line of thinking. Revisit the rhetorical parts, consider the overall approach, and think globally about the ideas, organization, and voice of your first draft.

6-2 Revise for ideas and organization.

Make sure the ideas are fully developed and the organization is logical. The ideas in the first draft should be complete and clear. The organization should lead readers logically from one point to the next.

6-3 Revise for voice and style.

Check to see if the voice sounds informed and authoritative. The voice should convey the writer's interest and commitment to the topic. For academic writing, use an academic style that is clear and easy to follow. Use these tips:

- **Avoid personal pronouns** (*I, we, you*) in most academic writing. These words are okay in personal writing, such as in narratives.
- **Avoid jargon and define technical terms.**
- **Use a formal voice** with a serious tone and careful word choice.
- **Remove excess modifiers** such as *mostly, likely, truly*.
- **Use active voice for most sentences.**

6-4 Address paragraph issues.

Take a close look at your paragraphs for focus, unity, and coherence. Follow these guidelines:

- **Remember the basics.** A paragraph should be a concise unit of thought; it should include a controlling idea and supporting details.
- **Keep the purpose in mind.**
- **Check for unity.** A unified paragraph is one in which all the details help to develop a single main topic or achieve a single main effect.
- **Check for coherence.** When a paragraph is coherent, the parts work together. A coherent paragraph flows smoothly because each sentence is connected to others through the use of repetition and transitions.
- **Check for completeness.** The sentences in a paragraph should support and expand on the main point. If your paragraph does not seem complete, you will need to add information.

6-5 Revise collaboratively.

Find a peer or a group of peers to review your writing. As the writer, introduce the draft and solicit honest responses. Reviewers should make constructive comments in response to the writing.

6-6 Use the writing center.

A college writing center or lab employs trained advisers to help you develop and strengthen a piece of writing.

KEY TERMS

6-3

voice the way writing sounds, revealing the writer's feelings about all parts of the communication situation

personal pronouns words such as *I, me, you, your, she, it* that take the place of nouns and other pronouns

technical terms specialized vocabulary of a subject, a discipline, a profession, or a social group (also known as "jargon")

qualifiers words or phrases that are added to another word to modify its meaning, either limiting it or enhancing it

active voice construction in which the subject of the sentence performs the action of the verb

passive voice construction in which the subject of the sentence receives the action of the verb

LEARNING OBJECTIVES

7-1 Adopt strategies for polishing your writing.

Edit your writing so that it is clear, concise, energetic, varied, and correct. Start by reviewing the overall style of your writing.

7-2 Combine short, simplistic sentences.

Consider one of the following strategies for combining short, simplistic sentences into longer, more detailed sentences:

- **Use a series** to combine three or more similar ideas.
- **Use a relative pronoun** (*who, whose, that, which*) to introduce subordinate (less important) ideas.
- **Use an introductory phrase or clause.**
- **Use a semicolon.**
- **Use correlative conjunctions.**

7-3 Expand sentences to add details.

Expand sentences when you edit so as to connect related ideas and make room for new information. You can expand sentences by creating cumulative sentences or expanding the details, using adjectives and adverbs, phrases, or clauses.

7-4 Edit sentences for variety and style.

Effective sentences provide variety for readers in the following ways:

- **Openings:** Start some sentences with the subject and other sentences with phrases or clauses.
- **Lengths:** Use medium-length sentences for most material. Create short sentences for impact. Use long sentences for complex ideas.
- **Kinds:** Use statements to give information, questions to engage readers, and commands to call readers to action.
- **Types:** Use simple sentences for straightforward information; compound sentences to connect ideas equally; and complex sentences to show a special relationship between ideas.
- **Arrangement:** Place the main point in different parts of the sentence.

7-5 Eliminate wordiness.

Eliminate wordiness by (1) cutting deadwood, (2) eliminating redundancy, (3) cutting unnecessary modifiers, and (4) replacing long phrases and clauses.

7-6 Avoid vague, weak, and biased words.

Exchange vague nouns and verbs for specific ones. Replace jargon and cliches. Use plain English. Avoid biased words.

7-7 Edit and proofread for correctness.

Correct errors in spelling, mechanics, usage, grammar, and form. (See Part 3: Handbook for specific rules.)

KEY TERMS

7-2
series a list of three or more items

7-3
cumulative sentence a sentence made of a general "base clause" that is expanded by adding modifying words, phrases, or clauses

7-4
parallel structure presenting the coordinated elements of a sentence should be are written in the same grammatical form.
nominal constructions noun form of a verb (*description* for *describe*)
expletives filler phrases such as *there is* and *it is*

7-5
deadwood irrelevant information and obvious statements that add nothing to a sentence
redundancy unnecessary repetition

7-6
jargon language that is overly technical or difficult to understand
cliches overused words and phrases that give the reader no concrete picture
obfuscation fuzzy terms that make simple terms sound more profound, or make false ideas sound true
euphemisms overly polite expressions that avoid stating an uncomfortable truth
doublespeak phrasing that deliberately seeks either to hide the truth from readers or to understate the situation
ambiguity statements that are open to multiple interpretations
bias an expression that betrays a prejudice

LEARNING OBJECTIVES

8-1 Format your writing.

A good page design makes your writing clear and easy to follow. Follow these tips:

Formatting

- **Keep the design clear and uncluttered**.
- **Use the designated documentation form.** Follow all the requirements outlined in the MLA or APA style guides.

Typography

- **Use an easy-to-read serif font for the main text.** For most types of writing, use a 10- or 12-point type size.
- **Consider using a sans-serif font for the title and headings.** Use larger type, perhaps 18-point, for your title and use 14-point type for any headings.

Spacing

- **Follow all requirements for indents and margins.**
- **Avoid widows and orphans.**

Graphic Devices

- **Create bulleted or numbered lists** to highlight individual items in a list.
- **Include charts or other graphics.** Graphics should be neither so small that they get lost on the page, nor so large that they overpower the page.

8-2 Create a writing portfolio.

There are two basic types of writing portfolios: (1) a working portfolio in which you store documents at various stages of development, and (2) a showcase portfolio with which you share appropriate finished work.

The documents that follow are commonly included in a showcase portfolio:

- A **table of contents** listing the pieces included in your portfolio
- An **opening essay or letter** detailing the story behind your portfolio (how you compiled it and why it features the qualities expected by the intended reader)
- A **specified number of—and types of— finished pieces**
- A **cover sheet** attached to each piece of writing, discussing the reason for its selection, the amount of work that went into it, and so on
- **Evaluation sheets or checklists** charting the progress or experience you want to show related to issues of interest to the reader

KEY TERMS

8-1

serif font typography with "tails" at the tops and bottoms of the letters

sans-serif font typography without "tails" at the tops and bottoms of the letters

orphan a single line of a new paragraph at the bottom of a page

widow a single word or short line at the top of a page carried over from a previous paragraph

8-2

writing portfolio an archive of your writing

LEARNING OBJECTIVES

9-1 Understand how to read personal essays.

Personal essays blend narration, description, and reflection.

- **Narration:** Well-written narratives are stories that include characters, dialogue, action, and settings.
- **Description:** Effective descriptive passages offer precise details that help readers thoughtfully experience the topic through description and sensory details. In addition, figurative language such as metaphors, similes, and symbols commonly enrich the text.
- **Reflection:** Strong reflective passages relay the writers' observations and insights regarding the nature, impact, and value of their experiences.

The following checklist questions can guide your reading of personal essays:

- ✔ Why does the writer care about the topic, and how is he or she affected by it?
- ✔ What ideas or themes evolve from the story? Explain.
- ✔ Are the characters' actions and dialogue believable and consistent?
- ✔ Is the description concise, precise, informing, and engaging?

9-2 Understand how to use anecdotes.

One common narrative is the anecdote—a brief story that enlivens your writing while introducing a topic or illustrating an idea.

9-3 Establish setting, describe people, and narrate action.

Personal essays often cite details to help you visualize places, people, and events. Direct dialogue reveals personalities and feelings.

9-4 Reflect on an experience.

The meaning of an experience can be enhanced through the author's observations and insights about the experience.

9-5 Use narration, description, and reflection to write a personal essay.

1. **Select a topic.** Consider an experience that gave you insights into yourself.
2. **Get the big picture.** Freewrite or brainstorm about the experience.
3. **Probe the topic and reveal what you find.** Ask questions about the experience.
4. **Get organized.** List the main events in chronological order.
5. **Write the first draft.**
6. **Review the draft.** Read your essay for truthfulness and completeness.
7. **Get feedback.** Ask a classmate to read your paper and respond to it.
8. **Improve the ideas, organization, and voice.**
9. **Edit and proofread your essay.** Check for sentence issues, word choice, correctness, and page design.
10. **Publish your writing.**

KEY TERMS

9-1

narration to tell a story

dialogue conversation that indicates who characters are and what they think

description precise details that help readers experience, often through details related to the senses

reflection observations and insights regarding the nature, impact, and value of an experience

9-2

anecdote brief story that introduces a topic or illustrates an idea

LEARNING OBJECTIVES

10-1 Understand how to read definition essays.

Definition essays clarify and deepen readers' understanding of a term—whether the term refers to something concrete or abstract. To understand a definition essay, examine how the writer conveys the term's denotative (or literal) meaning, its connotative (or suggested) meaning, and its etymological (or historical) meaning. The following checklist questions can guide your reading of definition essays:

- ✔ Precisely what does the writer claim about the term's meaning?
- ✔ Is the definition current, relevant, complete, and clear?
- ✔ Is the definition accurate in terms of its past and current usage?

10-2 Define a term through distinction from related terms.

Some definition essays are organized by first analyzing a common definition that the author finds inadequate, and then developing a new more scholarly definition.

10-3 Define a term by examining denotation and connotation.

Definition essays may analyze a term using its literal and suggested meanings.

10-4 Define a term through etymology.

Definition essays may explain the meaning of a term by examining the term's historical meaning.

10-5 Define a term through cultural and philosophical analysis.

Definition essays may explain the meaning of a term by analyzing the term's cultural and philosophical impact.

10-6 Write, revise, and edit an extended definition.

1. **Select a topic.** The best topics are abstract nouns, complex terms, or words connected to a personal experience.
2. **Identify what you know.** Explore your connections with the word.
3. **Gather information.** Research the word's history, usage, and form.
4. **Compress what you know.** Write a formal, one-sentence definition that satisfies the following equation:

   term = larger class + distinguishing characteristics
5. **Get organized.**
6. **Draft the essay.** Use the opening to get the reader's attention and introduce the term. Use the middle to explain exactly what the word means. Use the closing to review your main point and close the essay.
7. **Improve the ideas, organization, and voice.** Revise as needed.
8. **Edit the essay.** Check for sentence issues, word choice, correctness, and page design.
9. **Publish the essay.**

KEY TERMS

10-3

denotation literal (or concrete) meaning

connotation suggested (or abstract) meaning

10-4

etymology historical meaning

CHAPTER REVIEW

Classification

LEARNING OBJECTIVES

11-1 Understand how to read classification essays.

Classification essays break a topic into individual items or members that can be sorted into clearly distinguishable groups or categories. Classification groups should follow three principles: (1) consistency, (2) exclusivity, and (3) completeness. The following checklist questions can guide your reading of classification essays:

- ✔ Does the writer's classification scheme effectively explain the order of this topic for the target audience?
- ✔ Are the categories consistent, exclusive, and complete?
- ✔ Do the writer's classification strategies help you understand the subject?

11-2 Devise a suitable classification plan.

Classification distinguish the components of a group by sorting them into distinct categories.

11-3 Create categories that are consistent, exclusive, and complete.

Using the same criteria in a consistent manner throughout the sorting process helps create groups that are exclusive and complete.

11-4 Title categories clearly.

Classification groups should be sorted and titled clearly.

11-5 Illustrate distinctive and shared traits of categories.

Illustrate distinctive and shared traits by citing examples that show how the classification scheme helps readers understand a complex topic.

11-6 Write, revise, and edit a classification essay.

1. **Select a topic.** Pick a topic that is characterized by a larger set of items or members that can best be explained by ordering them into categories.
2. **Look at the big picture.** Consider classification criteria.
3. **Choose and test your criteria.** Make sure the criteria are consistent, exclusive, and complete.
4. **Gather and organize information.** Use a classification grid to show distinct groups.
5. **Draft a thesis.** State the topic and identify the classification scheme.
6. **Draft the essay.** Use the opening to introduce the thesis and give your criteria for dividing the subject into categories. Use the middle to examine each category. Use the closing to tie together the classification scheme.
7. **Improve the ideas, organization, and voice.** Revise as needed.
8. **Edit the essay.** Check for sentence issues, word choice, correctness, and page design.
9. **Publish the essay.**

KEY TERMS

11-1

consistent the same criteria are used in the same way when sorting items into groups

exclusive each group is distinct

complete all individual items or members of the larger body fit into a category with no items left over

11-3

classification criteria the factors or principles used to create consistent, exclusive, and complete categories

LEARNING OBJECTIVES

12-1 Understand how to read process essays and instructions.

In process writing, an author breaks a process into a clear series of steps and then explains how and why those steps lead to a specific outcome. Depending on the writer's purpose, audience, and topic, process writing usually takes one of two forms: an essay that describes and analyzes the nature and function of a process, or a set of instructions that tells readers precisely how to do the process. The following questions can guide your reading of process writing:

✔ Does the essay clearly identify the process, outline its stages, explain individual steps, and (if appropriate) discuss causes and effects?

✔ Do the instructions clearly and accurately explain the process, the materials needed, the steps required, and the necessary precautions?

✔ Does the document use clear, precise language and define unfamiliar terms?

12-2 Understand and use signal terms.

In instructions, writers use signal terms to help users complete a process safely and successfully.

12-3 Study and use chronological structure.

Ordering steps chronologically and linking them with transitions help readers understand individual steps and the process as a whole.

12-4 Describe and analyze steps in a process.

Process essays analyze how and why a series of steps comprise a process.

12-5 Write, revise, and edit a process essay.

1. **Select a topic.**
2. **Review the process.** Use a process-analysis chart to organize each step in the process in chronological order.
3. **Research as needed.** Discover what steps are required, what order the steps follow, how the steps are done, what outcome the process produces, and what safety precautions are needed.
4. **Organize information.** Revise your process-analysis chart as needed.
5. **Draft the document.** For process essays, the opening should Introduce the topic, give an overview of the process, and explain why the process is important. The middle should describe the steps in order using transitions. The closing should summarize the process and restate key points.

   For instructions, the opening should summarize the process's goal and list any materials and tools needed. The middle should describe the steps. The closing should explain follow-up action.
6. **Improve the ideas, organization, and voice.** Revise as needed.
8. **Edit the essay.** Check for sentence issues, word choice, correctness, and page design.
9. **Publish the essay.**

KEY TERMS

12-2
signal terms specific words that that indicate special care is needed for success and safety (*Note, Caution! Warning!*)

12-3
chronological structure details organized according to time

CHAPTER REVIEW

13

Comparison-Contrast

LEARNING OBJECTIVES

13-1 Understand how to read comparison-contrast writing.

Writers compare and contrast subjects in order to understand their similarities and differences. The following checklist questions can guide your reading of comparison-contrast essays:

- ✔ Why is the writer comparing these topics? Is the goal to stress similarities, differences, or both?
- ✔ How does the comparison speak to specific readers?
- ✔ What features or traits of the topics are compared? Why?
- ✔ How does the writer present the topics and the criteria for comparison?
- ✔ What conclusion does the writer develop through analysis?

13-2 Use subject-by-subject or trait-by-trait organization.

Some essays compare and contrast subjects based on traits. Other essays deal with one subject fully before dealing with the other subject.

13-3 Cite details to support and clarify compare-contrast claims.

Writers may use details, anecdotes, and keen observations to support compare-contrast claims.

13-4 Use comparison-contrast strategies to analyze, illustrate, or define concepts.

Writers commonly enrich their writing by combining compare-contrast strategies with other strategies such as classification or cause-effect.

13-5 Write, revise, and edit a compare-contrast essay.

1. **Select a topic.** Pick two subjects that have a solid basis for comparison.
2. **Get the big picture.** Brainstorm a list of traits for each subject.
3. **Gather information.** Research the subjects.
4. **Draft a working thesis.** Write a sentence that states the essential insight about the similarities and/or differences between the topics.
5. **Get organized.** Decide whether you will compare your two subjects trait by trait or subject by subject.
6. **Write your first draft.** For trait-by-trait organization, the opening should introduce the subjects and offer a thesis. The middle should compare and/or contrast the two subjects trait by trait. The closing should summarize the key relationships. For subject-by-subject organization, the opening should introduce the subjects and offer a thesis. The middle should discuss the first subject, then analyze the second subject. The closing should summarize similarities, differences, and implications.
7. **Get feedback** regarding your thesis, logic, and organization.
8. **Rework your draft** for ideas, organization, and voice.
9. **Edit your essay** for sentence issues, word choice, correctness, and design.
10. **Publish the essay.**

KEY TERMS

13-1

comparison criteria specific points of comparison that writers use to analyze two subjects

subject-by-subject organization first dealing with one topic fully and then the other

trait-by-trait organization comparing topics side by side, feature by feature

WWW.CENGAGEBRAIN.COM/LOGIN

14 CHAPTER REVIEW
Cause-Effect

LEARNING OBJECTIVES

14-1 Understand how to read cause-effect writing.

In a cause and effect essay, a writer analyzes and explains the causes, the effects, or both the causes and the effects of a phenomenon. As you read essays using cause-effect reasoning, identify the problem or phenomenon addressed and the cause-effect logic. The following checklist questions can guide your reading of cause-effect essays:

- ✔ Is the writer's rationale for writing informed, reasonable, and convincing?
- ✔ Who is the intended audience, and does the essay present all the information that they need to understand and respond to the analysis?
- ✔ Is the topic clearly identified and explored as a phenomenon?
- ✔ Is the thesis clear, and is the argument free of logical fallacies?
- ✔ What claims does the writer make regarding causes and effects, and are the statements sufficiently limited, focused, and logical?
- ✔ Are supporting details well researched, relevant, and strong?

14-2 Make limited and logical cause-effect claims.

To build a convincing cause-effect analysis, writers need to start with reasonable, measured claims about cause-effect links.

14-3 Support cause-effect reasoning with relevant, reliable evidence.

Writers should support cause-effect claims with documented evidence.

14-4 Avoid logical fallacies.

The reasoning should be transparent, unified, and free of logical fallacies such as bare assertion (188), false cause (189), and false analogy (190).

14-5 Write, revise, and edit a cause-effect essay.

1. **Select a topic.** Choose a topic and analyze its causes, its effects, or both.
2. **Narrow and research the topic.** Do preliminary research to distinguish primary causes and effects from secondary ones.
3. **Draft and test your thesis.** Create a thesis that introduces the topic along with the causes and effects you intend to discuss.
4. **Gather and analyze information.** Test your analysis to avoid mistaking a coincidence for a cause-effect relationship.
5. **Get organized.** Develop an outline that lays out your thesis and argument in a clear pattern.
6. **Use your outline to draft the essay.** Show how specific causes led to specific effects, citing examples as needed. Use transitions to connect ideas.
7. **Get feedback** regarding the strength and clarity of your argument.
8. **Revise the essay,** focusing on ideas, organization, and voice.
9. **Edit the essay for clarity and correctness.**
10. **Publish your essay.**

KEY TERMS

14-1
cause-effect reasoning a series of statements that are used to reach a conclusion about the link between causes and effects

14-2
claim a debatable statement that should be arguable, defendable, reasonable, understandable, and interesting

14-4
logical fallacies fuzzy or false forms of reasoning

LEARNING OBJECTIVES

15-1 Understand how to read literary analyses.

Analyzing a literary text is a critical, interpretive process. With a literary analysis, your primary research is reading, rereading, and thinking through the literary text itself in order to develop a sound, insightful interpretation.

The following questions can guide your reading of literary analyses:

- ✔ Does the essay writer understand the elements of the literary form, its distinguishing a qualities, and how to assess those qualities?
- ✔ Does the essay explore nuances such as ironies, motifs, symbols, or allusions?
- ✔ Does the essay have a clear thesis and logical claims supported by relevant evidence?
- ✔ Is the tone informed, respectful, and honest?

15-2 Identify approaches to literary analysis.

Literary texts can be interpreted through different critical approaches or schools. Here are the four basic approaches:

1. **Formalist criticism** focuses on the literary text itself, especially its structure and genre.
2. **Rhetorical criticism** is audience-centered, focused on the "transaction" between text and reader.
3. **Historical criticism** focuses on the historical context of the literary text, including its author.
4. **Ideological criticism** applies ideas outside of literature to literary texts.

15-3 Analyze a short story.

An analysis of a short story may focus on characters, plot, symbols, and diction.

15-4 Analyze a poem.

An analysis of a poem may focus on how the poem is structured, what it expresses, and how its ideas might relate to your life.

15-5 Understand and use literary terms. (See a list of literary terms on the other side of this card.)

15-6 Write a literary analysis.

1. **Select a topic** (a literary work with which you are familiar).
2. **Understand the work** (read or experience it thoughtfully).
3. **Develop a focus** (choose one of the four critical approaches).
4. **Organize your thoughts** (outline points of your key insight, or thesis).
5. **Write the first draft** (include an opening, middle, and conclusion).
6. **Improve the ideas, organization, and voice** (revise as necessary).
7. **Edit and proofread the essay** (check terms, sentences, and mechanics).
8. **Publish your essay.**

KEY TERMS

15-1

formalist criticism literary analysis that focuses on the literary text itself, especially its structure and genre

rhetorical criticism literary analysis that is audience centered, focused on the "transaction" between text and reader.

historical criticism literary analysis that focuses on the historical context of the literary text, including its author

ideological criticism literary analysis that applies ideas outside of literature to literary texts

15-5

anecdote brief story that introduces a topic or illustrates an idea

LITERARY TERMS

Antagonist is the person or thing actively working against the protagonist, or hero.

Climax is the turning point, an intense moment characterized by a key event, discovery, or decision.

Conflict is the problem or struggle in a story that triggers the action.

Denouement is the outcome of a play or story.

Diction is an author's choice of words.

Exposition is the introductory section of a story or play. Typically, the setting, main characters, and themes are introduced, and the action is initiated.

Falling action is the action of a play or story that follows the climax and shows the characters dealing with the climactic event or decision.

Figure of speech is a literary device used to create a special effect or to describe something in a fresh way.

Genre refers to the type of literature based on its style, form, and content.

Imagery refers to words or phrases that a writer uses to appeal to the reader's senses.

Irony is a deliberate discrepancy in meaning or in the way something is understood.

Plot is the action or sequence of events in a story. It is usually a series of related incidents that build upon one another as the story develops.

Point of view is the vantage point from which the story unfolds.

Protagonist is the main character of the story.

Resolution (or *denouement*) is the portion of the play or story in which the problem is solved. The resolution brings the story to a satisfactory end.

Rising action is the series of conflicts or struggles that build a story or play to a fulfilling climax.

Setting is the time and place in which the action of a literary work occurs.

Structure is the form or organization a writer uses for her or his literary work. A great number of possible forms are used regularly in literature: parable, fable, romance, satire, and so on.

Symbol is a person, a place, a thing, or an event used to represent something else. For example, the dove is a symbol of peace.

Theme is the statement about life that a particular work shares with readers.

Rhythm is the ordered or free occurrences of stressed syllables in poetry. Ordered or regular rhythm is called *meter*. Irregularly patterned rhythm is called *free verse*.

Stanza is a division of poetry named for the number of lines it contains

Verse is a metric line of poetry. It is named according to the kind and number of feet composing it.

POETRY TERMS

Alliteration is the repetition of initial consonant sounds in words such as "rough and ready."

Blank verse is an unrhymed form of poetry that follows an iambic pentameter.

Foot is the smallest repeated pattern of stressed and unstressed syllables in a poetic line.

Refrain is the repetition of a line or phrase of a poem at regular intervals, especially at the end of each stanza.

Strategies for Argumentation and Persuasion

LEARNING OBJECTIVES

16-1 Understand how to build an argument.

Step 1: Consider your audience, purpose, and topic.
- Identify your audience and purpose.
- Generate ideas and gather solid evidence.
- Develop a line of reasoning.

Step 2: Make and qualify your claim.
- Draw reasonable conclusions from the evidence.
- Add qualifiers.

Step 3: Support your claim.
- Support each point in your claim with solid evidence.
- Identify logical fallacies.

Step 4: Engage the opposition.
- Make concessions, develop rebuttals, or use appropriate appeals.

16-2 Prepare your argument.

Argumentative writing requires a clear line of reasoning with each point logically supporting your argument.

16-3 Make and qualify your claims.

An argument centers on a claim. A claim is a conclusion drawn from logical thought and reliable evidence. Unlike a fact and an opinion, a claim can be debated. To develop supportable claims, avoid all-or-nothing, extreme claims; avoid obvious or trivial claims; and use qualifiers to temper your claims.

16-4 Support your claims.

A claim stands or falls on its support. To develop strong support, select and use evidence. When using evidence, follow these tips:
1. **Go for quality and variety, not just quantity.**
2. **Use inductive and deductive patterns of logic.**
3. **Reason using valid warrants.**

See pages 186–187 for a list of different types of evidence.

16-5 Identify and avoid logical fallacies.

Fallacies weaken an argument by distorting an issue, sabotaging an argument, drawing false conclusions, misusing evidence, or misusing language.

16-6 Engage the opposition.

Make concessions, develop rebuttals, and consolidate your claim.

16-7 Use appropriate appeals.

To appeal to your audience, your argument should (1) build credibility, (2) make logical appeals, and (3) focus on readers' needs.

KEY TERMS

16-1
argument a series of statements arranged in a logical sequence, supported with sound evidence, and expressed powerfully so as to sway your reader or listener

16-2
line of reasoning a clear, logical sequence of ideas supporting an argument

16-3
claim a debatable statement that should be arguable, defendable, reasonable, understandable, and interesting
fact a statement that can be checked for accuracy
opinion a personally held taste or attitude
qualifiers words or phrases that make claims more reasonable

16-4
inductive reasoning works from the particular toward general conclusions
deductive reasoning starts from accepted truths and applies them to a new situation so as to reach a conclusion about it
warrant the often unspoken thinking used to relate the supporting reasons to the claim

16-5
logical fallacies bits of fuzzy, dishonest, or incomplete thinking

16-6
concessions recognition of an argument's limits and the truth of other positions
rebuttal an argument aimed at a weak spot in an opposing argument

LEARNING OBJECTIVES

17-1 Understand how to read position papers.

Position papers should exhibit these qualities:

- **Informed Writing:** The writer has researched the topic thoroughly and understands it fully, including positions other than his or her own.
- **Logical Writing:** The writer presents the topic objectively, describes alternative positions fairly, and takes the position supported by the best evidence and strongest logic. The writer avoids logical fallacies.
- **Engaging Writing:** Rather than quarreling or pontificating, the writer converses with readers by making reasonable concessions, rebutting opposing arguments, and consolidating or refocusing claims.

The following questions can guide your reading of position papers:

- ✔ What is the topic, and is it debatable, stated fairly, and addressed fully?
- ✔ What are the writer's claims, and are they supported by reliable evidence?
- ✔ Is the overall argument clear, unified, and free of logical fallacies?
- ✔ Is the tone measured, reasonable, and free of manipulative language?

17-2 Develop sound claims with reliable evidence.

A convincing position is built on sound, measured claims supported by clear, reliable evidence.

17-3 Make concessions and rebut opposing arguments.

Position papers make claims, support them, and rebut opposing arguments.

17-4 Make effective appeals.

A sound argument involves using appropriate appeals to credibility, logic, and emotion, while avoiding a wide range of logical fallacies.

17-5 Write, revise, and edit a logical position paper.

1. **Select a debatable topic.**
2. **Take stock.** What is your current position on the topic?
3. **Get inside the issue.** Investigate all possible positions on the issue and research as needed. Develop reasoning that supports your position.
4. **Refine your position.**
5. **Organize your argument and support.** Choose from the organizational option listed under the "key terms."
6. **Write your first draft.** Use the opening to seize the readers' attention and supply background information that they need to understand the issue. Use the middle to deepen, clarify, and support your position statement, using solid logic and reliable support. Use the closing to make a direct or indirect plea to readers to adopt your position.
7. **Improve the ideas, organization, and voice.** Revise as needed.
8. **Edit your essay.** Check for sentence issues, word choice, correctness, and page design.
9. **Publish your essay.**

KEY TERMS

17-5

traditional pattern introduces the issue, states the position, supports it, addresses and refutes opposition, and restates the position

blatant confession places the position statement in the first sentence

delayed gratification describes various positions on the topic, compares and contrasts them, and then takes and defends a position

changed mind explains how and why the writer changed her or his mind on an issue

winning over addresses readers' concerns by anticipating and answering their objections or questions

LEARNING OBJECTIVES

18-1 Know how to read an appeal for action.

Persuasive writing can urge readers to act on something. When reading an appeal to act, look for the following:

- **Compelling Argument:** The writer accurately describes the issue, convinces readers of its importance, and calls for action that is doable and effective.
- **Logical Argument:** The argument is based on reliable evidence; and the argument avoids logical fallacies such as half-truths, unreliable testimonials, attacks against a person, and false analogies.
- **Mature Voice:** The writing sounds informed and genuine; it includes no manipulative appeals, quarrelsome language, or demeaning accusations.

The following questions can guide your reading of persuasive essays:

- ✔ What is the issue, and what action is requested to address it?
- ✔ Who are the intended readers, and what capacity to act do they have?
- ✔ Are the writer's claims accurate, compelling, and logical?
- ✔ Is the argument's tone informed, genuine, and respectful?
- ✔ Is the writing convincing—does it move readers to act?

18-2 Describe a debatable issue.

Some persuasive essays ask readers to reconsider what they value.

18-3 Make clear and rational claims, supported with reliable evidence.

Martin Luther King, Jr.'s, "I Have a Dream" speech is a powerful example of an appeal for action.

18-4 Use an informed and mature voice.

Persuasive essays should use an informed, mature voice that is passionate but not manipulative or attacking in nature.

18-5 Write, revise, and edit an essay persuading readers to act.

1. **Select a topic** that is debatable, significant, current, and manageable.
2. **Choose and analyze your audience.**
3. **Narrow your focus and determine your purpose.**
4. **Generate strong ideas and reliable support.**
5. **Organize your thinking.** Make a compelling claim that points toward action. Review the evidence, and develop your line of reasoning.
6. **Write your first draft.** In the opening, raise the issue, help the readers care about it, and state your claim. In the middle, develop support and a line of reasoning. Also use appropriate logical and emotional appeals. In the closing, restate your claim and call your readers to act.
7. **Improve the ideas, organization, and voice.** Revise as needed.
8. **Edit your essay.** Check for sentences, word choice, correctness, and design.
9. **Publish your writing.**

KEY TERMS

18-1

expert testimony insights from an authority on a topic

half-truths a logical fallacy that contains part of but not the whole truth

attacks against a person a logical fallacy that directs attention to a person's character, lifestyle, or beliefs rather than to the issue

false analogy a logical fallacy that makes an analogy that is vague or unrelated to the central argument

appeal a request or plea directed to the audience

LEARNING OBJECTIVES

19-1 Understand how to read problem-solution essays.

Problem-solution writing aims to describe a problem accurately, to present workable solutions, and to explain the strengths and weaknesses of each. When reading problem-solution writing, look for the following:

- **Accurate Description:** The writer correctly describes the problem and its direct or indirect impact on readers. The writing also describes all reasonable solutions, including details about their history, successes, and failures.
- **Thorough Analysis:** The writer carefully analyzes the problem, each solution, and why the recommended solution is the best choice. The writer supports all claims with reliable data and logical reasoning.
- **Rational Argument:** The writer's claims and appeals for action are thoughtful, stated in objective terms, and presented in a measured, informed voice.

The following questions can guide your reading of problem-solution writing:

- ✔ What is the problem, what is its history, and why should it be resolved?
- ✔ What is the solution, how does it resolve the problem, and with what side effects?
- ✔ What action does the writer call for, and is it effective, realistic, and cost effective?
- ✔ Are the writer's arguments reasonable, well documented, and free of fallacies?

19-2 Describe the problem and solution.

Descriptions of problems and solutions should be accurate and free of fallacies.

19-3 Analyze the problem.

To analyze a problem, the writing may trace its history, causes, and effects.

19-4 Analyze a persuasive argument.

A problem-solution argument should be supported with logical appeals linked to readers' needs and values.

19-5 Write, revise, and edit a problem-solution essay.

1. **Select and narrow a topic.** The problem should be real, serious, and currently—or potentially—harmful.
2. **Identify and analyze your audience.**
3. **Probe the problem.** Define the problem; determine the problem's seriousness; analyze causes; explore context; and think of creative solutions.
4. **Choose the best solution.** Brainstorm and evaluate solutions.
5. **Outline your proposal and complete a first draft.** Describe the problem, offer a solution, and defend it using strategies that fit your purpose and audience.
6. **Improve the ideas, organization, and voice.**
7. **Edit and proofread the essay.**
8. **Publish your essay.**

KEY TERMS

19-1

claim a debatable statement that should be arguable, defendable, reasonable, understandable, and interesting

appeals for action a request or plea for action directed to the audience

SPECIAL CONSIDERATION

Problem-solution writing has four potential audiences: people responsible for the problem, decision makers with the power to adopt a solution, people affected by the problem, and a public seeking information about the problem.

LEARNING OBJECTIVES

20-1 Understand academic research.

The research process involves getting started, planning, conducting research, and developing the results.

20-2 Initiate the process.

To get started, you need to (1) understand the assignment, (2) select a topic, (3) build research questions, and (4) develop a working thesis. Your research will focus on a main question, the main issue you need to address. After you have confirmed the main question, develop a working thesis using this formula:

$$\text{a limited topic} + \text{a tentative claim, statement, or hypothesis} = \text{a working thesis}$$

20-3 Develop a research plan.

Consider different methods of research when developing a research plan.
- **Background research:** Initial investigations of key ideas and concepts related to your topic
- **Primary research:** Firsthand research in which you carry out interviews, observe the topic in action
- **Library research:** Scholarly library resources such as journals and periodicals
- **Internet research:** Scholarly Web sites and databases

20-4 Consider possible resources and sites.

When researching your topic, use a wide range of quality resources, as opposed to relying exclusively on information, substantial or not, from a few Web sites.

20-5 Distinguish types of sources.

Information sources can be primary, secondary, or tertiary.

Primary sources are original sources, providing firsthand information on a topic.
- *Upside:* Primary sources produce information precisely tailored to your research needs, giving you direct, hands-on access to your topic.
- *Downside:* Primary research can take a lot of time and many resources.

Secondary sources present secondhand information on your topic—information at least once removed from the original.
- *Upside:* Scholarly secondary sources offer quality information in the form of expert perspectives on and analysis of your topic. Secondary sources can save you plenty of research labor while providing you with extensive data.
- *Downside:* The information that you find may be faulty or filtered through a researcher's bias.

Tertiary sources present thirdhand information on your topic.
- *Upside:* Tertiary sources are typically easy to find, easy to access, and easy to read. They can provide starting points for more advanced research.
- *Downside:* Because of the distance from the original source, these sources lack the reliability and depth necessary for college-level research projects.

KEY TERMS

20-2
main question the main issue a researcher wants answered
working thesis a preliminary answer to your main research question, the focus of your research

20-3
Library of Congress classification a system of classification used in most academic and research libraries
artifact any object made or modified by a human culture and later discovered

20-5
primary resource an original source providing firsthand information on a topic
secondary resource a source of information prepared by someone studying primary information
tertiary resource a source of information prepared by someone studying secondary resources

21 CHAPTER REVIEW
Doing Your Research

LEARNING OBJECTIVES

21-1 Learn keyword searching.

The goal of a keyword search is to find quality sources of information. To realize the best sources, employ these strategies:

- **Get to know the database.** What material does the database contain? What time frames? What are you searching—authors, titles, subjects, full text? What are the search rules? How can you narrow the search?
- **Use a shotgun approach.** Start with the most likely keyword. If you have no "hits," choose a related term.
- **Use Boolean operators to refine your search.** When you combine keywords with Boolean operators you will obtain better results.

21-2 Conduct primary research.

Consider employing these strategies to obtain firsthand information: (1) surveys, (2) interviews, (3) observations, (4) experiments, and (5) analysis of texts and artifacts.

21-3 Do library research.

The college library offers four basic resources for your research projects.

- Librarians
- Collections (books and other materials housed within the library)
- Research tools (online catalogs, print indexes, and subscription databases)
- Special services (interlibrary loan, the reference desk)

21-4 Use books.

When researching books, use strategies for locating and scanning information.

21-5 Find periodical articles.

Periodicals are publications or broadcasts produced at regular intervals. One type of periodical is a journal, which provides specialized scholarly information for a narrowly focused audience. Online databases allow you to search for scholarly journal articles. College libraries subscribe to database services.

21-6 Understand the Internet.

Besides the Internet, your college's network will likely give you access to the library and other local resources.

21-7 Find reliable free-Web information.

Your library may sponsor a Web site that can help you access quality resources in various disciplines and connect to other virtual resources.

21-8 Evaluate online sources.

Review the assignment for restrictions on Web resources. Use sites sponsored by legitimate groups; and be aware of a site's bias, currentness, and quality of information and writing.

KEY TERMS

21-1
Boolean operators words or symbols used to search databases

21-2
survey/questionnaire a set of questions created for the purpose of gathering information from respondents about a specific topic
observation noting information received in person through the senses
inspection the purposeful analysis of a site or situation
field research an on-site scientific study
closed questions questions that can be answered with a simple fact or with a yes or a no
open-ended questions questions that require elaborate answers

21-3
collections the materials housed within a library
subscription databases online services that, for a fee, provide access to hundreds of thousands of articles
Library of Congress call numbers a set of numbers and letters specifying the subject area, topic, and authorship or title of a book

21-4
appendixes sections (in a book) that provide additional or background information
bibliographies lists of works that cover a particular subject
directories references that provide contact information
indexes searchable lists of resources on various topics
abstracts summaries of resources

LEARNING OBJECTIVES

22-1 Evaluate your sources.

Use this rating scale to target reliable sources ("10" is the highest reliability).

10. Scholarly Books and Articles
9. Trade Books and Journal Articles
8. Government Resources
7. Reviewed Official Online Documents
6. Reference Works and Textbooks
5. News and Topical Stories from Quality Sources
4. Popular Magazine Stories
3. Business and Nonprofit Publications
2. List Server Discussions, Blog Articles, Talk Radio Discussions
1. Unregulated Web Material
0. Tabloid Articles (print and Web)

You can test the reliability of any source by examining the benchmarks found on the reverse side of this card.

22-2 Create a working bibliography.

A working bibliography lists sources that you have used or intend to use. Compiling this list helps you track your research, develop your final bibliography, and avoid plagiarism.

22-3 Take notes effectively.

- System 1: Paper or electronic note cards . . . Establish one set of cards for your bibliography. On a second set of cards, take notes on sources.
- System 2: Copy (or save) and annotate . . . Mark up source material (photo copies or digital versions) with your thoughts, ideas, and questions. Highlight key points.
- System 3: The computer notebook or research log . . . Take notes on one source at a time. Use codes in your notes to identify which information in the notes relates to which topic in your outline.
- System 4: The double-entry notebook . . . Divide pages vertically. In the left column, record bibliographic information and take notes on sources. In the right column, write your responses.

22-4 Summarize, paraphrase, and quote.

Summarizing condenses in your own words the main points in a passage. Summarize when a source provides relevant ideas and information on your topic.

Paraphrasing puts a whole passage in your own words. Paraphrase passages that present key points, explanations, or arguments that are useful to your project.

Quoting records statements or phrases from an original source word for word. Quote nuggets only—statements that are well phrased or authoritative.

KEY TERMS

22-1
reliability evaluation of a source based on credibility, accuracy, and timeliness
reviewed official online documents Internet resources posted by legitimate institutions—colleges and universities, research institutes, service organizations
unregulated Web material personal sites, joke sites, chat rooms, special-interest sites, advertising and junk email (spam)

22-2
working bibliography a list of sources that you have used or intend to use in your research

22-3
annotate underline or highlight important passages in a text and make notes in the margins

22-4
summarize to condense in your own words the main points in a passage
paraphrase to put a whole passage in your own words
quotation a word-for-word statement or passage from an original source

Working with Your Sources (Cont.)

RELIABILITY TEST

Use these benchmarks to evaluate print and online sources for reliability.

Credible Author

Is the author an expert on this topic? What are her or his credentials, and can you confirm them?

> **Web test:** Is an author indicated? If so, are the author's credentials noted and contact information offered (for example, an email address)?

Reliable Publication

Has the source been published by a scholarly press, a peer-reviewed professional journal, a quality trade-book publisher, or a trusted news source? Did you find this resource through a reliable search tool?

> **Web test:** Which individual or group posted this page? How stable is the site—has it been around for a while and is the material current, well documented, and readily accessible?

Unbiased Discussion

A biased source may be pushing an agenda in an unfair, unbalanced, incomplete manner. Watch for bias toward a certain region, country, political party, industry, gender, race, ethnic group, or religion. Be alert to connections among authors, financial backers, and points of view.

> **Web test:** Is the online document one-sided? Is the site nonprofit (.org), government (.gov), commercial (.com), educational (.edu), business (.biz), informational (.info), network related (.net), or military (.mil)? Is this organization pushing a cause, product, service, or belief? How do advertising or special interests affect the site?

Current Information

A five-year-old book on computers may be outdated, but a forty-year-old book on Abraham Lincoln could still be the best source. Given what you need, is this source's discussion up-to-date?

> **Web test:** When was the material originally posted and last updated? Are links live or dead?

Accurate Information

Check the source for factual errors, statistical flaws, and conclusions that don't add up.

> **Web test:** Is the site information rich or poor—filled with helpful, factual materials or fluffy with thin, unsubstantiated opinions? Can you trace and confirm sources?

Full, Logical Support

Is the discussion of the topic reasonable, balanced, and complete? Are claims backed up with quality evidence? Does the source avoid faulty assumptions, logical fallacies, and unfair persuasion tactics?

> **Web test:** Does the page offer well-supported claims and helpful links to more information?

Quality Writing

Is the source well written? Is it free of sarcasm, derogatory terms, clichés, catch phrases, mindless slogans, grammar slips, and spelling errors?

> **Web test:** Are words neutral or emotionally charged?

Positive Relationship with Other Sources

Does the source disagree with other sources? If yes, is the disagreement about the facts themselves or about how to interpret the facts? Which source seems more credible?

> **Web test:** Is the site's information logically consistent with print sources? Do other reputable sites offer links to this site?

Design and Visual Resources

Are graphics well designed and informative or merely decorative? Are they manipulative in any way? What do they include or exclude? And do they contain information from a reliable source?

> **Web test:** Are pages well designed? Is the site easy to navigate?

LEARNING OBJECTIVES

23-1 Avoid plagiarism.

Plagiarism is using someone else's words, ideas, or images so that they appear to be your own. Follow these strategies to avoid plagiarism:

- As you research, take orderly notes and maintain an accurate working bibliography. Carefully summarize, paraphrase, and quote material.
- As you write, carefully credit all material that is quoted, summarized, or paraphrased from another source. For quoted material, use quotation marks. For summaries and paraphrases, signal where borrowed material begins and ends (see reverse side of this card for more information).
- After you write, compile a complete, accurate works-cited or reference list with full source information for all borrowed material in your writing.

23-2 Avoid other source abuses.

Here are other source abuses to avoid:

1. Using sources inaccurately
2. Using source material out of context
3. Overusing source material
4. "Plunking" quotations
5. Using "blanket" citations
6. Relying heavily on one source
7. Failing to match in-text citations to bibliographic entries
8. Violating copyrights

23-3 Use sources well.

See the reverse side of this card for a review of how to integrate and document sources in research writing.

23-4 Write a research paper.

1. **Review your research materials.** Is the information complete or at least sufficient for the project? Is the information reliable and accurate?
2. **Revisit your research questions and deepen your thesis.** Improve your thesis by using one or more of these strategies: (1) use richer, clearer terms; (2) introduce qualifying terms; or (3) stress your idea through opposition.
3. **Organize your work effectively.** Use an appropriate organizational pattern.
4. **Develop your first draft.** Start by gaining your reader's attention, establishing a common ground with your reader and the topic, and offering your thesis. Use the middle to develop your thesis by presenting each main point separately, expanding upon points logically, and integrating source material. Close the paper by reviewing or tying together important points, reinforcing your thesis, and drawing a conclusion.
5. **Revise your first draft.**
6. **Edit your paper.**
7. **Design your paper.** Make certain that your paper follows the appropriate style (MLA and APA are the most common).

23-5 Follow a model.

Review the sample MLA model on pages 277–286.

KEY TERMS

23-1
plagiarism presenting someone else's work or ideas as one's own
documentation crediting sources of information through in-text citations or references and a list of works cited or references
academic transcript the permanent record of educational achievement and activity
working bibliography list of the sources that you have used or intend to use in your research

23-2
context the set of circumstances in which a statement is made; the text and other factors that surround a specific statement and are crucial to understanding it
"plunking" quotations failing both to introduce quotations and to provide a follow-up
"blanket" citations making the reader guess where borrowed material begins and ends

23-3
attributive phrase a group of words that indicates the source of an idea or a quotation
ellipsis a set of three periods with one space preceding and following each period; a punctuation mark that indicates omission of material

USE SOURCES WELL

To use research effectively in your writing, you need to show (1) what information you are borrowing and (2) where you got it.

INTEGRATE SOURCES

Use sources to deepen and develop your thesis.

Managing Your Sources

Here's a pattern you can follow to make sure you control your sources, rather than letting them control you:

1. State and explain your idea, creating context for the source.
2. Identify and introduce the source, linking it to your discussion.
3. Summarize, paraphrase, or quote the source.
4. Provide a citation in an appropriate spot.
5. Comment on the source by explaining, expanding on, or refuting it.
6. When appropriate, refer again to a source to further develop the ideas it contains.

Incorporating Quotations

When using quotations, work them into your writing as smoothly as possible, paying attention to style, punctuation, and syntax. Use enough of the quotation to make your point without changing the meaning of the original. Place quotation marks around key phrases taken from the source.

DOCUMENT SOURCES

Carefully document where that source material comes from.

Identifying the Start

- *First Reference:* For the first reference to a source, use an attributive statement that indicates some of the following: author's name and credentials, title of the source, nature of the study or research, and helpful background.
- *Subsequent References:* For subsequent references to a source, use a simplified attributive phrase, such as the author's last name or a shortened version of the title.
- *Other References:* In some situations, such as quoting straightforward facts, simply skip the attributive phrase. The parenthetical citation supplies sufficient attribution.

Identifying the End

- *Quotations and Ideas:* Closing quotation marks and a citation, as shown in the following example, indicate the end of a source quotation.

  > As the "Lifestyle Costs" study concludes, when greenhouse gases, air pollution, and oil insecurity are factored into the analysis, alternative-fuel vehicles "offer lower LCCs than typical new cars" (Ogden, Williams, and Larson 25).

- *Longer Quotations:* If a quotation is longer than four typed lines, set it off from the main text.
- *Changing Quotations:* You may shorten or change a quotation so that it fits more smoothly into your sentence—but don't alter the original meaning. Use an ellipsis within square brackets [. . .] to indicate that you have omitted words from the original.

  > In their projections of where fuel-cell vehicles are heading, Ogden, Williams, and Larson discuss GM's AUTOnomy vehicle, with its "radical redesign of the entire car. [. . .] In these cars, steering, braking, and other vehicle systems are controlled electronically rather than mechanically" (24).

- *Using Brackets:* Use square brackets to indicate a clarification, to change a pronoun or verb tense, or to switch around uppercase and lowercase.

  > As Ogden, Williams, and Larson explain, "[e]ven if such barriers [the high cost of fuel cells and the lack of an H2 fuel infrastructure] can be overcome, decades would be required before this embryonic technology could make major contributions in reducing the major externalities that characterize today's cars" (25).

LEARNING OBJECTIVES: MLA STYLE

24-1 Learn the basics of MLA documentation.

The MLA system involves two parts: (1) an in-text citation within your paper when you use a source and (2) a matching bibliographic entry at the end of your paper. In the example below, "Anna Hutchens" and "(449)" tell the reader that

- the borrowed material came from a source by Anna Hutchens.
- the specific material can be found on page 449 of the source.
- full source details are in the works-cited list under the author's last name.

1. In-Text Citation in Body of Paper

As Anna Hutchens puts it, there is an "absence of a policy framework and institutional mechanisms that promote women's empowerment as a rights-based rather than a culture-based issue" (449).

2. Matching Works-Cited Entry at End of Paper

Hutchens, Anna. "Empowering Women Through Fair Trade? Lessons from Asia." *Third World Quarterly* 31.3 (2010): 449-67. *Academic Search Premier*. Web. 18 Jan. 2012.

24-2 Identify source material through in-text citations.

In MLA, in-text citations typically follow these guidelines:

1. Refer to the author (plus the work's title, if helpful) and a page number by using one of these methods:
   - Last name and page number in parentheses
   - Name cited in sentence, page number in parentheses
2. Present and punctuate citations according to these rules:
   - Place the parenthetical reference after the source material.
   - Within the parentheses, normally give the author's last name only.
   - Do not put a comma between the author's last name and the page reference.
   - Cite the page number as a numeral, not a word.
   - Place any sentence punctuation after the closed parenthesis.

24-3 Develop bibliographic entries.

In MLA, a works cited page lists the sources used in the paper. Follow the guidelines for creating a works-cited list on pages 297–298.

24-4 List books and other nonperiodical documents.

Review pages 300–307 for citation examples for learning objectives 24-4–24-7.

24-5 List print periodical articles.

24-6 List online sources.

24-7 List other sources.

24-8 Follow format guidelines for MLA.

The MLA system offers guidelines for format and page layout (see side bar.)

KEY TERMS: MLA STYLE

24-1

MLA the Modern Language Association; the professional organization that sets style decisions for English and humanities disciplines

24-2

in-text citation a reference within the text of a research report, indicating the origin of summarized, paraphrased, or quoted material

24-8

works-cited list in an MLA paper, a list of sources cited within the paper, arranged alphabetically by author's last name

MLA Formatting

Here are some basic formatting guidelines for MLA papers. More detailed instructions appear on pages 308–311.

Pagination

Number pages consecutively in the upper-right corner, one-half inch from the top and flush with the right margin (1 inch from the edge of the page). Type your last name before the page number.

Spacing

Margins: Set margins top and bottom, left and right, at one inch, with the exception of the page numbers (one-half inch from top).

Line Spacing: Double-space the entire paper— including the heading and works-cited entries, as well as tables, captions, and inset quotations.

Works-Cited List

Start the list on a new page immediately after your paper's conclusion. Continue the pagination.

LEARNING OBJECTIVES: APA STYLE

24-1 Learn the basics of APA documentation.

APA documentation involves two parts: (1) an in-text citation within your text whenever you incorporate a source and (2) a matching bibliographic entry in a "References" page at the end of your text. In the example below, "Pascopella, 2011, p.32)" tells the reader that

- The borrowed material came from a source authored by Pascopella.
- The source was published in 2011.
- The specific material can be found on page 32 of the source.
- Full source details are in the reference list under the surname Pascopella.

1. **In-Text Citation in the Body of the Writing:**

   In newcomer programs, "separate, relatively self-contained educational interventions" (Pascopella, 2011, p. 32) are implemented to meet the academic and transitional needs of recent immigrants before they enter a mainstream English Language Development (EDL) program .

2. **Matching Reference Entry at the End of the Paper**

   Pascopella, A. (2011). Successful strategies for English language learners. *District Administration, 47*(2), 29-44.

24-2 Identify source material through in-text citations.

In APA, in-text citations typically follow these guidelines:

1. Refer to the author, date of publication, and a page number (when citing a specific part) by using one of these methods:
   - Last name and publication year in parentheses
   - Name cited in sentence, publication year in parentheses (page number included in this example)
2. Present and punctuate citations according to these rules:
   - Clearly indicate where cited material begins and ends.
   - List authors in text by last name only.
   - Include the publication date in parentheses.
   - Give any page numbers as numerals, not words.
   - In parentheses, separate author name, date, and any page numbers with commas.
   - Use *p.* for a page number and *pp.* for multiple pages.

24-3 Develop bibliographic entries.

In APA, a reference page lists the sources used in the paper. Follow the guidelines for creating a references page on pages 298–299.

24-4 List books and other nonperiodical documents.

Review pages 300–307 for citation examples for learning objectives 24-4–24-7.

24-8 Follow format guidelines for APA.

The APA system offers guidelines for format and page layout (see sidebar.)

KEY TERMS: APA STYLE

24-1
APA the American Psychological Association, which publishes a manuscript style for the behaviorial and social sciences

24-2
documentation notations in text, pointing to outside sources of information

26-4
DOI digital object identifier, intended to ensure an electronic source can be found even if its online location changes

24-8
reference list in APA style, a list of all sources referred to in a paper or article

APA Formatting

Here are some basic formatting guidelines for the body of APA papers. More detailed instructions appear on pages 312–321.

Margins:

One-inch margin on all four sides of each page (one and one-half inches on the left if the paper will be bound).

Line Spacing:

Double-space throughout.

Page Numbers:

Place your running head and the page number flush left and flush right respectively, at the top of each page, beginning with the title page.

Headings:

All topics of equal importance should have headings of the same level, or style.

LEARNING OBJECTIVES: GRAMMAR

25-1 Noun
A noun is a word that names something: a person, a place, a thing, or an idea. Proper nouns are capitalized; common nouns are not capitalized.

25-2 Pronoun
A pronoun is a word that is used in place of a noun. Each pronoun must agree with its antecedent in number, person, and gender.

25-3 Verb
Verbs are classified as action, auxiliary (helping), or linking (state of being).

25-4 Adjective
Adjectives, including the articles (*a, an, the*), describe or modify a noun or pronoun.

25-5 Adverb
An adverb describes or modifies a verb, an adjective, another adverb, or a whole sentence.

25-6 Preposition
A preposition is a word (or group of words) that shows the relationship between its object (a noun or pronoun following the preposition) and another word in the sentence.

25-7 Conjunction
A conjunction connects individual words or groups of words.

25-8 Interjection
An interjection is a word or phrase that communicates strong emotion or surprise.

LEARNING OBJECTIVES: SENTENCES

26-1 Subjects and Predicates
Sentences have two main parts: a subject and a predicate. The subject is most often a noun or a pronoun. The predicate contains a verb.

26-2 Phrases
A phrase is a group of related words that functions as a single part of speech. A phrase lacks a subject, a predicate, or both.

26-3 Clauses
A clause is a group of related words that has both a subject and a verb..

26-4 Sentence Variety
There are five kinds of sentences: declarative (make statements); interrogative (ask questions), imperative (give commands), exclamatory (communicate strong emotion or surprise), or conditional (express two circumstances).

KEY TERMS: GRAMMAR

25-1
proper noun names a specific person, place, thing, or idea
common noun a general name for a person, place, thing, or idea

25-2
antecedent the noun or pronoun that a pronoun refers to or replaces

25-3
active voice (of verb) indicates that the subject of the verb is performing the action
passive voice (of verb) indicates that the subject of the verb is being acted upon or is receiving the action

25-6
prepositional phrase includes the preposition, the object of the preposition, and the modifiers of the object

KEY TERMS: SENTENCES

26-4
simple sentence contains one independent clause
compound sentence consists of two independent clauses
complex sentence contains one independent clause and one or more dependent clauses
compound-complex sentence contains two or more independent clauses and one or more dependent clauses

CHAPTER REVIEW
Sentence Errors

LEARNING OBJECTIVES

27-1 Subject-Verb Agreement

The subject and verb of any clause must agree in both *person* and *number*. *Person* indicates whether the subject of the verb is *first*, *second*, or *third* person. *Number* indicates whether the subject and verb are *singular* or *plural*.

27-2 Pronoun-Antecedent Agreement

A pronoun must agree in number, person, and gender with its antecedent. The antecedent is the word to which the pronoun refers.

27-3 Shifts in Sentence Construction

A shift is an improper change in structure midway through a sentence.

27-4 Fragments, Comma Splices, and Run-Ons

- A **fragment** is a phrase or dependent clause used as a sentence. It is not a sentence, however, because a phrase lacks a subject, a verb, or some other essential part; and a dependent clause must be connected to an independent clause to complete its meaning.
- A **comma splice** is a mistake made when two independent clauses are connected (spliced) with only a comma. The comma is not enough: A period, semicolon, or conjunction is needed.
- A **run-on sentence** is actually two sentences (two independent clauses) joined without adequate punctuation or a connecting word.

27-5 Misplaced and Dangling Modifiers

- **Misplaced modifiers** are descriptive words or phrases so separated from what they are describing that the reader is confused.
- **Dangling modifiers** are descriptive phrases that tell about a subject that isn't stated in the sentence.

27-6 Ambiguous Wording

- An **indefinite reference** is a problem caused by careless use of pronouns. There must always be a word or phrase nearby (its antecedent) that a pronoun clearly replaces.
- **Incomplete comparisons**—leaving out words that show exactly what is being compared to what—can confuse readers.
- **Unclear wording** is wording that has two or more possible meanings due to an unclear reference to something elsewhere in the sentence.

27-7 Nonstandard Language

Nonstandard language is language that does not conform to the standards set by schools, media, and public institutions. It is often acceptable in everyday conversation and in fictional writing, but it is seldom used in formal speech or other forms of writing. (See examples in the sidebar.)

KEY TERMS

27-7

colloquial language wording used in informal conversation that is unacceptable in formal writing

double preposition *off of, off to, from off*

substitution using *and* in place of *to*, or *of* in place of *have*

double negative a sentence that contains two negative words used to express a single negative idea

slang — informal language, characterized by "buzz" words such as *way cool* or *my bad*

LEARNING OBJECTIVES: PUNCTUATION

Use the checklists on this card to edit for punctuation and mechanics.

Have I used...

____ 1. **periods** after sentences other than questions?

____ 2. **question marks** after direct questions?

____ 3. **commas** between the clauses of a compound sentence?

____ 4. **commas** between items in a series?

____ 5. **commas** after introductory phrases?

____ 6. **commas** to separate equal adjectives?

____ 7. **commas** to separate nonrestrictive phrases and clauses?

____ 8. **hyphens** to join numbers indicating a range?

____ 9. **quotation marks** around direct quotations and titles of short works?

____ 10. **end quotation marks** following periods and commas but preceding semicolons and colons?

____ 11. **italics** for titles of long works?

____ 12. **apostrophes** to indicate missing letters in contractions?

____ 13. **apostrophes** to form possessives (but not possessive pronouns)?

LEARNING OBJECTIVES: MECHANICS

Have I ...

____ 1. **capitalized** first words in sentences and full quotations?

____ 2. **capitalized** proper nouns and adjectives?

____ 3. **capitalized** languages, ethnic groups, nationalities, and religions?

____ 4. **capitalized** these words in titles—the first, the last, and all others, except articles (*a, an, the*), short prepositions, *to* in an infinitive, and coordinating conjunctions (*and, but, or, nor, for, so, yet*)?

____ 5. **formed plurals** by adding an *s* after most singular nouns and adding *es* after those ending in *sh, ch, x, s,* or *z*?

____ 6. **formed plurals** of compound nouns by adding *s* or *es* to the most important word in the compound?

____ 7. **spelled out numbers** from one to one hundred?

____ 8. **used numerals** for decimals, percentages, pages, chapters, addresses, dates, statistics, numbers used with abbreviations, and phone and identification numbers?

____ 9. **checked spelling** using a spell checker and dictionary?

KEY TERMS: PUNCTUATION

28-2
ellipsis (three periods) used to show that one or more words have been omitted in a quotation

28-7
hyphen used to make some compound words

28-8
dash used to set off nonessential elements for emphasis

28-12
diagonal (also called a slash) used to form a fraction or between two words to indicate that either is acceptable

28-13
brackets used before or after words that are added to clarify what another person has said or written

KEY TERMS: MECHANICS

29-4
abbreviation shortened form of a word or a phrase

29-5
acronym a word formed from the first (or first few) letters of words in a set phrase

initialism similar to an acronym except that the initials used to form this abbreviation are pronounced individually

LEARNING OBJECTIVES

30-1 Parts of Speech

- **Nouns** are words that name people, places, and things. Count nouns refer to things that can be counted. They can have *a*, *an*, *the*, or *one* in front of them. Noncount nouns refer to things that cannot be counted. Do not use *a*, *an*, or *one* in front of them.
- **Verbs** show action, link words, or accompany another verb as an auxiliary or helping verb.
- **Adjectives** describe or modify a noun or pronoun. An adjective comes before the noun it modifies.
- **Adverbs** describe or modify a verb, an adjective, another adverb, or a whole sentence. An adverb answers questions such as *how, when, where, why, how often*, or *how much*.
- **Prepositions** combine with a noun to form a prepositional phrase, which acts as a modifier—an adverb or an adjective. *In, on, at,* and *by* are four common prepositions that refer to time and place.

30-2 Sentence Basics

Simple sentences in the English language follow five basic patterns:

- Subject + Verb
- Subject + Verb + Direct Object
- Subject + Verb + Indirect Object + Direct Object
- Subject + Verb + Direct Object + Object Complement
- Subject + Linking Verb + Predicate Nominative (or Predicate Adjective)

30-3 Sentence Problems

- **Double negative:** A sentence that contains two negative words used to express a single negative idea
- **Subject-verb agreement:** The subject and verb of any clause must agree in both *person* and *number.*
- **Omitted words:** Do not omit subjects or the expletives *there* or *here.*
- **Repeated words:** Do not repeat the subject of a clause or sentence. Also do not repeat an object in an adjective dependent clause.

30-4 Numbers, Word Parts, and Idioms

- **Numbers:** A period is used to express percentages (5.5%, 75.9%) and the comma is used to organize large numbers into units (7,000). Commas are not used in writing the year (2015).
- **Prefixes, suffixes, and roots:** Learning word parts and their meanings can help you learn unfamiliar words.
- **Idioms:** These phrases are used in a special way and must be learned as a whole. American English includes several common idioms. (See page 384–385.)

KEY TERMS

30-1

collective nouns nouns that name a whole category or group and are often noncount nouns

two-way nouns nouns that can be used as either count or noncount nouns, depending on what they refer to

specific (definite) article *the* is used to refer to a specific noun

indefinite article *a* or *an* are used to refer to a specific noun

progressive- or continuous-tense progressive- or continuous-tense verbs express action in progress

30-2

intransitive verb a verb that does not need a direct object to express a complete thought

transitive verb a verb that needs a direct object to express a complete thought

direct object names *who* or *what* receives the action

indirect object names *to whom* or *for whom* the action was done

linking verb connects the subject to the predicate noun or predicate adjective